Harvard East Asian Series 14

THE UNITED STATES AND THE
FAR EASTERN CRISIS OF 1933–1938

The East Asian Research Center at Harvard University administers research projects designed to further scholarly understanding of China, Korea, Japan, and adjacent areas.

THE UNITED STATES AND
THE FAR EASTERN CRISIS OF
1933-1938

FROM THE MANCHURIAN INCIDENT
THROUGH THE INITIAL STAGE OF THE
UNDECLARED SINO-JAPANESE WAR

DOROTHY BORG

HARVARD UNIVERSITY PRESS
CAMBRIDGE, MASSACHUSETTS

1964

Preparation and publication of this volume was aided by a grant from the Ford Foundation.

PREFACE

The reasons for undertaking the present study need no elaborate explanation. It was felt that much had been written about American Far Eastern policy in connection with the Manchurian incident and the events of the years immediately preceding Pearl Harbor. In contrast, however, little attention had been paid to the development of that policy in the mid-1930's. Yet here was a point in time when Japan and China were involved in a continuous struggle which had profoundly important implications for the United States.

In approaching the material which forms the basis of this volume the writer sought to emphasize the aims of American policy and the methods by which the United States government attempted to achieve these aims. The conflict between Japan and China passed through two phases in the period under review. In the first, which extended from the end of the Manchurian crisis in 1933 to the Marco Polo Bridge incident in July 1937, Japan tried to obtain control of China through the use of nonmilitary—or what today would be called "cold war"—tactics. By 1936 it looked to many American officials as though her efforts were proving so successful that most or all of China might soon pass under the domination of the Japanese. The main theme throughout chapters I and IX is that, faced with this situation, the primary goal of the United States was not—as has sometimes been contended—to champion China but rather to prevent the threat of war between the United States and Japan from increasing. Many members of the Roosevelt administration believed that the occurrence of such a war in the not too distant future was, if not a probability, at least a decided possibility. They were alarmed by the resurgence of anti-American feeling in Japan that had resulted from the Manchurian crisis. Moreover they were convinced that, incited by their military leaders, the Japanese might try to expand not only beyond China but beyond the mainland of Asia on to the islands of the west Pacific including those which belonged to the United States. Theoretically the Roosevelt administration might have adopted any one of three methods to reduce the likelihood of a conflict between the United States and Japan. It might have sought to appease the Japanese; it might have opposed them; or it might have refrained from any action. As will be seen it chose the third course.

HISTORY

In the phase of the Sino-Japanese struggle that started with the Marco Polo Bridge incident, Japan obviously ceased to rely upon nonmilitary pressures and resorted to an all-out use of force. As a result, the United States government felt that an entirely new situation had been created analogous to that which had existed at the time of the Manchurian and Ethiopian crises. In short, Japan was defying the entire movement for the maintenance of world peace upon which so much of the hope of peoples in all nations had centered since 1919. Support of that movement became the chief objective of the administration in Washington. Linked closely with this aim was the desire to prevent the spread of war from Asia to Europe, where Hitler and Mussolini were increasingly threatening the security of Great Britain and France. Chapters X to XVI deal to a large extent with the question of how far the United States government was willing to go toward checking Japanese aggression. There is a popular belief that the administration wished to take strong action against Japan, following the outbreak of the Sino-Japanese conflict, and was only deterred from doing so by the force of isolationism throughout the United States. The writer has attempted to show that the facts do not lend themselves to any such simple interpretation. Many elements were involved which it has been necessary to consider in detail. Foremost among these were the views of the President, the Secretary of State, Congress, and certain organized groups and publications representative of various segments of public opinion. Still, as events unfolded it became evident that whatever the reasons the net result was that the administration did not depart basically from the course it had chosen earlier.

The writing of this book was made possible because of the assistance, both direct and indirect, rendered by many people. The author's appreciation of their help is, however, too deep and in many instances too personal to be expressed in a formal preface. No attempt will be made here, therefore, to do more than mention the few persons who undertook the special task of reading either all or parts of the manuscript so that it might be possible to benefit from their criticisms.

The manuscript was read in its entirety by John K. Fairbank and Ernest R. May while the writer was associated with the East Asian Research Center at Harvard. Chapters dealing with specialized subjects were reviewed by experts with an intensive knowledge of the issues involved: chapters III, VIII, and XVI on naval questions, by Louis Morton; chapter IV on our silver policy as it affected China, by Sir Frederick Leith-Ross, Herbert Feis, and Arthur N. Young; chapter VII on the views of American officials concerning the Chinese

Communists and the Sian incident, by O. Edmund Clubb, Harold C. Hinton, Benjamin I. Schwartz, and James C. Thomson, Jr.; the sections of chapter IX on economic developments in China, by Franklin L. Ho; and chapter XV on the Japanese efforts at reaching a settlement after the outbreak of war in China in 1937, by F. C. Jones.

The part of the book which deals with President Roosevelt's "quarantine" speech went through several stages. An earlier version, which eventually appeared as an article in the *Political Science Quarterly*, was discussed in some detail with Professor William L. Langer, Frank Freidel, and Arthur M. Schlesinger, Jr., at Harvard and with Herman Kahn, then director of the Franklin D. Roosevelt Library, at Hyde Park. Subsequent drafts, written in a further effort to solve certain political and legal questions, were commented upon by Judge Philip C. Jessup and by Oliver J. Lissitzyn of the Public Law Department of Columbia.

While the above were consulted they may not agree with all the points in the final text. In any event the full responsibility for this volume essentially rests with the author.

DOROTHY BORG

New York, New York
1963

CONTENTS

THE UNITED STATES AND
THE FAR EASTERN CRISIS OF
1933-1938

FROM THE MANCHURIAN INCIDENT
THROUGH THE INITIAL STAGE OF THE
UNDECLARED SINO-JAPANESE WAR

CHAPTER I | THE MANCHURIAN INCIDENT AND THE TANGKU TRUCE

REVIEW OF THE STIMSON PERIOD

As President Roosevelt was elected to office in November 1932 the Manchurian crisis was drawing to a close. The Lytton Commission, which had been appointed by the League of Nations to investigate the Sino-Japanese dispute over Manchuria, had delivered its report to the Council of the League which was scheduled to consider it in late November.

No one was watching developments at Geneva with more intense interest than Secretary of State Stimson in Washington. Stimson, with all the vigor and earnestness that formed such an impressive part of his personality, believed in the broad principles that constituted the foundations of the internationalist movement which had developed in the 1920's. In contrast to the general view of American isolationists that this country should remain aloof from the affairs of others, the Secretary felt that the ultimate aim of every nation should be the establishment and maintenance of universal peace and that this goal must be achieved largely through international cooperation. Furthermore, he thought that, since the World War, the internationalist movement had made substantial progress by the conclusion of various multilateral treaties foremost among which were the Covenant of the League of Nations, the agreements that emerged from the Washington Conference of 1921-1922, and the Pact of Paris, otherwise known as the Kellogg-Briand Pact. Stimson looked upon these treaties as in effect forming a peace system that reflected the postwar efforts to solve the problem of world peace through a number of different though interrelated approaches. He regarded Japan's attack upon Manchuria as the first great test of this system and therefore as an event that had immeasurably grave and far-reaching implications. Consequently since the start of hostilities between Japan and China a little over a year earlier, the Secretary had personally directed the conduct of American diplomacy.

Even before the Lytton report had been received at Geneva, Stimson had begun to show signs of concern over the trend of developments. In late September in a message to Hugh Wilson, our Minister in Switzerland, who frequently represented the United States in League circles, Stimson said that he had been reading stories in the newspapers to the effect that the League was looking to America for "leadership" which would enable it to devise a policy once the findings of the Lytton Commission were known.[1] If such an attitude was in fact prevalent at Geneva, the Secretary declared, American officials should do their best to discourage it. The responsibility for shaping a policy must rest with the League. It was far better for a group of fifty-six nations, such as the League represented, to settle upon a line of action and then ask a single other state to adopt the same course than vice versa. If the members of the League approached the American government with constructive suggestions, it would no doubt accept them. Recalling a memorandum of October 5, 1931, which had embodied his views on the subject of the United States' relations with the League in regard to the Sino-Japanese conflict, Stimson asserted that his opinions had in no way changed.[2]

In short, since the commencement of the Manchurian incident, the Secretary had grappled with the problem of the relationship of the United States to the League in dealing with the Sino-Japanese conflict. Stimson was determined to cooperate with the League in attempting to meet Japan's challenge to the international peace structure but he had periodically insisted that the initiative in taking action should be assumed by the League. His main arguments were that, by virtue of the Covenant, the League possessed the proper machinery for the handling of international disputes and that, as a collective body, it could act with greater impunity than any individual nation. The United States, he felt, must proceed independently of the League both because it was a nonmember and because many Americans were opposed to any close association with Geneva; at the same time it should primarily support such positions as members of the League, without prior reference to Washington, had decided to take.

Even a cursory look at the record indicates that Stimson's thesis that America should follow and not lead the League was constantly disregarded throughout the Manchurian crisis not only by the statesmen of other nations but also by the Secretary himself.[3] China, it will be recalled, immediately after the Mukden incident, which gave rise to the Manchurian conflict, appealed its case to the League under Article XI of the Covenant. The Council, which happened to be in session at Geneva, met from September 19 to 30 in an effort to settle the controversy. On September 30 it passed a resolution which, among other matters, committed the Japanese to withdraw their troops as rapidly as possible from the area they had occupied following the Mukden incident. The Council then recessed with the understanding that it would meet again in mid-October to consider the situation as it existed at that time, the hope being that in the interval conditions would have improved to the point where no further action by the League would be necessary. But instead of withdrawing, the Japanese armies advanced further into Manchuria. Moreover, on October 8 a squadron of Japanese planes bombed the city of Chinchow, far from the scene of hostilities, thereby shocking a world which still regarded aerial attacks upon civilian centers as unjustifiable acts of brutality.

In the first days that the Council was in session on the Manchurian crisis, Norman Davis telephoned to Stimson from Geneva to relate his impressions of developments there.[4] Davis, an important figure in both Democratic and Republican administrations throughout the 1920's and 1930's, had served under President Wilson and was well known for his profound and unqualified devotion to the ideas of internationalism that Wilson had tried to realize at the end of the World War. It is not surprising, therefore, that Davis told Secretary Stimson that he felt the Sino-Japanese controversy presented an unparalleled opportunity for American collaboration with the League which might not only result in the settlement of the Sino-Japanese dispute but also in the establishment of an invaluable precedent for American participation in the international effort to further the cause of world peace. Specifically, Davis recommended that an American representative should sit on the Council while it debated the Sino-Japanese issue. Stimson said that this was impossible as the Council was operating under the terms of the Covenant to which the United States was not a party. He felt that the League should exercise its authority to the fullest in order to restore peace and that, for the time being at least, the United States should limit itself to providing the League with diplomatic and moral support. Stimson added, however, that if there were indications that the League might prove unable to cope with developments, the United States might take some more direct action such as joining with the other interested powers in invoking the Kellogg-Briand Pact or the Nine Power Treaty of which, in contrast to the Covenant, it was a signatory.

As the Council appeared to be making excellent progress toward finding a solution to the Sino-Japanese controversy throughout its

September session, the Secretary adhered to his idea of restricting himself to actions which would strengthen the League's hand.[5] But, like most of the rest of the world, he was outraged by the bombing of Chinchow, which he felt indicated that the situation was getting out of control. Therefore, after expressly obtaining the consent of the President, Stimson in confidence suggested to the Council that, upon reconvening in mid-October, it might discuss the question of invoking the Paris Pact; he furthermore intimated that, if invited, the American Consul at Geneva—Prentiss Gilbert—would be authorized to participate in the deliberations.[6] As most of the Council members wanted, above all, to establish the closest possible contact with the United States, they were more than eager to extend an invitation to Gilbert. But the Japanese, who held a seat on the Council, raised unexpectedly vigorous objections, and the United States quickly became the target of an abusive propaganda campaign in the Japanese press. In the end, the Council overruled the Japanese and on October 16 Gilbert took his place at the Council table.

At the last moment the Secretary personally telephoned to Gilbert to make absolutely certain that he fully understood the instructions which had been sent him.[7] Gilbert was "to keep modestly in the background" indicating that he was in no way assuming the status of a Council member. He could enter into the discussions when they touched upon the possible invocation of the Paris Pact but otherwise he was to refrain from taking any part in the proceedings. Moreover, even in regard to invoking the pact, the initiative for raising this issue was to be left to the League. On this point the Secretary was adamant, declaring repeatedly that the initiative must under no circumstances whatever be "sent back" to Washington and that the recent show of anti-American feeling in Japan made it "doubly important" for the United States not to be pushed into a position of leadership which would seem to "array this country . . . vis-à-vis Japan."

Secretary Stimson's idea that Gilbert could stay "modestly in the background" proved to be decidedly unrealistic. It was widely felt at Geneva that Gilbert's appearance at the Council table should be treated as a great occasion, since it might mark the end of American isolationism. A special meeting was called by the Council on October 16 to greet Gilbert, and when he arrived the room was filled to overflowing with a hushed, expectant crowd. Aristide Briand, then President of the Council, made a warm, welcoming speech. But as Gilbert in reply read a prepared statement, based upon the Secretary's instructions, it quickly became evident that his participation in the Council's activities would fall far short of the hopes that had been raised. Still the Council moved ahead rapidly and on the following day its members, excepting Japan and China, decided that their governments should invoke the Kellogg-Briand Pact by reminding the Japanese and Chinese of their obligations under the terms of that agreement to seek a settlement of their dispute by peaceful means. Notes were subsequently sent to Japan and China by individual signatories of the pact, including the United States.[8] The business relative to the pact having thus been completed, Secretary Stimson cabled Gilbert to leave his seat at the Council table and resume the position he customarily occupied in the Council room as an observer.[9] While Stimson seems to have taken for granted that the members of the Council realized from the outset that Gilbert would withdraw, once a decision had been reached concerning the Paris Pact, this turned out to be far from the case. Briand himself, Lord Reading, who as Foreign Secretary was representing Great Britain on the Council, and Sir Eric Drummond, the able Secretary-General of the League, all hastened to assure Stimson that Gilbert's retirement would be interpreted as a "rebuff" to the League and would be "disastrous."[10] A long argument ensued in which Stimson maintained that "the last thing in the world" he wanted to do was embarrass the League; but neither did he want to arouse fresh antagonism to the United States in Japan nor did he wish to alarm the American public by establishing a closer contact with Geneva than he could justify. Finally, with scarcely suppressed irritation, the Secretary agreed to allow Gilbert to attend one more public meeting at the Council table.

Nevertheless, Stimson was not unduly discouraged by the difficulties which had developed from his attempts at cooperation with the Council and was determined to adhere to his policy of re-enforcing any moves made by the League and, whenever necessary, participating in any action taken in connection with the Pact of Paris and the Nine Power Treaty. In regard to the League, his policy was put to a somewhat severe test when, at the close of its October session, the Council adopted a resolution calling upon the Japanese to withdraw their forces from the occupied areas before November 16, the date of the next Council meeting. For the Secretary disapproved of fixing a time limit which, in his opinion, the Japanese would in all probability ignore, thereby putting the League in an exceedingly awkward position. Still he went as far as he felt he could, in good conscience, toward supporting the League's resolution.[11]

As mid-November approached and the Council was preparing to reconvene in Paris, the Secretary again decided to appoint an American representative to cooperate with the members of the Council in case further action under the Kellogg-Briand Pact seemed advisable. But this time he chose an internationally known figure, General Charles G. Dawes, who was not only a former Vice President of the United States but was currently Ambassador to Great Britain. In discussing his appointment with Dawes initially, Stimson emphasized in particular that the general had the prestige plus "the personality and good horse sense" to be able to deal with the members of the Council without allowing himself to be pushed into the forefront of the scene.[12] Prentiss Gilbert's presence at the last Council meeting, the Secretary declared, had been treated with such elaborate ceremony by the League that much more significance had been attached to it than was originally intended. General Dawes replied that he thought he could "handle" that part of the assignment and that he would "lay low." It was thereupon decided that Dawes would confer with individual members of the Council informally and would not attend any sessions of the Council.

On arriving in Paris, the general encountered more difficulties than he expected. On November 14 he telephoned the Secretary to say that the question of whether he would appear at the Council meetings was uppermost in everyone's mind and like Banquo's ghost confronted him "both in the halls of the mighty and on every street corner."[13] Briand was insisting that if the United States refused to cooperate with the Council as closely as heretofore, the League's prestige would be greatly damaged. The Secretary agreed that General Dawes might find it necessary to sit with the Council on the same terms as Prentiss Gilbert or, in other words, when the Kellogg-Briand Pact was under discussion. Subsequently, however, the general decided against participating in any of the Council's formal deliberations and instead conducted an endless series of private conferences with the members of the Council and other interested officials in his own establishment at the Ritz.

By mid-November the situation had deteriorated far more than had been generally anticipated. The Japanese, utterly defying the appeals of the League and the United States for the cessation of hostilities, had launched an extensive military campaign which took their armies hundreds of miles beyond their base in South Manchuria. After a three-day battle in the first week of November, the Chinese forces in the north were virtually destroyed and on November 18 the Japanese occupied Tsitsihar, the capital of Heilungkiang. At the same time there were indications that the Kwantung army was also beginning to move southward in an operation which looked as though it might be directed against the city of Chinchow.

On the day after the fall of Tsitsihar, General Dawes telephoned to Stimson again for instructions.[14] There was reason to believe, he said, that the Council might consider the application of economic sanctions against Japan, in which case he would undoubtedly once more be urged to join in the discussions. However he felt more strongly than ever that the United States must pursue its course independently of the League and was even in favor of issuing a public statement to that effect. The Secretary agreed and authorized Dawes to give a statement to the press on the following day.[15] Stimson, moreover, declared that the administration in Washington was not prepared to impose economic sanctions on Japan as it believed that even measures such as an embargo were a "step to war."[16] On the other hand, it would not "interfere through the fleet with any embargo by anyone else" though this was a matter which he was inclined to believe should be kept secret until after the Council had made its decision.

At this point the situation in the Far East seemed to improve unexpectedly. Perhaps as the result of a strong protest from Washington, the drive of the Japanese armies toward Chinchow stopped. The Japanese also made various diplomatic moves which suggested that they might be ready to consider a settlement. As a consequence, talk of sanctions ceased and on December 10 the Council adopted a resolution which provided for the commission of inquiry that was to be headed by Lord Lytton. Stimson immediately expressed his approval of the League's action publicly.[17] Further, he agreed to the appointment of an unofficial American representative to serve on the commission and, on the request of Briand, suggested Major General Frank McCoy.

With the establishment of the Lytton Commission, the first phase of the Manchurian crisis came to an end. Ostensibly at least, the League of Nations had taken the leadership among the powers interested in preserving the postwar peace system in an attempt to find a solution to the Sino-Japanese controversy. The second phase was to start almost immediately, and in it Secretary of State Stimson was to seize the initiative which he had so far insisted belonged to the League.

Within less than forty-eight hours after the Council decided to establish a commission of inquiry, the Japanese Cabinet was driven from office. Throughout all the difficulties of the preceding months, Secretary Stimson had maintained the hope that Baron Shidehara, the Foreign Secretary, long known as the chief exponent in Japan of a conciliatory policy toward China, would eventually be able to restrain the extremist factions, who were behind the activities of the Kwantung army, and negotiate a reasonable settlement with the Chinese.[18] In fact, Stimson had repeatedly urged the League to refrain from exerting any strong pressure against the Japanese government on the grounds that nothing should be done which might weaken the position of the moderate faction that was in power. The fall of the cabinet therefore seemed to Stimson a disastrous event which completely altered the picture in the Far East.

The men who took over the Japanese government were indeed far more militant than their predecessors and quickly decided to support the Kwantung army in its expansionist adventures. Within a few weeks, that army resumed its march southward and on January 2, 1932, occupied Chinchow, thereby destroying the last vestige of Chinese authority in South Manchuria. The loss of Chinchow angered Stimson especially because late in November he had been assured not only by Baron Shidehara but also by the Japanese Minister of War and the Chief of Staff that the capture of Chinchow was not even being contemplated.[19]

Faced with these developments, the Secretary concluded that the long-drawn-out process of trying to persuade the Japanese to agree to a peaceful settlement had been futile and that, as he colorfully expressed the matter, it was time to "wind it up with a snap."[20] He therefore decided to implement a proposal, advanced by President Hoover in early November, to the effect that the United States might issue a statement—comparable to the declaration made by Secretary Bryan in 1915—refusing to recognize any changes brought about by Japanese aggression in Manchuria in violation of certain treaties.[21] The idea of reaffirming the nonrecognition doctrine appealed to Stimson primarily as a means of strengthening the peace system by the use of a moral sanction. For he felt that it would demonstrate that while the peace-loving nations of the world might not be prepared to stop acts of aggression by military or economic measures neither were they willing to condone them by accepting their consequences. Moreover, he entertained some hope that an explicit indication of moral censure might serve to persuade the Japanese to abandon their lawless methods.[22]

Still it was evident that if a reassertion of the nonrecognition doctrine was to attain any such far-reaching aims it should not be undertaken by the United States alone but by many governments representing a large part of the public opinion of the world. At the same time, delay seemed inadvisable since the situation appeared to call for some quick, decisive move. Stimson, in conjunction with the President, therefore decided to issue a unilateral declaration immediately but to frame it so broadly that any nation which so desired could follow suit. This necessitated associating the principle of nonrecognition, not just with agreements related to China (as in Secretary Bryan's pronouncement), but with some appropriate treaty that had been universally accepted. The most obvious treaty was the Kellogg-Briand Pact. As a consequence, on January 7, 1932, the Secretary issued the famous note to Japan and China in which he proclaimed the so-called "Stimson doctrine," asserting that the United States "does not intend to recognize any situation, treaty, or agreement which may be brought about by means contrary to the covenants and obligations of the Pact of Paris."[23]

Years later, in writing of the nonrecognition note in *On Active Service*, McGeorge Bundy stated,

With the publication of this note the United States, with Stimson as its spokesman, stepped to the forefront of the nations opposing aggression, and from this time onward, until his retirement from office fourteen months later, Stimson was the outstanding advocate of collective condemnation of Japan.[24]

The American Secretary of State had undoubtedly "stepped to the forefront of the nations opposing aggression" but this was at best a hazardous position and it was made more hazardous by the failure of other governments to support him. Like many people of his era, Stimson had an abiding faith in the ability of the United States and Great Britain to solve many of the problems which threatened the stability of the world, if they would only work together. The Secretary therefore looked to the British to endorse his January 7 statement, after which he thought other countries would fall in line. But the British issued a communiqué which the Secretary regarded as an outright rebuff, although the Foreign Office insisted then and forever after that no rebuff had been intended.[25] In any event, the British made no further move nor, perhaps due to their example, did any other government.

The Secretary's effort at leadership had therefore resulted in leaving the United States "out on a limb." Worse was to come, however. In late January, the situation in the Far East again took an unexpected turn with the outbreak of fighting in Shanghai. The Chinese had for some time been conducting an anti-Japanese boycott in that city which was increasingly effective. Tension rose, leading to clashes between Chinese and Japanese civilians. The Japanese government responded by re-enforcing the military detachment which they normally maintained in the International Settlement at Shanghai. As a result of further friction, the local Japanese commander delivered an ultimatum to the Chinese on January 27 demanding the closing of the headquarters of the boycott associations. Although the Chinese complied, the Japanese moved some of their troops into Chapei, a district bordering on the Settlement which was occupied by the Nineteenth Route Army. To the surprise of the Japanese, the Chinese put up a highly effective resistance. Fighting continued for more than a month, during which period the Japanese constantly sent new detachments to the Shanghai area until their forces reportedly numbered around 70,000. Finally, at the beginning of March, the Nineteenth Route Army was compelled to withdraw and the hostilities ceased.

The military events at Shanghai were paralleled by diplomatic efforts to achieve a settlement. Immediately after the outbreak of hostilities, China appealed to the League for assistance. The Council took action at Geneva and also at Shanghai, where it worked through a committee of consular officials representing six nations. Stimson permitted an American representative to cooperate with this committee. But, more importantly, he drafted a plan which he hoped would furnish the basis for a settlement and persuaded the British to join with him in submitting it to the Chinese and Japanese. The plan was, however, rejected by the Japanese on February 4.

The Council's attempts to terminate the dispute dragged on throughout February but were no more successful than Stimson's. Discouraged, the Chinese asked to have their case transferred from the Council to the Assembly of the League. A special session of the Assembly was held in the early part of March during the course of which a Committee of Nineteen, consisting of members of both the Council and the Assembly, was organized to continue the efforts at conciliation. Being a nonmember of the League, the United States was not represented on the Committee of Nineteen. The subsequent negotiations for settlement were, however, largely conducted at Shanghai in a conference in which the American Minister, Nelson T. Johnson, participated together with the Ministers of Great Britain, France, and Italy. The negotiations were long and exceedingly difficult but the terms of an armistice agreement were finally drawn up and approved by the Assembly. On May 5, 1932, the agreement was signed by representatives of China and Japan in the presence of the four Ministers who had taken part in the negotiations. At the end of May, the last Japanese troops, which had been sent to Shanghai during the hostilities, sailed for home.

However, long before the concerted effort of the powers had restored relatively peaceful conditions in Shanghai, Stimson had made another major move on his own initiative. On February 9, Nelson

Johnson had cabled that, according to a Reuters report, Japanese officials in China were thinking of asking the Western nations to participate in a "moral program rather than political" to solve the China problem.[26] The scheme allegedly involved the creation of a demilitarized zone about 20 kilometers wide around each of the principal ports of China, notably Shanghai, Hankow, Canton, Tientsin, and Tsingtao. The Japanese were said to have admitted that any such arrangement would violate the principles of the Nine Power Treaty but they contended that, since that treaty had been on trial for ten years and had failed, it was time to adopt new principles. The signatories of the Washington agreements—so their argument ran— had hoped that, free from outside interference, China would develop into a strong national state but, on the contrary, it had remained so disorganized as still to be little more than "a geographical name"; for the sake of the Chinese themselves, as well as the rest of the world, the foreign powers should therefore espouse a policy of intervention.[27]

Commenting upon the Reuters story, Johnson said that, before lending itself to a discussion of any such program, the United States government would, in his opinion, do well to consider its possible effect upon the Chinese. The situation of Americans in China would be "dangerous in the extreme" if the Chinese should "get into their heads" that America was in any way siding with Japan. "I feel certain," the Minister declared, "that the time is ripe for another disaster similar to the Boxer uprising unless we walk carefully with these sorely exasperated people." Johnson suggested that, instead of allowing the Japanese to implicate us in their "sinister" attempt to dismember China, we should issue a statement reaffirming the principles of the Nine Power Treaty.

Johnson's cable made a deep impression upon Secretary Stimson and apparently did much to encourage him to pursue a course upon which he had already started.[28] The Secretary had reacted sharply against Japan's repudiation of his initial proposal for a settlement, on February 4, and had about decided that he would not engage in any further efforts to conciliate the Japanese. For one thing, he had become convinced that negotiations with the Japanese were futile. But beyond that he was afraid of making some move which would be interpreted as condoning Japan's acts of aggression, thereby weakening the position which the United States government had taken in its nonrecognition note of January 7. Far from being prepared to weaken this position, the Secretary was rapidly arriving at the conclusion that the Japanese attack on Shanghai offered him an opportunity to strengthen it. For in contrast to the assault on Manchuria, which seemed a remote area of the world to most Westerners, the attack upon Shanghai had aroused a feeling of horror and revulsion in the nations of Europe as well as in America. It seemed possible, therefore, that if the United States issued another statement, comparable to that of January 7, it could obtain some of the support which had been so universally withheld from its earlier pronouncement.

On February 8, Secretary Stimson talked the situation over with President Hoover who expressed approval of the idea that the United States should "again test" European willingness to cooperate with America in the use of the nonrecognition doctrine.[29] It was agreed that if a new note were issued, it should be based upon a specific refusal to recognize changes resulting from violations of the Nine Power Treaty as well as the Paris Pact. The Secretary was eager to invoke the Nine Power Treaty because of his belief that, together with the Covenant of the League and the Kellogg-Briand Pact, the Washington Conference agreements formed the foundation of the postwar peace structure.[30] Moreover he thought it well to see that the public was informed that the Japanese were violating not only the more general principles contained in the pact but also the definite commitments embodied in the Nine Power Treaty.

In addition, Stimson wanted to invoke the Nine Power Treaty because he was convinced that it held "a special historical sanctity for China" which looked upon it as a "shelter and protection." A reaffirmation of its principles by the United States would encourage the Chinese at a moment when they were desperate and would also be a means of expressing the great sympathy which the American people felt for the Chinese people. Furthermore, it would serve our own interests in China by preserving the goodwill which the Chinese had always felt for the United States. Nelson Johnson's message was especially important in that it impressed upon the Secretary the need to take some immediate step to retain the goodwill of the Chinese in order to forestall a wave of antiforeignism in China which might include Americans.

On the afternoon of February 9, Stimson virtually reached the conclusion that he would definitely issue a statement reiterating the nonrecognition doctrine and applying it to violations of both the Nine Power Treaty and the Kellogg-Briand Pact. While, as earlier, he wanted to move quickly, he nevertheless decided on this occasion to make every possible effort to secure the cooperation of the British. The Secretary felt very deeply that if England and America acted together they would provide the leadership necessary to induce other countries to support the nonrecognition doctrine and, in addition, would be able to reassure the Chinese of their good faith.

On February 11, Stimson took up the task of trying to persuade the British to participate in his plan and for the next four days he engaged in a series of trans-Atlantic telephone conversations with Sir John Simon who had been made British Foreign Secretary in October.[31] Stimson explained at the outset his reasons for wanting to issue another statement and stressed the great importance that he attached to obtaining the collaboration of the British. Sir John Simon, on his part, said that his government was "most anxious" to cooperate with the United States. Nevertheless he indicated that England was in a somewhat different position from America in that it was a member of the Council of the League and would "have to be careful not to seem to be deserting the Council" which was itself engaged in considering the Sino-Japanese controversy. On February 12, Stimson sent the Foreign Secretary a tentative draft of a statement that he hoped Great Britain and the United States might release jointly. After discussing the draft with the Prime Minister, Sir John telephoned Stimson to say that he wanted to re-emphasize his government's desire to work in close association with the United States. He hastened to add, however, that the British felt the best procedure would be for Great Britain to persuade the Council of the League to make public a declaration to the effect that it would not recognize any changes brought about in violation of article X of the Covenant; the British could then participate in the Council's declaration while the United States made a separate statement which, following the Stimson draft, would deal with violations of the Paris Pact and the Nine Power Treaty.[32] Stimson objected at once to the procedure proposed by the British, declaring that unless England was willing to act in conjunction with America the entire scheme would lose its effectiveness. He further insisted that, for the reasons he had stated in the beginning, it was more important in the existing situation to invoke the Nine Power Treaty and the Kellogg-Briand Pact than any provisions of the Covenant of the League.[33] Finally, Stimson suggested that the British should sign "two papers," one together with the rest of the Council members, the other alongside of the United States. Despite the Secretary's vehemence, no decision was reached before the end of his talks with Sir John Simon on February 15. But on the following day, an official of the United States Embassy in London telephoned Stimson to inform him that Sir John had left for Geneva, where he expected to issue a nonrecognition note in common with the other members of the Council after which, to all appearances, the British did not intend to take any further action.[34] The Secretary replied that the British had "let us down," a statement which marked the end of his efforts to obtain their cooperation.

The British have always insisted that Stimson misunderstood their position. They say that their attitude was defined in a Foreign Office memorandum, given to our embassy in London the day that Sir John Simon departed for Geneva, which asserted,

It is thoroughly understood that the question whether other Powers can join in the American document is still in suspense. Sir John Simon has already told Mr. Stimson how keenly the British Government wished to keep in close cooperation with America over the whole field of the Far Eastern crisis and he is hopeful that the adherence of the Powers now at Geneva to the declaration proposed to be made by the Council of the League . . . might predispose those of them who are signatories to the Nine Power Treaty to associate themselves with the American démarche also.[35]

The British contention has been therefore that Sir John Simon had decided that, following the Council declaration (which was, in fact, issued on February 16), he would try to obtain the support of the other signatories of the Nine Power Treaty for Secretary Stimson's statement and that the British government was still considering a joint démarche when Stimson dropped the issue. But this explanation never satisfied Stimson. In the first place, he felt that in seeking to round up the other signatories of the Nine Power Treaty, the British were inviting the kind of delay that he wanted to avoid in view of the urgency of the situation. But, far more important, he believed that the British did not want to join the United States in assuming a role of leadership which inevitably incurred certain risks and that they had therefore decided to use various devices which would enable them to act in conjunction with a group of powers. Three years later, in a confidential memorandum to the Foreign Office in which he reviewed the controversy that had arisen from his talks with Sir John Simon in February 1932, the Secretary directly charged that at a time of world crisis in the Far East when the United States "thought it the wisest and most effective policy to walk openly hand in hand with the British Commonwealth of Nations and officially offered to do so, Great Britain preferred to take refuge in the inconspicuousness of . . . action" among a "flock" of nations.[36]

Whether justifiably or not, Stimson therefore felt left "out on a limb" by the British for the second time. Nevertheless he continued to take the lead among the nations concerned with the Sino-Japanese dispute and on February 23 published his well known letter to Senator Borah.[37] In this he appealed to other governments to adopt a nonrecognition policy based on the Pact of Paris and the Nine Power Treaty which he described as "harmonious" agreements through which the "conscience and public opinion of the world" could speak out in favor of an international system governed by law instead of force. In addition, in a classic restatement of the principles of the Nine Power Treaty, the Secretary declared in essence that the American people were still committed to the idea that China must be given the fullest opportunity to develop into a "modern and enlightened" state, free from outside interference, and that they had an "abiding faith in the future of the people of China." Stimson thus placed himself squarely in opposition to the expressed view of the Japanese that the principles of the Nine Power Treaty should be frankly discarded and that outside intervention was necessary for the good of the Chinese themselves. But the Secretary went even further and indirectly threatened Japan. For he intimated that since the treaties concluded at the Washington Conference of 1921 had been designed as interdependent parts of a whole, the violation of any one of these agreements tended to nullify the others; consequently, if Japan disregarded the Nine Power Treaty, the United States might feel that it was no longer bound by the Washington Naval Treaty and related agreements which had imposed severe restrictions upon our naval power in the Pacific.[38]

Stimson's appeal to other governments to adopt a nonrecognition policy for the first time received really substantial support when on March 11 the Assembly of the League, without dissent, adopted a resolution declaring that it was "incumbent upon the members of the League not to recognize any situation, treaty or agreement brought about by means contrary to the Covenant . . . or to the Pact of Paris."[39] After the passage of this resolution the activities at Geneva were largely limited to the efforts of the Committee of Nineteen to restore peaceful conditions at Shanghai until the end of May when this objective was attained.

Meanwhile, in Manchuria a Declaration of Independence had been proclaimed and the new state of "Manchukuo" had been formed. Nevertheless, the summer of 1932 was a period of relative quiet, while all the nations concerned with the Sino-Japanese conflict waited for the Lytton Commission, which was still conducting its investigations in the Far East, to finish its report. The report was finally made public on October 2.[40] This date roughly marks what for our purposes may be termed the third and last phase of the Manchurian crisis

1932

when the League rather than the United States government again ostensibly became the spearhead of diplomatic activity. For Stimson, the shift back to Geneva presented a well-defined problem. On the one hand, he wanted to avoid a recurrence of the situation which had arisen during the first phase of the Manchurian crisis, when he felt that the League had attempted to push, first, Prentiss Gilbert, and, then, General Dawes to the fore so that it could shirk its own responsibilities. Indeed, in this respect matters were worse than ever, since the intervening period had demonstrated that once America moved into an advance position, it was likely to find itself left there in splendid but unwanted isolation. Stimson therefore, as indicated at the outset of this chapter, returned to the formula that the initiative in dealing with the Sino-Japanese controversy rightfully belonged to the League, which possessed the machinery for the handling of international disputes, and that the American government was prepared to support the League but only after the nations at Geneva had already decided upon a course of action. On the other hand, the Secretary believed that the experience of the last months had shown that the members of the League were—as he stated in his diary—like a "flock of sheep" that scattered unless the shepherd constantly herded them in.[41] And since the United States alone seemed to have the courage to serve as shepherd, he felt that he must constantly prod the League into action, albeit as inconspicuously as possible.

Stimson welcomed the Lytton report as a "magnificent achievement."[42] While he admired its scope and thoroughness in general, he noted certain points in particular: that the commissioners emphasized the vital importance of protecting the existing peace system from encroachments; that they rejected every major argument advanced by Japan in justification of its aggression in China; and that they opposed the "maintenance and recognition" of the new regime in Manchuria and recommended the establishment of a government consistent with the sovereignty and administrative integrity of China. To the Secretary, these points suggested that the League should immediately adopt the Lytton report, which would amount to an outright condemnation of Japan, and, on the basis of the commissioners' findings, apply the nonrecognition policy to "Manchukuo."[43]

As might have been anticipated, the League did not move either as quickly or as decisively as Stimson wanted. The Council met on November 21 to consider the Lytton report and, after a week's discussion, referred it to the Assembly. The Assembly held a special session, in early December, in which many of the smaller nations advocated the adoption of the report and warned the larger powers, who appeared reluctant to act, that unless they were willing to uphold the principles of the Covenant, the League in its existing form could not survive.[44] In the end, the Assembly decided to submit the entire issue to the Committee of Nineteen, which was to try to bring about a settlement between Japan and China by conciliation. If its efforts failed, the Committee was to draw up proposals for further action, which were to be based on the Lytton report, and present them to the Assembly as soon as possible.

Stimson reacted strongly against the whole idea of engaging in any further efforts at conciliation. In a number of dispatches to Norman Davis and Hugh Wilson at Geneva, he said that when the original effort to settle the Sino-Japanese dispute by negotiation had failed he himself had resorted to the "more drastic method of principle" and that he did not propose to "go back and begin over again on conciliation."[45] Moreover he thought the League was merely trying to dodge the real issues by pretending to believe that a committee of conciliation could "accomplish anything effective" and that it was displaying "cowardice."

Meanwhile Stimson was becoming increasingly concerned about the possibility that the incoming administration in Washington would reverse the policy which he had been following in regard to the Manchurian crisis. The Secretary therefore visited Roosevelt early in January and discussed the Far Eastern situation at length. As a result, he felt confident that the President-elect shared his views and that American policy would be the same in the future as in the past.[46]

In the days following Secretary Stimson's talk with Roosevelt, events seemed rapidly to be moving toward a showdown. The Committee of Nineteen which had recessed in December was scheduled to reconvene on January 16. The chances were that it would soon decide to break off its efforts at conciliation, which to date had been wholly unsuccessful, and move on to the final stage of its task: recommending to the members of the Assembly what stand they should take as a consequence of the findings of the Lytton report. On January 10, Paul Hymans, who was president of both the Assembly and the Committee of Nineteen, informed Stimson in strictest confidence that there was every indication that the British and French were not prepared to take any strong stand against Japan; moreover that this was known to the Japanese who also seemed convinced that the United States government would not take any action since the present administration would soon go out of office.[47] Whether Hymans was correct or not in his estimate of Japanese opinion, the

Japanese certainly sought to impress upon the State Department that, under no circumstances, would they give ground at Geneva and that it was in the interests of other nations not to oppose Japan's policy in Manchuria. The Japanese ambassador in Washington had a long talk with Stanley K. Hornbeck, Chief of the Department's Division of Far Eastern Affairs, in which both men spoke with unusual frankness. To quote Hornbeck's official account:

> . . . the Ambassador said . . . that he would like to know what was going to be the attitude of the American Government when the League resumes its discussions. Mr. Hornbeck said that . . . the American Government is not a party to the discussions at Geneva and the Japanese Government is a party to those discussions: the important question is that of the attitude in which the Japanese Government may approach the renewal thereof . . . The Ambassador said that, however the matter may be looked at, the Japanese Government cannot make any change in the position which it has taken. He then went on to say that he wished that the world would close its eyes and turn its back and keep still, give Japan a chance to work the thing out in her own way, let her demonstrate the wisdom and success of her policy of restoring order in Manchuria and developing that area; Japan would make Manchuria prosperous; trade with Manchuria would increase; the United States would profit by it; in particular, there would be an increase in demand for American cotton and probably a demand for machinery and industrial supplies; the population of Manchuria would increase rapidly; the world would have reason to be pleased. Mr. Hornbeck said that the suggestion that the world close its eyes and turn its back amounted to asking the League of Nations to forget the Covenant, the whole world to forget the multilateral treaties; everybody to forget the efforts which have been made during recent years to substitute new methods for old in connection with the settling of international disputes . . . He said that he regretted, as he believed would all friends of Japan in this country, that Japanese thought should be traveling along that line . . ."[48]

To Secretary Stimson the situation as it was developing pointed primarily to the necessity of getting the League to adopt a firm position *vis-à-vis* Japan. The newspapers for some time had been commenting upon the silence of the United States government in regard to the Far Eastern crisis and speculating as to whether the present administration was about to alter its policy or whether it was perhaps loathe to say anything because it had been told confidentially that Roosevelt intended to follow a different line of action.[49] Therefore, just before the Committee of Nineteen was to resume its meetings, Stimson sent long messages to the British and French governments and to the authorities at Geneva assuring them that the policy of the current administration remained unchanged and that there was "every reason to believe" it would be continued by the new administration.[50] The Secretary stated further that since the League had jurisdiction over the Sino-Japanese case, it should exercise it, and that the United States government could not interfere without irritating the Japanese and provoking criticism at home. Yet Stimson went on to say that the Japanese were insisting that they could not make any concessions and were even asking the world to "close its eyes" and "turn its back" for an indefinite period while they worked out the situation in the Far East in their own way. Such a demand could only be conceded "at the expense to the world of a shameful abandonment of principles, stultification of treaty provisions and peace machinery, and, on the part of the League, complete loss of face." In his opinion, the Secretary declared, the League was in the position of a Court of Equity which, having commissioned a Master to make a report of the findings, had now received the report and must proceed to the task of approving it after which it should logically apply the "judgment of non-recognition . . . to Manchukuo."

In the end the action of the League accorded with the Secretary's wishes. The Committee of Nineteen soon acknowledged that its efforts at conciliation could not succeed in the face of Japan's intransigence. On February 21 it submitted to the Assembly an impressive report, based upon the work of the Lytton Commission, which placed the responsibility for the hostilities in Manchuria and Shanghai upon the Japanese and recommended the evacuation of the Japanese troops from the territory that they had taken in Manchuria. At the same time the report made a wide variety of proposals, one of which was that Japan and China should open negotiations for the sake of establishing a new regime in Manchuria under Chinese sovereignty.[51] Meanwhile the members of the League were to continue not to recognize the existing regime in Manchuria "either *de jure* or *de facto*." On February 24, in an atmosphere laden with the feeling that an event of extraordinary significance was taking place, the Assembly met and adopted the committee's report. The Japanese delegate, after making a brief but bitter speech, walked out of the meeting. This sensational gesture was followed within a few weeks by Japan's formal withdrawal from the League.

Stimson believed that the Assembly's action marked a "great day when for the first time in history the united group of nations" had "condemned morally another great nation."[52] His first thought was to issue a press release in support of the Assembly's stand but he was almost prevented from doing so by President Hoover.

Hoover, who had continuously opposed the use of anything but moral sanctions against Japan, had been alarmed by a message, received the day before the Assembly meeting, from Ambassador Grew in Tokyo, in which Grew suggested that even moral sanctions were creating an amount of hostility toward the United States in Japan that might explode into the war which the President wanted, above all, to avoid.[53] Grew had taken up his post in Tokyo in the early summer of 1932 and throughout the following months had sent the State Department numerous cables describing what he termed the "tornado" of anti-American propaganda gripping Japan.[54] The main points that the Ambassador made were: that the Japanese government was determined to go through with its Manchurian venture "regardless of foreign opposition of whatever nature"; that, through propaganda, it was creating a war psychology comparable to that which the German government had built up in 1914; and that this war psychology was specifically directed against the United States while the part that the nations of the League were playing in regard to the Manchurian crisis was disregarded. Grew asserted also that the Japanese were convinced that the United States was itself planning a war against Japan and that it was motivated by a desire to get "absolute control of the Far East" although it pretended to be concerned over the threat to the world peace machinery presented by Japan's actions in China. In September the ambassador forwarded to Washington a long report on the "great increase in anti-American feeling" in Japan which included some startling information, as in the following passage:

The press and many associations have repeatedly warned the United States against meddling in the Manchurian affair. As the time for the publication of the League of Nations report draws near, these warnings are more frequent. In addition to this, the number of articles and books dealing with the possibility of a war with the United States have increased in number. Many of them, from the facts and figures they contain, clearly show that the writer at least has an understanding with the Army and Navy Departments, if not access to their files. All of them deal with the possible war in the Pacific and Manchuria's connection therewith, under such titles as 'What effect will the Manchurian Affair have on the War in the Pacific?' 'Japan's Invasion of the Philippines,' 'Japanese Invasion of Hawaii,' 'Blowing Up the Panama Canal,' 'Air Raid on Alaska,' etc. Fifteen of the leading magazines have carried 36 such articles since the first of the year and, to our knowledge, 13 books on this subject have appeared . . . eight in 1932. One of the latest has gone through 50 editions, while two others have had 20 editions . . . The articles in the newspapers enlarging upon American interference in Japan's schemes . . . must run into the thousands.[55]

In October the dispatches from the Embassy in Tokyo received support from General McCoy, who on arriving in Geneva recounted to American officials there the impressions that he had received while working on the Lytton Commission in the Far East.[56] The general stated that, in his opinion, only "good luck" had so far prevented the occurrence of some incident which would so inflame the "fanatical sentiment against the United States" in Japan as to have serious repercussions in America and "perhaps create a situation which could not be controlled." He also supported Grew's frequently expressed view that the hostility of the Japanese, whether in government circles or throughout the country, was being channeled against the United States. When asked whether he could suggest any way of remedying the situation, General McCoy said that he could not.

It was against this background that Grew sent to Washington his cable of February 23 which so alarmed President Hoover.[57] Reviewing the factors which he believed should be taken into consideration by the United States government before deciding upon any move in respect to Japan, the ambassador asserted that the Japanese were "fully prepared to fight rather than to surrender to moral or other pressure from the West" and that the "moral obloquy of the rest of the world" only served to strengthen their determination. Any tendency on the part of the Japanese government to compromise would almost certainly result in assassinations, if not in internal revolution. With great earnestness Grew warned,

. . . it may be said that a large section of the public and the Army has been led by military propaganda to believe that eventual war between the United States and Japan or Russia and Japan or both is inevitable. The military and naval machines are in a state of high efficiency and are rapidly being strengthened. They possess complete self-confidence and arrogance. The Navy is becoming more bellicose. In the present temper of the Army and Navy and the public there is always the risk that any serious incident tending to inflame public opinion might lead Japan to radical steps without counting the cost thereof.

The "foregoing" views, the ambassador added, represented the opinion of all the principal members of his staff, as well as most of his diplomatic colleagues and other foreigners in Tokyo.

Because of Ambassador Grew's wire, the President, upon receipt of the news of the Assembly's action on February 24, suggested to Stimson that it might "relax a considerable amount of present tension" if the United States publicly declared that it would not "ever engage in sanctions other than that of public opinion."[58] Stimson replied that he did not believe any such declaration would have the effect the President desired and that, unless we supported the position that the League had with so much effort adopted, the nations represented at Geneva would feel that we had "let them down." In the end Hoover yielded, and on February 25 the State Department issued a statement endorsing the stand which had been taken by the Assembly.[59]

The action of the Assembly and the United States did not succeed in mitigating Japan's policies in any way. Not only did the Japanese withdraw from the League, they also embarked upon a new military campaign in China which was designed to conquer the province of Jehol and bring the Japanese armies down to the Great Wall itself. As the terrain of Jehol was exceedingly mountainous and therefore easy to defend, the Japanese forces expected to have trouble in advancing and planned their operations on a relatively large scale. The Chinese armies, however, collapsed almost immediately so that the province fell to the Japanese within less than two weeks. Japanese troops occupied Chengteh, the provincial capital, on the day that Roosevelt was inaugurated as president in Washington.

In the first months of the Roosevelt administration confusion prevailed in the State Department.[60] The President was inevitably absorbed in his attempt to solve the problems created by the economic depression, the enormity of which overshadowed all else. Cordell Hull appeared to those around him to be bewildered by the complexity of his new responsibilities and to cling to the habit, characteristic of a politician, of parceling out his time to miscellaneous callers bent upon furthering their own interests. The only expert on international affairs with ready access to the Secretary was Norman Davis, a fellow Tennessean and old friend, upon whose advice Hull was to rely heavily throughout the next years.[61] As to the State Department staff and the Foreign Service, most of the higher officials— whether in Washington, Geneva, Tokyo, or Peiping—who had been closely associated with developments related to the Sino-Japanese conflict during the Hoover regime were retained by the Roosevelt administration. It was these men who soon showed that the Manchurian crisis had left them with a deep sense of disillusionment.

This disillusionment first became apparent during the course of several interrelated episodes which occurred in the spring of 1933. Hoover, during his term in office, had been anxious to get Congress to pass legislation that would give the President the authority to prevent the export of arms and ammunition to any country or countries he might designate in case of war or a threat of war.[62] Beginning with 1932, he was particularly interested in using such authority himself in connection with the dispute between Paraguay and Bolivia over the Chaco. At the outset, Congress took the position that if the United States adopted an arms embargo and other nations refused to follow suit, American munitions manufacturers would be placed at an unfair disadvantage. This solicitude for our munitions makers is remarkable when compared with the attitude adopted after the Nye investigations started less than two years later; nevertheless it was sufficiently strong at this time to postpone action by the administration. Finally, in January 1933, Hoover asked Congress to confer upon the President the power "in his discretion to limit or forbid shipment of arms . . . in cases where special undertakings of cooperation can be secured with the principal arms-manufacturing nations." A resolution in keeping with the President's request was unanimously passed by the Senate on January 19 and thereafter introduced into the House, where it was referred to the Committee on Foreign Affairs.

Stimson appeared before the committee and addressed himself not only to the problem of the munitions makers but also the entire question of neutrality.[63] This was an issue which, as his audience well knew, had become a very important factor in his thinking. In the preceding August, the Secretary had given a speech, entitled "The Pact of Paris—Three Years of Development," which had attracted world-wide attention largely because he asserted that the pact had completely altered the old concept of neutrality based upon the idea that a neutral must not take sides between belligerents. Stimson's thesis was that, since the pact declared that a resort to war was illegal, any nation found to be an aggressor was essentially a "lawbreaker" and as such could not claim the right to be treated impartially.[64] In speaking to the Committee on Foreign Affairs, the Secretary related this theory to the resolution under discussion by stating that the United States government would not impose an arms embargo exclusively on one of the nations that was party to a dispute unless a "comprehensive group of important states," after investigation and consultation, had pronounced that nation the aggressor. In that event, the United States would be freed from the traditional obligations of a neutral and, indeed, if a general embargo were declared, would "practically" have to participate in order to preserve its "national dignity and standing as a peaceful nation."

The committee was only partially persuaded by Stimson and before long the House adjourned.[65] When Congress reopened in February, President Hoover, in a special message, again urged the enactment of legislation similar to that which he had suggested earlier, but there was scarcely time to consider the matter before his term came to an end.

In the first hectic week that the Roosevelt administration was in office, it was decided to continue the policy started by Hoover.[66] A special message to Congress was drafted comparable to President Hoover's, but the draft was set aside immediately after its completion on the grounds that a presidential pronouncement would place too much emphasis upon the whole embargo question and that it would therefore be better to write letters to the chairman of the two foreign relations committees on Capitol Hill. The letters were dispatched, but no sooner had they reached their destination than they were recalled by the State Department for fear that they were too strong and might arouse antagonism. It was thereupon announced that the Under Secretary of State would testify before the House Committee, which had already begun to consider a new arms embargo resolution, but subsequently his appearance was canceled.

This unusual display of indecision looked for a moment as though it might be decidedly costly.[67] Taking advantage of the delay caused by the administration's vacillation, the House Committee, which contained some of the most vocal isolationists in the country, held hearings consisting mainly of testimony provided by certain eminent jurists who were probably the most impassioned believers of their time in classical concepts of neutrality. But—again in remarkable contrast to the events which were to occur shortly thereafter—the appeals for a strict neutrality had little effect upon the House, which on April 17 passed the arms embargo resolution by a vote of 253 to 19.

Meanwhile the British had made a wholly unexpected move.[68] On February 27, Sir John Simon announced in Parliament that the British government would temporarily forbid the export of munitions to both Japan and China until such time as it had consulted with other governments to determine whether they would enter into some sort of an international agreement. The British measure was adopted under pressure from different political groups at home which under the stimulus of the League's acceptance of the Lytton report and the Japanese military campaign in Jehol, were criticizing their government for not taking further action. For the most part their demands were for an arms embargo, but they differed sharply in the kind of embargo they wanted. The believers in vigorous efforts to stop aggression wished, for example, to cut off shipments of munitions to Japan alone as a form of sanctions, while those who were pacifist-minded advocated the cessation of all trade in implements of war whether to the Japanese or the Chinese. Government spokesmen in Parliament persistently argued that, in any event, an embargo was useless if undertaken solely by the United Kingdom, a point which was generally conceded. The same spokesmen, however, seemed unable to convince their hearers that there was little chance of obtaining the cooperation of other countries, especially the key country—the United States— which had as yet not even passed legislation that would give the President the authority to proclaim an embargo. To be doubly certain of its position, the British government had asked Stimson whether the United States would join in a ban on munitions and the Secretary had affirmed that it could not do so until and unless Congress provided the President with the necessary powers.[69] He had indicated furthermore that the State Department was generally opposed to an embargo because, if it were enforced against both sides in the conflict, it would injure the Chinese and not the Japanese, who were well supplied with armaments, and if it were applied against Japan only it would probably result in the Japanese engaging in retaliatory measures such as declaring a blockade of the China coast. The decision of the British government to forbid the export of arms pending the opportunity to explore whether an international agreement was possible seems therefore to have been motivated by a desire to demonstrate conclusively to its domestic critics that other nations were not prepared to cooperate in an embargo and that the whole idea of an embargo was impractical.

Whatever their motives, the British proceeded to initiate discussion of an arms embargo by asking the reconstituted Committee of Nineteen to consider the question. Following the endorsement of the Lytton Report, the Assembly had decided to appoint a committee to follow developments in the Far East and aid the members of the League to concert "their action and their attitude among themselves and with nonmember states."[70] To fulfill these purposes, the Committee of Nineteen was enlarged and given the title of Advisory Committee, and the United States was asked to cooperate in its work. One of the first acts of the Roosevelt administration was to authorize Hugh Wilson to participate in the meetings of the committee without, however, the right to vote and with the explicit understanding that Wilson's attendance must not be regarded as impairing the freedom of the United States to act independently.[71]

As the discussions in the Advisory Committee were getting underway, the British government on March 13 lifted its embargo, stating that informal inquiries had revealed that there was no prospect of reaching an international agreement on the export of arms to the Far East in the near future but that it intended "vigourously to pursue the conversations" which were beginning at Geneva in an effort to arrive at an understanding.[72] But no understanding was ever reached, and from the viewpoint of American officials the discussion in the Advisory Committee seemed largely a repetition of the discouraging experiences which they had had in cooperating with other nations throughout the Manchurian crisis. At the end of March, Wilson cabled to the State Department that his impression of the debates in the committee was that the other powers would not make any move in relation to an arms embargo unless Congress passed legislation enabling the President to act; even then, the arms-producing states would wait until Roosevelt had adopted a specific policy after which they would merely follow suit.[73] The State Department promptly answered, in no uncertain terms, that the United States government did not intend to "assume the role of mentor to the League" which evoked the reply from Wilson that "Nothing was further from my mind than to urge such a course."[74]

The fact of the matter was that on the day of his initial cable to Washington Wilson had written a friend in the State Department discussing the whole question of America's adopting "the role of mentor" toward other nations in respect to the Far East. However, to understand his comments fully, it is necessary to consider for a moment various developments which were taking place in connection with the Disarmament Conference that was also currently meeting at Geneva.

The Disarmament Conference had opened in February 1932 and remained in session until July, at which time it recessed for six months.[75] A whole series of plans had been advanced by various nations, including the United States. For the most part, the proposals were designed to solve two major problems: security and the reduction and limitation of armaments. The French, haunted by memories of the disasters of 1914, refused to enter into a disarmament agreement until the other powers guaranteed them against attack by signing some sort of security pact which would strengthen the already existing peace machinery. The Germans, on the other hand, were opposed to more security arrangements and insisted upon the immediate negotiation of a convention on armaments which would have the effect of freeing them from the provisions of the Versailles Treaty that had reduced their military strength far below that of the victorious powers.[76] By the time the conference reconvened in February 1933, the differences between the French and Germans had been accentuated by the rise of Hitler to power. Nevertheless, the French again submitted a plan with provisions for disarmament and for treaties of mutual assistance. The latter were once more opposed by the Germans and their supporters. In an effort to break the deadlock, Prime Minister Ramsay MacDonald went to Geneva where he appealed to the members of the conference to "turn the tide of fear" which was quickly rising in Europe by making a contribution to disarmament and the whole problem of the "organization of peace." At the same time the British offered a compromise program that contained some of the disarmament features recommended by the French but substituted for the French treaties of mutual assistance a consultative agreement which provided that, in case of a violation of the Kellogg-Briand Pact, the signatories of that pact would confer to determine which of the parties to the dispute was guilty of aggression. The question of what action should be taken against the aggressor was left open but the presumption was that some sort of military or economic sanctions might be applied.

Wilson's letter to Washington was written shortly after the British plan had been put forward and was based on the idea that, as a result of the Disarmament Conference and the Manchurian crisis, the United States should take a new look at its foreign policy.[77] Wilson felt that events had shown that the "conscious" desire to "build up a machinery for the maintenance of peace, a machinery for the prevention of war, a machinery to make warfare too hot for aggression" was "all concentrated" on the European continent; no comparable interest in the organization of peace existed in Asia, or the Americas, or—so far as was known—in Africa. Experience had, however, also demonstrated that for the European nations to run the risks involved in instigating international action against an aggressor, the trouble must occur within the European continent where their "immediate and vital interests" were involved. In "any action outside the Continent of Europe the United States" would "inevitably be maneuvered into being the initiator in reality if not in form." Under these circumstances, if the United States wanted to contribute to the strengthening of the peace machinery and still avoid the dangers inherent in assuming the leadership of any movement against an aggressor, it should adopt a regional approach which would enable it to commit itself to certain policies in the event of war in Europe while remaining uncommitted if hostilities broke out elsewhere. Concretely, Wilson suggested that the United States government should assist in solving the security problem by offering to sign a treaty pledging that, in case of a breach of the peace in Europe, it (a) would confer with the European states along the lines proposed by the British, and (b) would not, by insisting upon its neutral rights, "obstruct any collective action these states might elect to adopt against an aggressor." In practice this would mean that the United States would forego its right to trade with the nation being subjected to sanctions.

Wilson subsequently presented his views to Norman Davis, who had just arrived in Geneva to serve as the new head of the United States Delegation to the Disarmament Conference appointed by President Roosevelt. Davis and the other American delegates were immediately willing to accept Wilson's suggestions.[78] In addition, they felt that a regional approach should also be used to solve the disarmament problem. Their argument was that any realistic estimate of the situation must recognize that the United States was greatly hampered in its efforts at disarmament by its position in relation to Japan. For America could not accept restrictions on certain aspects of its military power—especially its land and air strength—unless the Japanese were willing to adopt analogous measures, which, for the present, was obviously not likely to be the case. On the other hand, conditions in Europe could not be stabilized until the European nations had reduced their armaments to a substantial degree. The best solution seemed therefore to be, first, to negotiate a universal disarmament treaty, embodying points that lent themselves to general agreement, and, thereafter, to conclude regional treaties, limited to the European states, which would contain provisions that were too drastic for the Japanese to endorse.

In mid-April Davis sent a number of long and unusually carefully reasoned dispatches to the President and the Secretary of State outlining the delegation's ideas about a security pact and universal and regional disarmament agreements.[79] Roosevelt was, however, still too preoccupied with monetary and other financial and economic questions to do more than reply that he believed that, since a treaty had to go to the Senate, Davis' proposals concerning a security pact should take the form of a declaration which would have the validity of a Monroe Doctrine.[80] Some ten days later, Roosevelt discussed the entire situation at the Disarmament Conference with Prime Minister Mac-Donald, who had arrived in Washington on an official visit.[81] Much to the distress of the experts in the State Department who were working on the Disarmament Conference, the President and the Prime Minister conducted their conversations in private except for the presence of Sir Robert Vansittart of the British Foreign Office. Precisely what transpired seems never to have become known to the State Department, but it was immediately apparent that MacDonald was attempting to persuade the President that to adopt a regional approach would be a mistake. As the State Department experts themselves were thoroughly convinced of the soundness of this approach, they did their best to counteract the Prime Minister's influence but found it impossible to see Roosevelt under circumstances that allowed for frank talk. In the end, the President wired Davis that he intended to "make another genuine effort at a universal approach to both disarmament and security" but that if this failed he would proceed within the more limited scope that Davis had been advocating.[82]

The upshot was that, as far as the reduction and limitation of arms were concerned, the United States government for the most part supported plans that had already been submitted at Geneva.[83] But in dealing with the security issue, the administration decided to take an unusually important step and authorize Davis to make a statement based upon his proposal for a security pact; however, the proposal was to be altered so as to conform to the President's desire to give it the character of a Monroe Doctrine and his insistence upon a universal approach. Accordingly, on May 22, in a speech before the Disarmament Conference, Norman Davis made the announcement which was to be so frequently quoted in the future,

In addition I wish to make it clear that we are ready not only to do our part toward the substantive reduction of armaments, but, if this is effected by general international agreement, we are also prepared to contribute in other ways to the organization of peace. In particular we are willing to consult with other states in case of a threat to peace, with a view to averting conflict. Further than that, in the event that the states, in conference, determine that a state has been guilty of a breach of the peace in violation of its international obligations and take measures against the violator, then, if we concur in the judgment rendered as to the responsible and guilty party, we will refrain from any action tending to defeat such collective effort which these states may thus make to restore peace.[84]

From the viewpoint of our Far Eastern policy, the significance of the episode which culminated in Davis' statement is that the administration was prepared to make a major contribution to the peace system but that the disillusionment over the Manchurian crisis was sufficiently great to bring American officials close to limiting that contribution to Europe.

Davis' declaration undoubtedly marked one of the greatest advances toward internationalism made by the United States in the period between the two world wars.[85] But it was immediately followed by a retreat into isolationism. The arms embargo resolution which had been passed by the House in mid-April was still pending in the Senate. On May 10, Key Pittman, as Chairman of the Committee on Foreign Relations, had sent Secretary Hull a letter informing him that the Committee members had raised certain questions concerning the resolution.[86] Besides expressing continued concern over the possible effect of the resolution upon our munitions makers, the senators felt that if the President had the authority to stop the shipment of arms exclusively to one side of a conflict he might use his power in a way that would involve us in hostilities. They also contended that the nations at Geneva, having just accepted the Lytton report which amounted to a denunciation of Japan, might ask the President to join them in forbidding the export of arms to the Japanese which would create an "embarrassing situation." On May 17, a member of the State Department in a secret session of the committee, read a long statement in support of the resolution.[87] In respect to the Far East, the statement declared that the administration had no intention of taking any action against the shipment of arms to Japan if only because it was convinced that the chief result would be a Japanese blockade of the China coast. The senators may well have been persuaded, but if so they quickly changed their minds. For only a few days after Davis delivered his speech at Geneva, the Foreign Relations Committee amended the resolution to provide that, if the President decreed an embargo, it would have to be applied against both sides in a war, equally. As Hull asserted in a letter to the President, the amendment was "directly in conflict" with the policy enunciated by Norman Davis.[88] Whether, if that policy had been put upon a regional basis, the senators would have been more likely to accept the amendment in its original form is an interesting question in view of the far-reaching consequences of their decision which obviously opened the door to the rigid neutrality laws of the mid-1930's.

In any event, the disillusionment arising out of the Manchurian crisis was not solely reflected in the discussion over the wisdom of adopting a regional policy. It received what was perhaps its most bitter expression in the private writings of the two foremost representatives of the United States in the Far East: Minister Johnson in Peiping and Ambassador Grew in Tokyo.

Nelson Johnson had come to Peiping as Minister in 1929 after four years of service in Washington as head of the Far Eastern Division of the State Department. His letters from Peiping to friends at home were full of political comments which tended to fall into the category of the philosophical or of the earthy, shrewd, and realistic. It was in the latter vein that, in January 1933, he wrote to his friend and colleague Stanley Hornbeck in Washington to say that he saw no possibility of either the United States or the League powers being able to bring about a settlement between Japan and China in the present mood of the Japanese militarists.[89] The Japanese were perpetually giving assurances that they would not initiate any further hostilities against China, but as soon as the Chinese did anything whatever, the Japanese charged them with provocative action and embarked upon "punitive" measures. Not mincing his words, Johnson declared,

Personally, I am thoroughly disgusted with the whole hypocritical mess that the Japanese have made of the . . . League machinery, the Washington

Treaty and the Kellogg Pact. They have used every bit of the machinery that implied a certain standard of international sportsmanship until the whole business is a stench in the nostrils.

At about the same time the Minister wrote in a similar tone to one of the sponsors of the Kellogg Pact, former Secretary of State Kellogg, who had been Johnson's superior when he was chief of the Far Eastern Division.[90] After reviewing the events of the Manchurian crisis in great detail, Johnson stated in conclusion,

All of this makes me feel very much discouraged over the future in respect to the League Covenant and the Washington Treaty of 1922 and the Kellogg Pact. It seems to me that it is all very well to talk about public opinion and its effect; but when I was a boy in Oklahoma the only influence that had any effect on the gentlemen who used to come to town on Saturday, get drunk, and then take command of the streets with their guns, was a public opinion that was willing to step out in the street equally armed with a gun and do some shooting. Perhaps there is no parallel. But I have a feeling that in so far as Asia is concerned the Japanese have within the past years made ashes in the mouths of every thinking European out of the League machinery, the Washington treaties, and the Kellogg Pact.

Over two years later, in another letter to Kellogg, Johnson said that he was still convinced that the idealism which had inspired the Kellogg Pact could not prevail unless the people who held these ideals were "prepared to go and shoot it out with the drunk who now confuses our thoughts."[91] Indeed the one benefit that Johnson felt had been derived from the Manchurian crisis was that it had revealed conditions as they actually existed. In an exchange of views with Tyler Dennett, he wrote that, as a result of the entire Manchurian affair,

We know where Japan stands, we know where the East stands, and we know our own minds. Our people know that we live in a world in which the kind of thing that was provided for by the Covenant of the League, the Washington settlements, and the Kellogg Pact is utterly useless and impossible . . . It is a disillusion; it is terrible, but real. We owe thanks to the Japanese for awakening us to the realities of the situation.[92]

Ambassador Grew's opinions were primarily expressed in his diary, which he wrote in installments that were circulated among a small group of people, including some members of the State Department. In January 1933, having been in Japan for about half a year, Grew settled down to take stock of his own views on the Manchurian crisis. At the beginning he recorded that from a purely practical point of view he felt there was much to be said in favor of the occupation of Manchuria by the Japanese.[93] The new government of "Manchukuo" would probably establish law and order in an area which was presently in a state of chaos, having been subjected to the rule of "rapacious" Chinese warlords and continuous "internecine strife." Moreover, properly administered, "Manchukuo" would serve as a buffer state which would stop the spread of Bolshevism eastward. On the other hand, the Japanese conquest of Manchuria could scarcely be reconciled with ethical considerations such as the necessity of safeguarding the peace structure of the postwar world. Grew declared that he favored the idea of "passive punishment" of Japan and believed that if the signatories of the Kellogg Pact stuck together in their determination not to recognize the fruits of aggression a long step would have been taken toward providing the moral sanctions which the Pact envisaged.

But less than two months later, when the League endorsed the Lytton report, Grew declared, in a new installment of his diary, that he had changed his mind as he felt he was bound to do "from time to time on maturer thought and consideration."[94] The more he had mulled over the developments related to the Manchurian crisis, the more he had been inclined to question whether the peace machinery which the world had been trying "so earnestly and painstakingly to erect these last fourteen years" was "basically sound . . . or rather basically practical." He had ceased to think that the Kellogg Pact or any similar agreement could be effectively supported by moral sanctions. When a nation was "beset with a war psychology" the moral obloquy of the rest of the world would only tend to strengthen, not weaken, its warlike temper, as witness the situation in Japan. The ambassador stated further,

Then if moral ostracism is ineffective, or likely to be ineffective, what more can we do? How can we implement the Kellogg Pact? Certainly not by force of arms, which would be contrary to the very principle for which the Kellogg Pact stands. The great war to end wars has signally failed in that particular purpose. If other world wars are the only method of protecting our peace structure, then we had better abandon that structure here and now, because civilization itself will be in jeopardy. Severance of diplomatic relations would be futile unless followed by other steps. Arms embargoes are generally ineffective in practice. In the present case they would simply aid the aggressor. There remains an economic and financial boycott. Probably futile in practice. In the present case, an economic boycott would simply cause Japan to occupy those parts of China whence needed supplies could be obtained, with the resultant risk of a general world conflagration. Financially Japan cannot even now obtain a loan abroad . . . but she still carries on.

The ambassador concluded that the existing peace machinery was "magnificent in theory" but "ineffective in practice" and that it was

ineffective because it was "superficial." It should concern itself with
the "facts, conditions, and circumstances" that led to international
conflicts and not with attempting to deal with those conflicts by
collective action after they had already erupted.

In general it may be said that the disillusionment evident among
American officials, following the Manchurian incident, resulted primarily from what was widely regarded as the ineffectiveness of the
existing peace system. Men like Johnson and Grew concluded that
the events of the Manchurian incident had not only shown that the
peace structure was ineffective but had demonstrated that the whole
internationalist effort to solve the problem of establishing and maintaining world order was virtually bound to prove futile. Other
American officials such as, for example, Norman Davis, while retaining
their faith in the internationalist movement were nevertheless discouraged about the possibility of developing a peace system capable
of preventing or curtailing military aggression in the Far East or,
in fact, in any area outside of Europe. Apart from the weakness of
the peace structure, there was also a strong sense of disillusionment
in Washington as a consequence of the attempt of the United States
to cooperate with other nations in the settlement of the Manchurian
crisis. To most members of the State Department it seemed as though
the ceaseless controversy which had taken place between the interested governments over the question of initiative and leadership
could only mean that if America participated in any international
action related to the Far East, it would find itself in the position
of having to assume most of the responsibility irrespective of its
own best interests.

TENTATIVE STEPS TOWARD A NEW POLICY

Following the occupation of Jehol in early March, the Japanese
armies paused for a moment before launching a new offensive. But
in April they began to move southward once more and, despite unexpectedly strong Chinese resistance, took some of the passes along the
Great Wall. By the third week in April there were strong rumors,
however, that the Japanese did not want to advance any further
immediately and would concentrate on trying to destroy the Chinese
military units in the Great Wall area. On April 19, the Japanese
Chargé d'Affaires at Peiping called on the British Minister, Sir Miles
Lampson, whose skill as a negotiator was well known, and asked whether
he would assist in attempting to arrange for an armistice.[95] On the
following day a prominent Chinese, who was close to Wang Ching-

wei, then Premier of the Nanking government, came to see Sir Miles with the same request. The British Minister indicated that he wished to talk the matter over with his American colleague but that he would consider the possibility of mediating between the Chinese and Japanese if the Premier would state the terms that the Nanking government was willing to accept. Shortly thereafter, Sir Miles received word from the Chinese Minister of Foreign Affairs to the effect that he was not interested in any effort at mediation but thought that the foreign powers should warn the Japanese that if they advanced into China below the Great Wall they would be inviting international complications. Minister Johnson thereupon cabled the State Department that, since the Chinese officials could not agree among themselves, he and Sir Miles had concluded that it would be unwise for Great Britain and the United States to take any action in regard to mediation.

Yet the question of mediation was again raised in early May when Wang Ching-wei instructed the Chinese Minister in Washington to find out whether the United States would not make some move toward ending the Sino-Japanese hostilities.[96] A long talk ensued between Minister Sze and Stanley Hornbeck, in which the latter received the impression that the Chinese still did not have any definite plans but were primarily clinging to the hope that President Roosevelt would offer either to assume the role of mediator or to take the lead in organizing a movement among the large powers to call upon the Japanese to stop their advance into North China. In addition, toward the middle of May a cable was received from the United States Ambassador in Rome stating that Mussolini had told him with "great emphasis" that, in his opinion, Japan presented a greater threat to international peace than any other nation and that if she gained control over China (which he appeared to regard as almost inevitable) the "whole world would be menaced."[97] On the basis of Mussolini's assertions, the suggestion was made within the State Department that the United States government might urge the Italians to initiate a joint effort, on the part of Italy, England, France, and America, to settle the conflict in North China.[98]

Hornbeck discussed the North China situation in a number of long memoranda addressed to the Secretary.[99] These memoranda were characteristic of many which were to follow and which formed part of a large body of similar documents that Hornbeck wrote while in office. Inclined to drive himself tirelessly into analyzing every aspect of any important problem with which he was confronted, Hornbeck in his communications to the Secretary customarily set forth in detail all the arguments which he felt justified the particular policy he was recommending. In connection with the situation in North China, Hornbeck's main proposal was that Japan's military aggression in that area should be allowed to run its course; "given time," he said, "the flood tide of her invasion will reach its height and the ebb will follow." Among the points which he made in support of this proposal was that, if left unchecked, Japan's advance in North China might at least help to achieve that which the Manchurian crisis had not been able to accomplish: the enlightenment of other governments and peoples concerning the importance of the existing peace system and the extent to which Japan was damaging that system.[100] ("Enlightenment with regard to this matter," Hornbeck wrote, "comes slowly. Some people learn by observation, reasoning, and the use of the imagination. Others learn only by experience.") Concerning the United States, Hornbeck's main argument was that a settlement in North China might be detrimental to the United States as it would enable the Japanese to consolidate their position on the continent of Asia and prepare for their next move—"either further coercion of China, or conflict with Russia, or conflict with the United States." "In the long run," Hornbeck declared, "our interests would be best served by a complete exposure of Japan's program, her strength and/or weakness, and as complete as possible involvement of herself in the situation" in North China.[101] In respect to China, Hornbeck's most important contention was that the conclusion of a Sino-Japanese agreement would involve "a capitulation on the part of China in terms of recognition of the new *status quo* in Manchuria and a pledge to refrain from any further efforts to upset the *status quo*." China was "between the devil and the deep sea: the devil being the prospect of further military adversities and the deep sea being the potential conclusion of a disastrous 'peace'."

Hornbeck also considered the question of what the United States should do if the powers decided that instead of letting Japanese aggression in North China run its course they would interfere to prevent further hostilities through mediation or otherwise.[102] Above all, he felt, the United States should not take the initiative in regard to any cooperative action. The initiative should be left to the League or to such nations as Great Britain, France, and Italy—"we are in a position of jeopardy," he said, "in relations with Japan more delicate than is theirs."[103]

Hornbeck stated specifically in his memoranda that he was expressing not only his own opinions but also those of other officers in the Far Eastern Division. In general, the division was rapidly achieving a greater influence within the administration at this time than it had exercised under Stimson. Hornbeck's memoranda were sent to the President who apparently was in agreement with them. As a consequence, no action was taken by the United States in regard to the situation in North China. Reference was, however, made to that situation in a statement issued on May 19 by Roosevelt in conjunction with Dr. T. V. Soong.[104] Dr. Soong had come to America for a brief visit en route to the World Economic Conference to be held in England in June and had urged once more that the United States "do something" to end the fighting in North China. The joint statement, nonetheless, was confined to the category that the President in his more irreverent moods liked caustically to characterize as "completely pious." The passage dealing with the North China situation read:

We agree that economic stability cannot be achieved without political tranquility and that economic disarmament can be attained only in a world in which military disarmament is possible. It is our ardent hope that peace may be assured and that to this end practical measures of disarmament may soon be adopted. In this connection our thoughts naturally have turned to the serious developments in the Far East, which have disturbed the peace of the world during the past 2 years. There the military forces of two great nations have been engaged in destructive hostilities. We trust that these hostilities may soon cease in order that the present effort of all the nations of the world to re-establish political and economic peace may succeed.

Meanwhile the Japanese armies had renewed their offensive in North China and pushed down into the open plains below the Great Wall, where the Chinese military front collapsed. The Chinese themselves counted their casualties at some 30,000 and admitted frankly that they were at the end of their resources. The day that the Roosevelt-Soong statement was issued the Japanese forces reached a point only thirteen miles north of Peiping. On the same day Nelson Johnson cabled from Peiping that an airplane, believed to be a Japanese bomber with "bombs in racks," had circled over the city for half an hour.[105] The department answered that in its opinion this incident or any similar incident might properly form the basis of a protest by the diplomatic body but that Johnson should "take no initiative in the matter." On May 22 the Minister cabled again to say that the Japanese occupation of Peiping seemed imminent but that, since the Chinese were retiring in an orderly fashion without fighting, the local American community did not appear to be in danger. Within a few days, however, Johnson reported that the hostilities in North China had ceased and that the Japanese and Chinese military were trying to agree upon the terms of a truce. But until the time that the truce was announced a week later he was unable to obtain any further information. The negotiations, as he told Washington, were conducted in the "strictest secrecy" and the Chinese officials who were involved were obviously afraid that the slightest contact with the foreign legations might stop the discussions, as the Japanese had indicated that they would not tolerate any third party interference.

The atmosphere which surrounded the negotiations that took place at Tangku and resulted in what became known as the Tangku Truce was vividly described in contemporary accounts in the *New York Times*.[106] The Chinese delegates were so terrified of being assassinated by some of their countrymen, who were enraged at the thought of another surrender to Japan, that they went to "absurd expedients" to conceal their activities. After "many days of evasions, mystifications, and forthright denials that any plan was afoot" the Chinese finally met with the Japanese to draw up the terms of an agreement. On the morning of May 31, when the agreement was to be signed, the town bristled with Chinese troops, standing with drawn weapons to ensure the safety of the Chinese negotiators.

The Japanese, evidently grimly determined to impose humiliations upon the vanquished, sent a Major General to countersign with a Chinese Lieutenant General and also arranged the venue forcing the Chinese delegates to leave their luxurious special trains and proceed afoot across the narrow, dusty roadway to enter the Japanese barracks to sign the final terms of capitulation.

The Tangku Truce has appropriately been called the "charter of Japan's later aggressions in North China."[107] Those terms of the truce that were made known to the public provided for the establishment of a demilitarized zone, some 30 to 40 miles wide, between the Great Wall and a line running across Hopei just north of Peiping. No Chinese troops were to be permitted in this zone and order was to be kept only by a Chinese police force. The Japanese could at any time, through the use of airplanes or other means, verify whether these provisions were being observed. The Chinese armies were to withdraw immediately south of the zone, after which the Japanese troops were to withdraw to the Great Wall. The truce did not, however, affect the Japanese garrisons which, by virtue of the Boxer Protocol, were stationed at points that were to be included in the demilitarized territories. Moreover, it contained secret terms which stated that the police force, whose function was to be the maintenance of order, would have to be made up of units "friendly" to Japan, which in reality meant that they would be amenable to the wishes of the Japanese. In effect the truce gave the Japanese a hold on almost all of Hopei above the Peiping-Tientsin area, which enabled them throughout the next years to exercise military, political, and economic pressure against both the local administrations in North China and the Nanking government in an effort to secure ever greater control over the entire Chinese nation.

Even after the conclusion of the Tangku Truce, the United States government adhered to its policy of remaining inactive and in no way protested to the Japanese. In fact, Ambassador Grew was at this time engaged in trying to ease the tension between the United States and Japan. Grew and the embassy staff in Tokyo, perhaps even more than the State Department in Washington, continued to fear the possibility of a conflict between the United States and Japan. In May, the ambassador had written the Department again concerning the extent to which the Japanese nation was ready for war.[108] Grew declared that the American people would probably be shocked if they realized the excellence of the Japanese military machine which, taken in its entirety (land, sea, and air forces combined), was in his opinion the most complete, the best coordinated and balanced, and therefore on the whole the most powerful fighting instrument that existed anywhere in the world. While Japan's armed forces might not be able to draw upon enough industrial strength to stand the strain of a protracted, large-scale war, for a "quick, hard push" they had no equal. Moreover, they were supported by a people fired with national ambition and possessed of an unbounded capacity for courageous self-sacrifice. As to a potential enemy, the hostility of the Japanese was still focused upon America primarily because they remained convinced that the United States stood in the way of their natural expansion upon the continent of Asia.

While, in this and other dispatches to the Department, Ambassador Grew was stressing the dangers involved in the existing state of America's relations with Japan, he had also, with the unusual conscientiousness that characterized all his undertakings, been devoting himself for some time to the task which was to absorb so much of his thought and energy throughout the next years: seeking to avert war between Japan and the United States by the creation of a genuine friendship between the two countries. His aim was to wipe out the hostility between America and Japan that had resulted from the Manchurian crisis and (in line with his general theory about the best means of avoiding international conflicts) to forestall the development of new causes of irritation by establishing an atmosphere of good will in which friction would be unable to thrive. As a consequence, in his public statements Grew increasingly emphasized the theme of international friendship, especially of friendship between Japan and the United States. For example, in an article written for the *Japan Times* (which is reprinted in the Ambassador's book *Ten Years in Japan* under the heading "The Revolution in Diplomacy and Japanese-American Relations") he said,

The future of American-Japanese relations . . . is not a matter of concern only to our two countries. For our own welfare, peace, and prosperity we must certainly strive to ensure the continuance of the friendly relations between Japan and the United States, but in addition we have a larger duty—a duty which we owe to all the nations of the world. This duty is to develop the coming Pacific Era as an era of peace and friendly cooperation, rather than one of bitterness and strife . . .

It should not be at all difficult for our two nations to live in peace and harmony and to cooperate. Economic interests, which in the past history of the world have been the cause of many conflicts, are, in our case, complementary rather than antagonistic . . . Other interests, which jingoists in both Japan and the United States are constantly bringing forward as possible causes of conflict, can undoubtedly be reconciled by patient study and a mutual spirit of helpfulness.

I can see no reason why the coming Pacific Era, whose destiny lies so largely in our hands, should not be one of peace and friendliness, consecrated to the promotion of the welfare of the world, and it is in our combined power to make it so.[109]

By the summer of 1933 Grew felt that the tension between America and Japan was decreasing. On June 8, the first anniversary of his arrival as ambassador in Japan, he cabled the Secretary, "There seems to have been a noticeable improvement recently in the Japanese attitude toward the United States."[110] While it was, of course, possible that the current "wave of good feeling" would be undermined by the Japanese military through a new "broadside of anti-American propaganda," nevertheless it looked as though "constructive and probably lasting headway" had been made. In his diary the ambassador expressed similar views and added, "I am glad to have remained here long enough to see this improvement . . . I think it will last unless unforeseen incidents or developments occur to injure it. Certainly there is a very great change since a year ago."[111] A few weeks later he recorded with satisfaction that during the course of an interview the Emperor granted to an American visitor, he had significantly remarked that American-Japanese relations were far better.[112]

As the summer drew to a close, a new event took place which Grew believed augured especially well for the future. Koki Hirota, known as a political moderate, was appointed Japanese Foreign Minister. Grew was particularly pleased by his initial reception by Hirota for reasons which are evident from the account of their meeting that appears in the ambassador's diary:

Hirota received me with warmth, clasping my hands in both of his and in the course of our short talk he said that the cornerstone of his policy would be the development of better relations with the United States and that this, in fact, was the primary reason why he had accepted the appointment which had come to him as a complete surprise. I am convinced from his manner that he meant it. I said that so far as I could see, one of the chief impediments to good relations between our countries was the press, which constantly stirred up distrust and suspicion on totally illusory grounds. He replied, "We shall talk all that over together."[113]

On October 2, Grew returned to resume his conversation with the Foreign Minister.[114] Hirota reiterated that he wanted the best possible relations with the United States and asked the ambassador's opinion of the advisability of sending a good will mission to America for the sake of explaining Japan to the American people and establishing a better climate of public opinion. Grew said that he did not believe that such a mission would serve any real purpose, since the American people were fundamentally friendly to Japan and would continue to be so if they were not subjected to irresponsible attacks from the Japanese press. Hirota asked pointedly whether Grew had observed any anti-American articles in the newspapers since the Foreign Minister had assumed office, to which the ambassador responded in the negative.

Grew described his conversations with Hirota in detail in a cable to the Secretary of State.[115] Hull in reply expressed his warm approval, saying, "The report of satisfactory recent contacts and probabilities for the future between Hirota and yourself is of great gratification to me."[116] The Secretary suggested that the conversations be continued but agreed with Grew that any project for a Japanese good will mission to the United States should be discouraged. On the other hand, he thought that the ambassador might point out that the authorities of "Manchukuo" were apparently embarking upon a policy of discrimination against American and other foreign commercial interests in Manchuria. If the Japanese government would use its influence to prevent such practices it would "contribute more than any gesture of goodwill mission" toward the end which both the American and Japanese governments wished to achieve: the improvement of relations between their two countries.

Subsequently Ambassador Grew told Hirota that he had informed Washington of the tenor of their previous talks and that the Secretary was "greatly pleased."[117] Apparently the Foreign Minister felt sufficiently encouraged to send Hull an informal message upon the occasion of the appointment of a new Japanese Ambassador (Hiroshi Saito) to Washington in February 1934. The message which, together with the Secretary's reply, was made public in both Japan and the United States, began with the statement:

It is significant that ever since Japan and the United States opened their doors to each other exactly eighty years ago, the two countries have always maintained a relationship of friendliness and cordiality.[118]

The Foreign Minister went on to say that he was firmly convinced that any question that existed between Japan and the United States could be amicably solved when approached in a conciliatory spirit and a good understanding on the part of each nation of the other's position. He then declared,

I can state with all emphasis at my command that the Japanese nation makes it its basic principle to collaborate in peace and harmony with all nations and has no intention whatever to provoke and make trouble with any other power.

It is the sincere desire of Japan that a most peaceful and friendly relation will be firmly established between her and her great neighbor across the Pacific, the United States. And to this end I have been exerting my best efforts since I took the post of Foreign Minister.

I am happy, therefore, to avail myself of the occasion of the arrival in your country of Mr. Saito, the new Ambassador, to lay before you, through him, Mr. Secretary, my thoughts as to the necessity of promoting our traditional friendship as above.

Hull replied that he had "not failed to note, with gratification, Your Excellency's effort to foster friendly relations with other powers" and that he himself wished to provide the "fullest possible measure of cooperation" toward the furtherance of this effort. He expressed full agreement with the view that all issues between Japan and the United States were "readily susceptible to adjustment by pacific processes." In addition the Secretary said,

You state emphatically that Japan has no intention whatever to provoke and make trouble with any other power. I receive this statement with special gratification . . .

I shall of course be glad to receive through the Ambassador of Japan to the United States . . . any suggestions calculated to maintain and to increase the friendliness and cordiality which have constantly marked since the conclusion of our first treaty the relations between our two countries.

The Secretary's reference to the adjustment of disputes by pacific means and the pronounced enthusiasm with which he welcomed Hirota's assurances that Japan would not create international difficulties in future seemed an obvious reminder that the American government had not entirely forgotten the immediate past. Otherwise Hull's statement was in accord with the marked trend within the

State Department toward attempting to establish our relations with the Japanese upon a less precarious basis.

While this trend was the direct result of the opinions held by officials in Washington and in our embassy in Tokyo, it did not conflict with the views maintained by Nelson Johnson in Peiping. Johnson, in contrast to Grew, was not inclined to express his ideas in any regular reports to the State Department but rather in long speculative letters to friends, often his colleagues in the Far Eastern Division, and in official memoranda that amounted to essays on broad questions such as "The American Mind," and "The Chinese Mind."[119] Prominent among the subjects which formed the basis of his writings was America's role in Asia. In dealing with this topic, he customarily started with the assumption that the one consideration which should guide the conduct of America's policy in the Far East was the furtherance of its own national interests in the Pacific area. In a characteristic letter, written to Roy Howard of the Scripps-Howard newspapers in 1933, Johnson, after stating that he had been in the State Department for twenty-six years, dealing with America's relations with Asia, said,

> Throughout this time it has been to me a source of somewhat melancholy reflection that, in so far as the American public is concerned, conditions in this part of the world appear to be debated publicly and privately solely in terms of what might be called pro-Japanese or pro-Chinese . . .
>
> I have always tried to keep before me the conviction that there is a distinctly American interest at stake which can be neither pro-Chinese nor pro-Japanese but which must have a single eye to the . . . effect of developments in the East . . . upon the future interest of America.[120]

Johnson went on to indicate just what he thought constituted the "distinctly American interest at stake" in the Pacific area:

> I conceive the interest of America in the Pacific Ocean and in all that goes on in that area . . . as being a very real and fundamental interest. In the first place, we cannot shut our eyes to the fact that China and Japan are our neighbors . . . and that with our long coastline on the Pacific we are naturally interested in the Pacific Ocean as a means of communication between us and Asia—a common sea whereon our ships must freely come and go. We cannot shut our eyes to the fact that the great population of Asia offers a valuable outlet for the products of our industries and that as our industries develop we will be more and more interested in cultivating an outlet for them.
>
> It may be that we have come by accident into possession of the Philippines, but . . . rightly or wrongly we adopted a certain attitude toward these oriental peoples for whose future we became responsible. We have said to them and to ourselves that we would give them an opportunity to develop to the point where they might take over their own government . . . If we carry out this promise, . . . whatever we make of them, it will be an American enterprise, peculiarly American, peculiarly the product of Ameri-

can idealism, in the future of which we shall continue to be interested as a father must be interested in the career of his son long after the son has left the family nest. These I conceive to be real and tangible and understandable American interests.

In short, Johnson believed that the two problems in the Pacific area that were of direct concern to the United States were the expansion of our trade with Asia and the preservation of the freedom of the Philippines once they had achieved independence. Concerning the origins and the future of our interest in these problems, the Minister had a semihistorical, semipsychological theory which he liked to expound with the following elaborations.[121] Americans did not differ from the people of other countries except for certain traits of mind which they had inherited from their pioneer forefathers. These forefathers were men who had battled with an untamed wilderness over a long period of years during which, deprived of all material advantages, they had conceived an appreciation of the comforts of life above that belonging to other, longer settled, peoples. Hence when an American traveled abroad today he felt something like contempt for those who lacked such mechanical aids as automobiles and washing machines, with which he was surrounded at home. But the pioneer had also learned to help others less fortunate than himself, thus giving rise to the altruism that characterized America as a nation. It was this altruism which explained the American missionary movement that had flowered in the Far East and the American undertaking to sow the seed of idealism in the Philippines.

However, while strengthening their own altruistic tendencies, these same pioneers had also developed along acquisitive and practical lines. They had put young America upon the sea, built a fleet of sailing ships which had no superior, and established trading houses on the China coast equal in importance to those of any nation. Later in their history, they had trekked West and created the greatest empire the world had ever known. During these years of expansion at home, the commercial energy of the country had been drained from overseas enterprises while, in contrast, the activities of the missionaries had come to the fore. But the aggressive spirit of the pioneers remained in the blood of the nation. It was a vital heritage which, for too long, had been forgotten and which, in future, must be obeyed. "It is possible," Johnson declared in a passage which he repeated on several occasions, "that we are on the threshhold of a new period of American international relations—a period characterized by the acquisitive, practical side of American life rather than its idealistic and altruistic side."[122]

Johnson even went so far as to say in a memorandum to the State Department that "for these interests [that is, our trade in Asia and the security of an independent Philippines] we will be and must be prepared to fight."[123] But while all this had a decidedly belligerent sound, Johnson, always inclined to let nature take its course in political matters, was not likely to urge Washington to put his theories into practice. Moreover, the Minister did not think that the time had come for the United States to reassert itself in the Pacific area. During the early stages of the Manchurian crisis, he was concerned over the damage which the Japanese were indirectly inflicting upon the United States in their efforts to destroy the peace system set up by the major postwar agreements. However, once disillusionment had set in and he had discarded the peace system as an issue, Johnson concluded that "whether China rules Manchuria, or whether Japan rules Manchuria, or whether Russia rules Manchuria" was a matter with which America was "not concerned."[124] Similarly, when Japan invaded North China, the Minister took the position that the United States had little at stake although, if the Sino-Japanese conflict continued, its interests might eventually be affected. On the day after the signing of the Tangku Truce, Johnson wrote a letter to Hornbeck full of unhappy forebodings.[125] "What next?" he asked. With the establishment of the demilitarized zone provided for by the truce, the Japanese could in future do "anything and everything" to threaten the peace of North China. Furthermore, they had undisputed control of Manchuria and Jehol and would undoubtedly soon conquer Chahar and possibly Suiyuan. The Nationalist armies, driven back by the better equipped Japanese troops, were scarcely likely to rally since the Nanking government was itself torn by dissension among its leaders and could exercise no authority. Concerning America's connection with these events, the Minister said,

None of this concerns us directly. It probably does not mean the loss of a dollar from an American purse. On the contrary, the development of this area under Japanese enterprise may mean an increased opportunity for American industrial plants to sell the kind of machinery and other manufactured goods that will be needed where so much energy is being displayed.

The only thing that is of concern to the United States . . . is the extension of Japanese influence through China and along the coast of China so as to set up a barrier past which we and our ships must go if we seek intercourse with China's ports or people. That is a situation closely related to our future attitude in regard to the Philippine Islands. Sooner or later the increased prestige of Japan in China . . . must give us cause to wonder just what our position in the Pacific is to be. These are matters which will not concern us at the present time but in the years to come I am sure that they will.

Johnson was, therefore, not inclined to raise any objections to the administration's decision to refrain from interfering in the situation which had developed in North China. There was, in fact, no dissension within the State Department as officials, looking back upon the past with profound discouragement and forward to the future with considerable anxiety, began to reassess our policy in the Far East. The idea of promoting the movement for the establishment of world order was by tacit agreement in the process of being set aside—whether temporarily or permanently remained to be seen—and officials were for the most part asking themselves how they could safeguard the United States against an aggressive and antagonistic Japan. The initial impulse in Washington was to avoid any action for the present. Ambassador Grew, on his part, sought to embark upon the more positive task of attempting to lay the foundations for friendly relations between the United States and Japan and, in his first efforts, he received the support of the Secretary of State.

THE BACKGROUND

The theory underlying the Nine Power Treaty was that the development of a strong China was essential not only for the Chinese themselves but for the international community as a whole. As far as the interest of the non-Chinese world was concerned, it was argued that China, weak, divided, and economically backward, had long been an area in which most of the large powers had sought territorial gains or economic advantages that had brought them into conflict with each other. If peace was to be preserved in East Asia it could therefore only be maintained by a Chinese government powerful enough to defend itself against aggression and to ensure equality of opportunity to all countries by enforcing the principle of the Open Door. It was perhaps this line of reasoning more than any other that led the signatories of the Nine Power Treaty to pledge themselves to abstain from any further interference in China's affairs so as to give the Chinese nation a chance to realize its potentialities. In the years following the Washington Conference it had therefore been taken for granted that the outside world had a large stake in the internal development of China.

Through the early part of the 1920's, China was little more than a battleground for the armies of warlords who were struggling with each other for supremacy.[1] In 1923 Dr. Sun Yat-sen, in conjunction with a mission of Soviet advisers sent from Moscow, reorganized the Kuomintang turning it into a highly disciplined administrative machine supported by a well trained army. Dr. Sun's thesis was that China had to pass through three revolutionary stages in order to fulfill its national destiny: first, the unification of the country was to be effected by military means through the Kuomintang forces; secondly, the nation was to learn self-rule and to carry out a program of economic reconstruction under the tutelage of the Kuomintang; and finally, the processes of government were to be transferred to the people themselves with the adoption of a constitution. Although Dr. Sun did not live to see his plan put into operation, the military phase of the revolution was actually inaugurated with the launching of the Northern Expedition in 1926 and was officially proclaimed at an end when the Nationalist armies, under the direction of Chiang Kai-shek, conquered Peking in the late spring of 1928 and changed the name of that city to Peiping.

With the capture of Peking, China was—in theory at least—prepared to embark upon the experiment of transforming itself into a strong nation. In accordance with Dr. Sun's ideas, a Nationalist regime was established at Nanking in which the supreme power remained in the hands of the Kuomintang while the government, which had been formed in 1927, was to function under the stewardship of the party. In the autumn of 1928 the government was reorganized through the promulgation of an Organic Law so that it was thereafter based upon a system of five yuans, known as the Executive, Legislative, Judicial, Examination, and Control Yuan.

The tasks which the new regime faced were admittedly enormous. Politically, to be successful, it had to extend its authority over a far larger part of the country since, despite the fact that the unification of China had been officially declared, Nanking actually controlled no more than five provinces which lay in the area of the lower Yangtze. The remaining provinces were, for the most part, ruled by political or military leaders who wished to retain their actual, if not nominal, independence and could often do so because they had large regional armies at their command or because they lived in remote sections of the land in which it was difficult for any central government to enforce its power. Economically, as Dr. Sun had long and emphatically insisted, a vast program of reconstruction was needed to expand the existing transportation and communications facilities, develop the country's industries, and create a modern financial system capable of producing the revenues necessary for the conduct of the government's manifold activities. Throughout the vast countryside of China, the appalling condition of the peasantry was crying for betterment, presenting a problem almost as complex as it was urgent. Far-reaching improvements were also required in respect to such fundamental matters as education, public health, and the administration of justice. After its inception, the regime at Nanking addressed itself to a wide range of the issues with which it was confronted with consequences that, during the period under discussion in this study, were to be very differently assessed by outside observers concerned with the question of the creation of a strong China.

Immediately after the close of the Northern Expedition, it looked as though China had at least a chance of enjoying a period of peace. But there were two obvious sources of potential friction. One was the desire of various warlords and military leaders for power which had led them to contend with each other in the past and which, it was generally recognized, might well drive them to try to overthrow the new Central government in the future. The most important of the northern warlords were Feng Yu-hsiang, known as the "Christian General"; Yen Hsi-shan, the Governor of Shansi; and Chang Hsueh-liang who, following the death of his father in June 1928, had assumed control of Manchuria.[2] However, since Feng and Yen had joined forces with the Nationalist armies during the Northern Expedition and Chang Hsueh-liang had declared his allegiance to the Nanking government, it seemed possible that, for the time being at least, there would be no major conflicts in the north. In the south, on the other hand, where the Kwangsi generals led by Li Tsung-jen exercised great influence, there were from the beginning signs of restiveness at having to submit to the authority of the Nationalist regime.

The second likely cause of dissension was the rivalry between leaders of the Kuomintang, especially Chiang Kai-shek, Wang Ching-wei, and Hu Han-min. Wang and Hu had developed a personal antipathy to each other during the years when they were both prominent disciples of Dr. Sun Yat-sen. Wang, talented but opportunistic and mercurial, had subsequently become the spokesman of the Leftist faction in the Kuomintang and in 1928 was no longer cooperating with the Nationalist government. Hu, who in contrast to Wang was noted for his sincerity and a dogged dedication to the task at hand, headed the Rightist group in the Kuomintang and became the first chairman of the Legislative Yuan. Chiang Kai-shek, on his part, had the advantage of being supported by the best military contingents in the country and, with the establishment of the Nationalist regime became the key figure in both the party and governmental structure and consequently the real center of power.

Peace lasted only until the spring of 1929, when the troops of the Kwangsi generals entered into open conflict with the government's armies which defeated them. The Kwangsi revolt was followed by another minor rebellion in the south in which Wang Ching-wei participated. When this also proved abortive, Wang allied himself with Feng Yu-hsiang and Yen Hsi-shan, who had decided to break with the Nanking government which, through its increasing strength, seemed to menace their own positions. In the summer of 1930 intensive fighting took place and a new government, which claimed to be the legitimate government of China, was set up at Peiping under the leadership of Wang Ching-wei and Yen Hsi-shan. Both the military and the political ventures in the north soon collapsed, however, as Chang Hsueh-liang, coming to the rescue of Nanking, subdued the Feng-Yen forces and recaptured Peiping.

Yet stability was still far from having been achieved and further dissension developed in the following year. A conflict of opinion between Chiang Kai-shek and Hu Han-min led to the latter's arrest at Nanking in March 1931. Two months later Wang Ching-wei was instrumental in establishing another separatist government, this time at Canton, where he had the cooperation of other Leftist leaders and the Kwangsi generals. With the outbreak of the Manchurian crisis, negotiations were opened between the regimes at Canton and Nanking for the sake of effecting at least a semblance of unity in the face of Japanese aggression. The Leftists, who had persistently opposed Chiang Kai-shek on the grounds that he was virtually wielding dictatorial powers, forced the Generalissimo to relinquish much of his authority. They also insisted upon the release of Hu Han-min, who subsequently came to Canton where he died in 1936, having repeatedly refused to return to Nanking despite pleas from various quarters. The negotiations between Canton and Nanking finally led to an agreement to form a coalition consisting of Chiang Kai-shek, Hu Han-min, and Wang Ching-wei, but partly because of Hu's reluctance to go back to the capital, the coalition never actually came into being. Instead, in the early part of 1932, Chiang resumed primary control of the government and Wang Ching-wei accepted the post of Chairman of the Executive Yuan which, except for a brief interval, he retained throughout the next years.[3] The Kuomintang leaders who remained at Canton participated in the organization and operation of a Southwest Political Council which maintained a semiautonomous status.

In addition to the conflicts within the Kuomintang itself, the Nanking government was engaged in a determined effort to exterminate the Chinese Communists. In 1927 the Kuomintang had expelled the Communists from its ranks thereby severing the ties established by Sun Yat-sen in 1923. The Communists, driven underground, managed to develop bases in the interior and by the end of 1931 had set up a Chinese Soviet Republic in Kiangsi with Mao Tse-tung as chairman. In December 1930, Chiang Kai-shek began the first of his historic Annihilation Campaigns against the Communists, which he interrupted in 1932 but resumed in the following year.[4]

While engaged in the fifth Annihilation Campaign in the autumn of 1933, the Nationalist government was faced with still another outbreak of hostilities which occurred in Fukien province. The Nineteenth Route army, which had achieved nationwide fame for its gallant resistance to the Japanese at Shanghai in 1932, revolted against Nanking and, joined by other disaffected elements, created a People's government in Fukien. The proclaimed aims of the rebel forces were to resist the Japanese and to establish democratic rule in China. For a moment it looked as though the Communists would unite with the new People's government which might have substantially strengthened their position.[5] This threat to the Nanking regime did not materialize, however, and the Generalissimo's armies quelled the Fukien revolt by January 1934.

In the early 1930's outside observers, as has been suggested, held widely varying opinions concerning the developments which were taking place in China.[6] The views that received the most publicity were those expressed by the Lytton Commission in its report on the Manchurian crisis. In a section of the report devoted to recent events in China, the commission took the position that China was a "nation in evolution" and that all facets of its national life had to be judged accordingly.[7] The commission showed great sympathy for the Kuomintang and faith in the ability of the Nationalist regime to carry out the aims of the tutelage period, provided China was left free from outside interference. Thus, it declared that after the close of the Northern Expedition the Kuomintang had been prepared to put into effect far-reaching plans for the political and economic reconstruction of China but had been prevented from doing so by various factors which stood in the way of the unification of the country. Although the commission included in these factors the dissension within the Kuomintang itself, it put decidedly more emphasis upon the obstacles to centralization presented by the warlords and the Communists. While admitting that, as the tutelage period proceeded, China had presented a spectacle of "political, social, intellectual and moral disorder," the commission suggested that, granted a state of profound national transition, extreme confusion was "unavoidable." In effect it chided China's "impatient friends" for being disappointed in the accomplishments of the Nationalist regime and stated that "in spite of difficulties, delays and failures," considerable progress had in fact been achieved. On the credit side, the commission cited in particular the financial reforms which had been initiated since 1928 by T. V. Soong as Minister of Finance, enumerating specifically the efforts which had been made to establish a central banking system, balance national receipts and expenditures, supervise and improve the collection of provincial revenues, and obtain the cooperation and support of the Chinese business community. For all these undertakings, the commission declared, the authorities at Nanking were entitled to credit; no doubt they had failed in many things but they had "already accomplished much." In the final section of the report, containing its conclusions, the commission spoke even more positively of the attempts at reconstruction which had been made by the Nationalist regime as bearing "much promise of success."

The opinions expressed behind the scenes by the American Minister in China fell far short of reflecting the optimism of the Lytton Commission. In February 1933, Johnson sent a dispatch to Washington for the stated purpose of informing the State Department of his personal views.[8] Johnson asserted that, at the beginning of the tutelage period, the Kuomintang had had a virtual monopoly of all political power as well as of the judiciary, education, and the press, but that its efforts at preparing the country for self-rule had been "largely barren" with the result that its prestige was presently at a "low ebb." Having failed to take advantage of its exceptional opportunities, the Kuomintang had lost the support of the people and, divided against itself, was not likely to regain the power that had once made it so important. The government, as distinguished from the party, had given little evidence of having a "constructive mind of its own," and had "allowed affairs to drift more or less aimlessly." It did not have sufficient military strength to defeat decisively the armies of the warlords whose most solemn pledges to support the Nationalist regime had proved worthless. Nor did it have the loyal and disciplined troops necessary to overcome the Communists militarily. Moreover, the authorities at Nanking had only recently paid attention to the economic and agrarian aspects of the communist problem. Famines, floods, civil wars, and other misfortunes had driven millions of peasants to desperation so that they had become an easy prey of Communist propagandists who glibly promised relief from intolerable conditions. The "shadow of Bolshevism" would lie over parts of China until a "thoroughgoing program of rural economy" had improved the lot of the masses and an efficient administration had produced a sense of security throughout the land.

Yet, Johnson asserted, despite these discouraging factors any impartial observer had to admit that perceptible progress could be seen in certain directions and that, when allowance had been made for the exceptional intricacy of the tasks confronting a national government crippled and impoverished by years of internecine strife, there was "no ground for undue pessimism." The admittedly transitory and provisional character of the Kuomintang regime in itself explained many of its failures. It might be confidently expected that in time whatever dictatorship China might require would be less obtrusive. The need for adequate financial resources for normal requirements was being fully recognized. T. V. Soong had displayed great skill in restoring confidence in China's credit, which was all the more remarkable as a financial breakdown had seemed inevitable.

About a year later, in order to bring his earlier communication up to date, the Minister sent another dispatch to Washington, in which he wrote at the outset that at no time in his experience had he felt the domestic political situation to be "so discouraging."[9] The Kuomintang, he said, was becoming "increasingly impotent" as its leadership, still divided, had "deteriorated." The declining power of the Central government had been transferred to General Chiang Kai-shek but there seemed "little if any hope" that he could unify the country. The eleven provinces of the South, West, and Northwest remained practically independent of Nanking and the five provinces of North China were only loosely supervised by appointees of Chiang at Peiping. Most of the provinces were controlled by militarists who gave nominal allegience to the Central government but treated it with the utmost cynicism, regarding their troops as their own concern and contributing little if any revenue to the National Treasury. The revolution, begun twenty-two years ago with the fall of the Manchus, had scarcely touched the great mass of the people except where "communism (so-called)" had undertaken to settle some of the problems of the peasantry. Those who had had an interest in government at the outset of the tutelage period had "suffered disillusionment" and expected "no real good" from their present leaders. Only a few recent trends could be regarded as hopeful. The Central government now appeared to realize the importance of economic and agrarian developments for political stability although it had done "nothing significant"; there was a wider realization among the people of need for reform but it was defeated by disappointment; substantial progress had been achieved in such phases of social welfare as education, local sanitation, and public health; "amazing construction work" was being undertaken in the port cities but, until those cities felt the mutual need for unity, the political situation would remain unaltered; attempts were being made to reconcile the Kuomintang leaders at Nanking with those in the South but there was little likelihood that anything approximating an understanding would be reached.

In personal letters, especially those written in the winter of 1933-1934, Johnson kept reiterating that conditions in China were "very discouraging" and constantly returned to the point that the crux of the matter lay in the "deterioration" of the leadership of the Kuomintang which had left the party without the courage to make the major decisions necessary to carry out its original objectives.[10] If a genuine leader could be found, he wrote on one occasion, either in the camp of the Kuomintang or of the "so-called Communists," a great advance would have been made toward unifying China and building a strong country. Although such many-sided comments tend to defy any generalizations, it may perhaps be said that the Lytton Commission felt that the failures of the Kuomintang could be ascribed to the complexity of the problems at hand while its achievements promised well for the future and that, in contrast, Johnson believed that the Kuomintang was suffering from some inner corrosion which accounted for its many difficulties in the past and which there was some, but not much, hope of arresting.

Johnson's pessimistic views were re-enforced by a report written by Clarence E. Gauss, then Counselor of Legation at Peiping and later Ambassador to China, who went on a brief mission to Nanking in the autumn of 1934 and sent the Minister an account of his impressions of conditions in the capital.[11] Gauss declared that he was struck by the lack of vigor in the Nationalist government and by the fact that the impulse of the revolution was dead, extinguished largely by incessant and bitter factional disputes. The revolutionary zealots now took refuge in the comfort of public office and concerned themselves less with the welfare and progress of the country and more with their personal fortunes and jealousies. The government had no substantial program and merely followed a policy of drift. Chiang Kai-shek dominated the entire scene to a degree that could not be realized when viewed from Peiping. It was not a healthy or happy situation and there was evidence of discontent, discouragement, and criticism, but no one in office would dare lift his voice in opposition.

The position taken by Hornbeck was somewhere in between that of the Lytton Commission and Nelson Johnson. At the time that the Roosevelt administration came into office, Hornbeck wrote a long memorandum on "What the President and Secretary of State may at this moment need, or may wish, to know with regard to China and American-Chinese relations."[12] In this he referred to many positive aspects of the Kuomintang's record. At one point he stated that the Nationalist regime, despite constant attacks from its foreign and domestic enemies, had managed to extend its mandate throughout the country as, for example, in its efficient operation on a nationwide scale of the customs, salt, and postal services. In other parts of the memorandum he spoke of the "remarkable success" achieved by T. V.

Soong, in relation to such matters as balancing the budget, and expressed the view that China was making steady economic progress and that the highly pessimistic reports to the contrary were largely a result of Japanese propaganda. In connection with the communist problem, Hornbeck declared that the Nationalist regime, while continuing its military campaigns against the Red armies, was also attempting to better the political and economic conditions which were essentially the cause of communism and had within the last year adopted constructive measures designed to improve the welfare of the peasants. On the negative side, Hornbeck asserted that the Chinese leaders, both political and military, had "not yet given evidence of having arrived at any position of unity or solidarity among themselves." However, he added that in making this statement he did not wish to "imply or impute blame." It was his belief that

everybody who intelligently observes and studies Far Eastern affairs must realize that China is passing through a period of internal revolution in the nature of what is frequently referred to as a "five-fold" revolution and that it stands to reason that there must be differences of opinion among her leaders and people and there must be internal political contests over a considerable period of time.

A few months later, Hornbeck returned to the problem of the conflicts within the Kuomintang in a conversation with Dr. T. V. Soong.[13] According to Hornbeck's own account, after much time had been devoted to reviewing the situation in China, Dr. Soong said that, in the light of all that had been discussed, the future for China looked gloomy. Hornbeck responded with the statement that more would depend upon one question than any other: could the predominant individualism, which prevailed among the Chinese and appeared so conspicuously in the constant dissension among their leaders, be overcome? He then asked Soong whether the spirit of nationalism had not yet reached a point in China where an appeal might be made by some Chinese leader to all other Chinese leaders to lay aside their differences and to make concessions to each other so that they could cooperate in a program of reconstruction. Whether correctly or not, Hornbeck received the impression that Soong thought that only China's businessmen and financiers were as yet prepared to work unitedly for the good of the country. In any event, both Hornbeck and Soong concluded that it would be a long time before order and an effectively functioning government could be established in China. In general, therefore, Hornbeck seems to have been considerably less critical of the Kuomintang than Johnson but more doubtful of its ability to solve its problems than the members of the Lytton Commission.

From the above, it is evident that, as relative peace was restored between Japan and China following the Manchurian incident and the Tangku Truce, the question of the capacity of the Chinese to effect the internal development of their country seemed to many to be hanging in the balance. Moreover it was widely felt that upon the solution to this question depended, not only the future of China but the stabilization of the Pacific area as envisaged by the signatories of the Nine Power Treaty. According to the schedule outlined by Dr. Sun Yat-sen, the period of political tutelage was already well advanced and time was pressing upon the Kuomintang to show that its efforts at national reconstruction were achieving the desired end. Western officials, well aware that China was passing through a critical phase in its history, were watching the activities of the Kuomintang closely, responding with a mixture of hope and discouragement. It was against this background that the Japanese were to proclaim the Amau doctrine which amounted to an attempt to prevent the rehabilitation of China by warning the West not to provide the Chinese with assistance. Since the Amau doctrine involved as important issues as the Tangku Truce, and moreover constituted a more direct challenge to the West, it was bound to provide a further test of the Roosevelt administration's policy.

THE AMAU STATEMENT OF APRIL 1934

In 1924, in his famous lectures on the *San Min Chu I*, Dr. Sun Yat-sen told his countrymen that China was ground down by the economic exploitation of the large powers to a point where it was reduced to a level even below that of a colony, for its people were "not slaves of one country but of all."[14] Nevertheless, Dr. Sun continued to maintain the thesis that he had set forth two years earlier in his book, *The International Development of China*, namely, that in order to transform itself into a modern state, China should make use of foreign capital and foreign technical assistance even though he assumed that much of this outside help would have to come from the major powers. China, he argued, could not achieve such immense goals as industrialization without receiving substantial aid at least at the outset. As to the powers, he hoped that they would see that the only means of avoiding a general war in the Far East was to abandon their competitive struggle for the domination of China and support the Chinese effort at reconstruction.

Dr. Sun's idea that China's reconstruction would have to be brought about in collaboration with other countries became an integral part of the Kuomintang's policies. Even before the establishment of the Nationalist regime, the Peking government obtained the help of the League of Nations in planning a health program in China.[15] At Peking's request, medical studies of far-reaching significance were undertaken by League experts in 1922 and Dr. Ludwig Rajchman, the Director of the Health Section of the League, visited China in 1926. Rajchman's trip had no immediate consequences owing to the chaotic conditions which inevitably prevailed in China during the years of the Northern Expedition. But shortly after its assumption of power, the Nanking government invited not only Rajchman but Sir Arthur Salter, the Director of the Economic and Financial Section of the League, and Robert Haas, the Director of the Communications and Transit Section, to come to China for consultation. The outcome of the visit of these prominent League officials was that the Chinese government decided in the spring of 1931, first to create a National Economic Council, which would serve as a central planning commission for the economic reconstruction of China, and thereafter to appeal to the League for assistance to be rendered partly through the council and partly through other agencies of the Chinese government.[16] Dr. T. V. Soong accordingly asked the League to agree to certain measures. These included sending experts to China who would help to plan and carry out various parts of the government's reconstruction program; arranging for the training of Chinese specialists who would be required for the more extended work of reconstruction in later years; designating an officer to keep the Chinese government in contact with the relevant technical organizations at Geneva; and aiding in the development of the Chinese educational system. In June the League acceded to Dr. Soong's request, with the result that the Chinese government entered into a period of technical collaboration with the League which in its first phase (1931-1933) was conducted on an informal basis.

The National Economic Council lost little time in asking the League for technical assistance for the improvement of China's highways.[17] The Chinese had long placed a great deal of emphasis upon the necessity of building an adequate system of communications and in the more recent past Sun Yat-sen had drawn up an elaborate scheme for the development of China's railways. It was felt that, without such a system, no central government could hope to establish national unity or defend the country from outside aggression, as it did not have any efficient means with which to move troops from one area to another.

Moreover, modern methods of transportation were regarded as essential for the expansion of trade and the development of the economy throughout the agrarian districts of China which was urgently required to raise the level of living of the peasants. After the advent of the Nationalist government, grandiose schemes were evolved for the construction of a network of railways in China. But, lacking funds, the plans could not be implemented. Under these circumstances, the National Economic Council decided to devote itself to the more modest task of expanding the country's highways. For the work which it undertook subsequently, it requested and obtained from the League the services of two European engineers. A policy was developed for the planning of highways upon a scientific basis which, in so far as possible, would do away with the existing practice of constructing roads haphazardly without any regard for national needs.[18] The council encouraged the building of roads by local authorities and itself undertook to link together some of the more important local highways so that they connected a number of provinces. In addition, studies were made to ascertain such matters as what types of roads were best suited to certain areas of China and the kinds of vehicles that were most serviceable.

In the early part of the summer of 1931, the National Economic Council also asked for the help of the League in securing foreign experts to make studies of certain water conservation problems.[19] Flood control was considered a particularly pressing issue, as in the past China had periodically been subjected to devastating floods. Indeed, in August 1931, before the League had had a chance to carry out the National Economic Council's request, the worst flood in China's history occurred in the Yangtze Valley. In this emergency, the authorities at Nanking again sought assistance from the League which sent one of its most experienced field workers to China to head the National Flood Relief Commission that had been created to deal with the situation. The commission not only sought to bring all possible relief to the population of some twenty-five million affected by the flood but undertook to build dikes, the length of over 7,000 kilometers, to contain the Yangtze and its tributaries. It was estimated that, at the peak of the commission's activities, over a million persons were employed in the construction of these dikes.

The Chinese government, in addition, turned to the League for technical cooperation in two other phases of its reconstruction program: health and education.[20] A three-year health plan was adopted which involved, among other items, the establishment of a Central Hospital and Central Field Health Station. The latter, which began to function in 1931, was planned on a broad scale consisting of nine different departments including a department of bacteriology, chemistry, medical relief and social medicine, maternity and child care, industrial health, and health education. The station energetically undertook to bring its services into rural areas where medical aid had hitherto been wholly lacking. In the conduct of the three-year plan, the Chinese National Health Service and the Health Committee of the League collaborated closely and continuously. In the field of education, the help which Dr. Soong had requested in his original appeal to the League was provided in the form of a mission dispatched to China by the International Institute of Intellectual Cooperation in order to make a study of the Chinese educational system. The mission, whose members included R. H. Tawney of London University and Dr. Carl Becker, formerly Prussian Minister of Education, was accompanied by the Director of the International Institute and by an official representative of the Secretary General of the League. The conclusions of the mission were embodied in a report which in effect presented a thoroughgoing plan of reform for the Chinese educational system aimed in particular at the establishment of a far larger number of primary schools, a radical alteration in the curriculum of the secondary schools, and a much more intensive concentration on the training of teachers.

Last but most fundamental of all, the Chinese sought aid from Geneva in the solution of their agrarian problem. In 1932, through an arrangement made between the League and the National Economic Council, Professor Carlo Dragoni, who had been Secretary General of the International Institute of Agriculture at Geneva, made a survey of agrarian conditions in China.[21] The council had originally asked for an expert who would outline a program which might provide the basis for a policy of agrarian reform. But Dragoni soon concluded that only the Chinese themselves could undertake such an herculean task, as it demanded the kind of intimate knowledge of the nation and its peoples that no outsider could acquire. Nevertheless, in the spring of 1933 Dragoni submitted a report to the National Economic Council in which he made certain recommendations concerning means of increasing the area of arable land and the yield from land already under cultivation in China and of improving the system of land tenure and the general economic conditions of the farmer. On the latter point he stated that the betterment of the farmer's position called for the solution of a number of problems, the most important of which were

the concentration of landownership in certain regions and the excessive rents of farms operated by tenants, the smallness of many farms and fields, the exorbitant rates of interest on lands granted to farmers, the unsatisfactory conditions of marketing agricultural produce, the excess of taxations, and the lack of communications.[22]

Concerning the general attitude of the peasant, Dragoni warned that it was essential "to devise and resolutely to apply" agricultural policies which would prevent the "growth of discontent among the peasantry" lest the Chinese peasants reach the end of their patience, as the Russian peasants had done, and take action "which would gravely endanger social and political stability."[23] Before Dragoni left China, a Rural Reconstruction Committee was established by the National Economic Council, at his suggestion, which as one of its first projects undertook to find means of encouraging the development of the movement for rural cooperatives in China.[24] In addition to Dragoni's study, the National Economic Council, through the medium of the League, had several surveys made, with a view to rehabilitating two of China's key industries—cotton and silk.[25]

As the technical collaboration between China and the League progressed, it attracted considerable attention. Admittedly the League's operation in China was a modest one, confined to only a few aspects of China's reconstruction and limited, to a considerable extent, to making studies and offering advice. Nevertheless, it was regarded by many as having at least great potential significance. If that work were expanded, it was said, China would be able to effect her economic development through an international organization which functioned disinterestedly, thereby avoiding the danger that foreign aid would lead to foreign exploitation.[26] It was even quite frequently suggested that the League, in addition to enlarging the scope of its technical assistance to China, should, through an international loan or some other means, undertake to finance an extensive reconstruction program for the Chinese.[27] On the other hand, there were those who criticized the League's activities in China. Some felt that the League experts who had made studies for the Chinese government, although for the most part men of unusual attainments, lacked experience in economically backward countries and consequently drew up plans that were wholly unsuited to conditions in China.[28] Others took positions similar to that of Nelson Johnson who stated that no plans, however sound, could produce significant results since the Nationalist regime did not have leaders who commanded sufficient support among the Chinese people to take the necessary measures.[29]

The Lytton Commission in its report emphatically reaffirmed the thesis that a strong China was essential for the maintenance of peace in the Far East. In addition it stated that in the sphere of economic development the best means of strengthening China was through international cooperation, as China herself had neither "the capital nor the trained specialists necessary for the unaided accomplishment of her national reconstruction."[30] The Assembly of the League in its own report of February 24, 1933, not only endorsed the Lytton Commission's views but declared even more positively that "temporary international cooperation in the internal reconstruction of China, as suggested by the late Dr. Sun Yat-sen" was a prerequisite for peace in the Far East.[31]

Partly as a result of the position taken by the Lytton Commission and the Assembly, the Chinese government decided in the early spring of 1933 that, on his forthcoming trip to the World Economic Conference in London, Dr. T. V. Soong should appeal to the League for further technical assistance and should try to obtain funds for reconstruction purposes. Consequently, on June 28, while in Europe, Soong addressed a letter to the Council of the League in which he stated that the Chinese government was about to enter upon a new phase of its reconstruction work that would be devoted to the conduct of an intensive program in a few provinces which were to serve as models for the rest of the nation.[32] Soong asked the Council to agree to a "continuous collaboration" with his government in this effort and, in particular, to appoint a technical agent who would be stationed in China to coordinate the activities of the various League experts in that country and who would serve as a liaison officer between Nanking and Geneva relative to matters of technical assistance.

In response to a request from Soong for quick action, the Council met on July 3 and created a special committee to take all necessary measures in respect to technical cooperation between the League and the Chinese government.[33] The committee, as constituted, consisted of the President of the Council and the representatives of eight nations: Great Britain, France, Italy, Germany, Czechoslovakia, Spain, Norway, and China. With the United States specifically in mind, the committee was empowered to invite the representatives of other states to take part in its proceedings. The reason for establishing the committee was officially defined as being to provide a medium whereby the various interested governments would be more directly associated with China's effort at reconstruction than in the past when the National Economic Council and similar Chinese agencies had merely dealt informally with the technical organizations of the League.[34]

On July 14, Joseph Avenol, the newly appointed Secretary General of the League, sent Hull (who was himself in London attending the World Economic Conference) an *aide-mémoire* in which he stated that the special committee which had just been created would hold its first session on July 18.[35] The business of the meeting, Avenol said, would be to name a technical agent, as proposed by Soong, and to outline the principles by which the committee should be guided so that its operations could be maintained on an entirely "non-political" basis. Avenol stated further that technical cooperation with China was considered to be a "matter of international importance" and, as such, had been strongly recommended by the Lytton Commission and endorsed in the Assembly report of February 1933, which had been accepted by the American government. Granted these circumstances and granted the fact that the United States was already a member of the League Advisory Committee dealing with the Sino-Japanese dispute, it was hoped that an American representative could be present at the session on July 18.[36]

Secretary Hull immediately referred Avenol's message to the State Department in Washington with an urgent request for suggestions as to what action, if any, to take.[37] In its reply—evidently drafted in the Far Eastern Division—the Department said that it had not been previously informed of the creation of the special committee and that it was inclined to believe that the stamp of the American government's approval was being sought for a program which the League had developed in China during the past two years without any consultation with the United States.[38] It might be that the program was such that the Department could advisedly approve it and contribute to its advancement. But it might be otherwise. The Department therefore felt that the United States should avoid becoming "definitely or conspicuously committed" until it knew the "set-up" and that it should confine itself to sending an unofficial observer to the meeting of July 18. After the observer had reported and the League had asked for definite collaboration from the United States in the conduct of its program and after more information had been obtained about the character and contents of that program, the United States could decide whether or not it was in a position to cooperate. On the general question of the value of strengthening China through the kind of methods proposed by the League, the Department stated in conclusion:

Incidentally the Department favors in principle the idea of . . . [technical] collaboration and is inclined to believe that a satisfactory program for such collaboration, well carried out, would give greater promise on the side of constructive effort by the powers toward diminishing causes of conflict in the Far East than has appeared in connection with any other of the many possibilities canvassed in that connection in recent years.

The first session of the special committee was held in Paris on July 18 according to schedule. The United States embassy in France cabled the State Department subsequently that one of its staff had attended the meeting strictly in the role of observer.[39] The proceedings had been "brief." Rajchman had been "unanimously appointed" technical agent. The future work of the committee had been discussed and "considerable emphasis" had been put on the fact that it must be "entirely technical, impartial, and nonpolitical."[40]

When news of the action taken by the special committee reached China, Nelson Johnson wired Washington that, in his opinion, Rajchman's appointment would "doom" the League's program "to the suspicious attention and opposition of the Japanese."[41] Indeed, if the State Department, despite its high estimate of the potentialities of an international technical aid program, had initially approached the special committee with caution, it was likely to be even more cautious after the meeting of July 18. For the Japanese had developed an intense dislike of Rajchman during the Manchurian crisis when he was in China, officially involved in the technical work of the League but allegedly also privately engaged in political activities in support of China against Japan. It seemed quite possible, therefore, that—as Johnson indicated—Rajchman's designation as the council's technical agent would make the League program in China a political issue despite the special committee's insistence on the "nonpolitical" character of its undertakings.

But the "Rajchman question" (as it came to be called), as well as the whole League program, was to prove only one facet of the effort to strengthen China which was soon to be opposed by the Japanese. True to the decision made by the Chinese government in the early spring of 1933, Dr. Soong attempted to obtain financial in addition to technical assistance for China on his trip abroad in connection with the World Economic Conference. On his way to London, Soong made arrangements with the Reconstruction Finance Corporation in Washington for a U.S. $50 million credit. A somewhat similar credit had been advanced by the United States Federal Farm Board in 1931 for the sake of helping the Chinese government to pay the costs entailed in the construction of dikes following the Yangtze flood disaster. Fourfifths of the R.F.C. credit was to be devoted to the purchase of American cotton by the Chinese government while the rest was to be used for buying American wheat and flour. The credit was to be repaid in three years with five per cent interest and various taxes were pledged as collateral.[42] The United States government stated officially that the purpose of the credit from its point of view was to aid the

American economic recovery program by disposing of surplus stocks.[43] The Chinese government, on its part, announced that it would sell the cotton and wheat and use the proceeds for "productive purposes." The Legislative Yuan, in agreeing to the credit, stipulated specifically that any funds derived by the Chinese government from its arrangements with the R.F.C. should be employed solely for such ends as the development of industry, agriculture, and communications.[44]

In Europe, Dr. Soong embarked upon a considerably more elaborate venture in his search for financial support for China's economic reconstruction.[45] His plan was to create what he called a consultative committee which, within the immediate future, would obtain further credits for China and, in the long run, would provide sufficient funds to undertake certain large industrial and railroad projects and settle China's outstanding foreign obligations. The consultative committee was to be made up of prominent financiers and businessmen, divided evenly among Chinese and foreigners. The foreigners were to be appointed by the Chinese and were to consist of about three Americans, an equal number of Englishmen, a Frenchman, and an Italian. No Japanese was to be included. As a by-product of this scheme, Soong hoped that the consultative committee would eventually take the place of the international Banking Consortium organized in 1920 to assist the Chinese government in any plans for reconstruction that required extensive financial support.[46] Soong's desire to replace the Consortium stemmed partly from his opposition to any agency which would serve as an instrument for Japanese participation in the reconstruction of China and partly from his sympathy with the widespread criticism of the Consortium which had always existed among the Chinese. The Chinese had not only refused to recognize the Consortium but had repeatedly attacked it as a monolithic institution which wanted to control all of China's external financial operations and to strengthen the hold of foreigners on China's economy.[47] The consultative committee was therefore designed to leave paramount power in the hands of the Chinese.[48]

As a first step toward the organization of a consultative committee, Dr. Soong succeeded in persuading Jean Monnet—who was later to become one of the architects of economic development in Europe— to act as chairman for the committee and to go to China for that purpose.[49] Next, Soong extended invitations to serve on the committee to Thomas W. Lamont of J. P. Morgan and Company, who was head of the American group of the Consortium, and Sir Charles Addis of the Hongkong and Shanghai Banking Corporation, who was head of the British group. At the same time he sent a letter to Secretary Hull explaining his idea of a consultative committee and expressing the hope that the United States government would be "sympathetic" to the effort which China was making toward reconstruction.[50] Hull forwarded Soong's letter to Washington with the comment that the Japanese were reportedly "closely observing these economic cooperation plans of China with the view of lodging objections to the course of other nations in that connection if any ground at all" could be found.[51] Lamont and Sir Charles Addis, on their part, decided to write to Daisuke Nohara, the representative of the Japanese group of the Consortium, to sound out that group's opinion. Nohara replied that the Japanese, perhaps more than any other people, were eager to help in the rehabilitation of China, but that they believed assistance should only be given to the Chinese "in such manner and at such time" as afforded hope of bringing about "harmonious relations" between China and other countries.[52] With regard to the proposed consultative committee, the Japanese group felt that it was "impossible to conceive" that such a committee, set up in the form suggested (that is, without Japanese participation), could be "authoritative and effective in view of the special position and influence of Japan in the Far East." Moreover, the constitution of the committee might "easily produce a feeling of irritation" in Japan which could lead to "untoward relations" between Japan and China that would disturb the peace. Also, if the representatives of some of the countries associated with the Consortium were, as suggested, members of the consultative committee, trouble might arise between the committee and the Consortium which could even result in the latter's disruption. For all these "very potent reasons" the Japanese group, to its regret, felt compelled to say that it viewed "with apprehension and disfavor the creation of the Consultative Committee contemplated."

According to Dr. Soong's account of subsequent developments, before the end of his trip to Europe he saw Lamont and found him "naturally" more concerned with the problems of J. P. Morgan and Company than with those of the Chinese Minister of Finance.[53] Lamont had indicated that he was not inclined to join the consultative committee and had "frankly" stated that he had to take into consideration the opposition of the Japanese as his firm was a banking representative of Japan's and did a good deal of business in that country.[54] Addis, on the other hand, had expressed a willingness to serve on the committee but intimated that he was delaying making any final decision at the request of the British Foreign Office, which wanted no more trouble with Japan. According to Lamont's account, he personally was convinced from the beginning that no plan involving substantial foreign aid for the reconstruction of China could be successful without the support of the Japanese.[55] He had consequently decided that his actions in respect to the consultative committee should, to a large extent, be guided by the opinions of his Japanese colleagues in the Consortium. Lamont also maintained subsequently that Addis had shared his views. In any event, the entire episode ended with both Lamont and Addis refusing to accept membership on the proposed consultative committee which in turn led Dr. Soong to shelve the whole idea of bringing such a committee into being.

Whatever Dr. Soong's successes or failures in obtaining financial support, his activities in the United States and Europe gave rise to a wave of violent protests on the part of the Japanese. On July 25, the Counselor of the Japanese Embassy in Washington, Toshihiko Taketomi, engaged Hornbeck in a long conversation. Hornbeck's official record of this talk states that Taketomi started with the assertion that the Japanese were "unfavorably impressed" with the special committee for technical cooperation between the League and China partly because the powers were embarking upon a project for aiding the Chinese from which Japan was excluded.[56] Taketomi thereupon launched into a lengthy discourse about "Japanese psychology and temperament" which ended in his saying that the Japanese people did not think the time was "ripe for the powers to be engaging in an enterprise of assistance to China" as their doing so made "things more difficult for Japan." Chiang Kai-shek and his "group at Nanking" had for some time been indicating that they were in favor of coming to an agreement with the Japanese. T. V. Soong and "his group" were, however, firmly set against such an agreement and were therefore applying for aid abroad which, by increasing the self-confidence of the Chinese people, would stiffen their opposition to Japan. Japan wanted to reach an understanding with China and the world "ought not to make it more difficult for her to do so." Upon being asked what kind of an understanding the Japanese had in mind, Taketomi replied that Japan wanted "peace on the basis of the *status quo*." At this point Taketomi "abruptly" inquired as to whether the United States government had received "definite assurance" that the proceeds of the R.F.C. credit would not be employed by the Nanking government for political ends. In response Hornbeck said that the Legislative Yuan had adopted a resolution to the effect that the credit should be used for productive purposes only and that some good faith was necessary in such transactions. The conversation closed as follows:

Mr. Taketomi then reverted to the subject of the League's effort to assist China. He said that it was ill-advised and ill-timed. Mr. Hornbeck asked what Mr. Taketomi thought the world should do. Mr. Taketomi replied that the world should desist. Mr. Hornbeck remarked that the League has been working on the project for several years, that it has a number of its experts already in China and that its most recent step has apparently been directed to the coordinating of the work of these experts; thus the project has a certain momentum; when something has gained momentum there are certain alternatives: there can be a certain amount of deflecting as regards direction or there can be a putting on of brakes or an attempt to come to a complete stop; what did Mr. Taketomi think should be done? Mr. Taketomi said that the thing should be "stopped." He thought that the League should let the matter alone and that if the League persisted the United States at least should let it alone. Mr. Hornbeck asked whether that did not amount to a suggestion that the world, in deference to Japanese susceptibilities and opinions and/or policies, should give up its own views (almost unanimously held among the nations) and abandon its wish and effort to be of assistance to an important and numerous population, the Chinese, who are struggling with a great variety of what to them are new and difficult problems. Mr. Taketomi said that it amounted to practically that.

Two weeks later, the Japanese ambassador referred to the R.F.C. loan during the course of a call on Secretary of State Hull.[57] The ambassador declared that China planned to sell the cotton and wheat purchased on credit at a discount and use the proceeds for all kinds of purposes which might seriously affect Japan. He expressed the "earnest hope" that the United States government would "keep these phases in mind" and would in future consult with Japan before taking any steps that might concern her interests. Hull replied that as far as the American government was concerned, the aim of the R.F.C. transaction had been to dispose of surplus stocks in order to help the price situation within the United States, which had become "intolerable"; any intention of exercising an adverse influence upon Japan's affairs had not been "remotely in mind." The ambassador, however, indicated that he was opposed not only to the R.F.C. agreement but also to the activities of the League of Nations and "similar proceedings" recently instituted in Europe for furnishing China with assistance. In this connection he repeatedly expressed his gratification that Lamont and other members of the Consortium did not seem inclined to take part in the current movement for the reconstruction of China.

The ambassador subsequently re-enforced his remarks to Secretary Hull by instructing Taketomi to give Hornbeck a fuller explanation of Japan's position in regard to the proposed consultative committee. Taketomi, consequently, told Hornbeck that the Japanese felt that the plan for a consultative committee was "objectionable" and that they were opposed to it for the same reasons that they were opposed to the League's project for technical assistance in China, that is, they were convinced that any effort to strengthen China would only encourage the Chinese to "persevere in an attitude of hostility to Japan" and they objected to any scheme from which they were excluded.[58]

In addition to protests made by Japanese officials without the knowledge of the public, the Japanese engaged in a press campaign in which they openly attacked the League and the United States for helping China.[59] All the charges that Rajchman was intensely and actively pro-Chinese and anti-Japanese were revived and it was constantly asserted that under Rajchman's leadership the newly created special committee for technical cooperation between the League and China would be fashioned into a political weapon for use against the Japanese. A spokesman of the Japanese Foreign Office was widely quoted as saying that, in view of Rajchman's appointment as the council's technical agent in China, Japan must be "prepared to take steps" for the protection of her interests should the special committee, by political maneuvers, seek to undermine her position on the mainland.[60] The Japanese press also carried the text of instructions dealing with the question of foreign financial aid to China, which had allegedly been sent by the Japanese Foreign Office to its embassies in the principal countries of Europe and the United States.[61] The instructions said that, in view of T. V. Soong's current activities, embassy officials should "remind government authorities, political parties, business leaders and financial groups of the Powers" that funds advanced to China were "apt to be misused for military purposes to oppose Japan and Manchukuo"; in addition, they should state that, if a situation developed in which China actually made such misuse of funds, the Japanese government would take drastic action against the Chinese, as it had in the case of Manchuria, and would hold the powers furnishing aid to China "partly responsible for the recurrence of the Sino-Japanese trouble." In relation to the R.F.C. credit in particular, the Japanese made much of the fact that the dissident Kuomintang faction in South China had cabled the State Department objecting to the credit on the grounds that it would be used by Chiang Kai-shek, T. V. Soong, and their followers to buy arms in order to wage war against their rivals.[62] The Japanese persistently claimed that the position taken by the South China leaders showed a "promiscuous supply" of money to China would only foment civil war in that country thereby disturbing the "peace of the Far East." They likewise charged that the R.F.C. credit could not be purely "commercial" as, in view of China's failure to meet all her previous financial obligations, it was evident that it would not be repaid. This argument led some the foremost newspapers in Japan to speculate on what political or military concessions the United States had received in return for granting the credit.[63]

The reaction of the Far Eastern Division of the State Department to the developments connected with Dr. Soong's efforts to obtain financial support for China is evident from a variety of documents written by members of the division at the time. Soong was to return to the United States for a brief visit on his way home from Europe in August 1933 and it was known that he wanted to see Roosevelt. The assumption within the Far Eastern Division was that Soong wished to discuss the question of financial and other aid for China. The division, consequently, prepared a number of memoranda for the President's use.

One of these memoranda, entitled "The Fifty Million Dollar Credit to China," constituted a warning to the President that the R.F.C. credit—which had been negotiated without the approval of the State Department—was creating serious difficulties in regard to our policy in the Far East.[64] The division stated that the British group in the Consortium had informed the other groups that, in its opinion, the credit violated the spirit, if not the letter, of the Consortium agreement.[65] The argument advanced by the British had been that, at the time the Consortium was formed, the various groups involved had been assured of the complete support of their governments and that therefore competition from any of those governments in providing China with financial assistance was not to be expected. The Japanese group had endorsed the objections raised by the British and had, in addition, expressed the fear that the proceeds of the credit would be used for the purchase of arms, thereby "fostering further political strife in China." The credit had also been criticized by the semi-independent faction in South China. Moreover many people believed that the Chinese government would not be able to sell the cotton and wheat profitably in which case the moral benefit that might have accrued to the United States government from the entire arrangement would have been lost.

In a second memorandum, the division asserted that Soong would undoubtedly endeavor to enlist American support for the technical program of the League in China.[66] The Japanese, however, had demonstrated recently that they objected to that program. Under these circumstances, the division felt that "we should assume a favorable attitude in principle toward the League's effort"; at the same time, "in connection with the actual giving of any encouragement to the Chinese to expect assistance from the American Government," we should take the opportunity, afforded by China's request for aid, to suggest that the Chinese government make a more effective attempt to pay the debts which it owed to the United States and its nationals. Appended to this memorandum was another, marked "Outstanding Claims Against the Chinese Government," which said that, in the view of the Far Eastern Division, the Chinese government had long exhibited a "lamentable lack" of desire to even seriously consider its financial obligations to American citizens. As a result, the problem of claims had become urgent, not only because of the inherent rights of the Americans concerned, but also because the Chinese government was constantly hypothecating, for new purposes, revenues which should be devoted to the service of debts owed to American creditors. An attempt should therefore be made to impress upon Soong the importance which the United States government attached to the Chinese government's settling its obligations.[67]

After Dr. Soong's arrival in the United States, at the beginning of August, Hornbeck had several long conversations with him during which it became evident that Soong was primarily interested in raising money in this country for the consultative committee which he still hoped to organize.[68] In relation to the problem of obtaining funds, Hornbeck spoke at length and most emphatically about the difficulties which the United States and other countries had experienced as a result of loans that had been extended to China in the past. He asserted that, in his opinion, the only way to reawaken American interest in loans to China would be for the Chinese government to demonstrate that it was making some concrete progress toward settling its outstanding obligations; what the creditors wanted, Hornbeck declared, was "performance." On the subject of debts, Soong confined himself to the remark that the consultative committee would take care of China's commitments. On the other hand, he dwelt in detail upon the developments that had taken place in connection with his plan for a consultative committee while he was in Europe. At the time Soong was speaking, Addis and Lamont had not yet responded formally to the invitation to serve on the consultative committee and Soong was under the impression that Addis would accept and that Lamont would not. He therefore expressed the hope that the American government would use its influence on his behalf to obtain banking assistance in the United States. Hornbeck sought to discourage this idea by remarking that it must be understood that the administration was not likely to attempt to drive American bankers into any project for international financing. On being asked what he thought in general of establishing a consultative committee, Hornbeck said that it might be a useful step but that various considerations would have to be taken into account. The Japanese would certainly do their utmost to thwart the committee's activities. Furthermore, the feasibility of creating such a committee would depend to a considerable extent upon the attitude of some two or three men in a few countries. Much might hinge upon obtaining Lamont's approval if only because of the influence which his attitude would have upon others. Hornbeck on his part inquired whether Soong's scheme for a consultative committee could not be linked with the Consortium as that body represented powerful interests and powerful governments. But Soong rejected this suggestion, saying that his plan, if successful, would mean the end of the Consortium which had always been anathema to the Chinese.

In sending a record of the above conversation to Hull, Hornbeck attached some written comments to the effect that Soong was naturally more intent on obtaining new loans for China than on taking care of old obligations.[69] Consequently, Hornbeck asserted, there seemed no occasion for optimism concerning the settlement of outstanding claims. Moreover, in respect to new loans, Soong was evidently determined to make arrangements whereby foreign powers and their nationals would furnish China with assistance but would not exercise any supervision over her political and economic development so that all control would remain in the hands of the Chinese.[70]

A few weeks later (August 25), Hornbeck in another memorandum to Secretary Hull, commented upon the proposed consultative committee further, this time from the point of view of Japan's opposition. Referring to Taketomi's protests against both the League's technical program in China and the plan for a consultative committee, Hornbeck declared that, in his opinion, "we should not allow ourselves to be substantially influenced by these manifestations of the Japanese Government's attitude. The fact, however, of these approaches should serve to put us on guard." Concerning the consultative committee in particular, Hornbeck wrote: "There is no reason why we should not, and there is sufficient why we should, take an attitude favorable toward the project." It might "well be doubted" whether such an undertaking as Soong had in mind would prosper sufficiently rapidly to become a "definite 'issue'" in the near future. If a consultative committee were organized, it would probably have to concentrate at first on meeting China's existing obligations and obtaining credits rather than on soliciting "substantial and definite financial assistance on a large scale." The Japanese, in all likelihood, were not apprehensive about any immediate foreign aid to China. What they feared was the growth of the influence of T. V. Soong in China and abroad. They regarded him as an obstacle to the "consummation of their plans" especially for forcing upon the Nanking government the conclusion of a formal agreement favorable to Japan. Admittedly anything which tended "to strengthen China must have a proportionally weakening effect as regards the policy of Japan to put over Japan's program." Nevertheless, the only means of "creating conditions of stability in the Far East" was to strengthen China. This course had been advocated in the preamble of the Nine Power Treaty. "That preamble," Hornbeck stated, "was and is directly in line with the traditional policy of the United States." We should therefore "continue to adhere to the principles therein laid down, disregarding, though not failing to take account of, Japan's unique present (and expressed) dissent from these principles and her efforts to dictate to the rest of the world a tacit or express abandonment of them."

It is apparent, therefore, that in general the Far Eastern Division was critical of the R.F.C. credit but continued to approve of the purposes of the League program in China and was not averse to Dr. Soong's plan for a consultative committee. It felt obliged, however, to approach the entire question of aid to China with caution and limited itself to suggesting that before looking for more financial assistance the Chinese government should discharge the financial responsibilities to foreign creditors which it had already incurred.

Following his talks with Hornbeck, T. V. Soong went to see the President at Hyde Park, where he discussed his difficulties in obtaining American support for his consultative committee.[71] Roosevelt suggested a number of persons who might be helpful, including John Pelley, President of the New York, New Haven, and Hartford Railroad. The President's proposal led to Pelley's obtaining a six months leave of absence from his board in order to make a survey of the Chinese railway system. But before the arrangements had been completed Pelley sought the advice of Lamont who said that the Chinese Government already had plenty of information about the nation's railroads in its possession and could readily make them profitable if the revenues were not absorbed by warlords.[72] Presumably as a result of Lamont's views, Pelley did not proceed to China.

Soong, therefore, departed from the United States without having achieved his goal as far as the consultative committee was concerned. A few months after his return to China, he resigned as Minister of Finance, reportedly because of pressures from various quarters including the Japanese.[73] Although the project for a consultative committee had by this time been set aside, Jean Monnet went to

China at Soong's request and, during the course of the ensuing winter engaged in the organization of a banking syndicate which became known as the China Development Finance Corporation. The corporation was inaugurated in June 1934 at which time it issued a statement declaring that it was entirely Chinese "in conception, capital, and direction" and that its over-all objective was to serve as an "instrument for the organized reconstruction of China."[74] Although Chinese in character, the corporation was not designed to exclude foreigners from its operations but, on the contrary, to arrange for the financing of any suitable enterprise with both foreign and Chinese money. Thus it sought to attract foreign capital to China and to provide Chinese with a means for investing accumulated funds. In connection with the latter point, the corporation proposed to develop an investment market in China and, in other ways, modernize China's financial practices. While the corporation itself had a capital of only CN $10 million it was set up to engage in a wide variety of activities (beginning with railroad rehabilitation) and was regarded by Monnet himself as having almost unlimited possibilities.[75]

During the winter of 1933-1934, the League program of technical aid for China also made some progress. League experts continued to help the Chinese in the solution of problems related to road construction, water conservation, health, and education.[76] At the same time, the League participated in the National Economic Council's experiment of conducting an intensive program of rural reconstruction in a few provinces. Studies of conditions in Kiangsi and Chekiang were undertaken by members of the council staff in conjunction with representatives of the League's technical organizations. These studies, like the more general survey done by Professor Dragoni earlier, dealt with many aspects of China's agrarian problem.[77] The work in Chekiang was carried out under the chairmanship of Sir Arthur Salter, who in February 1934 also wrote a report for the Chinese government of his impressions of the existing state of the Chinese economy, in which he included suggestions for changes in policy.[78] The League experts did not, therefore, confine themselves to a consideration of technical questions but discussed fundamental political, economic, and social issues. The broad outlook which thus characterized the League program in China was probably in part because of the influence of Rajchman who as technical agent demonstrated a feeling for and understanding of the entire Chinese scene that was regarded as exceptional among foreigners.[79] Rajchman had returned to China after his appointment as technical agent and remained there until the early spring of 1934, when he departed for Geneva to make his first comprehensive report on the League's technical work in China to the special committee. It is noteworthy that in this report Rajchman stressed the necessity of placing less emphasis upon sending foreign experts to China and devoting more attention to bringing Chinese specialists to the West. Rajchman's belief was that the help which foreign advisers could give China was essentially ephemeral while the development of a group of Chinese leaders through study and experience in the West would produce permanent and much more significant results.[80]

Of the various attempts which were made to provide China with technical and financial assistance, the R.F.C. credit encountered the greatest difficulties. In December 1933, the Chinese government decided to give the National Economic Council greater power and to subsidize its activities through proceeds derived from the sale of the wheat and cotton obtained through the R.F.C. credit. But, for a number of reasons, the authorities at Nanking found it impossible to sell as much cotton as originally planned.[81] As a consequence, in March 1934 the credit was reduced to U.S. $20 million by agreement between the Chinese and American governments.[82]

Assistance in technical and financial matters for China's reconstruction was, however, not the only form of foreign aid sought by the Chinese. Chiang Kai-shek was determined to create a professional, modern army.[83] For this purpose he turned to Germany where, owing to the limitations imposed upon the armed forces by the Versailles Treaty, high officials who otherwise would have been in the service of their country were free to engage in undertakings elsewhere. At the Generalissimo's invitation General von Seeckt, the former commander-in-chief of the Reichswehr, spent three months in China in 1933 during which time he drew up a plan that was used as a blueprint for the reorganization of the Chinese army. Besides dealing with purely military problems, von Seeckt placed the utmost emphasis upon the question of industrialization, insisting that the creation of a powerful army was impossible without the simultaneous development of an efficient economic system. In the spring of 1934, von Seeckt returned to China as the head of a German military mission which was to assist in the practical application of many of his own recommendations.

Chiang Kai-shek was also concerned with the building of an air force and, during the Manchurian crisis, appealed to the United States to send a number of qualified Americans to China to organize and operate a school for the training of military aviators.[84] The United States War Department, with the concurrence of the State Department, rejected this appeal largely on the grounds that it would be unwise for the United States to become involved in any such project in view of the conflict between Japan and China. Subsequently, however, the Chinese government arranged with Colonel John Hamilton Jouett and some thirteen other American aviators, all of the United States Reserve Corps, to come to China to help in the establishment and direction of a military aviation school at Hangchow. The arrangements between the Chinese government and the Jouett group were made through the United States Department of Commerce without the knowledge of any of the other branches of the United States government.[85] The State Department only learned of the matter when Colonel Jouett and his associates applied for passports. It thereupon expressed its disapproval of the entire transaction to the Department of Commerce. But in view of the fact that all the aviators involved had already signed contracts with the Chinese government, they were permitted to proceed to China. The school at Hangchow was soon in operation and, by the end of 1933, Colonel Jouett was credited with having played a major part in the development of an embryo Chinese air force which was regarded as very promising.[86] By this time, however, the Italian government had decided to enter the field of military aviation in China and on the personal urging of Mussolini the Chinese agreed to accept an Italian Air Mission which was to be supported by funds from the Italian Boxer Indemnity.[87] The mission arrived in China in October 1933 and its commander, General Lordi, was appointed chief aviation adviser to the Chinese government six months later. The position of the American group seemed therefore threatened, if not doomed, unless it received some effective support from Washington.[88]

The Nanking government not only sought foreign aid in the development of aviation for military purposes but also for commercial uses. In 1931, two large companies were formed, the China National Aviation Corporation, a Sino-American concern, and the Eurasia Aviation Corporation, a Sino-German enterprise. Foreign participation in both military and nonmilitary aviation in China was closely tied in with the sale of foreign airplanes to the Chinese. Despite keen competition in effecting such sales, the United States took first place in 1933 when her exports to China of aircraft and related equipment more than quadrupled those of the previous year.[89] This sharp increase was presumed to be partially a result of the efforts of the United States Department of Commerce, which had been actively engaged in promoting American aviation trade with China.[90]

After the summer of 1933 the outburst of indignation on the

part of the Japanese against foreign aid to China had quieted down. The ensuing calm was temporarily broken, however, at the time that the Chinese government announced that the National Economic Council was empowered to undertake a larger program which would be supported through the R.F.C. credit. Taketomi again called on Hornbeck to say that the R.F.C. credit continued to make "a very bad impression" in Japan and that his government hoped that if and when the question of extending the credit arose, thought would be given to its "general effect upon American-Japanese relations."[91] Also, during the midwinter session of the Japanese Diet, various members of the Lower House charged the United States government with sending "many aviators to China as instructors," in order to build up a powerful air force, and with attempting to establish control over all phases of China's aviation as a threat to Japan. The Japanese press had, indeed, from time to time published lurid articles about American military activities in China including an elaborate story of a secret Sino-American aviation treaty including three chapters and seventeen articles, all set forth in detail.[92] Attacks upon the United States in Japanese newspapers had, moreover, often involved the claim that America was seeking military bases in China and was equipping the Chinese army with all kinds of Western arms in order to serve her own selfish ends.[93]

It was not until April 1934, however, that Japanese opposition to foreign aid to China was renewed in a manner that transformed it into an issue of major international importance. The events that took place were so peculiarly confused that it was some time before foreign officials were able to piece together even a moderately coherent account.[94] The facts as ascertained by the American embassy in Tokyo were that during the course of a press conference on April 17, a foreign correspondent asked Eiji Amau, a spokesman for the Japanese Foreign Office, to explain the position of the Japanese government in respect to the aid being furnished to China from abroad. Amau went to his files and produced a paper which seemed to the reporters to contain instructions that had recently been sent to the Japanese Minister in China. After translating the document orally, Amau explained that his translation was unofficial but that the document itself had been approved by Hirota. Later on the same day, he issued a statement to the Japanese press which was labeled "unofficial." However, in reply to questions from some American journalists, Amau said that the statement "could be considered as official" and that a summary would be sent to Japanese diplomatic officers in other countries to be conveyed to the governments to which they were accredited "if necessary." He also promised to provide the correspondents with a written English translation which he delivered to them on April 19 but which was again stamped "unofficial." Subsequently, at the request of Secretary Hull, the Japanese Ambassador gave the State Department a copy of instructions which had been sent to the Japanese Minister in China by Hirota some time earlier and which presumably had provided the basis for the Amau statement.

The State Department in Washington initially sought to get an authoritative text of the Amau declaration and to find out whether it had been made with the consent of the Japanese Minister of Foreign Affairs. Further investigation revealed that no authoritative text existed. But it also quickly became apparent that this fact in and of itself was not of major importance as the various statements, oral and written, which had been made by the Japanese were so similar in substance as to leave no doubt of their basic meaning.[95] Despite variations in language they all proclaimed that Japan had a special responsibility for the maintenance of peace in East Asia and therefore did not always agree with the views of other nations in respect to China. While Japan desired to see the Chinese preserve their national integrity, restore order, and achieve unification, history had demonstrated that such objectives could only be attained through China's own independent efforts. Japan must consequently oppose any operations undertaken by the foreign powers in the name of technical and financial assistance to China and any projects such as detailing military instructors or military advisers to China or supplying the Chinese with war planes. These assertions were re-enforced in the instructions which had been sent to the Minister in Peiping by the following concluding paragraph:

From the point of view above stated, we think our guiding principle should be generally to defeat foreign activities in China at present, not only those of a joint nature but those conducted individually, in view of the fact that China is still trying to tie Japan's hands through using the influence of foreign Powers.

The issue of whether the Amau declaration had been made with Hirota's approval was raised by the Foreign Minister himself in a highly confidential interview with Ambassador Grew on April 25.[96] Hirota stated that Amau had acted without his knowledge and had given the world a "wholly false impression" of Japan's attitude. Various foreign activities had tended to disturb peaceful conditions in China, and Japan was naturally very much interested in those conditions owing to her nearness to China. But Japan intended to observe the provisions of the Nine Power Treaty. For his own part, he was trying to follow the policy of the Emperor and was seeking to "achieve with all countries, and especially with the United States, relations of friendliness." The chauvinists in Japan wanted to pursue a more aggressive foreign policy but, as long as he had the support of the Emperor, he would adhere to his present course even though that should mean his assassination.

Grew was clearly moved by the Minister's remarks and prepared to believe that he had not sanctioned the issuance of the Amau statement.[97] In a letter in which he described his interview with Hirota to the State Department the Ambassador said, "In such a case one can only be guided by one's personal impressions. My impressions of his sincerity were quite clear."[98] Nevertheless, Grew soon concluded that whether or not the Foreign Minister had consented to the Amau declaration in advance was beside the point as the declaration represented the policy that the Japanese were determined to follow and, given the state of public opinion in Japan, Hirota could not repudiate it and remain in office.[99] If the principles which Amau had enunciated were carried out, Grew thought that they would place China "in a state of tutelage under Japan" but he did not believe that any immediate measures would be taken owing to Hirota's desire for moderation.

Yet, even if Grew's assumption that Hirota neither initiated nor supported the Amau statement were correct, the question remained as to why Amau himself had made such a pronouncement at this particular time. In general it was thought that Amau had probably acted as a result of pressure from the Japanese militarists and a rising tide of anxiety in Japan about the increasing evidence of foreign aid to China.[100] The Japanese seemed especially concerned over the activities of Jean Monnet and Rajchman. There had been many rumors to the effect that Monnet was organizing an international banking syndicate which would serve as a means for the reentry of foreign capital—especially American capital—into China on a large scale. Moreover, Monnet and Rajchman were known to be close friends and the Japanese tended to assume that they were collaborating in an effort to obtain extensive support for China in Europe and the United States.[101] Rajchman was scheduled to give his first important report on the League's work in China to the Special Committee at Geneva in late April and there was widespread speculation as to whether he would urge the League to undertake a greatly expanded program involving both technical and financial assistance in China's reconstruction. In any event, the technical aid that the League was currently according the Chinese was ostensibly bearing fruit, and the interchange between Chinese and Western personnel, which the League was encouraging, seemed to the Japanese to be giving the Nanking government an increasingly dangerous Occidental orientation. In addition, the Japanese were aroused by the news that General von Seeckt had returned to China with a military mission and that foreign participation in the development of Chinese aviation was showing a marked upward turn.[102]

Within the State Department in Washington, the days following the Amau declaration were filled with a steady stream of incoming and outgoing messages. Ambassador Grew was busy furnishing the Department with information but offered no suggestions as to the course the United States government should follow. Nelson Johnson, on the other hand, cabled the Department that, in his opinion, the administration should not let the Japanese pronouncement "pass unchallenged" as it ran "directly counter to the spirit and letter of the Nine Power Treaty."[103] In accordance with his whole concept of American policy in the Far East, the minister declared: "It is not China's independence that interests us so much as our independence of action in the Pacific both now and in the future." Johnson warned that the mere assertion of a doctrine such as Amau had enunciated might be a sufficient threat to prevent the Chinese from purchasing American airplanes and other articles to which the Japanese objected, thus damaging our trade relations with China. He also urged the Department to consider that, upon our retirement from the Philippines, the neutrality of those islands would be of "questionable value" in the face of Japan's attitude toward the Washington treaties as demonstrated by the Amau statement.

On April 21 the United States embassy in London cabled the State Department that the British press and public opinion were greatly concerned over the Amau declaration and that Sir John Simon had told Ambassador Bingham that he took a "most apprehensive view" of the Japanese move.[104] Sir John had furthermore stated that, as soon as all the facts were established, he wished to exchange opinions with the State Department as he believed the situation called for close Anglo-American cooperation. Two days later the Department instructed Ambassador Bingham to inform Sir John that it would "give careful consideration to any suggestions or proposals" he wished to make.[105] At the same time the ambassador was to say that the administration in Washington was willing to do its part "toward the safeguarding of the common interest" but that it would not do more than its part. Hornbeck stated additionally in a talk with the British ambassador in Washington that, although the adoption of parallel policies by several governments had the advantage of giving the semblance of a common front, the American government "did not intend to assume or be placed in a position of leadership in initiating proposals for joint or concurrent action."[106] The question of undertaking cooperative measures was, however, dropped by the British themselves who, in apparent contradiction to their initial stand, decided to act individually and to limit themselves to asking Tokyo for a clarification of the Amau statement with a view to determining, in particular, its relationship to the provisions of the Nine Power Treaty.[107]

The Far Eastern Division of the State Department had felt from the outset that, in light of all the confusion surrounding the developments in Japan, it should take its time in formulating a policy for the United States. But, on learning of the course the British had decided to pursue, the Assistant Chief of the Division, Maxwell Hamilton, suggested that the United States should refrain from taking any notice of the Amau declaration and should merely "carry on business as usual."[108] Hamilton argued that the other powers evidently did not intend to raise any strong objections to the Amau declaration; consequently, if the administration were to respond with a statement of its own or make any similar move, it would only put America back in the position that it had occupied during the Manchurian crisis, when it had persistently registered its opposition to Japan's actions in advance of all other nations. Hamilton saw no reason for the United States to "stick out its neck" and become the spearhead of a movement directed against the Japanese. American interests in China, he said, were not any more important than—if as important as— the interests of Great Britain, Russia, and France. Moreover, in dealing with a military people like the Japanese, words would have no favorable effect unless they were accompanied by a manifest determination to enforce them if necessary. The United States neither was nor should be prepared to use force against Japan at this juncture.

In the end, however, the Far Eastern Division decided that, as the Japanese had spoken out vigorously and the British had at least raised the issue of the Nine Power Treaty, the American people would expect their government to make some sort of statement.[109] An aide-mémoire was therefore drafted in the division and approved by the Secretary.[110] It was deliberately worded to be as nonprovocative as possible in order not to invite a controversy with Japan so that no reference was made to the Nine Power Treaty nor were any arguments advanced on China's behalf. In general, the Far Eastern Division felt that the importance of the communication must lie in the fact of its being issued rather than (as Hornbeck stated) in the "vigor or lack of vigor, the completeness or lack of completeness of its content."

The *aide-mémoire* was delivered to the Japanese on April 29 and made public by the State Department on the following day.[111] It declared at the outset that, in view of the recent indications of Japan's attitude toward the rights and interests of other countries in China, the American government, wishing to adhere to the "tradition of frankness" that had prevailed in its relations with the Japanese government, desired to reaffirm its own position. The relations of the United States with China, as well as with other nations, were governed by generally accepted principles of international law and the provisions of treaties. The United States was associated with China or with Japan or with both in multilateral treaties related to the Far East and "in one great multilateral treaty" to which practically all the countries of the world were parties. Entered into by agreement, treaties could lawfully be modified or terminated but only by processes to which its signatories had given their consent. The statement went on to say,

In the international associations and relationships of the United States, the American Government seeks to be duly considerate of the rights, the obligations and the legitimate interests of other countries, and it expects on the part of other governments due consideration of the rights, obligations and the legitimate interests of the United States.

In the opinion of the American people and the American Government, no nation can, without the assent of the other nations concerned, rightfully endeavor to make conclusive its will in situations where there are involved the rights, obligations and the legitimate interests of other sovereign states.

The American Government has dedicated the United States to the policy of the good neighbor. To the practical application of that policy it will continue, on its own part and in association with other governments, to devote its best efforts.

At a press conference on May 1, the Secretary of State gave an off-the-record talk on the *aide-mémoire* and appealed to the correspondents to refrain from writing the kind of stories that would antagonize the Japanese.[112] It was the policy of the United States, Hull said, to cooperate with the efforts and professed desire of the Japanese government to strengthen the traditional relations of friendship between the two countries. To carry out this policy as successfully as possible, the administration in Washington felt that the less the agitation created over any differences that arose between Japan and America the easier it was to settle those differences in a "spirit of better understanding and harmony." It would therefore be most helpful to both countries if people in the United States, instead of trying to "seek out and rake together" reports of an unfriendly nature, would emphasize the spirit of such communications as the letters which he (Hull) had exchanged with Hirota in February. The *aide-mémoire* which had just been issued was a "statement of principles, attitudes and one might say of intentions" which governed the course of the American government in the conduct of its foreign affairs. This statement had a "message for China and other countries as well as Japan."

Shortly after his press conference, Hull asked the Far Eastern Division to review the policy of the United States toward China for the purpose of determining whether it should in any way be altered for the sake of avoiding friction with Japan.[113] As a result in mid-May the division presented the Secretary with a memorandum containing suggestions in regard to the granting of American financial and military aid to China in future. In connection with the question of financial aid, the memorandum declared that various considerations must be taken into account. The Japanese had attacked the $50 million cotton and wheat credit as violating the spirit, if not the letter, of the Consortium. There appeared to be some validity to this contention. Moreover the credit had been detrimental to the interests both of China and of the United States. Coupled with the difficulties which had arisen over the R.F.C. transaction was the fact that the Chinese government had a long history of defaulting on the payment of its obligations and currently was heavily in debt to American creditors. In view of these circumstances, the memorandum asserted, it was felt that the American government and its agencies should refrain from according any further financial assistance to China in any form whatsoever. (A marginal note indicated that an exception could be made in case of international action.)

In respect to military assistance, the memorandum argued that Japan's charges against the United States were unjustified. The American instructors at Hangchow, it said, were in no way connected with the American government except possibly through the holding of commissions in the reserve corps. Of the arms and munitions of war (exclusive of aircraft) which had been supplied to China from abroad during the year 1933, America's share had been no more than one quarter of one per cent. Furthermore, under existing regulations no arms or munitions could be exported from the United States to China without a license from the State Department which examined every application with great care. While admittedly America had taken the lead in 1933 in the shipment of aircraft and accessories to China, a relatively small portion of this equipment had been for military purposes. In any case, the volume of trade in such articles was insufficient to justify any apprehension on the part of the Japanese that China was effectively preparing for an armed offensive against them; indeed, Japan was fully aware of the fact that, from a military standpoint, China was all but impotent. Nevertheless, the memorandum stated, certain measures should be taken to avert any future controversy between America and Japan over the issue of military aid to China. Whenever and wherever possible, the United States government should discourage American citizens from offering direct help to the Chinese armed forces. The administration should also seize every opportunity to make known to the public that the American aviators who were currently serving as advisers in China were acting solely in a private capacity. In addition the State Department should continue to exercise rigid control over the exports of arms and munitions to China and should make no attempt to foster such exports.[114]

Only two days after the above memorandum had been given to Secretary Hull an occasion arose to apply concretely the recommendations of the Far Eastern Division which were related to financial assistance to China.[115] A cable arrived in Washington from Professor James Harvey Rogers who had gone to China at the request of Secretary of the Treasury Henry Morgenthau, Jr., to obtain a first-hand view of conditions.[116] Rogers reported that he had just spent some time with H. H. Kung who had suggested that the United States should give China a loan, the proceeds of which would be spent on projects such as highway construction and water conservation, that would serve to accelerate the growing movement toward the unification of China; Kung was shortly to submit proposals for satisfactory security provisions. Rogers urged that consideration be given in Washington to meeting Kung's request on the "assumption that a unified China is of high importance to the United States."[117] Hornbeck, however, strongly advised Hull to persuade the Treasury to instruct Rogers not to engage in any further discussion of the entire subject of loans. In a detailed communication to the Secretary he restated the Far Eastern Division's position against furnishing China with any form of financial assistance and also presented further arguments in support of its stand. It should be borne in mind, he wrote, that the existing situation in China differed but little from that which had prevailed for many years and that "even an approximate rehabilitation of that vast country" was "not likely to occur for decades to come." The Japanese had, moreover, declared their opposition to any foreign government's giving the Chinese any "political loans." In view of the "known weakness" of China's financial structure which was "such that no private banking institution would under existing circumstances consider seriously the granting of further loans to China," other nations as well as Japan would in all likelihood "consider as political any further loans made or credits extended to China by the United States."

Whether as a result of action by Secretary Hull or for some other reason, Dr. Kung's proposal was set aside and, for the time being, there appears to have been no further discussion in Washington of either financial or military help to China. Meanwhile, however, the Japanese Consul General at Geneva, Masayuki Yokoyama, had made a formal statement to the press which was similar to the Amau declaration but specifically designed as an attack upon the League for providing the Chinese with technical assistance.[118] After issuing the statement, Yokoyama told Prentiss Gilbert that he was about to inform Avenol that the Japanese government would regard as "inimical acts" any measures undertaken by the League's technical organizations which did not conform to Japan's expressed policy in the Far East.[119] Yokoyama referred in particular to the fact that Rajchman was to present his first comprehensive report to the special committee at a meeting to be held on May 17 and declared that he understood the report would involve suggestions which were "either implicitly or explicitly" antagonistic to Japan.

In a subsequent talk with Gilbert, Avenol said that many rumors were current concerning Rajchman's alleged political activities and that he might have to take steps to "clarify" the situation. Gilbert received the impression that the Secretary General was intimating that if Rajchman were shown to have exceeded the scope of his mandate from the League, it might become necessary to repudiate him.[120] On the other hand, Avenol declared that the special committee must continue its program of technical cooperation with China which he described as a "modest" and "wholly appropriate" undertaking.

The "Rajchman question" rapidly became more acute. As the time drew near for the meeting of the special committee on May 17, there were rumors that the Japanese would tender formal charges against Rajchman. High government officials in Tokyo were quoted in the Japanese press as saying that the special committee would avoid reappointing Rajchman (whose first term in office was about to expire) in order to avert further friction with Japan.[121] Western newspaper correspondents at Geneva came to feel that a failure by the special committee to support Rajchman would amount to a complete abandonment by the League of any effort to oppose the Amau doctrine and Japanese aggression in China in general. The correspondents therefore made a deliberate attempt to bring the "Rajchman question" before the public with the result that leading newspapers in the West paid considerably more attention to it than would otherwise have been the case.[122] Even the London *Times,* which had put the best possible light on the Amau declaration, came out in defense of Rajchman and declared that the Chinese government had the right to seek help in any way it deemed necessary.[123]

The United States government, on its part, decided that it must not become involved in any dispute with Japan over the Rajchman issue. On May 10, the State Department instructed Ferdinand L. Mayer, an American official at Geneva, to attend the May 17 session of the special committee serving, as previously, in the capacity of an unofficial observer.[124] However, in case there were indications that the committee intended to take formal notice of Japan's allegations against Rajchman, Mayer was to inform the Department immediately and refrain from attending any further meetings until specifically authorized to do so. On May 15, Sze called on Hornbeck to say that the Chinese government was "very much concerned" over the forthcoming session of the special committee which it felt was of "vital importance to China."[125] The Minister urgently expressed the hope that the American government would take an "active" part in the committee's deliberations but Hornbeck indicated very plainly that any such expectations were bound to be disappointed.

In the end the problem of Japan's opposition to Rajchman was not raised at the meeting of May 17. During the course of the summer, however, Rajchman was informed by the authorities of the League that, for "administrative reasons" he could not retain his position as technical agent in China and at the same time remain Director of the Health Section of the League.[126] Faced with this choice, Rajchman decided to give up his post in China. Granted the events which had taken place earlier, it was believed at Geneva that, regardless of any administrative difficulties which might have arisen, the League had acted primarily as a result of direct or indirect pressures exercised by the Japanese.

In view of the many difficulties that had developed in respect to foreign aid for China's reconstruction, Hornbeck attempted to reassess the entire situation in the summer of 1934. In a detailed exposition of his views submitted to the President and Secretary Hull, he asserted that there was little likelihood of establishing order and peace in China unless the Chinese government engaged in an extensive program for the development of communications, industries, trade, et cetera, that would substantially improve economic conditions throughout the country.[127] But, since such a program was essentially costly, the question was how to finance it. Hornbeck stated further,

. . . for such endeavor the Chinese Government has no funds. It has often been pointed out that the Chinese Government expends an undue proportion of its revenues upon military equipment and activities. If that be a fact, the pointing it out and complaining of it as a fact does not alter the equally or more important fact that for purposes of substantial constructive effort on the economic side the Chinese Government does not possess funds. Moreover, it is also a fact that the revenues of the Chinese Government are not extensive, and further a fact that the taxpaying capacity of the Chinese nation is not great, and finally a fact that, from the historical point of view, it has not been the practice of nations to finance large scale economic developments from current revenues. The economic developments which are called for in China can be carried out only by a process of borrowing by the Chinese Government. That Government cannot borrow at home the amounts necessary: the capital simply is not available in China. This points to the desirability, to the advantage both of the Chinese and of the world, for international financing in relation to China.

Hornbeck went on to say that the Japanese had opposed the efforts of other countries to help China; at the same time, other nations would undoubtedly object to being excluded from any enterprise to aid the Chinese which might be fostered by Japan. The "way out" of this impasse was to resurrect the "idea of joint and collective assistance to China" which could be realized through an instrument that was already in existence—the Consortium. The groups that made up the Consortium represented the only powers that might have enough spare capital to provide the Chinese with the amounts needed for any large effort at economic development. And while admittedly these groups had not made loans to China in the past, this was partly because the Chinese themselves had not been willing to appeal to them, a situation which might hopefully be altered.

Specifically, Hornbeck suggested that he should be authorized to discuss the relevant aspects of the Consortium with Lamont who was about to sail for Europe where he intended to talk over Consortium matters with some of his associates in London.[128] In this connection, Hornbeck stated in an accompanying letter to the Secretary,

If authorized and instructed to see Mr. Lamont, I would like to be able . . . to say to him that you and the President, although you have not had occasion to make any intensive study of the Consortium proposition, and although you do not wish to be committed or to be brought into discussions of the matter at this stage, are not adversely disposed in regard to the Consortium and its possibilities as an agency for cooperative action; to say that this Administration would like, in case the British, the French, and the

Japanese Governments are already of that inclination, to see the Consortium agreement kept alive, in the thought that it may have future value; to say that in whatever may be done with or by the Consortium, this Administration would not wish, for the present at least, that the American Government or the American banking group take a position of leadership; to say that we believe that the leadership should be taken by the British or the Japanese; and to say, in brief, that with an open mind as regards future possibilities, which possibilities will need to be carefully explored and sympathetically dealt with, the attitude of the Administration with regard to Consortium possibilities is one of good will and watchful optimism.

With Secretary Hull's consent, Hornbeck subsequently made a statement to Lamont by telephone along the lines indicated above.[129] The essence of his remarks was that the administration would "prefer to see at this time no change with regard to the life of the Consortium"; in other words, the administration hoped the Consortium would not disband but at the same time was "not ready to suggest activity." Concerning the future Mr. Hornbeck said,

When there becomes available more and clearer evidence with regard to what really are Japan's intention and plan of procedure with regard to China and the Far Eastern situation in general, everybody will be in a better position to judge with regard to what seems possible and practicable on the part of other countries.

Lamont agreed to sound out the views of his colleagues in the Consortium but intimated that he might have difficulty in persuading his American associates to follow the policy Hornbeck had outlined.[130] For a large part of the American group had been showing an increasing inclination to withdraw from the Consortium on two grounds: first, that membership entailed expenses (such as the maintenance of an office) which, however small, yielded no tangible results; and, second, that even if the Consortium ultimately engaged in loans to China, the Securities Exchange Act, which had just been passed in the United States, would prevent most of the interested American banks from floating any portion of the loans.[131] To all appearances Lamont himself was skeptical about the value of keeping the American group in existence, partly for the reasons just mentioned and partly because he had become discouraged about the situation in China. None of the evidence at hand indicates that Lamont was at this time as bitterly disappointed over developments in China as he was to become later.[132] But a letter which he wrote to Nelson Johnson in November 1933 suggests that even then he regarded political and economic conditions in China as too unpromising to make foreign aid practicable.[133] Furthermore, Johnson's reply to this letter could only have tended to convince Lamont of the correctness of his views.[134]

The Minister said in effect that foreign bankers could not assist the Nanking regime until assured of adequate protection for whatever investments they made in China; "Chinese leadership" was, however, unable to provide the necessary safeguards and certainly neither Europe nor America was prepared to "substitute itself for the Chinese Government in the exercise of the responsibility of policing the country and making things secure for capital."

Aside from any personal preferences he may have entertained, Lamont was evidently anxious to carry out the administration's wishes.[135] At a meeting of the managing committee of the American group in 1934, he explained in confidence that, in the view of the Department of State, the "present would be an inopportune time for active consideration of Group dissolution." He thereupon recommended that the issue of disbandment be "held entirely in abeyance," a suggestion with which the group concurred.[136]

In conclusion, a résumé of the administration's most important actions following the Amau declaration may serve to bring out the nature of the policy that it had adopted. First, an officer of the Far Eastern Division recommended that the United States should not lead the other nations in opposing Japan—as it had during the Manchurian crisis—but should proceed on its customary course as though nothing had happened. Next, the State Department told the British that it would consider a proposal for parallel action submitted by others but would not put forth any plan of its own. Upon the failure of the British to make any suggestions, Hull issued a unilateral statement which was, however, worded to create as little friction as possible between the United States and Japan. Immediately thereafter the Secretary asked the press to refrain from stirring up trouble between America and Japan and instructed the Far Eastern Division to explore the possibility of making changes in our China policy that might serve to obviate difficulties with the Japanese. The Far Eastern Division thereupon recommended that the administration should not provide the Chinese with any further financial aid and should adhere to the circumspect procedures which the State Department had been advocating in respect to various forms of military assistance. The recommendations concerning loans—which were based on various considerations though the main one was to avoid arousing further hostility in Japan—were put into effect at once. Meanwhile, in an evident attempt to avoid quarrels with the Japanese on other fronts, the State Department remained aloof from the controversy between Japan and the League. In the end the administration decided that capital for China's reconstruction would have to come from both the West and

Japan and that the best means of obtaining funds would be through the Consortium. The State Department consequently exerted its influence to keep the Consortium intact but, at the same time, did not expect that organization to engage in any activities for the present and was actually opposed to the American group's initiating any move.

The administration therefore followed a remarkably consistent course. It might have renewed the Stimsonian effort to champion the movement for world order as the Amau doctrine was a clear violation of the Nine Power Treaty; but it did not do so.[137] Instead the State Department sought to avoid increasing the dangers which already existed in the relations of the United States and Japan and decided, not only to refrain from making any move that might provoke the Japanese, but for the most part to remain relatively inactive. The administration's policy in respect to the Amau doctrine consequently was dominated by the same considerations that determined its policy at the time of the Tangku Truce suggesting that its ideas were taking definite form.

As the Roosevelt administration shaped its course in the Far East, in all probability it assumed that it had the support of the press. According to the testimony of officials who were in a position to know, the Far Eastern Division of the State Department attempted to follow the editorial policies of only a few leading newspapers.[138] A study of eight such newspapers, undertaken by Lawrence I. Kramer, Jr., at Harvard University a few years ago, gives an indication of the impression likely to have been created by a small sampling of publications representative of a cross-section of political opinion and of different geographic areas.[139]

At the end of the Manchurian crisis, the internationalist newspapers surveyed by Kramer all believed that the main issue involved in the situation in the Far East was the preservation of the world's peace machinery. A good expression of their point of view appeared in an editorial in the *San Francisco Chronicle*—entitled "The League Must Act or Quit"—written at the time that the Committee of Nineteen was about to consider the position it wished to assume in respect to the Lytton report:

We could stand a surrender on Manchuria if China and Japan can. But a surrender of the new machinery of organized peace throughout the world would set us back before 1914 and make the stupendous sacrifices of the great war fruitless. That is too high a price to pay, even for the friendship, which we all desire, of Japan.[140]

As to the type of action the internationalist papers wanted the League and the United States to adopt on behalf of the peace system, the *Milwaukee Journal* called for the severance of trade relations with Japan to bring her to "her knees."[141] The *Chronicle* favored a "concerted refusal to lend money or sell munitions to Japan."[142] The *Cleveland Press* advocated economic and financial sanctions against Manchukuo.[143] The *Christian Science Monitor* urged an arms embargo against the Japanese and seemed to lean toward the idea of a boycott if the world was prepared to make the necessary sacrifices.[144]

When it became evident, however, that the Manchurian crisis was over, the attitude of the internationalist journals changed markedly. Even more than the State Department itself, they assumed that since the effort of the League and the United States to safeguard the peace structure had failed, the whole question of the maintenance of the peace system had for the present ceased to be a live factor in the Far Eastern situation. Moreover they tended to feel that, apart from this question, the Sino-Japanese conflict did not involve any issue of vital importance to the United States. In contrast to the great emphasis which they placed upon the Manchurian crisis up until the moment of Japan's decision to withdraw from the League, the internationalist papers paid little attention to the Tangku Truce, either overlooking it entirely or treating it as a matter of no direct concern to America.[145] The *Cleveland Press* and the *San Francisco Chronicle* carried no editorials on the truce. The *Los Angeles Times* made only a few comments on what it termed "New Oriental Complications."[146] The *Christian Science Monitor* contented itself with hoping that Japan was now satiated and would seek to consolidate its gains in Manchuria and Jehol without invading China proper.[147] *The New York Times* alone published two editorials on the truce but in both intimated that the concessions which the Chinese were being forced to make to Japan were their own affair and that China had better adjust herself to the situation as it had developed.[148] All in all the mood of the internationalist press does not seem to have differed radically from that of the isolationist Hearst publications which, in reference to the events leading up to the Tangku Truce, declared,

Let the Japanese decide to set up new states and governments in Asia if they choose, while the Chinese decide to resist or not to resist. All that is not OUR business. It interests us. We SYMPATHIZE. But it is NOT OUR CONCERN.[149]

Admittedly the American press might have championed China's cause at the time of the Tangku Truce irrespective of whether the United States itself had a stake in the Sino-Japanese conflict. But even the internationalist papers studied by Kramer exhibited little of the concern for China customarily ascribed to the American people. On

the contrary, toward the close of the Manchurian crisis they repeatedly
stressed the existence in China of "warlordism," disunity, and lack of
order, and stated that many of Japan's complaints against the Chinese
were justified.[150] On March 2, when the Chinese armies were retreating in Jehol, *The New York Times* declared,

> . . . when we say China, what do we mean? The military developments
> of the past few days show that we cannot mean a strong and united gov-
> ernment with the people solidly behind it. The old internal divisions and
> jealousies and enmities have shown themselves again, even in the face of
> the advancing Japanese armies. The chief of the nominal Chinese Govern-
> ment at Nanking has almost ostentatiously refused to join the defense of
> Jehol against Japanese arms. It is the old Chinese story of one war lord
> distrusting another and seeking to undermine or defeat him. So long as this
> is true it is obvious that China does not answer to the definition of a "nation"
> as contemplated in the Covenant of the League of Nations.[151]

A few weeks later the editor of the *San Francisco Chronicle* asserted
that China had made a "vast nuisance" of itself "to Japan and to the
peace and order in the Far East" and that the American people had
only been willing to overlook this fact because Japan's "flouting" of
the peace treaties had obscured all else in their eyes.[152]

In general the American press seems to have given far greater
coverage to the Amau declaration than to the Tangku Truce, presumably because Amau openly challenged the western powers.[153]
However, in keeping with their earlier attitude, most of the internationalist papers in Kramer's study took the position that since the
maintenance of the world's peace structure was no longer under discussion, the United States had no interest in the Far Eastern situation
which was sufficient to warrant opposing Japan. In fact, some of the
publications which had been the staunchest advocates of firm action
against the Japanese during the Manchurian crisis now urged the
adoption of a conciliatory policy. The *Milwaukee Journal*, which had
called for economic sanctions against Japan in February 1933, suggested after the Amau statement that the United States should recognize Japan's special political, social, and economic interests in China
and should limit itself to undertaking, by "friendly" persuasion, to
induce the Japanese to discharge their responsibilities toward China
"in accordance with international thought."[154] The *Christian Science
Monitor*, which had also favored a strong stand against the Japanese
in the final phase of the Manchurian crisis, proposed "collaboration
between Japan and the League committees to determine jointly what
kinds of technical aid in China can be given without raising military
dangers and what kinds will actually be harmful . . . to real peace-
making."[155] Similarly, the *Cleveland Press* in contrast to its previous

advocacy of sanctions against Manchuria, appealed to the United States government to pursue a policy of caution, in light of the Amau doctrine, and commented that: "In the end, if Japan is determined to dominate China, only China herself can prevent it."[156] The *Los Angeles Times* envisaged the possibility of conditions in China deteriorating to the extent of requiring the establishment of a protectorate but went no further than to indicate that the Japanese should not be given sole control.[157] *The New York Times* and the *San Francisco Chronicle* expressed strong indignation at the Amau statement on the grounds that it was a breach of treaties to which Japan was a party.[158] But on the side of action the *Times* merely supported the general idea of Anglo-American consultation and the *Chronicle,* with great earnestness, warned Washington against becoming the "spearhead" of a movement which might "concentrate Japanese resentment on America alone."[159]

The two isolationist papers—the *Chicago Tribune* and Hearst's *San Francisco Examiner*—that formed part of Kramer's survey, were naturally opposed to any intervention by the United States in the Sino-Japanese conflict even during the Manchurian crisis.[160] After that crisis, both papers sought to present "the case for Japan."[161] While this was no surprise as far as the *Tribune* was concerned, Hearst's departure from his customary virulent anti-Japanese policy occasioned some astonishment and led historians later to speculate on whether his attacks upon Japan in the past had stemmed from a desire to be sensational rather than from any genuine hostility.[162] Be that as it may, the Hearst press actually defended the Amau doctrine arguing that, because of population pressures, the Japanese needed "*lebensraum*" and urging the American people to try to understand Japan's problems "sympathetically."[163] In contrast, the *Chicago Tribune* criticized the Amau doctrine and asserted that Japan had no right to interfere with trade between China and western countries.[164] However, the *Tribune* abandoned this negative attitude almost immediately, perhaps in part because even such outstanding representatives of business opinion as the *Wall Street Journal* and the *Journal of Commerce* were not willing to deviate from their generally favorable approach to Japan despite the threat to the "open door" implicit in the Amau statement.[165] On April 28, the *Wall Street Journal* wrote that the Amau declaration

. . . presaged as far as now appears no new policy of further expansion or tangible action on the part of Japan. It protested a little more strongly than was courteous American aid to "civil" aviation. That was its sole impingement upon actual western activities.[166]

A few weeks later, the *Wall Street Journal* expressly supported continuance of the Roosevelt administration's "unobtrusive policy of non-interference" in the Sino-Japanese controversy and, according to Kramer, "seemed quite willing to concede the Far East to Japan as a sphere of influence."[167] The *Journal of Commerce*, commenting on the Amau statement, implied that, in view of Japan's achievements in Manchukuo, a worse result might befall China than to come under Japan's domination.[168]

In general, the only objections to the Amau doctrine raised in the newspapers, noted above, were that it undermined the principle of the sanctity of treaties and disregarded the rule of the "open door." Little attention was paid to the question of the possible reconstruction of China and the implications for the West of Japan's evident determination to prevent such an eventuality.[169] In this respect the thinking in both the internationalist and the isolationist newspapers differed sharply from that of the State Department. But there were few differences concerning the fundamental point of the pursuance of a policy which, in so far as possible, would avoid friction between the United States and Japan.

A VITAL ASPECT OF HULL'S POLICY

Soon after the Amau declaration a strange episode took place in Washington which involved several significant talks between Secretary Hull and Ambassador Saito. Perhaps because of what the Japanese government regarded as the "friendly" nature of the *aide-mémoire* addressed to it by the State Department following the Amau pronouncement, Saito decided that the time might be ripe for a Japanese-American rapprochement.[170] As a result, in mid-May he indicated his wish for a "highly" important and confidential conference with the Secretary of State. Insisting upon the utmost secrecy, he asked to see Hull at the latter's home, rather than his office, and requested the Secretary not to take any notes of their talk or communicate anything about it to the Japanese government. Hull, though somewhat amused by the ambassador's melodramatic air of being about to embark upon a mysterious undertaking designed to produce epoch-making consequences, agreed to receive him in his apartment on May 16 but said nothing about the matter of recording their discussion. The Secretary did, in fact, in accordance with the customary State Department procedures, write an official account of his conversation with Saito immediately after their interview.[171]

In this account Hull stated that, at the outset of their meeting, the ambassador said that he wanted to talk over different problems which existed between the United States and Japan, to see if they could not be "simplified" in order that the two countries might attain a "perfect and permanent . . . understanding and friendship." Saito thereupon handed the Secretary a document which began with the sentence: "These are entirely my private thoughts." Hull, after glancing at the paper, remarked that he would study it and communicate his views to the ambassador in a few days. Saito, however, continued the conversation, observing that the Japanese people had been led to believe that, in the past, America had sought to checkmate almost all of their moves in the way of "progress externally"—a phrase which the Secretary construed to mean "political and military expansion." Hull replied that "we were living in a highly civilized age" and that the United States was exerting every effort "to condemn, repudiate, and discard any and every practice, policy or utterance" that might give reasonable ground for complaint to any other people. As an example he asserted that the Roosevelt administration was abandoning the "irritating and trouble-breeding methods" that the United States government had at times applied to the countries of Latin America; "human progress," the Secretary declared, "called for just such reforms."

Hull went on to speak of the changes which had occurred throughout the world in the last few decades. Only a short time ago, he said, an American citizen (Wiley Post) had stepped into an airplane and sailed away, flying over Japan and around the globe, to alight within eight days in the place from which he had started. Until recently, England, with the Channel between her shores and the European continent, had felt entirely secure from any ordinary interference; but now a fleet of 2,000 bombing planes could, with perfect ease, fly from many of the capitals of Europe and blow London off the map. Twenty years ago, "no human being with the wildest stretch of imagination could have visualized the smallest part of the amazing changes that had taken place . . . during this period and only the Lord could begin to visualize the even more startling changes that might reasonably take place during the next twenty years."

From the transformations which the world was undergoing, the Secretary drew the lesson that, as international life became more complex, "greater responsibilities and duties" essentially devolved upon "the more highly civilized nations." This enabled him to make what was obviously intended to be the main point of his comments:

I stated that this meant that since there were no two more highly civilized countries than Japan and the United States, their own self-preservation, as well as their world responsibility, called for the utmost breadth of view and the profoundest statesmanship that their biggest and ablest statesmen could offer; that, faced with these unprecedented problems and conditions, it was all-important that his statesmen and mine should be broad-gauged enough to understand each other's problems and conditions, as well as those of the world, and to have the disposition and the will to deal with them in such capable manner as would avoid misunderstanding or material differences and promote both national and world progress; and that in no other way could countries like Japan and the United States, which were at present the trustees of the greatest civilization in history, make such showing as would give them a creditable place in the future history of the world. I said that, of course, Great Britain and other countries had their wonderful civilization, which I was not even remotely minimizing, but that Great Britain in particular was at present, and would be perhaps for some time to come, deeply engrossed with the serious and dangerous political, economic, and peace problems in Western Europe.

Three days later the Secretary had a talk with Saito in his office, which was actually a continuation of their previous meeting. According to Hull's record, Ambassador Saito said that he had just received a message from his government to the effect that Hirota had not heretofore replied to the American *aide-mémoire* on the Amau declaration because Grew had assured him that no answer was expected; the Foreign Minister wished now, however, to express his appreciation of the way in which the State Department had acted.[172] The Secretary remarked that the *aide-mémoire* had been issued in a "respectful and friendly spirit" as a "comprehensive statement" of the "rights, interests, and obligations" pertaining to the United States and other countries under the provisions of the Nine Power Treaty, the Kellogg Pact, and international law in general. Hull inquired as to whether the Japanese government differed with any of the basic affirmations in the *aide-mémoire*. The ambassador replied that it did not, but that his government felt it had "a special interest in preserving peace and order in China." The Secretary recorded at this point:

I remarked that . . . I saw no reason whatever why our two countries should not, in the most friendly and satisfactory way to each, solve every question or condition that existed now or that might arise in the future. I then said that, in my opinion, his country could conduct its affairs in such a way that it would live by itself during the coming generations or that it might conduct its affairs even more profitably and at the same time retain the perfect understanding and the friendship of all civilized nations in particular; that my hope and prayer was that all the civilized nations of the world, including Japan, should work together and in a perfectly friendly and understanding way so as to promote to the fullest extent the welfare of their respective peoples and at the same time meet their duties to civilization and to the more backward peoples of the world; and that my government would always be ready and desirous of meeting his government fully half-way in pursuing these latter objectives.

The Secretary stated further that he would be entirely frank and say that there was considerable speculation everywhere as to the reasons for the Japanese government's singling out "the clause or formula about Japan's claiming superior and special interests in the peace situation in Eastern Asia." Many people wondered whether this phrase had "ulterior or ultimate implications partaking of the nature of an overlordship of the Orient or a definite purpose to secure preferential trade rights." The ambassador protested that his government had no such implications in mind. Hull in return said that many countries were contemplating an increase in their military strength because of the state of the world and that Japan and Germany were widely regarded as chiefly responsible for this development; if it were generally understood that the Japanese government had no "overlordship intentions," as the ambassador asserted, then Japan would "not be the occasion for armament discussion." This illustrated, the Secretary declared, what he had said earlier: countries must make a special effort to understand each other and statesmen must be ready at all times to correct "trouble-making rumors or irresponsible or inaccurate statements calculated to breed distrust and misunderstanding and lukewarmness between nations"; never in history had it been so important for the "few existing civilized countries of the world to work whole-heartedly together." At the end of the passage in which he related the foregoing, Hull wrote:

I said that in this awful crisis through which the world was passing, debtors everywhere were not keeping faith with creditors in many instances; that sanctity of treaties, in Western Europe especially, was being ignored and violated; that this was peculiarly a time when our civilized countries should be especially vigilant to observe and to preserve both legal and moral obligations; and that my country especially felt that way, not only on its own account but for the sake of preserving the better and the higher standards of both individual and national conduct everywhere.

The theme which persistently recurred throughout Hull's comments was that Japan should cooperate with other nations in an "understanding" and "friendly" way and, in general, should fulfill her responsibilities as one of the "trustees" and foremost leaders of the civilized world. In talking in these terms to Saito, the Secretary evidently wished to emphasize his desire to be conciliatory toward the Japanese. But Hull's remarks also involved another element which was to play an exceedingly important part in his conduct of diplomacy and which he himself was to explain in detail in connection with an episode that occurred later.[173] The essence of the matter was that the Secretary believed, with a conviction too profound to be influenced by any external factors, that most of the basic problems of international relations could be solved by moral education. To him, part of the task of an enlightened statesman was therefore, whenever and wherever necessary, to impress upon others their obligation to live up to the precepts which he felt should govern all human behavior. In his statements to Saito, the Secretary was trying to awaken the conscience of the Japanese and, in all probability, he entertained a very real hope that his efforts would produce concrete results.

The document that the Japanese ambassador had left with Hull at their first meeting formed the basis of a third conference on May 29 which was again held under the conditions of secrecy that Saito had requested.[174] The document consisted primarily of a proposal for the issuance of a joint Japanese-American declaration of policy. It maintained that some government action should be taken to dispel the strong, though unjustified, suspicions that existed between the United States and Japan. America, it said, feared that Japan had aggressive designs on the Asiatic continent and might even be "courting war" with the United States; Japan, on the other hand, felt that America was trying to prevent her from achieving her national aim—which was "nothing but the establishment of peace and order in the Far East"— and was encouraging China to take a "defiant attitude" toward Japan. The joint declaration was to contain three articles. In the first, the two signatories were to assert their willingness to cooperate with each other in the promotion of trade to their mutual advantage and in securing the principle of the Open Door in the Pacific area. In the second, the Japanese and American governments were to state that they had "no aggressive designs whatever," to renew their pledges to respect the territorial possessions and rights and interests of the other, and to reaffirm their determination to "maintain a relationship of peace and amity." The third provision was to read:

Both Governments mutually recognize that the United States in the eastern Pacific regions and Japan in the western Pacific regions are principal stabilizing factors and both Governments will exercise their best and constant efforts so far as lies within their proper and legitimate power to establish a reign of law and order in the regions geographically adjacent to their respective countries.

The memorandum concluded with the assertion that if a joint declaration of this character were made, all war talk would immediately be silenced, the psychology of men would undergo a change, and whatever differences arose between the United States and Japan would be capable of easy solution. Furthermore, China would begin to perceive that she could "no longer rely upon her time-honored policy of setting one power against another."

In replying to Saito's memorandum the Secretary made a formal statement, the substance of which appears in notes that he later submitted to President Roosevelt.[175] These indicate that, in respect to the ambassador's proposed joint declaration, Hull said in effect that he was inclined to question, in principle, the value of bilateral declarations of policy. In his view, the numerous countries which make up the family of nations had in recent years been drawn so closely together that each was essentially the neighbor of all. Consequently, every nation had substantial contacts with many nations and its rights and obligations tended accordingly to become general. But the conclusion between any two countries of a special agreement along political lines suggested that the signatories had common interests and objectives not shared by, or open to, others. The American people had always been adversely disposed toward the theory and practice of political alliances and, while the United States was party to a considerable number of treaties with regard to policies, these treaties were largely multilateral agreements.

The full meaning of the Secretary's comments is apparent when taken in conjunction with the chapter in his memoirs in which he deals with developments in the Far East during his first years in office.[176] Beginning with the spring of 1934, Hull says, Japan repeatedly suggested direct agreements of a general political character (such as nonaggression pacts) between Washington and Tokyo; if we had entered into any such agreements it "would have made us a kind of silent partner in Japan's aggressions."[177] In other words, Hull was opposed to any joint political declaration by the American and Japanese governments because he thought it would imply a particular closeness between their countries which in turn would suggest a moral endorsement by the United States of Japan's actions, both past and future.

In his statement to the Japanese ambassador, Hull in addition specifically rejected the idea implicit in the third article of the declaration suggested by Saito. The idea was obviously that which the ambassador and Secretary Hull had discussed earlier, namely, that Japan had "special interests" in the maintenance of peace in Eastern Asia which gave her the right to strive for a position of "overlordship of the Orient," including exclusive trading privileges. Since the Secretary felt that any bilateral declaration of policy issued by the United States and Japan would, in effect, make us a party to the acts of the

Japanese, he was certain to object to a joint statement involving Japan's doctrine of "special interests" with all of its connotations. Nor was Saito's notion that the Japanese would, on their part, recognize America's "special interests" in the establishment of peaceful conditions on her side of the Pacific, conducive to improving the situation in the Secretary's eyes.[178] In the notes which he sent to Roosevelt, Hull stated that the gist of his remarks to Saito concerning the draft of the third provision as presented in the ambassador's memorandum was:

Neither the Government nor the people of the United States have conceived that it is a right or a duty or an intention of the United States to establish a reign of law and order in regions geographically adjacent to this country. We would not wish to make assertion of that right or to entertain such an objective now or in future. It would be impossible for me to give encouragement to Japan toward the assertion by it of such a right or the prosecution by it of such an intention in regions geographically adjacent to it. The tendency among nations today is, it seems to us, away from rather than toward such concepts and practices.

Hull asserts in his memoirs that for the United States to have agreed to any provision, such as Saito desired, would have meant "giving our blessing" to Japan's conquest of China and other neighboring countries and to her prohibiting trade between the West and the territories under her control.[179]

On sending his account of his interview with the Japanese ambassador to Roosevelt, the Secretary stated that there were indications that Saito might appeal to the President in a final effort to realize his plan of a Japanese-American declaration of policy.[180] Secretary Hull reminded Roosevelt that Viscount Ishii had similarly appealed to President Wilson in 1917 which had led to the conclusion of the "Lansing-Ishii Agreement—which Agreement resulted in no end of confusion and embarrassment." "I feel that it is highly desirable," Hull said, "that you give the Ambassador no encouragement." The President in reply congratulated the Secretary on the "magnificent" position he had taken in his meeting with Saito and added, "If Saito comes to see me I want you to be there."[181] Shortly thereafter the ambassador did pay a visit to the White House at which Hull was present. But the call proved to be a routine one, the occasion for which was the ambassador's temporary return to Japan. Saito had apparently accepted the fact that the stand taken by the Secretary in their last talk was irreversible.

Hull's replies to Ambassador Saito demonstrated an aspect of the Secretary's policy the importance of which can scarcely be overestimated. As indicated in the discussion of the Amau declaration, the

Roosevelt administration was in the process of forming its Far Eastern policy and, gropingly but with increasing determination, was adhering to the view that it must seek to prevent any further deterioration of the relations between the United States and Japan. It had therefore shown a marked desire to avoid any active involvement in developments in the Far East. In addition, Hull had attempted to introduce a more conciliatory note into his dealings with the Japanese government through his exchange of messages with Foreign Minister Hirota. When it came to his interviews with Saito, the Secretary continued his effort to be conciliatory. But in responding to the ambassador's request for a joint statement of policy, Hull showed that, while he might be willing to refrain from action and even to be cordial in his relations with the Japanese, there was a point beyond which he would not go for the sake of avoiding difficulties with Japan: he would not make any affirmative move which could be construed as a willingness on the part of the United States to give Japan its moral support.

Following the Amau incident, American officials were quickly compelled to turn their attention away from the economic factors involved in our Far Eastern policy toward the naval factors. The Japanese press had long been proclaiming that 1935, when the next naval conference was scheduled to be held, would be the "dangerous year" for Japan, in which her relations with the West would be strained to the utmost. Grew had often warned the State Department that every bit of good will we could create for ourselves in Japan would be needed once the naval conference started.

THE NAVAL MEETINGS OF 1934 AND 1935

Ever since the Washington Conference of 1921, the United States had repeatedly sought to obtain further naval limitation among the powers.[1] The naval treaty, which had been signed at the Washington Conference, had established limits or so-called ceilings on tonnages for two classes of ships—capital ships and aircraft carriers—the tonnages of the British, American, and Japanese fleets, respectively, being fixed in accordance with the famous 5:5:3 ratio. After a number of abortive efforts to attain further agreement, the London Treaty of 1930 was signed, providing ceilings for small cruisers, destroyers, and submarines. The United States had, however, not built up to its ceilings and had instead undertaken a policy that was often described as "disarmament by example." This policy reached its height during the Hoover administration when, owing to President Hoover's aversion to rearming, not a single new ship was authorized. The consequence was that by the time that Roosevelt became President, the United States fleet was far below the limits allowed it by the existing treaties while the Japanese fleet was close to filling the quotas which it was permitted.

Roosevelt's own views about the navy had changed startlingly since the days during the first World War when, as Assistant Secretary of the Navy, he somewhat flamboyantly advocated a big fleet.[2] After the war, Roosevelt supported the general internationalist movement for the establishment of world order. In 1920, as candidate for Vice President, he stumped the country for the League of Nations. And when he became convinced that America's entry into the League was politically impractical, he turned to the idea of naval limitation even before the Washington Conference was proposed. He was wholly in sympathy with the results of that conference and in 1923 published an article which amounted to an appeal to the American people to reconsider their attitude toward Japan in the light of the Washington Conference treaties.[3] There was no reason, he said, to maintain the old idea that war with Japan was inevitable; we should, on the contrary, base our future thinking on the "assumption of peace." The Washington treaties had created a "naval strategical dead-lock" in the Pacific by reducing the Japanese and American navies to a point where neither could successfully carry on a war in the waters of the other. In 1928, Roosevelt published another article, this time attacking the Coolidge administration for supporting a large naval bill in Congress.[4] What was needed, Roosevelt declared, was a "wholly new approach" to naval problems. It should be recognized that there was no need for a large navy—"only the most excited Admirals" would seriously consider the possibility of an invasion of the United States by sea. There should be "unofficial, friendly 'chats around the table'" to devise a means of further realizing the "splendid ultimate ideal of the Naval Limitation Treaty." However, if such means were going to be found "the leadership of the American President" and the vision of his Secretary of State would have to be "of a very different order."

When Roosevelt became President he had many reasons, besides his own sincere and even passionate desire for peace, to advocate further naval limitation. The hideous burden imposed upon the world by the economic depression made the expenditure of huge sums on armaments by all the big nations even more questionable than in normal times. For technical reasons it was hard to push the construction of the American Navy beyond a certain pace so that even the attainment of the level allowed the United States fleet by the treaties might not be an easy matter. In addition, there was the vital factor of public opinion. A powerful group in Congress had long opposed any naval expansion and had no intention of changing its mind. It possessed an impressive ally in the church groups and peace societies which had been extraordinarily active in the 1920's.[5] Moreover, it was generally assumed that the American people, by instinct and conviction, were in favor of almost any form of arms limitation and, as far as naval problems were concerned were—as the General Board of the Navy commented in one of its reports to the President—"listless and without understanding."[6]

The fact that Roosevelt wanted further limitation of armaments did not mean, however, that he approved of "disarmament by example." In other words he objected to a "big navy" policy but he also objected to a policy which left the United States with a navy that was weak relative to those of other countries. Three days after his inauguration he let it be known that his administration was in favor of using some of the special funds, provided for in the National Industrial Recovery Act, for the construction of new ships. In early 1934, he favored the introduction into Congress of the Vinson-Trammell bill which requested approval of a program that would bring the navy up to the quota allowed by the Washington and London treaties. On the other hand, he continued to advocate disarmament and, on signing the Vinson-Trammell bill after its passage through Congress in March, specifically stated that it had been and would be the policy of his administration to favor the "limitation of Naval armaments" and that it was his "personal hope" that the naval conference of 1935 would "extend all existing limitations and agree to further reductions."[7] While there can be no question as to the genuineness of this statement, it was no doubt also made because the Vinson-Trammell bill had met with considerable opposition in Congress, where it had touched off a large-scale foreign policy debate.[8] The senators who wanted only disarmament and were opposed to any kind of rearmament, led by Senator Nye (who called the bill the "national bluff, bluster, and bully bill"), had mustered their forces and again demonstrated their strength.[9]

The 1935 conference had been provided for in the London Naval Treaty of 1930 on the grounds that the treaty would expire in 1936 and that a conference should be held to work out a new agreement unless the powers decided otherwise. It was also possible that the Washington Naval Treaty would come to an end in 1936 as, according to its terms, any of the signatories could declare in December 1934 that the treaty would be terminated two years later. There had long been indications that the Japanese might take such action and moreover that, in negotiating a new treaty, they would insist upon parity with the British and American navies instead of being willing to continue the inferior ratios which they had accepted at the London and Washington conferences.

The stories that the Japanese might demand parity worried the British to such an extent that Prime Minister MacDonald in the early spring of 1934 suggested to Norman Davis, who was then in London, that the British and Americans might meet in advance of the 1935 conference to iron out their differences in order to present a common front in case the Japanese actually made such a demand.[10] Shortly thereafter Davis left England for home and on April 28 took up the matter with the President and Secretary Hull in a talk at a luncheon at the White House.[11]

According to Davis's record of this talk, he himself said that he was inclined to think that, in view of Japan's violations of the Nine Power Treaty, we should not negotiate a new agreement with the Japanese as the mere fact that we were willing to negotiate would seem to condone their previous actions. The President replied that on the contrary we should, in his opinion, make every effort to reach an understanding with the Japanese and that we should "propose a new treaty for ten years on the present ratios but with say a general reduction of twenty percent; that if Japan should refuse that then we should offer to renew the Treaty just as it is for a period of five years; that if Japan then refused that she would be on the defensive and England and the United States and perhaps also France and Italy could proceed to sign a treaty . . . with a provision for parity between the British and ourselves, the level of which would go up or down depending upon what Japan might do."

In the end, it was decided that Davis, after attending the Disarmament Conference at Geneva in May, should go to London to hold informal naval talks with the British on the basis of the policy which the President had outlined. This plan was followed and the naval talks were opened in June. Prime Minister MacDonald announced almost immediately that, if a new treaty was to be negotiated in 1935, the British would unfortunately have to ask for a considerable increase in cruisers.[12] As this was a demand which the British had made at previous naval conferences and which had created bitterness between the British and American navies, Davis was exceedingly surprised.[13] Moreover, as he told the British, he felt he could not possibly entertain a proposal which involved an increase in armaments instead of a decrease such as the President was suggesting. The American people were averse to rearming and no such proposal could conceivably be presented to the Senate.

Throughout the following weeks MacDonald, Baldwin (at this time the real power behind the Prime Minister), and Simon sought to explain the British position.[14] They said that the international situation had completely changed since the naval conference of 1930, when England and America had a single common problem: Japan. Hitler had risen to power in the meantime and so far all international efforts to restrain him had failed. Great Britain was therefore confronted with a rapidly rising crisis in Europe—a crisis which, to the United States, was "relatively academic." If England could depend on American help in the Pacific, she would feel quite differently. But the United States had shown, during the Manchurian crisis, that she was unwilling to take any strong action against Japan and since then her Far Eastern policy had become an increasingly uncertain factor as evidenced by her withdrawal from the Philippines. Under these circumstances, the British were convinced they would have to be able to deal alone with the situations in Europe and Asia, though the former must come first. There was one thing which could alter the picture, however, namely, if the United States were willing to arrive at an understanding with Great Britain on a policy of cooperation in the Far East. Even then, to command the confidence of the British people, such an understanding would have to be embodied in an agreement ratified by the Senate.

Davis said at once that an agreement which would amount to an Anglo-American alliance was out of the question.[15] In general, he seems to have been puzzled by the fact that the British attitude had changed so radically since MacDonald first broached the subject of naval conversations to him only a few months earlier.[16] A possible explanation was one which Ambassador Bingham had already advanced in connection with the shift in British policy following the Amau declaration, namely that the British government, alarmed by the rapid deterioration of conditions in Europe (a deterioration which had been further hastened by the collapse of the Disarmament Conference in May), had suddenly decided to avoid all measures which might give the appearance of the formation of an Anglo-American front for fear of provoking the Japanese. Another possible explanation —which the State Department, on the basis of rumors in the press, had as early as May suggested to Davis—was that the British had arrived at the conclusion that the only way to protect their interests in the Far East, while meeting the threat of Germany in Europe, was to effect a *rapprochement* with Japan or even renew the old Anglo-Japanese alliance. (Hull thought that the British might attempt to get an agreement with Japan "on policy in China in return for England's support of or acquiescence in Japan's claims to naval parity.")[17] Davis felt that, in any case, his talks with the British were at an impasse and, contrary to his usual resourcefulness in overcoming every obstacle, he had no suggestion to make as to how to proceed.[18]

The President, however, had not lost the optimism which Davis normally shared with him. Roosevelt's first thought, on hearing that the British wanted an increase in naval strength, was that he might issue a "dramatic appeal" to the public to support his efforts to obtain a further limitation of naval armaments.[19] But he decided that to make such a move was premature and instead sent a confidential message to Prime Minister MacDonald repeating his proposal for a renewal of the existing naval treaties with a twenty per cent reduction and saying that "it is still my thought that the difficult situation of modern civilization throughout the world demands for the social and economic good of human beings a reduction in armaments and not an increase."[20] The President added that he was fully aware of the "pressure exercised by Navy Departments and Admiralties" but hoped that "those in high authority" would work with him to progressively bring about naval reductions. At the same time he asked Davis to impress upon the British that his proposal did not represent a "bargaining position" but a "deep conviction" that a new naval treaty must, at the very least, hold the naval strength of the various powers down to the existing levels.[21]

Although the President's appeal was strong, it did not succeed in swaying the British. The Prime Minister sent Roosevelt a letter in which he said that he shared the President's sentiments but it was "not a question of desire but of realistic need." Whether it was possible to effect a standstill agreement or naval reductions depended entirely on conditions. Britain had serious risks in Europe and in Asia; he would be delighted to cut the navy by "ten, twenty, or thirty per cent" if some way were found to cut those risks proportionately.[22]

MacDonald's letter made it quite clear that Davis had been correct in feeling that a stalemate had been reached which could not be resolved for the present. It was therefore decided, late in July, that further discussions should be postponed until the autumn. The Japanese (who at the last minute had been invited to London by the British to participate in the naval talks) had just sent word that they would not be able to come for some months, probably October, so that it seemed best for Davis to go home and return at that time.[23]

In September, matters grew considerably worse when Hirota privately informed Ambassador Grew that the Japanese government had definitely decided to denounce the Washington Naval Treaty in December which meant that it would automatically be terminated in two years. Grew nevertheless felt that the situation was not entirely hopeless and that the Japanese might be more conciliatory than expected when they arrived in London. He did not think that what he termed the "fire-eating nationalists" who ruled the Japanese navy, or even the Japanese people themselves, would want to make concessions but he believed they might be forced to do so because of the fact that Japan could not afford the cost of a naval race.[24]

As time for the renewal of the London talks approached, the President reaffirmed his stand on naval limitation. In early October Admiral Standley, who as Chief of Naval Operations was about to accompany Norman Davis back to England, asked the President whether he would consider a slight increase in tonnages if necessary to reach an understanding with the British and the Japanese.[25] Roosevelt answered with a decisive "No" and added, even more decisively, that he would not present a treaty to the Senate or the American people which contained one ton more than the totals in the existing agreements. The United States, he said, had consistently worked for land and naval disarmament and should continue to do so.

Still, the President's very determination not to agree to an increase in armaments looked as though it might create difficulties of its own. For it was likely to result in his rejecting all manner of proposals advanced by the British and Japanese which might make him seem, in the eyes of the public, responsible for blocking the conclusion of a new naval agreement. To protect himself as far as possible against the development of such a situation, Roosevelt decided to give Davis a letter to take with him to London with the understanding that it would be used if a moment arose when it seemed necessary to explain the American position to the world in a dramatic form.[26] A letter was consequently prepared by the State Department which embodied what was called Roosevelt's "philosophy of disarmament." It primarily expressed the President's belief that further naval reduction was essential but could only be achieved on a proportional basis in accordance with the existing ratios. Roosevelt, however, characteristically rejected the Department's draft as sounding like "just another diplomatic document" and rewrote it himself so that it would put the American case on a "clear cut and high plane" in language which could be understood by the "man in the street" from "one end of the land to the other."

The naval talks opened in London in October with the British, Americans, and Japanese all present. It was decided to conduct the discussions on a bilateral basis, that is to say the representatives of no more than two nations were to attend any one meeting. From beginning to end, the State Department in Washington resented this procedure, feeling that it put the United States at a disadvantage by enabling the British to give the impression that they were playing the role of "honest broker" in an effort to bring together the Japanese and Americans who were made to look as though they were continuously at odds with each other and unwilling to reach an understanding.[27]

At the first meeting between the Japanese and Americans, the Japanese declared flatly that they would not negotiate a new treaty at the 1935 conference unless it was agreed that the Japanese fleet would be given parity with the British and American navies.[28] They argued that the existing ratios did not give Japan sufficient security and, moreover, constituted a stigma of inferiority which the Japanese people were no longer willing to endure and which damaged their prestige throughout Asia.

By way of countering the Japanese arguments, Davis said he would like briefly to review the history of the ratios. The various nations which had assembled at the Washington Conference in 1921 had decided to limit their navies in accordance with the principle of equality of security by which they meant that each country should have sufficient naval strength in relation to the others for defensive but not for offensive purposes. It was on this basis that the 5:5:3 ratio had been allotted to England, America, and Japan, the assumption being that Japan did not need parity because the areas she had to defend were so much smaller than those of Great Britain and the United States. Although the 5:5:3 ratio had consequently been considered fair at the time, England and America had also agreed to the nonfortification provisions of the Washington Naval Treaty in order to make the Japanese feel freer from the possibility of attack. In addition, an effort had been made to remove the causes of friction which were most likely to precipitate an attack and, as a result, the Nine Power Treaty had been signed. The provisions of the naval and political treaties concluded at the Washington Conference were therefore interdependent and, taken as a whole, constituted a system which furnished a basis for peace in the Pacific area. Japan had heretofore believed that this system gave her adequate safety and in no way damaged her prestige. The United States could not see that anything had happened which would justify the Japanese in changing their minds.

The arguments advanced by the Japanese and American delegations at their first meeting were to be repeated over and over again by both sides during the following weeks. The positions of Japan and the United States were therefore clear from the beginning of the naval discussions. But the attitude of the British remained uncertain. Davis told the President that, although he was convinced that the British would not agree to parity with Japan, he thought they might be willing to accept a slight increase in the Japanese ratio.[29] Roosevelt replied on November 9, in an unusually impatient letter which he appears to have written personally, that Davis should impress upon "Simon and a few other Tories . . . the simple fact that, if Great Britain is even suspected of preferring to play with Japan to playing with us" he would feel compelled in the interests of American security to "approach public sentiment in Canada, Australia, New Zealand, and South Africa in a definite effort to make these Dominions understand clearly that their future security is linked with . . . the United States."[30] "You will best know," Roosevelt concluded, "how to inject this thought into the minds of Simon, Chamberlain, Baldwin, and MacDonald in the most diplomatic way."

Davis did not act upon the President's letter for, by the time it reached him he felt the situation had changed sufficiently not to require such drastic treatment.[31] As Davis interpreted developments, when he had arrived in London there had been what he termed a "small, willful group of men," a minority of extreme Tories in the Cabinet, who wanted—as Hull had predicted—to make some sort of deal with Japan, especially as they had become convinced that the United States would never pledge itself in any formal agreement to cooperate with Great Britain in the Far East. They hoped that they could negotiate some arrangement with the Japanese which would, for the time being at least, preserve the *status quo* in the Pacific and perhaps stave off the realization of a German-Japanese alliance. They were supported by the business interests in Great Britain that wanted in so far as possible to protect their stake in the Far East and especially in China. They had, moreover, expected to have additional support from the strong antiwar elements in England that were inclined to favor almost any form of international conciliation. But events had turned out differently. The British people had been surprisingly critical of Japan's insistence on parity. And Smuts and other Dominion leaders who were currently attending a conference in London had, both publicly and in private meetings with members of the British government, emphatically declared that Great Britain must not adopt any policy that would interfere with Anglo-American unity. The extreme Tories had therefore gained few adherents. In addition, they themselves had been startled by the extravagance and inflexibility of the Japanese demands which suggested that to try to make a deal with Japan would be a costly proposition with uncertain results. Their interest had been further dampened by the promulgation of an oil monopoly law in Manchukuo, which was adopted over repeated British and American official protests, and was obviously designed to drive the American and British oil companies out of that area. As a consequence of all these matters, men such as Simon and Chamberlain had decided that they would not enter into any agreement with Japan without the full knowledge and approval of the

United States and that their main objective must be the maintenance of friendly relations with America. Whether or not this interpretation of Davis' was correct, he himself was firmly convinced that the tide had turned and that he would, throughout the rest of the naval talks, have British support. Indeed, he told the British with remarkable frankness that he was staking his whole reputation upon his belief that they were not going to let the United States down.

Nevertheless, the fact remained that there were differences between the British and American attitudes toward the naval discussions that were bound to make themselves felt. As the talks had progressed, the British had become more and more impressed with the idea that, if all attempts at negotiating a new treaty failed and naval limitation therefore ceased to exist, the results would be disastrous for England— even more disastrous than for the United States because British interests in the Far East were so much greater than ours. They therefore decided that some sort of agreement, even if it contained only minor restrictions on the naval power of its signatories, would be better than no agreement at all. Consequently, on November 14 they proposed a plan to Davis which became known as the "middle course" because it was intended to steer a way between the extremes of renewing the Washington and London treaties without change (as the President had suggested) and of making no effort to achieve any sort of understanding.[32] The "middle course," as outlined by the British, was to contain: (1) provisions for qualitative limitations on naval armaments (without quantitative limitations such as formed the basis of the existing treaties); (2) restrictions on fortifications similar to those in the Washington Naval Treaty; and (3) a pledge from each of the signatories to notify the other before laying down any new ships.

The President himself seems to have thought for a while that it would be better to reach some kind of understanding with the Japanese, no matter how limited, than to have no understanding at all.[33] For even before the British suggested the "middle course" he told Hull that if all else failed he wanted to negotiate an agreement which would assure full publicity on all naval construction and the mere existence of which would be "conducive" to more naval limitation in the future.

Secretary Hull did not, however, want to consider any middle-of-the-road solution and apparently succeeded in winning the President over to his point of view.[34] Hull felt that Japan's desire to terminate the Washington Naval Treaty symbolized an even greater issue, namely, her apparent determination to destroy the entire system of interdependent agreements which had been negotiated at the Washington Conference, especially the Nine Power pact. As a consequence, the Secretary believed that if the United States entered into a new treaty with the Japanese, which did not embody the main principles incorporated in the Washington Conference agreements, it would in effect be sanctioning Japan's destruction of those agreements. Hull therefore instructed Davis to try to persuade the British to drop the idea of the "middle course" and to continue the London talks on the basis that England and America would only consent to a renewal of the existing treaties. If the Japanese persisted in refusing to negotiate even under these conditions, the Secretary thought that Great Britain and the United States should stand their ground and terminate the talks, sending the Japanese representatives home "empty-handed."

In advocating what was sometimes called the "empty-handed theory," Hull was largely prompted by his desire to maintain the moral position of the United States as he saw it. But he also hoped to achieve more concrete results. Grew had continued to cable that the Japanese could not afford a naval race and had advised the Secretary that if he did not make any substantial concessions to Japan during the London meetings the Japanese government would in all probability gradually arrive at the conclusion that, in order to rescue itself from an impossible situation, it would have to advance some compromise proposals of its own.[35] Hull felt, therefore, that to send the Japanese back from London entirely "empty-handed" would serve to bring about the results Grew envisaged and might, moreover, set in motion a wave of hostility amongst the Japanese people against their government for having pursued a policy which ended in failure.[36]

The Secretary also believed that to terminate the London talks squarely on the issue that the Japanese were abandoning the Washington Naval Treaty and the principles upon which it was based would help to revive the somewhat flagging support which the American people were giving to the administration's naval policy. Throughout the first weeks of the London meetings the American press seemed, with extraordinary unity, to be approving the President's position that the ratios had to be maintained for the sake of the security of the United States and that Japan's demand for parity had no sound or logical basis. But as the meetings dragged on there was inevitably more criticism and in late November Senator Nye made a speech championing Japan's position and attacking the administration for launching a "crazy, insane" naval race which would ultimately ruin the United States financially. The Secretary consequently felt that a "lot of loose pacifist thought in the country" was perhaps being awakened and that, to avoid trouble, it would be wise to focus the attention of the American people on the main issues in the naval controversy.[37]

Davis, on being informed of the "'empty-handed' theory," said that he thought it would be more advisable to cooperate with the British in exploring the possibilities of getting agreement on the "middle course." Both he and Admiral Standley believed that the British proposal would be of decided value in helping to avoid an arms race.[38] Furthermore, all the American representatives at the London meetings agreed that the preservation of Anglo-American unity was vital to world peace and more important than remaining—as one of them put it—"'simon pure' in principle."[39] But as the Secretary did not change his mind, Davis explained Hull's point of view to the British at a long meeting on December 4. As he stated the matter, Hull felt it would be wrong to enter into discussions about an entirely new naval treaty with the Japanese "as though nothing had happened." The Japanese were, in fact, demolishing the whole system upon which peace in the Pacific was founded and such discussions would essentially imply "tacit" approval of their actions.[40] Simon and MacDonald contended that no such implication was involved and that, in any case, there was no use in pinning guilt on the Japanese government (or "tying a can" on it, to use Davis' phrase) for terminating the naval treaties when it had the legal right to do so. They declared further that in their opinion if the Japanese representatives went home "empty-handed" they would not be discredited in the eyes of their own people, as Hull expected, but would be acclaimed as heroes who had rid their country of all naval restrictions and asserted its equality with the west. The Japanese extremists would gain ground and Japan would thereafter reject any proposal for naval limitation. Sir John Simon stated that the "worst thing of everything" would be to make naval limitation impossible in the future.

After much discussion the British finally agreed, for the sake of maintaining Anglo-American unity, to accept Hull's plan. Furthermore, at Hull's insistence, the British and Americans dragged out the London talks until December 19.[41] The object of this was to bring the final session of the London meetings as close as possible to the day (December 29) when Japan was scheduled to denounce formally the Washington Naval Treaty so that it would be clear to the public that the London meetings had broken down because of Japan's action.[42]

Formal notification by any signatory of the Washington Naval Treaty that it had decided to terminate that treaty had to be given to the United States which was charged with the responsibility of informing the other governments involved. On December 29, Ambassador Saito therefore went to Hull's office to present the necessary papers.[43] As the ambassador approached the musty but impressive old

State Department building, he found a crowd awaiting him outside. Whether intentionally or not, he created the impression that he was relishing his task. But on this occasion Hull was in no mood to be cordial. He merely accepted the documents which Saito handed him with a curt and expressive "Very well, Sir," and concluded the interview.

A few hours later, the Secretary issued a press release which restated the American case for the preservation of the naval treaties with emphasis upon the reasons for retaining the ratios and which ended with the assertion that the objectives of the Washington Conference of 1921 were "still fundamental among the objectives of the foreign policy of the United States" and that the administration would "unswervingly" hold to the "high purpose" of seeking their realization.[44] The President, more concerned with naval limitation than with our Far Eastern policy, as he had obviously been from the beginning, told correspondents in an off-the-record press conference that he believed Americans should keep their "mouths shut" about the naval problem and not antagonize any country "by thought, word, or deed."[45] A correspondent asked whether this meant that the President still thought some naval agreement might be reached, to which Roosevelt replied with great feeling: "I hope so, I hope so."

A study of the group of leading publications that have already been cited suggests that the newspapers were, in any case, anxious to be conciliatory and avoid, in the words of the *Christian Science Monitor*, "spanning the Pacific with hate."[46] The *Chicago Tribune* went to the extreme of urging the administration to say officially that as Japan's denunciation of the naval treaty was quite legal and her motives entirely understandable, the United States had no "hard feelings."[47] The Hearst editorials were again surprisingly mild and for the most part merely stated that they deplored the fact that Japan had left us with no alternative but to build competitively a navy which would be adequate for our defense.[48]

The 1935 naval conference, which took place in December of that year, had much more of a universal and much less of a Far Eastern slant than the talks of 1934. There were several reasons for this. The conference was not just attended by the three powers that had been at the 1934 meetings but, in addition, by the other signatories of the Washington and London naval treaties: France and Italy. Moreover, the conference was completely overshadowed by the Italian-Ethiopian crisis which gathered force during the summer of 1935 and reached its height in October and November with the outbreak of full-scale war and the imposition of sanctions upon

Italy by the League. These events had the most serious repercussions in the United States, among them being the passage of the first of the neutrality laws of the 1930's which was pushed through Congress by Nye and his isolationist colleagues who, as a result of the famous investigation into the activities of munitions manufacturers, were riding high on the crest of a wave of publicity.[49]

Even before the conference started, Roosevelt had resigned himself to the fact that in the light of the Italian-Ethiopian situation and all that that entailed, he would not be able to get the kind of a naval treaty he wanted, namely, one which severely restricted the naval strength of the nations involved. He had therefore decided that, if worst came to worst, he would try to obtain a stop-gap agreement which would prevent a naval race until a better opportunity presented itself to negotiate a genuinely satisfactory treaty.[50] He consequently instructed Norman Davis to read, at the opening session of the 1935 conference, the letter which he (the President) had written over a year earlier that was intended as a ringing appeal to the "man in the street" to support Roosevelt's program of a renewal of the Washington and London treaties with a 20 per cent reduction of the tonnages that they allowed.[51] Davis was to make every effort to negotiate a new treaty on the basis of this program. However, if as anticipated these efforts failed, he was to try to reach a temporary agreement which would provide for qualitative limitations and other restrictions that would lessen the risk of naval competition. Should it prove impossible to attain even this modest objective, he was to seek an arrangement with the British which would avert an Anglo-American naval race and which would serve as a constant example to the rest of the world of the advantages of naval limitation thereby acting as a stimulus to the achievement of some future agreement between all the large naval powers. Both the President and Davis were, however, optimistic about the possibilities of concluding a temporary multilateral treaty because they thought that all the nations involved preferred naval limitations to the dangers and economic burdens of all-out competition.

Unfortunately the conference—which by coincidence opened on the day that the Hoare-Laval agreement appeared in the press—showed that the President and Davis' hopes were unjustified.[52] The Japanese at once renewed the demands which they had made during the 1934 naval talks and frankly stated that they had in no way changed their position. Subsequently, they refused to consider any proposal for a limited treaty with qualitative and similar restrictions and indeed were entirely unresponsive to all of the suggestions made by the other powers. On January 14, Davis cabled the Secretary that the "jig was up" by which he meant that the Japanese had definitely decided to quit the conference.[53] This they did on the following day.

The departure of the Japanese presented the other delegations with the problem of whether to continue the conference or go home. Davis wired the President that he was in favor of continuing and attempting to negotiate a treaty with the British, French, and Italians.[54] There was, he said, a general feeling among the delegates that the Japanese had no intention of starting a naval race and had only taken an unreasonable and unyielding position in order to satisfy public opinion at home. If this proved correct, it was quite possible that if the remaining powers arrived at an understanding the Japanese would ask to be included later. Roosevelt not only agreed with Davis' views but allowed his expectations to revive to the point of thinking that a four-power treaty might be concluded which would retain the ceilings on tonnages in the existing naval agreements; but Davis told him that was "out of the question."[55] Indeed, as matters turned out, it took three months to negotiate a treaty which included little more than qualitative restrictions on armaments and a pledge to exchange information on plans for construction.

The treaty was presented to the Senate in May 1936.[56] As it was regarded as totally innocuous, it was adopted after only a two-hour debate without a dissenting vote. Most of the senators who expressed an opinion voiced their disappointment at the treaty's accomplishing so little to further the cause of disarmament. At the same time, however, Congress passed the largest peacetime naval appropriation bill in American history to carry forward the program which had been approved by the Vinson-Trammell Act.

Throughout the long series of naval meetings held from 1934 to 1936 the United States tried therefore to obtain naval limitation primarily as a result of the persistent and vigorous efforts of President Roosevelt. As far as Japan was concerned, the administration attempted from the outset to negotiate an agreement with the Japanese which would be based on the principles of the Washington Naval Treaty and would provide for naval reduction or, failing this, would freeze the *status quo*. Although the Japanese insisted that any arrangement which perpetuated the existing ratios would endanger their security, all the evidence suggests that American officials genuinely believed that an agreement such as the administration was trying to obtain would not only safeguard Japan but would actually work to her benefit more than to that of the United States. In short, while the main objective of American policy was to achieve further naval limitation, the administration felt that the methods it was pursuing could not possibly be regarded as provocative by the Japanese on any reasonable basis.

However, as the Japanese never became reconciled to the American point of view, the United States was faced with the question of whether to enter into a new agreement with Japan which was limited to a few aspects of the naval problem and was not related to the principles upon which the Washington Conference treaties had been founded. In all likelihood the President would have been willing to negotiate such an agreement. But Secretary Hull objected on the grounds that doing so would imply that the United States was prepared to sanction Japan's disregard of her existing commitments, especially those which she had undertaken as a signatory of the Nine Power Treaty. While, therefore, at Hull's insistence the administration took a firm moral stand on behalf of the Nine Power Treaty, it also indicated that it was not likely to defend that treaty against Japanese violations by any vigorous action. For the main argument which spokesmen for the United States advanced in the naval talks with Japan was that it was essential to maintain the principles of the Washington Naval Treaty because they established equality of security. However, since equality of security meant primarily that the Japanese and American fleets had been reduced to the point where they were only strong enough to protect their home territories, the preservation of the Washington Naval Treaty made the enforcement of the Nine Power pact exceedingly difficult. The policy the administration pursued during the naval meetings seemed therefore to indicate that it expected on the one hand to adhere to the moral position, foreshadowed in Secretary Hull's talks with Ambassador Saito, of withholding approval from Japan's actions and on the other to avoid any semblance of challenging Japan.

POLICY MEMORANDA

Immediately after the close of the American-British-Japanese naval meetings in 1934, Grew mailed the Secretary of State a policy memorandum to which he himself attached the greatest importance.[57] "I wanted it," he recorded in his diary, "to 'take'—like vaccination." The Ambassador consequently dated the memorandum December 27 to conform to his "only superstition" which was that twenty-seven was his lucky number since many important occasions in the life of his family, including his own and his daughter's birthday, fell on the twenty-seventh of the month.

The theme which formed the basis of Grew's communication to the Secretary was that the Japanese might at any time go beserk and that our Far Eastern policy should be primarily directed toward safeguarding against such an eventuality. To quote, Grew said that it was necessary for people in the United States to

realize the expansionist ambitions which lie not far from the surface in the minds of certain elements in the Army and Navy, the patriotic societies and the intense nationalists throughout the country [i.e., Japan]. Their aim is to obtain trade control and eventually predominant political influence in China, the Philippines, the Straits Settlements, Siam and the Dutch East Indies, the Maritime Provinces and Vladivostok, one step at a time, as in Korea and Manchuria, pausing intermittently to consolidate and then continuing as soon as the intervening obstacles can be overcome by diplomacy or force. With such dreams of empire cherished by many, and with an army and navy capable of taking the bit in their own teeth . . . we would be reprehensibly somnolent if we were to trust to the security of treaty restraints or international comity . . .

I may refer here to my despatch . . . of December 12, 1933 . . . That despatch reported a confidential conversation with the Netherlands Minister, General Pabst, a shrewd and rational colleague with long experience in Japan, in which the Minister said that, in his opinion, the Japanese navy, imbued as it is with patriotic and chauvinistic fervor and with a desire to emulate the deeds of the Army in order not to lose caste with the public, would be perfectly capable of descending upon and occupying Guam at a moment of crisis or, indeed, at any other moment, regardless of the ulterior consequences. I do not think that such an insane step is likely, yet the action of the Army in Manchuria, judged from the point of view of treaty rights and international comity, might also have been judged as insensate. The important fact is that under present circumstances, and indeed under circumstances which may continue in future . . . the armed forces of the country are perfectly capable of overriding the restraining control of the Government and of committing what might well amount to national "hari-kari" in a mistaken conception of patriotism.

Nor, Grew went on to say, was there much likelihood of Japanese liberals serving as a brake upon the military as so many Americans—"speaking and writing academically on a subject which they know nothing whatever about"—seemed to expect. The idea that there was a "great body of liberal thought" which, though dormant since 1931, would emerge and assume control if it received a little foreign encouragement, was "thoroughly mistaken." The liberal thought was there but "inarticulate and largely impotent" and in all probability would remain so for some time to come.

Given these circumstances, Grew declared, the administration should try to adhere to the "policy of the good neighbor." This was a matter of the tactful conduct of day-to-day diplomacy for the "ultra-sensitive-ness of the Japanese," arising out of a marked inferiority complex manifested in the garb of an equally marked superiority complex, made the manner and method of dealing with controversies assume a significance and importance often out of all proportion to the nature of the controversy itself.

Behind the conduct of day-to-day diplomacy, however, must lie, above all, military preparedness. The United States had, as a nation, taken the lead in international efforts to restrict and reduce armaments. It had hoped that the movement would be progressive but the condition of world affairs since the Washington Conference had not afforded fruitful ground for such progress. Therefore, Grew said, unless the United States wanted to subscribe to a "Pax Japonica" and all which that would entail, it must build its navy as rapidly as possible to treaty strength and if the Washington Naval Treaty expired must continue to maintain the present ratio with Japan regardless of cost, "a peacetime insurance both to cover and to reduce the risk of war."

In conclusion, Grew eloquently summarized his views:

Theodore Roosevelt enunciated the policy "Speak softly but carry a big stick." If our diplomacy in the Far East is to achieve favorable results, and if we are to reduce the risk of an eventual war with Japan to a minimum, that is the only way to proceed. Such a war may be unthinkable, and so it is, but the spectre of it is always present and will be present for some time to come. It would be criminally shortsighted to discard it from our calculations and the best possible way to avoid it is to be adequately prepared, for preparedness is a cold fact which even the chauvinists, the military, the patriots, and the ultra-nationalists in Japan, for all their bluster . . . can grasp and understand . . . again, and yet again, I urge that our own country be adequately prepared to meet all eventualities in the Far East.

By a curious coincidence, Hornbeck had sent the Secretary a memorandum on January 3, 1935, before Grew's reached Washington, in which he wrote,

I ventured a few weeks ago to state what I thought should be in broad outline the policy of the United States with regard to the Far East. I said,
"That which should be the policy of the United States with regard to the Far East can readily be summed up in one sentence: (a) to act with justice and with sympathy, as a 'good neighbor' . . . (b) to speak softly; and (c) to carry a big stick."
I still think and shall continue to think that the points (a), (b) and (c) set forth in that sentence should stand as the cardinal principles by which we should be guided at every step in our conduct of "Far Eastern relations" during the critical year which lies ahead.[58]

Hornbeck had set forth his views concerning American policy in various memoranda related to the naval meetings. The first of these, written in May 1934, stressed the point which formed the essence of Ambassador Grew's letter to the Secretary: that there existed a danger of war between the United States and Japan and that it was, therefore, essential to develop America's naval power.[59] In this connection Hornbeck said,

There are in the Far East three oriental powers: Japan, Russia and China. There are possessed in important measures of territory in Eastern Asia and the western Pacific three occidental powers: Great Britain, France and the Netherlands.

There are, however, in and on the Pacific Ocean, facing and faced by each other on that ocean, two *great* powers, and only two: the United States and Japan . . .

With regard to many matters, the concepts and the methods of the Japanese people and those of the American people differ; with regard to some, they are in definite and obvious conflict. For example, the American people have throughout their history shown a tendency to exalt the authority of international law, of treaties, of formal international agreements, and to deprecate and discourage possession and use of military force. (Note: We have fought a great deal, and we will fight; but in principle we are opposed to fighting.) The Japanese people have had until recently no familiarity with international law or treaties or international agreements; they have shown themselves in late years a [sic] little disposed to regard such as of high authority; and they have always placed high value upon possession of military weapons and processes of direct display and use of force.

. . . Whatever may be our strategy and tactics, it is a fact that, after China and Russia, this country has more reason than has any other for apprehension with regard to the use which Japan may make of the military equipment which that country possesses or acquires. The Japanese army is a menace to Russia and China. The Japanese army and navy are a menace to China. The Japanese navy is a menace to us. Great Britain, France and the Netherlands have reason to fear that Japan may impair their interests or drive them from the Far East. They have little reason to fear an assault by the Japanese upon their home territories. They are powers in but not powers on the Pacific Ocean. We are both in and on that ocean . . .

The maximum of insurance which we can take out against injury to ourselves by and from Japan lies along the line of naval construction. The Japanese speak and understand the language of force . . . the soundest course for us lies on the line of possessing naval strength such that the Japanese will not dare to take the risk or resort to force against us.

In his memorandum of January 3, 1935, Hornbeck not only spoke again of the threat to American security presented by Japan but injected considerable urgency into his comments by stating at the outset,

I venture to express the opinion that in the field of foreign relations the most important problem confronting the United States for the year 1935 is that of relations with Japan.

In the field of relations between the United States and Japan we are confronted with a much more obvious possibility—I do not say probability—of war than in the field of relations with any other country.

Throughout the memorandum Hornbeck continued to advocate the creation of a powerful navy as the most effective way of preventing an attack by Japan. At the same time he declared that while we "should unquestionably have a 'big stick,'" we did "not need to wave it or to talk about it." On the other hand, we should not "go out of our way" to make gestures of "good will" to Japan or to China; we should be "neither more cordial or less cordial" toward either of these two countries than toward other nations.

In another memorandum, written a few months later, Hornbeck recommended in effect that the United States government should continue to maintain the moral distinction, which the Secretary had been making, between engaging in an affirmative act that might imply support of Japan or refraining from action in the face of Japan's infringements of the rights of other nations.[60] The memorandum dealt in general with the question of the position which the United States should take in regard to the maintenance of the principles of the open door and the integrity of China. The United States, Hornbeck stated, had never undertaken to "*guarantee*" these principles. It had seen them impaired but had not used force on their behalf; it knew that they were about to be impaired further but it had no intention of using force. At the same time, Hornbeck went on to say,

we have no right to take action in authorization of their impairment . . . It may be that Japan will be able to have her way in and with regard to China. That possibility creates no warrant for a taking of sides by us with Japan and against China . . . We may have to, we may even wish to acquiesce. It does not follow that we must *give assent* . . .
Authorization, assent, acquiescence, diplomatic opposition and *opposition by force* are all separate and distinct things.

Joseph Grew's memorandum of December 27 and Stanley Hornbeck's of January 3 had an unusual reception in the State Department. The policy officers of the Far Eastern and West European Divisions, after reading Grew's communication, attached a note to it saying that they were "in full concurrence with its content." The Secretary of State, the Under Secretary, and other members of the Department's staff wrote to commend Grew. (The ambassador observed in his diary that he had never known a Secretary of State to write a personal letter of comment concerning a single dispatch and that his remarks had received all the consideration in Washington he had hoped for.) Hull sent both the Grew and Hornbeck memoranda to the President, together with a letter in which he said that he was "absolutely in accord" with the views expressed "with regard to the present situation and the importance of American naval preparedness." The Secretary added that he would like "at some time in the near future" to discuss with Roosevelt "ways and means for bringing these matters discreetly and in confidence to the attention of certain members of the Congress." Grew, on his part, was pleased that Hornbeck had written a memorandum similar to his own. "It is amusing and very gratifying," he noted in a diary entry, "to see how our minds work alike."

The memoranda which resulted from the naval meetings therefore revealed the amount of anxiety over the possibility of war with Japan that existed among American officials concerned with the making of our Far Eastern policy, an anxiety which no doubt had been increased by the naval discussions. These officials were henceforth to place much more emphasis upon the need for a larger navy. For the rest the tenor of the memoranda and the acclaim which they received from members of the State Department suggested that there was substantial agreement within the administration upon the wisdom of adhering to the course that the United States government had been pursuing in the Far East since the time of the Tangku Truce. However, in view of later developments, it should be noted that there was a difference between Ambassador Grew's and Hornbeck's comments that went unobserved at the time. Grew advocated the "tactful conduct of day-to-day diplomacy." By this he meant, as both his previous and subsequent dispatches show, that through a tactful treatment of the Japanese it might be possible to develop a spirit of good will between the United States and Japan which would furnish the basis for the establishment of genuinely friendly relations. Hornbeck, in contrast, recommended that the United States should maintain the same cordiality in its contacts with Japan as with other countries but that it should not engage in any unusual efforts to solicit the good will of the Japanese.

CHAPTER IV

THE UNITED STATES
SILVER POLICY AND THE FAR EAST

During the years 1934 and 1935, when the naval talks were taking place, new economic problems arose in the Far East which, differing from those discussed heretofore, involved the direct impact of the United States silver policy on the financial structure of China.

A change in the American silver policy which had been under discussion for some time was taking final shape just as the agitation over the Amau Doctrine was dying down. In early 1934, the group in Congress, which represented the silver-producing states and which was led by such powerful senators as Pittman of Nevada, decided to make a determined effort to obtain legislation designed to raise the dollar price of silver; the law was to require the United States government, through engaging in an extensive silver-purchasing program, to increase its holdings of the metal. As a result, Congress entered into a long debate on such legislation during which there was considerable discussion of the effect that an American silver-purchasing program might have upon China, the only large country still on a silver standard. Some congressmen argued that the consequences would be beneficial to China as a rise in the price of silver would increase the dollar value of her own stocks of the metal and thereby increase her buying power. Others declared that, if the world price of silver was higher than that prevailing in China, the metal might be drained from that country to an extent that would undermine the Chinese currency system. It was primarily in order to get further information about the financial situation in China, which might serve to settle this dispute, that Secretary Morgenthau sent Professor James Harvey Rogers to China in the spring of 1934.[1] However, the silver senators were only angered by Morgenthau's action, believing that he was engaging in delaying tactics in the hope of forestalling legislation. They consequently redoubled their efforts to get a law passed, with the result that the Silver Purchase Act was adopted by Congress in June, several months before Rogers' return from China. The Act authorized the

Secretary of the Treasury to buy silver until it constituted one fourth of the total United States monetary stocks of silver and gold.[2]

As early as February 1934, when the debate in Congress was just getting under way, the Chinese Bankers Association and the Chinese and foreign Shanghai General Chambers of Commerce all cabled President Roosevelt warning that if Congress really fulfilled its threat of legislation China would probably have to abandon its silver standard and adopt a managed currency.[3] Within a few months after the Silver Purchase Act was passed, these predictions seemed already on the road to realization as, between June and September, the monthly export of silver from China had increased sevenfold. In August, and again in September and October, H. H. Kung asked the administration in Washington whether it could not provide China with some kind of relief.[4] When Hull plainly indicated that there was little the administration could do, the Nanking government itself took action and, in the middle of October, imposed a heavy export tax on silver.[5]

During November, the legitimate export of silver from China declined sharply but there was evidence of an increase in smuggling. To discourage this new development, Secretary Morgenthau persuaded the President to stabilize the world price of silver around $0.55 per ounce for the time being. Nevertheless, early in December Dr. Kung again appealed for assistance saying that as there was still a disparity between the value of silver inside and outside of China, the metal was bound to leave the country by legal or illegal means.[6] He inquired whether the United States government would agree either (1) to announce that it would not pay more than $0.45 for silver bought from abroad or (2) to give the Nanking government a credit or otherwise cooperate in facilitating a reorganization of the Chinese currency system.

The Under Secretary of State sent Kung's message to the President together with cables from prominent American businessmen in Shanghai, who said that if foreign aid were not provided the entire Chinese economic structure might collapse within a few months and that there was already a serious amount of anti-American feeling in China directly attributable to our silver policy. He added a note of his own suggesting that, in view of the situation which seemed to be developing in China, the President might want to reconsider the administration's policy.[7]

The rest of December was in fact devoted to an intensive reconsideration of policy in an attempt to find the best way of answering Kung's appeal. A memorandum was written in the State Department by Nelson Johnson, who was in Washington on a short trip home, and by Herbert Feis, the Department's economic adviser.[8] The memorandum stated in essence that our silver policy was indeed, as the Shanghai businessmen were proclaiming, damaging our relations with the Chinese. The Chinese felt that the President had promised T. V. Soong and others that the United States would assist in China's reconstruction while the administration was actually undermining the Chinese economy and turning a deaf ear to requests for aid. As to Kung's references to the reorganization of China's currency, the Chinese government would scarcely be able to effect such a reorganization by itself without inviting disaster, as it lacked the necessary administrative power. On the other hand, if the United States or any other single country extended credits to China or otherwise cooperated in effecting monetary reforms, it would in all probability find itself drawn more and more deeply into China's internal affairs, let alone having to deal with Japanese opposition. In any case, the best solution appeared to be to do away with the causes of China's financial difficulties, the principle cause being the United States government's silver-purchasing program. That program should be suspended or, if for whatever reasons this proved impossible, the administration should follow Kung's suggestion and announce that it would not pay over $0.45 for silver.

A far more elaborate memorandum was prepared by the Treasury Department with the aid of Jacob Viner and others, on the basis of which the Treasury arrived at the opposite conclusion from the State Department.[9] It felt that, in view of the attitude of Congress, the administration would have to continue its silver-purchasing program but that it should refrain from any action which would drastically increase the price of silver until the United States had advanced a credit to the Chinese government for currency reorganization.

Although there were almost daily meetings between State and Treasury officials, their differences were not resolved and were finally taken up at a joint meeting with the President. A scheme was worked out which involved keeping the world price of silver around $0.55 and buying silver inside China only at that price and only from the Chinese government on terms which were mutually acceptable.[10] As the scheme was intended to change our silver policy at least sufficiently to stop the flight of silver from China and had nothing to do with currency reorganization, it was more in line with the State Department's than with the Treasury's views.

But whatever ground the State Department gained, it lost in record time. A note incorporating the new program was sent to the Central

Bank of China on December 18.[11] It, however, included a proviso to the effect that the program could be terminated "at any time on one week's notice." The note was confidential but stories appeared in the American press saying that the administration, in response to a request from Nanking, had agreed to slow up its purchase of silver. The stories so aroused the silver bloc in Congress that the President and Morgenthau felt compelled to notify the Chinese government on December 31 that the plan, which had been instituted only two weeks earlier, would have to be terminated. At the same time they urged Nanking to send a representative to the United States to discuss China's financial problems.[12]

The Chinese consequently arranged to have Dr. Soong leave for America in late January.[13] But this scheme was also to come to nothing. The State Department (which was not informed about the note of December 31 until after it had been sent) felt that Soong's visit would essentially end in failure since the administration had nothing concrete to offer.[14] It feared that failure might result in forcing the Chinese off the silver standard which, in turn, might bring about the very situation that the Department had been trying to avoid: the United States' having to choose between allowing chaos to develop in China or aiding the Chinese in a way that might involve us in serious trouble with Japan and perhaps even in difficulties with the Chinese themselves. The State Department's opposition to Soong's visit was unexpectedly re-enforced by Senator Pittman who declared that Soong should not come to this country unless it was understood in advance that he would not raise any questions about our silver policy. The senator's objections appear to have been the factor which made the President decide to drop the whole issue.[15] In the end, the Chinese were told that Soong's trip seemed unnecessary, as any proposals they had to make could just as well be forwarded by cable.[16]

In January, a new element was injected into the situation in China. There were widespread rumors that the Japanese had decided to take advantage of the precarious position in which the Chinese government found itself as a result of the financial emergency in China in order to strike a bargain with Nanking.[17] The Japanese were said to have proposed a Sino-Japanese rapprochement which would involve the Nanking government's promising to rid itself of all western "interference" in its affairs, in return for which the Japanese would provide a loan.

These rumors were given an alarming amount of substance by two messages which were sent to Washington—one by Dr. Soong, the other by Willys Peck. Soong's message was an extremely forceful plea for acceptance of a new set of proposals which the Chinese Ministry of Finance was about to submit to the United States government.[18] Soong said that in his opinion the Chinese currency system was heading for a breakdown "possibly in March, probably in April, certainly before June." The result would be the complete destruction of the country's banking system and finances so that the whole authority of the central government would be undermined. While this would obviously be hard to cope with under any circumstances, under existing conditions it might be disastrous in view of the fact that the Japanese were "pressing for a showdown . . . in order to dominate China." The Nanking government might well be forced to choose between accepting a Japanese loan, "under onerous political and economic conditions," or watching the establishment of new provincial governments in the North, virtually under Japanese jurisdiction. Japan's new efforts to control China had such wide implications that aid to China should be considered, not just as a matter of saving the present Chinese government or even safeguarding the nation's economy, but as essential to the peace of the world.

Peck reported that Kung had paid him a visit to appeal for support from Washington for his new proposals during which he apparently expressed precisely the same ideas as Soong.[19] But the most significant part of Peck's cable was his own analysis of the general situation in Nanking. Chinese leaders, he said, who usually talked very freely about Japanese oppression of China, were being abnormally reticent. The most likely explanation was that the Nanking government was considering adopting a "policy of submission to and collaboration with Japan" but wanted to keep the matter secret until it was an accomplished fact. It was "certain" that there were leaders in the government who were advocating such a policy on the basis that the aid which China had hoped to obtain from the United States showed no signs of materializing. These same leaders might already have succeeded in persuading Chiang Kai-shek to listen to Japan's overtures.

Soong's and Peck's messages were sent by the State Department to the White House again with a note from Phillips which said that our silver policy was contributing to China's weakness in a way that the Japanese were capitalizing on to the fullest extent.[20] In short, it had become evident that our silver policy was not only hurting China and damaging our relations with the Chinese but might also drive the Nanking government into a diplomatic surrender to Japan.

It was against this grim background that the new Chinese proposals arrived in Washington. They stated that China wanted to adopt a currency based on gold as well as silver and would like to know whether in order to make this possible the United States would advance a loan of $100 million and a credit of equal value to be used in case of emergency.[21]

The Chinese plan was discussed at a meeting of State and Treasury Department officials on February 14.[22] The meeting went poorly from the start. The Secretary and Under Secretary of the Treasury were present but neither Hull nor Phillips could attend and Morgenthau found it difficult to arrive at decisions with State Department officials whose rank was in no way equivalent to his own. Hornbeck, who had been designated to present the State Department's views, read the draft of a reply which the Department wanted to send to Nanking.

The draft was based on the idea that the administration should say neither "no" nor "yes" to the Chinese request.[23] To say "no" would further discourage officials and perhaps make them wonder more than ever whether they should not submit to the Japanese. To agree would be inadvisable for the reasons which had repeatedly been emphasized, that is, to give China a loan or credit for currency reorganization would involve us in "uncontrollable responsibilities in the Far East" and put us in the dangerous position of having to meet Japanese opposition. The best solution, therefore, was to make a counter-proposal.

The counterproposal, as incorporated in the draft reply, consisted of suggesting that Nanking submit the plan which it had presented to Washington to several other governments that had "in the past shown themselves most interested in projects dealing with Chinese financial problems" (a phrase which was clearly intended to include the Japanese).[24] The American government would then cooperate with the other governments—as well as with the Chinese themselves—in exploring the possibilities of aiding China on a collective basis.

On hearing the State Department's draft, Morgenthau said at once that it was meaningless and would "get us nowhere." The matter should not be dealt with by international action—we should "go it alone." The invitation to Soong should be renewed and the negotiations left to the Treasury which was prepared to push ahead "aggressively" with plans for assisting China. Hornbeck replied that the issue was not purely a monetary one (which would have justified its being handled exclusively by the Treasury) but involved "very definite political factors." Unless invited to participate, the Japanese would oppose any attempt by the United States or any other country to provide China with a loan or to help in her reconstruction. The meeting ended with a general recognition that, as Morgenthau said, the State and Treasury Departments were "at opposite poles" and further discussion was therefore useless.

A few days later, Morgenthau and Hull talked over the State Department draft with the President.[25] Morgenthau received the impression that the President was trying to tell Secretary Hull to leave the negotiations with the Chinese in the hands of the Treasury. If so, Hull did not understand and the only action which Roosevelt took subsequently was to ask the State Department to tone down the draft reply. He thought that it went too far toward committing the administration to consult with other countries on aid to China and that it could be interpreted as approving the $100 million loan and credit in principle.[26] As a consequence, the reply, which was delivered to the Chinese on February 26, contained only the somewhat cryptic statement that "the American Government . . . ventures to inquire whether the Chinese Government had given thought to the possibility of presenting this outline [Kung's proposals] . . . simultaneously to the governments of those foreign powers—of which the United States is one—which have in the past manifested interest in projects relating to Chinese financial problems."[27]

The discussion over the reply to the Chinese showed that the differences between the State and the Treasury Departments had entered a new phase. State Department officials had for a long time clung to the hope that the President and Morgenthau could be persuaded to change our silver policy in order to avoid any further injury to China. By February they had, however, decided—not without some bitterness—that it was necessary to proceed on the assumption that Roosevelt and Morgenthau would not do anything which might result in a conflict with the silver senators. They had, therefore, fallen back upon what they regarded as the best alternative: a policy of helping China in cooperation with other countries including Japan.[28]

The second phase of the dispute centered upon this policy. The general confusion was increased by constant clashes of personality which at times obscured the more fundamental political differences that were involved. The greatest difference was that Morgenthau was exceedingly critical of Hull's whole Far Eastern policy which he regarded as far too conciliatory toward the Japanese. He was irritated because he believed the State Department was blocking his every move out of an inordinate fear of angering Japan. He thought that, if trouble between the United States and Japan was coming, it would come anyhow and that to try to postpone it was useless.[29]

State Department officials, on the other hand, felt that they were as deeply sympathetic as anyone to China, but that Morgenthau was possessed of a romantic notion of rescuing the Chinese, which involved unjustifiable risks. In other words, the State Department believed that for the United States to "go it alone" in aiding China was to fly in the face of the Amau Doctrine and it was as convinced as ever that American interests did not warrant any such procedure.

The President himself seems at times to have favored the Treasury Department, at times the State Department. In all probability neither was offering any solution which really satisfied him. What he wanted, as he himself made very clear, was some wholly new idea that would provide a way out of the situation which would offend neither the silver bloc in Congress nor the Japanese.[30]

By mid-February, the conflict within the administration had obviously created a deadlock. But at this juncture, the State Department found an unexpected ally in the British. The Chinese had also appealed to the British for a loan which the Foreign Office had refused on the grounds that a loan would, at best, only give the Chinese temporary relief.[31] Nevertheless, the British were very concerned about the possibility of an economic collapse in China and in late February suggested to the Japanese, American, and French governments, trying to work out some plan for collective aid to China.[32] The British said that, if these three governments and the Chinese themselves would cooperate, they would be glad to canvass the possibilities for helping China. They felt, however, that any economic program would only be effective if preceded by an easing of tensions in the Far East which required a Sino-Japanese détente.

Phillips immediately told the British ambassador in Washington that the State Department was also in favor of the idea of joint aid to China and warmly welcomed the British government's taking the initiative in this respect.[33] The only question was whether a Sino-Japanese détente should not come after, rather than before, the grant of assistance to China. The Department was afraid that if the Chinese had to come to an agreement with the Japanese under existing conditions they would be forced to accept exceedingly unfavorable terms.[34]

Phillips subsequently (on March 4) endorsed the British proposal in a press release and in oral statements to the Chinese Minister and Japanese ambassador in Washington.[35] The first reports of the Japanese reaction to the British plan were mixed. Grew cabled that Hirota had spoken of the plan in very friendly terms but that Amau had made various remarks to the press which sounded both resentful and belligerent.[36] The Japanese newspapers were for the most part hostile and were insisting that the British were merely trying to inject themselves into the situation in the Far East to prevent China from accepting assistance from Japan to the exclusion of the Western powers. In Washington, Ambassador Saito went so far as to say that he doubted whether Hirota had really meant to indicate that he approved the British suggestion.[37] The Chinese, on their part, declared that they would gladly participate in any international project designed to find a means of solving their monetary problems.[38]

On March 28, Sir Warren Fisher of the British Treasury announced that the British government had decided upon a concrete scheme which consisted of sending a financial expert to China to be attached to the British Legation for a brief period.[39] It hoped the three other interested governments would take similar action so that the experts could collaborate in studying the financial emergency in China and in working out possible remedies for its solution.

Sir Warren's explanation to Ray Atherton (the Counselor of the American embassy in London) of the motives behind the British plan indicate that British policy in the Far East was still very much as Norman Davis had described it during the naval negotiations of 1934.[40] Sir Warren said that Hitler would undoubtedly plunge Europe into war within at least the next ten years; that Germany was already 70 per cent prepared; and that the British government would soon have to awaken its people to the dangers that lay ahead and to the need for rearmament. Under these circumstances, the British wanted to maintain the *status quo* in the Pacific so that the Far East would not develop into another area of conflict and the Open Door in China would be preserved for British interests. They hoped that, if the plan for discussions between financial attachés of the various powers was successful, it would lead to a consideration of political issues, especially those between China and Japan, on a diplomatic level. A habit of interchange of thought might thereby be established inconspicuously and the Japanese might lose some of their apprehension of the West and return to a cooperative policy. Sir Warren frankly admitted that before the British plan was finally evolved, he had talked over many aspects of it with the Japanese ambassador, Tsuneo Matsudaira, who was consequently giving it his full support and felt his government was likely to accept it.

Nothing was, however, heard from the Japanese government and the British proposal was quickly obscured by other developments. The world price of silver, which had started to rise from a level of about $0.55 in February, suddenly soared and reached a peak of $0.81 by the end of April. The impact upon China was severe and the State Department was concerned again about the possible out-break of anti-American feeling.[41] Matters were scarcely improved by the spectacular bankruptcy of the American-Oriental Banking Corporation and other large interests held by F. J. Raven, an American, in Shanghai. The Chinese, apparently in despair over the American silver policy, made some badly needed changes in their banking system which for the first time gave the Nanking government control over an appreciable amount of the silver inside China.[42] In addition, a "gentlemen's agreement" not to participate in the export of silver was concluded between the foreign and Chinese banks in Shanghai.[43] Unfortunately, smuggling continued so that more than 173 million ounces of silver were reportedly taken out of China illegally during 1935 in contrast to 15 million for the year before.[44] On the political side, the Japanese, in June, forced the Chinese to accept the famous Ho-Umetsu agreement which amounted to another major surrender in North China.[45]

Nevertheless, the British pushed ahead with their plan for financial consultation, apparently feeling that despite the renewed hostility engendered by the conflict in North China they would make a final, supreme effort to persuade the Japanese to abandon their ideas of aggression and expansion and adopt a more conciliatory and cooperative attitude.[46] On June 9, the British took the quite sensational step of announcing that they were sending their foremost economic adviser, Sir Frederick Leith-Ross, to Peiping as financial attaché. At the same time they inquired whether the other interested governments had as yet appointed any financial attachés of their own to go to China.[47]

Again there was no reply from the Japanese, which was a source of considerable concern to both the British government and the State Department. The Chinese indicated strong approval of the British move and begged the United States government to appoint a financial expert to work with Leith-Ross. But the administration in Washington deferred taking any action because the State and Treasury Departments could not agree. Morgenthau was opposed to the British plan partly because of his feeling that any program for aiding China which required Japanese participation was not likely to succeed, as the Japanese would probably not cooperate, and that we should therefore act independently without concerning ourselves too much over Japan's reaction. However, he had an even more immediate cause of worry, which was that if a group of economists reviewed the situation in China, they were likely to recommend drastic changes in our silver policy which, in view of the inevitable opposition of the silver senators, he would be unable to make.[48] The State Department, on the other hand, wanted to participate in the British plan because it believed in—and was indeed already publicly committed to—the idea of helping China on a collective basis. Moreover, State Department officials felt very strongly that, leaving all other aspects of the problem aside, we ought if possible to cooperate with the British in order to maintain Anglo-American unity in the Far East.[49]

As weeks of discussion passed, the State and Treasury Departments drew, if anything, further apart. In July, Sir Frederick Leith-Ross announced that he would leave for China in August, traveling by way of Canada, and a British official suggested to Morgenthau that the American government might like to avail itself of the opportunity to talk to Sir Frederick. Unfortunately the suggestion was made at a moment when relations between the British and American Treasuries were strained so that Morgenthau was unwilling to invite Leith-Ross to Washington or to agree to any American official's meeting him elsewhere.[50] The State Department repeatedly appealed to Secretary Morgenthau to change his mind and Phillips finally proposed going to Toronto himself to sound out Leith-Ross on his mission to China.[51] But Morgenthau felt that it was inappropriate for the Under Secretary of State to make such a trip to contact "a British official, who was only fourth or fifth in order of rank." Phillips replied that he knew nothing about Sir Frederick's "numerals" but that he was, in fact, one of Great Britain's "most important officials." Nevertheless, nothing came of the matter and Sir Frederick went through Canada without consulting with anyone from the Treasury or State Departments.

The State Department's intense desire to talk with Sir Frederick was, to some extent, based upon a new development. In July the press was again full of rumors of an Anglo-Japanese rapprochement. The British were, at this time, still canvassing the other governments in preparation for the naval conference to be held in December. It was known that Leith-Ross was going to stop in Japan on his way to China and the press predicted that he would pave the way for Anglo-Japanese negotiations on naval and economic problems. Hornbeck felt the situation to be so serious that he urged the Secretary of State to again take up with the President the issue of sending a financial attaché to China.[52] If we took no action, he said, the British might feel, as they had tended to in the past, that they could not shape their Far Eastern policy in accordance with "an unassured, an uncertain and a not-to-be-relied upon willingness to cooperate on the part of the United States." They might, consequently, turn to the Japanese and make some agreement which was not to our liking. If so, we would have only ourselves to blame.

In the end, the President decided to drop the whole issue of the financial emergency in China, hoping it would somehow take care of itself. In June, the silver senators had renewed their pressure on the administration. Senator McCarran wrote a public letter to Morgenthau protesting the decline of the world price of silver from the April high of $0.81. A few weeks later, forty-six senators addressed a similar protest to the President. Shortly thereafter, a resolution was introduced into the Senate calling for an investigation of the administration's conduct of our silver policy. Beset with these difficulties at home, Roosevelt undoubtedly had no more desire than Morgenthau to have a group of economists attract further attention to the damage which our silver policy was doing in China when he felt in no position to take any remedial action.[53]

In so far as the story of the Leith-Ross mission can be pieced together from American sources, Sir Frederick left England with only the broadest instructions: he was not to suggest a loan to China unless the other interested nations would participate; he was to assure the Japanese that Great Britain was not trying to challenge Japan but rather to cooperate with her.[54] Sir Frederick remained in Tokyo longer than originally planned in the hope of finding out what the Japanese attitude was toward helping China by collective action. The Japanese, however, revealed nothing, and he proceeded to China in late September where he found the financial situation on the verge of disaster. In several interviews during October, he told Nelson Johnson that he had about come to the conclusion that it was impractical to adhere to the "London view" that an improvement in Sino-Japanese relations should precede any program of aid to China as the hostility between the Chinese and Japanese was too great to be resolved.[55] He said he had recommended certain reforms to Nanking, especially further changes in the banking system and a centralization of the note issue, and had asked the Japanese whether, if these reforms were instituted, they would join in giving China a small loan. However, he also stated frankly that he doubted whether Nanking had the administrative power to carry through the technical measures which might be involved in a currency reorganization.

Sir Frederick's doubts were fully shared by Johnson who, as already noted, had expressed similar views much earlier. Johnson had been somewhat more optimistic in the spring when the Chinese government had obtained control over a larger proportion of the silver stocks in the country. He had, in fact, with very friendly directness urged Chinese officials to adopt some currency policy of their own, arguing—in line with his comments to Lamont the year before—that China would be much more likely to get help from others if she first did something to help herself.[56] But by autumn Johnson had again become discouraged and on October 9 wrote Secretary Hull that he did not believe that the Chinese government would, within any "foreseeable future," possess enough police to enforce the regulations necessary to stabilize the monetary situation.[57] Nor was Johnson anxious to cooperate with the Leith-Ross mission, as he felt the British were really intent on saving their interests in China and Hong Kong from the threat presented by the Japanese and by America's silver policy without much regard for the welfare of others.[58]

The outlook was indeed bleak when, on November 3, under extreme pressure from a new wave of smuggling in the North, the Chinese government took matters into its own hands and published the famous currency decree which nationalized silver and ordered its exchange for legal tender notes issued by three government banks. The chaos, which had so frequently been predicted, did not ensue, in part no doubt because the American and British governments were exceedingly sympathetic to the Chinese move and provided substantial support. The British did what they could to overcome the obstacle presented by the existence of extraterritoriality which prevented the decree from applying to foreign nationals. The Foreign Office in London approved a so-called King's Regulation prepared by British officials at Shanghai, to be issued on the day that the Chinese currency law was to go into effect, which aimed primarily at getting the British banks to conform to the law. This move was important because of the magnitude of British interests in China and was widely acclaimed by the Chinese.[59]

American support was largely provided by the Treasury. In the last week of October, the Chinese government asked Morgenthau if he would buy 100 million ounces of silver in order to pave the way for an eventual reorganization of the Chinese currency. Morgenthau immediately agreed, feeling that at last a situation had arisen which, being purely monetary in character since it involved neither loans nor credits, he could handle with a minimum of consultation with the State Department.[60] Negotiations were already under way when the Chinese issued the currency decree of November 3. Morgenthau thought the Chinese had "gone off half cocked" but nevertheless consented to continue the negotiations.[61] Difficulties developed when the Chinese refused to tie the yuan to the United States dollar, partly out of fear of Japanese opposition. Secretary Morgenthau felt the issue was a vital one because—to quote one of the best accounts of these events—"he was obsessed by the thought that he might finance China only to see her turn to sterling" and suspected that the British were maneuvering to establish a sterling bloc in Asia.[62] A further problem arose in that the British informed Morgenthau that Hong Kong also wanted to abandon silver and sell 100 million ounces to the United States. It looked therefore as though the American Treasury would have to buy large quantities of silver from the Far East at the current world price, which was high. Morgenthau suggested to the President that perhaps the best solution was to let the world price drop but Roosevelt rejected this idea on the grounds that it was politically impractical. Roosevelt himself proposed buying only 20 million ounces of silver from China, which though a relatively small amount would be enough to help her temporarily, and thereafter awaiting further developments. He was also willing to forego linking the yuan to the dollar especially as the State Department had never favored such an arrangement, fearing that it would tend to involve the United States in any trouble that developed out of the reorganization of China's currency system.

An agreement was reached with the Chinese on November 13.[63] At the last minute, as a result of a desperate appeal from Nanking, the President agreed to purchase 50 million instead of 20 million ounces of silver. Strong strings were attached to the proceeds which the Chinese were to derive from the sale. The funds were to be deposited in New York and the Chinese had to promise to use them exclusively for the stabilization of China's currency. The United States Treasury representative at Shanghai (Professor J. Lossing Buck) was to be kept fully informed about the use of the funds and about monetary developments in China throughout the next year. The purpose of these conditions was to ensure the proceeds not being diverted to military ends and to provide the U.S. Treasury with sufficient information about the silver situation in China to guarantee against sudden surprises such as the dumping of large quantities of silver by the Nanking government on the world market. In addition, it was specifically understood that the mere existence of the agreement was to be kept secret, presumably in order to avoid Japanese opposition. The Japanese were exceedingly angry about the new Chinese currency law and were doing everything in their power to prevent its successful operation.[64] Their anger was, however, mainly directed against the British government and against Sir Frederick Leith-Ross in particular, as they were convinced, despite repeated denials on his part, that he had instigated the new monetary measures.[65] Even when, owing to the leakage of information to the press, Morgenthau admitted in February that he had bought 50 million ounces of silver from the Nanking government, the Japanese continued to berate Leith-Ross rather than the American Treasury which they apparently regarded as having conducted no more than an ordinary monetary transaction.[66]

The silver senators also accepted the Treasury's agreement with the Chinese without violent protest. This was perhaps a foregone conclusion, as Senator Pittman had been consulted throughout the negotiations. Moreover, some of the leading silverites in Congress were undergoing a change of heart and by December arrived at the conclusion that they would not object to a decline in the world price of silver as long as the domestic price was kept at a relatively high level. As a consequence of their attitude and of various other factors, Morgenthau, who was himself utterly disenchanted by this time with the entire silver program, persuaded the President to let the world price of silver fall so that between December and January it dropped from $0.65 to $0.45.[67] This amounted to a reversal of our silver policy as far as foreign countries were concerned.

Early in 1936, Secretary Morgenthau, partly in response to requests from the Chinese for the purchase of more silver, decided to ask Soong to come to Washington so that they could discuss the whole Chinese financial situation directly.[68] According to Morgenthau's account, Secretary Hull objected to Soong's visit, believing that it would touch off a controversy with the Japanese. The President, however, overruled Hull and moreover appears to have stated that the negotiations should be handled exclusively by the Treasury. As matters turned out, Soong was unable to come to the United States because of political complications at home, but in April the Chinese government sent in his stead K. P. Chen, a well-known Shanghai banker. The State Department seems to have known very little about the Chen mission, which perhaps heightened its anxiety.[69] In any case, after hearing rumors that Chen intended to ask for a reinstatement of the canceled portion of the R.F.C. cotton and wheat loan, the Department cabled Johnson to impress upon the Chinese government that Chen was coming to discuss "monetary matters" but should not entertain any hopes in respect to "loans or credits."[70]

Chen spent six weeks of peaceful and fruitful negotiations with the Treasury. Secretary Morgenthau seems increasingly to have taken the position that the United States should strengthen China even, if necessary, at the expense of alienating the Japanese. The Chinese on their part kept asserting that if other countries did not stop the Japanese soon the Japanese would attack them ultimately and be in a far better position to do so having gained control of China.

An agreement was finally concluded in the middle of May. It carefully avoided making any references to "loans" or "credits" and stated that the United States would provide China with "dollar exchange" for the sake of stabilizing her currency. The sum involved in the dollar exchange was not mentioned in the agreement but actually the Treasury undertook to furnish the Chinese with $20 million against a deposit of 50 million ounces of silver.[71] To avoid difficulties with the State Department, the agreement was signed on behalf of the Chinese Ministry of Finance and the United States Treasury (rather than the United States government). In addition, Morgenthau arranged with Chen to buy 75 million ounces of silver from China, on a monthly basis, for nine months. On May 19, Secretary Morgenthau issued a public statement which confined itself to saying that the Treasury "in accordance with its silver purchase policy" was prepared to buy "substantial amounts of silver" from China and also to make available "dollar exchange for currency stabilization purposes."[72] This time the terms of the transaction were successfully kept secret.

Hull and Phillips apparently approved the arrangements. One can safely assume that their reasons for doing so were very similar to those given by Hornbeck in an advisory memorandum when his opinion was asked:[73]

With regard to the plan of the Treasury for an agreement . . . for purchases of silver, it is believed that this Department will need to regard that matter as essentially Treasury business.

Our principal concern, of course . . . is . . . that of the political effect in the Far East, including the reactions of the British and the Japanese Governments. It is a definite feature of our Far Eastern policy at present that (1) we do not wish to inject new elements of irritation into that situation; (2) we do not wish to assume new responsibilities of initiative or leadership in regard to matters of general international interests in the Far East; (3) we favor cooperation with Great Britain and do not wish to give Japan ground for contention that she is being discriminated against or being deliberately left out in the cold. It is believed that the proposed arrangements in this case give no warrant for criticism or objection by the British and/or the Japanese.

In sum, after all the endless delays and frustrations, the discussions and conflicts, a way had been found to repair some of the damage inflicted on China by our silver-purchasing program while keeping our Far Eastern policy intact. Every effort was made to furnish China with assistance in a manner that would not violate the letter—if not the spirit—of the Amau doctrine and to minimize the importance of the Chen-Morgenthau agreement. As a result, the Japanese continued to concentrate their attacks on Sir Frederick Leith-Ross whom, as Grew said, they regarded as the real culprit "responsible for the financial and political machinations in China which were undermining Japan's stabilizing influence in that allegedly misguided country." The British, on their part, insisted to the very end that, while they were ready to give China a loan, or some other form of financial aid, they would not act without the approval and preferably the participation of Japan and the United States.[74] Consequently, Anglo-American cooperation in the Far East was also maintained intact although the British must have felt sorely tried by the behavior of the Roosevelt administration, which at times was erratic to the point of being hard to believe.

CHAPTER V | FURTHER JAPANESE
ENCROACHMENTS ON CHINA

Throughout 1935 the events connected with the impact of our silver policy upon China were paralleled by the heightening of the crisis between China and Japan. From January to June and again from September to the end of the year the Japanese redoubled their efforts to extend control over China.

JANUARY TO JULY 1935

In January 1935, it will be recalled, the State Department received numerous communications from China—including urgent messages from high Chinese officials—indicating that the Japanese were attempting to take advantage of the financial situation in that country to force the Nanking government to enter into a rapprochement with Japan. The terms of the rapprochement, it was asserted, would involve such far-reaching concessions on the part of the Chinese that in future China would be entirely under the domination of Japan. Following January 1935 the dispatches of American Foreign Service officers in China continued to be filled with reports of the activities of Japanese diplomats at Nanking.[1] Representatives of the Japanese Foreign Office were known to be engaged in an extraordinary series of conversations with Chiang Kai-shek, Wang Ching-wei, and other leaders of the Chinese government. The purport of the talks remained secret but as far as could be ascertained they centered around Japan's demand for a rapprochement.

When the first rumors that the Japanese were exerting new pressures on Nanking reached Washington, the Far Eastern Division addressed a memorandum to Hull asserting that it assumed the stories had some validity.[2] The division suggested that the United States should watch events closely, expect its own "course of action" to be negative, and refrain as far as possible from comment while not cultivating the impression that it was indifferent to the "possibilities and implications" of developments. Secretary Hull sent the memorandum to the President with the comment that he was inclined to follow the advice it contained.[3] The President expressed his approval, stating that he thought "our immediate course should be to watch closely all evidence, reports, rumors, etc." and be prepared to ask for official information from both China and Japan if and when the situation warranted.[4]

In the ensuing months the State Department became increasingly disturbed over the dispatches from China. At the end of March the Department cabled Nelson Johnson that as "developments of far-reaching importance" were evidently taking place between Japan and China, it would like his estimate of the situation.[5] In response the Minister wrote several long memoranda in which he discussed a variety of factors, historical and otherwise, that had a bearing upon Sino-Japanese relations.[6] Concerning recent events the Minister declared that in his opinion Japanese policy in China had entered upon a new phase in January 1935 which reflected the division that existed within the Japanese government. The Japanese military, who constituted the "party of force" in the conduct of Japan's foreign affairs, had been responsible for the Manchurian incident and had continued to direct Japanese policy in China since 1931. While they remained in control of that policy they had become disillusioned with their venture in Manchuria, which was not yielding the economic benefits they had expected. The military had therefore decided to give the Japanese Foreign Office and industrialists, who together formed the more liberal element in Japan, an opportunity to try to win economic concessions from the Nanking government by the use of diplomacy rather than force. As a result, since January 1935 representatives of the Foreign Office had been engaged in an effort to bring about a rapprochement with Nanking. The activities of the Japanese in regard to a rapprochement were, however, only part of a more general attempt to get underway a policy of so-called economic "cooperation" between Japan and China the purpose of which was to secure "the development of China as a market for Japanese produce and as a source of raw materials for Japanese factories." According to confidential information given to the legation by Chinese officials, the Japanese had so far presented the Nanking government with only one formal "demand" which was that all anti-Japanese agitation in China must be suppressed. At the same time, however, the Japanese were "pressing the Chinese very hard" to work out a plan for economic "cooperation" in North China. They had made certain proposals which included: the joint development by Japan and China of the cotton growing areas of North China; the construction by the Japanese of a railway which would give them access to and virtual control over the coal fields of Shansi; and the organization of a Sino-Japanese company with the right to operate air lines in China's northern provinces.

Johnson left no doubt whatever of the implications which, in his judgment, Japan's policy of economic "cooperation" had for China and the West. The Japanese, he thought, driven by the necessity of finding a solution to the acute economic problems with which they were confronted at home, were determined to obtain economic control over China which would inevitably entail political control. To rid themselves of all competition, they would eradicate every vestige of western influence in China and stifle every attempt on the part of the Chinese to further their own economic growth. Following the pattern which they had established in Formosa, Korea, and Manchuria, the Japanese would substitute themselves for the ruling class in China. To extract raw materials for their own use they would take over the management of much of China's industrial and agricultural production and rely upon the Chinese, with their almost inexhaustible supply of cheap, intelligent, and industrious labor, to work the mines, till the soil, et cetera. Similarly, to develop China as a market for their manufactured products, the Japanese would assume administrative positions within the Chinese government which would enable them to establish and maintain the peaceful conditions essential for the conduct of trade. Moreover, the Japanese would furnish the police force necessary for the preservation of law and order in China.[7]

Johnson also sought to estimate the Chinese side of the developments which were currently taking place in the relations between Japan and China.[8] In a memorandum written at the end of March, he told the State Department that on a recent trip to Nanking he had found that the response of Chinese officials to Japan's insistence on a rapprochement and economic "cooperation" was "one of frightened acquiescence." The Chinese government, he believed, would comply with the wishes of the Japanese since it did not have the power to resist Japan and felt it could not expect help from abroad. Throughout April and the early part of May, Johnson and members of his staff reported to Washington that perhaps for the first time in China's history Chinese officials were acquiring a "sense of the realities." In the past they had always relied upon a strategy of feigning surrender in order to circumvent and overcome the enemy. But in the existing situation they recognized that equivocation was useless, that in fact their government was "helpless" and could "do little but delay, and then not for too long, in meeting Japanese desires." As the weeks went by, Johnson himself became convinced that there were many signs that the Nanking regime was preparing to give in to Japan. In particular he was impressed by the conciliatory attitude being demonstrated toward the Japanese by the foremost leaders of the Chinese government, including Chiang Kai-shek, Wang Ching-wei, Sun Fo, and even T. V. Soong, who for so long had seemed almost the embodiment of anti-Japanese sentiment. On May 9, Johnson wrote the Department that Chinese officials were increasingly uniting "in the belief that, in the present critical situation and in the improbability of assistance from Western nations, 'friendship' with Japan" was "practically inevitable." As to the reaction of the Chinese people to the recent developments in Sino-Japanese relations, Johnson said that little public comment could be expected because of the tight controls which the government exercised over the press. However the Chinese intellectuals in the Peiping area showed "acquiescence in or resignation to the inevitableness of Japanese domination over China for the next generation or two."

The State Department had also asked our embassy in Tokyo for an assessment of the intense diplomatic activity which had characterized Japanese policy in China since the beginning of 1935. The embassy expressed its complete agreement with Johnson's view that the Japanese military were giving the Foreign Office a chance to demonstrate what it could accomplish through diplomacy.[9] As to the motives of the military, the embassy felt that it was necessary to look to Japan's relations with the Soviet Union.

The embassy had for several years attempted to follow the course of Japanese-Russian relations closely and to keep the State Department abreast of developments by providing it with reports regularly every two weeks.[10] These reports indicate that in early 1933 the embassy was immensely concerned over the possible outbreak of war between Japan and the Soviet Union. It did not expect the Russians to precipitate such a war since they were obviously intent upon solving their domestic problems and attaining at least a modicum of security by improving their international status. The embassy did, however, fear that Japan might attack the Soviet Union at some time in the relatively near future, in all likelihood in the year 1935, when the Japanese government would have completed plans which were then in progress for the modernization of its army. The Japanese—the embassy thought—would not postpone action much beyond 1935, as any delay would operate in favor of the Russians who were already energetically carrying out an extensive program for the construction of a network of communications, fortifications, air bases, et cetera, and the strengthening of their armies in the Far East.

But, contrary to its expectations, the embassy gradually became very hopeful that war between the Soviet Union and Japan would be averted. According to the analysis of developments progressively presented in its reports, the Russians managed to improve the situation on their western front by negotiating agreements with various European countries so that they were in a far better position to cope with Japan. Even more significantly, the Russians proved far more successful than had been anticipated in building up their military power in the Far East. As a result, by 1935 they were "telling Japan" in the only language it could understand (the language of force) that the "door to the north" was locked and that any future Japanese expansion would have to be directed into China or southeast Asia. But while the Soviet Union therefore made great strides forward, Japan also achieved impressive gains. In 1933 the Japanese military, to all appearances, decided to allow the Foreign Office to take charge of the conduct of Japanese-Russian affairs until such time as the Japanese army was prepared to engage in a venture against the Soviet Union. Hirota thereupon adopted a policy of trying to settle, item by item, the concrete problems which were creating difficulties between Japan and the U.S.S.R. and devoted himself in particular to negotiating the purchase of the Soviet rights in the Chinese Eastern Railway. Although the negotiations met with many obstacles, Hirota brought them to a successful conclusion in the early part of 1935. In doing so, he in effect carried to its culmination the movement which the Japanese military had started in 1931 of forcing the Russians to abandon Manchuria completely, leaving the Japanese in exclusive control of that area. Thus a "chapter in the relations between Soviet Russia and Japan" had been brought to an end as a balance of power had been established between the two countries in the Far East which, barring some new turn of events, went far to preclude any conflict within the foreseeable future.[11]

In the embassy's view it was the close of this "chapter" in Soviet-Japanese relations and the satisfactory results of Hirota's negotiations with the Russians that were leading the Japanese military to give the Foreign Office the opportunity to see what it could achieve through diplomacy in dealing with the Chinese. Grew was, however, no more optimistic than Johnson about the current trend of Sino-Japanese affairs. In a letter written to the State Department on May 3, the ambassador asserted in substance that, while the Japanese Foreign Office believed in peaceful methods and in contrast to the army was desirous of avoiding war, its objectives differed little from those of the military.[12] Moreover, Grew declared with the utmost emphasis that there was no evidence whatever to suggest that the guidance of Japanese policy in China was "passing from the military to the civilian"; on the contrary, it was apparent that the military were "still the strongest single element in Japanese affairs."

Grew's estimate of the continuing pre-eminence of the military in the Japanese government was amply borne out by events which occurred before the end of the month. These events were in part touched off by an episode which must be considered for a moment in connection with United States relations with China. On May 9 the Japanese Foreign Office notified Grew that it was about to raise the Japanese Legation in China to the grade of an embassy. The Foreign Office expressed a willingness to delay action, however, if the United States wished to take a similar step simultaneously.[13] On being informed of the matter, the Far Eastern Division of the State Department advised the Secretary of State to give serious consideration to taking advantage of the Japanese offer.[14] The division asserted that the status of the United States Legation had not been raised in the past because of the additional expense involved in the conduct of an embassy and because China's position, both internally and internationally, was "so unsettled" that there was no justification for making a gesture which "under ordinary circumstances would signalize satisfactory progress." However, if the Japanese raised the rank of their legation and the United States did not follow suit, the result might be to increase the ill will toward America which had already been generated in China by our silver policy. After referring the issue to the President, it was decided to consult with the British with a view to working out some parallel course. But on inquiry, the State Department learned that the British had already agreed to simultaneous action with the Japanese.[15] The upshot was that on May 17, Japan, Great Britain, and the United States announced that their missions in China would henceforth have the grade of embassies.[16] Unfortunately, however, Great Britain and the United States reaped little benefit from this move. For, apparently at the instigation of the Japanese Foreign Office, a few days before May 17 Rengo published a statement to the effect that the Japanese government was about to raise the grade of its legation in China and had so informed London and Washington. Consequently, as Grew remarked in a dispatch to the State Department, the announcements of May 17 merely created the impression that the United States and Great Britain were "following in the footsteps of Japan through force of circumstances."[17] The United States was, moreover, put in an especially unfavorable position, for, while the new Japanese and British ambassadors presented their credentials at Nanking in mid-June, Johnson was forced to wait until mid-September largely because his appointment had to be confirmed by the Senate.[18] Although this delay was inevitable, it was criticized in China as an indication of lack of interest in that country's affairs thereby leading to the increase in ill will which the State Department had been most anxious to avoid.

Within the context of Japan's relations with China the episode involving a change in the status of the legations was important in that it aroused the anger of the Japanese military against the Foreign Office. As far as American Foreign Service officers could ascertain, there were various reasons for the reaction of the military.[19] The Foreign Office had acted without prior consultation with any of the military leaders who were therefore faced with a *fait accompli*. Certain sections of the army believed that Hirota was adopting too friendly an attitude toward the Chinese in his effort to secure a rapprochement, and that no significant concessions should be made to Nanking without demanding a *quid pro quo*. And the military as a whole disliked the idea that with the establishment of an embassy at Nanking the Foreign Office would have a representative in China, in the person of the ambassador, who outranked any Japanese army officer stationed in that country. Moreover in general the time seemed ripe for drastic measures. In the autumn of 1934 the Nationalist troops had finally succeeded in driving the Communists out of their stronghold in Kiangsi. The Communists had thereupon embarked upon their historic Long March and the Generalissimo was currently in the southwest deeply involved in trying to stop the advance of the Red armies. At any rate, whatever the motivating causes, at the end of May the military resumed control of Japan's policy in China.

Information concerning the events which followed was made available to the State Department by a steady flow of reports from its representatives in China and of news stories which appeared in the press in this country and in the foremost English language publications in China, such as the *North China Daily News* and the *China Weekly Review*.[20] According to these accounts, the first sign of renewed activity on the part of the Japanese military was the issuance of a statement by Major Takahashi, the Japanese Military attaché at Peiping, and Colonel Sakai, Chief of Staff of the Japanese army in North China.[21] The statement asserted that the two Japanese officials had called on General Ho Ying-chin, who was then serving as chairman of the Peiping branch of the Military Council, and had protested against certain conditions in North China which they declared violated the Tangku Truce. They had charged in particular that the Chinese authorities were fomenting trouble in the demilitarized zone and sanctioning anti-Japanese activities which had led to the murder of two Chinese editors of a pro-Japanese newspaper at Tientsin on May 3. "Should this state of affairs be allowed to keep up," it was said, "the Japanese Army would be confronted with the necessity of again advancing beyond the Great Wall and further with the necessity of including Tientsin and Peiping in the demilitarized zone."

Immediately after the publication of this statement it was widely rumored that Colonel Sakai and Major Takahashi had secretly presented General Ho with a number of demands. What purported to be lists of the demands were cabled abroad by foreign correspondents in China and were repeatedly wired to the State Department by its representatives at Peiping and Nanking.[22] The lists on the whole were remarkably similar and indicated that the Japanese were insisting upon the elimination of all officials from Hopei who were not sympathetic to Japan, all governmental and semigovernmental organizations that the Japanese regarded as inimical to their interests, and all troops to which the Japanese objected which consisted of the remaining units of the northeastern armies in Hopei and two divisions of the central government forces. That the substance of the Japanese demands was as reported by the press and American Foreign Service officers in China was virtually confirmed when, in the second week of June, Ambassador Grew notified the State Department that a liaison officer from the Japanese Ministry of War had called upon the United States Military attaché in Tokyo, evidently under instructions to deliver a "special message."[23] The highlight of the message was that compliance with the "general Army demands" would "remove from North China the troops, anti-Japanese organizations and individuals considered objectionable" by the Japanese and ensure their replacement by pro-Japanese officials and gendarmerie for the preservation of order that were acceptable to Japan.

Meanwhile all accounts of developments within China indicated that the Chinese were complying with the wishes of the Japanese.[24] General Yu Hsueh-chung, the Governor of Hopei, who controlled the northeastern troops in the province and was a prime object of Japanese hostility, was transferred to the Kansu area. The Mayor of Tientsin was replaced by a pro-Japanese official as were many other government and party leaders in Hopei. The provincial government was moved south from Tientsin to Paotingfu. Orders were given for the dissolution of all branches of the Kuomintang and affiliated organizations through which the Nanking regime normally carried out its local operations. Troop movements were undertaken on a large scale and it was presumed that the evacuation from Hopei of all the armed forces to which the Japanese were opposed would be completed by the end of June. In addition on June 10, in an effort to suppress all anti-Japanese activities, the Nanking government issued a "goodwill mandate" in which it exhorted the Chinese people to be "friendly" in their attitude toward other countries and, under threat of punishment, forbade "words or actions" likely to provoke ill will or otherwise obstruct the conduct of international relations. The Japanese military, on their part, continued to put pressure on the Chinese by stationing troops at strategic points north of the Great Wall.

By the second week in July, the Chinese had gone so far in meeting the desires of the Japanese that it was assumed that the crisis in North China was over. However, on June 9 Colonel Sakai and Major Takahashi paid a second visit to General Ho Ying-chin. On emerging from the interview, the two Japanese officials told reporters that the Nanking government appeared to be "seeing the light" and accommodating itself to Japan's policies; but if, contrary to present indications, Nanking should ultimately prove intransigent, the situation would be "exceedingly grave."[25] The newspaper correspondents were unable to obtain further information but assumed that the Japanese officers had repeated the demands which they had made earlier but probably presented them in the form of an ultimatum which involved compliance within a specified time.

Confidential accounts of what had taken place were given to Minister Johnson in Peiping by an emissary of General Ho Ying-chin's and to George Atcheson, a member of the United States Legation, at Nanking by the Chinese Vice Minister for Foreign Affairs. According to these accounts, Colonel Sakai and Major Takahashi had, as the press had supposed, reiterated their previous demands in their interview with General Ho on June 9.[26] They had not, however, issued an ultimatum on that day but had returned on the following day to tell General Ho that he would have to give them a favorable reply by noon of June 12. General Ho had explained in great detail that the Chinese government had already fulfilled their demands or else was in the process of doing so. He received the impression that they were satisfied. But, on the contrary, they returned within twenty-four hours and handed him a "memorandum" which they insisted he must sign. The "memorandum" not only contained the old demands but several new ones, the most important of which was that in the appointment of any officials in North China the Chinese authorities should consult the Japanese.

Atcheson in informing the Department of his talk with the Vice

Minister, said that the latter had "stated that the Chinese Government would be pleased to learn the attitude of the American Government in respect to the developments in North China which he had just described."[27] Atcheson declared further that the Vice Minister's account appeared to him "fair and honest, subject to criticism chiefly in its understatement."[28] It seemed, however, "generally the policy of the Chinese Government to minimize matters in respect to the current situation"; moreover, the most recent press reports suggested that the Japanese military were now denying that they had presented General Ho with any fresh demands. These might possibly be hopeful signs.

The day after Atcheson's cable arrived in Washington (June 15), the British ambassador came to see Under Secretary of State Phillips.[29] Sir Ronald Lindsay remarked gravely that the British Foreign Office regarded the situation in North China as "very serious and that it clearly invoked the Article of the Nine Power Treaty stipulating consultation between the signatories of that treaty." The Foreign Office had already instructed its ambassador in Tokyo, Sir Robert Clive, to ask the Japanese whether they had, as reported, demanded that Nanking agree to appoint officials in North China only after consultation with Japan and, if so, to point out that such a demand violated the Nine Power Treaty. Speaking under instructions himself, Sir Ronald wanted to know whether the State Department would take similar action through Grew. Phillips replied that the Chinese Vice Minister for Foreign Affairs had "discussed the matter with our representative in Nanking yesterday" and inquired in regard to the American government's attitude toward developments but that the State Department had not yet given any reply. The Under Secretary went on to say that the situation seemed to be "changing from hour to hour," that "the reports coming in from various sources were conflicting," and that yesterday's dispatch from our representative in Nanking had noted some hopeful signs. The Department therefore felt that the atmosphere was "cloudy and uncertain" and was "waiting for it to become a little clarified before considering the advisability of action vis-à-vis the Japanese." Sir Ronald responded by expressing the hope that, if the United States government were going to act, it would do so promptly and not delay "for example, until next week."

A few hours after Sir Ronald's talk with Phillips, the Japanese ambassador called upon the Secretary of State.[30] Because of the significance which the State Department subsequently attached to this interview, the Secretary's own version of it as related in a dispatch to Ambassador Grew and Minister Johnson assumes considerable importance:

. . . the Japanese Ambassador called on me . . . and stated that this morning he had received a cable from the Japanese Foreign Minister expressing a desire that the Ambassador make known that there was nothing in all of the many reports, rumors, and despatches coming out of China except an effort of the Japanese to have carried out two or three more or less minor things . . . I at once replied that I was very much gratified to have this information directly from the Foreign Office of the Japanese Government. I said that with such a mass of rumors and reports it was exceedingly important that the Japanese Foreign Office was taking these steps to keep the situation clarified; that the press of this and other countries is naturally filled with more or less alarming reports and comment that is undesirable from every standpoint. I said that lack of clarification by the Japanese Government might lead to representations from the parties having treaty rights and obligations and it would therefore be helpful if the Japanese Foreign Office continued to take action toward clarifying the situation.

Grew meanwhile had a number of conversations with his British colleague in Tokyo which he reported to the State Department.[31] The British ambassador, he said, had already expressed his government's concern over the developments in North China to the Japanese Foreign Office twice during the first week of June. The Foreign Office assured him that Japan had no intention of demanding the inclusion of Peiping and Tientsin in the demilitarized zone and that the Kwangtung army could not move south of the Great Wall without imperial sanction. The British ambassador had thereupon received instructions to inquire whether the Japanese government had endorsed a demand by the military that the Chinese appoint no officials in North China without their consent. In view of the assurances already given him, Sir Robert Clive had decided to postpone any action on his own part and had sent his Counselor of Embassy to make the inquiry set forth in his instructions. The counselor had talked with a member of the Japanese Foreign Office who had "ridiculed" the idea that the Japanese government would endorse any such demand but had said that the Japanese military had indicated to the Chinese the "advisability of only appointing officials friendly to Japan." Sir Robert intended to see Foreign Minister Hirota within a few days. In the meantime he had, however, told his government that, in his opinion, the Nine Power Treaty should only be invoked as a last resort because of the "irritation" which its invocation would arouse in Japan. Grew added, "I agree with this opinion."

On June 17 Sir Ronald Lindsay paid a second visit to the Under Secretary of State at the latter's request.[32] Phillips read to him the dispatches which had been received from Grew and stated that since Ambassador Clive had not, in fact, made representations along the lines of his instructions, there was no need for the State Department to give any immediate reply to the question Sir Ronald had raised previously concerning the United States government's making representations. Phillips then said that the Japanese ambassador had given "certain information to the Secretary" and proceeded to read aloud Hull's account of his talks with Saito that is quoted above. In conclusion, according to his own record, the Under Secretary explained,

. . . in the circumstances, we [in the State Department] did not feel that we were in a position to make any representations as yet to the Japanese Government; that, in view of the conflicting reports which were coming from China and Japan, it was apparent that we did not have a clear knowledge of the situation; that, in any event, we felt that we must proceed with the utmost caution and that this was evidently the judgment of our respective Ambassadors in Tokyo.

In the course of his remarks Phillips told Sir Ronald Lindsay that he would like to "keep closely in touch" with him on "all aspects" of the North China crisis. A memorandum of the Under Secretary's, dated July 1, indicates, however, that he did not discuss the events in North China with the British ambassador again until almost two weeks later, at which time he made clear that the State Department had definitely decided not to take any action.[33] Phillips wrote,

During the British Ambassador's call upon me yesterday I referred to the exchange of views which he and I had had with respect to the situation in North China. I reminded him that he had brought a message from the Foreign Office inviting this Government to take certain steps in Tokyo along the lines of the British action; that Ambassador Clive had apparently not carried out fully his instructions . . . ; at the same time the Japanese Ambassador in Washington had given the Secretary of State assurances, which I reminded the Ambassador I had already read to him. I said I assumed that, since we had heard nothing more from him [the Ambassador], his Government had decided to let matters rest without taking any further action in Tokyo. I said that, in view of the assurances which we had received and the attitude of the Chinese Government itself, we had come to the same conclusion . . .[34]

I reminded Sir Ronald that we were always desirous of cooperating with the British in this situation and that I mentioned it now only to reiterate that the views of both our Governments seemed to be running along the same lines.

Actually, although the British had not notified the State Department, presumably because Grew had reported on the matter, Sir Robert Clive had had a further interview with the Japanese Foreign Minister as planned.[35] Ambassador Clive had not invoked the Nine Power Treaty. He had, however, again inquired about the situation in North China. Hirota, in conformity with the statement made earlier by a member of his staff, had asserted that the Japanese military were not insisting upon the right to pass on the appointment of officials in North China but that it would "of course" be unfortunate if any officials with "anti-Japanese proclivities" were chosen to replace those to whom the military had objected. In addition, the Minister had reaffirmed that Japanese troops could not advance beyond the Great Wall without imperial sanction and had stated that "no alteration of Japan's policy in China was envisaged."

Even though Sir Robert Clive did not resort to the Nine Power Treaty, the Chinese—in marked contrast to the views which had been expressed by Phillips—believed that there was a decided difference between the policies of the American and British governments toward the North China crisis and were critical of the course which the United States had followed. Their criticism was no doubt in part based upon the response which the State Department had finally made to the Chinese government's inquiry concerning its views on the situation in North China.[36] For on June 18 a spokesman for the Department had told the Chinese Minister in Washington that the United States was not "contemplating taking any action." In any event, early in July George Atcheson cabled from Nanking that he had been told by a "ranking official" of the Chinese government that, during a recent government meeting at which the reaction of the foreign powers to developments in North China had been discussed, the Acting Minister for Foreign Affairs had "made a point of stating that the American Government had shown a very cold attitude to China in these difficulties and that the British Government had been the most sympathetic."[37] The State Department's reply to Atcheson involved an interesting defense of its position.[38] Stating that the substance of its message should be communicated to the Acting Minister if the occasion arose, the Department said,

After your telegram arrived, the Department mentioned to the Chinese Minister informally the story of the statement of the Minister for Foreign Affairs alleging a "cold attitude" on the part of this Government toward difficulties recently experienced by China and the Chinese Minister said that he had had similar information.

The Department told the Chinese Minister that the American Government's attitude and position with regard to treaty rights and obligations was in no way altered; . . . that while the American Government had been actuated by the belief that no useful purpose would be served by making charges either directly or through the press, it had taken steps which had seemed to it appropriate and feasible; that the situation has called for tactful handling and the American Government has refrained from public statements; that the Department has reasoned that the situation would only have been made more acute had the American Government appeared to intrude into the controversy; that the American Government has received certain assurances of which it has made careful note; that the American Government intends to attempt to exert its influence quietly and unobtrusively to avoid giving any countenance to measures or situations contravening any legitimate interests or treaty rights and to continue to keep in contact with the other interested powers; that the courses followed by the American and British Governments have apparently been on parallel lines; and that in the light of the foregoing the Department finds without warrant in fact any allegation that it had shown a "cold attitude."

Although in the early summer of 1935 the crisis in Hopei was the focus of attention, a very similar situation occurred in Chahar in the latter half of June.[39] The background in brief was that the Japanese, anxious to strengthen their position in relation to Soviet-dominated Outer Mongolia, had been attempting to gain a firmer hold on Inner Mongolia since their conquest of Jehol in 1933. They had first created a large Mongol province in Manchukuo in the hope of inducing the Mongols of Chahar and Suiyuan to break away from Chinese rule and amalgamate with their neighbors. But the Princes of Inner Mongolia, while antagonistic to the Chinese government, had not been prepared to submit to Japanese control and in 1934, after prolonged negotiations with Nanking, had set up an autonomous regime which retained certain ties with China. The Japanese had thereupon decided to use more vigorous methods and in January 1935, as a result of an armed clash on the Chahar-Jehol border, had annexed a substantial strip of territory on the Chahar side of the boundary. A few months of quiet had followed, but they proved to be no more than a prelude to the crisis which developed in June. On June 13, Nelson Johnson informed the State Department that an incident had taken place in Chahar which the Japanese might use to further "their efforts to separate Inner Mongolia from China."[40] The incident involved the brief detention by the Chinese military of four Japanese officers traveling in Chahar who, according to the Chinese, lacked passports and other essential documents but, according to the Japanese, were held illegally. During the ensuing days, American officials in China, as well as the press, reported many rumors to the effect that the Japanese were insisting upon a formal settlement of the incident and that negotiations were underway between General Chin Teh-chen, a member of the Chahar Provincial Government, and Major General Doihara, representing the Kwantung army. On June 26, Ambassador Grew told the Department that he had been reliably informed that an agreement had been reached orally which would be signed in a few days. It allegedly consisted of nine provisions, which he enumerated.[41] The provisions were obviously similar to the demands that the Japanese had made in Hopei, in that they included the dismissal from office of Sung Che-yuan, the Chairman of the Chahar Provincial Government, and various other officials; the disbanding of all local Kuomintang headquarters and "anti-Japanese organizations"; and the removal from Chahar of certain specified troops. They furthermore involved the creation of a broad demilitarized zone in Chahar.[42] On June 27, Johnson cabled Washington that Doihara had announced a settlement of the Chahar incident and that, although the terms had not been made public, they were understood to be as reported by Grew.[43] Similar terms were published in the press almost immediately and it was widely presumed that in all essentials they were accurate.[44]

The Hopei crisis itself in all probability was formally terminated with the conclusion of an understanding between General Ho Ying-chin and Major General Umetsu, commander of the Japanese North China Garrison, on July 6. In this understanding General Ho seems to have committed himself in writing to fulfill the Japanese demands that he had already accepted verbally and to a large extent executed. While there were many rumors at the time of the signing of a so-called "Ho-Umetsu Agreement," they were denied by Chinese officials. In March 1936, an American Foreign Service officer was, however, given a document in the strictest secrecy, which purported to be the text of the agreement and which had every indication of being genuine.[45]

Johnson continued to provide Washington with his estimate of developments between Japan and China until the end of the crisis in Hopei. On June 17, the Minister sent the State Department a message which he was to refer to later as representing his fixed opinion.[46] Johnson said he questioned the value of inviting the attention of the Japanese Foreign Office to "obvious contraventions" of the Nine Power Treaty. Japanese policy, in his view, was being determined by the Kwantung army without consultation with the Foreign Office. Any suggestion that the United States and Great Britain "dared comment adversely" upon the activities of the Kwantung army would only infuriate its leaders and probably incite them to renewed aggression. While Johnson was therefore in complete accord with the State Department's decision not to make any representations to Tokyo, he also continued to place the utmost emphasis upon the gravity of the situation in North China. When informed of the Japanese ambassador's interview with Hull, the Minister pointed out that Saito's assurance that the Japanese were only asking the Chinese to carry out "two or three more or less minor things" was decidedly at variance with the established facts.[47] In a number of long dispatches written in early July, in which he reviewed the recent developments in Hopei and

Chahar, Johnson stated in effect that the Japanese had succeeded in compelling the Chinese to fulfill all the major demands which had been reported.[48] The "immediate aim" of the Japanese military seemed to be the creation of a regime in North China nominally under Nanking but staffed with Chinese officials "friendly" to Japan. The ultimate aim was, to all appearances, "the expansion of control over China, with the elimination of any effective military opposition in China, to facilitate Japanese exploitation of the Asiatic mainland."

As to the likelihood of the Japanese achieving their ends, Johnson reminded the Department of the pessimism concerning the future he had expressed in discussing Japan's policy of economic "cooperation" with China. He saw no reason, he declared, to change his point of view. As a result of events in Hopei and Chahar, an "atmosphere of gloom and fear" permeated the offices of the Chinese government to an extent that could scarcely be appreciated unless one had constant contact with those offices and the men who headed the various departments. No Chinese official felt secure. At any moment the visiting card of a hitherto unheard-of Japanese major or colonel might be presented, which meant that he was in for an interview with a man whose slightest opinion might become the "active policy" of the Japanese military. So real was the fear which the Japanese had succeeded in breeding in the minds of the Chinese that they could obtain anything they wanted. "I expect," the Minister asserted grimly, "to see Japanese activities, political and economic, increase in China from now on . . . The Japanese Army is determined to break China to its will, whatever the consequences may be."

Grew also strongly supported the State Department's decision not to make any representations in regard to the North China crisis. In his opinion—the ambassador told the Department in a message sent in June—the remarks which the Secretary of State had made to Ambassador Saito during the course of their interview had "adequately and admirably covered the situation" so that no additional action was at present called for.[49] At the same time, Grew's comments on the developments in North China reflected much the same concern as Johnson's.[50] The ambassador clearly indicated that he believed that the Japanese military had not only succeeded in ridding North China, especially the Peiping-Tientsin area, of "all organized elements hostile to Japan" but had also secured the political control necessary to prevent any similar elements gaining a foothold in that region in the future.[51] Moreover, while refraining from any definite predictions, he expressed the view that the Japanese military might well proceed to attempt to transform North China into "an autonomous state friendly to Japan" or to create "a vast Manchuria-North China empire" under the control of the Japanese.

In any retrospective look at the record of American policy toward the growing struggle between Japan and China, in the period that extended from January to July 1935, certain parallel developments should be kept in mind. It was precisely at the outset of this period that the very similar memoranda written by Ambassador Grew and Hornbeck concerning the possibility of a Japanese-American war were submitted to the State Department.[52] These memoranda, it will be recalled, touched off a deep chord of agreement among officials in the Department and were forwarded to the President by Hull with a note containing a strong personal endorsement. Memoranda dealing with the same subject in equally forceful terms continued to be written by American officials during the next months. In March, for example, Hornbeck sent a long communication to the Secretary in which he reiterated his conviction that the views of the peoples of the United States and of Japan were in many vital respects in conflict.[53] Hornbeck emphasized, as he had earlier, that the Japanese had comparatively little respect for the concept of law and were willing to try to attain their aims—above all the aim of creating a great empire— through reliance upon the "politik of force." The ideas and objectives of the Japanese being what they were, he declared, there was "substantial likelihood" that "barring unpredictable political accidents or acts of God," the time would come "within the next few years" when Japan would "feel strongly moved to defy the United States and cross swords with us." Hornbeck asserted, furthermore, that there was no way of guaranteeing that the Japanese would "not embark upon an aggression against us." Writing with evident feeling, he stated that "no conceivable concessions" on the part of the United States would have any "conclusive effect" in deterring Japan; even if the United States "gave up all thought of overseas commerce, even if American interests and American nationals withdrew or were withdrawn from the Far East, even if the United States endeavored to make itself a hermit nation," the fact remained that the psychology of the Japanese was one of "adolescent imperialism" and that war might prove unavoidable. In short, the memoranda of the period of January to July 1935 showed that a very genuine fear of an armed conflict between the United States and Japan persisted within the State Department. Moreover, as has been seen, this fear influenced the State Department's conduct of policy in regard to the silver problem in China so that, as in the past, the administration refrained from any action that might seem provocative to the Japanese.

The record of American policy toward the Sino-Japanese conflict in the early months of 1935 seems to fall naturally into two stages, the first dominated by the attempts of the Japanese Foreign Office to secure a rapprochement with China, the second by the activities of the Japanese military in North China.[54] In the earlier stage, Nelson Johnson, and other American officials in a position to observe events in China closely, came to the conclusion that the Japanese Foreign Office was engaged in a determined effort to initiate a policy of economic "cooperation" with China in order to develop China's economy as a complement to and adjunct of Japan's. They believed that such a policy was bound to entail the destruction of China's independence and the ousting of all western interests from China in complete violation of the principle of the Open Door. The views expressed by Johnson and members of his staff, together with similar opinions advanced by leading Chinese officials, inevitably had a disturbing effect in Washington. But at the very beginning of the talk of a Sino-Japanese rapprochement the President and the State Department had agreed upon the advisability of following a "negative" or passive course, and there is no indication that they ever reconsidered this decision.

In the second phase of American policy, the theme which ran through the reports of the United States Foreign Service officers in both China and Japan was that the Japanese military were successfully insisting upon the exclusion from Hopei of all elements opposed to them; that the activities of the military were part of a renewed effort to extend their control over North China; and that, in all probability, the Japanese intended in one way or another to alienate the northern provinces from the rest of China. In this phase, the question of taking action was raised in Washington by the British and the Chinese, the British specifically suggesting that the United States should cooperate with them in making representations to the Japanese Foreign Office. It is doubtful whether the State Department at any point seriously contemplated accepting the British proposal. Phillips, as spokesman for the Department, first told Ambassador Lindsay that the administration wanted more time to observe developments, then stated frankly that the State Department wished to proceed with the utmost caution, and finally asserted that the Department had decided to "let matters rest" without taking any action in Tokyo. The only noteworthy move which the United States government made at this time consisted of

Secretary Hull's comments to Ambassador Saito at their meeting of June 15. Presumably the State Department had mainly these comments in mind when, in reply to the Chinese charge of adopting a "cold attitude," it said that the United States had taken steps to meet the situation which it regarded as "appropriate and feasible." The underlying meaning of the Department's reply to the Chinese criticism seems in fact to have been that the United States believed in conducting its policy "quietly and unobtrusively" through just such confidential and friendly interchanges as had taken place between the Secretary and the Japanese ambassador.[55]

The State Department advanced a number of explanations for its policy. It repeatedly asserted that it did not want to make representations at Tokyo or adopt any similar measures because the situation in North China was too confused and because Ambassador Saito had assured Hull that the reports of renewed friction between Japan and China were without foundation. However, it seems reasonable to assume that these assertions were little more than excuses such as are customarily fabricated to smooth the wheels of diplomacy.[56] Except for a few relatively minor points, the accounts of events in North China were unusually consistent and the reports of American Foreign Service officers were based upon so many excellent sources that their validity could scarcely be doubted. But the Department also advanced an argument which undoubtedly represented a view widely held by American officials, namely, that any protests made by the United States in regard to Japan's activities in China would only incite the Japanese military to further aggression. Beyond that, it seems evident that throughout the period under discussion the administration continued to adhere to the kind of "negative" or passive policy that stemmed from its whole approach to the situation in the Far East, an approach to which it manifestly remained committed.

JULY TO DECEMBER 1935

As the summer of 1935 advanced there was a growing belief in China that the Japanese would immediately proceed to capitalize upon their gains in Hopei and press for the establishment of an autonomous regime for the five provinces of North China. Much speculation centered upon the question of what course Chiang Kai-shek intended to pursue. Throughout the critical days of June, which ostensibly ended in the Ho-Umetsu Agreement, the Generalissimo had stayed in the Southwest. Although his troops had not succeeded in arresting the advance of the Red armies, he had turned the presence of central government forces in the southwestern area to his advantage. Using the power which their proximity inevitably gave him, he had reorganized the local governments and armies in Kweichow and Yunnan so that these provinces were brought under the authority of Nanking. He had thus made progress in the unification of China, some twelve out of twenty-three provinces now being to a large extent under Nanking's control. The absence of the Generalissimo from the capital during the developments between China and Japan in June had however accentuated the increasingly important fact that his intentions in regard to the Japanese remained unknown. In August he returned to Nanking and it was hoped that he would clarify his position but he did not do so. American Foreign Service officers repeatedly reported to Washington that two schools of thought existed in Chinese circles, one of which maintained that Chiang Kai-shek would continue to support a policy of conciliation toward Japan while the other insisted that he would not retreat any further and would, if necessary, resist the Japanese armies with force.[57] A vital aspect of the problem was whether the Nanking regime could survive the political pressures inside China if it did not take a firm stand against Japan.

From late September on, the dispatches from China indicated that the officials of our embassy (now raised from the status of a legation) felt that the Japanese were preparing to take some drastic measures. On September 24 Major General Tada, the commander of the Japanese garrison in North China, called a press conference at which he issued a pamphlet that constituted a sensational attack upon both the Western powers and the Chiang Kai-shek regime.[58] The pamphlet declared that Japan had been entrusted with the divine mission of emancipating the people of the Orient from the white races. It accused Chiang Kai-shek and his associates in the Nanking government of forming a new capitalistic military class that was determined to exploit the Chinese people. But at the same time it charged the Generalissimo with being pro-Russian and questioned his sincerity in seeking to attempt to exterminate the Chinese Communists. The pamphlet claimed that, in any event, communism was spreading in China and was consequently menacing all of East Asia. If the Nanking regime would not or could not cope with it, then that regime must be destroyed. The Chinese should recognize that the only real solution to their problems lay in collaboration with Japan. A new program should be inaugurated by the Japanese government to create a "paradise of co-existence and mutual prosperity" between Japan and China and the first steps should be taken in North China.

The Tada pamphlet evoked such a storm of criticism that representatives of the Japanese government took great pains to disclaim it.[59] Nevertheless, American officials felt that it reflected activities which were taking place behind the scenes in Tokyo. At the beginning of October it was rumored that the Japanese Ministries of War, Navy, and Foreign Affairs had buried their differences and agreed upon a new policy toward China.[60] Conferences of Japanese officials stationed in China were held thereafter in which the policy decided upon by the Ministries was presumably explained.[61] On October 29 Major General Tada issued a statement asserting that the Chinese authorities had not carried out the promises which they had made in June to eliminate all anti-Japanese organizations from North China.[62] The statement accused the Chinese of bad faith and demanded "prompt and vigorous action." Within the next days, according to information received from reliable sources by the American embassy at Peiping, arrests were made of many Chinese, including outstanding educators who were suspected by the Japanese of belonging to patriotic organizations hostile to Japan.[63]

Meanwhile, at the end of October, at least part of the new policy agreed upon by the Ministries in Tokyo was revealed. It became known that Chiang Tso-pin, the Chinese ambassador in Tokyo who was about to return home, had had a long interview with the Japanese Foreign Minister. Although no information was made public officially, through unofficial sources it was established that during the course of the interview Hirota had outlined three points that were to govern Japan's policy toward China and, if possible, to form the basis for negotiations with the Nanking government.[64] These points, which were to become well known as Hirota's three principles, were said to be that China must agree to (1) enter into an alliance or collaborate with Japan for the suppression of communism in Asia, (2) abandon the policy of playing one "barbarian tribe" (foreign nation) against another, and (3) establish economic "cooperation" between Japan, Manchukuo, and China.[65] In commenting upon Hirota's principles to the State Department, Ambassador Johnson observed that in his opinion acceptance of them by the Nanking government would "place China almost completely under Japanese control."[66] He repeatedly returned to an analysis of the three points maintaining the position that, if implemented, the first would result in China's being forced to consent to the stationing of Japanese armies on its soil ostensibly to combat communism; the second would lead to the supervision by Japan of China's foreign policy and finances; while the third would entail the economic penetration of China by Japan along the lines he had already discussed at some length.

News of Japan's three-point policy touched off some of the pent-up anger against the Japanese which the Chinese had so far largely held in check. As a consequence, on November 1 a Chinese reporter shot at and seriously wounded Wang Ching-wei, who was generally re-garded as the leader of the pro-Japanese faction within the Nanking government.[67] The assault upon the Chinese Premier in turn had strong repercussions in Japan, where it was looked upon as a renewed outburst of anti-Japanese sentiment. The situation between Japan and China became even more strained when, a few days after the at-tempted assassination of Wang, Nanking published its famous cur-rency decree nationalizing silver and introducing currency reforms. As already related, the Japanese were strongly opposed to the decree and sought to prevent its being carried out successfully. Conditions were therefore such that the Japanese would under any circumstances have been likely to bring their efforts to create an autonomous North China to a head. But it was widely believed that they were especially anxious to do so because the Italian-Ethiopian conflict had arrived at a point where it was engrossing the energies of all the major powers thereby affording Japan an opportunity to proceed with a free hand.[68]

Beginning in mid-November, events followed each other rapidly. American Foreign Service officers sought to supplement the news coverage in such papers as the *New York Times* by providing the Department with whatever confidential information was available. From press stories and off-the-record accounts, there emerged a pic-ture of the Japanese attempting, through a mixture of military and political pressures, to induce the leaders of the North China provinces to found an autonomous regime which would only maintain nominal ties with Nanking.[69] Although the Japanese themselves insisted that the movement for the autonomy of North China was entirely an out-growth of the will of the local population and in no way instigated by the Japanese military, few observers believed them. Japanese troops were known to be concentrating north of the Great Wall.[70] Major General Doihara was busily engaged in trying to negotiate with offi-cials in North China, primarily Sung Che-yuan, who, with the consent of the Japanese, had been appointed Garrison-Commander of the Peiping-Tientsin area, and Hsiao Chen-ying, who had replaced Sung as chairman of the Chahar Provincial Government.[71] On November 18, Hsiao held a press conference in which he said that Major General Doihara had declared that an announcement of the new autonomous regime must be made on November 20 or else the Japanese forces at the Great Wall would enter Hopei and establish an entirely inde-pendent North China linked with Manchukuo. The next day Hugh Byas, the *New York Times* correspondent in Tokyo, stated in a front page article in that paper that foreign observers in Japan were convinced that North China would go the way of Manchuria before the week was over. American Foreign Service officers at Peiping and Nanking doubted whether the North China leaders had as yet come to an agreement concerning the autonomous regime but expected them to do so by November 20 or shortly thereafter.

To the astonishment of all observers, November 20 and the succeeding days brought no drastic change in North China. Major General Doihara's plans had apparently misfired. What actually occurred behind the scenes was and remained something of a mystery. Many onlookers believed that Major General Doihara had overplayed his hand and misjudged the extent to which the North China leaders were willing to cooperate with him; also, it seemed possible that he had exceeded his instructions.[72] Willys Peck told the Department that in his opinion the most plausible explanation was one given to him by a Chinese official who said that Chiang Kai-shek had received intelligence reports to the effect that the Japanese cabinet was still divided on how far to go in supporting Major General Doihara's schemes.[73] The Generalissimo had consequently decided to hazard "calling Doihara's bluff" and had ordered Sung Che-yuan to discontinue negotiations with the Japanese. The Japanese government, on its part, had concluded that it was not prepared to carry out Major General Doihara's threats of military invasion.

Nevertheless, Major General Doihara's activities in North China were by no means in vain. On November 24 Yin Ju-keng, a Chinese official who had been serving as chief administrator in the demilitarized zone and who was notoriously pro-Japanese, issued a declaration proclaiming that henceforth the zone would be ruled by a body to be called the East Hopei Anti-Communist Autonomous Council.[74] The council was to be independent of Nanking and to pave the way for a federation of the North China provinces. Yin explained that this move was necessary because the Nanking government had made disastrous errors in the conduct of both its foreign and financial policies and had encouraged class conflict so that China was now being subjected to the "terrors of Communism." The new autonomous regime, though containing a population of only about five million, was economically important, as it possessed valuable coal mines including those belonging to the Sino-British Kailan Mining administration.

Meanwhile Chiang Kai-shek and the Japanese ambassador at Nanking, Akira Ariyoshi, had opened negotiations on the basis of Hirota's three principles.[75] The negotiations reportedly went badly but subsequently the Nanking government undertook various measures apparently designed to appease the Japanese including the appointment of Ho Ying-chin as resident representative of the central government at Peiping.[76] These measures were still not sufficient to deter the Japanese military from renewing their attempts to detach the northern provinces from the rest of China by trying to persuade other officials to follow in the footsteps of Yin Ju-keng. The Japanese hoped in particular that they could induce Sung Che-yuan to initiate an independent regime for Hopei and Chahar. They consequently renewed their military movements north of the Great Wall and sent additional troops to Peiping and Tientsin.[77] On November 27 Japanese forces seized and temporarily occupied a strategic railroad junction at Fengtai. On November 30 the United States embassy at Peiping cabled the Department that it was inclined to think that Sung would soon break away from Nanking. The following day the *New York Times* carried a two-column headline on its front page which stated, CHINESE IN NORTH GIVE UP, CONCLUDE AUTONOMY PLAN, WILL DETACH TWO PROVINCES.

At this juncture the Nanking government decided to send General Ho Ying-chin to the north to see if he could work out some sort of compromise solution. General Ho engaged in secret conversations with Japanese and local Chinese officials but American Foreign Service officers felt that he had little chance of achieving any success. At the end of the first week of December, Ambassador Johnson informed the Department that General Ho had arrived in Peiping without any proposal for a settlement and was therefore contributing nothing helpful to the situation.[78] As a result, the autonomy of Hopei and Chahar appeared "to be nearer and practically inevitable."

But as matters developed, General Ho did manage to prevent the complete severance of Hopei and Chahar from Nanking.[79] An agreement was reached whereby a political council was to be organized for the administration of Hopei and Chahar. The council was to enjoy a high degree of autonomy. Nevertheless, ostensibly at least, the conduct of its foreign, financial, and military policies were to remain in the hands of the central government. Moreover the members of the council were to be appointed by Nanking.

The new Hopei-Chahar Political Council was scheduled to be inaugurated on December 16. But opposition developed through the revival of the student movement which had been dormant in China since the Manchurian crisis. On December 9 our embassy in Peiping wired the Department that about six hundred students from Tsinghua and Yenching were trying to enter the city, the gates of which had been closed against them, while over a thousand students were gathering in front of General Ho's residence to hold a mass meeting "against the autonomy movement traitors and Japanese imperialism."[80] Throughout the remainder of December the students' activities continued to be the center of attention. The student movement spread from Peiping to many of the other large cities of China where mammoth demonstrations were conducted, re-enforced by extensive strikes. In Shanghai the students commandeered two trains and proceeded toward Nanking exhorting the people along the way to oppose the Japanese and compel the Chinese government to resist Japan's attempts to bring about the autonomy of North China. The police proved unable to control the situation with the result that the government proclaimed martial law in Shanghai, Nanking, and Hankow. But, despite their dramatic efforts, the students did not achieve their immediate objective of preventing the establishment of the Hopei-Chahar Political Council. In order to avoid further inciting the students, the government did, however, postpone the inauguration of the council for a few days and conducted the inaugural ceremonies without prior announcement in semisecrecy.[81]

At the close of the year, American Foreign Service officers in China felt that there was little to relieve the negative aspects of the developments they were witnessing. In its semiannual report for the last six months of 1935, the embassy at Peiping wrote that despite the gains which Chiang Kai-shek had made in the Southwest the situation in China appeared at the end of December "to be even more precarious than at the end of the first half of the year."[82] Reiterating the thought Ambassador Johnson had expressed earlier, it referred to the "inevitability of the loss to the National Government of North China" and asserted that the formation of the Hopei-Chahar Political Council must be regarded as a "significant step" in the direction of the separation of the five northern provinces from Nanking. Johnson, writing to Hornbeck, stated that he was convinced that the Japanese military had embarked upon a well-considered plan to gain control of China and would proceed until they had reached their objectives.[83] Similarly, in a letter to former Secretary of State Stimson, the ambassador declared that the Japanese would carry out their schemes of expansion in Asia as there was no force in the East capable of resisting them.

There were times during the autumn of 1935 when Johnson expressed the hope that the Chinese intellectuals were abandoning their defeatist attitude and would try to rally the nation against Japan. He was especially impressed by Hu Shih and Chiang Monlin, then

Chancellor of the National University of Peking, who at considerable personal risk were openly advocating the assumption of a strong stand against Japan.[84] The ambassador also admired the students for their activities. Following the student demonstrations in December he wrote to Roy Howard that the students represented "a new thing in China," a group consciously trained to be nationalistic, welded together by pride in China's past and confidence in its future. This pride and confidence had been "terribly shaken" by Japan's encroachments on China and the students were doing their "pathetic best" to arouse the government and the people to oppose the Japanese. While Johnson believed that so far the students had won widespread sympathy, he nevertheless regarded it as only a matter of time before some incident occurred which would turn popular sentiment against them. In fact, by the end of 1935 he had again become, as he himself said, "a good deal discouraged" about the likelihood of China's achieving unity by any means.[85] Furthermore he remained very skeptical about the possibility of the Nanking regime's undertaking any genuinely effective program of national reconstruction and in general building up the country internally. Willys Peck, writing to Stanley Hornbeck in early 1936 referred to talk of the Chinese government's introducing a Five-Year Plan and said that in his own and Nelson Johnson's opinion there was "little reason for optimism."[86] In an unusual outburst of feeling, Peck declared,

"Too late, too late, the Captain cried . . ." Where are the foundations for this superstructure? Where is the smoothly-moving machinery in the Capital, operated by conscientious, intelligent and patriotic officials? Unfortunately one must reply that these and numerous other results which should have followed the "free and unembarrassed opportunity" granted for at least nine years by the Washington Conference Treaty are lacking.

Under these circumstances, Peck concluded, it hardly seemed probable that China would be able to cope with "such an energetic neighbor as Japan."

In terms of American policy toward the crisis in the Far East, the summer of 1935 had produced a few events worth noting. In midsummer Ambassador Grew came home on a five months leave of absence. Before departing from Tokyo he paid a farewell visit on Hirota during the course of which he asked whether the Foreign Minister would like to express any views which he, Grew, might convey to President Roosevelt and Secretary of State Hull.[87] By way of reply Hirota recalled that on taking office he had said that the improvement of relations between Japan and the United States was to be the "cornerstone" of his policy. While relations had been difficult two years ago, the Minister asserted, they were now "distinctly good" and he saw "no reason whatever" for their not remaining so.

One may surmise that in transmitting Hirota's message upon his arrival in Washington, Grew again emphasized his own belief that the United States should continue to work for the betterment of Japanese-American relations. Certainly this belief, which was so central to his thought, must have found prominent expression in the conversations that, according to his diary entries, he had with the President, Secretary Hull, and leading members of the Far Eastern Division of the State Department.[88] If one reads between the lines of these diary entries, Grew seems to have found general agreement with his opinions in Washington. Of the President he recorded that Roosevelt had been "quite affectionate" and during their "three talks" had said that the fact that he had not written to the ambassador "very often was a compliment as it meant that no mistakes had been made."

In late summer the Chinese Minister of Finance made an effort to sound out Nelson Johnson on the subject of American policy.[89] Dr. Kung sent Arthur H. Young, a prominent American adviser to the Chinese Ministry of Finance, as his emissary to enter into a "preliminary" conversation with Johnson because Young had enjoyed a long friendship with the ambassador. Young said that because of continued pressure from Japan the Chinese government was faced with "the probable early necessity" of making a decision which might result in an alliance between China and Japan that would involve the extension of Japanese control over the whole of China according to the pattern established in "Manchukuo." In the event that the Chinese government reached such a decision Young wanted to know what the reaction of the United States would be. Johnson replied that he was of course in no position to make a statement concerning the possible reaction of the American government. In his succeeding remarks, however, the ambassador made little effort to conceal his own opinion which was that, in the light of the whole trend of American policy in the Pacific, the United States could not be expected to take any strong stand against Japan.[90] Somewhat later Willys Peck was asked by the Chinese Vice Minister for Foreign Affairs about the attitude of the United States government toward the activities of the Japanese military in North China.[91] Peck replied that Washington had not specifically defined its views in any recent communications but that, in his estimation, the dominant purpose of the American government was to avoid the danger of being involved in any war.

In so far as the above events reflected the thinking of American officials they suggest the prevalence among them of a tacit assumption that the conduct of our policy in the Far East would continue along the lines already established. It is not surprising therefore that as the North China crisis erupted into the particularly acute phase which developed in the autumn of 1935 the question of taking action was again first raised by the British. On November 20, the day on which the independence of North China was ostensibly to be proclaimed, Sir Ronald Lindsay inquired of Under Secretary Phillips as to what decision, if any, the American government had arrived at in regard to the new regime in North China.[92] Phillips replied that the picture in North China was unclear and the United States government consequently had not reached the point of making a decision.

While the Under Secretary's answer recalled the remarks he had made when Sir Ronald Lindsay had approached him in regard to the North China crisis in June, on this occasion the British reacted differently and proceeded without further reference to the United States government. On November 26 the Foreign Office in London instructed its chargé in Tokyo to inform the Japanese government that it was concerned over the reports of Japanese activities aiming at the administrative separation of North China and "would welcome a frank statement of Japanese policy and assurances that no action is being taken or intended at variance with the principles laid down in the Nine Power Treaty."[93] The British chargé delivered this message to the Japanese Vice Minister of Foreign Affairs who retorted by repeating the standard Japanese claim that the autonomy movement in North China was indigenous and had no connection with Japan.[94] At the same time the Vice Minister ostentatiously refrained from taking any notice of the British government's reference to the Nine Power Treaty with the patent intention of administering what was subsequently referred to in the State Department as a "diplomatic snub."

The British having protested to Tokyo, the administration in Washington was faced with the problem of whether to follow suit. Before reaching any conclusion concerning this matter, the State Department asked Ambassador Johnson and Edwin L. Neville (our chargé in Tokyo who was replacing Grew during the latter's leave of absence) for their recommendations. Johnson replied in substance that he was still of the opinion that to make any representations at Tokyo might have the adverse effect of inciting the Japanese military to increase their aggression. Furthermore, Japan's manipulation of the autonomy movement in North China was only part of a larger plan which she was determined to pursue.[95] Unless the Nanking government agreed to submit to Japanese control by accepting Hirota's three principles, the Japanese would continue to promote the autonomy movement in North China. Once autonomous regimes were established, they would be urged by Tokyo to invite Japanese troops and advisers into their areas "to combat communism and organize finances." In the end, Japan would identify what was left of Nationalist China with communism and would even "include therein Chiang Kai-shek and the Kuomintang." No one was in a position to stop this scheme unless it was the Chinese themselves, and whether they had achieved sufficient unity to offer effective resistance was doubtful.

A copy of Ambassador Johnson's dispatch reached Tokyo before Neville had sent his own comments to the Department. In his response to Washington, Neville emphasized at the outset that he was in general agreement with the ambassador's views.[96] He went on to say that to be effective any questioning of Japan's policy would have to be backed by superior military power and that ineffective protests would certainly be useless and might be "positively harmful." While stating that he did not feel competent to discuss the details of Japan's plans in regard to China, Neville declared that the Japanese undoubtedly intended to become the dominant force in Asia and would go as far as possible at the moment dealing with future situations as they arose. Meanwhile, the United States must face the fact that the only people who in the long run could deal effectively with the Japanese in China were the Chinese themselves. "I cannot see," Neville wrote, with exceptional candor, "where any interest of the United States (except that of endeavoring to maintain the Nine Power Treaty) would be served by laying ourselves open to a rebuff by protesting on behalf of a people who apparently are incapable of political action and unwilling to make any sort of common cause against what they complain of as aggression."

On December 2, in a memorandum to the Secretary of State, Hornbeck outlined the course which he believed the United States government should follow.[97] He advised Hull against making any representations at Tokyo. His main arguments rested upon the same basic premises as those advanced by Ambassador Johnson and Neville and were in essence: that diplomatic protests only ran the risk of angering the Japanese military; that the Japanese army would "work its will in North China" unless it encountered "the resistance of force to force"; and that neither the United States nor any other country, excepting China, had any thought of resorting to force. In addition,

Hornbeck maintained that there was no need for the United States to make any representations. The British had done so but had not suggested or implied that we should follow their example. Many American newspapers had commented editorially on the recent events in North China, saying that they furnished further evidence of Japan's imperialistic ambitions and were a serious threat to the interests of other nations and the cause of peace; but "in practically no case" had they expressed the opinion that action by the United States was called for.

While arguing against making representations, Hornbeck nevertheless urged the Secretary not to remain entirely silent. To say nothing whatever, he thought, might create the impression that we were "indifferent" to the developments in North China and might lay us open to the criticism that there was "inconsistency between our manifestation of concern in regard to the Italian-Ethiopian situation and our lack of manifestation of concern in regard to the Chinese-Japanese situation." Moreover, we might be charged by the British with having adopted a wholly unresponsive attitude unless we displayed some sympathy for the action they had taken. At "all times," Hornbeck wrote, in deciding upon the courses of action with regard to Far Eastern matters, we should keep in mind that where common interests were involved cooperation or parallel action on the part of the American and British governments had potentially great advantages.

In conclusion, Hornbeck recommended that the Secretary make a statement to the press (the text of which had already been drafted by the Far Eastern Division) and that representatives of the State Department explain the administration's position informally to the British. Both proposals were adopted and, at a press conference on December 5, Hull read a statement of our Far Eastern policy, the second he had issued during his term in office, the first being the pronouncement made following the Amau declaration.[98] The Secretary began as follows:

There is going on in and with regard to North China a political struggle which is unusual in character and which may have far-reaching effects. The persons mentioned in reports of it are many; the action is rapid and covers a large area; opinions with regard to it vary; what may come of it no one could safely undertake to say; but, whatever the origin, whoever the agents, be what they may the methods, the fact stands out that an effort is being made—and is being resisted—to bring about a substantial change in the political status and condition of several of China's northern provinces.

The Secretary then asserted that unusual developments in any part of China were rightfully and necessarily of concern not alone to the government and people of China but to all the "treaty powers" of which the United States was one. In North China, the United States had treaty rights and treaty obligations pertaining to a considerable number of American nationals, some American property and substantial American commercial and cultural activities. The United States government was closely observing events in that area in the belief that political disturbances produced economic, social, and other dislocations that made difficult the enjoyment of such rights and obligations. Hull finished by saying,

The views of the American Government with regard to such matters not alone in relation to China but in relation to the whole world are well known. As I have stated on many occasions, it seems to this Government most important in this period of world-wide political unrest and economic instability that governments and peoples keep faith in principles and pledges. In international relations there must be agreements and respect for agreements in order that there may be the confidence and stability and sense of security which are essential to orderly life and progress. This country has abiding faith in the fundamental principles of its traditional policy. This Government adheres to the provisions of the treaties to which it is a party and continues to bespeak respect by all nations for the provisions and treaties solemnly entered into for the purpose of facilitating and regulating, to reciprocal and common advantage, the contacts between and among the countries signatory.

Even contemporary observers who had no occasion to study the matter in detail noted a resemblance between Hull's statement of December 1935 and his earlier pronouncement.[99] A close examination of the texts reveals such a marked similarity that one may assume that, like its counterpart, the December 1935 statement was drafted with the idea of being as nonprovocative as possible in the eyes of the Japanese. Indeed, the drafters not only adhered to the rule, followed previously, of avoiding any semblance of championing China and any mention of the Nine Power Treaty but—as Secretary Hull points out in his memoirs—even deliberately refrained from making any direct reference to Japan.[100] The statement essentially amounted to another declaration of American rights and obligations in China and of the principles which the United States believed should be observed in the conduct of international relations throughout the world.

In order to realize Hornbeck's proposal in respect to the British, an advance copy of the Secretary's statement was given to the British ambassador in Washington with an explanation of its purposes.[101] The ambassador was also told that, if the occasion warranted, the United States government would take some further action and that it hoped to carry on free and frank exchanges of information with the British government.

The expectation which had been prevalent among American officials that our Far Eastern policy would remain the same seemed therefore justified in the latter part of 1935. As at the beginning so at the end of the year the administration adhered to the belief that it should maintain a passive policy but not appear indifferent to Japan's encroachments upon China. Consequently the State Department continued to avoid taking such action as making representations at Tokyo while the Secretary issued his statement of December 5. The decision to issue this statement was largely reached as a result of two considerations: first, as in the aftermath of the Amau declaration, the British had already protested to Tokyo so that the State Department wished to make some move; second, confronted with a renewal of the North China controversy at a time when the Italian-Ethiopian crisis was at its height, the Department wanted to make clear its concern over the emergence of any situation that involved a disregard by other nations of the principles to which the United States had always proclaimed its adherence.[102]

As earlier, the administration seems to have been under the impression that its policy conformed with the opinions held by a substantial segment of the public. Hornbeck stated that "great numbers" of editorial writers had commented on the North China crisis but that almost none had advocated action by the United States. Kramer, in his sampling of the press, reached similar conclusions.[103] He found that newspapers which had paid little attention to Japan's activities at the time of the Tangku Truce were keenly interested in the struggle for North China in 1935. They tended however to treat that struggle as a "Far Eastern problem" in which the United States would not and should not become involved. The general attitude revealed by the editorials cited by Kramer seems to have been most frankly and vigorously expressed in connection with an episode which took place in February 1936.

During the early part of 1935 a resolution had been introduced into the Senate asking for an investigation of Japan's policy in Manchuria in order to determine whether it violated treaties to which the United States was also a party.[104] Pittman, as Chairman of the Senate Committee on Foreign Relations, referred the resolution to the Secretary of State for comment. Hull replied that in his judgment it would be unwise to start an investigation which would in all probability cause "a considerable amount of ill-advised public discussion" of issues which would profit by "a period of quiet consideration rather than of agitation and contention." At the end of June, a similar resolution was introduced into Congress in regard to Japan's policy in North China and was again sent by Senator Pittman to Secretary Hull who responded in the same vein as previously.[105]

Nevertheless, in February 1936 Senator Pittman unexpectedly delivered a violently anti-Japanese speech on the floor of the Senate that was designed to provoke all the "agitation and contention" which the State Department wished to avoid.[106] The reaction of many of the leading newspapers in the United States seems to have been unusually sharp. Quoting the comments of the *New York Times* at some length, Kramer says that they furnish the "key" to the *Times'* policy in regard to the situation in North China in the mid-1930's:

> Mr. Pittman is unfortunately not the first chairman of the Senate Foreign Relations Committee to take his responsibilities lightly, or to forget what they are. But none has ever made a more improper or provocative attack on a friendly nation than that of Senator Pittman on Japan. Conceding that there was an element of truth in his charges what did he hope to gain by such a speech? His reckless remark that our "only" answer to Japan's Far Eastern policy would be "dominating naval and air forces" can merely serve to rouse resentment in Japan and to strengthen the hand of its military party.
>
> Why was the Senator so angry? Partly, it seems, because his heart bleeds for justice to the Chinese and partly because he wants to continue to sell them American goods. He implies that he is willing to go to war, if necessary to protect our legitimate foreign trade with them and the Open Door. This willingness may not be shared by all Americans, particularly when they recall that our sales to China last year were less than 2% of our total sales abroad.[107]

The *Los Angeles Times* in an editorial entitled "A Speech Out of Turn" declared similarly that the senator's attack upon the Japanese had done no good and might end by doing a great deal of harm. It stated, furthermore, "It is not true that Japan's Chinese policy necessarily threatens any substantial interest of the United States; what happens on the Asiatic mainland is very little practical concern of ours." The *Christian Science Monitor* reaffirmed the stand which it had taken in a series of editorials in June 1935, in which it maintained that to admonish Japan repeatedly would only aggravate the situation in the Pacific, that America's interests in Asia were far from sufficient to warrant any effort to oppose the Japanese by force, and that it would be "quixotic" to expect Western nations to rush to the aid of China while that country could not achieve unity even "in the face of a foreign foe." The *Milwaukee Journal* also indicated that while, in its opinion, Japan's seizure of China was reprehensible, there was no reason for "especially wasting sympathy" on the Chinese, as their inability to govern themselves was "partially responsible for their present predicament." In any case the *Journal* thought it was essential to recognize that other nations, including the United States, would not fight to preserve China's integrity. "Jingoistic outbursts" such as Senator Pittman's could therefore only have the effect of playing into the hands of the Japanese military. The *San Francisco Chronicle* alone of the papers Kramer studied, although disapproving Senator Pittman's speech, generally advocated the administration's taking a strong stand on behalf of American "rights" in the Far East even, if necessary, to the point of going to war. In addition, the *Chronicle* was the only publication, whether internationalist or isolationist, to demonstrate definite sympathy for China. Among the isolationist papers the *Chicago Tribune* denounced Senator Pittman's address in keeping with its whole policy which during the North China crisis of 1935 had taken the form of insisting that Japanese domination would not hurt American interests in that country and might even benefit them by awakening the "dormant China market."

AMERICAN POLICY AND A CHANGING FAR EAST

One of the results of the intensification of Japan's forward push into China in 1935 was that it caused American officials to speculate about whether the time was not fast approaching when the United States would have to recognize that vast transformations had taken place in the Far East and frankly consider the changes, if any, it wished to make in its policy. Of the various reflections committed to paper, none were so brilliantly expressed as those contained in a memorandum— still referred to from time to time by members of the State Department—submitted to the Secretary of State by John Van Antwerp MacMurray in November 1935.[108] MacMurray had been American Minister to China from 1925 to 1929. Home on leave from his post in Riga in the autumn of 1935, he indicated his concern over the drift of events in the Far East and requested permission to devote several months to writing a memorandum on our relations with China and Japan which might furnish some practical guidance for the future. The product which emerged was to a large extent an analysis of the developments which had taken place during the time when MacMurray served in China. We need not enter into the historical sections of the MacMurray memorandum here except for one point which invites comment.[109] While Minister in China, MacMurray had become bitterly, almost passionately, critical of the activities of the Chinese and especially of the nationalistic, antiforeign movement which he felt, under the direction of the Kuomintang, had taken the form of an unrestrained and outrageous defiance of the treaty powers. The memorandum showed that MacMurray's views had in no way altered and, among other matters, had led him to look upon Japanese aggression in the 1930's with a measure of tolerance. MacMurray maintained that Japan's attack upon Manchuria and her subsequent encroachments on China were to a large extent the result of long years of provocation on the part of the Chinese and were therefore understandable, however much they lacked moral justification. But, despite this measure of tolerance, when he reached the point in his memorandum of considering the future, MacMurray suggested a Far Eastern policy for the United States that deviated little from that which the administration was currently following. His thesis, in very rough outline, was that China was falling under the "shadow of Japan's domination" and that the United States should proceed on the assumption that in all probability the whole of China would gradually pass under the control of the Japanese. We, the American people, should therefore realize that for us China had ceased to be a "land of opportunity" or even "a primary factor in the Far East" and that, in contrast, Japan had become of "paramount interest."[110] As to the exact nature of American policy, the United States could follow one of three courses: First, it could oppose the Japanese with all the power at its command. This course was, however, scarcely worth consideration since, if pursued consistently and with determination, it would almost inevitably lead us into war with Japan. Such a war would entail sacrifices and risks on our part and "gain us no benefits."[111] Indeed, our major purpose in the Far East should be to avoid being drawn into hostilities with the Japanese. Second, the United States could assent to or even participate in Japan's encroachments on China. But to do so would essentially involve the surrender of principles that had traditionally underlain our policy not only in the Far East but throughout the world. Third, the United States could "take a passive attitude . . . avoiding all positive action" and "conceding nothing" from the ideals of conduct it had always professed. MacMurray suggested that the administration should adopt the third course as "obviously the wisest." If—as appears to have been the case—he did not recognize how closely it corresponded to the policy which was already in effect, the explanation may well lie in the fact that throughout the preceding eventful years he had been out of touch with the deliberations on the Far East that had taken place in the inner councils in Washington.[112]

About two months after MacMurray had presented his memorandum to the Secretary, Norman Davis, who was in London attending the naval conference, reported to the State Department a conversation which he had had with Sir Robert Craigie, then British Under Secretary of State for Foreign Affairs and soon to become the British Ambassador to Japan.[113] Sir Robert had said that, according to confidential information he had just received, Chiang Kai-shek was in the process of negotiating a nonaggression pact with the Japanese. Should such a pact be concluded, it was Sir Robert's view that Great Britain, the United States, and Japan ought to enter into a tripartite nonaggression pact of their own which would have the advantage of furnishing the Japanese with some political justification for signing a naval agreement that would provide for the maintenance of the *status quo*.

Sir Robert's idea of a tripartite pact never received any official support. It did not meet with the approval of Anthony Eden, who had recently been appointed British Foreign Secretary. Nor was it welcomed in Washington where the President had stated on a number of occasions that he would not consider a nonaggression pact which did not include all of the nations of the Pacific area.[114] However, the State Department sent Norman Davis' account of his talks with Sir Robert Craigie to both Ambassador Grew and Ambassador Johnson for comment.[115]

Grew told the Department at once that in his opinion it was most unlikely that Japan and China were engaged in any negotiations such as Sir Robert had described.[116] Several weeks later in a long letter to the State Department which was clearly the result of much reflection, the ambassador discussed the broad issues which he felt had been raised by Sir Robert Craigie's suggestion for a tripartite nonaggression pact.[117] Very like MacMurray, Grew took the position that as Japan seemed well on the way to extending her control over all of China, the United States would soon be compelled to "seriously reconsider" its whole outlook and policy in the Far East. Grew's main argument was that it was constantly becoming more "impracticable" for the United States to deal with Japan on "a legal, moral, or idealistic basis" or, in other words, on any of the bases upon which "the policy and acts of the United States in the Far East" were traditionally founded. Nevertheless, the United States should not "scrap its time-honored beliefs"; rather it should seek supplementary means of protecting its rights and interests in Asia from Japanese interference while continuing to conduct its relations with a view to reducing existing tensions. Seen within this context, the negotiations of a tripartite agreement such as Sir Robert Craigie had proposed had its advantages and its disadvantages. On the one hand, it might serve as an additional means of safeguarding our rights and interests. On the other, a nonaggression pact would inevitably imply our tacit acceptance of the *status quo* on the mainland of Asia and to that extent "condone" Japan's seizure of Manchuria and encroachment on North China. In view of the moral implications of such a pact, its disadvantages would seem to outweigh its advantages. However (Grew made this point three separate times for emphasis), although a nonaggression pact between America, Great Britain, and Japan might not seem desirable, the embassy believed that the United States should lose no opportunity to explore every avenue that might lead to some variety of political agreement or agreements which might furnish us with essential safeguards without any sacrifice of principle. But any agreement or agreements that were devised should be limited in time and restricted to an attempt to restrain Japan in one direction or another. For it had become evident that the situation in the Far East, perhaps to a greater degree than in any other part of the world, was "not static but decidedly dynamic" and therefore did not lend itself to any permanent, over-all solution such as the Nine Power Treaty was intended to provide.

Johnson also told the State Department that he doubted whether any negotiations of the kind Sir Robert Craigie had indicated were in progress between Japan and China.[118] Nevertheless he went on to say in substance that he regarded the conclusion of such a pact or some sort of an alliance between Japan and China as decidedly within the realm of possibility. For the only alternative to a Sino-Japanese armed conflict was the formation of an alliance which, as it would essentially be characterized by the relations of a "master to a slave" rather than of two equal parties, would constitute a surrender by the Chinese. Johnson stated further that admittedly, if an alliance were consummated, it would create a new situation in the Far East. But he was not in favor of the United States' trying to anticipate the new situation either by an effort to champion China or to enter into an agreement with Japan however great the likelihood that American policy would eventually have to be readjusted. Apparently apprehensive that Washington might misunderstand his position, the ambassador declared,

> I do not want to be considered as one who believes that the American Government should bestir itself to use force to save China from probable Japanese conquest. . . . I do not wish to be considered as one who clings to a belief in the permanence of the status here and who therefore is unwilling to accept new developments with all that they imply and unprepared to entertain new understandings more in keeping with the new state of affairs. But it seems to me that it is not we who should take the initiative and abandon the past at this moment. . . . Little or no harm will come to us if we await the outcome for the initiative lies with China.

Despite his willingness to "entertain new understandings," Johnson, in contrast to Grew, did not believe that the United States could achieve any practical benefits from a nonaggression pact with Japan. His point was that the great powers were divided between the "have" nations—Russia, Great Britain, and the United States—and the "have-nots"—Germany, Italy, and Japan—and that the conflict over the world's resources between the two groups was too fundamental to allow them to make "common cause." Speaking of the "have-not" nations, Johnson said, "I would as soon make an agreement with a starving family next door whereby we would mutually undertake not to seize one another's bread, as enter into an arrangement with any or all of these three countries not to aggress on one another's interests." Moreover, Johnson went even further and asserted that he had to confess that, under the existing circumstances, he did not see any basis for agreement with the Japanese.

The most important aspect of the views noted above is that the officials who held them shared the belief that the world might soon be confronted with a Japanese-dominated China and at the same time did not favor any important change in American policy. There was no disposition to oppose Japan. On the contrary the discussion centered largely on whether the United States could reach some understanding with the Japanese. Ambassador Grew, who had obviously given most thought to the matter, believed that the United States might arrive at some limited agreement or series of agreements with Japan which would provide a degree of security for American interests in Asia. In addition, however, he laid down the condition that the United States should only become party to an arrangement that did not violate the principles of international conduct which it had always sought to uphold. But unless and until Grew was able to suggest some concrete way of meeting this condition, he was not likely to get much response from the administration in view of the importance which it had clearly indicated it attached to moral considerations.

At the beginning of 1936 the trend toward the subjugation of China by the Japanese seemed, if anything, to be accelerated by new developments. The famous mutiny of February 26 took place in Japan. The mutiny was the outcome of a prolonged struggle between two groups in the Japanese army—the Control Faction and the Imperial Way Faction—and constituted a final supreme effort on the part of the latter to seize power through a *coup d'état*.[1] Before dawn on February 26, some 1,500 soldiers led by the so-called Young Officers, who dominated the Imperial Way Faction, occupied various strategic buildings in Tokyo and, carrying out a well planned program of terrorism, assassinated a number of high government officials.[2] Later in the day the insurgents, abandoning their violent methods, sought to win the people over to their side by peaceful persuasion. But perhaps in part because of the brutality of the acts which they had already committed, they were unsuccessful. Meanwhile loyal troops, who had been ordered by the army to put down the revolt, marched into the city and within a brief time forced the rebels to surrender.

While the failure of the mutiny virtually eliminated the Imperial Way Faction from Japanese political life, it increased the power of the army as a whole, which gained in prestige partly by virtue of the fact that it had itself subdued the rebels and brought the crisis to an end. Indeed, it soon became evident that one of the primary results of the mutiny was that the army would, for the time being at least, control the policies of the government in Tokyo and that the civilian officials would have to play a subsidiary role.[3]

The first person to experience the full effect of the army's increase in power was Foreign Minister Hirota who, following the mutiny of February 26, was asked to assume the premiership and form a new cabinet. Hirota announced the setup of his cabinet early in March but was forced to renege on several appointments owing to the army's objections.[4] In addition, the Control Faction, now the dominant force in the army, compelled Hirota to accept its political program which involved sweeping reforms in domestic affairs and an aggressive foreign policy that aimed at the establishment of Japanese hegemony over Asia through what was vaguely called a "positive diplomacy."

On March 9 Hirota issued a statement to the press in which he outlined his basic policies and emphasized the phrase "positive diplomacy." This led Ambassador Grew, on his first visit to the new Premier, to ask Hirota whether he could explain what was meant by that term.[5] Hirota said that "positive diplomacy" was only to be applied to the Soviet Union and China and would mainly involve an intensification of the policies which the Japanese government had for some time been pursuing in relation to those two countries. So far as Soviet Russia was concerned, the army was dissatisfied with the great difference between the Soviet forces in Siberia and the Japanese forces in Manchukuo and wished the latter to be built to a point more nearly approximating the Soviet armies across the border. With regard to China, the Japanese government intended to enter into negotiations on the basis of the three points which it had already enunciated. Hirota also took the occasion to reassure Grew that the maintenance of good relations with the United States would be the "cornerstone of his foreign policy" as it had been during his tenure of office as Foreign Minister.

In keeping with Hirota's comments, negotiations based on Hirota's three principles were opened between the Chinese and Japanese governments at Nanking in the middle of March.[6] They were conducted on the Japanese side by Hachiro Arita, who had just been appointed Ambassador to China. They made little progress, however, and were almost immediately broken off as Arita was recalled to Tokyo to take up the post of Minister for Foreign Affairs which Hirota himself had retained for a time together with the premiership.

But the lapse of the negotiations did not mean even a temporary cessation of Japanese activities in China. Throughout the spring of 1936, the Japanese sought to promote extensive smuggling operations in North China as an additional means of putting pressure on the Chinese to accede to their wishes.

The Japanese had opened the door to widespread smuggling through the demilitarized zone in the summer of 1935.[7] As already related, the smuggling of silver out of China through the zone had assumed critical proportions earlier in that year and had been an important factor in undermining the Chinese currency system. In June, following an incident in which two Japanese silver smugglers were injured in an attempt to escape from customs authorities near the

Great Wall, the Japanese disarmed all customs officers in the East Hopei area. In September, the Japanese demanded the removal of all Customs Preventive vessels from within the three-mile limit off the East Hopei coast. Subsequently, when the customs authorities tried to apply (outside the three-mile limit) the right given them by Chinese law to search mercantile vessels within twelve miles of the Chinese coast, the Japanese declared that they would treat any such proceeding as an act of piracy upon the high seas. As the customs authorities were in no position to resist the Japanese, their work on land was greatly curtailed and they virtually ceased to function at sea. Smuggling, chiefly carried on by Japanese and Koreans, increased by leaps and bounds and flourished especially between Dairen and various points along the shore of the demilitarized zone.

While smuggling was therefore a highly successful business by the end of 1935, the customs authorities were still operating to some extent in East Hopei where they formed the one remaining obstacle to the unhampered flow of illicit trade. In order to remove this obstacle, the Japanese, in the early part of 1936, persuaded the new puppet regime of Yin Ju-keng to levy its own taxes on imports into the demilitarized zone at approximately one quarter of the rate required by the Nanking government. As a consequence, smuggled articles were thereafter treated as legal and duties were collected by the East Hopei Tax Office whose representatives received the protection of the Japanese gendarmerie which was under the direction of the Kwantung army. If any official of the Chinese Customs Administration sought to intervene, he was bodily assaulted—a situation which led to a whole series of incidents in which such officials were seriously injured.

The illicit goods which were brought into East Hopei included a wide variety of articles. At first the cargo was taken to Tientsin and from there transported to places in North China. But as stocks accumulated, the smuggled commodities were drained off into the Yangtze Valley area, flooding the markets of such cities as Hankow and even Shanghai.

During much of the spring of 1936, American Foreign Service officers reported to Washington almost daily concerning the smuggling activities in China. The importance which they attached to those activities stemmed from a number of causes. American traders were increasingly insistent that if the smuggling operations continued all legitimate commerce in China would be ruined. The Chinese Customs Administration was already experiencing a serious loss of revenue which, unless arrested, was bound to affect the servicing of foreign loans.[8] Moreover, in the opinion of Ambassador Johnson and his staff, the Customs Administration seemed headed for a breakdown which, should it occur, would almost inevitably produce acute economic and eventually political disorder in China, depriving the Chinese of any power they had to resist Japan.[9]

But, despite the seriousness with which they viewed developments, our embassies in China and Japan did not suggest taking any action, nor does Washington seem to have contemplated doing so. Once more, however, the initiative was assumed by the British. The British government was in fact under considerable pressure to do what it could to alleviate the situation.[10] Even segments of the British public customarily sympathetic to Japan were aroused by the smuggling operations in China, since they constituted a threat to the large British economic stake in that country and to the Chinese Customs Administration, with which the British had for so long had such close and important associations. The British government therefore undertook to register strong objections with the Japanese. On May 2, Sir Robert Clive protested to Foreign Minister Arita concerning the damage being done by the smuggling operations in China and stated that the Japanese authorities, far from seeming disposed to curb these activities, were reportedly encouraging them.[11] A few days later Arita handed the ambassador a formal memorandum denying that Japan had any connection with the smuggling in China and placing the blame solely upon the Nanking government. That government, it declared, invited illicit trade by imposing unreasonably high import taxes and was unable to collect customs duties in the north because it had alienated the local authorities by refusing to allow them to retain a part of the revenue with which to defray their administrative expenses. Thereafter the Japanese deliberately limited themselves to a constant repetition of these contentions. The British consequently became increasingly outspoken. In talks with Japanese officials in June, Sir Robert Clive said that the Japanese government could not expect the rest of the world to accept the naïve statement that Japan had nothing to do with the smuggling in China and that the British government, on its part, definitely did not accept it.

The British appealed to the United States to protest to Tokyo following Sir Robert Clive's initial talk with Arita.[12] Grew was thereupon instructed by the State Department to speak to Arita informally along the same lines as the British ambassador.[13] On two subsequent occasions the State Department told the embassy in Tokyo to raise the issue of smuggling with the Japanese Foreign Office again and point out the damage being done to American interests. But apparently no protests were made comparable in vigor to those of the British.

In the middle of June, Shigeru Yoshida, who had recently been appointed Ambassador to Great Britain, came to the United States, where he had an interview with Secretary Hull. Grew had already reported that, in a conversation with him, Yoshida had complained that the population problem in Japan was becoming increasingly difficult and that foreign countries should realize the seriousness of the situation.[14] Yoshida had maintained that the solution for Japan lay principally in the direction of finding outlets for her trade and in giving her subjects the opportunity to follow that trade. When questioned, he said what he had in mind was "peaceful penetration."

Presumably moved in part by Grew's report, the Secretary told Yoshida that in frankness he wished to say that many persons in the United States had the impression that Japan sought "absolute economic domination, first of eastern Asia, and then, of other portions as she might see fit."[15] The ultimate result would be political and military as well as economic domination which would entail the exclusion of countries like the United States from trading with the territories under Japanese control. The Secretary continued with the statement that

. . . this presented a serious question to first-class countries with commercial interests in every part of the world, for the reason that, for instance, my country stood unqualifiedly for the principle of equality of commercial opportunity and industrial right in every part of the world; and that it would be strange and impracticable for my country to stand for this doctrine with the announcement always that it qualified same by applying it to only one-half of the world and one-half of the world's population.

The Secretary asserted that, in his judgment, there was no reason why countries like Japan, the United States, and England could not "in the most amicable spirit and with perfect justice and fairness to each" agree to abide by the worldwide principle of commercial and industrial opportunity. Where differences existed, they could be resolved by the statesmen of the three powers sitting down together and conferring until they found a way for reasonable adjustments. Such a procedure would eliminate "90% of all occasions for friction." No single country would be able for a generation to supply the capital of many millions of dollars needed by China and similar Asiatic localities. But if three or four major powers furnished whatever capital they had available, the purchasing power in China and elsewhere would be increased so as to afford a market for most of the goods that the various interested nations had for sale.

Hull then spoke of his trade agreements program, itself founded upon the concept that the principle of equality of opportunity must form the basis of commercial relations. The Secretary, as was well known, attached immense importance to this program believing that the recovery of world trade, which was its objective, might not be "an absolute panacea against war" but was nonetheless an "indispensable cornerstone for the edifice of peace."[16] Stated somewhat more specifically, he was convinced that an adequate flow of trade between nations was essential for the improvement of economic conditions throughout the world and that while the betterment of those conditions might not in and of itself create peace it was a prerequisite to any lasting political settlement of international differences. In his tireless efforts to promote his reciprocal trade agreements program, Hull in his talks with foreign statesmen often went out of his way to explain the vital contribution which he felt it should make to the welfare of the world. He entered long and earnestly into such an explanation in his conversation with Yoshida. During the course of his remarks, the Secretary emphasized in particular the great benefits that would accrue to the Japanese if his movement for the recovery of international trade was successful and achieved its immediate end of restoring "some 20 billions of dollars" of international commerce.[17]

Hull seems to have intended his interview with Yoshida to be entirely cordial, as he repeatedly emphasized that he was speaking "in the friendliest possible spirit" and that he had a "high opinion and personal regard" for the Japanese people and especially for their statesmen. In general, his comments do not appear to have been planned but rather to have been governed by his impulse to seize all possible occasions to speak on behalf of the cause of peace and the means of attaining peace. The Secretary was essentially trying to impress upon Yoshida that Japan, as well as every other nation, should attempt to solve its economic problems through international cooperation instead of through short-sighted unilateral action which could only lead to further conflict.

Japanese statesmen on their part continued to indicate their satisfaction with the course of Japanese-American relations. When in August Ambassador Grew made the rounds of Japanese officials to say goodbye, before leaving on another visit to the United States, Prime Minister Hirota expressed his great appreciation of the policy which President Roosevelt had followed in regard to the Far East.[18] Foreign Minister Arita stated in the same vein that America's relations with Japan were proceeding "very well" and that Roosevelt's policy appeared to be different from that of his predecessor.

In the early part of 1936, the reports of American Foreign Service officers in China not only emphasized the smuggling situation but other developments as well which were detrimental to China in her struggle with Japan. In May the Japanese greatly increased the number of troops in the Peiping-Tientsin area that were under the command of their North China garrison.[19] Furthermore, the Japanese military evidently remained determined to detach the northern provinces from the rest of China. In response to their pressures, General Sung Che-yuan progressively introduced a greater degree of autonomy into the administration of Hopei and Chahar through such measures as the assumption of control over financial, communications, cultural, and other organs which had theretofore been under the direction of the National Government.[20] By June, General Sung reportedly had made up his mind to proclaim the independence of Hopei and Chahar but at the last moment was prevented from doing so by some of his subordinates who remained loyal to Nanking. In August a new phase of Japan's "positive diplomacy" seemed to be unfolding in North China. Shigeru Kawagoe, who had succeeded Arita as Japanese ambassador in China, was attempting with the support of the Japanese military to get General Sung and other authorities in the North to agree to a program of economic "cooperation" with Japan. The program was in general the same as that which the Japanese Foreign Office had allegedly been advocating for some time in that it involved the construction by the Japanese of railroads in North China, the joint development by Japan and China of mines and of agricultural areas, especially cotton-producing areas, and the establishment of a Sino-Japanese aviation corporation which would serve to weld all of North China into an economic and political unit connected with Manchukuo.[21] Arrangements for the building of two railroads were said to be well advanced. The opinion of the American embassy concerning these developments was succinctly stated in its review of conditions in China for the first half of 1936, in which it said that "practically all major developments of the six months were factors working for the disintegration of China."[22]

Nevertheless the dispatches of American Foreign Service officers also dealt with some events which were operating in favor of strengthening China in relation to Japan. The student demonstrations of 1935 were followed by a wave of nationalist, anti-Japanese activities that spread rapidly throughout the country. Partly as a result of the continuing agitation of the students, patriotic groups were organized in many parts of China to participate in a National Salvation Movement aimed at arousing the mass of the people to put pressure on their leaders to resist the Japanese.[23] At the end of May representatives of fifty such groups met at Shanghai and inaugurated an All China Federation of National Salvation Unions which issued a statement calling for the end of internal strife in China and the formation of a National Salvation Movement against Japan that would include all political factions. It seemed therefore as though a genuine popular demand was arising for the unification of China to resist Japan.

In addition, in the spring of 1936 a situation developed which, though at first threatening the country with further disruption, in the end helped to bring about its consolidation. The communist armies that had engaged in the Long March had gradually and with indescribable difficulty made their way to the Northwest where they settled on the land available to them, which consisted largely of barren terrain. In February 1936 communist groups advanced into Shansi with the announced purpose of marching through that province to establish contact with the Japanese armies so that they could engage in a war of resistance against Japan.[24] Initially it seemed as though they might gain converts as a consequence of their anti-Japanese slogans which could only have led to augmenting the divisive tendencies within China. But the Shansi campaign of the Communists proved short-lived. Central government forces were sent against the communist troops which were compelled to retreat to their strongholds in the Northwest. The Generalissimo thereupon made use of the presence of his armies in Shansi, as he had earlier in Kweichow and Yunnan, to extend his authority over an area where he had so far enjoyed little power.

Following the abortive Shansi campaign, a far more serious conflict arose in the Southwest which brought the nation to the verge of a major catastrophe but ultimately also contributed to its unification.[25] The Southwest Political Council had continued to rule in Kwangtung and Kwangsi maintaining the semiautonomous status of those provinces although the council itself was officially an organ of the central government. The breach between the Southwest faction and Chiang Kai-shek had never been healed, owing to many points of dispute the most important of which was probably that the leaders of the Southwest objected to the constant centralization of more and more power in the hands of the Generalissimo. The chief leaders of the Southwest were Generals Li Tsung-jen and Pai Ch'ung-hsi of Kwangsi, who had long played an important part in Chinese political life, and General Chen Chi-tang of Kwangtung, known as an old-style militarist. During the spring of 1936, the tension between the Southwest and Nanking mounted until in early June the Southwest Political

Council announced that the Kwangtung-Kwangsi armies were being mobilized to embark upon a northern expedition. Ostensibly, at least, the expedition was not directed against the Nanking government. The Southwest leaders declared repeatedly that their sole objective was to go north so that they could fight the Japanese and that they were only assuming the initiative because the Nanking government itself refused to take any action to save the country from Japan. As a demonstration of their sincerity, they renamed their armies the Anti-Japanese National Salvation Forces and invited the Nanking government to cooperate with them. Nanking, for its part, massed its troops within striking distance of Kwangtung and Kwangsi. Throughout most of June and early July it looked as though a large-scale civil war could not be averted.

The Southwest leaders did not, however, receive the support they expected. Generals Li and Pai were mistrusted as it was thought that, despite their official pronouncements, they were largely motivated by their strong dislike of the Generalissimo and were really determined to overthrow the Nanking regime. Since the destruction of that regime raised the specter of plunging the country into chaos and thereby playing into the hands of the Japanese, Generals Li and Pai found themselves increasingly opposed by all the elements in China that had joined in the growing demand for unity in the face of Japanese aggression. Moreover in mid-July the Central Executive Committee of the Kuomintang met with the determination to find a solution to the situation which would favor the National Government but would, if possible, be peaceful. As a result of the committee's efforts, the Southwest Political Council was abolished and Chen Chi-tang, whose troops were in any case rapidly defecting to Nanking, was dismissed from office and fled the country. In the middle of August, Chiang Kai-shek went to Canton where he introduced drastic administrative and other reforms designed to integrate Kwangtung with the parts of China already under his control. Considerable political skill was used in the treatment of Generals Li and Pai on the theory that, in view of the national prestige which they possessed, even their nominal allegiance would be a valuable asset to the Nanking regime. They were therefore offered posts in the government which they could not refuse without openly breaking with Nanking thereby running the risk of incurring more popular displeasure and perhaps eliminating themselves permanently from the political arena. In late September a settlement was reached which allowed Kwangsi more political independence than had been left to Kwangtung but provided for the reorganization of the Kwangsi military forces and their enrollment as national troops under the jurisdiction of the Nanking government.

Even before the conflict between Kwangsi and Nanking had been finally resolved, however, a series of incidents had occurred which further indicated that the determination to defy Japan was spreading among the Chinese people.[26] In August the Japanese sought to reopen a consulate general at Chengtu which they had closed at the time of the Manchurian crisis. The people of Chengtu objected on the basis that the city was not a treaty port and engaged in mass demonstrations which led to the stoning of a Japanese official in the streets and the killing of two Japanese newspaper men. At the beginning of September a Japanese was murdered at Pakhoi and the Japanese officials who were sent to investigate the case were forcibly prevented from landing. Some two weeks later, a Japanese policeman was shot to death while on duty in the Japanese concession at Hankow. On September 23 four Japanese bluejackets were attacked in Shanghai, one of whom was killed and two injured. The latter incident led to the landing of Japanese marines in Shanghai who for a while took up defensive positions behind barbed wire entanglements in Hongkew and Chapei.

As already indicated, the attitude of the American embassy toward the general situation in China at the time that most of the above events were taking place was exceedingly pessimistic. Concerning the more positive developments, in so far as can be judged by the documents now available, the embassy did not regard the emergence of the National Salvation Movement as a factor of major significance.[27] In contrast, the consulate general at Tientsin was decidedly impressed by the activities of the National Salvation Movement, believing that it was gradually creating an articulate public opinion which was demanding resistance to Japan with a vigor that was already having its effect upon Nanking.[28] In regard to the results of the Shansi campaign, while the embassy felt that the Generalissimo had scored a gain in extending his control over Shansi, it viewed the gain as a very minor one relative to the losses which he was simultaneously suffering in North China at the hands of the Japanese.[29] As to the conflict between the Southwest and the Nanking government, the embassy for a long time shared the widespread belief that large-scale fighting would break out which would result in the complete collapse of all authority in China and a consequent encouragement to Japan to engage in further aggression.[30] In late July, however, Willys Peck reported a general feeling in official circles at Nanking that Chiang Kai-shek had "outwitted" his enemies, Generals Li and Pai, and that the consolidation of the central government's position in the Southwest was assured.[31] Nevertheless the embassy appears to have thought that the over-all situation in China had not undergone any substantial change. Nelson Johnson, for example, stated in a letter to Silas Strawn in late August that conditions in China were "about as chaotic as ever."[32] Furthermore, in the same month writing to Malcolm Simpson of J. P. Morgan and Company, the ambassador expressed the opinion that Chiang Kai-shek's policy had always been to placate the Japanese, short of signing a treaty granting their demands, and that this policy remained unaltered.[33] "In short," Johnson declared, "Chiang is not going to resist if the Japanese take what they want."

The series of incidents involving attacks upon Japanese led the Japanese government at Tokyo in mid-September to redouble its efforts to implement its "positive diplomacy." Demanding redress for the events which had taken place at Chengtu and Pakhoi, Ambassador Kawagoe entered into a series of conversations with Foreign Minister Chang Chun beginning September 15. The substance of their talks was theoretically secret but the Chinese Vice Minister for Foreign Affairs kept the British and American embassies informed.[34] According to his account, Kawagoe had not limited himself to attempting to negotiate a settlement of the incidents at Chengtu and Pakhoi but had immediately advanced various far-reaching proposals. These involved the reorganization of the five provinces of North China and their economic development through Sino-Japanese "cooperation"; collaboration between the Chinese and Japanese armed forces for the suppression of the Communists in China which entailed the stationing of Japanese troops on Chinese territory; and an agreement by the Nanking government to appoint Japanese advisers, including military advisers, to be given controlling positions in the Chinese army.[35] The Chinese Minister for Foreign Affairs had replied that he was willing to discuss some of the Japanese proposals but that the Chinese government regarded the suppression of the Communists as a purely internal problem which was not a fit subject for diplomatic negotiations.[36] Moreover, General Chang had asserted that he would only enter into an exchange of views on the other issues raised by the Japanese ambassador on terms which fully recognized China's rights as an equal and sovereign state. During the third interview, on September 23, the Foreign Minister had adopted an even firmer tone and stated that, if there was to be any genuine improvement in Sino-Japanese relations, Japan would also have to meet certain conditions. The conditions which he specified were a cancellation of the Tangku

Truce, elimination of the autonomous regime in East Hopei, and Japanese assistance in the abolition of smuggling in North China. As a result of General Chang's remarks, the atmosphere at the meeting had become markedly strained and the conversations were broken off for the time being.

Almost a month passed before the Chang Chun-Kawagoe talks were resumed. Meanwhile in an effort to circumvent General Chang, Kawagoe had an interview with the Generalissimo. He received little satisfaction, however, as Chiang Kai-shek referred him back to the Foreign Minister. At the same time an officially inspired statement was issued by the Chinese press which declared that China still entertained the hope of breaking the deadlock with Japan but that if all attempts at negotiation failed she would "make her last sacrifice in a last effort to maintain her independence." Chinese public opinion, it was said, had reached the point where it would "not tolerate the Government accepting humiliating terms in order to preserve peace."[37]

The Japanese ambassador and the Chinese Foreign Minister reopened their talks on October 19. According to official Chinese sources, Kawagoe devoted his time almost exclusively to reasserting the Japanese proposal for collaboration between Japan and China to crush the Communists. He was, however, friendlier than earlier and suggested negotiating an agreement on the basis of general principles and leaving the details to be threshed out by military experts later. But if Ambassador Kawagoe ever had any chance of getting General Chang to consider such an agreement, it soon became evident that unexpected events were working against him.

A very dangerous situation had been developing in Inner Mongolia, where following the Chin-Doihara agreement, the Japanese had substantially increased their influence.[38] In February 1936 a split occurred in the Inner Mongolian Autonomy Council, which had been established in 1934 and still retained its connections with Nanking. Prince Teh, who was head of a movement for the creation of a wholly independent Mongolian state, set up a government in Chahar to which the Mongols of that province adhered while a new political council was created by the Nanking government for the Mongols of Suiyuan. Prince Teh's faction veered increasingly toward the Japanese who inevitably used it for their own purposes. In November, instigated by the Japanese, a force of Chahar Mongols and pro-Manchukuo "irregulars" attacked Suiyuan with the aid of Japanese airplanes. The invaders were soon driven back by the armies of the Provincial government under Fu Tso-yi with re-enforcements from Nanking. On November 24 General Fu's troops captured Pailingmiao which had served as a base of operations for the insurgents. Thereafter the invasion collapsed.

The most surprising and significant result of the Chinese victory at Suiyuan was its effect inside China. The defense of Suiyuan became a popular issue around which the Chinese rallied, enormously increasing the outcry throughout the country for resistance to Japan. The hardening of opinion, at least among the articulate segments of the public, had an immediate influence upon the Chang Chun-Kawagoe talks. On December 3, Ambassador Kawagoe handed General Chang an *aide-mémoire* reviewing their discussions to date.[39] The Foreign Minister returned the memorandum on the grounds that it indicated that he had gone further in meeting the Japanese point of view than was in fact the case. The talks were thereupon terminated.[40]

In retrospect it would seem that for our embassy in China the autumn of 1936 marked a turning point in the Sino-Japanese struggle. Perhaps for the first time in many years the embassy saw genuine cause for optimism in the Chinese scene. In a report written at the end of December, the embassy asserted that whereas the outstanding developments during the first half of 1936 had increased the precariousness of China's position, those of the second half had produced the opposite effect.[41] Enumerating the elements which in its opinion had "definitely tended to unify and strengthen" China, it stated that the Suiyuan campaign had played a vital part in that it had "evoked an amazing manifestation of nationalism." Ambassador Johnson himself seems first to have thought, in October 1936, that Chiang Kai-shek might abandon a policy of placating Japan. After a trip to Nanking in the middle of that month, Johnson wrote Hornbeck that he had "gathered . . . that Chiang and all those with him were prepared to meet force with force."[42] Their feeling, he said, was that, although Japan was more powerful, China was in a position to make things so difficult and costly for the Japanese that in the end Japan would be the greater loser; moreover they were convinced that in any case resistance was their "only hope for support from the Chinese people and from the Chinese military." From then on he spoke of the Chinese as having decided to fight if necessary.[43]

The one moment in which Washington was in any significant sense involved in the developments between Japan and China in the latter half of 1936 was before the events occurred which American officials felt provided grounds for a measure of optimism in respect to China. In late September when the Chang Chun-Kawagoe talks were first broken off, the British government concluded that the situation was very precarious and sought to impress its concern upon both the Chinese and the Japanese.[44] The British ambassador at Nanking was instructed to urge upon Chinese officials the necessity of preventing, if possible, any recurrence of incidents involving assaults upon Japanese such as had taken place in various Chinese cities. At the same time Sir Robert Clive was told to call on Foreign Minister Arita and officially express his government's desire to see relations between Japan and China established upon a genuinely peaceful basis. The British version of the ambassador's interview with the Foreign Minister indicates that, after delivering his government's message, Sir Robert devoted himself to attempting to get across to Arita the one argument which he felt might have some effect upon the Japanese. Speaking personally, the ambassador dwelt upon the likelihood that if Japan put too much pressure upon Chiang Kai-shek to accept far-reaching demands, the Generalissimo might resort to armed resistance "with consequences so serious that no one could foresee the end." The Minister said that he recognized this risk but intimated that the Japanese government regarded the "anti-Japanese agitation" in the northern part of China—especially in the areas under the influence of Feng Yu-hsiang and Chang Hsueh-liang—as a threat to the safety of Manchukuo, which it could not tolerate. When in response Sir Robert observed that there were usually two sides to every quarrel,[45] Arita replied "'somewhat ominously' that 'the Japanese could not be expected to give consideration to the Chinese point of view.'" The Minister added, however, that the proposals made to General Chang Chun were "not unconditional demands but were subject to discussion."

The British, who were showing a marked tendency to become increasingly involved in Far Eastern affairs and to proceed independently, limited themselves to merely informing the State Department of the action which they had taken.[46] In Nanking, however, the Vice Minister for Foreign Affairs asked Willys Peck whether the American government would not follow the British example and urge moderation at Tokyo.[47] In addition, the Vice Minister remarked that Peck might have heard a comment being made by "many persons" to the effect that in the present crisis Great Britain and the United States had reversed the position that they had adopted "during a similar crisis in 1931 and 1932." In Washington, Ambassador Sze called on Secretary Hull also to inquire whether the United States would not make an approach to the Japanese government similar to that of the British.[48] The Secretary wrote in a record of his conversation with Sze,

I replied that we are following developments in relations between China and Japan with care and genuine interest; that we very much regret the serious conditions; that we will give every attention and consideration to each phase as it develops; that we are mindful of all phases; that in thus giving attention it will be necessary for us to avoid any step which might do more harm than good.

At this point the ambassador—Hull went on to say—asked about the attitude of the United States in the event of a clash between China and Japan. "I replied again," the Secretary noted, "that our country is, of course, intensely interested in peace and that we earnestly hoped no clash will occur."

As was perhaps implicit in the Secretary's remarks, the United States had not yet made up its mind what action, if any, it wished to take. On being questioned by the French ambassador on the same day (October 2) that the Secretary spoke with Sze, Maxwell Hamilton asserted that the State Department had not yet reached any decision as to whether to take steps along the lines followed by the British.[49] The Department felt, Hamilton said, that because of the position of leadership which the United States had assumed during the Manchurian crisis the American government "had to move perhaps more circumspectly than other governments" lest any diplomatic measures it adopted have "an adverse rather than a good effect" in Japan.

Meanwhile the Department had consulted Erle R. Dickover who was in charge of the United States embassy in Tokyo, as Ambassador Grew was still in the United States. Partly as a result of Dickover's recommendations, it was decided that an officer of the embassy should, in informal conversation, convey to the Japanese Vice Minister for Foreign Affairs that the United States government was watching the situation between Japan and China "constantly and with interest."[50] The officer was to speak as though upon his own initiative, to make no reference to the British démarche, and to take every precaution to avoid any possible publicity. He was to say that the embassy had for some time been reading the press reports of the differences between the Chinese and Japanese governments with concern but had refrained from approaching the Japanese Foreign Office out of fear that some undesirable publicity might ensue; however, the press reports had now assumed so serious a tone that the embassy deemed it advisable to seek authoritative information that it could transmit to Washington.

Dickover, who was in the hospital at the time, seized upon the opportunity afforded by a visit from the Vice Minister to talk with him personally in the strictest privacy.[51] Subsequently Dickover cabled the Department that the Vice Minister had told him that the discussions between General Chang Chun and Ambassador Kawagoe were "in no respect like the twenty-one demands" and that the Japanese had "no intention of using force" to get the Chinese to agree to their desires. The only demand on which Japan would insist was the suppression of anti-Japanese agitation. Other matters were simply to be made a part of negotiations that were to be "based on Hirota's three points." Upon receipt of Dickover's dispatch, the Department sent him a statement which was to be read to the Vice Minister. The statement declared primarily that the United States government "sincerely" appreciated the information provided by the Vice Minister which contributed "toward an understanding of the present state of relations between Japan and China" and that it was "especially gratified" to receive assurances that Japan wanted to solve its differences with China by diplomacy. The United States government, it was also said, would follow developments as they unfolded "with solicitude."

Foreign Minister Arita had originally begged Sir Robert Clive not to let Nanking know of the British government's approach to the Japanese government.[52] But rumors of the ambassador's call on Arita became sufficiently general for the Japanese Foreign Office to resort to the somewhat unusual gesture of announcing publicly that Sir Robert had not made any official representations to the Japanese government and that, furthermore, no representations had been made by the United States. While the British nevertheless informed Nanking of Sir Robert's conversation with Arita, the United States government decided to fulfill the Japanese desire for secrecy on the grounds that by doing so its actions were more likely to have a "constructively helpful" influence in Tokyo. The Department was concerned, however, lest its silence at Nanking prejudice its relations with the Chinese government. It therefore sent Ambassador Johnson and Willys Peck a dispatch containing certain comments which it was suggested they might use in answering any questions concerning American policy put to them in confidence by Chinese officials.[53]

The comments amounted to a large extent to a repetition of the remarks made by American officials in July 1935 in response to the Chinese criticism that the United States had displayed a "cold attitude" toward Nanking during the latest phase of the North China crisis.[54] The most important point made was that the United States would continue to try to exert its influences on the current controversy between Japan and China "quietly and unobtrusively," the inference being that the administration intended to adhere to the policy which it had been maintaining. A notation in Ambassador Grew's diary suggests that in fact the continuation of our policy was largely being taken for granted in Washington at this time.[55] For in reference to a trip to the capital in early October, the ambassador gives an account of an interview with Roosevelt and several meetings with Hull which shows that neither the President nor the Secretary indicated any dis-position to discuss our relations with the Far East or even Far Eastern affairs in general. Concerning the Secretary, Grew wrote that in talk-ing with Hull he had attempted to "pilot" the conversation on to a consideration of our future policy in the Far East but that "he [Hull] had invariably started off on his idealistic trade theories."

In December Hornbeck sought to furnish Peck with some guidance concerning the broader aspects of the problem of what to say to Chinese officials.[56] Peck had written to the Department stating that he hesitated to press Chinese officials for information concerning their difficulties with Japan because he was under the impression that the administration wanted him to "carefully avoid any implication of a joint American-Chinese interest in China's struggle against Japanese encroachment."[57] Hornbeck's reply led him into a discussion of both the aim and the conduct of American policy. The core of his argument was that in dealing with Chinese officials American officials found themselves in a situation which was "full of difficult angles." The United States wished to keep out of war. It believed that to intrude in the quarrels of others was inconsistent with this objective. It was therefore determined not to make any gesture which could be inter-preted as "taking sides" and, in general, strove to remain on good terms with all countries. At the same time a strong sentiment existed in the United States for those who attempted to keep the peace and against those who were ready to resort to aggression. In relation to China, American officials were therefore faced with a dilemma. For, on the one hand, they feared that the impression might be created that this country was lacking in a feeling of friendly sympathy for China; but, on the other hand, they wanted to avoid expressing sym-pathy in a manner which might lead the Chinese to expect more sup-port from the United States than we were inclined to give. Hornbeck suggested that it was perhaps a useful device to think of the relation-ship of America and China as being in some respects comparable to that of two friends, one of whom happened to be stronger and to have a greater capacity for self-reliance than the other. The first friend natu-rally desired the one who was less fortunate to progress. But it was often the lesson of life that the best help that could be offered to others was to encourage them to develop the qualities which enabled them to be independent. The Chinese seemed in the past few years gradually to have sensed the value of these qualities and tried to achieve them. There was therefore at least one thing that American officials could appropriately point out in their conversations with Chinese officials, namely, that it was our policy—and moreover had long been our policy as evidenced by the leading role we had played in the formulation of the Nine Power Treaty—to rely on the belief that the Chinese were capable of creating and maintaining a well-ordered state.

Fundamentally Hornbeck was saying that as our primary purpose was to avoid war with Japan the support that we extended to China could not, in our own national interests, go much beyond a reaffirmation of confidence.[58] As had already become evident, a policy such as Hornbeck had in mind was not inclined to satisfy Chinese officials. A few months later (March 1937) Chiang Kai-shek in a talk with Ambassador Johnson, referred to a "widespread impression among Chinese to the effect that the United States seemed to be less ardently interested in the Far East while the British were showing a growing interest."[59] The Generalissimo twice repeated the hope that the United States would "keep pace" with Great Britain's current concern with the Far East as the stability of the Pacific area depended upon its doing so.

The Japanese, on the other hand, continued to express their approval of American policy. The Foreign Minister told Grew, on the ambassador's return to Tokyo from the United States, that the Japanese government had been gratified by the attitude of the United States toward the Chang Chun-Kawagoe negotiations.[60] In addition, shortly thereafter Amau sought to impress upon Grew his government's satisfaction with the state of American-Japanese relations and the improvement which they had undergone during the two or three previous years. Grew, at the end of 1936, wrote in a long report to the Department that relations between Japan and the United States were progressing well and that there was no good reason to believe they would "not maintain their present satisfactory status for some time to come."

In its final weeks, the year 1936 was to witness what was perhaps the most dramatic event of the entire period under consideration: the Sian incident. It seems evident that up to the time of the Sian incident, the Roosevelt administration had followed a policy in the Far East which it had worked out with great care and maintained throughout many critical developments. Moreover, there appeared little likelihood that it would depart from this policy unless conditions in the Far East underwent a radical transformation. If the trend toward the extension of Japanese control over China by gradual encroachment continued, there was—as already suggested—no indication that the United States would alter its aims or its strategy. On the other hand, if the movement within China toward unity and resistance to Japan increased, the United States might be faced with a very different situation from that with which it had been dealing. There was a possibility that, confronted with a China markedly growing in power and determination, the Japanese might abandon or modify their present policies. Or, on the contrary, they might feel compelled to accelerate their efforts to gain control of China before the Chinese were in a position to put up a better defense. These and other eventualities were the subject of speculation among American officials. On the whole, however, they were largely interested in the immediate future and the question, which they regarded as still unanswered, of whether the improvement in conditions in China was temporary or permanent.

An additional event occurred toward the end of 1936 which was also looked upon as an unpredictable factor. On November 25 Germany and Japan concluded the Anti-Comintern Pact.[61] The published part of the text declared that the signatories would exchange information concerning the activities of the Comintern within their borders and would collaborate in the adoption of whatever countermeasures were necessary for their own protection. It was also asserted that other nations would be invited to participate in the treaty. In addition, the pact contained secret articles which provided that, in case of an unprovoked attack by the Soviet Union on one of the signatories, the other would not engage in any action that would have "the effect of relieving the position of the U.S.S.R." Moreover the assent of both parties to the treaty was necessary in case either wished to enter into a political agreement with the Soviet Union.

The negotiation of an understanding between Japan and Germany had long been the subject of much rumor, leading to the assumption that it would amount to an alliance involving military commitments. Two days before the announcement of the agreement the Japanese Vice Minister for Foreign Affairs went out of his way, as he himself stated, to prevent its giving rise to a misunderstanding with the United States.[62] The Vice Minister informed Dickover confidentially of the conclusion of the Anti-Comintern Pact and assured him that it did not contain secret military provisions or in any way constitute an alliance. He furthermore declared emphatically that the Japanese government would not allow itself to be drawn into European politics through the pact nor did it intend to join any bloc of nations—"such as a fascist bloc."

The popular reaction to the Anti-Comintern Pact proved remarkably hostile even in Japan itself where the agreement was opposed on the grounds that it would seriously damage Japan's relations with other countries, especially with the Soviet Union. The Japanese government made every effort to present the treaty in the best possible

light and repeated the assurances in public that had been given to
Dickover in private. However there seemed little inclination in the
United States, as in other countries, to take the Japanese government's
words at their face value. A survey of American newspapers, made
at the time, states that a wide cross section of the press showed more
interest in the announcement of the Japanese-German pact than in
any other event in the winter of 1936-1937.[63] The "outstanding" feature
of the editorials reviewed was a "complete disbelief" that the pact
"meant what it said." Speculations about the real content of the treaty
varied considerably but there was general agreement that it represented an entente between two totalitarian states of "well-known
territorial ambitions" and was therefore bound to add substantially to
the heavy feeling of apprehension which already existed among the
democratic nations. On an official level Grew informed Washington in
early December that the consensus of opinion among his diplomatic
colleagues in Tokyo was that the German-Japanese accord included
a secret military understanding.[64] The ambassador indicated that his
own view was that, irrespective of the precise nature of the treaty, it
reflected a reorientation of Japan's policy which would probably
result in the strengthening of its ties with Germany.[65] In all, the year
1936 as it drew to a close appeared to be leaving a legacy of great
uncertainty as to future developments.[66]

CHAPTER VII | VIEWS OF AMERICAN
OFFICIALS ON THE CHINESE COM-
MUNISTS AND THE SIAN INCIDENT

The period of the Sian incident culminated in the Kuomintang-Communist rapprochement of September 1937. Inevitably this rapprochement appeared much less significant at the time than it does today,
for it was virtually impossible to foresee that the Communists would
gain control of all of mainland China in the postwar years. However,
in view of the fact that they have done so and that they have become
a major factor in the foreign policy of the United States, it seems
pertinent to consider here the attitude of American officials, not only
toward the understanding reached by the Communists and the
Kuomintang in 1937, but also toward the whole subject of Chinese
communism in the years preceding that understanding.

THE CHINESE COMMUNISTS FROM THE EARLY 1930's
THROUGH THE LONG MARCH

Information concerning the Chinese Communists was exceedingly difficult to obtain in Nationalist China after the Communist movement
was driven underground following the revolution of 1925-1928.[1] The
communist areas in the interior were largely sealed off from the rest
of China and, although the Central Committee of the Chinese Communist Party functioned in Shanghai for some years, it was forced by
the rigorous measures of the Kuomintang police to move to Kiangsi
in the early 1930's. The circulation of communist publications—
whether printed in China or abroad—was banned, so that the main
sources of published information consisted of heavily censored reports
concerning the Communists in the Nationalist press or of articles in
periodicals that were occasionally smuggled in from the communist
districts in China or from the Soviet Union. Before the recognition of
the Soviet Union by the United States, the American Legation at
Peiping on occasion received from the American Legation at Riga

copies of translations of articles, printed in the USSR, that had a bearing upon the Communist movement in China. Also at times American Foreign Service officers were able to obtain data about the activities of the Chinese Communists from American missionaries or other American nationals living or traveling in the interior of China. Beyond this, however, they had no special sources of information.

The scarcity of material concerning the Chinese Communists was reflected in the official dispatches to the State Department from China in the winter of 1930 when the first annihilation campaign started.[2] One typical dispatch stated that the so-called "communist" soldiers in the interior were in fact only bandits. The Chinese Communist Party, it was said, while it had remained in being surreptitiously after 1927, had dwindled to a point where it consisted of no more than a handful of intellectuals that were wholly divorced from the ostensibly "Red" armies. The latter existed, not by virtue of any political convictions but as a result of the maladministration of the Kuomintang, which was driving the peasants into such desperation that they were willing to engage in almost any form of violence to overthrow organized authority and replace it throughout the country with organized banditry.

The brief dispatches sent in 1930 were supplemented in 1931 and 1932 by two long reports on Chinese communism written, respectively, by a consul at Shanghai, who had been in Canton during the 1925-1928 revolution, and a vice consul at Hankow, who had been in China no more than three years. Both studies were done on a voluntary basis and their authors were apparently the only two men in the American diplomatic service in China at the time who were attempting to follow the Communist movement in detail. The writer of the Shanghai report died in 1932, leaving solely the Hankow officer to carry on this work. The latter was—as far as it has been possible to ascertain—the only American Foreign Service officer in China able to read both Chinese and Russian. From 1932 to the time of the Kuomintang-Communist rapprochement of September 1937 he appears to have been alone in his efforts to supply the State Department with first-hand material (official documents, et cetera) on the Chinese Communists and to provide some consistent analysis of their activities.

The 79-page study of the Chinese Communists, which was done in Shanghai, was largely based upon communist publications of the 1925-1928 vintage, on documents which had been seized from Communists in Shanghai by the police, or on official Kuomintang reports.[3] These sources were sufficient to allow the author to correct the impression that the Red armies consisted only of bandits and to state that, on the contrary, they probably numbered several hundred thousand well-disciplined soldiers many of whom were expertly trained in guerrilla tactics. The nature of the source material did not allow, however, for any description of the Soviets which had been established in the interior of China. The study therefore limited itself to a discussion of the activities of the Chinese Communist Party in Shanghai, which it portrayed as the instrument by means of which the Soviet Union (referred to as the "Arch Enemy") was attempting cold-bloodedly and fanatically to achieve domination over all Asia and ultimately over the whole world. The objective, it was said, was to create such chaos in China that China would cease to exist as a market for western nations which would thereby themselves be driven into a state of bankruptcy that would make them an easy prey to communist penetration.

Only about half of the study was devoted to communism, however, the rest consisting of comments upon the Kuomintang. The Kuomintang armies, it was asserted, existed for the "sole objective of plundering the people." For the past fifteen years, under various guises and pretexts, they had systematically looted the country until it was on the verge of complete disorganization; yet the "orgy" continued "even under the so-called enlightened beneficent rule of a central national government." The "Dictator of the Dictatorship" was himself engaged in waging a series of annual wars with other military groups for the control of the nation so that the revenues were dissipated "to the complete stultification of any measures looking to the alleviation of the oppressive system of militarism that . . . spawned over the country." Under these circumstances, it was concluded, the Kuomintang would never be able to keep China from coming under the control of Russia or else of Japan (as was currently happening in Manchuria). These assertions led the author to present his main thesis which was that if China was to be saved the Western powers would have to intervene and establish a government that would give the Chinese people an opportunity to live and enjoy the fruits of their labors in peace.

On reaching Washington, the above study was given the rating of "excellent" by the Far Eastern Division on the grounds that it showed a "thorough investigation" of a timely subject of importance and an "unusual understanding of Chinese affairs."[4] This action by the Division was in itself an indication that its knowledge of Chinese communism was exceedingly scanty. For in retrospect it is evident that the Shanghai report provided a painfully inadequate picture of the Chinese Communists and was indeed little more than a presentation of some loosely reasoned theories about the whole Chinese situation.

The report on the Chinese Communists which was sent from Hankow (in April 1932) consisted of 123 pages.[5] It strongly emphasized in the introduction that owing to the impossibility of obtaining adequate information concerning the Communists in Nationalist China the author had been compelled to make a number of assertions which could not be fully documented. Reliance, it was said, had for the most part been placed upon the *Peking and Tientsin Times* and the *Ta Kung Pao* although communist and other materials had been used wherever feasible. An inspection of the footnotes shows that the writer had employed copies of some issues of *Inprecorr, Pravda,* and other Soviet publications which had somehow slipped by the Nationalist police; articles in the *China Forum,* a radical journal published by an American, Harold Isaacs, in Shanghai; and a variety of other sources including a pamphlet by Yang Chien (then Assistant Director of the National Research Institute in China) and an account of Chinese communism prepared by the Japanese government for the Lytton Commission. The two last named items were of particular importance as they contained an unusual amount of information about the Soviet districts in Kiangsi and other parts of China.[6]

Indeed, in contrast to the Shanghai study, the Hankow report dealt extensively with the activities of the Chinese Communists in the interior. It stated that there were currently seven large Soviet areas in China (shown on an accompanying map) and that, if the districts under the influence of the Red armies were included, the Chinese Communists controlled about one-sixth of China. It noted that governments had been established in the various Soviet districts and that an over-all Provisional Government of the Chinese Soviet Republic had been created at an All-China Conference of Soviets held at Juichin in November 1931. It sought to give a general idea of the manner in which the Soviet administrative system functioned, emphasizing in particular that it placed all authority in the highest organs of government so that every phase of the life of the community and the individual was centrally controlled. The changes which had been affected in family relations, the status of women, religious practices and education (including the manner in which the school program sought to disseminate the teachings of Marx and Lenin) were touched upon though only briefly treated. Considerable space was, however, devoted to the agrarian program of the Communists—especially their land confiscation policy and their abortive attempts at collectivization—the data being drawn from a document prepared for the use of communist discussion groups that had been picked up accidentally by a dyke worker in Nationalist territory.

The report took for granted that close relations existed between the Chinese Communist Party and the Comintern. It stated emphatically, moreover, that the views of the Chinese Communists were based upon the same orthodox Leninist tenets as those of Communists elsewhere and that those persons, whether Chinese or foreign, who doubted this fact were following a will-o'-the-wisp which, if widely pursued, would prove "completely disastrous."

However, the main emphasis in the report was not upon the international aspects of the Chinese Communist movement but rather upon that movement within the context of the Chinese scene. As in the Shanghai report, as much attention was devoted to a discussion of the Kuomintang as of the Communists, and indeed the picture which emerged was that the development of the Communist movement in China depended primarily not upon its own inherent qualities but upon the character of the Kuomintang. The concept which governed all parts of the report was that the vast mass of the peasant population of China, ground down by extreme poverty, was involved in an ever-widening revolutionary upsurge that could only be stopped by economic means. So far, it was said in substance, the Kuomintang had been either unwilling or unable—or both—to relieve the economic misery of the country and unless it succeeded in doing so the Nanking government would itself be driven from power. In that case, the social upheaval throughout the country would continue and there might ultimately emerge in China some sort of communist or socialist government. The major issue was therefore whether the Kuomintang would find within itself the capacity to cope with the situation with which it was confronted or whether through oppression, incompetence, and corruption it would channel the spirit of revolt throughout the nation in an increasingly radical direction.

Despite many deficiencies (judged by later standards) and more than a few errors, the Hankow report provided a considerable amount of information.[7] It was in fact so well regarded by the American consul general at Hankow that he sent it to the legation at Peiping and most of the consulates in China. Many responses were received expressing an unusual degree of appreciation, the most important reply being that of Nelson Johnson who said that he was especially interested in those parts of the report which indicated that the growing wave of revolution in China would only be arrested by an improvement of economic conditions and that he hoped the author of the report would continue his studies of Chinese communism.[8]

The report met with a different reception in Washington, however. Apparently the Far Eastern Division of the State Department was considering giving it the rating of "excellent" when the East European

Division, which at that time contained the Department's specialists on the Soviet Union, objected that it only deserved a "rating of good." The East European Division explained its position in a memorandum to the Far Eastern Division in which it asserted primarily that the statements made in the report concerning the Chinese Soviets and the Chinese Communist Party were not based upon adequate source materials.[9] A person making a study of communism in China, it declared, should examine the publications in that country of such organizations as the Chinese Communist Party and the Pan Pacific Trade Union, and many others, and should check the information in them with noncommunist sources. Events, conditions, policies, and so forth, concerning which there was unanimous agreement, should be segregated from those lacking in such agreement. By analyzing his materials in this fashion, the writer would be in a position to make assertions in regard to the aims and policies of the communistic elements in China based upon quoted sources and to set forth—with similar use of sources— the means which these elements employed and the successes which they attained in putting their policies into effect.

The memorandum of the East European Division is especially significant for the light that it throws upon the manner in which that division itself was operating. In short, it suggests that its members were so exclusively European-oriented that they did not recognize the difficulties involved in obtaining communist materials in China and thought of the situation as being analogous to that in the Soviet Union.[10] This, despite the fact that in the introduction to the Hankow report its writer had especially pointed out the handicaps under which he—and essentially any other American Foreign Service officer attempting to report on communism from China—labored.[11]

But if the East European Division's memorandum reflected a lack of understanding of the situation in China, another episode occurred during this period which demonstrated an equal lack of comprehension on the part of the Far Eastern Division of the subject of communism. In 1933, the vice consul, who had written the Hankow report, began to forward to the Department copies of the *Chinese Workers Correspondence*, a mimeographed sheet which, he explained, was the official English language organ of the Chinese Communist Party. In April 1934, at his instigation, the consulate general at Hankow sent a dispatch to the Department enclosing an issue of the *Chinese Workers Correspondence* that contained Mao Tse-tung's now well-known report on the progress of the Chinese Soviet Republic to the Second National Congress of the Chinese Soviets which had been held in January.[12] The dispatch opened with the statement that "This report, in the opinion of this office, constitutes the most authoritative available expression of the ideology and aims of the Chinese Soviets" and went on to make a few further comments. When this communication reached Washington, it was given to a briefing officer in the Far Eastern Division who, as was customary, attached a note to it for the guidance of higher officials in the division among whom it was then circulated. "I suggest," the note said, "that the covering dispatch be read. The lengthy enclosure would be of interest to a student of Soviet propaganda but is of no particular interest to F.E."[13] Apparently no exception was taken to these remarks by other members of the Far Eastern Division and the briefing officer continued to attach almost precisely the same memorandum to subsequent issues of the *Chinese Workers Correspondence* even though they contained such documents as an order to the Red armies to march northward issued by Chu Teh on August 1, 1934.[14]

At the same time it should be said that the East European Division did come to realize the value of the material in the *Chinese Workers Correspondence* and, soon after the receipt of the copy containing Mao's speech, asked the consulate general at Hankow to forward a full file and all future numbers of the periodical to Washington.[15] The consulate general replied that this was impossible as the publication was illegal in China and could only be obtained intermittently by roundabout means. Nevertheless, it supplied the Department subsequently with whatever issues came into its possession that contained items of significance. These issues were regularly sent by the Far Eastern to the Eastern European Division, as were almost all dispatches from China that had anything to do with the subject of communism. They were in turn routed back by the East European Division but almost invariably without comment.[16] As a result, the China specialists in the Department did not receive the benefit of the knowledge which the Soviet specialists had of Communist affairs. This lack of adequate intercommunication between the two divisions proved to be a very serious matter, as will be discussed in detail later.

In China itself the next important chapter in the reporting on Communism by American Foreign Service officers came with the Long March.[17] Quantitatively the accounts of the Long March were impressive, 150 dispatches being sent in the period alone which began with the Red armies moving out of Kiangsi in October 1934 and ended with their arrival in northwest Szechwan in the following June. But qualitatively the accounts left much to be desired, consisting almost entirely of meticulously detailed descriptions of the route which the communist forces were traversing. The information supplied was to all appearances largely gathered from the press, official communiqués, and talks with Nationalist officers. The purpose of the reports was (a) to apprise the State Department of the major events taking place in each consular district and (b) to provide data which might be useful in case the Red armies created a situation that threatened the security of American nationals residing in the provinces through which the troops were passing or otherwise infringed upon the rights of United States citizens.[18] The dispatches were usually sent by the local consulate in the area where the communist troops were at the time and consisted of relatively brief cables or written statements that were supplemented by monthly reports, a section of which was devoted to the Chinese Communists. The monthly reports all followed the same pattern, being based upon an outline which had been furnished to Foreign Service officers in China by the Department in March 1933.[19] The instructions that went with the outline stated specifically that the monthly reports were intended to supply officials in the Department with a bird's-eye-view of developments in China—political, commercial, legal, and others—so that they should be as factual and as brief as possible. It was further asserted that if a Foreign Service officer wished to make "detailed comments or analyses" he could send them in separate dispatches. However, the record bears testimony to the fact that such comments and analyses were most infrequent.

It is both impractical and unnecessary to attempt to summarize extensively here the information concerning the Long March contained in the many dispatches forwarded to the Department. But the following brief account may give the reader a more concrete impression than can be derived from the foregoing paragraph.[20] The early reports dealt with the activities of the armies of Ho Lung and Hsiao K'o until the time of their junction in October 1934. The evacuation of Kiangsi by the main body of the communist forces under Mao Tsetung and Chu Teh was predicted in advance and it was first assumed that they would attempt to join Ho Lung in Hunan. This idea was soon discarded, however, in favor of the theory that they would try to fight their way through to northern Szechwan, where Chang Kuo-t'ao and Hsu Hsiang-ch'ien had already established a Soviet, in order to create a large communist base which would be in direct touch with the Soviet Union through Sinkiang. The advance of the Red armies westward was described in a long report written in December, which contains the following passage that is typical of the vast majority of the dispatches on the Long March:[21]

Drive into North Kwangtung and South Hunan.
The westward trek of the Reds has continued. On November 2, their

penetration into North Kwangtung resulted in their capture of Yanfa . . . The Reds were enabled to capture Chengkow, Changkiangshu, Kiufengshan, and Pingshek . . . thus breaking the line of communications between Lokshong and Chenhsien in south Hunan. Another route of the Red armies had in the meantime been advancing westward via Jucheng, southeast Hunan, and the coordination of these two movements resulted in the capture of Ichang, South Hunan, on or about November 10 . . .

Advance Through South Hunan into North Kwangsi.

It was necessary for the Reds to move rapidly toward their immediate objective, west Hunan, in as much as two Nanking Army Corps . . . had entered Hunan in mid-November and were en route to Hengyang. The Hunan divisions under Wang Tung-yuan and T'ao Kuang combined their forces at Ichang on November 18 . . . The Reds . . . again divided into two routes, one proceeding southward toward Linhsien, Kwangtung, the other continuing westward toward Ningyuan in South Hunan . . .

Kianghwa and Taohsien in South Hunan were the next hsien cities to fall to the Reds, and between November 20 and November 25 a strong force of Reds entered northeast Kwangsi via Yungankuan, Wenshih, and Lunghukuan.

After the Red armies entered Kweichow, most of the reporting was done, for the time being, by a vice consul at Yunnanfu who, in the same detailed manner, described the diversionary tactics engaged in by the Communists in Kweichow and later in Yunnan, their subsequent spectacular crossing of the Yangtze, and their union with Chang Kuo-t'ao and Hsu Hsiang-ch'ien at Mowkung in June. When the major part of the communist forces left Mowkung, later in the summer, their advance was followed by the consulate general at Hankow. For a while the dispatches from Hankow referred to Chu Teh's forces as having accompanied the main armies northward but eventually this error was corrected. The consulate general for the most part provided descriptions of the tribal areas through which, according to the statements of the Nationalists, the Red troops passed and gave whatever information was available concerning their final trek into Kansu and North Shensi. Some data were supplied on the Communists already in the northwest, especially on Liu Tzu-tan and the Soviet which had grown up under his leadership.

The dispatches on the Long March as a whole seem to indicate that the chief point of dispute concerned itself with the question of how large a communist force escaped from Kiangsi.[22] In December 1934, a discussion arose between a United States representative stationed at Peiping and the author of the Hankow report who had by this time become Third Secretary to the legation. The former took the position that the Red armies had suffered such severe losses on leaving Kiangsi that probably only "small bands of Reds" remained, so that the Communists were virtually eliminated as a serious threat to the government. The latter contended that, on the contrary, a substantial part of the communist forces had broken through the ring of National-ist soldiers surrounding Kiangsi and that, in future, the Communists would be an even greater menace to the Nationalists than theretofore, having demonstrated an extraordinary capacity to overcome all op-position. The opinion expressed by the Third Secretary was supported by his superior officers and was undoubtedly shared by other Amer-ican officials in China. But the idea that the strength of the Com-munists was so depleted after their exit from Kiangsi as to make them a negligible factor persisted even after the Long March was completed and influenced the thinking of many foreign observers in China.

The highlight of the very few dispatches which dealt with anything other than the military side of the Communist movement during the Long March was an account written by the vice consul in Yunnanfu in June 1935, which sought to review some of the more important aspects of the passage of the Communists through the southwest provinces.[23] The communist troops, it was said, were everywhere pre-ceded by political agents who indoctrinated various groups in the population so that, on many occasions, a battle had been won or a city taken even before the soldiers arrived. In a city in Kweichow, for example, communist cells had been organized among the tailors, barbers, and engravers, who, on the arrival of the Red armies outside the city walls, had started a riot within the city which so demoralized the defense that the Communists entered without encountering any resistance. The Communists, it was further stated, could "readily have swollen their ranks to several times their numbers had they so desired." But they generally accepted only such persons as were useful to them, believing that any large increase in their forces would only be undertaken at the expense of their mobility and effective-ness. The Red armies were described as relatively small, probably numbering no more than 50,000, but as exceedingly powerful owing to their strong morale. They had, it was asserted, an "almost fanatical unity of purpose," a spirit of dedication and disinterestedness that had not been seen in any large body of armed forces in China since the early days of the T'aiping rebellion. The report also declared that the leadership of the Red armies was in the hands of men of unusual ability who had been seasoned by years of hardship and, in support of this fact, it gave brief biographical sketches of about a dozen prominent Communists.

Any account of the reports on the Long March would, however, give a very distorted impression indeed if it did not make clear that the major interest of American Foreign Service officers was not in the Long March itself but in the effect of the advance of the communist armies upon Nationalist China. In the early stages of the Long March, most of the dispatches were filled with a kind of cynical despair over the manner in which the southern provinces were meeting the challenge of the communist forces. In one typical dispatch it was said,

The practically unopposed parade of the Communists, numbering at most 60,000 men, poorly equipped, underfed, and worn out from years of fighting, through territory defended by some 200,000 better outfitted, better nourished, and fresh troops representing the provinces of Kwangtung, Kwangsi, Hunan, and Kweichow, is but a pathetic commentary on the hopeless disorganization, petty rivalry, and general inefficiency characteristic of this part of China.[24]

On various occasions it was stated that the head of the provincial government was rumored to have made an agreement with the Communists which enabled them to pass through his area unmolested as long as they left his personal interests intact. In other instances it was reported that the provincial authorities refused to resist the Communists for fear that if any extensive military operations ensued the central government would send its troops into South China which would result in curtailing the power of the local officials. Even more startlingly, it was asserted that the provincial governments were at times so jealous of each other that they preferred to engage in an interprovincial conflict to having their troops unite to fight the Communists.

Nevertheless, as time went by the tone of despair became tempered with a substantial degree of optimism. It was felt that although the Generalissimo had not been able to exterminate the Communists by military action he was indirectly turning the Long March to his own and his government's advantage. The reconstruction movement which the Generalissimo and Madame Chiang Kai-shek introduced into Kiangsi after the expulsion of the Communists, in which American missionaries participated, was regarded by many Foreign Service officers as an exceedingly hopeful measure. And, as related previously, when in the wake of the Long March Chiang Kai-shek visited such provinces as Kweichow and Yunnan and reorganized their administrations and their armies so as to bring them under the control of the central government—for the first time since the establishment of the Nanking regime—it was believed that China was, at long last, advancing a step toward national unity.[25]

By the end of the Long March, the situation in regard to the reporting by American Foreign Service officers was therefore one in which no more than a single Foreign Service officer was attempting to follow the Chinese Communist movement consistently and to provide the State Department with information which might lead to an understanding of various aspects of that movement. For the rest, the reporting which had been meager increased greatly during the Long March but, with rare exceptions, did little more than fulfill the Department's requirements of sending dispatches relating outstanding events (especially those affecting American interests) in any given consular district and consequently limited itself to military developments. As to the situation in Washington, the Far Eastern Division had clearly not yet achieved a sufficient awareness of the significance of communism in general to evaluate the importance of the activities of the Chinese Communists. Furthermore, the Far Eastern Division was receiving little assistance from the Soviet experts in the Department who were themselves not following developments in China closely, perhaps feeling that this was the concern of their colleagues who specialized in Chinese affairs.

THE UNITED FRONT POLICY

The united front policy was proclaimed, it will be recalled, at the 7th Congress of the Third International, which was convened at Moscow in July 1935. The main speech was delivered by Dimitrov, who stated that the immediate aim of the Communist parties of all nations must be to "wipe fascism off the face of the earth" and that, in order to achieve this purpose, they should cooperate in a united front with other political groups and parties even to the point of entering into coalition governments if necessary. At the same time, Dimitrov made clear that the ultimate objective of the Communist movement had not altered and remained the overthrow of capitalism throughout the world. As to the colonial and "semi-colonial" countries, Dimitrov asserted that in these areas the united front should take the form of an "anti-imperialist united front" which, in China, was to assume the task of fighting the Japanese and their Chinese "henchmen"—meaning Chiang Kai-shek and other leaders of the Kuomintang.[26]

Following Dimitrov's speech, many other important addresses on the united front policy were delivered at the congress, among them one by Wang Ming (Ch'en Shao-yü), the chief representative of the Chinese Communist Party in Moscow, who not only proclaimed the necessity for establishing a united front in China but called for the creation of a united front government and army:

In my opinion and in the opinion of the entire Central Committee of the Communist Party of China, our tactics should consist of a joint appeal with the Soviet Government of China to all parties, groups, troops, mass organizations, and to all prominent political and social leaders to organize together with us an All China United People's Government of National Defense and an All China United Anti-Japanese National Defense Army.[27]

At the same time Wang Ming gave no indication that the Chinese Communist Party intended to depart from Dimitrov's thesis that the united front strategy did not mean that the Communists were altering their ultimate aims. Indeed, in an enlarged version of his speech, printed subsequently, he discussed at length the eventual establishment of Soviet power in China and warned against any repetition of the "opportunism" which had led party moderates, such as Ch'en Tu-hsiu, to defeat the revolution of 1927.[28]

That the China specialists in the State Department could have learned much about the proceedings at the 7th Congress from easily accessible sources is evident from a survey of only a few of those sources. The events of the 7th Congress were admittedly not well covered in the American press, even the *New York Times* devoting no more than one sentence (at the end of an article on page 10) to Wang Ming's discourse on China.[29] But a large part of the proceedings were published in the London edition of *Inprecorr*, following the congress, and before the end of 1935 English translations of the main addresses, including those of Dimitrov and Wang Ming, had been printed in pamphlet form by the Workers Library Publishers in New York which advertised that they could be bought "from your nearest bookstore" or by mail from the publishers' local post office box.[30]

Furthermore, the United States embassy in Moscow supplied the East European Division of the State Department with a great deal of information about the congress, including long dispatches containing its own views of the united front policy.[31] Even before the congress opened, Ambassador Bullitt told the Department that he was convinced that the united front policy did not signify any abandonment by the Communists of their ideas of world revolution but was merely part of a maneuver of "reculer pour mieux sauter."[32] The Soviet Union, he said in substance, wanted the Communist parties in the democratic countries to use the united front policy to mobilize those countries against the fascist nations for the protection of the USSR. Not only did Moscow hope thereby to avoid attack but it wished to gain for itself a period of peace in which it could build up its strength to such proportions that it would ultimately be able to pursue its goals almost without challenge. The day after the 7th Congress ended, Bullitt cabled the Department again to say that its proceedings had only confirmed his previous opinions and to urge the President to make a speech to the American people which would leave them in no doubt as to the true nature of the united front policy.[33]

In addition to the material on the 7th Congress, there was in the year following the congress a considerable amount of equally available material concerning the application of the united front policy to China. During the winter of 1935-1936, Wang Ming published five articles in the London edition of *Inprecorr,* three of which were reprinted as parts of a longer article in a special Chinese number of the New York edition of the *Communist International.*[34] In these he not only reaffirmed the statements he had made at the 7th Congress but carried the concept of a united front policy in China further in two important respects. In an article entitled "Replies to Chief Arguments Against the Anti-Imperialist Front in China" (published in the January 11 issue of *Inprecorr*) he suggested a so-called "united front from above" instead of, as previously, a "united front from below"—that is to say, a united front which would include, rather than exclude, Chiang Kai-shek and the whole top leadership of the Kuomintang.[35] In another article, called "Changes In All Spheres Of Our Work," he proposed a variety of extensive modifications in the foreign and domestic program of the Chinese Communist Party in order (a) to make cooperation with western countries possible so that the full energies of the united front would be directed against Japan, and (b) to conciliate various classes of Chinese society, such as the *petit bourgeoisie* and even the rich peasants and some landlords, in the hope of securing their participation in the united front.[36] As earlier, however, Wang Ming did not imply that either the "united front from above" or the proposed alterations in the Chinese Communist program were intended as an abandonment of the objectives which had long been maintained by the Chinese Communists and, indeed, he concluded his article in the *Communist International* with a passage which scarcely left open to doubt that the Chinese Communist Party was and intended to remain an orthodox member of the world communist movement. Proclaiming that the Chinese Communist Party should assume the initiative in forming a united front, Wang Ming declared,

Only the Communist Party of China . . . a party equipped with the doctrine of Marx-Engels-Lenin-Stalin, the party which today relies upon the Soviet Government . . . the Party which is a section of the Leninist Communist International . . . the Communist Party of China alone, which organically links up its struggle with the revolutionary struggle of the proletariat and people of Japan, of the whole East, of the whole world . . . only a party of this kind . . . can set for itself such a historic task.[37]

In addition to carrying Wang Ming's articles, *Inprecorr* and the *Communist International* printed some of the important pronouncements of the united front issued by the leadership of the Chinese Communist Party in China. Thus they published the first really significant declaration of a united front policy made by the Central Committee of the Chinese Communist Party, namely, the statement of mid-June 1935, issued while the Red armies were still in North Szechwan, in which it was said that the "sole path of salvation" for China lay in the establishment of a united front to fight "Japanese imperialism and Chiang Kai-shek."[38] Subsequently they published the August 1, 1935, manifesto of the Central Committee which was the first formal appeal of the Central Committee to the Chinese people to participate in a joint government of national defense and which rapidly became famous in communist circles and was repeatedly referred to in articles such as Wang Ming's.[39] In March 1936, *Inprecorr* carried the text of an interview that it was said Mao Tse-tung had given to a correspondent of the "Red China News Agency" in which he was quoted as having declared that "if Chiang Kai-shek really means to take up the struggle against Japan, then obviously the Soviet government will extend to him the hand of friendship in the field of battle against Japan"—an apparent veering toward a "united front from above."[40] In the same month of March, the Central North Bureau of the Chinese Communist Party issued a manifesto which outlined modifications that were being made in the policies of the Chinese Communist Party that clearly paralleled those advocated by Wang Ming in his "Changes In All Spheres Of Our Work." A copy of the manifesto appeared in the August issue of *China Today*, a left-wing periodical issued in New York, and was at the same time forwarded to the State Department from China by the Foreign Service officer who had been supplying the Far Eastern Division with whatever Chinese communist documents he had been able to procure.[41]

There was therefore sufficient material at hand to bring out the main points concerning the united front policy which were that that policy had been proclaimed by the Comintern to apply to all communist parties; that it was primarily designed to encourage the democratic nations to form a protective ring around the Soviet Union; and that whatever form it took—including united fronts "from above" and "changes in all spheres" of the communists' programs—it would in all probability still be a temporary tactic.

To all appearances, however, the Far Eastern Division did not avail itself of the sources of information at hand. Part of this was perhaps because of the lack of sufficiently close intercommunication between the Far Eastern and the Eastern European sections of the State Department, which has already been emphasized. Many of the reports concerning the 7th Congress furnished by the United States embassy in Moscow to the East European Division were not relayed to the Far Eastern Division. The practice seems to have been to relay only those dispatches which dealt directly with China—a practice which could scarcely fail to give an inadequate picture of the united front policy as a whole.[42] Moreover, while the members of the East European Division undoubtedly saw Wang Ming's articles and the pronouncements of the Chinese Communists, referred to above, they do not appear to have brought them to the attention of officers in the Far Eastern Division. The latter on their part do not seem (as might be expected) to have read such publications as *Inprecorr* and the *Communist International* on their own initiative, judging first by the reception given to the dispatches concerning Wang Ming's articles which were sent from China and secondly by the lack of guidance furnished to American Foreign Service officers in China on the whole subject of the united front policy. Both these matters, however, belong to the part of the story which is related to the reporting on the united front done by American officials in China.

* * * *

Many aspects of the reporting on the united front done by representatives of the United States in China can best be understood if seen in conjunction with the ideas which were prevalent among foreigners in general in China at the time, as American officials almost inevitably reflected some of the views of the foreign communities in which they were living. Thus it is pertinent that many foreigners in China reacted to the first indications that the Chinese Communists were advocating a united front with a feeling of incredulity. This was illustrated when, in the middle of the summer of 1935, the appeal for a united front, which had been issued by the Chinese Communist Party from North Szechwan in June, was circulated anonymously among foreigners in Shanghai, leading to the publication by the *China Weekly Review* of a long article under the title of "Red Ghosts, Japanese Propaganda, or Has the Silly Season Started?"[43] The title was explained by the thesis of the article which was that, as everyone knew that the Chinese Communist Party had ceased to exist after the Red armies left Kiangsi and that the Communists themselves had been all but destroyed, the appeal for a united front must have been issued by ghosts or else the "silly season" had set in—unless (it was added) the appeal was a piece of Japanese propaganda directed at keeping the communist "bogey" alive so as to provide an excuse for Japanese aggression in China.

The latter idea—namely, that the communist menace in China was an invention of the Japanese which they had fabricated to suit their own purposes—became especially widespread among foreigners in the months after the establishment of the communist forces in the northwest as the Japanese launched a particularly violent propaganda campaign, proclaiming the necessity for a Japanese "crusade" to stamp out communism in China. That Ambassador Johnson himself shared this idea is suggested by a passage in a letter which he wrote to Roy Howard in December 1935:

The new stereotype which the Japanese will use and which will justify intervention in China has been invented. It is the word "communist." Just as every man who armed and who offered any opposition to the Japanese in Manchuria was a bandit in 1931 and 1932, so all Chinese offering opposition to Japan in China will become "communists." This is a word which the newspaper correspondents will telegraph home to the press from now on. It is a clever word to use because all the world now hates the communist who is associated in the newspaper public's mind with one who is against God, private property, and organized government.[44]

However, while Johnson apparently tended at this time to believe that the communist threat was largely a propaganda weapon of the Japanese, some of his staff were evidently inclined to accept—or at least not to reject—the idea that the Communists were a menace because they were powerful opponents of the government but not because they were Communists. In February 1936 the embassy forwarded a report to Washington, written by an American official outside of the diplomatic service, which stated that the Chinese Communists could "hardly be said to represent pure Communism" but should be regarded more as "outs" or banished enemies of the Kuomintang militarists as their leaders consisted of the men who had been associated with the Chinese Communist Party during its alliance with the Kuomintang in the 1920's. Nevertheless, it was further asserted, their leaders were expert organizers, dangerously capable of staging a major revolution. In dispatching this report, a member of the embassy staff appended a note which stated that it was a "thoughtful and intelligent" account of the Chinese Communist movement. (It may be added parenthetically that the report was likewise marked by the briefing officer in the Far Eastern Division in Washington as containing "worthwhile" observations on the Chinese Communists.)[45]

As to the united front policy itself, little further consideration was given to it by foreigners in China until the spring of 1936, when the Red armies undertook their abortive excursion into Shansi. One of the best reports of the campaign was sent to the Department by the consulate general at Tientsin at the end of March and was at the same time circulated among various other United States consulates in China.[46] The report stated that the Communists were allegedly insisting that their sole objective in entering Shansi was to "burrow a road" through that province in order to establish a fighting front with the Japanese troops in North China and that they were appealing for a united front to "oppose Yen Hsi-shan and Chiang Kai-shek and then fight Japan." The interpretation put upon these developments by the consulate general was that the Communists were attempting to capitalize on the growing wave of nationalistic and anti-Japanese feeling in China in order to gain adherents.

A few weeks later, the *Shanghai Evening Post and Mercury* (which, as already noted, usually reflected views prevalent in the American business community in Shanghai) published an account in its news columns of Wang Ming's "Changes In All Spheres Of Our Work"— which it had somehow obtained from *Inprecorr*—with an accompanying editorial which stated that the Chinese Communist Party had evidently decided to adopt a "new" policy that called for a united anti-Japanese front in foreign affairs and a more moderate domestic program.[47] The theme of the editorial was in keeping with the opinion expressed by the Tientsin consulate general in that it declared that the Chinese Communists were being motivated by a desire to make use of the emerging patriotic and anti-Japanese sentiment in China in order to "sell" themselves to the Chinese people. The actions of the Communists, the *Post* asserted, proved that they were not, as some people in Shanghai insisted upon believing, merely an "outrageous gang of robbers concerned only in pillage and murder" but were considerably smarter than that. Like "America's Republicans and Democrats" they had sorted over the issues to find those with the greatest popular appeal and had changed their program accordingly so that it contained some "very intelligent notions" which were not "primarily communist at all, but open to anyone." While it could hardly be said that the Communist Party would "overnight become, say, the Democratic Party of China," nevertheless, in view of its new policy, it seemed only "sound judgment to regard it as a potential real Opposition Party."

The text of both the editorial and news article in the *Post* was forwarded to the Department on April 17 by Clarence E. Gauss (then Consul General at Shanghai), who added a comment to the effect that the idea that the Chinese Communists had decided upon a "new" orientation of their policy so that it would henceforth be directed chiefly against Japan was perhaps given substance by the manner in which the communist armies were conducting their Shansi campaign as described by the Tientsin consulate general.[48] On the same day Willys Peck cabled from Nanking that the *Post* had published parts of an "article said to have been written by one Wang Ming, 'leading member of the Internationale in Moscow' and to have appeared (date not given) in the London *International Press Correspondence*, 'official organ of the *Communist Internationale.*'"[49]

According to the article, Peck went on to say, the Chinese Communists had adopted a "new" policy which involved the concentration of their efforts against Japan and the establishment of more normal relations with other so-called imperialist countries. Such a policy would, he asserted, be a complete reversal of that which had hitherto been followed by the Communists but would nevertheless be a logical development in the light of the existing strained relations between the Soviet Union and Japan because it would tend simultaneously to build up possible resources against Japan and to strengthen the communist cause in China by supporting and playing upon the anti-Japanese feeling among the Chinese people. Moreover, although the principles of the "First International"[50] were opposed alike to the furthering of democratic institutions and nationalistic ambitions, nevertheless Russian communist advisers had for their own ends espoused "bourgeois democratic" aims in China in 1927 and, if the reported present plan to direct Chinese communist strength against Japan was a fact, the change in policy appeared to be a reversion to past techniques.

The dispatches from Gauss and Peck, together with the clippings from the *Post*, were circulated upon their arrival in Washington among the China specialists in the Department with a note drawing attention to the main points in Wang Ming's article in a manner which suggests that the article had not as yet been seen by those specialists. This, moreover, was apparently assumed to be the case by the East European Division which, in returning Peck's cable to the Far Eastern Division, noted that his summary of the content of Wang Ming's article was "accurate in substance" and further furnished the reference to the volume and page number in *Inprecorr* where the article could be found. Some weeks later, the Far Eastern Division sent the full text of Wang Ming's article, as it had appeared in *Inprecorr*, to Peck and Gauss with the comment that the "Department understands that *International Press Correspondence* is, in fact, a publication of the *Communist International.*"[51] This comment was presumably elicited by the abundance of quotation marks in the passage from Peck's cable quoted above which implied that he was uncertain about the nature of

Inprecorr and indeed the phraseology of the Far Eastern Division's answer (even allowing for the customary tortuousness of diplomatic terminology) would seem to raise the question of whether some members of the Division did not share part of this uncertainty.

In any case, no real guidance, of the kind to which reference has been made, was given to American Foreign Service officers in China. Specifically, nothing was said to indicate that Wang Ming's article was not an isolated statement but part of a series of interrelated addresses, articles, manifestos, and other pronouncements, which showed that the united front policy was neither "new" nor peculiar to China and that its very nature was such that any modification of the Chinese communist program was far more likely to be a diversionary measure, as Peck had indicated, than a permanent change in the character of the Chinese Communist Party which would qualify it to become a "real Opposition Party."

In the months following the Shansi campaign and the publication of Wang Ming's article by the *Post*, there were few references in the reporting of Foreign Service officers in China to the united front policy of the Chinese Communists. In fact, as during the summer of 1936, the nationalistic feeling throughout China mounted and the country suddenly showed signs of genuine unification under the leadership of Chiang Kai-shek, what little attention might otherwise have been accorded to the Communists by foreigners in China was diverted by the new sense of excitement over the progress which Nationalist China was unexpectedly making.

Yet the midsummer of 1936 marked a great quickening in the tempo of the united front movement in China. On August 25, the Central Committee of the Chinese Communist Party issued its now famous "Open Letter Addressed to the Kuomintang" in which it officially and decisively announced its willingness to adopt "a united front from above" policy. This manifesto was not printed in *Inprecorr* or the *Communist International* or (as far as the present writer can ascertain) in any other publication which was equally accessible in the West, until about five months later, by which time the text had been sent to the Department from the embassy at Peiping.[52] However, an article by Wang Ming written in celebration of the 15th anniversary of the Communist Party of China, which did appear in *Inprecorr* in September 1936 and was reprinted in the *Communist International* in the following month, made many of the same points.[53] Thus it was said that the Chinese Communists were prepared to come to an agreement with Chiang Kai-shek for the establishment of a united front and that if an All Chinese Democratic Republic was formed, with a parliament to be elected by universal suffrage, the Chinese Soviet districts would participate in the parliament and introduce "the same kind of political and administrative regime" in their territory as would govern the rest of China.

Again the *Shanghai Evening Post and Mercury* managed to pick up Wang Ming's article in *Inprecorr* and published an account of it in its issue of October 31.[54] The account asserted at the beginning that Wang Ming had shown "beyond peradventure" that the Chinese Communist Party had "thrown overboard its former policy of revolutionary struggle for the overthrow of the Kuomintang" and was "now seeking civil peace at any price in order to rally the entire country for resistance to Japan." After quoting Wang Ming at some length, it concluded with the statement that the Chinese Communist Party was, in effect, announcing its readiness to "liquidate" the so-called Soviet districts in the interests of a united front.

The news item in the *Post* was apparently the first intimation that American Foreign Service officers in China had of the possibility that the Chinese Communists might agree to a "united front from above." For in August the Foreign Service officer who had been following Chinese Communist developments as closely as the situation in China permitted sent the Far Eastern Division a letter in which he specifically stated that the Chinese Communists, while seeking to cooperate with other groups in China, were continuing to lump the leaders of the Kuomintang together with the Japanese and were referring to the former with such epithets as "running dogs of Japan" and "Chinese rascals and treasonous thieves."[55] As earlier, however, the Department provided no guidance though, as has been related, Wang Ming had published an article in January favoring a united front, inclusive of Chiang Kai-shek, and Mao had stated in an interview two months later that he was prepared to "extend the hand of friendship" to Chiang Kai-shek if the latter arrived at a decision to oppose the Japanese.

The account of Wang Ming's 15th anniversary article in the *Post* was again mailed by the consul general at Shanghai to Washington, where it was again circulated in the Far Eastern Division in a manner which would indicate that it had not been seen there previously.[56] This time, however, the Far Eastern Division did not respond by sending the full text in return, an omission which was of importance because the original contained passages such as the following which had not been quoted in the *Post*:

Finally the success of the new policy of the Chinese Communist Party is assured by the fact that the liberation struggle of the Chinese people is led by the Leninist Communist International, at whose helm stands the tried comrade-in-arms of the great Stalin, the banner-bearer of the struggle against fascism and war, the pride of the world Communist movement, our own Dimitroff. This struggle is led by the International which is inspired by the one who faithfully continues the work of Marx, Engels and Lenin, the genius and strategist of the world revolution, the leader and teacher of toiling mankind, the banner of the victory of world communism, our Stalin.[57]

In short the passages which had not appeared in the *Post* served to reaffirm that, irrespective of the form which the united front policy of the Chinese Communists might take, that policy remained an integral part of the larger united front movement of the whole orthodox communist world.

On November 19, the Foreign Service officer who had sent all the other communist documents to the Department forwarded a copy of the August 25, 1936, manifesto and two interviews that Mao Tse-tung had given to Edgar Snow (who had just concluded his famous four months' visit to Communist China) on the subject of the united front policy.[58] While these documents were exceedingly important for the light which they threw upon the type of agreement that the Communists were prepared to make with Chiang Kai-shek, they did not throw much light upon the nature or purpose of that policy. Moreover, they were not likely to have any strong immediate impact upon the thinking of most American officials whether in China or Washington. For at the time that they were sent from China the eyes of most foreigners in that country were fixed upon the effect which the Suiyuan campaign was having in rallying the Chinese people behind their government. The reports of American Foreign Service officers were therefore filled with speculations as to the influence which the new-found strength of the Chinese people might have upon the Sino-Japanese crisis. As far as officials in Washington were concerned, the documents did not arrive until December 15, at which time they were completely overshadowed by the news of the kid-naping of Chiang Kai-shek at Sian that had taken place a few days earlier.

In retrospect it would seem, therefore, that the situation concerning the coverage of the Communist movement in China, which had prevailed among American officials at the time of the Long March, remained essentially the same up to the Sian incident. The military aspects of the Shansi campaign and other military activities of the Red armies continued to be reported in detail.[59] But on the political side only one Foreign Service officer showed any more than an inter-mittent interest. Even at such central listening posts as Nanking and

Shanghai, officials only learned of the united front policy long after it had come into existence and then obtained their information accidentally from the local *Shanghai Evening Post and Mercury* which, somewhat ironically, was the American businessman's newspaper in China. In addition, in Washington the Far Eastern and the East European Divisions continued, each for its own reasons, to fail to supply Foreign Service officers in China with the information concerning the united front movement that was available in the west. This failure made it far more difficult for Foreign Service officers to see the united front activities of the Chinese Communists in the international context which was necessary for a genuine understanding of them. While Willys Peck's comments on Wang Ming's article show that he stressed the international aspects of the united front policy in China, nevertheless his approach was not typical of that of other Foreign Service officers or of foreigners in China in general. The tendency of most foreign observers was to look inward and not outward beyond China's borders and therefore to regard the united front policy of the Chinese Communists as though it were an indigenous problem which could be understood entirely in terms of the Chinese scene. As the speed and intensity of political developments in China increased, this tendency increased correspondingly and was to reach a new peak as a result of the Sian incident.

THE SIAN INCIDENT

The Sian Incident burst upon a world which was preoccupied with the romance of Mrs. Simpson and King Edward VIII, and the latter's decision to abdicate the throne of England. On the morning of December 12 (the day that Chiang Kai-shek was kidnaped), the *New York Times* announced in large headlines on its front page that "Edward" had delivered his farewell speech and departed from England to join Mrs. Simpson, who had spent the day in taking an automobile ride. On December 13, the predominating headline in the *Chicago Tribune* was "Edward Gone" while only a subhead stated that the "Chinese Dictator" had been captured by a "War Lord."

Rumors concerning the situation in the northwest had indeed been in circulation in China for some months prior to the kidnaping of the Generalissimo. As early as the autumn of 1935, Chang Hsueh-liang and his Tungpei (northeastern) armies had been ordered into Shensi to fight the so-called "remnants" of the Red troops that were just moving into the northwestern provinces. Shortly thereafter, stories began to spread to the effect that the Tungpei soldiers, far from attempting to "annihilate" the Communists, were fraternizing with them. In July it was widely reported from Shensi that Chang Hsueh-liang and some of his Tungpei officers had met at a conference in which they decided to suspend all hostilities against the Communists and to take a much firmer stand on the issue of opposing Japan. It was generally thought that the Young Marshal was being motivated partly by his strong sense of patriotism and well-known liberal tendencies and partly by the fact that his troops, homeless, ill paid, and "exiled" by the Nanking government to one of the most barren areas of China, wanted to fight their way back to their native territory. While some of these rumors were repeated in the official dispatches to Washington from China, American Foreign Service officers did not emphasize the situation in the northwest and moreover presented conflicting accounts which may have left the Department unnecessarily badly prepared for the events which took place at Sian.[60]

As it is difficult to recall the manner in which the story of the Sian incident was currently revealed to the world, the following is a brief account based upon reports that were printed at the time in various English language publications in China and in some outstanding newspapers in the United States.[61]

The Generalissimo, together with many of his best generals and closest advisers, had gone to Sian in the first week of December. On December 12 it became known that early in the morning of that day the Generalissimo had been kidnaped at Sian by Chang Hsueh-liang and General Yang Hu-cheng, who was the Pacification Commissioner of Shensi and the Commander of the Hsipei (northwestern) armies. Few facts were available concerning the way in which the Generalissimo had been seized, but there were rumors that some of his personal bodyguard had been killed and it was apparent that all of his entourage would be detained at Sian.

The Nanking government immediately clamped down a strict censorship on news. Nevertheless, correspondents learned that Chang Hsueh-liang, in cooperation with other leaders of the so-called Shensi rebels, had issued a telegram to the central government making eight demands which they wanted fulfilled before releasing Chiang Kai-shek.[62] In the early stages of the Sian incident, garbled versions of these demands were circulated both in Nationalist China and abroad. But even from such versions it was evident that the rebels were primarily insisting upon the adoption by Nanking of a definite policy of resistance to Japan and the formation of a united anti-Japanese front which would include both the Kuomintang and the Communists.

For several days after the seizure of the Generalissimo, many newspapers carried reports (apparently emanating from Japanese sources) which stated that Chiang Kai-shek had been killed. However, W. H. Donald, the Generalissimo's Australian adviser who was also a close friend of the Young Marshal's, had flown to Sian on December 14 and it became known a few days later that he had telephoned to Nanking to say that the Generalissimo was alive, in good health, and, although under forcible detention, was being comfortably housed and generally well treated. Shortly thereafter the story went the rounds that Chang Hsueh-liang was paying constant visits to the Generalissimo, assuring him of his loyalty and urging him to enter into negotiations on the basis of the eight demands. According to this tale, the Generalissimo had refused to talk to the Young Marshal until the latter had inadvertently addressed him with a term customarily reserved for superiors only. Chiang Kai-shek had then said that if Chang Hsueh-liang was willing to admit his authority, he should release him; but if, on the contrary, the Young Marshal regarded him as his hostage, he should shoot him. A long discussion reportedly followed which ended in Chiang Kai-shek's writing a letter in the presence of the Young Marshal that was taken to Nanking on December 18 by one of the Generalissimo's most trusted advisers who was currently also being held at Sian. The adviser was in addition commissioned by Chang Hsueh-liang to ask the central government to send a representative to Sian to enter into negotiations for the Generalissimo's release.

Meanwhile, one of the most spectacular developments of the crisis was the reaction of the country to the Generalissimo's arrest. Reports from all over China indicated that the Chinese people were stunned by Chang Hsueh-liang's action and that the entire nation was profoundly shaken by the news of Chiang Kai-shek's capture. It was thought that perhaps some of the local factions, such as the Kwangsi-Kwangtung group, would seize the opportunity to defect from the Nanking regime and attempt to overthrow it, but this did not prove to be the case.

At the same time it became known, shortly after the kidnaping of the Generalissimo, that Madame Chiang Kai-shek, supported by some members of her family, notably T. V. Soong, were at odds with many of the leaders of the central government. The latter, immediately after the Sian coup, ordered the Nationalist armies to move northward for an attack upon the rebels. Their position (according to their own public statements) was that, while they recognized that war between Nanking and the rebels might entail the murder of the Generalissimo by his captors at Sian, the maintenance of the authority of the government was more important than the life of any one individual. They therefore believed in quelling the revolt by force rather than yielding to any of the Young Marshal's demands or even entering into negotiations with him. Madame Chiang, on the other hand, allegedly urged that the safety of Chiang Kai-shek was vital to the country's welfare and that an effort should be made to secure his freedom by peaceful means even if some concessions were necessary.

The military side of the discussion was temporarily resolved when Chiang Kai-shek's letter arrived from Sian for it demanded a cessation of all hostilities for about a week, at which time, the Generalissimo asserted, he would probably be in Nanking himself. On the political side, the government remained adamant, however, refusing the Young Marshal's request to send a representative to Sian to conduct negotiations. Finally permission was granted for T. V. Soong to go to Sian, not as a delegate of the government but in a private capacity as a member of the Soong-Chiang family. Soong arrived in Sian on December 20 and returned to Nanking on the following day but refused to say anything to the press other than that he was optimistic about the possibility of a peaceful settlement. On December 22, it was announced that Soong had again flown to Sian, this time with Madame Chiang Kai-shek. A brief period of silence followed in which it was assumed that some sort of negotiations were taking place in order to bring about the Generalissimo's liberation. On December 25, without prior warning, the General and Madame appeared in Nanking, to be followed by the Young Marshal himself. According to all accounts, there was unrestrained rejoicing throughout the country at the resolution of the crisis and the Generalissimo's safe return to the capital. News stories not only from the large cities but also from towns and villages throughout China described widespread popular demonstrations the genuineness of which was not open to question.

As far as the possible role of the Communists in the Sian incident was concerned, reference was repeatedly made in the press to the fraternization which had taken place between the Tungpei and Red armies prior to the Generalissimo's capture and to Chang Hsueh-liang's alleged sympathy for the Communists and their united front policy. Much attention was also paid to the fact that the Young Marshal's demands emphasized cooperation between the Kuomintang and the Communists in a united front against Japan. At one stage of the incident, fear was expressed that the communist armies would march on Sian from the northwest and join forces with the Tungpei and Hsipei troops thereby adding to the military strength of the rebels. But it was not until after the Generalissimo's return to Nanking that outside observers began to suspect that there had been communist leaders at Sian at the time that Chiang Kai-shek's release was being negotiated.

As to the international aspects of the events at Sian, considerable space was devoted in the newspapers to the charges and counter-charges which Japan and the Soviet Union leveled at each other. Many of the early press dispatches concerning the incident were written by foreign correspondents in Tokyo owing to the censorship imposed within China by the Nanking government. As a consequence, emphasis was put upon the attitude of the Japanese government which announced as early as December 12 that, in its opinion, Chang Hsueh-liang was merely acting as a "tool of Moscow" and that the Shensi rebellion was being directed by representatives of the USSR who were at Sian. Subsequently it was reported that a member of the Soviet Union's embassy in China (Ivan Spilwanek) had made a formal visit to the Chinese Foreign Office to deny the Japanese allegations and to state that, far from instigating the Sian rebellion, the Soviet Union was opposed to it.[63] At the same time, *Tass* obtained as wide a circulation as possible of two editorials, published in *Pravda* and *Izvestia* on December 14, which virtually accused Chang Hsueh-liang of being a Japanese agent—all appearances to the contrary— and of fomenting civil war in China in order to bring about the collapse of the united front movement and all other forms of resistance to Japan.[64]

The dispatches of American Foreign Service officers during the Sian incident added nothing of importance to the information which was provided by the press and was generally available in China at the time.[65] In fact, the Department obtained so little information from its representatives in China, after the outbreak of the incident, that the Acting Secretary of State cabled the embassy on December 16 that he found it "very embarrassing" to have received virtually no communications and that he wanted to have at least one bulletin a day.[66] American officials in China, on their part, felt that they did not wish to pass on to Washington the welter of unconfirmed rumors that were going the rounds in China and that it was impossible to get the true story of what was taking place as members of the Nanking government were, as far as could be determined, in the dark themselves.[67]

Concerning the conduct of American policy during the time that the Generalissimo was under detention, the suggestions for action came entirely from Washington. As Hull was at the Buenos Aires Conference, the decisions within the administration were taken by the Acting Secretary of State, Judge R. Walton Moore, in consultation with the President.[68] Two days after the kidnaping of the Generalissimo, Judge Moore cabled to Nelson Johnson at Nanking:

There may exist or may arise an opportunity for appropriate use of influence by the representatives of foreign governments in the best interest of all concerned. It stands to reason that interference with the normal functioning of the National Government in China, especially if this should involve procedures of unlawful violence among and against high officials and perhaps a domestic military conflict, would impair and impede the progress which China has been making toward establishing political stability and economic well-being, would impose new hardships on the Chinese people, would create a new menace to foreign lives and property and interests in general in China, and would add to the danger of international conflict in the Far East. The situation, therefore, is of concern to the world. It is, as you know, the policy of this Government not to interfere or intervene in the internal affairs of foreign countries. At the same time we cannot be indifferent to developments anywhere which jeopardize the interests of nations which are earnestly seeking political and economic stability and which may inject new hazards into a situation already delicate. We are not prepared at this moment to say or to suggest that any action might appropriately be taken by this or other governments in relation to the situation under reference; but we will be carefully observing developments therein and studying the question of possible helpful action.[69]

The ambassador replied on December 16 that the situation was still "exceedingly obscure," owing to lack of information about the purposes of Chang Hsueh-liang.[70] He had, however, conferred with his British, French, and German colleagues and, while all of them regarded conditions as critical, none were prepared to recommend any action. Subsequently, Johnson took the position that in general it would be better for all concerned if the Chinese government were able to find a solution to the situation for itself without bringing in the foreign powers.[71]

Nevertheless, the administration in Washington continued to hope that it might find some means whereby it could "contribute helpfully and without impropriety" toward averting the "tragic developments" and the further political disturbances that might result from the events at Sian.[72] But it never managed to formulate any plan and the only proposal which was made was advanced by the British on December 18. The British were under the impression that negotiations had been conducted at Sian and had been concluded and that Chang Hsueh-liang was, in all probability, prepared to release the Generalissimo if only a means could be found to guarantee his own personal safety.[73] They therefore suggested that the American, Japanese, French, and Italian governments should join them in seeking to make some arrangement for transporting the Young Marshal by air from Sian to Tientsin or Shanghai, whence he could readily depart from China. After prolonged consultations, the various governments concerned, with the exception of the Japanese, agreed to accept the British plan which was submitted to Dr. H. H. Kung on December 24.[74] But as the Generalissimo and Chang Hsueh-liang arrived in Nanking on the following day, there was obviously no need to consider the possibility of the powers rendering any assistance.

Both during and after the Sian incident, American officials in Washington and in China sought to interpret the motives behind the actions of Chang Hsueh-liang and his supporters and their likely consequences. On December 15, Stanley Hornbeck wrote a memorandum to Judge Moore in which he stated that, although it was possible that Chang Hsueh-liang's demands for resistance to the Japanese and cooperation with the Communists were "in some degree" genuine, in all probability the Young Marshal was using these issues to appeal to the "patriotic and radical sentiment" in China as a "blind" for the "more realistic" purposes of obtaining more money, better territory, and other similar benefits for himself and his troops.[75] "It is essentially," Hornbeck asserted, "an old Chinese warlord's game of taking advantage of a situation to improve personal fortunes." As far as the international aspects of the events at Sian were concerned, Hornbeck said that various charges of Russian and Japanese influence had been made but no evidence to support such charges had been forthcoming. It therefore seemed quite possible that the entire affair rested upon "personal and financial considerations."

In a later memorandum written on December 22, which was sent to the President, Hornbeck declared that irrespective of the factors which might have motivated the Sian incident the net result would to all appearances be constructive, assuming that a peaceful solution was reached and the Generalissimo emerged from Sian alive.[76] For the Sian affair had, he asserted, evoked an extraordinarily widespread protestation of loyalty for Chiang Kai-shek on the part of Chinese officials, both civilian and military, and of the Chinese public in general so that the Generalissimo's prestige was greater than ever and the cause of unification of China was being substantially advanced.

In China itself the American Foreign Service officer who expressed himself most decisively on the Sian incident was Ambassador Johnson. In the midst of the incident, the ambassador wrote a letter to Roy Howard in which he stated that it was hard to understand what Chang Hsueh-liang could have in mind in capturing the Generalissimo.[77] However, he said, the Tungpei soldiers were known to have been full of bitterness and discontent ever since they had ignominiously been driven from Manchuria by the Japanese, and in all probability they had put pressure on Chang Hsueh-liang to do something to better their position as a result of which he had acted like a "first-class Chicago gangster." In January, some weeks after the Generalissimo's release, Johnson wrote in much the same vein to William Castle, ascribing the Sian incident to the low morale of the Tungpei armies "under a sick leader who had been a narcotics addict and was the son of a bandit father."[78] But by February the ambassador had apparently come to believe that the events at Sian were not so much the result of the temper of the Tungpei troops as of the personal qualities of Chang Hsueh-liang, especially the irresponsibility and vanity which, it was said, characterized him. For in a letter written in early February to Hornbeck, who had asked for the ambassador's post-mortem assessment of the Sian coup, Johnson said,

Personally, I am inclined to believe that it was nothing more than a kidnaping indulged in by Chang Hsueh-liang and his friend Yang Hu-cheng for the purpose of compelling Chiang Kai-shek to give complete recognition to their talents. Just a kidnaping. As you know, I have always felt that the confusion and complications which we ascribe to the Chinese mind are very much the product of our much more complicated brain.[79]

The ambassador went on to state that he believed Chang Hsueh-liang had persuaded himself that his suddenly devised kidnaping would be welcomed by a large part of the Chinese people owing to the fact that he had overestimated the amount of sentiment throughout the country which was in favor of war with Japan and was in sympathy with the Communists and other Leftists. Surprised when he did not receive the support from the public he expected, the Young Marshal had felt that he must take some action or his very life would be in jeopardy. He had consequently escaped from Sian, taking with him the Generalissimo and Madame Chiang.

It would appear that at least in some respects other high American officials in China agreed with the ambassador's interpretation of the Sian incident. Gauss, for example, believed at the outset that the whole affair rested upon the desire of the Tungpei armies to have some of their grievances remedied and that a "few million dollars" would win back their loyalty. He seems to have maintained this view to the end as he telegraphed to the Department late in December to say that negotiations were being conducted at Sian by T. V. Soong for the purpose of buying off the rebels, following which the revolt would collapse.[80]

As to the consequences of the events at Sian, American Foreign Service officers apparently thought for some time after the incident that the mere fact that a revolt had broken out constituted a serious setback to the cause of unity in China. Ambassador Johnson in particular held this view, stressing frequently that the Sian incident had been a "terrible blow" to the pride of the Chinese people who had begun to feel that they were at last achieving some semblance of solidarity. As time went by, however, Johnson began to take the same position as Hornbeck, namely that, in the last analysis, the detention of the Generalissimo had been of advantage to the Chinese people in that it had revealed to them the depth of their own desire for national unification. By the middle of the spring of 1937, the ambassador, in both his official dispatches and his private correspondence, spoke constantly of the progress toward unity which the Chinese were making and he referred increasingly to the Sian incident as having been a major step in that advance. While his attitude toward the unification of China will be discussed in more detail later, a quotation from a letter which he wrote to Lamont in May 1937 may serve here as a pertinent example:

Up to Sian, Chiang Kai-shek stood alone in his efforts to bring unity out of chaos in China. But Chiang had many of the failings which characterized Woodrow Wilson. He was a lonely, cold, ruthless man who had no friends; he was unable to give his confidence; he was hated by those who believed him ambitious to be a dictator. Nevertheless he received their grudging support because they generally recognized no man in China equalled him in ability to command adherence. When Chang Hsueh-liang seized him at Sian, he issued a call which should have been popular . . . However, people did not listen to him; they turned against him and called him traitor. And why? Well, I think this was because Chang's act in seizing the person of Chiang Kai-shek suddenly made of Chiang Kai-shek a symbol of all that the Chinese people wanted most, namely, unity.[81]

Thus it can be said in summary that there was a belief among United States officials that the kidnaping of the Generalissimo did not involve any strong political and social forces but was the consequence of relatively superficial factors. Initially, there was considerable anxiety in Washington owing to the fear that, if Chiang Kai-shek were killed at Sian, the Chinese nation would again be torn by civil war and revert to a state of virtual chaos. At the same time, Ambassador Johnson entertained the hope that the Nanking government could extricate itself from the situation and generally felt that it should be left to do so. Almost no thought was given to the role which the Chinese Communists might be playing and few questions were asked about the role of the Soviet Union. The main significance of the events at Sian was assumed to be their effect upon the movement for unity among the Chinese people. As has been suggested at the end of the last section, the sheer drama and rapidity of the developments in China tended, to an ever increasing extent, to focus the attention of foreigners upon the Chinese scene itself and, above all, upon the question of whether or not the process of unification would continue until China became an integrated and effective nation. It was in this atmosphere that the negotiations between the Kuomintang and the Communists took place, after the Sian incident, leading to the agreement of September 1937.

The Kuomintang-Communist Negotiations

The events immediately following the Sian incident were scarcely less spectacular than those which had taken place earlier. The Young Marshal was sentenced to ten years imprisonment and then pardoned. But despite the pardon he remained the prisoner of the central government and has to date, in fact, never regained his freedom. Chiang Kai-shek, on his part, issued a statement of self-condemnation in which he blamed the Sian mutiny on his own personal weaknesses and offered his resignation to the government, which it rejected. Early in January he retired to his home at Fenghua where he remained until the middle of February.

It was generally assumed by the public that, while at Fenghua, the Generalissimo was trying to reach some major policy decision which he would announce subsequently.[82] Immediately after Chiang Kai-shek's release from Sian, rumors had begun to circulate in China to the effect that, official statements notwithstanding, he had not been freed unconditionally but had been compelled to make various promises to his captors. Outstanding among such pledges, it was said, was a commitment to cooperate with the Communists and adopt a firmer anti-Japanese policy. There were even some stories to the effect that certain communist leaders had been at Sian and entered into the negotiations between Chiang Kai-shek and the commanders of the Tungpei armies. In the weeks following the Sian incident, there was therefore some speculation as to whether the Generalissimo might be secretly continuing his talks with the representatives of both the Tungpei forces and the Communists, at Fenghua, in an effort to arrive at an agreement on the basis of whatever understanding had been threshed out between them at Sian.

Matters came to a head in mid-February when the CEC (Central Executive Committee) of the Kuomintang met in plenary session. During the course of the meeting a message from the Communists was presented to the CEC stating that, if the central government abandoned its policy of civil war and devoted itself to the task of coping with external aggression, the Communists would: (1) change the name of the Red Army to the "National Revolutionary Army" and place it under the command of the Military Affairs Commission; (2) change the name of the Soviet Government to the "Special Area Government of the Republic of China"; (3) realize democracy in the Soviet districts; and (4) suspend the enforcement of their land confiscation policy so as to concentrate upon the national program of resistance to Japan. The CEC at first ignored the Communists' communication but on the last day of the plenary session (February 21) passed a resolution which seemed on the surface only one more bitter denunciation of the Communists. But in reality it left the door open for negotiations on condition that the Communists would abolish the Red Army and incorporate it into the national forces; dissolve the Soviet Government; stop all Communist propaganda which was in conflict with Sun Yat-sen's three principles; and abandon the class struggle.

Little was known to the general public about the developments which occurred after the plenary session. But unconfirmed stories, again often stemming from Japanese sources, which appeared in some of the English language newspapers in China during March and early April stated that negotiations were conducted between representatives of the Generalissimo and the Communists at Sian for the purpose of reaching an agreement on the basis of the principles that had been enunciated during the plenary session by both sides. In May there were further press reports which asserted that an understanding had been reached or was about to be reached. Interest for the most part centered upon the fact that the terms allegedly provided for the Red armies being placed under the command of the central government. Despite these accounts in the press, no official statement was made by either the Kuomintang or the Communists until September when the Communists issued a manifesto listing the changes they were making in their policies in order to cooperate with the Kuomintang in resistance to Japan—changes which were similar to those which had been proposed to the CEC at its plenary session. The Generalissimo responded with a pronouncement of his own welcoming the Communists' declaration. This interchange of communications received little publicity at the time, however, as it was completely overshadowed by the events of the Sino-Japanese war which was by then in full swing.[83]

As soon as the possibility of a Communist-Kuomintang rapprochement began to be discussed, it received considerable attention in the English language press in China and it may be assumed that the views of two outstanding publications, the *North China Daily News* and the *China Weekly Review,* reflected the opinions of many foreigners. As early as the beginning of January 1937, the *News* took the position that unity was essential for China and that the Kuomintang should therefore make every effort to reach an understanding with the Communists. The *News* discussed the pros and cons of this thesis in many subsequent articles and editorials.[84] Intensely pro-Chiang Kai-shek and equally intensely anti-Communist, it persistently stated that, if the government entered into an agreement with the Reds, it must in no way compromise its integrity but should insist upon the Communists giving up whatever communistic ideas they possessed and abandoning their "foreign insignia and battle-cries" and other "such exotic paraphernalia." The *News,* however, argued much of the time that there was a good chance of the Communists meeting these conditions. The Chinese Communists, it said, whatever their misdeeds, were nevertheless "Chinese citizens and by no means wanting in patriotism." Moreover, they had no genuine connection with "urban" Communist theoreticians as the Chinese Reds were in reality no more than a group of "outlawed adventurers" who had evolved certain agrarian policies (some of which had much to be said for them) by the trial-and-error method during the long years of harsh experience to which they had been subjected. In addition, there was good reason to suppose that the Chinese Communists were sincerely ready to "return to the Kuomintang fold" in that, according to all reports, they were tired and dispirited as a consequence of the hardships they had suffered, and had therefore lost all "initiative and capacity for resistance." Nevertheless, as the summer of 1937 advanced and the Kuomintang-Communist negotiations still seemed to be producing no agreement, the *News* at times became discouraged and felt that the Chinese Communists were, after all, confirmed Communists who would not depart from their radical principles. But in September, when the terms of the Kuomintang-Communist understanding were finally announced, the *News* stated with satisfaction that China had purged herself of communism, the issue being solved by the Communists themselves, who had subordinated their forces and their program to those of the Kuomintang for the "better consolidation of national unity."

The fact that the *North China Daily News* was willing to consider a Kuomintang-Communist agreement favorable was indeed an extraordinary demonstration of the extent to which the thinking concerning the communist problem in China had changed in some sections of the foreign community since the 1925-1928 revolution.

For, as the *China Weekly Review* pointed out in a long editorial devoted to this subject, the *News* some ten years earlier had led a virtual crusade to break up the Kuomintang-Communist alliance.[85]

The attitude of the *China Weekly Review* itself, following the Sian incident, was fundamentally the same as that of the *News*, namely that the unification of China was vital to the welfare of the country and that the so-called "remarriage" of the Kuomintang and the Chinese Communist Party was therefore essentially desirable.[86] J. B. Powell agreed with the *News* further in that he thought the Communists were ready to abandon their "political isms" out of a genuinely patriotic feeling. While he conceded that Moscow might be advising the Chinese Communists to divest themselves of the radical aspects of their program in order to form a united front in China which would oppose Moscow's main enemy in the Far East, that is, Japan, Powell nevertheless felt that Moscow's advice one way or the other made no difference. The "inspiration," he said, which was leading the Chinese Communists to cooperate with the Kuomintang was the same nationalistic inspiration that had determined the Kwangsi-Kwangtung group and other rebellious elements in China to join hands with Nanking.

As far as American Foreign Service officers were concerned, their first reaction to the rumors of a Kuomintang-Communist agreement was, as one consular official stated to the Department, that these rumors were "fantastic." But as time went by and the talk of an agreement persisted, American officials attempted to get inside information. Although for a while they obtained only conflicting stories, just before the plenary session of the CEC, a high Kuomintang official told Ambassador Johnson that the government was ready to reach an understanding with the Communists who had agreed to abandon their "principles and ideals" in favor of a reconciliation with Nanking. In succeeding months, other members of the National government, on at least two occasions, spoke with apparent frankness of the progress of the negotiations with various United States officials.[87]

The reporting to the State Department by American Foreign Service officers, on the Kuomintang-Communist rapprochement, was exceedingly meager and, as was customary, it was for the most part limited to the passing on of purely factual information. Yet there were some important communications from the embassy which, when supplemented by other documents, furnish substantial insight into Ambassador Johnson's own point of view.

Following the CEC plenary session, Johnson recorded in an official memorandum that he had paid a call on Wang Ching-wei during the course of which he (Johnson) had said that "There was reason for gratification in that the Communist troubles seemed to have been effectively dealt with and the Communists themselves seemed to have been willing to cooperate with the Government."[88] Writing to a friend of this interview subsequently, the ambassador stated that Wang had appeared "skeptical" of any attempt at whole-hearted collaboration with the Communists and added,

I think however that there is a growing feeling among the Chinese that the Communists are a force which must be reckoned with in the future development of China; that they represent a living spirit which should be brought into the picture if possible.[89]

As the spring of 1937 advanced, Johnson was, as has been indicated, more and more deeply impressed with the growing solidarity of the Chinese people. In a dispatch to the Department in May he discussed at length the manner in which Chiang Kai-shek had in his opinion become what he repeatedly referred to as the "living symbol of unity," in the minds of the Chinese people.[90] At the same time he stated that the Chinese people had themselves undergone such a profound change in recognizing the need for unification that, even if the country were deprived of the Generalissimo's leadership, the various factions in China (among which he seemed to include the Communists) would hold together. In June he wrote again in a similar tone and asserted that the resolution of the enmity between the Kuomintang and the Southwest militarists and the fact that the Kuomintang and the Communists were, to all appearances, about to establish a working arrangement, were "certain indications" of the extent to which the Chinese people, however heterogeneous in spoken language, physique, temperament, and political beliefs, had come to realize the necessity of cooperating in forming "a real nation under effective government."[91]

In short, Johnson seems to have shared the view that a Kuomintang-Communist understanding was to be welcomed in the national interest and that the factor which had impelled the Communists to propose such an understanding was that, like all other political groups in China, they had been affected by and become part of the wave of nationalism that was sweeping the country. There is no reason to suppose that Ambassador Johnson did not believe that the Communists were still Communists. But it is very likely that his attitude, in so far as it was defined, was analogous to that of a future ambassador to China—John Leighton Stuart—who, according to the *China Weekly Review*, said in an address at Yenching in February 1937 that "there are very few Chinese who are communistic first and Chinese afterwards; they are Chinese first and Communistic afterwards."[92]

The dispatches on the Chinese Communists which were sent to the State Department from China, following the Sian incident, were however supplemented by reports from a wholly new source, namely, the United States embassy in the Soviet Union. In June 1936 the embassy had initiated a series of memoranda on "Soviet Relations with Far Eastern Countries." But, in keeping with the general tendency on the part of the Soviet specialists in the administration to overlook China, the memorandum had been limited to the relations of the USSR with Japan and Manchukuo. However, following the Sian incident George Kennan, who was currently writing the memoranda, informed the State Department that he would like henceforth to include a section on Soviet-Chinese relations. Consequently until his reassignment to Washington, in the summer of 1937, he reported regularly on Moscow's connections with both the Nanking government and the Chinese Communists.[93]

Kennan's fundamental thesis was that the objective of Moscow in regard to China was to build up that country so that it would be an effective shield for the Soviet Union against Japan. The Kremlin, he said, was therefore willing to conciliate Nanking, even to the point of making "enormous concessions in dogma," and might go so far as to enter into an alliance with Chiang Kai-shek in spite of its intense dislike of him. If it did so, it would not, however, expect to furnish Nanking with more than a minimum of positive or material aid, even in case of a Sino-Japanese war, but rather would limit itself to "patronizing" offers of moral support from one "democratic" nation to another as it had under similar conditions in other countries in the past.

Kennan thought further that, on the active side, the policy of the Soviet Union would be directed toward encouraging China to fight Moscow's battles against Japan through the use of the Chinese Communists and the united front policy. As the Kuomintang-Communist negotiations for an agreement proceeded, Kennan warned in effect, that the key to the activities of the Chinese Communists lay not in China but in Moscow. There was every indication, he declared, that the policies of the Chinese Communist Party, the Communist International, and the Soviet government were being well coordinated and were "in fact only integral portions of the policy of the Moscow Communist Party leaders." The latter's aim was, to all appearances, to obtain as a *quid pro quo* for Chinese Communist support of the Nanking government, the elimination of the pro-Japanese elements in that government thereby turning China into an effective weapon against Japan. In addition, it was hoped to enhance Soviet influence in China proper by securing the legalization of the Chinese Communist Party to open the way for its reintroduction into the inner councils of the Kuomintang according to "the ancient tactics of the Wooden Horse of Troy." By way of emphasizing even further the degree to which the Chinese Communist efforts to form a united front with the Kuomintang reflected the wishes of Moscow, Kennan forwarded an article of Wang Ming's which appeared in *Bolshevik* in mid-April. The article, Kennan asserted, showed definitely (for anyone who still had doubts on the subject) that the policy which was currently being followed by the Chinese Communist Party not only enjoyed "the full approval and support of Moscow but was probably laid down in the Kremlin." In the first place, the appearance of the article in *Bolshevik*, the organ of the Central Committee of the All Union Communist Party, left "not the faintest shred of doubt" that it had the Kremlin's sanction. Secondly, the fact that the article itself expressed approval of the Chinese Communist policy meant that the Chinese Communists were being backed and perhaps directed by the Moscow leaders as the latter had never shown any inclination to speak favorably of the activities of any communist faction abroad over which they did not have control.

Kennan was therefore providing some of the international orientation that had been lacking in the reports of the American Foreign Service officers from China. Looking at the Chinese scene from the outside in, not as one immersed in China's problems, he saw the Chinese Communists as Communists first and foremost and as Chinese long afterwards. Far from believing that their effort to establish a united front with Nanking was patriotically motivated to assure China's consolidation and welfare, he regarded the united front in China as primarily a creature of the Soviet Union which was itself prepared to play China off against Japan regardless of the cost to the Chinese people.

After Kennan's return to the United States, the embassy in Moscow not only continued to provide the Department with information on Sino-Soviet affairs in its monthly summaries of the Soviet Union's relations with the Far East but, at Kennan's instigation, supplemented those summaries with cabled dispatches on important developments between China and the USSR.[94] Whether the reports which were received from the Moscow embassy resulted in any officials in the Far Eastern Division in Washington and any American Foreign Service officers in China viewing the Chinese Communist movement in a wider perspective than theretofore, it is impossible to say without examining the documents in the State Department files for the years which stretch beyond the boundaries of this study. However, it must be remembered that, during the period of the Sino-Japanese war, most American Foreign Service officers in China worked under near-chaotic conditions so that there were many obstacles to intercommunication. Moreover, while foreigners had an access to the Chinese Communists which they did not have earlier, all problems in China were completely overshadowed by the war itself so that the most important question concerning the Kuomintang-Communist issue appeared more than ever to be whether the two factions could maintain sufficient unity to continue resistance to Japan. In retrospect it therefore seems especially unfortunate that American officials as a whole did not achieve a genuine understanding of the Chinese Communist movement in the prewar years. On the other hand, it must be recognized that the atmosphere of the times militated against attaining any such understanding. Not only was the significance of the Chinese Communist movement generally underestimated, but so little was known about the Chinese Communists by foreign observers that ideas— even among foreigners living in China—fluctuated from believing that the Communists constituted a powerful threat to the Nanking government to believing that they were a factor of no importance, and from regarding them as puppets of Moscow to assuming that they were almost wholly divorced from the Soviet Union and the Comintern. That the ideas which were held did not depend upon the political outlook of the holder is evident from the fact that the most conservative and rabidly anti-Communist foreign publications in China were among the foremost to express the view that the Chinese Communists were not really Communists but were, in the last analysis, only Chinese patriots. For American officials to have gained real insight into the Chinese Communist movement would therefore have required rising above the general level of political thinking of the times and this, for the most part, they understandably did not do.

The Washington Naval Treaty, as already related, came to an end in December 1936. But even before this date arrived, in the autumn of 1936, the British Foreign Office suggested that Great Britain, Japan, and the United States should enter into a new agreement the sole purpose of which would be to prolong the life of Article XIX of the treaty, which provided for the maintenance of the *status quo* in regard to fortifications and naval bases on their insular possessions in the Pacific.

As the British proposal was only part of a series of developments concerning the vital question of military defenses on the Pacific islands, it seems advisable to recall some of the highlights of the history of Article XIX and a few related agreements. Before the Washington Conference of 1921 the United States Navy, believing that our greatest weakness in the Pacific lay in a lack of naval bases, had had plans to build a naval base at Guam and a subsidiary base in the Philippines.[1] These plans had been discussed in Congress and had created considerable anxiety in Japan. It was therefore rumored that the Japanese delegates would come to the Washington Conference prepared to seek a treaty that would prohibit the powers from further fortifying their islands in the Pacific in exchange for which the Japanese would consent to certain limitations being imposed upon their navy. In anticipation of such an eventuality, the General Board of the United States Navy warned the administration against making any commitments which would prevent the American government from constructing bases in its Pacific territories and indeed recommended not even entering into a discussion of this subject. Nevertheless, when, as it turned out, the Japanese did propose that Great Britain and the United States agree to maintain the *status quo* on fortifications and bases in the Pacific, in return for Japan's consenting to the 5:5:3 ratio, Hughes decided to disregard the advice of his naval experts and negotiate on the basis of the Japanese suggestion. The Secretary apparently felt that the importance of establishing the 5:5:3 ratio outweighed other considerations and, in addition, he was influenced by the fact that the American delegation at the conference was convinced that Congress would not vote the funds necessary to make such islands as Guam and the Philippines defensible in case of war.[2] As a consequence, Article XIX was inserted in the Washington Treaty.[3] At the same time, Hughes sought, insofar as possible, to make sure that Japan would refrain from engaging in military preparations not only on the islands specifically mentioned in Article XIX but also on the former German islands which had been given to Japan under mandate by the signatories of the Versailles Treaty.[4] In accepting the mandate, Japan had definitely pledged herself not to undertake military construction or establish bases on the mandated territories.[5] Secretary Hughes obtained a renewal of this pledge in a treaty signed with Japan in February 1922.[6] Furthermore, in order to have some means of checking, by first-hand observation, whether the Japanese were living up to their promises, Hughes made various arrangements which committed the Japanese to permit American vessels and American nationals to visit the islands.[7]

According to statements made years later by Captain Zacharias, an American Naval Intelligence officer, the United States Naval Intelligence office at Tokyo (at which he was stationed for a time) began to suspect that Japan was arming the mandated islands in the early 1920's. Lacking sufficient trained personnel to dispatch as observers, it suggested to the authorities in Washington that it might be well to have United States naval vessels stop at the islands on "courtesy calls" of the type which were customarily paid to foreign ports.[8] Captain Zacharias asserts that, while the Navy accepted this suggestion with enthusiasm, the State Department discouraged it, for fear of creating trouble with Japan, and made no more than "half-hearted efforts" to get permission for naval vessels to visit the islands—efforts to which the Japanese paid little attention.

In any event, prior to the Roosevelt administration, the last of the attempts to obtain entry into the mandates for United States naval vessels was made in 1929.[9] In the spring of that year, again at the Navy's urging, the State Department asked the Japanese whether a United States destroyer, which was then on its way home from the Far East, could stop at certain unopened ports (that is, ports normally closed to foreign trade) in the mandated islands. The Japanese indicated their opposition and the State Department dropped the issue without protest. A few months later, the Department inquired as to whether American naval vessels engaged in obtaining hydrographic information could from time to time call at unopened ports and harbors in the mandates.[10] In an obvious attempt to avoid controversy, the Department stated that it was not raising the legal question of the right of the Japanese to exclude ships from such places; but, it added, it did wish to point out that the United States government had always accorded the privilege of visiting similar areas, situated on United States territory, to the ships of foreign governments and that it would appreciate having this courtesy reciprocated. After considerable delay, the Japanese replied that they did not want United States naval vessels to call at the mandated islands unless Japanese officials were present and that such officials only went to many parts of the islands on the infrequent occasions when routine tours of inspection took them there. Edwin Neville, then United States chargé at Tokyo, explained to the Department that the Japanese feared that the natives in the mandates might become panicky at the sight of a foreign man-of-war so that the presence of a Japanese official was desirable to keep order; moreover, the Japanese felt that it would be "decidedly impolite" not to have a representative on the spot to accord an official welcome to the ship of a foreign government visiting a region under Japanese jurisdiction. Again the Department made no protest and abided by the wishes of the Japanese throughout the next years.

The next development concerning the fortification of the mandated islands, including the right to visit them, took the form of charges in the press that the Japanese were preparing the islands for possible use in case of war.[11] As a result of these charges, the members of the Permanent Mandates Commission of the League of Nations carefully cross-examined the Japanese representative, Ito, who appeared before them at their regular meeting in November 1932.[12] The chairman of the commission pointed out that the Japanese had failed to allude to the execution of the military and naval clauses of the mandate in any of their annual reports for the preceding seven years and that the budget indicated that Japan was spending over three times more on "harbor improvements" in the islands than earlier. A naval base, the chairman continued, was not necessarily self-evident and could be disguised as harbor works;[13] it was therefore of the "greatest importance" for Japan to show conclusively that the projects she was undertaking were simply for commercial use and generally to refute the charges being made against her.

Not only did Ito seek to reassure the commission by stating that the rumors concerning Japan's activities in the mandates were unfounded, but the Japanese government itself sent the commission a letter reinforcing Ito's assertions.[14] Nevertheless, the commision was obviously not satisfied as, despite the protest of one of its members, it deliberately recorded in its final report the fact that the question of Japan's violation of the nonfortifications provisions in the mandate had been raised.[15] Moreover, two years later (in November 1934) the commission renewed its interrogation of Ito declaring that the rumors concerning naval and air bases in the Japanese mandates were still persistently appearing in the press.[16] The chairman observed that Ito had constantly urged the commission to treat these rumors with "circumspection" but that the commission would like to have information which showed conclusively that the reports were "pure fabrication." As the commission was in no position to send observers to the spot, the chairman suggested that it would be advisable, in the interests of the mandatory itself, to have foreign warships visit the mandated islands at the first opportunity. Further, the commission's report for 1934 asserted very specifically that it was not satisfied with the explanations which the Japanese had given to prove that the expenditures for the islands were only for civil and commercial purposes and that it would like to have "further particulars" furnished at next year's annual meeting.[17] Since, however, the Japanese did not clarify the situation, some of the members of the commission went out of their way to show, by the unusual sharpness of their tone in interrogating Ito again at the 1935 meeting, that their doubts concerning the arming of the mandates were not dissipated.[18] William Rappard, one of the best known members of the commission, said, for example, that he would be glad to know why the Japanese government was so carefully passing regulations concerning the conditions under which the islands could be visited; the commission was not used to such legislation which seemed to reflect a strong desire to keep the "inquisitive at a distance." Ito replied that the commission would never understand Eastern problems if it sought to judge them from a Western standpoint for "'East is East and West is West, and never the twain shall meet'"; the members of the commission should not press their judgments too far. To this Rappard responded that of all the Orientals who had ever come to Geneva, none had shown a more complete understanding of Western institutions than Ito, so that the philosophical considerations he was advancing came as something of a surprise.

The idea that the Mandates Commission was, and remained throughout the 1930's, suspicious of Japan's activities in the mandates was not an obscure matter. The reports and the minutes of the commission's meetings were all published and accounts of them often appeared in American newspapers such as the *New York Times* which, for instance, on December 24, 1934 carried on its front page the headline, "League Board Criticizes Japan On Mandate; Finds Reply As To

Policy Is Unsatisfactory."[19] In addition to the commission's suspicions, the United States government was itself receiving information, through its representatives in Japan, which indicated that the Japanese might be fortifying Yap, Saipan, and Palau.[20] While the information was admittedly not conclusive, it was sufficiently impressive to lead Grew to write in his diary in March 1933 that there was "abundant first-hand evidence" that Japan was engaging in military preparations on the mandated islands and that the whole problem of fortifications on the islands was "full of potential dynamite" and might "yet cause as much trouble as Manchuria."[21]

Nevertheless, the Roosevelt administration approached the subject of access to the mandated islands very cautiously.[22] The first time the issue was raised with Ambassador Saito was in June 1934 when the latter was about to depart for a brief trip home. During the course of a casual conversation which ranged over a variety of subjects, Hornbeck mentioned the problem of access by foreign vessels, especially naval vessels, to the mandated islands.[23] Hornbeck explained that in the past Great Britain, the United States, and other foreign governments had demanded such access but had always been refused and that the United States Navy Department continued to draw the State Department's attention to this matter from time to time. It therefore seemed to him (Hornbeck) that it might be useful for the ambassador to find out, during his trip to Tokyo, whether anything could be done to remedy the situation "without creating excitement or ill feeling"; if so, a cause of suspicion on the part of foreigners toward Japan would have been removed and good will and confidence created. On his return from Japan some months later, Saito reported to Hornbeck that he had talked with the naval authorities in Tokyo and that, according to his understanding, they were prepared to grant any request for foreign naval vessels to cruise among the mandated islands freely and enter any port they wished.[24]

No request was made by the State Department, however, until two years later.[25] In June 1936 Secretary Hull wired Grew saying that there had for some time been a strong undercurrent of suspicion that both the United States and Japan were fortifying their possessions in the Pacific, contrary to their treaty commitments.[26] The United States had therefore made a point of granting various requests of the Japanese to have their naval vessels visit closed harbors in Alaska and the Aleutians in the hope that, if Japanese naval officers saw these areas at first hand, they would be convinced that the United States was not doing anything which ran counter to the Washington Naval Treaty; unfortunately the Japanese had not reciprocated in kind.

While it was understandable, the Secretary continued, that the Japanese government might not wish to "give any countenance to irresponsible allegations" that it was arming the Pacific islands, nevertheless the fact that suspicion of its activities persisted was breeding distrust between Japan and America, clearly an unfortunate situation for which a solution should be found. Concretely, Hull suggested that Grew should inform the Japanese Foreign Office that the U.S. destroyer *Alden* was about to leave for its Asiatic station and that an invitation by the Japanese government to the *Alden* to visit some of the closed ports in the mandated islands would have a very good effect on American-Japanese relations.

Grew replied that he doubted whether the Secretary's proposal would produce the desired results.[27] As the Japanese had repeatedly refused to give American naval vessels access to the mandates in the past, they would undoubtedly do so again. If this should prove the case, the fact that Japan had rebuffed the United States might find its way into the press which would only serve to intensify suspicion on both sides of the ocean. Indeed, Grew asserted, the only benefit that in his opinion could possibly be derived from reopening the issue of visiting the mandates was that it would force the Japanese to restate their position which might be useful in case any discussion of the fortifications issue took place after the expiration of the Washington Naval Treaty; in other words, if a "showdown" was wanted, the Secretary's proposal would no doubt be of service.

Hull's response indicated very clearly, however, that he had no desire for a "showdown."[28] There was no connection, he stated emphatically, between his suggestion concerning the *Alden* and any discussion of Article XIX of the Washington Treaty which might arise in future. His suggestion stemmed from two considerations only: the administration wanted to see something done toward alleviating suspicion and improving the relations between Japan and the United States; and the Navy was increasingly considering the possibility of refusing permission to Japanese ships to enter certain American harbors if the Japanese persisted in denying access by our ships to the mandated islands. "Would it not be better," the Secretary asked, "for them [the Japanese] to take some step toward preventing such a possible development?" However, Hull added, it was not the Department's "thought to make of the matter an issue." Grew was not to present the Department's suggestions regarding the *Alden* as an idea conceived in Washington but rather as a scheme which had occurred to him personally and which he was advancing on his own initiative. This procedure would, moreover, have the advantage of minimizing the risk of publicity and also the risk of a definite refusal or rebuff by the Japanese.

On July 8, Ambassador Grew spoke to the Japanese Foreign Minister concerning the *Alden* in accordance with his instructions.[29] As a month went by with no comment from the Japanese government (other than that its various ministries were studying the plan), it became obvious that, in preference to giving an unfavorable answer, the Japanese were letting the issue die by default.[30] By way of expressing its displeasure, the administration in Washington on August 7 refused to allow a Japanese government training ship to stop at a harbor in Hawaii which was not listed as a port of entry.[31] Perhaps hoping that this refusal had constituted enough pressure to persuade the Japanese government to reverse its position, the Department a few days later asked for permission to have the U.S.S. *Gold Star* visit Saipan, Truk, and Palau on certain dates which were specifically listed, but its request was rejected.[32] The Department thereupon in mid-September instructed Grew to inform the Japanese Foreign Office orally that the schedule of the *Gold Star* had been changed.[33] Grew was to say that, in view of the repeated indications by the Japanese government of its willingness to have American ships enter the open ports of the mandated islands, the Department assumed that the initial objections of the Japanese to the visits of the *Gold Star* must have been caused by some inconvenience attached to the dates that had originally been stipulated. In response to Grew's approach, the Foreign Office replied with a note to the effect that it was unable "for various reasons" to consent to the proposed trip of the *Gold Star*.[34] At the same time the Japanese turned down a similar request from the British, stating that any call by British naval vessels at the open ports of the mandates would be "inconvenient for some time to come."[35] During 1937, the State Department on two separate occasions again asked whether a visit by the *Gold Star* to Saipan, Truk, and Palau would be "agreeable" to the Japanese and was again told that it would not.[36]

In view of the fact that talk about Japan's arming of the mandates was already prevalent in the 1930's, one might expect to find that the subject of fortifications and bases in the Pacific had played a major role in the naval negotiations of 1934 and 1935. But only one discussion of the matter took place, consisting of a brief and highly inconclusive exchange between Sir John Simon and Norman Davis.[37] The British did, however, raise the question of renewing part of Article XIX in connection with the plan, known as the "middle course," which they proposed as a solution of the naval impasse.[38]

The British idea, insofar as it was defined to Davis, was that Great Britain and the United States should agree to maintain the "provisions for nonfortification of bases in the Far East" on condition that there be an "additional provision granting the right of full and free inspection."[39]

After the naval conference the issue of military defenses on the Pacific islands was set aside until the autumn of 1936 when, as related at the outset of this chapter, the British advanced a new plan for the continuation of Article XIX after the Washington Treaty lapsed. Victor Mallet, the British chargé in Washington who conveyed the plan to the State Department, said that the Japanese had indicated several months earlier that they were prepared to consider the renewal of Article XIX.[40] The British government, after studying the matter, had arrived at the conclusion that the article ought certainly to be preserved but in a manner which would allow "more freedom to bring up to date and extend existing fortifications." Mallet explained in confidence that his government felt it was "most imperative" to "modernize" its fortifications at Hong Kong.

The British suggestion was discussed at a meeting called for that purpose on September 11, which was attended by Norman Davis and nine officials of the State, War, and Navy Departments.[41] The military implications of the proposal were considered first, the issue being whether the United States did in fact want to fortify its islands in the west Pacific in which case, as Davis put the matter, it had "better let the treaty go by the board" and free its hands. Speaking respectively for the Army and the Navy, Major General Embick and Admiral Standley indicated that the military services did not expect to establish further defenses in the territories covered by Article XIX. The talk centered mainly on the Philippines, concerning which General Embick said most emphatically that in the event of war they would be a detriment to the United States and that "Corregidor was merely a refuge, a place where the flag might be kept flying." The meeting then took up the political aspects of the British plan. Eugene H. Dooman, representing the State Department, read a prepared statement which opened with a long excerpt from the minutes of the Washington conference that was intended to clarify the original purpose of Article XIX. Thereafter, the statement set forth the following thesis: It was entirely clear from the record, it asserted, that the status quo on fortifications and bases had been agreed to by the United States at the Washington Conference as a concession to Japan. Whether the issue of military defenses in the Pacific was still as important as in 1922 was of course a "purely technical question." At the same time the interest that the Japanese were demonstrating in the renewal of Article XIX showed that it remained significant in their eyes. It was also clear that Article XIX had been only one item in a comprehensive agreement, involving not only military but political problems, which had been reached at the Washington Conference as a result of point-by-point bargaining. To proceed at this stage to separate a single factor—especially a factor which represented a concession by the United States— and set it up in an independent treaty without receiving compensations would be unwise. Important alterations were taking place in the Far East so that approximately ten years hence America would be faced with a totally new set of conditions at which time it might wish to negotiate another general settlement comparable to that which had resulted from the Washington Conference.

Norman Davis, serving as chairman of the meeting, also advanced certain political considerations. He indicated that he was puzzled by the motives of the British in suggesting the renewal of Article XIX and felt that perhaps they were being influenced by Ambassador Yoshida who was seeking a rapprochement with Great Britain with the expressed intention of trying ultimately to extend it to the United States.[42] Davis declared that in his opinion, if the United States allowed itself to be drawn into negotiations over Article XIX, it would soon be confronted with a request from the British and the Japanese for a tripartite nonaggression pact. Since the administration was opposed to such a pact, it should be wary of entering into any formal discussions. In addition, Davis took a position that was closely associated with that which Secretary Hull had so adamantly maintained during the naval talks of 1934. In essence he contended that the administration should not conclude a new agreement with the Japanese, which was limited to a few of the many provisions that made up the Washington Conference treaties, because to do so would suggest that the United States viewed with tolerance Japan's repudiation of the other provisions.

All those present at the meeting of September 11 fully concurred with the opinions expressed by both Dooman and Davis. As a result an oral reply was given to the British chargé that was actually based upon a written note, handed to him in confidence, which rejected the British plan.[43] The arguments advanced were largely those which had been set forth in Dooman's memorandum. At the same time, however, it was emphatically stated that in communicating its decision not to join with the British and the Japanese governments in a renewal of Article XIX, the United States government wished it "clearly understood" that it had "no desire to alter" and "no present intention of altering" the status quo in fortifications in the Pacific. Moreover, the British were assured that although the United States government could not at present see that it would derive any benefits from the renewal of Article XIX, it would be glad to consider any additional comments the British might care to make. But as nothing further was heard from the British, matters were allowed to rest.

However, about two months later a new suggestion concerning fortifications and bases in the Pacific was made from an unexpected source, namely, President Roosevelt. On November 16, 1936, the President stated at a Cabinet meeting that he would like to initiate a plan for the neutralization of the Pacific islands. The occasion for this was that Roosevelt was about to leave for the Pan American Conference at Buenos Aires, where he expected to conclude a series of agreements for the maintenance of peace in the Americas. These, he hoped, would pave the way for the negotiation of similar understandings in other parts of the world that would serve to relieve the ever-increasing international tension. In his diary entry of November 20, Secretary Ickes, referring to Roosevelt's comments at the cabinet meeting, wrote,

He said that if we were successful in reaching some sort of an understanding on peace and disarmament at the Buenos Aires Conference, we might later try for something of the same sort in the Pacific Ocean. This would be an ambitious program. He did not go much into details, but he suggested a possible agreement for the disarmament of practically everything in the Pacific except Japan, Australia, New Zealand, and Singapore. This would leave the Philippines, Shanghai, Hong Kong, the Dutch East Indies, British North Borneo, and other important places neutralized. The question was raised whether, as a condition for such an agreement, Japan might not ask us to disarm in Hawaii, but the President made the point that Hawaii is only about one-third of the way to Japan and that such a request would not be reasonable. He said that he would be willing to disarm so far as American Samoa is concerned. Then the question of Alaska came up, and in that connection the President said that we would be willing to except from fortifications that portion of Alaska nearest Japan.[44]

Toward the end of January, Ickes recorded that the President had again spoken to him about the "possibility of a neutralization policy of the Pacific on the part of the Great Powers" on a "couple of occasions."[45]

The President apparently did not forget his neutralization scheme, for in February he asked the State Department to explore the idea of neutralizing the Pacific islands and to furnish him with a memorandum. The result was an exceedingly long memorandum, drafted in the Far Eastern Division, which started by saying that as the concept of "neutralization" was very vague, it had best be discarded in favor of the more specific concepts of nonaggression and mutual pledges to respect each other's rights; and that the term "Pacific islands," being also very broad, needed definition.[46] On the latter point it stated that fifteen countries owned islands in the Pacific, of which the following would have to be included in any neutralization agreement: the United States, Great Britain, Japan, the Netherlands, France, Australia, and New Zealand. Some nations with relatively small holdings might be excluded, although China and the Soviet Union were such essential parts of the whole political problem of the Pacific area that it would probably be unwise to omit them under any circumstances.

The memorandum then listed four separate types of neutralization agreements that could conceivably be applied in the Pacific. Three of these—initialed *A, C,* and *D*—were not dissimilar. *A* was an agreement by which the signatories pledged themselves to respect each other's rights in their insular possessions, including the mandates, in the Pacific. *C* had a larger geographic scope, as it extended these pledges to cover not only insular possessions but also "outlying dependencies" such as French Indochina and the Federated Malay States. *D* maintained the broader geographic scope but added to the obligation to respect each other's rights the idea of nonaggression in the form of a commitment not to use force for any purpose inconsistent with the principles of the Kellogg-Briand Pact. Agreement *B,* however, was quite different from the others in that it bound its signatories "to limit or refrain from erecting fortifications" in any of their islands in the Pacific—again including the mandates.

After listing these agreements, the memorandum went on to discuss each one in detail under the headings of "Considerations Pro" and "Considerations Contra." The arguments on the positive side remained much the same throughout, being largely (a) that the American people would welcome any international understanding for the maintenance of peace which did not demand more than moral (including diplomatic) support from the United States; (b) that those Americans who advocated what they loosely termed "withdrawal" by the United States from the Far East would obtain satisfaction from any neutrality agreement that reduced our responsibilities in the Pacific area; and (c) that the Japanese would be pleased with a neutralization proposal which indicated that the Occidental powers would hereafter rely solely on pledges as a means of protecting their island territories in the Pacific.

On the negative side, the memorandum distinguished between the three agreements that did not contain nonfortification provisions and agreement B, saying that whether or not to conclude any of the former was largely a matter of opinion as they were mainly "idealistic," whereas to surrender our right to fortify our islands in the Pacific (as envisaged in agreement B) entailed a concrete sacrifice of considerable significance. However, it was clearly indicated that the State Department itself was averse to all of the types of agreement under discussion. Various arguments were developed with considerable care but the one which recurred constantly throughout the memorandum was essentially a repetition of the thesis that had formed the substance of the comments read by Dooman at the meeting of the representatives of the State Department and the armed services on September 11. In one way or another, it was persistently asserted that the United States should not conclude a treaty in regard to any aspect of the Pacific area until the time arrived when conditions in the Far East had been stabilized and a comprehensive settlement could again be worked out involving concessions on both sides. The point was also made forcefully that the Japanese had repeatedly broken their treaty pledges in recent years and that any reliance upon their promises in their present mood would be extremely "hazardous." In addition, a number of secondary reasons were given for not entering into a nonfortification agreement, such as that the Japanese would probably want to include Hawaii in the agreement and that Great Britain, France, and the Netherlands might be reluctant to neutralize their territories in the Pacific.

On reading the Department's memorandum, Roosevelt responded with a note to Secretary Hull in which he made no effort to conceal his irritation. The President said in part,

This discussion is interesting and inclusive of much information but may I suggest that it does not fire one's imagination in favor of neutralization of the islands of the Pacific.

It is, for example, captious to object to the word "neutralization" and suggest the word "non-aggression" for the very simple reason that the laymen of all nations would understand what we were doing if we neutralize the islands of the Pacific against war being waged on them or from them by any of the powers owning them.

Secondly, I throw out agreement type A because it means nothing. "Mutual pledges to respect the rights of each signatory in their insular possessions and in their mandated islands in the Pacific" means, in the condition of the world today, exactly nil.

Agreement B, if you leave out the mutual pledges of non-aggression nonsense, does get us somewhere; "to limit or refrain from erecting fortifications in such islands." Why "limit or refrain"? Why not agree simply and definitely to erect no fortifications in such islands, and to remove all fortifications, armaments, munitions and implements of war from such islands? That does the trick . . .

The whole tenor of the argument is that this is not the time to do anything; that the proposal is merely idealistic and that an agreement would not be lived up to anyway.

In other words, taking it by and large, this argument all the way through is an argument of defeatism.

Being a realist, I wish you would let me have a talk with the author of this. Will you arrange it?[47]

There is no indication that the President did subsequently have a talk with anyone in the Far Eastern Division whose views as a whole the memorandum represented.[48] Nevertheless, the division prepared itself for possible future discussions with Roosevelt by seeking the opinions of Norman Davis and Ambassador Grew, both of whom agreed that the time was not yet ripe for a proposal such as the President had in mind. Grew was especially emphatic in declaring that, in his judgment, the "Considerations Contra" as outlined in the Department's memorandum far outweighed the "Considerations Pro."[49] Once again—the ambassador said—we would be entering into an agreement that we would scrupulously respect knowing that the Japanese would honor it only so long as suited their convenience; in fact they would regard the President's suggestion as a confession of "defeatism" and "moral weakness." Roosevelt was, however, a person who clung to his ideas with unusual persistence so that it is not surprising to find that he returned to his neutralization plan in a telephone conversation with Norman Davis just prior to the latter's departure for England at the end of March. Davis' record of this conversation states,

I . . . told him I thought the British were most likely to raise the question of non-fortification in the Pacific. He replied that I knew what his views were on this, which he explained some weeks ago, and that he was in favor of neutralization or non-fortification of the Philippines, Mandated islands, Dutch East Indies, etc. . . . Thus the only fortifications in the Pacific would be Singapore and Hawaii and Japan proper. He said that it was not his idea that the nations would guarantee to protect any territory against attack but that they would undertake not to fortify and not to use as a base any of the neutralized territory in case of war, and that they would not attack them. We agreed that I should discuss this entire problem with the British, which would be very helpful in reaching a definite conclusion later on.[50]

In England, Davis first spoke with Sir Alexander Cadogan, then British Under Secretary of State for Foreign Affairs, who said in effect that in his opinion it was useless to negotiate any new treaty of importance with the Japanese while they adhered to their present aggressive policies whereas, if they modified their policies, a neutralization agreement for the Pacific would be unnecessary.[51] Subsequently Prime Minister Chamberlain expressed very similar views and stated further that he would not be willing to demilitarize Hong Kong in return for any pledges by Japan until Japan's actions inspired more confidence in its good faith.[52] Anthony Eden alone adopted a positive attitude asserting that a plan "to make the Pacific a peace area" held considerable promise.[53] In the end it was decided that, if the United States government reached the stage of formulating any concrete proposal, it would confer with the British. This stage was never to be achieved, however, as the Sino-Japanese war broke out only three months later crowding all other developments off the Far Eastern scene.

Nevertheless, certain events which occurred subsequently are pertinent to a consideration of the administration's policy toward the strengthening of the defenses on the Pacific islands during the years under discussion. These events in turn have their roots in the past.

The strategic planners in the United States Army and Navy had long been convinced that, if this country became involved in a war, the enemy would in all probability be Japan.[54] It was thought that the conflict would be limited to the United States and Japan and that we would rely on naval operations. It was further believed that the navy would conduct an offensive war which meant that it must attempt to achieve supremacy in the west Pacific. But, since this could only be accomplished if the United States possessed adequate naval bases in that area, the question of bases assumed paramount importance. Consequently, as already related, at the time of the Washington Conference plans were being made for the construction of a major base at Guam to be supplemented by another in the Philippines.

With the incorporation of Article XIX into the Washington Naval Treaty, the army and navy were compelled to accept the fact that the *status quo* relative to bases and fortifications had, for the time being at least, been frozen and that their strategy would have to be designed accordingly. For almost two decades thereafter the Joint Board of the army and navy devoted most of its energies to successive revisions of the Orange plan, the blueprint for operations against Japan. In the early 1930's a serious controversy developed within the armed forces. While the dispute had many significant ramifications, the main point was that the navy clung tenaciously to the idea that, despite the enormous obstacles created by Article XIX, it could fight an offensive war against the Japanese. Doing so would, however, admittedly require the army's holding the Philippines, which possessed the only facilities in the west Pacific that would support a large naval force, until the navy battled its way across the Pacific to the Islands. The army on its part contended that the strategy advocated by the navy was wholly unrealistic. It was impossible, it said, for the army to defend the Philippines until the navy arrived, which might take several years, unless adequate bases and fortifications were constructed and the naval and land forces on the Islands were greatly augmented. But as it assumed that these conditions could not be met, the army recommended adopting defensive instead of offensive tactics and drawing a line from Alaska through Hawaii to Panama to serve as America's "strategic frontier."[55]

The army appears, however, to have favored an increase in bases and fortifications no less than the navy. It might therefore be supposed that after Japan denounced the Washington Naval Treaty a great deal of consideration would have been given to undertaking the military construction hitherto banned by Article XIX. But the available evidence suggests that this was not the case. The armed forces were inclined to view with extreme pessimism the possibility of getting Congress to vote the funds needed for extensive military installations. In their opinion the isolationist sentiment in the Senate and House was too strong and there was too much feeling that the United States should not adopt any measures that might provoke the Japanese. Moreover they believed that, as far as the Philippines were concerned, the Independence Act passed in 1934 provided all economically minded congressmen with a good reason for not approving any large investment in the defense of the Islands. For according to the terms of the Act, when the Philippines achieved full independence in 1946 they would acquire all United States military bases on their territory while the disposition of the United States naval bases was to be negotiated. The army and navy were therefore not likely to engage in vigorous demands for new fortifications and bases. Nor does the record indicate that either the President or the State Department wished to advance any proposal. As is apparent from the discussion of the British suggestion for the renewal of Article XIX at the meeting of September 1936, the United States continued to follow a policy of maintaining the *status quo*.

Indeed, instead of suggesting that the President and the State Department desired to take any action, the evidence points in the contrary direction. No move was made until the spring of 1938 at which time the initiative was taken not by the administration but by Congress. That body ordered the Secretary of the Navy to appoint a commission to examine the whole question of United States naval bases which led in turn to the establishment of the famous Hepburn Board. Perhaps even more importantly the recommendations made by the Board after months of labor—recommendations representing the Navy's point of view—were very much watered down by the administration in the bill, that as a result of the Hepburn Board's final report, it submitted to Congress.[56] The report urged construction work on twenty-five bases in an over-all budget of $326 million. But apparently under injunction from the Bureau of the Budget, which in the last analysis meant the White House, the navy cut this proposal to twelve bases at a cost of $94 million, a sum that was further reduced by the President to $65 million.[57] In addition the report went out of its way to emphasize the importance of building strong defenses on Guam. The administration's bill, however, did not ask for sufficient funds to fortify Guam, or even to strengthen its defenses substantially, but merely requested $5 million for minor engineering projects. Moreover, when questioned about the $5 million by members of the House and Senate naval affairs committee at hearings on the bill, administration spokesmen emphatically stated that they were not considering the development of Guam as a military base of any kind and that, if unforeseen changes in the international situation demanded their doing so, Congress would be informed. The President himself, on being asked about the bill by the press, said that the navy had a "beautiful idea" of improving defenses in our outlying possessions at a price of $500 million but that he was not bothering about long-range problems but merely looking to the next year during which no more than about $50 million would be spent; meanwhile international conditions might so change that it would be unnecessary to consider any broader program.[58] When requested at a press conference later to explain this matter further, the President at first hedged and then said he was willing to support the $5 million proposal but pointed out that it did not involve the "fortification" of Guam which he seemed to imply he would not approve.[59]

In the end the House of Representatives eliminated even the $5 million item from the administration's bill, an act which in later years gave rise to the charge that Congress was responsible for the failure to strengthen Guam that proved such a disastrous mistake after Pearl Harbor.[60] It seems evident, however, that Congress, the President, and the State Department must all share the blame. According to well-informed contemporary observers the $5 million appropriation for Guam did not have the support of the State Department from the beginning and was subsequently repudiated by the administration.[61] Years later Senators testified that, after its rejection by the House, the Senate did not consider the appropriation as a result of a request from the State Department and "after consultation with the President."[62] Following Pearl Harbor many congressmen, in telling their side of the story, said that they objected to the sum of $5 million as too small to accomplish anything and made the highly significant point that the administration never submitted any proposal to Congress designed to do more than effect relatively inconsequential improvements on Guam. It was openly stated in naval circles at the time that the "whole job of fortifying Guam" was killed because of the large expenditures involved and the "*sub rosa* opposition of the State Department."[63] Professors Langer and Gleason, who have had full access to the State Department files, in discussing the charges that have been leveled against Congress for not taking action in regard to Guam in 1939, state that "the truth of the matter was that complete fortification had not been contemplated and, more importantly, that it was primarily the President and the State Department who opposed even the modest construction envisaged."[64]

On the question of motivation, Professors Langer and Gleason assert that the reason for the President's and the State Department's attitude was fear that any effort to strengthen Guam might be regarded as a violation of the spirit of the Washington Conference treaties and a challenge to Japan. Other historians have taken the same position.[65] The idea that the administration and especially the State Department objected to the development of Guam as a major base because of the possible repercussions in Japan was in fact current in 1939.[66] It was furthermore felt that the Department's opposition increased when the news that Congress might authorize small construction projects on the islands proved sufficient to arouse violently antagonistic protests in the Japanese press. It may also be assumed that both President Roosevelt and Secretary Hull, always concerned over a possible conflict with Congress, did not want to run the risk of precipitating a controversy over an extensive program for the strengthening of our defenses in the west Pacific with the isolationists on Capitol Hill.

In general, the Roosevelt administration's handling of the problem of the Pacific islands formed an important segment of its Far Eastern policy. As far as the mandates were concerned, it is evident that the State Department deliberately refrained from probing into the question of military preparations because it wished to avoid a controversy with the Japanese. The Department's restraint was all the more striking as suspicions of Japan's activities were expressed not only by the public at large but by the Mandates Commission itself. In dealing with our insular possessions in the west Pacific, the administration decided to adhere to Article XIX even after the Washington Naval Treaty lapsed in 1936. This decision ostensibly ran counter to the fundamental wishes of the army and navy. While the published record does not throw any direct light on the thinking of the President or leading State Department officials at this time, nevertheless, given all the circumstances, it seems reasonable to suppose that their views did not differ in any significant manner from those which they held subsequently. In short, to all appearances President Roosevelt and Secretary Hull and his advisers were opposed to the construction of fortifications and bases in the west Pacific primarily for political reasons, foremost among which was the desire to avert trouble with Japan.

Besides the policy which was actually put into effect in regard to the Pacific islands, the administration considered the British proposal for the renewal of Article XIX and the President's neutralization plan. The British proposal was primarily rejected because of the objections raised by the State Department. The Department's line of reasoning was that it would be morally indefensible for the administration to enter into what was sometimes called a "piecemeal" treaty with Japan—that is to say, a treaty which involved only a small part of the broad settlement concluded at the Washington Conference. To sign such an agreement, it contended, would be equivalent to a declaration that the United States was prepared to accept Japan's violations of the principles incorporated in other parts of the Washington Conference settlement, especially the Nine Power pact. If the agreement were favorable to the Japanese, which would be the case if its provisions were similar to those of Article XIX, the implication that the United States was endorsing Japan's actions would be even stronger. Better, therefore, to await developments even if necessary for ten years. Ultimately the situation in the Far East would crystallize at which time the United States might be able to initiate negotiations for a new comprehensive settlement related to the Pacific area which would be based upon principles comparable to those that had been approved by the Washington Conference. However, the negotiations would essentially entail an elaborate process of trading concession for concession. Since the right to fortify our islands in the west Pacific might ultimately prove a valuable bargaining point, there was a practical as well as a moral reason for not signing a treaty with provisions similar to those of Article XIX.

As to the President's neutralization plan, Roosevelt, as already indicated, was moved to suggest this scheme because he was speculating upon the possibility of arriving at various regional understandings which might succeed in arresting the alarming trend of the international situation.[67] The neutralization pact outlined by the President, if put into effect, would have constituted a "piecemeal" agreement patterned on Article XIX. Its provisions were, however, far more drastic. For in contrast to the terms of Article XIX which were confined to the insular possessions of Great Britain, Japan, and the United States, they covered many other vital areas as, for example, the Dutch East Indies. Moreover, they required not just the maintenance of the *status quo* but the removal of all existing military installations and equipment as well as a promise not to use the territories involved for military purposes in case of war. State Department officials objected to the pact partly because in their judgment, it involved the same difficulties as the renewal of Article XIX and partly because it depended to such a large extent on the good faith of the Japanese. Although Roosevelt tried briefly to keep his neutralization plan alive, it seems to have been gradually abandoned by tacit agreement.

The net result of the agitation concerning the fortification of the Pacific islands was therefore that no measures were undertaken that might have seemed inimical to the Japanese nor was any treaty concluded that might have operated in their favor. The precept of inaction which the administration had so consistently applied in dealing with other aspects of the situation in the Far East was thus extended to the problem of strengthening the defenses on the Pacific islands. This precept was, moreover, not challenged except by Roosevelt's momentary effort to gain support for his idea of neutralizing the Pacific. Although his attempt was not successful, it was significant in that it further illustrated the tendency to look for a means, not of opposing the Japanese, but of reaching an understanding with them.

Throughout the first half of 1937 the reports of United States Foreign Service officers concerning conditions in China were increasingly optimistic. Nelson Johnson continued to emphasize the extraordinary success which the Chinese were achieving in their efforts to attain national unity. As the months went by, he also wrote the Department repeatedly about the remarkable economic activity apparent in so many parts of China. China, he said, had entered a "new era of economic development"; the National government was "pushing its program of economic reconstruction on all fronts, agricultural, industrial and communications." That program, he thought, was designed in accordance with one overriding objective: to bring the nation to the "highest possible point of efficiency" within a brief time so that it would be in a better position to meet an attack by Japan.[1]

The dispatches of our embassy in Tokyo on the other hand indicated that Japan was going through a period of considerable stress. In the autumn of 1936 the Hirota cabinet had approved a budget that involved unprecedented expenses, especially for the army and navy, and had introduced financial reforms which were to effect a large increase in taxes.[2] During the early part of the winter, the economic situation in Japan had seriously deteriorated. The public had reacted against these developments which, among other factors, led to attacks upon the Hirota cabinet by the political parties. As a result the cabinet was forced to resign in January. A brief interval followed in which the extremists in the army blocked the appointment of General Kazushige Ugaki as premier, partly on the grounds that he favored working with the civilian leaders. General Senjuro Hayashi finally undertook to form a new cabinet. While it was known that he had no very definite political philosophy, it was assumed that in general he would foster military rule.

In some respects, notably in the conduct of its foreign policy, the Hayashi government proved more moderate than had been expected. The post of Minister for Foreign Affairs was given to Naotake Sato, a career diplomat who had served for about twenty-five years in Europe and reportedly had considerable understanding of and sympathy for the Western point of view. In early March, Sato created a furor by delivering a speech in the Diet in which he advocated the adoption of a fresh approach to the whole subject of Japan's foreign relations. The Minister stated in effect that, contrary to the assertions of the chauvinists in Japan, the Japanese themselves had the ability to avoid a "crisis" (meaning war) at any time if they genuinely desired to do so. They should learn to respect the points of view of other nations and attempt to cooperate with them. As to Great Britain and the United States, Japan could improve her relations with those countries by altering her policy toward China. Henceforth, negotiations between Japan and China would therefore be conducted in a conciliatory spirit, and the Chinese would be dealt with upon a "basis of equality." On specific issues Sato mainly declared that the establishment of economic blocs—as, for example, between Japan and Manchukuo—was "premature." Under pressure from the cabinet, the Minister was compelled to qualify some of his statements. But he remained in office and during the course of the next months continued to reiterate many of the views he had initially proclaimed.

Paralleling these developments, the political parties, through their spokesmen in the Diet, continued their assaults not only upon the administration but the army itself. General Hayashi responded by arbitrarily dissolving the Diet and calling for an election on April 30. The election was a definite victory for the antigovernment factions. But it was not a popular endorsement of the two major parties whose position *vis-à-vis* the government was therefore not strengthened. Indeed the Hayashi cabinet showed its contempt for its opponents and for democratic procedures in general by remaining in office even after its repudiation by the voters.

The sheer complexity of these events left room for a variety of interpretations. But by the end of the spring of 1937 our embassy in Japan seems to have formed a fairly definite estimate of the situation.[3] It believed that the army had long been in control in Japan and that neither the activities of the political parties nor any other developments in recent months had impaired its position to any significant degree. The army, however, consisted of various groups of which the more moderate had for some time been in the ascendancy. It was these men who had brought General Hayashi into office and supported him.

In respect to Japan's foreign policy, the embassy's view was that all of Japan had been "thunderstruck" by the sudden and unexpected determination of the Chinese to resist Japanese aggression. The moderate military leaders had become convinced that the policy of the army extremists, with their insistence upon "expansion through active aggression," had been a dismal failure. They had moreover felt increasingly that, with the continuing growth of China's strength, the further pursuit of such a policy would invite war. They feared war because they recognized that, despite her military power, there was no assurance that in a prolonged conflict Japan might not suffer a disastrous defeat. As a consequence, the officers upon whom the Hayashi government depended had favored Sato's desire to put into effect a "policy of conciliation and friendship" toward China and toward other nations.

By May many of the reports both from our embassy in Japan and in China were emphasizing the marked turn for the better which had taken place in the situation between the Chinese and the Japanese. But there were differences of opinion as to whether this change would endure. A dispatch sent to the State Department from the embassy in Nanking in early May stated that there was "even a prospect that the Japanese policy of armed invasion of China" might be laid aside "for an indefinite period."[4] On the other hand, Grew asserted that he could not persuade himself that Sato would be able to do more than slow down the "expansionist tempo" of Japan's course.[5] The urge for expansion in Japan, he said, was like the incoming tide on the shore: a wave of aggression was followed by a period of retrocession, such as had set in for the present, but there would be another wave in time which would go further than its predecessor.

The picture presented to the State Department by United States Foreign Service officers therefore essentially indicated that, as far as the relations between China and Japan were concerned, the situation in the Far East was quieter than it had been for many years; that China was concentrating upon the rapid development of her national strength in order to be able to resist an attack from Japan if necessary; and that, to a large extent as a result of the progress which the Chinese were making, the Japanese had relaxed their pressures on China at least for the present.

Under these circumstances certainly one of the most important questions with which the United States was confronted in the spring of 1937 was that of American participation in China's economic reconstruction. However the policy of the United States government in this connection can only be understood in relation to the whole movement which had developed since the Amau declaration for the participation of Western private enterprise in China's rehabilitation.

In contrast to the attitude apparent in the United States government, the directors of the National Foreign Trade Council, a non-official organization, had begun to look upon China's efforts at reconstruction with considerable hope as early as 1934. They nevertheless recognized that, if American private enterprise was to play a significant part in China's economic growth, a solution would have to be found for some of the problems which were placing American businessmen at a disadvantage in China in relation to the businessmen of other nationalities. In particular United States manufacturers lacked adequate facilities for securing long-term credits which were necessary for the export to China of the capital goods that were essential to the carrying out of a reconstruction program. In comparison, their British counterparts could turn for assistance to such powerful institutions as the Hongkong and Shanghai Banking Corporation which, unlike the American banks in China, was itself empowered to engage in many different kinds of transactions and was also affiliated with a large credit organization.

Moreover by 1934 a number of European countries had already adopted the practice—which was soon to have a striking effect—of promoting exports to China through various forms of governmental aid. In 1930, for example, the British government had signed an agreement with the authorities at Nanking whereby the British Boxer Indemnity Funds (totaling about £11,000,000) were to be expended for the building of railways and similar public enterprises in China.[6] All of the materials needed for construction were to be purchased in Great Britain. Use of the Funds had begun in 1933 with the result that by the following year Great Britain was well on the way to becoming the largest supplier of railroad equipment to China, supplanting the United States which had hitherto held first place. In addition, the German government, eager to recapture its prewar share of the Chinese market, had begun to resort to such devices as export credit guarantees to encourage trade with China.[7] As a consequence, an important contract for the sale of railway material to the Chinese was concluded in 1934 by the German firm of Otto Wolff, in which the Reich government assumed most of the credit risk.

In the summer of 1934, the National Foreign Trade Council formulated a plan which involved the establishment of a syndicate of American firms interested in doing business in China and an American bank, supported by the United States government, which would be comparable in stature to the Hongkong and Shanghai Banking Corporation.[8] A meeting was held of the representatives of a number of large companies who expressed interest in the scheme but stated decisively that they would not assume any initiative. Subsequently, the council approached the Far Eastern Division of the State Department with a request for "authorization" for its plan. The division replied that in its opinion this particular project was impractical; furthermore, that China was still a "hazardous field" for new undertakings and that Japan's claim to a preferred position in China's economic development was a political reality that could not be ignored in any venture such as the council was proposing.

Nevertheless, the National Foreign Trade Council was not to be discouraged. Within a few months it began to organize an American economic mission which was to go to China to investigate that country's resources, industries, and trade, "with a view to possible American participation in their future development."[9] The chairman of the group was to be W. Cameron Forbes, whose family, through its association with the famous old trading house of Russell and Company, had played a dominant role in the American China trade of the 19th century. Forbes himself was regarded as eminently well qualified for the job at hand, as he had enjoyed a long career in both the business world and public life. The council wanted the total membership of the mission to be small but to consist of men of recognized competence in a variety of industries so that they would be able to make a broad assessment of the field. But even this relatively modest goal proved hard to attain owing to the slow response of the business community.[10] Members for the mission were still being recruited on the eve of the group's departure. Moreover the council had great difficulty in collecting the $50,000 which was regarded as the bare minimum needed to cover the mission's expenses although it appealed for contributions to some of the largest corporations in the United States.

The mission, which was called the American Economic Mission to the Far East, left the United States at the end of March. It was entirely unofficial in character although it had the State Department's "blessing." The Export-Import Bank had been asked to cooperate by sending a representative but had refused on the advice of the State Department. The Department had argued that any official association with the mission would be used by the Japanese to bolster their contention that American economic activity in China was primarily designed to realize the United States government's political aims.[11]

The mission's visit to China lasted about seven weeks.[12] As time went by, it became evident that Forbes as chairman was handicapped by a lack of knowledge of the Chinese political scene which, as he frankly acknowledged, led him into making some extraordinarily naïve blunders. However, he devoted himself with zeal to collecting as much information as possible and, together with a few of his associates, traveled extensively throughout the country interviewing its foremost leaders. The mission as a whole was greatly impressed by the signs of progress which it felt were evident in all parts of China. It moreover made its views known in a public statement in which it declared: "A vast change is coming over China; a modernization that as compared with ten or even five years ago, marks many centuries."[13] Forbes himself apparently left China convinced that he had a "very definite message to put across" to the United States government and its people, namely, that a "New China" was in the process of being created and that they should assist in its economic development.[14]

The Chinese leaders who talked with Forbes made a variety of concrete suggestions for the participation by American firms in China's plans for economic rehabilitation. Chiang Kai-shek stated that, in his opinion, American concerns should cooperate with the Chinese in the construction of a railroad in Szechwan and Yunnan and in the expansion of the tin industry in the latter province. Li Tsung-jen advanced various plans the most significant of which involved the development of the tin mines in Kwangsi through American enterprise. T. V. Soong and H. H. Kung discussed at some length with Forbes what in their opinion were the major deficiencies in the entire American business setup in China which made it difficult for American interests to play an important role in that nation's economic progress. They urged that action be taken to establish a large American trading house, a strong bank, and a credit organization which they felt would greatly improve the situation.

After his return to the United States Forbes, with the vigorous support of some of the other members of the American Economic Mission, undertook to initiate all of these proposals.[15] He made repeated trips to Washington in an attempt to enlist the aid of the highest officials in the State, Treasury, Commerce, and War Departments and even went to see the President whom he had long known personally. Wheels were set in motion to take over what remained of Russell and Company in order to create a trading house that might recapture some of the prestige which that firm had enjoyed in its heyday. A start was also made toward the organization of a bank, of the type that had been under discussion, which was to be backed by government and private funds. But both these projects were soon set aside owing to the emergence of obstacles which could not be overcome. Forbes himself was especially anxious to follow up the suggestion for the increase of tin production in South China and the development of railways essential for the export of that commodity as he was convinced that from the point of view of the United States it was vitally important to have access to further tin supplies for military purposes.

He therefore sought persistently throughout the next two years to awaken the interest of various American companies in the matter. At one time a mission was almost sent to China to survey the tin mines in Kwangsi. When this scheme did not eventuate, the United States Steel Corporation indicated that it might initiate some move but failed to do so before the outbreak of the Sino-Japanese War.

Of the various proposals considered, the establishment of a credit corporation came however to be regarded as the most important. In fact by mid-summer of 1935 the Chinese themselves had arrived at a point where they felt that American equipment was urgently needed to speed up the industrialization of China. They therefore decided to make an effort to form a credit structure which would facilitate its purchase.[16] As a result, a syndicate of seventeen leading Chinese banks drew up a tentative plan which they presented to C. H. French, a prominent American businessman in Shanghai. The plan was decidedly ambitious. French was to secure a loan of $150,000,000 in the United States. This money was to be reloaned by the syndicate for commercial and industrial projects in China on condition that all the foreign equipment which was employed would be obtained from American sources. Applications for funds were to be submitted to a local committee of American citizens in Shanghai which was to act as the agent for the American interests involved. According to the estimates of the syndicate this scheme, if realized, would succeed in doubling the rate of industrialization in China and would increase United States exports to China many times over.

French, who was about to go to the United States for a brief visit, undertook to investigate the possibilities of putting the syndicate's plan into effect. He discussed the project with members of the Far Eastern Division of the State Department in October. Subsequently he talked with executives of thirty of the most prominent manufacturing corporations in the United States and formed a committee which many of them joined. French drafted a plan for the committee's consideration that involved the organization of an American group, chosen to represent all segments of the capital goods industry, which was to cooperate with the Chinese banking syndicate. The group was to issue a series of debentures up to $150,000,000. French felt that the security, which the Chinese banks were prepared to offer, was excellent. Nevertheless he proposed that, in order to attract investors in the United States, payment of the debentures should also be guaranteed by the United States government and the American group to the extent of 80 and 20 per cent, respectively.

French failed, however, to achieve any concrete results. In November, at the suggestion of the committee, he sent his plan to the officers of the Far Eastern Division with the request that they submit it to any branch of the administration that might furnish the "desired assistance." But to all appearances the State Department did not want to become involved in the matter. For the Far Eastern Division replied that the Department was not in a position to say what agency of the government, if any, would be prepared to cooperate in furthering such an undertaking but that the business interests concerned might themselves discuss the matter with the Export-Import Bank or the Reconstruction Finance Corporation. Shortly thereafter, French left for Shanghai and the committee set aside his proposal in favor of a scheme which Forbes and his associates had for some time been trying to promote.

Forbes's plan was based on the idea of establishing a China Credit Corporation.[17] A sum of $10,000,000 was to be raised from private sources if possible; if not, it was hoped that up to 40 per cent of that amount would be furnished by the United States government. The Chinese government was to provide the rest of the capital as a way of settling the debts, estimated as in excess of $30,000,000, that it owed to American creditors. The creditors were to receive redeemable stock or some other form of security which the corporation was to issue. The capital was to be invested in enterprises which were essential to China's economic development with the stipulation that the purchase of all materials be made in the United States. Although this plan obviously had much in common with French's proposal (indeed both were patterned after the British Boxer Indemnity Funds), it was deliberately conceived on a much more modest scale. Also one of its main aims was to remove the obstacle to further American trade and investment in China created by the Chinese government's failure to meet its financial obligations.

Throughout the autumn of 1935, Forbes had continued to make the official rounds in Washington in the hope of securing support for the China Credit Corporation. On an unofficial level he obtained the approval of J. P. Morgan and Company. With the aid of Thomas Lamont he succeeded in January 1936 in convening a meeting of fifteen representatives of China's principal creditors which involved such concerns as the International General Electric Company, International Telephone and Telegraph Corporation, United States Steel Products Company, and Standard-Vacuum Oil Company.[18] Forbes told the meeting that the Chinese were making marked progress in the modernization of their country, that China consequently afforded "great opportunities" for trade, and that American businessmen were "standing on the platform watching the train go by." The meeting ended with the appointment of a subcommittee which under the chairmanship of Clark H. Minor, the President of International General Electric, undertook to study the plan for the formation of the China Credit Corporation.

For a brief period, the China Credit Corporation seemed to its promoters "in a fair way of realization." But within a few months even Forbes, who up to this time had displayed an unflagging enthusiasm, was showing signs of discouragement. Writing to a United States businessman in Shanghai he stated that no progress had been made by the subcommittee toward "really getting a group together."[19] No single corporation was willing to advance the money necessary to make a start toward establishing a credit organization. Even International General Electric, which had fairly large funds for the development of new projects in China, had "failed to come across with any substantial contribution."

As it had become increasingly evident that the business group was not likely to make any move on its own initiative, Forbes had appealed to the State Department for assistance. In an interview with William Phillips in April 1936 he sought to impress upon the Under Secretary that the various corporations with which he was in contact might well take action if they received some "help and encouragement" from official quarters; what was needed, he said, was "a favorable attitude on the part of the Department."[20] Phillips replied that the Department was decidedly pessimistic about American financial undertakings related to China.

Phillips' remark reflected the concern which existed in the State Department at the time over the problem of the payment by the Chinese government of the debts it owed to United States citizens. These debts consisted mainly of loans granted to China during a period that extended from 1910-1920. Officers of the Far Eastern Division had for some months been engaged in a controversy with the Chinese government over this issue and had frankly indicated that they regarded the attitude of the authorities at Nanking as extremely disappointing.[21] In early 1936 a new element was injected into the situation when the Chinese government announced that it had reached an agreement with a committee of British bondholders for an adjustment of loans, known as the Tientsin-Pukow railway loans, in which the British had important holdings.[22] The terms of the agreement were generally regarded as very favorable to the Chinese. Shortly thereafter Washington was informed that the Chinese had presented the British with a proposal, involving almost identical terms, for a settlement of the famous Hukuang railway loan, issued by the first Consortium, and that negotiations had been opened on this basis.

That the British government had had a hand in these developments was evident as Sir Frederick Leith-Ross was admittedly advising the British bondholders.[23] In fact, it would seem in retrospect that the British government had in all probability adopted a new policy toward the claims of its nationals against China following the Nanking government's currency reforms of November 1935. Briefly stated, the British appear to have concluded that the time had come to advance new loans to China; that little could be accomplished, however, until an understanding was achieved in respect to China's existing obligations; and that therefore the old loans should be adjusted even though the bondholders might have to make some important concessions.

In any event, the action taken by the Chinese and the British was not welcomed in Washington.[24] For it was felt that American investors, who held a substantial amount of Hukuang bonds, were being forced into the position of having to settle on the same terms as the British. And, as the Department explicitly stated, it believed that these terms involved "such extensive diluting of the creditors' rights" as to render them "unduly favorable to the debtor government." Moreover the Department feared that the Chinese would probably attempt to adjust the rest of their outstanding obligations on the same conditions. It therefore remained of the opinion that Nanking had little consideration for the interests of foreign investors and that the situation was decidedly discouraging from the point of view of embarking upon new financial undertakings in China.

The Department's over-all attitude toward Forbes's activities seems to have been that, if worked out with great care, some of his projects might ultimately bear fruit.[25] But in general United States officials continued to believe that American businessmen could not make any really extensive progress in China as long as the Japanese persisted in their determination to dominate the economic development of that country to the exclusion of others. Hornbeck, for example, writing to Nelson Johnson in July 1936 stated in substance that, in his estimation, China in some respects had reached the stage of becoming an attractive field for Western enterprise.[26] Japanese opposition, however, constituted a major obstacle and was likely to remain so within the near future. At the same time it was doubtful whether Japan had the resources fully to achieve China's reconstruction in the long run. The time might therefore come when American capital and technical skill would be needed in China more than at present. Meanwhile American businessmen would probably continue to share in China's trade. The United States government on its part should attempt through diplomatic means to protect what remained of commercial opportunity in China for Americans and wait patiently for the day when there might be new opportunities.

The apathy which Forbes encountered in the American business community and the pessimism of the State Department concerning Western participation in China's economic development contrasted sharply with the mood that seemed to be dominating official and business circles in some of the countries of Europe. There, as already intimated, the trend was toward becoming actively involved in China's rehabilitation plans. The Chinese themselves did their best to stimulate foreign interest especially in projects for railway construction.

At the beginning of 1936 the Chinese government embarked upon an ambitious program of railroad expansion. Its object was to create arteries of communication which would not only serve China in peacetime but would meet its needs in case of war with Japan. It seemed essential, therefore, to establish a network of lines south of the Yangtze as it was a foregone conclusion that any Sino-Japanese conflict would start in North China. The program was to be executed by Chang Kia-ngau, who had just been appointed Minister of Railways.

It was evident from the outset, however, that if China was to engage in any extensive railroad construction it would have to obtain aid from abroad.[27] On the other hand, Chang was determined not to enter into any arrangements which would revive the specter of foreign control of China's communications system. As a consequence, he decided, in so far as practicable, to adhere to the principle that had formed the basis of the contract which the Chinese government had concluded with the firm of Otto Wolff in 1934, namely, that foreign assistance should for the most part be limited to providing China with railway equipment and to financing the purchase of that equipment with long-term credits or so-called material loans.

In early 1936 an agreement similar to that of 1934 was entered into by the Chinese and Otto Wolff and was followed by another in which a German syndicate participated. In both instances, the major part of the risk was again borne by the Reich government. During the course of the year the Chinese and British signed two railway contracts which on the British side involved both private interests and, through the Boxer Indemnity Funds, the government. A French syndicate undertook to advance a loan for equipment to be used for the development of railroads in the Szechwan-Yunnan area, the region which the Generalissimo had discussed with Forbes in terms of American investment.[28] Analogous arrangements were made by a Belgian syndicate and a Czech corporation. By the end of 1936 railway loans amounting to Ch.$200,000,000 had been negotiated, a sum which was soon to be more than doubled.

The activities of the Germans and British were, moreover, not confined to the conclusion of railroad contracts.[29] In July 1936 a representative of Hitler visited China where he reached an understanding with the Nanking government that led to an exchange of German munitions and industrial supplies for metals, such as tungsten, needed for the Reich's rearmament program. Shortly thereafter, the British opened a special office of the Export Credits Guarantee Department of the Treasury in Shanghai for the sake of facilitating the sale of capital goods to China by British firms. This move was reportedly the result of recommendations made by Sir Frederick Leith-Ross who returned to England in the summer of 1936. At the same time Sir Frederick sought to encourage British businessmen to take part in China's economic development. Speaking at the annual dinner of the China Association in November, he declared that he was "definitely optimistic about China" and that he believed that "given a period of peace and good government China is going to be one of the biggest and best markets for our manufactures."[30]

Despite the growing involvement of European countries in China, the attitude of the State Department to all appearances remained unaltered at the end of the year. But as the spring advanced United States officials, both in Washington and in China, devoted an increasing amount of attention to the question of whether Americans should play a more active part in China's efforts at reconstruction.

In April Ambassador Johnson met with Willys Peck and the United States commercial and assistant commercial attachés at Nanking to discuss the "whole field of American enterprises in China, present and future."[31] There was apparently agreement on certain basic points: that China had entered a new era of economic development; that the policy of friendship inaugurated by Sato marked a definite, perhaps even permanent, change in Sino-Japanese relations; and that other countries, notably Great Britain, Germany, and France, had taken "unprecedented" action in extending long-term credits for railway materials to China.

In the light of these circumstances, Peck and the commercial attachés argued that the administration should support new ventures by American business in China. The assistant commercial attaché presented a plan for the establishment of a commission, under the auspices of the Export-Import Bank, to assist in promoting Sino-American trade. The commission was to consist of representatives of different departments of the United States government who were to operate in conjunction with the Shanghai American Chamber of Commerce. It was primarily to devote itself to an investigation of Chinese proposals for the purchase of American railroad equipment and other supplies with a view to expediting all promising transactions.

While Johnson thought the attaché's scheme had some merit, in the end he advised the State Department against endorsing it. His main contention was that American manufacturers and financiers had very little interest in going "any more deeply" into business in China. In addition, the ambassador viewed with distrust the current participation of the European powers in the railway and other projects being undertaken by the Nanking government. "Plus ça change plus c'est la meme chose" he wrote in one dispatch to Washington, indicating that in his opinion the European nations were jockeying for economic advantages in China in a manner which brought to mind some of the more unfortunate periods of their relations with that country.[32] He suspected that the British among others were driving a harder bargain in negotiating loans with the Chinese than appeared on the surface. As a consequence, he thought that if American businessmen attempted to assume an important role in China's economic development they would be joining a "game played by sharpers" in which they would be outwitted as in the past.[33]

Shortly after the meeting of United States officials at Nanking, Warren Lee Pierson, President of the Export-Import Bank, arrived in China for a brief visit.[34] The bank had received applications for aid in connection with the sale of railroad supplies to the Nanking government and Pierson wished to inspect conditions in China personally. It was stated in advance that he did not intend to make any decisions involving action by the bank during the course of his journey. But Pierson was very favorably impressed by what he saw in China and, presumably as a result, arranged on the spot for an Export-Import Bank credit of about $1,500,000 for the sale of locomotives to the Chinese Ministry of Railways by two American companies. The deal was admittedly a small one but, according to Chang Kia-ngau, was warmly welcomed by the Chinese as a sign that American capital was finally re-entering the field of railroad investment in China alongside of that of the European nations.[35]

Meanwhile the British were forging ahead. Some time during the autumn of 1936 Sir Charles Addis intimated to a representative of the Chinese Ministry of Railways in London that Great Britain was prepared to invest £10,000,000 in China's railroads.[36] This sum (raised to about £15,000,000 later) far exceeded any amount the Chinese had expected to obtain. In January 1937 Chang Kia-ngau approached the British with a definite proposal for a loan to aid in the construction of a railway in the southeastern part of China. The British pointed out that because of the terms of the loan they would have to offer a share to the other members of the Consortium. In response, the Chinese stated that they had always objected to the Consortium and in any event would not negotiate with an organization which included the Japanese.

The British Foreign Office thereupon sent a memorandum to the State Department explaining the situation.[37] In its present form, it declared, the Consortium seemed in fact to be "defeating its own object." It was preventing its members "from participating in the economic rehabilitation of China" and "impeding instead of assisting such rehabilitation." Under other circumstances His Majesty's government would have been willing to explore ways of reviving the Consortium agreement so as to take into account the changes which had occurred in the Far East. There was, however, obviously no prospect of obtaining the "good will" of the Chinese government even for a revised arrangement. Consequently, in the opinion of the Foreign Office, the Consortium "should now be dissolved by mutual consent."

Some months before these developments, rumors had already reached Washington to the effect that the British were inclined to think that the situation in the Far East demanded a breakup of the Consortium. Hornbeck had therefore written a long memorandum in which he restated his strong conviction that the Consortium should be maintained.[38] On this occasion he emphasized in particular that an abandonment of the Consortium would seriously undermine the principle of cooperative action on the part of the powers in their dealings with the Chinese government which, in turn, would have an adverse effect upon the future of American enterprise in China. Spelled out in somewhat greater detail, Hornbeck's thesis was that throughout the history of our relations with China the powers had alternated between following the principle of cooperative action and that of "free and unrestricted competition." During the periods when the latter had prevailed, American businessmen had stood little chance of succeeding in China owing to the more vigorous methods used by foreign nationals with the backing of their governments. The Consortium had been designed as an important instrument for the realization of the idea of cooperative action. If it went out of existence, American interests would find it increasingly difficult to hold their own to say nothing of making progress in China.

On receipt of the note from the Foreign Office, the State Department came to the conclusion, however, that it should not stand in the way of a British loan to the Chinese. It therefore drafted a reply to the British in which it assented to the dissolution of the Consortium but expressed its regret at having to make this move.[39] It moreover indicated that in the opinion of the United States government the principle of cooperative action, upon which the Consortium was based, should be retained. The draft was submitted to the President, who approved it after a private consultation with Morgenthau in which the Secretary said that he did not believe the maintenance of the Consortium would serve any "useful purpose."[40]

Following the dispatch of the State Department's reply to the British, the American group of the Consortium was informed that the United States government would not raise any objections to the termination of the Consortium agreement.[41] At the same time Hornbeck discussed with Lamont the "continuing value of co-operation"—in so far as it could be attained—by the banking interests of the four powers in the Consortium functioning with the general approval of their respective governments. As a result, Lamont drew up a rough outline of a new organization in which the same banking interests would be represented and read it before a meeting of the Executive Council of the Consortium in May.[42] The new organization was to be a "loosely knit Association" planned upon a very modest basis without regulations of any kind. Its members were to engage in frequent exchanges of views concerning important developments in China. They were, moreover, to proceed in accordance with a general understanding that, if one group undertook a financial operation in China it would offer a participation to the other groups provided "circumstances permitted." In order to avoid arousing the enmity of the Chinese, the new body was to make a wholly fresh start that would constitute a "complete cut-off" from the old Consortium.

The Executive Council apparently welcomed Lamont's idea of devising some means of further cooperation. But it was in no position to take action until the Consortium was dissolved, a matter which awaited the formal consent of the Japanese and French governments. As an interim measure the council passed a conditional resolution stating that none of the other groups would raise any objections if the British agreed to a loan for railway construction on the terms proposed by Chang Kia-ngau.[43]

The British not only concluded an agreement with the Chinese for the loan that had been under discussion but also for a further loan which was to be granted when the British group ceased to be bound by the Consortium obligations.[44] The agreements, which involved a total amount of £7,000,000 were signed after the outbreak of the Sino-Japanese War. Negotiations had already been started for a third loan of £8,000,000 but were discontinued because of the worsening of the military situation in China.

Besides seeking foreign aid for the development of their railways, the Chinese attempted in the early summer of 1937 to obtain assistance for the stabilization of their currency.[45] In June there were many rumors which indicated that H. H. Kung, who was then in London, was appealing for a large loan. On June 21 the British Foreign Office informed the State Department confidentially that it had decided to favor a comparatively small loan of 10 to 20 million pounds to be floated on the London market. The Chinese, on their side, had agreed to introduce a program of fiscal reforms of which the loan would be an integral part. The situation had now reached the stage when discussions were to be conducted between Kung and the British bankers. The Foreign Office strongly intimated that it hoped similar action would be taken by the United States government and American financiers.

In a memorandum to Secretary Hull, the Far Eastern Division urged that serious consideration be given to the British proposal.[46] It stated that Kung was expected in Washington in a few days and that the Department might suggest that he take up the matter with American financial interests. If he did so and if some specific scheme resulted, the administration should then consider it on its merits. A loan, the memorandum concluded, which paralleled that of the British "might lead to several advantages and disadvantages, both political and economic." What the administration's ultimate decision would have been remains in the realm of speculation as further discussion of this subject was also cut short by the Sino-Japanese War.

Despite the hostilities in North China, on July 9 Kung approached the Export-Import Bank with a request for credit facilities for the purchase of capital goods in the United States to assist "China for her program of construction with a view of building up her economic structure."[47] The Bank was to agree "in general principle" to the extension of credits up to $50,000,000 within the next two years. Each transaction was to be considered individually and the Bank remained free to give or withhold approval. At the beginning of August, the Chinese were informed that the bank was disposed to accede to their request but hesitated to make a formal commitment which, under the existing circumstances in the Far East, might soon prove meaningless. The Chinese responded with the suggestion that a total sum of only $10,000,000 should be considered for the present. The State Department told Warren Pierson that it favored a "prompt" acceptance of the Chinese scheme. But on August 11 the Executive Committee of the Export-Import Bank decided to postpone action indefinitely.

Kung also sought help from the United States Treasury in the form of more purchases of silver.[48] Secretary Morgenthau consulted the President who expressed the view that the Chinese were genuinely trying to build up their country internally and that the United States should support them. Consequently, Morgenthau arrived at an understanding with Kung on July 8 by which the Treasury agreed to buy the full amount of the silver that the Chinese were offering. Although the Marco Polo Bridge incident, which was to mark the beginning of the Sino-Japanese War, had already taken place, neither the Secretary nor Kung was as yet aware of what had happened.

One further question which requires some consideration arose during the months of relative quiet that characterized the relations of China and Japan in the spring of 1937. The question was essentially whether the United States should try to take advantage of the more conciliatory attitude of the government at Tokyo to explore the possibility of reaching an agreement with Japan.

The issue developed out of the activities of the British. In February, Secretary Morgenthau, with the consent of the President, sent a message to Neville Chamberlain (then still Chancellor of the Exchequer but already slated to become Prime Minister) asking for suggestions concerning possible ways of stopping the arms race which was currently undermining the economic system of most of the great powers and threatening to engulf a large part of the world in war.[49] Chamberlain responded with a long letter in which he stated with great frankness that the very existence of the British Isles was being threatened by Nazi Germany so that England could not consider any major reduction in armaments.[50]

At the same time Chamberlain intimated that there might be a means of affording the British government some relief in the Far East. His contention was that, as long as the conditions that had prevailed in recent years remained unaltered, Great Britain would have to be prepared to protect her position in Eastern Asia as far as her military capacities permitted. For in case of war between Germany and England, a hostile Japan would in all probability attempt to benefit from the situation by attacking British interests in the Pacific. However, there were signs that the Japanese were "contemplating a change in the direction of cooperation with other nations." Great Britain and the United States should therefore engage in an exchange of views on the "possibility of taking this opportunity to put relations between the U.S.A., Japan, and Great Britain on a footing that would ensure harmonious" collaboration in future.

As Chamberlain's letter dealt with broad issues of foreign policy, Secretary Morgenthau forwarded it to the State Department. The Department delayed answering for almost two months, perhaps in part for the sake of learning more of the British government's intentions.

In April, Norman Davis went to Europe on a trip which has already been mentioned in connection with the President's plan for the neutralization of the Pacific islands. While Davis's purpose in undertaking this journey was ostensibly to attend the International Sugar Conference, it provided him with a chance to serve as the President's unofficial emissary in sounding out the opinions of various European statesmen on the international situation.[51]

In the talks between Davis and Chamberlain, the latter explained his views somewhat more fully.[52] He said that he was opposed to concluding any treaties of fundamental importance with the Japanese as long as the militarists remained in control in Tokyo. Nevertheless, he favored making some sort of an arrangement which might serve as a basis for collaboration between Great Britain, the United States, and Japan. He expressed the firm conviction that the solution to the situation in the Far East lay in Anglo-American unity and that, if the Japanese government believed that the United States and England were "standing together in the Pacific," it would not cause any difficulties but would cooperate with them as it was now indicating a desire to do.

In the Foreign Office, Sir Alexander Cadogan told Davis that he was already engaged in informal conversations with Ambassador Yoshida concerning the possibility of opening negotiations for an agreement with Japan.[53] The initiative, he asserted, had been taken by the ambassador, who insisted that the Japanese militarists were losing ground and wished to abandon their aggressive foreign policy, especially in regard to China, which had only created "trouble and suspicion" with other countries. Yoshida had therefore repeatedly asked the British to allow him to invite his government to submit some concrete proposals for discussion. And, while he remained vague as to the form and content of the proposals he had in mind, they appeared to include provisions for improving Anglo-Japanese trade relations (presumably through the removal of British quotas against Japanese goods) and for assisting in the economic development of China through international collaboration.

Sir Alexander Cadogan stated further that the British had finally agreed to consider any suggestion the Japanese government wished to make concerning the reconstruction of China although they doubted that much would come of the matter. He added that in his opinion cooperation between Great Britain, the United States, Japan, and China in efforts to develop China economically might "help to insure peace and political stability in the Far East"—an idea which obviously conformed to Chamberlain's line of thought.

Around the middle of May, Yoshida told the British that the Japanese government was drawing up a plan which it would forward shortly. But Tokyo had still not been heard from when, at the end of the month, the Hayashi cabinet finally resigned. Within a few days Prince Konoye formed a new cabinet in which Hirota resumed his old position as Foreign Minister. The denouement of the story was that the Japanese decided upon the outline of an agreement which Ambassador Yoshida was to lay before the British as a basis for the opening of formal negotiations.[54] Although the record on this point, as well as many others, remains obscure, the outline was probably given to the British just before the Marco Polo Bridge incident. At any rate, a week after the incident the British Foreign Office told the authorities at Tokyo that it did not regard the present moment as "an opportune one" for holding Anglo-Japanese conversations looking toward the improvement of relations.[55]

While awaiting the Japanese proposals, British officials in private meetings with representatives of the United States government indicated their own views were scarcely any more clearly defined than at the time of Sir Alexander Cadogan's initial talk with Norman Davis.[56] Nevertheless, various startling rumors appeared in the press in the first part of May when it was learned that Ambassador Yoshida was engaged in preliminary discussions with the British Foreign Office relative to the possible negotiation of a treaty.[57] The treaty if concluded, it was alleged, would provide for the recognition by England of Japan's "special interests" in North China and might even involve an understanding to divide China into British and Japanese "spheres of economic influence." As a result of this development, the Chinese became sufficiently alarmed to ask the State Department to question the British.

The State Department did not believe that the newspaper stories had any basis in fact. Indeed it had already received assurances from the British on a number of occasions that they would "not consider any agreement that was not entirely acceptable to China" and that they would keep the United States informed in respect to the conversations being conducted with Ambassador Yoshida.[58] Nevertheless, the

Department took the precaution of instructing Ambassador Bingham to be "on the alert" for any evidence that the Foreign Office was considering a formal commitment attributing to Japan a "special position" in China.[59] If any such evidence emerged, the ambassador was to impress upon the British government that the administration in Washington would regard a commitment of this nature by any power as a "matter of concern" to the United States.

Beyond this, the Department decided on June 1 to reply to the letter which Chamberlain (now Prime Minister) had written to Secretary Morgenthau in March and to incorporate in its response a statement on the subject of attempting to reach an understanding with Japan at this time and on some of the related issues raised by the British. The result was a memorandum which was drafted with great care and received the personal attention of Hull who regarded it as a document of unusual significance.[60]

In the part of the memorandum that dealt with the Far East, the Department addressed itself at the outset to the problem of Anglo-American cooperation, which Chamberlain had so strongly emphasized, and defined the principles that, in accordance with its philosophy, must govern such cooperation. The interests of Great Britain and the United States in the Far East, it declared, had many aspects in common. In the event of the resort by any country to measures of aggression in that area, the United States government would attempt to afford appropriate protection to its legitimate interests but it was not in a position to state in advance what methods it would employ. It was the "traditional policy of this country" not to enter into any type of agreement that constituted or suggested an alliance. The governments principally involved in the Far East should constantly endeavor to exercise a "wholesome and restraining influence" toward safeguarding the rights of all concerned and toward preventing the development of friction and tension. The effectiveness of these efforts could best be promoted through consultation among the powers followed by action along parallel lines undertaken concurrently.

The Department then dealt with the specific situation at hand. Referring to Chamberlain's letter it said:

We note the statement that in the opinion of the British Government there are signs that Japan may realize that the recent trend of its policy has not been to its advantage and that Japan is contemplating a change in the direction of better cooperation with her neighbours in the Far East and with the powers which have great interests there. It appears to us that developments within and among the principal countries of the Far East are producing a trend toward or favourable to stabilization of the general situation there. We feel that with regard to Japan and China there are now actively at work within and between those two countries forces operating in the direction of peace. We are not oblivious to the fact that developments in the Far East may in due course call for the making of new political agreements but we are of the opinion that, if and when the time comes to proceed with the negotiation of such new agreements, the principles upon which they should advantageously be based could not deviate far from those to which the interested powers are already committed in treaties at present in existence.

The Department concluded by stating that in its opinion the most helpful contribution which the powers could make toward improving conditions in the Far East was to attempt to "cultivate goodwill and confidence," to promote "healthy trade relations," and to observe closely the "trend of events." The recent trend appeared to indicate that the peoples of the Far East were "approaching a state of mind" which would enable them to perceive by themselves that the "pathways of cooperation are the pathways of advantage."

In all, therefore, the movement toward the involvement of the West in China's rehabilitation had achieved genuine momentum by the summer of 1937. But, as was frequently observed at the time, the United States did not attempt to keep abreast of the other powers in taking part in this development.

On the side of business a few men, notably Forbes and his supporters in the National Foreign Trade Council, sought to infuse the American industrial community with their own vision of the vital importance of the United States' taking part in China's economic growth. Their argument was essentially twofold: that American private enterprise could, if it wished, have a great future in China; and that, for political as well as economic reasons, it should make a contribution toward the creation of a strong Chinese state. From the beginning to the end, however, the response of the American manufacturers remained disappointing. Nor is there any indication that the American financial group ever abandoned its negative attitude in respect to investment in China. Perhaps Lamont's willingness in the spring of 1937 to advocate a new association to follow the Consortium reflected some confidence that, contrary to his expectations, conditions in China were showing signs of promise. But there is nothing to suggest that the American banks, which were in a position to do so, were inclined to take action within the near future.

On the government side, the State Department was not prepared to adopt a policy, such as the British appeared to be pursuing, of encouraging private enterprise to engage in new ventures in China. Its hesitation was inevitably based upon many factors, but the most important remained its concern over Japanese opposition. It seems evident, however, that some change had occurred in the Department's attitude by the time of the Marco Polo Bridge incident, since it was willing to take under consideration the British proposal in regard to a loan. Undoubtedly officials in Washington were in part influenced by the continuing activity of the European powers in China and by their own belief that Japanese opposition was decreasing.[61] But the real shift came in the growing interest of the Export-Import Bank in the problem of American enterprise participating in China's economic development. Yet the bank's decision to make even an initial move, beyond the extension of relatively insignificant credits, came too late to produce any results. The only step taken consisted therefore of the monetary transaction concluded by Secretary Morgenthau.

As to the question, first raised by Chamberlain, of whether the time had come to reach some sort of an understanding with Japan, the State Department's reaction was obviously unfavorable. The implications of its exchanges with the British were, primarily, that the United States government remained adamantly opposed to considering any agreement which would violate or condone the violation of the principles of the Washington Conference treaties; that, as a result the Department saw no basis for entering into negotiations with the Japanese at present; and that when new accords were concluded, they should, in Hull's words, "be basically the same as the existing Nine Power and Four Power Treaties."[62] The Department also intimated that in view of recent developments it was not without hope that it might be possible to negotiate the kind of a settlement that it had in mind in the not too distant future. But any such hope was soon to be destroyed by the brutal reality of war, for the era of "peace," in which the Japanese had limited themselves to nonmilitary tactics, had come to an end.

UNDECLARED WAR IN CHINA

THE NORTH CHINA PHASE

The Marco Polo Bridge Incident and its Consequences

The increasing tension between the dictatorships and the democracies inevitably dominated all international relations by the summer of 1937 but the focus of attention in most Western capitals was upon Europe and not upon the Far East, where the situation was regarded as being relatively quiet. This condition of affairs was, however, sharply altered by the train of events that followed the Lukouchiao incident of July 7, 1937.

The immediate background to the incident was that the Chinese had become greatly concerned over the size and activities of the forces which Japan maintained in the Peiping-Tientsin area by virtue of the Boxer agreements.[1] It had been customary for the various signatories of the Boxer agreements to restrict their troops in North China to around 2,000 and to limit the field practices in which these contingents engaged to areas that were relatively distant from strategic centers in order not to arouse the concern of the Chinese. But by the summer of 1937 the Japanese had increased their forces to approximately 7,000 and had instructed them to engage in field maneuvers in the vicinity of Lukouchiao (or Marco Polo Bridge), which was an important railway junction only thirteen kilometers from Peiping.

Precisely what occurred on July 7, 1937, will probably always remain a mystery.[2] The Chinese claimed at the time that the Japanese had engaged in a mock attack on Wanping (a city near Lukouchiao) and during the course of the attack had demanded entrance to the city, alleging that one of their soldiers was missing. When entrance was refused, they opened artillery fire with the result that some 200 Chinese, who were part of the garrison defending Wanping, were killed or wounded. Subsequently, the Japanese troops received large re-enforcements and extended their operations to the immediate vicinity of Peiping. The Japanese, on their part, claimed that Chinese soldiers of the 37th Division of General Sung Che-yuan's army (the 29th Army) fired without provocation upon Japanese troops just north of the Marco Polo Bridge and that a temporary cessation of hostilities was arranged in order to open negotiations for a settlement of the incident but that the Chinese did not abide by the agreement or by an agreement made the next day for the mutual withdrawal of troops.

Wherever the truth lay, it was the developments which took place after July 7 that turned the Marco Polo Bridge incident into one of the memorable events of history, for there was nothing in the incident itself that made a major war inevitable. The following is a brief survey of these developments as they appeared at the time to United States officials.[3]

Early in the morning of July 8 a member of the American embassy at Peiping, sent to inspect the Marco Polo Bridge area, reported that desultory firing was still continuing but that the countryside was peaceful and the peasants were going about their affairs as usual.[4] The ambassador dispatched this report to Washington and added that Peiping itself was quiet and that there were no signs of troop movements on either the Chinese or Japanese side. On the following day, Grew wired that the prospects for a settlement of the incident seemed favorable and that the Foreign Office had stated that the firing by Chinese troops which had initiated the clash was apparently "not premeditated." On July 10 the ambassador wrote to Hornbeck that he was not greatly disturbed by the Lukouchiao incident because he did not believe any of the countries in the Far East were for the present "premeditating war," and while incidents might be irritating the chances were against their leading to serious troubles.[5]

The situation began to look more serious, however, when on July 11 rumors were printed in the press to the effect that the Japanese had presented the local authorities in North China with various demands which the Mayor of Tientsin, Chang Tsu-chung, had provisionally accepted in the absence of the Chairman of the Hopei-Chahar Political Council, General Sung Che-yuan. Sung had been in retirement in his home in Shantung for some two months in an apparent attempt to escape from the constant efforts of the Japanese to induce him to make more concessions to meet their wishes. The Japanese demands were said to consist of four requirements in all: the punishment of those responsible for the Marco Polo Bridge incident; the withdrawal of troops from the area in which the incident had occurred; the control of anti-Japanese activities in North China; and the enforcement of anti-Communist measures.[6] On July 13 a member of the Japanese embassy in China informed an American official confidentially that an agreement had in fact been signed on July 11 containing the terms which had appeared in the newspaper reports.[7] As any understanding had, however, ultimately to be accepted by Sung Che-yuan in order to be valid in the eyes of the Japanese, the negotiations shifted to Tientsin where General Sung arrived on July 12 from his Shantung retreat. From July 12 to 18 discussions continued between General Sung and the Japanese based upon the July 11 agreement.

In the meantime, Peck reported from Nanking on July 12 that he had been informed by the Chinese Foreign Office that the Japanese embassy was taking the position that North China was virtually independent and that the present difficulties must therefore be settled by regional authorities in the North without any interference from the central government at Nanking.[8] Since an acceptance of the Japanese thesis would have meant an acknowledgment of an autonomous North China, Peck stated, competent observers felt that the situation was moving toward war as the existence of the National government would be seriously jeopardized if it returned to its former policy of surrendering its northern territories rather than resisting Japanese aggression.[9] In the first place, the Generalissimo was believed to have pledged resistance to Japan as part of the settlement of the Sian revolt so that nonresistance would cause the alienation of the communist forces in the northwest who were in the process of being incorporated in the government's armies; secondly, the southwest "irreconcilables," Pai Ch'ung-hsi and Li Tsung-jen, who at best rendered little more than lip service to the government, would presumably demand Chinese military action or a new government; and thirdly, the position of the Suiyuan, Shansi, and Shantung authorities would be endangered by extensive Japanese control in Hopei and Chahar and they would also be expected to bring pressure upon the government to make a stand.

Meanwhile, American officials were getting reports of troop movements on both the Chinese and Japanese sides. On July 12 a member of the Chinese embassy in Washington told Stanley Hornbeck that Nanking had ordered six divisions to move northward toward Hopei.[10] Two days later the Chinese Minister for Foreign Affairs informed Peck that six divisions had already left Hankow by train and that others would follow.[11] The Japanese on their part announced that at a cabinet meeting on July 11 they had decided to dispatch re-enforcements to China.[12] Just what this announcement meant remained obscure, however. The Chinese claimed officially on July 15 that 20,000 Japanese soldiers had concentrated in the Peiping-Tientsin area.[13] But the confidential estimates of the American army and naval attachés in China and Japan indicated that fewer troops had been sent to China and none had gone from Japan proper but only from Manchuria and Korea.[14] Japanese Foreign Office officials, moreover, on several occasions made statements to members of the American embassy which were in line with the attachés' reports and gave assurances that no divisions would be sent from Japan unless there were further clashes between Japanese and Chinese forces.[15] Nevertheless, a sufficient number of Japanese re-enforcements continued to move into North China to create a highly explosive situation.

At Nanking, the Foreign Minister had sent an indirect message on July 12 to Ambassador Johnson at Peiping and to Sir Hughe Knatchbull-Hugessen, who happened to be vacationing at Peitaiho, asking them to come to the capital. Johnson decided against doing so largely on the grounds that he might be more useful in North China in case the situation there worsened.[16] He did not, in fact, arrive in Nanking until the Generalissimo personally requested him to do so at the end of July, which had the effect of cutting him off from the possibility of playing any significant part in the important events that took place before then.[17]

The British ambassador, on the other hand, returned at once to Nanking, where he plunged into the thick of developments. Politically, the situation was still that negotiations were continuing between General Sung and Japanese officials in the North with Nanking insisting that it would not recognize any agreement which had not been directly negotiated between the Japanese government and the central government of China. Militarily, the Japanese and Chinese troop movements were continuing, each side claiming that it was acting in self-defense. As early as July 12, however, the Chinese Minister for Foreign Affairs, in a discussion with the counselor of the Japanese embassy at Nanking, had proposed a mutual cessation of all military activities and the withdrawal of all armed forces to the positions occupied before the Marco Polo Bridge incident.[18] Sir Hughe Knatchbull-Hugessen seized upon this idea and was active in getting the Chinese to shape it into a proposal which he sent to James Dodds, the British chargé d'affaires at Tokyo, on July 16, for immediate transmission to the Japanese Foreign Office. Chiang Kai-shek, the ambassador told Dodds, wished to state formally that the Chinese government was prepared to stop all troop movements the next day (July 17) provided the Japanese would agree to do likewise and that the Chinese government was ready to enter into an arrangement thereafter for the restoration of the troops on both sides to their previous positions.[19] Dodds, in strict confidence, informed Ambassador Grew of this message for communication to Washington. Grew, in writing of the events of the summer of 1937 years later, declared that Sir Hughe's "very important communication . . . should not be overlooked in history, for had the Japanese desired to avoid the spread of hostilities a clear opportunity to do so was here presented."[20] As matters developed, the Japanese informed Sir Hughe that they could not act on the Generalissimo's "standstill" proposal because the entire issue of the Lukouchiao incident was a matter for the consideration of the local authorities in North China.[21]

On July 19 Chiang Kai-shek delivered a famous speech at Kuling in which he declared that the Chinese would not abandon the hope of peace as long as such hope existed to the slightest degree but that the time might come when they would reach the limit of their endurance.[22] If, the Generalissimo said, China allowed the Marco Polo Bridge to be occupied by force, the result would be that Peiping would be taken; the Peiping of today would then become a second Mukden, and Hopei and Chahar would share the fate of the northeastern provinces. If Peiping became a second Mukden, he asked, what was there to prevent Nanking from becoming a second Peiping? The safety of Lukouchiao was therefore a problem which involved the existence of the nation as a whole and whether it could be settled amicably would have much to do with whether the Chinese had reached the "limit of their endurance."

The Generalissimo then came to the heart of his message, which was that there were four points that formed the minimum basis for negotiations with the Japanese:

First, any kind of settlement must not infringe upon the territorial integrity and sovereign rights of our nation; second, the status of the Hopei and Chahar Council is fixed by the Central Government and we should not allow any illegal alteration; third, we will not agree to the removal by outside pressure of those local officials appointed by the Central Government, such as the Chairman of the Hopei and Chahar Political Council; and fourth, we will not allow any restriction being placed upon the position now held by the 29th Army.

At the same time an important exchange of communications was taking place between the Chinese and Japanese governments. On July 17 the assistant Japanese military attaché at Nanking handed the Chinese War Office a written memorandum to the effect that, if the National government in disregard of the Ho-Umetsu Agreement sent troops into North China, the Japanese military would take whatever measures they considered necessary and any eventualities which might develop would be the responsibility of the Chinese government.[23] On the same day a representative of the Japanese embassy at

Nanking left an *aide-mémoire* at the Foreign Office demanding the cessation of Chinese troop movements northward and an undertaking on the part of the central government to refrain from any interference with the negotiations underway locally for a settlement of the Lukouchiao incident.[24] According to information obtained by Peck from Japanese officials, the Japanese in delivering the *aide-mémoire* demanded a definite reply.[25] The Chinese sent a reply on July 19 which repeated in somewhat modified terms the proposal advanced earlier through Sir Hughe Knatchbull-Hugessen, stating that a definite date should be fixed jointly for the cessation of all military movements on both sides and for the withdrawal of all armed forces to their positions before the Lukouchiao incident.[26] Furthermore, the Chinese government asserted that it was willing to enter into diplomatic negotiations for a settlement of the incident through diplomatic channels but reaffirmed that any adjustment of questions of a local nature made by the authorities in the North must be subject to the sanction of the Chinese National government. The Japanese immediately proclaimed that the Chinese response was unsatisfactory as it did not meet the Japanese demands.[27] Grew cabled Washington that the Chinese reply had been sensationally displayed in the Japanese newspapers and that there had been editorials to the effect that Japan now had no choice but to "cross the Rubicon."[28]

Developments seemed, therefore, to have reached a new peak of tension. Sir Hughe Knatchbull-Hugessen consequently attempted once more to serve as a go-between, this time trying to convey to the Japanese the realities of the situation in China. On July 21 he telegraphed to Dodds:

> I feel that I must emphasize the extreme seriousness of the situation.
> It is quite clear that Chiang Kai-shek still desires a peaceful solution but that anything amounting to complete surrender to the present Japanese demands would bring about his fall . . . Position of the Central Government is that they are willing to negotiate with Japan through diplomatic channel on the present dispute in all its aspects and have offered arbitration and other methods of settlement but that they cannot commit themselves to blind acceptance of some local settlement which will destroy their position in the North once and for all.
> If the Japanese Government imagine that there is any element of bluff in the Chinese attitude they are making a great mistake.
> If the Japanese Government insist on settlement with the local authorities in North China to the exclusion of the Central Government they must realize that war will be inevitable.[29]

Despite many indications that the situation was worsening, there was evidence of optimism in Tokyo. On July 22 Foreign Minister

Hirota told Ambassador Grew that conditions in North China were steadily improving and that he was more hopeful than heretofore that a satisfactory settlement would be achieved.[30] General Sung had finally signed the July 11 agreement on July 19, and everything now depended upon its being carried out without obstruction from the central government. Hirota thereupon read the terms of the agreement to Ambassador Grew, which in general were the same as had been reported earlier but contained certain details that were not known, such as that the Japanese demanded,

Assurances for the future which comprise voluntary retirement of Chinese officials in North China who obstruct Sino-Japanese cooperation; expulsion of Communist elements from that district; control of the Blue Shirts and other organizations hostile to Japan; control of education in the schools; cessation of anti-Japanese propaganda.

These details scarcely seemed compatible with the four conditions the Generalissimo had laid down in his Kuling speech as the essential basis of any agreement with Japan as he had, for example, specifically asserted that there must be no "outside pressure" for the removal of local officials appointed by the central government in North China. Nevertheless he told Nelson Johnson after the latter's arrival in Nanking on July 25 that "out of a sincere desire for peace" he had acceded to the Japanese demands and withdrawn his opposition to a local settlement of the Marco Polo Bridge incident along the lines of the tentative agreement of July 11.[31]

For an exceedingly brief moment it looked to most American officials as though the crisis had passed. Frank P. Lockhart, counselor of the embassy, cabled from Peiping on July 25 that normal conditions had been restored to that region. Only a few hours after sending this message, however, he wired again to say that a new clash had occurred between Chinese and Japanese troops at Langfang, a railway station midway between Peiping and Tientsin. Almost immediately thereafter he reported that fighting had broken out in Peiping, where several hundred Japanese soldiers had allegedly tried to force their way through the gate in the West Wall. Some three days later it was evident that large-scale hostilities had started between the Japanese armies and General Sung's forces. General Sung departed from Peiping in effect leaving the city to the Japanese who took it without having to engage in any significant military operation. General Sung's troops were completely routed and did not even attempt to withstand the enemy except for a gallant though hopeless show of courage at Tungchow and Tientsin. The battle at Tientsin was especially destructive, the Japanese and Chinese engaging in intensive street fighting for several days while the Japanese bombed the city from the air and reduced many of its areas to ruin. Chaos ruled briefly but the Japanese soon gained complete control. On July 31 the United States consul general at Tientsin cabled to the State Department: "City quiet today." The Japanese had gained a major victory in North China.

The Attitude of the United States

Side by side with the reporting by American officials of the events following the Marco Polo Bridge incident went the conduct of American diplomacy.

It must be remembered that the clash at Marco Polo Bridge occurred at a time when the Western nations were deeply involved in the situation in Europe where the ever-increasing strength and drive for power of the dictatorships in Germany and Italy were becoming a vital threat to the democratic countries. Mussolini had only recently completed his conquest of Ethiopia; Hitler, having defied the last restrictions of the Versailles Treaty, was building up a vast military machine; and Germany and Italy combined were intervening in the civil war in Spain in a manner which, in itself, was endangering the security of much of Europe. In addition, as the international situation had deteriorated in the preceding years, the peace system, which at the beginning of the Manchurian incident was still the focus of hope for so many, had progressively grown weaker. Despite the efforts of Secretary of State Stimson and others, the Pact of Paris had not been transformed into an effective instrument for the outlawry of war. Japan's actions had made a mockery of the purposes of the Washington Conference agreements. The Italian-Ethiopian crisis, perhaps even more than the Manchurian crisis, had resulted in widespread discouragement over the ability of the League of Nations to serve as an instrument for the attainment of world peace. Also, within the United States, the isolationists, in the mid-1930's had acquired far more power than they possessed earlier. Faced with these conditions, President Roosevelt tried to find ways of checking the drift toward an armed clash in Europe and of reinvigorating the postwar effort to secure permanent universal peace through methods of international cooperation while not arousing the opposition of the isolationists. The President considered a variety of schemes which ranged from proposing new techniques of international cooperation for dealing with violations of the peace by vigorous collective action against an aggressor to suggesting remedies for the underlying causes of war such as economic distress. The President's plans will be discussed in detail in a later chapter. But it is essential to note here that the first concrete

attempt of his administration to develop a program for the maintenance of peace was undertaken in connection with the Buenos Aires
Conference of December 1936.[32]

The conference—called at the President's instigation—was ostensibly
intended to strengthen the system for the preservation of peace which
had gradually developed in the Americas. But before, during, and
after the conference, both the President and Secretary Hull repeatedly
stated that, in their opinion, the ultimate purpose of the meeting
was to adopt agreements that would form a comprehensive scheme
for the maintenance of peace which could be copied by the rest
of the world. In order to attract the attention of the whole world
to the conference, Roosevelt went to Buenos Aires himself to speak
at the opening session. A few days after he delivered his speech,
Secretary Hull gave his "Eight Pillars of Peace" address in which he
set forth eight principles and proposals that, he said, were in his
opinion "vitally important" for a "comprehensive peace program." The
first principle which he emphasized was that it was the responsibility
of every nation to educate its people in opposition to war and that
"every platform, every pulpit, every forum" should turn itself into
a "constant and active" agent to serve this end. The Secretary further
stressed the need for international cooperation, for the exchange of
ideas and information, and for a revitalization of respect for international law and the observance of treaties. Following the Secretary's
address, the conference remained in session for about three weeks
during which time it adopted sixty-seven agreements, declarations,
and resolutions dealing with such matters as international organization
for the maintenance of peace, the clarification of international law, disarmament, economic problems, and intellectual cooperation.

As we have seen, Roosevelt had some thought of proposing a
neutralization plan for the Pacific islands which would constitute a
peace venture in the Pacific that, although very different in character
from the Buenos Aires agreements, might help to supplement those
agreements; but his plan did not materialize. However, it is evident
from the record that Mr. Roosevelt was far more concerned in the
early summer of 1937 with the possibility of war in Europe than in
the Far East.

Indeed, as already suggested, in the period before the Lukouchiao
incident, attention in Washington was generally directed toward the
rapidly mounting hostility between the dictatorships and the democracies in the West, while the situation in the Far East was regarded
as relatively hopeful. Within the Far Eastern Division of the State
Department itself, a theory was developing to the effect that war

between China and Japan might be averted if China continued to build up its national strength, as Japan would be reluctant to attack a neighbor that showed signs of an ability to defend itself.[33] This point of view was expressed by Stanley Hornbeck and Maxwell Hamilton as late as July 10 (three days after the Marco Polo Bridge incident) at a luncheon meeting in Washington with Dr. H. H. Kung and Ambassador Wang.

According to the official memorandum of this meeting, Hornbeck commented at considerable length upon the fact that people who were returning from China almost without exception gave "glowing accounts" of the progress which that nation was making toward unity and economic rehabilitation.[34] However, Hornbeck went on to say that, as there were obviously still many difficulties to overcome, it seemed to him that China should continue its reconstructive efforts rather than "start arguments with foreign governments"; for, if China once attained sufficient power, her views would essentially be listened to in any dispute that might arise with another country. Kung replied that, while he recognized the force of Hornbeck's line of reasoning, he was nevertheless convinced that war with Japan was inevitable and although China was preparing for such a war, Japan was also preparing and was growing comparatively stronger with the passage of each year. Both Hornbeck and Hamilton dissented, asserting that China was developing along constructive lines whereas Japan was in many ways spending her energies destructively and, in the process, undermining her strength.

If this discussion did not seem academic on July 10, it must have appeared strangely so within a few days for by July 12 the reports of troop movements from both China and Japan indicated that the dispute over the clash at Marco Polo Bridge might well have disastrous consequences. Moreover, when the Counselor of the Chinese embassy was asked, during a call on Hornbeck, for his view of the situation he said, "I am afraid it means war."[35]

Given the gravity of developments, the Secretary of State was bound to take a far more active part in the conduct of policy than under normal circumstances. On July 12 the Japanese ambassador came to see Hull on his own initiative and read a memorandum to him which set forth the Japanese case in regard to the Lukouchiao incident and concluded with the assertion that the Japanese government had decided, as a precautionary measure, to dispatch additional troops to North China although it still hoped to attain a peaceful settlement through negotiation.[36] Hull's own memorandum of his conversation with the ambassador relates:

At the conclusion of the reading, I specially emphasized with approval the remarks of the Ambassador about the efforts of his government to work out a friendly settlement without war. I elaborated upon the futility of any other course and the awful consequences of war. I said that a great civilized first-class power like Japan not only could afford to exercise general self-restraint in such circumstances but that in the long run it was far better that this should characterize the attitude and policy of his government; that I have been looking forward with increasing encouragement to an early period when our two great nations in particular, while other important countries are hesitating to go forward and in fact are slipping backward fundamentally with respect to their economic and standard-of-living situations, would have the opportunity, as well as the great responsibility, for world leadership with a constructive program like the basic program proclaimed at Buenos Aires for the purpose of restoring and preserving stable conditions of business and of peace, which program I elaborated on; that no two great countries have rarely had such an opportunity in these respects as seems to be ahead for our two countries and that of course it means everything from this viewpoint, as well as others, that serious military operations should not be allowed to get under way.[37]

On the following day, the Secretary himself asked the ambassador to call, stating that he wished to keep in as close touch with events as possible. Again Hull recorded his own comments:

I proceeded then to say that to my country and government, the peace situation means everything and that naturally we are tremendously concerned in every aspect of the peace situation; that, whatever we say or do with respect to this Far Eastern crisis is prompted by the most impartial and friendly attitude towards all concerned; that amidst the confusion and fog in the Peking area it is not possible for us to discern just what is taking place and how . . . I then said that with respect to the general situation the question is whether anything could or should be consistently said or done from any agreeable source that might be helpful to all concerned; that my government, of course, is primarily and paramountly concerned in the preservation of peace and . . . would confine its interest and utterances to phases entirely within the range of its impartial, friendly attitude towards all alike; that in any event whatever it might now say, if anything, in an effort to be thus helpful, would stop entirely short of any question or phase of mediation.[38]

The Secretary's assertion that the United States intended to "stop entirely short" of mediation was clearly prompted by the fact that on July 12 the Chinese had asked both the American and British governments whether they would serve in some sort of mediatory capacity to settle the crisis.[39] Hornbeck had immediately advised Hull against agreeing to any form of mediation on the grounds that it would be unwise for the United States to take any step—for the moment at least—that went beyond indicating to both China and Japan that the administration in Washington would "look with great disfavor" upon the outbreak of hostilities in the Far East. Presumably influenced in part at least by Hornbeck's judgment, the Secretary had decided to tell the Japanese that he was not prepared to enter into the Sino-Japanese dispute to the extent of acting as a mediator. Further, after his talk with Ambassador Saito he proceeded to reject a British proposal which was partially designed to explore the possibility of Anglo-American mediation.

The British proposal was made in the form of an *aide-mémoire*, sent to the State Department on July 13, in which Eden asked Secretary Hull whether he would join with the British and French governments in urging moderation in Tokyo and in suggesting that the forces which Japan already maintained in China seemed sufficient to cope with the situation until a settlement of the Lukouchiao incident had been reached.[40] It was evident from the context of the note that one of the aims which Eden had in mind was to open an exchange of views with the Japanese in order to determine whether they would be receptive to the idea of mediation by any of the Western powers. The British proposal was regarded as so important in Washington that, although the Secretary only received it around nine in the evening, he immediately drafted a response (in consultation with Sumner Welles, Norman Davis, and Stanley Hornbeck); had the response approved by the President; and instructed Hornbeck to give it to the British ambassador before the night was over.[41]

The American reply stated that the Secretary had already seen representatives of the Japanese and Chinese governments on several occasions since the Lukouchiao incident and urged upon them "the importance of maintaining peace"; in substance, the United States government had therefore acted along the lines proposed by Eden— except that no reference had been made to the "possibility of mediation."[42] The United States government was, however, "heartily in accord" with the idea of the British making representations, such as Eden had outlined, and felt that in doing so the British government would be following a policy parallel to our own.

A memorandum written by Hornbeck subsequently states that he took the American reply to the British ambassador who read it "very carefully" and "then remarked: 'This means, I would understand, that the American Government is not prepared to join in representations at Tokyo and Nanking.'"[43] Hornbeck explained, under instructions, that the United States government desired to cooperate with the British but felt that "cooperation on parallel but independent lines would be more effective and less likely to have an effect the opposite of that desired than would . . . identical representations."

The ambassador, Hornbeck noted, "then read the memorandum again, maintained silence for some time, and then, with a smile, said that he understood." In short, the administration was attempting, albeit through singularly circuitous means, to convey to the British that it did not wish to become involved either in mediating the Sino-Japanese dispute or in joint action with any other power.

That Grew and Johnson approved the administration's rejection of the British proposal is not open to question. Grew wired on July 14 that a spokesman of the Japanese Foreign Office had indicated to an Associated Press correspondent that the Japanese government regarded the Lukouchiao incident as a matter for settlement between Japan and China and would consequently refuse any offer of mediation such as, according to stories in the press, London and Washington were contemplating.[44] Grew himself definitely advised the Secretary against making any tender of good offices. It was highly unlikely, he said, that the Japanese would react favorably to anything which amounted to an expression of the right of the Western powers to participate in Far Eastern affairs in view of the fact that one of the main objectives of Japanese foreign policy was to eliminate Western influence from eastern Asia. Moreover, he added,

we wish to point out that the improvement in relations between the United States and Japan, which are now better than they have been for a long time past, was made possible when the American Government transferred the emphasis of the actions taken by it in matters affecting relations between Japan and China from (a) endeavor to restrain the use by Japan of force to (b) the laying down of reservations of American rights in China. It is our opinion if there should occur an outbreak of organized hostility that we should continue to follow the course which our Government has followed during the past 4 years and should resort to protests against Japanese military action only in those circumstances where such protests might be expected not to aggravate the situation or when American citizens and property are molested or when humanitarian considerations make necessary an expression of American official opinion.

Two days later Nelson Johnson cabled that he fully agreed with the analysis of the situation set forth by Grew in the above message to the Department, a copy of which had been sent to Peiping.[45]

While the content of the notes exchanged between the British and American governments could scarcely have been known to either the Chinese or the Japanese, nevertheless, as early as mid-July, the idea seems to have gained ground in both Nanking and Tokyo that Great Britain was far more prepared to play a positive part in the crisis over the Lukouchiao incident than the United States. On July 16, the Chinese Vice Minister for Foreign Affairs remarked to Peck that the British government was being more active in the current dispute than the United States, thereby reversing the situation which had existed at the time of the Manchurian debacle.[46] A few days later the Japanese Vice Minister, in a discussion about the Chinese proposal to stop troop movements on July 17 (which had been transmitted through Sir Hughe Knatchbull-Hugessen), remarked pointedly that this proposal had reached him solely through the British and that no other government had taken action.[47] The Vice Minister then inquired even more pointedly "what the British Government had asked other governments to do and what they had replied." Dodds answered that the Foreign Office in London had urged the authorities in Washington to make representations in Tokyo similar to those of the British government but they had "not seen fit to do so."

However, despite the marked caution which Washington was displaying toward making any move that would embarrass the Japanese or would result in the administration's being drawn into joint action with other governments, Hull was deeply aware of the seriousness of the Far Eastern crisis and profoundly anxious to arrest its further development toward war. As has been seen, the Secretary had up to this time limited himself to pointing out to the Japanese the awfulness of war and to urging them to cooperate with the United States in effecting a program, such as the Buenos Aires program, that would lead the world back to international stability. In further pursuance of this course, the Secretary decided to issue a declaration that would, in essence, reiterate the Eight Pillars of Peace which he had proclaimed at Buenos Aires.[48] Consequently, with the sanction of the President, he made public a statement on July 16 which he himself felt to be of the utmost importance:

I have been receiving from many sources inquiries and suggestions arising out of disturbed situations in various parts of the world.

Unquestionably there are in a number of regions, tensions and strains which on their face involve only countries that are near neighbors but which in ultimate analysis are of inevitable concern to the whole world. Any situation in which armed hostilities are in progress or are threatened is a situation wherein rights and interests of all nations are or may be seriously affected. There can be no serious hostilities in the world which will not one way or another affect interests or rights or obligations of this country. I therefore feel waranted in making—in fact, I feel it a duty to make—a statement of this Government's position in regard to international problems and situations with respect to which this country feels deep concern.

This country constantly and consistently advocates maintenance of peace. We advocate national and international self-restraint. We advocate abstinence by all nations from use of force in pursuit of policy and from interference in the internal affairs of other nations. We advocate adjustment of problems in international relations by processes of peaceful negotiation and agreement. We advocate faithful observance of international agreements. Upholding the principle of the sanctity of treaties, we believe in modification of provisions of treaties, when need therefor arises, by orderly processes carried out in a spirit of mutual helpfulness and accommodation. We believe in respect by all nations for the rights of others and performance by all nations of established obligations. We stand for revitalizing and strengthening of international law. We advocate lowering or removing of excessive barriers in international trade. We seek effective equality of commercial opportunity and we urge upon all nations application of the principle of equality of treatment. We believe in limitation and reduction of armament. Realizing the necessity for maintaining armed forces adequate for national security, we are prepared to reduce or to increase our own armed forces in proportion to reductions or increases made by other countries. We avoid entering into alliances or entangling commitments but we believe in cooperative effort by peaceful and practicable means in support of the principles hereinbefore stated.[49]

Following its issuance on July 16, the Secretary sent this declaration to all the governments of the world with a request that they state their attitude by way of reply. As Hull himself relates in his *Memoirs:* "Sixty nations soon gave their full adherence to these principles. Ironically they included Germany, Italy and Japan."[50] The only critical comments came from Portugal, which observed that no objection could be raised against the "assertions, advices or wishes as a whole,, of the Secretary of State" as "everyone desires peace, everyone proclaims the sanctity of treaties and the faithful compliance therewith, everyone desires that there be less difficulties in international trade, and everyone wishes to have the burden of armaments removed or lightened"; difficulties arose, however, when nations passed from "the field of intentions into that of action" and a first step toward constructive work should be made by acknowledging the "inanity" of "entrusting the solution of grave external problems to vague formulae."[51]

The response of the Portuguese prompted the Secretary of State in writing his *Memoirs* many years later to set forth his reasons for placing such great store upon his July 16 declaration. Because of the extreme importance of understanding Hull's point of view toward this declaration, which was to form the cornerstone of his policy in the period following the outbreak of the Sino-Japanese war, his comments are quoted here in full:

Portugal's observation requires comment. In my narrative thus far I have given frequent statement to principles of international conduct which some persons might say come under the category of "vague formulae." I never lost an opportunity, in fact, to state and restate these principles in public speeches, statements, diplomatic notes, and conversations with foreign diplomats and visiting statesmen. To me there was nothing vague about them. They were solid, living, all-essential rules. If the world followed them, the world could live at peace forever. If the world ignored them, war would be eternal.

I had several purposes in mind in constantly reiterating these principles. One was to edge our own people gradually away from the slough of isolation into which so many had sunk. Another was to induce other nations to adopt them and make them the cornerstone of their foreign policies. Still another was to get peoples everywhere to believe in them so that, if aggressor governments sought war, their peoples might object or resist; and, if war did come, such peoples, having these principles at heart, would eventually swing back to the right international road.

To me these doctrines were as vital in international relations as the Ten Commandments in personal relations. One can argue that the Ten Commandments, too, are "vague formulae." But day after day millions of ministers of God throughout the world are preaching these formulae, and I believe there is untold value in this preaching. Society would lapse into chaos if the Ten Commandments were universally broken, just as international society lapses into chaos when the principles of right conduct among nations are widely disregarded.[52]

While Hull did not, at the time that he issued the July 16 declaration, give as detailed an analysis of his views as appears in the above paragraphs, nevertheless he sought to explain his purposes to newspaper correspondents at an off-the-record press conference at which the declaration was released.[53] Asked whether the declaration referred specifically to the situation in the Far East, the Secretary replied that it was intended for universal application and that he was striving "to arouse and promote the spirit of peace" wherever such action was calculated to be most helpful. Questioned about the policy of the United States toward the Sino-Japanese dispute in particular, Hull said he wished to emphasize that the administration had not as yet taken any action. After enjoining the correspondents to strict secrecy, he stated further that there had been various inquiries about the possibility of invoking the Nine Power Treaty but that he felt it would seriously damage the prospects of a peaceful settlement if officials, in this or any other country, stepped out "ahead of the game" and talked of invoking pacts while conditions in the Far East were still so confused that it was impossible to ascertain what was actually happening there.[54]

As already implied, the issuance of the American pronouncement of July 16 was an extension of the policy that the Secretary had been pursuing which amounted to implementing the first of the principles enunciated in his Eight Pillars of Peace, namely, that every government should exert its energies to the utmost to educate the people of the world in opposition to war.[55] The British, on their part, also continued to follow the course they had charted earlier and on July 20, when the situation between Japan and China seemed on the verge of reaching a disastrous impasse, again approached the State Department with a plan for a joint Anglo-American effort to effect a local settlement.[56] The British plan involved two points, namely that the American and British governments should jointly ask the Japanese and Chinese to suspend all troop movements and should put forward proposals in an attempt to end the existing deadlock.

Before responding to the British scheme, the Secretary at his own request had another interview (on the morning of July 21) with Ambassador Saito of which he cabled an account to Grew that was to be read by the ambassador to Foreign Minister Hirota in order to ensure the Japanese government's receiving a completely accurate report of the Secretary's comments.[57] As Hull himself related his talk with Saito, he reiterated many of the points which he had made in his earlier conversations with the ambassador. Thus he stressed that he was approaching both the Japanese and Chinese governments in a "spirit of genuine friendliness and impartiality" and would be glad to do anything to assist in a peaceful solution of the controversy, short of mediation; that he felt that war would prove disastrous, in the existing unsettled state of world affairs, to "all phases of human welfare and human progress"; and that general hostilities would jeopardize the "great objective and beneficent purposes of the program adopted at Buenos Aires including the eight-point pillars of peace proposal." In the latter connection, the Secretary handed the ambassador a copy of his July 16 declaration with the remark that it would "be most pleasing to us if the Government of Japan joined in carrying forward this great program." Immediately after his interview with Saito, Secretary Hull saw Ambassador Wang and spoke in much the same terms. He likewise cabled a summary of this talk to Nanking with a request to Peck to read it to the Chinese Minister for Foreign Affairs.[58]

Following these developments, the Secretary sent a reply to the British in which he declared that the administration in Washington felt that the policy thus far pursued by the American and British governments along parallel lines had been truly cooperative and that, in continuation of a common effort to avert hostilities, both governments should again, each in its own way, urge upon the Chinese and Japanese the importance of maintaining peace.[59] The Secretary further briefly described the remarks which he had made to the Japanese and Chinese during the course of the morning and asked whether the

British Foreign Office did not feel that it might usefully take similar action. Concerning the British plan for issuing an Anglo-American appeal for the cessation of all troop movements, the Secretary said that, as he understood the matter, the Chinese had already made such an appeal which the British had brought to the attention of the Japanese government but without favorable results. Concerning the second point which had been raised by the British—namely, that the British and American governments should jointly advance proposals for a settlement of the Lukouchiao incident—the Secretary remained silent.

The British seem to have done little further for the time being perhaps because in the third week of July the news from the Far East suggested that the crisis might be reaching an end.[60] It became known at this time that General Sung Che-yuan had accepted the terms which the Japanese had originally presented in the July 11 agreement and that the Nanking government had decided not to oppose his action.

If there was optimism in Washington over the turn of events in the Far East it was quickly dispelled when, on July 25, Nelson Johnson informed the State Department that he had just had an interview with Chiang Kai-shek who had declared that the crisis was by no means over and that the Japanese could be expected to approach the Chinese before long with a new set of demands which Nanking would inevitably reject.[61] The Generalissimo, Johnson stated further, had asserted with the greatest earnestness that the Japanese must be made to understand that China would "fight rather than make any further concessions" and had stated that the United States and Great Britain were the only powers in a position to bring this home to the Japanese government. Chiang Kai-shek had, in short, tried to impress upon him (the ambassador) that the "only way in which war between China and Japan could be averted would be by cooperative action by the United States and Great Britain along lines more vigorous than had hitherto been attempted."

The Generalissimo's appeal for a more vigorous Anglo-American policy (which he repeated to the British ambassador) evoked some significant comments from American officials. In a memorandum to the Secretary, Hornbeck stated that, in his opinion, there were two main issues involved in the Far Eastern crisis: the issue for the Japanese and Chinese was whether Japan would gain control of North China; while the issue for the Western powers, especially Great Britain and the United States, was whether to object to the pursuit of national policy by force, and if so, by what means.[62] In the present instance, he said, the United States and Great Britain, of course, found objectionable the prospect that the Japanese and Chinese were about to enter into serious hostilities. However, nothing short of a definite indication by one or more of the great foreign powers of a willingness to "throw some type of force into the equation" would have any appreciable effect upon the struggle for North China. As Great Britain and the United States were not ready to resort to force, other than that of moral suasion, whatever they did would be limited to the use of words which could not be expected to prove decisive. It was, consequently, the belief of the Far Eastern Division that "cooperative action by the United States and Great Britain along lines more vigorous than had hitherto been attempted" would not favorably influence developments—unless such action carried with it "some implication of a sanction."

Ambassador Grew likewise advised the Secretary against adopting a "more vigorous policy in collaboration with the British."[63] He did not think, he said, that any foreign diplomatic representations at Tokyo would have beneficial results; moreover, he agreed with the British chargé d'affaires who had told his government that, while it was true that the Japanese had a fixed policy of attempting to secure control of North China by successive stages, it was up to the Chinese themselves to decide when to resist. In his diary Grew wrote even more explicitly that to make representations, other than those related to the protection of American nationals, would only be regarded as "interference" by the Japanese and serve to aggravate the situation. He had found no one—he stated emphatically—whether on his staff or elsewhere, who had the slightest doubt of the soundness of this opinion.

Indeed, judging by some of his other diary entries, in the weeks following the Lukouchiao incident Grew became progressively convinced that the Western powers should take as little action as possible in relation to the Sino-Japanese dispute and therefore was increasingly enthusiastic about the manner in which Hull was conducting American policy and increasingly critical of the British. As early as July 14, he noted that "Humorists might find humor in the complete turning of the tables between 1931 and 1937. Then it was we who stepped out in front and the British who would not follow . . . In the present instance the Administration is playing its cards, or withholding them, with eminent wisdom." On July 17 he expressed his complete approval of the statement which Secretary Hull had issued the day before and added: "Whether it helps the situation or not it is a great deal wiser than direct representations which not only would not help but would harm by engendering irritation." Some ten days later he recorded: "The United States is still the fair-haired boy. I hope we can remain so and am making every effort to preserve that favorable position. What a change since 1931 and 1932!"[64] In the following month—on August 13—he returned to the theme of American policy and set forth his views in considerable detail:

It seems to me and to all of us here that the Japanese Government genuinely appreciates the attitude and action of our own Government since this trouble began. As we are going along we are adequately registering the importance of avoiding injury to American nationals . . . and other rights, and apart from that we are trying to be helpful . . . Every step that we have taken here has been taken without fanfare, quietly, courteously and with a minimum of publicity . . . The public, if not the Government, must have expected from the United States at least the possibility of a series of Stimsonian outbursts when the trouble started . . . As it gradually dawned on them that the present Administration in Washington has no intention whatever of following the now pretty well discredited course of action, pursued by us in 1931 and 1932, their own friendly attitude commensurately grew and today they take every little opportunity to show their appreciation . . . Whenever Hirota has occasion to write to me, he invariably inserts an expression of appreciation at the friendly attitude which the United States has consistently (during the present trouble) maintained towards Japan . . .

My point is that if we continue to play our cards as carefully and wisely as . . . up to the present, we are coming out of all this terrible mess with a prestige and genuinely cordial friendship on the part of Japan which we have not known for many a long day . . . If we in the Embassy, by our advice and recommendations to Washington (which are considerably listened to by Mr. Hull and SKH) and by our tactics . . . can contribute to the development of a genuine, as contrasted with a merely theoretical, friendship between the United States and Japan—a friendship thorough and sound enough to stand, without serious injury, the periodic knocks which it is bound to experience from time to time—then I shall feel that our work has been constructive and perhaps a satisfactory climax to a fairly long go of it in the profession of diplomacy.

On the subject of British policy, Grew expressed his opinions in various dispatches to the Department in which he spoke with a sharpness that was as a rule conspicuously absent from his comments. On July 29, he stated that the Japanese press had been closely examining the activities of the British since the Lukouchiao incident and had come to the conclusion that the British government was seeking a favorable opportunity to intervene in any military action which the Japanese might undertake and was attempting, for this purpose, to build a close association with the United States, the Soviet Union, and France.[65] On August 6 Grew told the Department in substance that he was surprised, not at the determination of the

British to resist within practicable limits the extension of Japanese influence in China, but at the "naïveté," "fatuity," and general ineptitude with which they were pursuing their aims which was resulting in the creation of an attitude of irritation, suspicion, and resentment on both sides that would color Anglo-Japanese relations for a long time to come.[66]

To cite statements made by Grew in August is, however, to advance beyond the unfolding of diplomatic events as so far related here. For almost immediately after the Generalissimo had warned Nelson Johnson against any easy assumption that the North China crisis was over, the Langfang incident occurred leading within a few days to the outbreak of the extensive hostilities in North China that resulted in the conquest of the Peiping-Tientsin area by the Japanese before the end of the month.

As soon as it became evident that the Japanese might attack Peiping and Tientsin, the British government and subsequently the American government urged the Japanese to refrain from proceeding with any military operations which would endanger the lives of British and American nationals, respectively, or would violate the rights of the foreign powers based on the Boxer Protocol and other international agreements.[67] In Washington, Secretary Hull, at a press conference, expressed the hope that both the Japanese and Chinese would exhibit restraint so that extensive hostilities in North China might be avoided.[68] In response to a question from a reporter concerning the attitude of the State Department toward Japan, the Secretary replied that relations between Japan and the United States had been thoroughly defined in the messages which he had exchanged with Hirota in 1934. As these messages had been expressions of marked goodwill, the Secretary was clearly trying to demonstrate the same friendliness toward Japan that he had carefully exhibited ever since the Lukouchiao incident had developed into a major crisis. However, perhaps for the first time since the crisis had started, an American official seems to have spoken in firmer tones to the Japanese, albeit behind the scenes. For Hornbeck relates that, in a talk with the counselor of the Japanese embassy on July 27, he said that any attack upon Peiping which endangered the lives of foreigners would have an "unfavorable reaction throughout the world" and that it would be "hard to convince the world that such action was called for by considerations of 'military necessity.' "[69]

As the fighting in North China actually got underway and appeared to be leading to a tragedy of the first magnitude, the British government for the third time approached the State Department in an effort to bring about some joint Anglo-American action which might stay the course of developments. Between July 28 and August 3, the British made various proposals, the final one being that the United States and Great Britain might offer their good offices (a) to provide neutral ground where Japanese and Chinese representatives might meet to enter into direct negotiations and (b) to smooth out any difficulties that might arise while the negotiations were being conducted.[70] The British suggested in addition that if the Japanese and Chinese governments agreed in principle to settle their differences through negotiation, then England and America might urge that no more Japanese troops should enter Hopei and no more Chinese central government troops be sent north. In presenting this plan to the State Department, the British, however, explained that if it was carried out it ought in their opinion to be made clear that it constituted a proposal for good offices and was in no sense intended as intervention.

There can be little doubt that the State Department was not genuinely in sympathy with the British plan. On July 29, in instructions to Grew, the Secretary again defined his policy and his definition certainly indicated that he did not want to go beyond the strict limits which he had been observing:

It is our intention as regards the general course of our diplomatic effort in regard to the present North China situation, not to make uncalled for and likely to be futile protests or gestures of interference; but, when, where and as it seems to us that action on this Government's part on behalf of peace or toward safeguarding lives of our nationals or calling attention to American rights and interests is warranted and may serve a useful purpose I shall be inclined toward taking such action.[71]

Grew, on his part, replied to the above message that he was "in complete concurrence and sympathy" with the policy which Hull had outlined and, in fact, "with every step thus far taken by the Department in connection with the present Sino-Japanese hostilities."[72]

Nevertheless, the State Department did not reject the British proposal of August 3 because, as it stated in a note to the Foreign Office, it believed that no possible course which might serve toward the maintenance of peace should be overlooked or omitted.[73] Instead it asked for time to consult with Ambassador Grew and suggested that the Foreign Office consult its own representatives in Tokyo.

On August 5 the Department therefore submitted the British plan to Grew, who replied, on the following day, that in his opinion much would depend upon the "method and manner" in which it was presented to the Japanese.[74] With the utmost emphasis, he advised the Department not to deliver the British proposal in the form of a diplomatic demarche but to authorize him to discuss the matter with Hirota in an "oral, confidential, semi-informal, and exploratory conversation" which, among other factors, would have the overwhelming advantage of ensuring an absence of publicity. The ambassador also suggested that the British chargé d'affaires might make a similar approach to Hirota but do so separately. He further asserted that, while he did not think that the British scheme was likely to be accepted in Tokyo under any circumstances, the situation was nevertheless not entirely hopeless and he felt that in any case no stone should be left unturned to avoid war. "I should like to feel," Grew said in concluding his cable, "that history will regard the record of American action in this most critical and pregnant period in Far Eastern affairs as exhaustive, unstintedly helpful and impartially correct."

Both the British and American governments accepted Ambassador Grew's recommendations.[75] As a result, Grew had an interview with Foreign Minister Hirota on August 10 in which he stated that the United States wanted to offer its good offices along the lines of the two points embodied in the British plan.[76] During the course of the conversation, the ambassador repeatedly stressed that he was talking in an "informal, confidential and exploratory way" both to forestall any possible publicity and to avoid "any semblance of interference" as his government only desired to be as helpful as possible. Hirota, on his part, informed Grew confidentially that direct negotiations with the Chinese had already been opened and that Ambassador Kawagoe had presented a "so-called 'plan'" for the adjustment of Sino-Japanese relations, to Kao Tsung-wu of the Chinese Foreign Office at Shanghai on the preceding day. Kao had immediately left for Nanking to submit the plan to Chiang Kai-shek. While Hirota did not reveal the details of the scheme, he did inform Grew that it contained demands for the cessation of anti-Japanese activities in China and for the establishment of good relations with Manchukuo. In regard to the situation in general the Minister seemed decidedly pessimistic and declared that, unless Chiang Kai-shek responded to the Japanese approach promptly and favorably, it would be very difficult to avert a general Sino-Japanese war. As to the United States' offer to be of assistance, Hirota declared that the most effective action the American government could take would be to persuade Chiang Kai-shek to make "some kind of proposal" (apparently meaning a counter-proposal to the Japanese plan) which might serve as a basis for negotiation.

On the day following Grew's talk with Hirota, the British chargé called upon the Foreign Minister and handed him a brief note containing the British offer of good offices.[77] According to Dodds' account to Ambassador Grew, Hirota read the document with the greatest care and then after a long pause (which Dodds estimated to have lasted "at least 5 minutes") remarked that it might be possible to take advantage of the British offer later. For the rest, Hirota spoke to the British chargé in almost precisely the same terms as he had spoken to Grew.

The embassy in Tokyo sent a report of the ambassador's talk with Hirota, not only to Washington, but also to Nelson Johnson at Nanking. The latter cabled the Department at once appealing to it, in issuing any further instructions, to take into account the difficulty with which he would be faced if he had had to urge the Chinese government to agree to a plan which included a demand for the elimination of all anti-Japanese activities in China.[78] Heretofore, Johnson said, whenever the Japanese had made such a demand they had extended it so as to include not only obvious anti-Japanese activities but the whole program of education used in Chinese schools and what the Japanese were "pleased to term communism."

A few days later Ambassador Johnson sent a supplementary message to the Department in which, for the first time since the Lukouchiao incident, he expressed his views on the subject of American policy:

The struggle between Japan and China ramifies into psychological, political and economic fields which are obscure. Although there can therefore be no infallible appraisal of its causes or outcome, I hesitatingly but from a sense of obligation submit my opinion that the Japanese military faction is forcing Japan along a road of compulsory piecemeal domination of China . . . It is my opinion that nothing can save China from the necessity of deciding sooner or later whether to oppose Japanese aggression with force or sink to the condition of a vassal state . . .

If serious hostilities occur between Japan and China, they will inflict untold damage on China and possibly Japan, but they may correct in China a tendency to rely on foreign aid and in Japan a belief in the profitable results of imperialist expansion.

In conclusion I believe a compromise truce at this juncture would merely postpone the inevitable decision whether China shall be dominated by Japan without resistance, and the urging of such a compromise by the United States would seriously impair the public stand we have taken against war and against violation of international agreements. It would follow from this conclusion that any representations to either party should be carefully noncommittal in regard to the fundamental issue and should be strictly confined to safeguarding of American interests unless frankly made on behalf of humanity or international morality.[79]

In reply to Johnson, the Secretary said that his analysis and opinions were helpful and were in general accord with the concepts prevalent in the Department.[80] But on the very day (August 13) that the Secretary sent Johnson this message, new developments obscured the question of the Chinese response to the Japanese proposals for a settlement. For hostilities broke out in Shanghai which proved to be the opening of a three months battle for the control of that city. Kao Tsung-wu consequently never returned from Nanking to resume his talks with Ambassador Kawagoe, upon which Hirota was placing his hopes for a settlement.

THE SHANGHAI PHASE

An uneasy peace had existed between the Japanese and Chinese in Shanghai ever since the conclusion of the Armistice Agreement of May 1932 which brought to an end the fighting between the Japanese and Chinese armies for the control of Shanghai during the Manchurian incident. The Armistice Agreement had provided for the withdrawal of the Japanese forces (known as the Japanese Naval Landing Party) to the areas in the International Settlement where they were customarily stationed and had stipulated that the Chinese forces should remain in their existing positions, about twenty kilometers toward the west of Shanghai, "pending later arrangements upon the re-establishment of normal conditions."[81] A Joint Commission, including representatives of the "friendly powers" that were assisting in bringing about the settlement, was to be established to serve in a kind of supervisory capacity in respect to the fulfillment of the agreement. In signing the truce, the Chinese had, however, made certain specific reservations the most important of which was an official declaration that nothing in the agreement was to be understood as implying "any permanent restriction of the movements of Chinese troops in Chinese territory."[82] At the same time they had announced the creation of a special Peace Preservation Corps which was to police the 20 kilometer zone into which the regular Chinese troops were not to return during the duration of the truce.

The "later arrangements" which were to be decided upon when conditions returned to normal were never brought into being, largely because the interested Western powers believed that the Japanese were trying to take advantage of the situation to turn the 20-kilometer zone into a permanently demilitarized area that would encircle the whole of Shanghai.[83] Because of the failure to take further action, there was considerable doubt as to whether the Armistice Agreement remained in effect. The Japanese, nevertheless, contended that it did and, for whatever reason, the Chinese not only refrained from openly challenging this contention but actually continued to observe the conditions laid down by the truce. As a consequence, up to the spring of 1937 the 20-kilometer zone remained free of all troops and was policed only by the Peace Preservation Corps which the Chinese voluntarily restricted to around 2,000 men permitted to carry no more than light arms.

In June of 1937 the Japanese called a meeting of the Joint Commission (which had not convened since its inception) at which they charged that the Chinese had expanded the Peace Preservation Corps so that it now consisted of 6,000 men equipped with artillery and tanks and that they were, furthermore, fortifying the "demilitarized zone" in "violation" of the 1932 Armistice Agreement.[84] The Chinese delegate at the meeting objected to the use of the term "demilitarized zone" on the grounds that there was no legal basis for the existence of such an area and in general asserted that the questions raised by the Japanese did not fall within the province of the agreement. The members of the commission who represented the Western powers, on their part, declared that they were not in a position to interpret the agreement and, as a consequence, no action was taken. Nevertheless it is evident from the confidential memorandum sent to the State Department by Nelson Johnson at this time that he at least believed that the Japanese were not justified in insisting that the 1932 truce had committed the Chinese to demilitarize the 20-kilometer zone but that he equally believed that it was useless for the Chinese to try to challenge the Japanese claim.[85]

The outbreak of war in North China inevitably increased the tension between the Chinese and Japanese in Shanghai. Toward the end of July, an incident occurred which almost led to a major clash between the Japanese Naval Landing Party and the Peace Preservation Corps.[86] No sooner had this matter been settled peacefully than news of the fall of Peiping and Tientsin convinced many people in Shanghai that hostilities would soon spread to the Yangtze region and, as a consequence, many Chinese began to flee southward or into the International Settlement, where they contributed to a rapidly rising sense of panic. On August 9 the situation was made more critical by another incident which occurred at the Hungjao Aerodrome, resulting in the death of two members of the Japanese Naval Landing Party and a Chinese sentry. But even before August 9, the Japanese government decided to send re-enforcements to the Landing Party, persuaded that the Chinese were still enlarging the Peace Preservation Corps and were in general engaging in military preparations in the "demilitarized zone."[87] The re-enforcements, consisting of 1,000 men and large supplies of arms and ammunition, arrived in Shanghai on August 11 where they joined the 2,000 marines that normally made up the Landing Party. On the following day, Nanking moved two of its crack divisions (numbering between 20,000 and 30,000 soldiers) into the Shanghai area, stationing part of them in the district which adjoined the section of the International Settlement that was occupied by the Japanese troops.[88] Early the next morning fighting broke out on several places along the line between the Chinese and Japanese forces leading to the prolonged struggle for Shanghai that ended in November.

A battle for Shanghai—a great Asian city, teeming at all times with a vast, poverty-stricken, wholly disorganized population—was bound to produce disasters tragically costly in human terms. The Japanese, trying to counterbalance the numerical inferiority of their forces, resorted at the outset to the shelling of Chinese troops with heavy guns which were stationed on warships that they had moored in the Whangpoo. The Chinese sought to put these guns out of commission by bombing from the air. But, suffering from lack of training and experience, the Chinese pilots were frequently unable to hit their targets and instead dropped their bombs within the city itself or on the boats of the neutral powers which were anchored close to those of the Japanese in the river. The most hideous catastrophe of all occurred on August 14—known thereafter as "bloody Saturday" in Shanghai—when bombs from Chinese planes landed first in the main street of the International Settlement and, secondly, in an area of the French Concession which, in addition to its usual inhabitants, harbored crowds of Chinese refugees. Even the normally colorless Annual Report of the Shanghai Municipal Council states in regard to the tragedy in the French Concession that the scene was "almost indescribable . . . the area covered with hundreds of dead and wounded, with mutilated and dismembered bodies scattered in all directions."[89] Over seventeen hundred civilians were killed and an even greater number were injured. Among the dead were three United States citizens, including Frank J. Rawlinson, the editor of the *Chinese Recorder*, who was one of the best-known Americans in China. A similar, though less extensive, disaster occurred again on August 23 when more bombs fell in densely populated parts of the settlement. The *Augusta*, the flagship of the United States Naval force at Shanghai, was also hit on several occasions and the *President Hoover*, a steamship of the American Dollar Line, was accidentally struck on August 30, resulting in the killing of two of its crew and the serious injury of several others.

For the neutral powers, the fighting in Shanghai essentially presented a two-fold problem of trying to avert an extensive Sino-Japanese war and attempting to safeguard the large foreign communities in the International Settlement and the French Concession together with the important economic interests which they represented. Even before the Hungjao incident Clarence Gauss, obviously intensely alarmed by the prospect of war in Shanghai, urged the State Department to propose a comprehensive plan for the neutralization of the city which would have involved the withdrawal of all Chinese and Japanese troops to a line some 10 miles beyond the Settlement and the Concession and the policing of the evacuated area by foreign forces.[90] This scheme came to nothing as the Department rejected it.[91] But as the likelihood of the Sino-Japanese conflict spreading to Shanghai increased, the Chinese themselves issued a warning, on August 8, to the effect that if the Japanese used the International Settlement as a base from which to attack the Chinese forces, the latter would take any measures they deemed necessary to protect themselves even if such measures meant engaging in military activities inside the International Settlement.[92]

From August 8 until the final outbreak of hostilities on August 12, the ambassadors of the various interested powers (Germany, Italy, Great Britain, France, and the United States) at Nanking and the Consular Body at Shanghai sought to obtain assurance from both the Chinese and the Japanese that they would exclude the Shanghai area from any possible warfare.[93] It soon became evident, however, that they were not likely to be successful as each combatant claimed that it had no control over the course of the crisis which was solely the outgrowth of the transgressions of the other.[94] As a consequence, on August 12 the State Department in Washington arrived at the conclusion that the best solution was to urge the Chinese to withdraw the forces which, to all appearances, they had for some time been introducing into the "demilitarized zone" established by the 1932 Agreement.[95] The Department reasoned that, regardless of the rights and wrongs of the matter, these troops were not needed for the maintenance of order and that their presence consequently implied a military purpose which served as an irritant to the Japanese and might provide them with an excuse for aggression. The Department's suggestion for withdrawal was, however, never presented to the Chinese government in part probably because it was outstripped by events and in part because the ambassadors at Nanking felt very strongly that it was impossible to ask the Chinese to remove their troops without simultaneously asking the Japanese to recall the re-enforcements which they had sent to augment the Naval Landing Party.[96]

Following the opening of hostilities on August 13, three major plans were advanced by representatives of the foreign powers to put an end to the warfare in Shanghai. The first of these was formulated by the consuls in Shanghai who proposed (1) that the Chinese should withdraw their regular army divisions to their former positions and remove the Peace Preservation Corps to a distance of some two miles from the International Settlement, leaving only police in the evacuated area and (2) that the Japanese should withdraw the re-enforcements and additional naval vessels, which they had sent to Shanghai, leaving only a "normal garrison" for the protection of their nationals.[97] The proposal of the consuls was supported by the State Department, which urged its serious consideration in both Nanking and Tokyo.[98] But in the end no constructive results were achieved as the Generalissimo wanted the powers to serve as "guarantors" to ensure the carrying out of the agreement by the Japanese (which the powers were unwilling to do) and the Japanese, on their side, insisted that they could not remove any of their troops from Shanghai as they were needed there to protect the Japanese community in the city which numbered around 20,000.[99]

The second plan was devised on August 16 by the five ambassadors at Nanking who had been working to find a solution to the Shanghai crisis from the beginning.[100] The plan was incorporated in a message sent by the ambassadors to their consuls at Shanghai which stated that the core of the problem was the presence of Japanese armed forces in the Shanghai area which was attracting danger to the life and property of the Japanese community. "The Japanese authorities," the ambassadors declared, "must make up their minds whether they are more interested in the presence of their armed forces or in the safety of their nationals." If the former, there was "nothing for it" but to fight out the issue. If the latter, the Japanese could be assured "most positively" that the best way of securing the safety of their nationals was to evacuate their armed forces from Shanghai subject to an arrangement whereby (a) the Chinese would withdraw their troops simultaneously and (b) other foreign forces would serve as a temporary protection while the Japanese removed their nationals from Shanghai until such time as the withdrawal of Chinese troops had been completed and the Shanghai Municipal Police had increased its complement of Japanese officers to a sufficient number (presumably around 100) to protect individual Japanese inside the Settlement from sporadic assaults by anti-Japanese fanatics.

The ambassadors' plan was rejected by the consuls who by this time had almost arrived at the conclusion that the situation was hopeless.[101] Gauss, in a brief but vividly descriptive cable sent to the

Department on August 18, stated that there were hundreds of thousands of Chinese refugees in the International Settlement and the French Concession who were in desperate need of aid and who were crowding the city so that the health and sanitation problems were becoming serious; public utilities were on the verge of breaking down; and rowdyism, looting, and street fighting were increasing.[102] Moreover, the whole of Shanghai might soon become a "field of desperate battle" in which case all foreigners might be compelled to leave.

Despite the negative attitude of the consuls toward the scheme which had been submitted to them by the ambassadors, the British decided to use it as a basis for another suggestion which became the third and final proposal submitted by foreigners to avert further hostilities in Shanghai. From the time the fighting in Shanghai had started on August 13, the British took an active part in the situation (comparable to that which they assumed in regard to the outbreak of warfare in North China) while the State Department in Washington continued its policy of strict restraint and impartiality. On the morning of August 13, Secretary Hull, in a talk with Ambassador Saito, laid down a thesis which he repeatedly emphasized thereafter, namely, that regardless of the argument over who was at fault, the world would hold Japan and China equally responsible if any extensive military conflict took place in Shanghai.[103] On the same day, Grew informed the Department that the British had protested at Tokyo against the possible use of Shanghai as a base of hostilities but that, in his opinion and in that of most of his colleagues, such representations would have no preventive effect and would only run the risk of provoking an antiforeign outburst in the Japanese press.[104] The next day Ambassador Grew cabled again to say that the British had presented the Japanese with another protest the text of which, as drafted in London, was so severe that Dodds had taken upon himself the responsibility of moderating it by omitting "such terms as 'preposterous' and 'glaring'" with reference to Japan's actions in Shanghai.[105] On August 16, Grew reported that the British had addressed a third message to the Foreign Office in Tokyo which in essence put the final blame for the developments at Shanghai upon the Japanese and urged the immediate withdrawal of the Naval Landing Party.[106]

On August 18, the British formally and publicly sent notes to both the Chinese and Japanese governments, which contained the proposal that was based upon the plan that had been worked out by the ambassadors at Nanking and which read as follows:

If both the Chinese and Japanese Governments will agree to withdraw their forces including men of war from the Shanghai area and will both agree that the protection of Japanese nationals in the International Settlement and on the extra-Settlement roads should be entrusted to foreign authorities, His Majesty's Government in the United Kingdom will be prepared to undertake the responsibility if other powers will join them in doing so.[107]

The British plan differed from that which the consuls had advanced (and which, as already stated, had received the support of the administration in Washington) in that it involved the active participation of the foreign powers. It indeed even went considerably further in this respect than the suggestion which had been made by the ambassadors for it envisaged placing the Japanese population in the Settlement under the protection of foreign forces for the duration of the crisis while the ambassadors had limited themselves to the idea of foreign troops assisting the Japanese in the removal of their nationals from the Shanghai area.

The day that Dodds presented the British note in Tokyo, Ambassador Grew told the Department that the Japanese Vice Minister for Foreign Affairs, in accepting the note, had stated that it was a "very important communication" which would have to be considered by his government but that he doubted whether the foreign powers had sufficient forces at their disposal in Shanghai to ensure the security of the Japanese community there and that moreover the Japanese government might find it difficult to entrust the protection of its nationals to other governments.[108] Later in the same day, the Department received a written inquiry from the British as to whether the United States government would participate in the British plan, to which the Department replied that, according to the reports of its embassy in Tokyo, the British proposal had "already been disposed of, adversely, by the attitude of the Japanese Government."[109] "However," the Department added, "toward avoiding any possible misunderstanding, it should not be expected that this Government would be favorably inclined toward any project envisaging military or police responsibilities over and above those which relate to the already existing missions of its armed forces now present in China."

On the afternoon of August 19, Grew advised the Department that the Japanese Vice Minister had that day informed the British chargé that Japan could not accept the British proposal but had qualified his statement with an assurance that the Japanese refusal was "only *pro tem* and might be reconsidered."[110] Clearly as a result of a similar communication from Dodds, the British addressed another note to the

State Department in which they asserted that, while the Japanese government had indicated "preliminary doubts," it had not yet given its final answer to the British plan and that the British Foreign Office earnestly hoped that the United States would be able to declare its readiness to cooperate.[111] To this the Department responded with a terse *aide-mémoire* which said that all available information "including reports received from American official sources" had only tended "conclusively to confirm" its original impression that the British proposal had already been disposed of by the negative attitude of the Japanese.[112] In handing the *aide-mémoire* to the British Ambassador, Stanley Hornbeck observed, ". . . we hoped that at no time would there be brought against us the charge that the project had come to nothing because of rejection of it by us or refusal on our part to cooperate."[113] In a subsequent interview with the British ambassador, Hornbeck explained that the administration's "impatience" with the British had been caused, not by their request for action or cooperation, but by the fact that they had approached us with a proposal which "seemed to us already to have been 'killed.'"[114]

But assuredly the Department did not want under any circumstances to participate in a plan such as the British were advancing. What else could be the meaning of its own statement, quoted above, to the effect that the United States government could not be expected to favor any scheme involving military or police responsibilities which went beyond the "already existing missions of its armed forces" in China? Moreover, following Hornbeck's interviews with the British ambassador, Secretary Hull cabled Grew (for his "strictly confidential information") that, while the British still seemed to entertain some hope of realizing their plan, the Department was opposed to it.[115]

A few days after the Department had replied to the British proposal for the second time, the Secretary of State decided to renew his efforts to focus the attention of the public upon the principles of international good conduct, originally incorporated in his Eight Pillars of Peace speech and reiterated in the July 16 declaration which he had sent to all the nations of the world, and to point up the necessity of applying those principles to the crisis in the Far East. Accordingly, he issued a press release on August 23 which, after referring to the dangers confronting the foreign community in Shanghai as a result of the outbreak of hostilities there, went on to proclaim:

> The issues and problems which are of concern to this Government in the present situation in the Pacific area go far beyond merely the immediate question of protection of the nationals and interests of the United States. The conditions which prevail in that area are intimately connected with

and have a direct and fundamental relationship to the general principles of policy to which attention was called in the statement of July 16, which statement has evoked expressions of approval from more than 50 governments. This Government is firmly of the opinion that the principles summarized in that statement should effectively govern international relationships.

When there unfortunately arises in any part of the world the threat or the existence of serious hostilities, the matter is of concern to all nations. Without attempting to pass judgment regarding the merits of the controversy, we appeal to the parties to refrain from resort to war. We urge that they settle their differences in accordance with principles which, in the opinion not alone of our people but of most peoples of the world, should govern in international relationships. We consider applicable throughout the world, in the Pacific area as elsewhere, the principles set forth in the statement of July 16. That statement of principles is comprehensive and basic. It embraces the principles embodied in many treaties, including the Washington Conference treaties and the Kellogg-Briand Pact of Paris.

From the beginning of the present controversy in the Far East, we have been urging upon both the Chinese and the Japanese Governments the importance of refraining from hostilities and of maintaining peace . . . In the light of our well-defined attitude and policies, and within the range thereof, this Government is giving most solicitous attention to every phase of the Far Eastern situation, toward safeguarding the lives and welfare of our people and making effective the policies—especially the policy of peace—in which this country believes and to which it is committed.

This Government is endeavoring to see kept alive, strengthened, and revitalized, in reference to the Pacific and to all the world, these fundamental principles.[116]

Unfortunately for Hull, his press release was issued on the day when, as already related, bombs from Chinese planes fell in a densely populated area of the International Settlement resulting in a disaster which was similar in kind, if not equal in scope, to the appalling catastrophe of August 14. The news from Shanghai therefore absorbed the attention which might otherwise have been paid by the newspapers to Hull's statement. According to those close to the Secretary, Hull had worked so hard to make his statement a success and had nurtured such high expectations of its beneficial effects that he was deeply disappointed at the denouement and, in the last week of August, wrote still another declaration based upon the Pillars of Peace which he was, however, dissuaded from making public by his advisers in the State Department.[117]

The issuance of the August 23 press release did not coincide only with further tragedies in Shanghai. Somewhat curiously it occurred on the same day that Generalissimo Chiang Kai-shek sent a message to the President and Secretary of the Treasury Morgenthau which was transmitted through the State Department. The message, which was incorporated in a dispatch from Professor J. Lossing Buck at Nanking who had just seen the Generalissimo, said:

I am truly disappointed that the United States did not cooperate with England in an attempt to avert the present crisis which could have been averted by joint representation to Japan and China. China and the world will long remember Simon's failure to cooperate with the United States in 1931 regarding Manchuria and now Britain will long remember the failure of the United States to cooperate. United States should not lose her prestige in the world as an upholder of international justice and if she will continue her Stimson policy the present conflict can be prevented also from extending to other countries including the United States. I do not want the United States to be dragged into the war, but I do look to her to maintain her position in the Pacific and to maintain peace there. It is not too late for action and I trust the United States to work out a just settlement for permanent peace.[118]

The unusually bitter tone of the Generalissimo's message plus the fact that it had been addressed to Morgenthau rather than to Hull was bound to stir up considerable agitation in the State Department. That it did so is apparent from a cable which was subsequently sent to Nelson Johnson instructing him to inform the Chinese Minister for Foreign Affairs that Chiang Kai-shek was evidently under a misapprehension in regard to American policy.[119] Johnson was to call attention to the texts of Secretary Hull's statements of July 16 and August 23 and to say that the American and British governments had been following parallel policies which were directed toward the same fundamental objective, namely, the preservation of peace. Ambassador Johnson was furthermore to tell Professor Buck that messages concerning questions of foreign relations ought to be referred to the agents most responsible for the conduct of foreign relations and that, in the United States, such officials were the Secretary of State and the President.

Chiang Kai-shek's urgent appeal for action by the United States was made during a period when there was considerable discussion, both in diplomatic circles and the press, of the possibility of a group of Western powers adopting some concerted measures to stop the hostilities in the Far East. The discussion was given impetus by the expansion of the warfare around Shanghai where, in the third week of August, the Japanese managed after a bitter struggle to land reenforcements that for the first time took the offensive against the Chinese armies. Moreover, the situation between the British and the Japanese was made worse by a dramatic incident in which two British embassy cars, that were traveling from Nanking to Shanghai, were sprayed with machine gun fire from a Japanese plane resulting in serious injury to Sir Hughe Knatchbull-Hugessen.[120] This in turn added gravity to rumors that England was trying to persuade the United States to issue a joint declaration vigorously condemning Japanese aggression in China. In an effort to forestall the administration's participating in any such declaration, Grew cabled the Department late in August in order to submit some of the views on the Sino-Japanese situation which characterized the thinking of the embassy in Tokyo and which he felt might be useful to the administration in reaching some decision about future policy.[121]

In essence, the ambassador declared that there were divergent opinions about the immediate responsibility for the hostilities in China but that the entire issue of responsibility no longer seemed of much practical importance. The really significant consideration was that the seeds of the present conflict had been sown long ago as it was evident that, once having conquered Manchuria, Japan would have to choose between abandoning the territory she had taken or gaining control over North China, and she was bound to choose the latter. In the embassy's view, the Japanese had probably originally wanted to achieve a local settlement of the Marco Polo Bridge incident or, failing this, to restrict the hostilities to North China. However, having been unsuccessful in both respects there could be "no question" but that the Japanese government, solidly supported by the public, was determined to see the war with China through to the end. Moreover, as a nation, the Japanese seemed completely confident in their ability to win an overwhelming military victory within a few months and never stopped to consider that, in all probability, it was only when the military victories were over and the Chinese armies virtually destroyed that the true war would begin in the form of "almost endless" guerrilla fighting. It was in the inability of the Japanese to visualize the long-range outlook that the embassy saw a "considerable risk" that Japan might emerge from the conflict in China shorn of much of her prestige and power.

As to American policy, Grew presented the embassy's views in the following significant formula: the embassy felt, he declared,

> that the fundamental objectives of the United States in the present situation should be: (1) to avoid involvement; (2) to protect to the utmost the lives, property and rights of American citizens; and (3) while reserving complete neutrality to maintain our traditional friendship with both combatants.

In line with his earlier writings, Grew emphasized the third point and especially one aspect of that point, the preservation of good relations between the United States and Japan. With reference to the possibility of the United States' issuing a statement in conjunction with Great Britain which would censure Japan, Grew declared that the embassy was of the opinion that any attempt to thwart Japanese policy in China by "manifestations of disapprobation on legal or moral grounds" would have no beneficial effect. If persisted in, they would merely tend to obliterate the elements of friendship on the part of Japan toward the United States that were daily being developed by the methods and manner of procedure which the administration had adopted during the existing crisis. (Concerning this part of his dispatch Grew commented in his diary: "In our opinion, American interests will best be served in future by a policy of dignified silence . . . in other words, the righteous indignation theme can now do no further good and should be soft-pedalled."[122])

Ambassador Grew's cable reached Washington on August 27, when the anxiety over the situation in the Far East was so great within the Department that Hull was holding meetings twice daily with his principal aides. Among those attending the meetings was Pierrepont Moffat, who was not only Chief of the Division of European Affairs but was also Grew's son-in-law, and consequently likely to be especially sensitive to the administration's reactions to the dispatches from Tokyo. Concerning the message received on August 27, Moffat recorded in his diary on that day that it had made a great impression upon the "powers-that-be" with its careful presentation of the embassy's opinion.[123] But on August 29 Moffat wrote that the temper of the American people was rising fast against Japan (although there was no disposition to get involved in the Far Eastern conflict) and that according to rumor, Senator Johnson of California, believing that both the State Department and the embassy in Tokyo were too pro-Japanese, was on the "war path" and trying to decide whether the moment was opportune to apply some sort of political pressure in order to change matters in the direction of his liking. "I fear," Moffat added, "that J.C.G.'s telegram emphasized too much the satisfaction of the Japanese at the course we have pursued thus far."[124] No one in Washington, he said, believed that it was possible for the United States to go through a major crisis provoked by Japanese aggression without causing Japanese resentment, most particularly because our policy in the Far East was only a segment of our foreign policy as a whole and had to be determined with respect to analogous situations elsewhere. The next day Moffat recorded that a reply to "J.C.G.'s telegram" was gradually being drafted in the Department and that, while there were differences concerning the manner in which it should be constructed, there was complete agreement that the embassy in

Tokyo would have to be "set right as to the way in which our minds are running."

The Department's reply, written in the first person as coming from the Secretary, was finally sent to Tokyo on the second of September. It stated in part:

This Government has endeavored in the current crisis to follow a course of absolute impartiality. We realize that manifestations of disapprobation on legal and moral grounds are not likely to bring the hostilities to an end. However, in shaping our course, it is necessary for us to have constantly in mind not only the possible serving of that objective, not only the possible effects of possible steps, upon Japan or upon China . . . but the attitude and wishes of our own people, the principles in which this country believes, the courses pursued by other countries, and various general and ultimate as well as immediate and particular objectives.

My statement of July 16 made clear the principles which are guiding this Government. . . . My subsequent statement of August 23 makes it clear that we regard these principles as applicable to the Pacific area. We consider those principles fundamental to a well-ordered existence of and in the society of nations. It is evident that neither Japan nor China in their present course of action are acting in accordance with those principles and that the course which Japan is pursuing is in direct conflict with many of them.

I am gratified to know that the Japanese have felt that our course has been indicative of a desire on our part to be fair and impartial. However, our first solicitude will have to be not for the maintenance of unqualified good will toward us by either or both of the combatants; it will have to be for the welfare of our own people and the broad interests and general policies of the United States; it will be guided by laws and treaties, public opinion and other controlling considerations. I share your view that among our fundamental objectives there should be (1) to avoid involvement and (2) to protect the lives, property and rights of American citizens. I doubt whether we can pursue those objectives and at the same time expect to pursue the third of the objectives [i.e. maintaining our "traditional friendship with both combatants"] which you suggest. I therefore do not feel that we should make it a definite objective to solidify our relations with either of the combatant nations.[125]

The dispatch went on to say that public opinion in the United States had been outraged by the actions of both the Japanese and the Chinese but had, in particular, become increasingly critical of Japan, especially since the incident which involved the shooting of the British ambassador near Shanghai. The administration did not wish, it was asserted, to give the Japanese the impression that we disapproved the course they were pursuing any less than the British did or indeed that we condoned it "in any sense whatever." Concerning the manner in which Grew was to represent the administration's position in Tokyo, it was said in conclusion:

I do not intend, in addressing either the Japanese or the Chinese authorities, to call names or to make threats; I heartily approve of the dignified and tactful manner in which you are conducting your approaches to the Japanese Government; but I desire that it be fully understood by the Japanese that this Government looks with thorough disapproval upon the present manifestation of their foreign policy. . . . I feel it desirable that you overlook no opportunity to impress upon Japanese officialdom the importance which we attach to the principles laid down in my statement of July 16 and the significance of my statement of August 23, and to suggest to them that by the course which she is pursuing Japan is destroying the world's good will and laying up for herself among the peoples of the world a liability of suspicion, distrust, popular antipathy and potential ostracism which it would take many, many years of benevolent endeavor on her part to liquidate.

The Department's criticism obviously came as a genuine shock to Grew who in a long and discursive letter (which contrasted sharply with the careful reasoning that usually characterized his communications) assured Hull that the embassy had not "for a single moment" advocated that the administration should "in any way or in any degree sacrifice American interests" in order to purchase Japanese good will.[126] He wished, he said, to explain further some of the fundamental considerations which had governed the line of thought presented in the embassy's previous dispatch of August 27:

1. We feel that in the present issue the Administration has acted with great wisdom and that your appeals of July 16 and August 23 and your various observations to the Japanese and Chinese Ambassadors have been high-minded, broad-visioned, statesmanlike pronouncements, fully called for and completely justified. They have beyond peradventure announced and established the position of the United States before the world, the American public, the combatants, international law and history.

2. While steadfastly maintaining our position in the world as the foremost exponent of the highest international ethics and principles, of disarmament and world peace, we feel that we can be of greater practical use in the world at large and the Far East in particular, and we can keep American interests on a sounder footing now and in future, if we aim, so far as practicable, to avoid unnecessarily sacrificing our present relations either with China or Japan than if we throw overboard our friendship with either.

3. The Japanese people, perhaps more than most people, are capable of long-remembered gratitude for what they consider friendly attitudes on the part of other nations and long-remembered resentment for unfriendly attitudes. Whatever we may think of the Japanese military machine, need we penalize our own future interests and perhaps our own future helpfulness in working for peace, by creating among the Japanese people a renewed antagonism against the United States? I know by personal experience, and bitter experience, how acute that antagonism was when I came here in 1932.

The embassy's telegram of August 27, Grew stated further, had centered "not about principle or policy or attitude but simply about method." The "main purpose" of the telegram had been to say that the embassy was in "most hearty accord" with the methods which the administration had been following and was in favor of adhering to them. "Our thought," Grew wrote, "lies not at all with what has been done but rather with what might be done in future." The embassy feared the adverse effects which would accrue if the Department changed its tactics and resorted to public censure of Japan either alone or, as rumored in the press, in concert with other powers. In his closing words to the Secretary, Grew frankly revealed his concern not only with the good will of the Department but also with that of history:

These comments go to you with great respect and certainly in no spirit of controversy. I do not like to send them in a formal dispatch but appreciate nevertheless the importance of having my general attitude made abundantly clear on the records, and it would therefore give me a feeling of satisfaction if you should be disposed to place this letter on the files of the Department in connection with and in elaboration of our telegram . . . of August 27.

Perhaps the most important immediate result of Grew's letter was that it stimulated Ambassador Johnson to express his views far more definitely than at any other time during the opening months of the Sino-Japanese war. A copy of Grew's communication to the Department did not reach Nanking until mid-November, by which time the fighting between the Japanese and Chinese was well advanced and Johnson (as he himself said) was in Nanking being subjected to the droning of Japanese airplanes overhead on their routine tours of dropping bombs upon the capital. Moreover, in the first week of November, the Brussels Conference had opened and embarked upon its effort to settle the Sino-Japanese conflict by international means. Johnson, in his response to Grew, however, made no mention of the conference but, speaking of the relationship of the United States to the Sino-Japanese crisis said instead,

I have just received and read your letter to the Secretary of September 15 and I want to tell you that your thoughts expressed in this letter and in the dispatches and telegrams, copies of which have come to me here, have been so much in line with my own that I sometimes feel that you read mine or I read yours. We certainly do not want to become involved in this struggle which is essentially one between the Japanese and the Chinese. We want to do what we can to protect American lives and save from the mess such rights as we can. We want to live in peace and friendship with both sides.[127]

As far as the Chinese were concerned, Johnson indicated that he alternated between a feeling of sympathy and a tempered, but genuine, irritation. It was hard, he said, sitting in Nanking and watching the advance of the Japanese upon the Asiatic continent, knowing that it meant the ultimate obliteration of Chinese independence, to "feel happy" about developments however much one might tell oneself: ". . . after all, the matter is of little or no concern of mine." On the other hand, he declared, "Certainly nothing makes me lose patience with my Chinese friends so quickly as when I hear them talk about the responsibility of America for aiding to preserve the independence and the integrity of China because we were conveners of the Washington Conference." As to the Japanese, Johnson stated that, difficult as it was to watch their activities and be friendly, he recognized the necessity of attempting to weather the current storm in the Far East in a way that would retain for the United States the good will of the Japanese as well as the Chinese peoples; for a far greater storm lay ahead once Japan had achieved dominance of the Asian side of the Pacific. Japan would destroy all American cultural influence in China; would reduce the International Settlement to nothing; would eliminate western trade with the Chinese; and, most serious of all, would eventually manufacture goods with cheap Chinese labor which, transported in cheap Japanese bottoms, would challenge us in our home market. The United States, Johnson asserted in substance, would need all the strength—from whatever source—it could muster to ride out this larger storm.

In short, Ambassador Grew and Ambassador Johnson held to the views which they had frequently expressed in the preceding years. Discouraged by the Manchurian crisis, they had progressively written off the possibility of achieving world peace by arresting wars through various forms of international cooperation. (Describing his own state of mind, Grew said that he had come to accept the idea that he lived in a "day and age of 'Real Politik.' "[128]) As a consequence, neither ambassador wished to see the United States deal with the hostilities that broke out in China following the Marco Polo Bridge incident as a breach of the peace that should be checked through the concerted efforts of many nations. Instead they hoped that the United States would continue to confine itself to safeguarding its own interests in the Pacific, a course which they believed entailed remaining aloof from the Sino-Japanese conflict and concentrating upon creating conditions that would make it possible to maintain America's position in the Far East while avoiding a clash with Japan. They therefore wanted the administration in Washington to limit itself to protecting its nationals in China and to refrain from any diplomatic involvement such as was inherent in the plans for mediation, or an offer of good offices, proposed by the British and in the vigorous protests made by the British in Tokyo. At the same time, both Grew and Johnson approved of Secretary Hull's statements of July 16 and August 23. However, their approval, to all appearances, was based upon the widely held assumption that the Secretary's pronouncements were largely designed to put the United States on record as still committed to the high ideals to which it had always proclaimed allegiance.

The Secretary, on the other hand, felt that once the Sino-Japanese controversy had again erupted into a major military conflict, it should be dealt with by the United States in terms of seeking to promote the postwar effort to eradicate war. Accordingly, the declarations of July 16 and August 23 were intended to accomplish more than merely to set the record straight. They represented an attempt on Hull's part, first, to lay down the principle that the outbreak of war anywhere was the responsibility of every nation and, second, to take action on the basis of that principle.[129] The action in which the Secretary engaged was to appeal to all governments to cooperate in awakening among their peoples a moral consciousness that would serve as a positive force for the restoration and maintenance of peace.

Hull did not, however, suggest going further than the adoption of measures that were essentially restricted to the type of moral education with which he had long been concerned. Moreover, these measures did not interfere with his conducting our policy toward Japan and China along much the same lines as theretofore. The passive course which he had been following was continued in his constant rejections of the British proposals for joint attempts by England and America to bring about a settlement of the Sino-Japanese dispute and his failure to advance any alternative plans of his own. The conciliatory attitude which he had often demonstrated toward the Japanese was also maintained for a substantial period after the outbreak of the Sino-Japanese conflict as manifested, for example, in the Secretary's repeated assertions that the United States viewed the two parties to that conflict with a feeling of friendliness and complete impartiality. At the beginning of September, Hull departed from his conciliatory attitude to the extent of urging Ambassador Grew to impress upon the Japanese that their conduct of hostilities in China was arousing strong indignation in the United States. It is significant, however, that this was the first move which the Secretary made to express disapproval of Japan's actions and that it was apparently made, in large measure, in response to the feeling within the administration that, as Pierrepont

Moffat said, the temper of the American people was rapidly rising. As public opinion, including congressional opinion, was repeatedly to have a vital influence upon the administration in the determination of its policy toward the Sino-Japanese conflict, it seems advisable to consider next the two problems which, in particular, became the center of controversy in the United States in the summer of 1937: the protection of American nationals in China and the question of applying the Neutrality Act to the hostilities in the Far East.

THE CONTROVERSY OVER THE PROTECTION OF
AMERICAN NATIONALS IN CHINA

The protection of American citizens in China had for many decades
involved peculiar circumstances unlike those related to the protection
of our nationals in other parts of the world. As a result of the Boxer
Protocol, the United States, since 1901, had maintained a Legation
Guard of marines at Peking and infantry troops at Tientsin which, in
case of another disaster such as had occurred during the Boxer
Rebellion, would seek to prevent the cutting off of communications
between the legation and the sea. In addition, the United States had
kept forces at Shanghai since 1927, when a contingent of marines had
been sent to the International Settlement to safeguard the Americans
residing there against a possible attack from the Chinese revolutionary
armies that were advancing on the Yangtze area.

Even before the Manchurian incident, the United States War Department suggested to the Secretary of State that it would be advisable to withdraw our troops from North China on the grounds that
they were a potential source of danger, as they might become involved
in any conflict that developed in that region.[1] Nothing was done at the
time but the War Department raised the question again in 1935
stating that, if Japan managed to establish pseudoautonomous governments in North China under her control, the presence of our forces at
Peiping and Tientsin might lead to the "gravest complications."[2] A
few months later, at the time that the United States legation in China
was raised to the rank of an embassy, the President himself urged
Secretary Hull to move the embassy to Nanking which would do
away with the ostensible reasons for maintaining American troops in
the North China area.[3]

Hull was, however, firmly convinced that the withdrawal of our
forces from North China at this time would expose our nationals to
attacks from the Japanese who were encroaching more and more upon

the territories around Peiping and Tientsin. The Secretary's views were re-enforced by a series of memoranda written by Stanley Hornbeck, who was vigorously opposed to altering the status of our forces in China.[4] Hornbeck argued primarily that to remove our troops would only incur further political hazards by inviting assaults upon our nationals and that while the administration should strive to put its relations with China on the same basis as its relations with other countries, nevertheless it was essential to recognize that China was still "in many respects a 'special' region" which had to be dealt with in "a special" manner. There was every reason, he said, for trying to keep up with the changes that were taking place in China but it would be a mistake to act "as though the situation had already been changed, and so completely changed as to be no longer special and call no longer for special agencies and methods."

As a result of the State Department's stand, the President dropped his request for a removal of the embassy to Nanking and the consequent withdrawal of American troops from North China. The situation at the time of the Lukouchiao incident was therefore that the United States had about 500 marines at Peiping, about 800 infantrymen at Tientsin, and a detachment of just over a thousand marines at Shanghai.[5]

Questions concerning the presence of these forces were raised by isolationist leaders in Congress soon after the outbreak of fighting following the Lukouchiao incident. On July 22 Representative Hamilton Fish announced to the press that he would seek legislation for the relinquishment of extraterritoriality in China in order to lessen the danger of the United States' being drawn into war and that he would appeal to the administration to recall our troops from Peiping and Tientsin.[6] Ten days later Fish made a typically isolationist speech in the House in which he defied all of his colleagues to mention a single good reason for the retention of American soldiers in China.[7] Instead of accepting Fish's challenge, Representative Coffee advanced the thesis that "American gunboats were on the Yangtze Kiang River to protect American oil interests which have heavy investments along that river." Fish stated that this was precisely the case and that, as the American people were aroused over the developments in the Far East, the time was propitious for the withdrawal of our boats and men from China. On the following day, Senator Lewis of Illinois made much the same speech in the Senate as Fish had made in the House.[8] He asserted that our soldiers were in North China because of the need to protect our interests there after the Boxer Rebellion but that a new China had emerged so that they were no longer needed. The administration should therefore remove them and, at the same time, advise our citizens in China to come home so as not to embroil us in any hostilities. On August 6 Senator Lewis introduced a resolution in the Senate calling upon the Secretary of War to state whether in his opinion it was advisable to leave a detachment of the United States Army in the Tientsin-Peiping war zone.[9] On August 9 Representative Tinkham of Massachusetts submitted a resolution to the House requesting the withdrawal of our forces from North China.[10]

No doubt in part because of these isolationist attacks, a spirited debate took place in cabinet meetings held by the President on August 7 and 13 in which the President and various members of the cabinet expressed considerable resentment over the fact that our forces had not been recalled from China at the time that Roosevelt had urged the State Department to do so.[11] Hull, on his part, reasserted his belief that extra protection had been needed to ensure the safety of our citizens in China and (as described by Ickes in his diary) was "quite strenuous in his argument and took pretty sharp exception" to the criticisms leveled against him. At the meeting of August 13 the President stated that he wanted some plan worked out to afford Americans a means of getting away from China and that he was "even in favor of going so far as to announce that any American who stayed in Shanghai was doing so at his own risk." Hull, however, deprecated taking so strong a position. Notwithstanding these disagreements, everyone agreed on one point, namely, that it was impossible to remove our troops from China under the existing circumstances.

When news reached the United States of the tragedies which occurred in Shanghai on August 14 and earned for that day the horrible name of "bloody Saturday," Senator Nye, in response to queries from the press, said that in his opinion all Americans should be evacuated from Shanghai immediately and our troops and vessels should be withdrawn.[12] Two days later, Senator Lewis made another isolationist speech in the Senate.[13] Referring to the announcement which had appeared in the morning press concerning the British plan for a settlement of the conflict in Shanghai that involved the active cooperation of the United States with England and other Treaty Powers, Lewis asserted,

I have on a previous occasion taken the liberty to address this honorable body recounting what I felt was the necessity for bringing home the American soldiers now in China . . .

Mr. President, I am moved to ask what is keeping our soldiers in China. Has it come to the point that there are those who are so audacious, whether in the Orient or in America, professing to be officers of the Government of the United States, who have pledged to England that we will keep our soldiers in China that they may participate in any conflict which may be necessary with regard to maintaining the property of England situated in China?

Senator Clark of Missouri, another leading isolationist, raised the point that not only our military but also our naval forces should be removed from China, with which Lewis agreed. The only other Senator who spoke upon this occasion was King of Utah, who referred to the possibility of international consultation to settle the Sino-Japanese conflict under the terms of the Four Power Treaty, the Nine Power Treaty, and the Kellogg-Briand Pact. Lewis decried the idea of being able to obtain any benefit from these treaties, saying that "they realized literally the expression . . . of Macbeth of the witches making the promise to the ear to break it to the hope." In conclusion he declared that "America must remain America, and for that she must remain American. All hands for all for peace—no American arms to any for war." A further statement concerning the withdrawal of American troops and nationals from China was made on August 17 by Representative Voorhis of California, who told the House that we had everything to lose and nothing to gain by keeping our marines in China and that American citizens should be given the choice of safe convoy home or remaining in China at their own risk.[14]

But to Americans in China the situation did not look as simple as it did to isolationist spokesmen in Congress. Following "bloody Saturday," American officials in Shanghai felt that their first obligation was to provide some sense of security for the American community in that city. Consequently, on August 15 Admiral Yarnell, who was at Shanghai as Commander-in-Chief of the U.S. Asiatic Fleet, asked the administration to send a re-enforcement of a thousand marines to the International Settlement.[15] As the admiral's request arrived at the time that Nye, Lewis, and Clark were demanding the evacuation of all Americans—whether civilian or military—from Shanghai, it seemed to the administration to present a delicate political problem.

It was Hornbeck who again took up the cudgels for the cause of protecting United States nationals in China. In a number of unusually forceful memoranda to the Secretary, Hornbeck argued in effect that in view of the seriousness of the situation at Shanghai and in view of the fact that the British and French had reportedly already decided to send re-enforcements to the Settlement, the United States would assume a "grave responsibility" and be "in an unenviable position from the point of view of world opinion" if it refused to comply with the request of its responsible officers on the spot.[16] He was not, he said, oblivious to the necessity of taking "political considerations within the United States" into account, but he believed that the dispatch of additional marines to Shanghai was essential to give adequate protection to American nationals and would also best serve the interests of the United States in the whole field of international relations.[17] He further urged the Secretary to take up the matter with the President at once and, if Roosevelt had any hesitation about meeting Admiral Yarnell's wishes, to ask him to consult with the State, Army, and Navy Departments before making any final decision.

The top officials of the State Department apparently unanimously supported Hornbeck's position.[18] Whether or not this had any influence upon the President, Roosevelt quickly arrived at the decision to authorize some 1,200 marines, then at San Diego, to proceed to Shanghai. It seems evident, however, that both the President and Hull were greatly concerned about how to break the news to the public that the United States was sending re-enforcements to China; they therefore maneuvered with care in order to arouse the minimum amount of isolationist criticism.

On August 17 the President, at one of his regular press conferences, gave the correspondents what amounted to an off-the-record lecture on the historical evolution of the special privileges which foreigners enjoyed in China.[19] Starting with 1831, when his grandfather "went out as a super cargo to China," Roosevelt sketched the chaotic conditions that had existed in China throughout the last century and the manner in which they had given rise to the establishment of treaty ports, the extraterritorial system, and the stationing of foreign troops at Peiping, Tientsin, and Shanghai. The purpose of the talk was clearly to impress upon his listeners that our troops were in China only as the result of an "inherited situation" and that our objective was to "get our marines completely out of China as fast as it is a practical thing to do." That the reporters themselves understood Roosevelt's intention is evident from the fact that news articles on the following day stated that the administration was afraid of being accused of intervention in sending troops to China and that, consequently, word had been "carefully spread" around Washington that the President was in favor of withdrawing our forces from China as soon as the time was ripe.[20]

On August 17 Secretary Hull also held a press conference which was regarded within the State Department as one of the best he had ever given. According to the press release issued subsequently the Secretary, after announcing that 1,200 additional marines would shortly depart for China, stated that the question of the degree of protection, if any, that the United States should give its nationals abroad was a "more or less misunderstood" subject albeit one about which even informed people might genuinely differ either partially or *in toto*.[21] Where American citizens, he said, were treated unfairly under the law of the countries in which they were residing, the United States made earnest representations. In other instances, such as in China, where American nationals were likely to be subjected to acts of violence from disordered groups suddenly sweeping across thickly populated areas, the United States had guards stationed at various points. The guards were there solely to protect our nationals and there was no occasion for any clash between them and the organized military troops of any country; the use of force was "entirely out of mind."

The Secretary was further described in the press release as saying,

. . . that we naturally found ourselves in between two extreme views. One was the view of extreme internationalism, which rested upon an idea of political commitments. We kept entirely away from that in our thoughts and views and policies, just as we sought, on the other hand, to keep entirely away from the extreme nationalists who would tell all Americans that they must stay here at home and that if they went abroad anywhere . . . and trouble overtook them and violence threatened, they must not expect any protection from their government. We could today order our guards to walk out of Shanghai and leave our 3,000 and more nationals who had not yet escaped to the mercy of the mob that was actually reported as threatening danger there today. That would mean that we would leave the British guards and the French guards and the guards of other nations who were there . . . to protect their nationals and ours while we moved out lock, stock and barrel and hastened back to within the water's edge . . .

We in no sense contemplated any belligerent attitude toward anybody. On the other hand, we frankly did not feel disposed, by leaning too far the other way, to give other countries a chance to suppose or to suggest that we were cowardly. If we wanted to be insulted fifty times a week, we only needed to let the impression be gained that we did not protect our nationals and that in no circumstances would we be disposed to protect them.

In short, Hull was setting forth the thesis, which he had long maintained, that it was part of the responsibility of the United States to protect its citizens in case of danger and that any failure to discharge that responsibility would only incur further difficulties. On the other hand, he was making every effort to convince the isolationists that our troops in China could not possibly become involved in a conflict with the armed forces of any other country and that in general he was pursuing a middle-of-the-road policy which excluded international commitments (presumably meaning in this instance commitments to Great Britain for positive action in the Far East).

The Secretary's comments naturally evoked editorial reaction in the press. Using as an example the eight leading newspapers whose editorial policies have been examined in connection with this study, it would seem that there were so many conflicting views on the withdrawal issue that neither the isolationist nor the internationalist press adhered to any particular line. Thus among the internationalist publications, the *New York Times* and the Scripps-Howard *Cleveland Press* both expressed approval of Hull's stand, the *Press* declaring that, while the American people wanted peace, peace could not be obtained by running away every time somebody said "'boo.'"[22] The *San Francisco Chronicle* stated similarly that even if risks had to be taken to protect our citizens and our interests in China, we should not desert them.[23] On the other hand, the customarily internationalist *Los Angeles Times* repeatedly and stridently called for the removal of our citizens and soldiers from China, using such editorial captions as "Bystanders Get Out," "Get Out Quick."[24] On the isolationist side, the *Chicago Tribune* demanded the withdrawal of *all* Americans from China, including Foreign Service officers, declaring that only by such stringent measures could we eliminate the risk of being swept into war by a wave of emotion following some massacre of Americans.[25] In contrast to the *Tribune,* the isolationist Hearst publications, while warning against the danger of incidents that might enflame American public opinion, endorsed Hull's middle-of-the-road position.[26]

If the press seems to have offered no more than scattered opposition to the administration's policy of protection, one segment of the public organized itself for a concerted effort to induce the United States government to withdraw from China—as Hull had said—"lock, stock and barrel." This segment consisted of six peace societies which occupied an important place in the extensive peace movement that existed in the United States in the 1930's. As after the Lukouchiao incident the primary objective of these societies was to obtain the enforcement of the Neutrality Act in the Far East, they will be discussed in detail in this connection.[27] They also concerned themselves, however, with seeking to achieve the withdrawal of all American troops and civilians from China and throughout July and August 1937 directed much of their individual propaganda effort toward this end.[28] At the end of August, they established a joint strategy board through which they conducted propaganda campaigns on a cooperative basis that attracted such widespread attention that they became a matter of major concern to the administration.[29] As Harold B. Hinton of the *New York Times,* who was very close to the State Department, wrote in a front page article on September 4, the administration recognized that the peace societies which were demanding the recall of Americans from China constituted only a small fraction of American opinion but it was nevertheless fearful of their impact upon the public.[30] Moreover, the activities of the six peace societies were re-enforced in early September by two other expressions of a popular desire for the evacuation of Americans from China. On September 2 the Veterans of Foreign Wars passed a resolution at their annual meeting requesting the administration to tell American citizens in China that they would only continue to receive protection for a limited period after which our troops in China would be brought home.[31] And on September 5 a Gallup poll was published in which the question had been asked: "Should we withdraw all troops in China to keep from getting involved in the fighting or should the troops remain there to protect American rights?" Fifty-four per cent of those who had answered had said, "Withdraw" and forty-six per cent, "Remain."[32]

The day that the Gallup poll appeared in the morning press the President, who was cruising on his yacht off the coast of Rhode Island, held a news conference in which, apparently without warning to anyone in the administration, he expressed the views that he had advanced at the cabinet meeting of August 13 only to evoke the disapproval of Secretary Hull. According to the stories of the correspondents who were present, Roosevelt said that Americans in China had been urged to leave that country and that, if they chose to remain, they did so "at their own risk."[33] The President further emphasized that naval facilities had been provided for the evacuation of Americans but that many were refusing to come home and that the situation was "an awful mess."

The President's remarks created what was described as an "uproar" among Americans in China. Referring to the accounts of his comments in the press, the *China Weekly Review* wrote: "Harrassed Americans with their nerves worn raw dodging accidentally or purposely misdirected shells and air bombs . . . literally 'blew up' when they read this."[34] The *New York Times* reported from China that business and missionary leaders were "stunned" by the President's statements and were sending messages of protest "by the hundreds" to Washington.[35] Among these was an expression of "unanimous disapproval" from the American Chamber of Commerce in Shanghai.[36] The *Shanghai Evening Post and Mercury*, presumably also reflecting the reaction of the American business community in Shanghai, printed four columns of interviews with local American citizens whose observations were described as so "untempered as to startle most non-Americans."[37] The tendency in general was to assume that the President had acted as a result of the pressures exercised by the peace groups in the United States together with isolationists in and out of Congress. The *China Weekly Review* was especially outspoken in accusing officials in Washington of being excited about the situation in China to a degree which verged upon "hysteria" and consequently scrapping long-established policies for the protection of its nationals in order to please pacifist and isolationist propagandists.[38] The *North China Daily News* wrote that the Americans in China explained the President's remarks by saying that he had felt compelled to make a gesture of appeasement toward the peace societies at home but that Americans in China were nevertheless determined to "stick to their guns."[39]

In the United States, the strategy board of the six associated peace societies attempted, not only to defend its members, but to take the offensive with a vigorous counterattack. Among many other matters, a telegram was sent to the President saying that Americans abroad might regard his order to withdraw from China as "cowardly" but that to Americans at home it seemed only common sense, as it sought to protect the interests of the nation as a whole instead of those of a few American citizens.[40] Nevertheless, the strategy board seems to have been unable to arouse much editorial reaction in the press.[41] Among the newspapers reviewed by Lawrence Kramer, only the *Los Angeles Times* expressed a view on the controversy over the President's statement, taking the position, which it had been advancing for some time, that Americans should "get out of China."[42]

Yet the administration clearly continued to keep its eye on those elements of the public which were attacking its withdrawal policy. Apparently acting as a spokesman for the administration, Senator Pittman, on August 23 right after the adjournment of Congress, launched a broadside against the administration's critics. In a speech delivered over the radio, he declared that the United States had missionaries and teachers, explorers and businessmen, in remote areas of China which could not possibly be safeguarded by either Chinese or Japanese police forces.[43] "The outcry," he stated, "coming even as it does from some intelligent sources that we should immediately withdraw our army and navy and leave our citizens in China without protection is cowardly and unpatriotic and reflects upon the dignity and glory of our country."

Only a few days after this broadcast, the administration was presented with a further dilemma by a request from Admiral Yarnell for additional cruisers to assist in the evacuation of Americans from China. Stanley Hornbeck, in another strong memorandum, urged the fulfillment of the admiral's request, declaring that "no outcries on the part of any part of our population" could justify an attempt "to close our eyes, to turn our back upon, or wash our hands of" the problems created by the existence of several thousand American citizens in China and the important interests which they represented.[44] However, according to Admiral Leahy, who was then Chief of Naval Operations in Washington, the majority of officials in the administration were opposed to sending additional ships to China, as they did not wish to evoke a storm of protest from the "peace advocates" in the United States and furthermore feared the effect upon Japan. Nevertheless, Admiral Leahy went to Hyde Park to recommend the dispatch of additional cruisers to the President. But whether out of concern for the "peace advocates" or because of some other consideration, the President refused to approve the recommendation.[45]

The State Department—perhaps largely owing to Hornbeck—had, on its part, stood its ground with relative firmness in regard to according protection to Americans in China but early in September when the campaign of the six peace societies was at its height, it sought to hedge its position by adopting a policy of extensive evacuation of American civilians not only from the war areas in China but from a large part of the country. On September 2, after reviewing the entire situation, it sent comprehensive instructions to its representatives in China which stated that while the future of the Sino-Japanese conflict was unpredictable, the hostilities seemed to be widening and might well be of long duration.[46] It therefore appeared to the Department that Americans in China must recognize that their normal activities were likely to be disturbed and that their lives might at any time be imperiled. This assertion, it was said, applied not only to Americans in large cities but also to those in smaller centers and even in remote parts of the country which might be subjected to air attacks by the Japanese. Moreover, as time went by government control was likely to decrease; disorders to become prevalent; and travel to grow hazardous if not impossible. American consulates throughout China were therefore to impress upon the American residents in their area that they should avail themselves of existing facilities to withdraw, as these facilities might not continue indefinitely and the United States government could not guarantee the safety of those who elected to remain in China under present conditions.

American representatives in China did their best to put the Department's instructions into effect but it is evident that, in common with many of their fellow citizens in China, they felt that the Department was laying down far too drastic a policy of evacuation. The consul at Tientsin, for example, wired Washington that he feared he would be unable to persuade Americans to withdraw from the Tientsin area unless the administration could provide him with information, not available on the spot, which indicated that withdrawal was essential.[47] He hesitated, he said, to make such representations to the Department but the effect of the issuance of an evacuation notification would be so great that he felt justified in asking it to reconsider the situation. Paul R. Josselyn, the Consul General at Hankow, was even more outspoken, as may be seen from the following passages taken from a message which he sent to Washington on September 18:

It is not 3 weeks since on the Embassy's instructions I sent my first warning to Americans in this Consular District advising them to withdraw from China. Since then that advice has been reiterated in two circulars and in many letters and personal interviews. Results are negligible.

The Americans to whom this advice has been tendered are not casual visitors free to concern themselves entirely with their own welfare. They are missionaries and merchants charged with duties and entrusted with the care of interests and property for which they are responsible to supervisors in China and the United States and . . . to many thousands of supporters and stockholders at home . . .

Our warning to all Americans to leave the country conveys an impression of indifference to our rights and interests that can serve us but ill. The implied assumption that China cannot protect our nationals is a blow to China's friendship . . . No such step has yet been taken or advised by any other goverment.[48]

As the above quotation indicates, the two groups which were most concerned with the question of withdrawal consisted of American missionaries and businessmen. On September 4 Secretary Hull sent a letter to the Foreign Missions Conference of North America (a coordinating agency involving about one hundred Protestant denominational mission societies) which was virtually the same as the instructions that the Secretary had sent to the embassy and consulates in China two days earlier.[49] A meeting of the available representatives of the member societies was held on September 8, at which the Secretary's letter was considered and a statement drafted that was subsequently circulated among all the North American Mission Boards. The statement was obviously intended to find some means, on the one hand, of enabling the administration to meet the criticism of those who were insisting that the presence of Americans in China was threatening to engulf the United States in war and, on the other, of permitting American missionaries in China to remain at their posts. Thus it was specifically asserted that missionary activities had to be undertaken, not only under favorable circumstances, but at all times; and that it was the duty of missionaries in China to conserve and carry forward their work despite existing conditions. At the same time sympathy was expressed with Hull's concern over the possible involvement of the United States in the Sino-Japanese conflict. It was said that only those missionaries should remain in China who could endure dangers and suffering and uncertainty and that mothers and children and those who, for physical or temperamental reasons were unsuited to hardships, should leave. It was further stated that the signatories of the statement shared the opinion, so strongly held by many of their countrymen, that every practicable step should be taken to prevent the United States from being drawn into war and that they therefore wished specifically to declare that they neither desired nor expected any injury suffered by their missionaries to be "made a cause of war or the threat of war."

The statement which emerged from the September 8 meeting set the tone for subsequent missionary policy. The missionary literature of the time is full of reports to the effect that the American embassy and consulates in China were issuing urgent warnings to missionaries to leave but that, while every effort was being made to give fair consideration to government pressure, relatively few missionaries felt free to desert their Chinese friends at a time when they were in special need of support.[50] It was subsequently estimated that even many of the missionaries, who felt compelled to leave the actual battle areas in China during the hostilities of the summer of 1937, returned as soon as conditions permitted and that missionary personnel in the early period of the Sino-Japanese war was reduced by no more than 10 per cent as compared to about 50 per cent as a result of the 1925-1928 revolution.[51] The stand of Catholic missionaries against a policy of evacuation was even firmer, as seen by the announcement of the Secretary General of Maryknoll on September 7 that, while the government's policy of withdrawal might apply to other American nationals, missionaries—like soldiers—must remain at their posts.[52]

Reference has already been made to the sharp negative reaction of American businessmen in Shanghai to the President's statement that Americans who elected to stay in China did so at their own risk. Subsequently the United States Chamber of Commerce passed a resolution declaring in the strongest terms that the United States government should grant the proper protection to the lives and interests of its nationals in China.[53] The American Commercial Attaché at Shanghai also took the position that American businessmen should not be urged to come home, stating in a report to Washington that the majority of American firms in China represented large and influential companies which were in a position to carry on financially, despite the disruptions caused by the Sino-Japanese conflict, and that it would in his opinion be "very poor" practice for them to withdraw from China sacrificing the goodwill and market contacts which they had established through years of pioneering efforts.[54]

Prominent among those who objected to what was widely termed the administration's policy of "wholesale" evacuation of Americans in China was Nelson Johnson who, as a result of the conflict between his own feelings and the necessity of following the Department's orders, became involved in a most unfortunate incident. Even before the Department had issued its comprehensive instructions of September 2, Johnson had apparently felt that the administration was going too far in urging Americans to pull out of China and had sent a cable of indirect protest to Washington which, of all the dispatches he wrote during this period, was perhaps the most frankly emotional. He said, in part,

It is not possible for us to withdraw from China all Americans now scattered throughout the interior. The result may well be that we shall find our nationals and their interests engulfed in the chaos which the Japanese seem ready and willing to create.

[But] sooner or later the world must, in my opinion, take cognizance of what is happening in China and act for its amelioration . . . If the powers fail to condemn this brutal, unscrupulous and merciless blotting out of Chinese Government control within its own territories the reaction within China may well be disastrous. Chinese ability or interest in protecting the interests and lives of foreign nationals may vanish . . .

Japanese pronouncements have justified more than a suspicion that Japan's present operations are actuated to a large extent by an ambition to replace western influence and interests in China with Japanese and it would seem that this rooting out of our vested interest demands attention simultaneously with our solicitude to avoid possible implication in the struggle. In fact, a too complaisant surrender now may precipitate a more violent effort at recovery later.[55]

Subsequently, on September 19, the Japanese government issued a warning that its air force might bomb Nanking on September 21 and that foreign officials and residents should voluntarily move into areas of greater safety.[56] Ambassador Johnson consequently went on board the U.S.S. *Luzon*, anchored off Nanking, on September 20, taking most of his staff with him. On departing from the embassy, he gave various newspaper correspondents the impression that he was acting under orders from the Department but was himself exceedingly unhappy at having to leave his office.[57] Actually the Department had left the question of withdrawal from the embassy to Johnson's discretion and the ambassador, once on board the *Luzon*, cabled the Secretary his reasons for deciding in favor of temporary evacuation:

The Department's instructions and the published statements of responsible American officials lead me to think that our Government has two principal objectives. The first is to ensure the safety of American citizens. The second is to avoid any situation which might involve the United States in the present conflict. The Embassy has urged on American citizens the policy of withdrawal from China to a point which has elicited protests from them that the danger does not justify withdrawal and that withdrawal means unwarranted abandonment of the rights and responsibilities of American citizens. To avoid possibility of injury to myself and my staff as a result of hostile operations which might place a strain on the relations of the United States with China or Japan, I decided on receipt of the warning of the Japanese . . . to withdraw with my staff . . . This I did in spite of extreme reluctance . . . My withdrawal from the Embassy premises has aroused the scarcely veiled resentment of the Chinese and the open disapproval of some of our citizens.[58]

The resentment and disapproval to which the ambassador referred was indeed intense and did not abate for some time despite his return to the embassy as soon as the bombing raid of September 21 was over. The *China Weekly Review* printed across the cover of its next issue: "U.S. Ambassador Remains at Nanking—On a Gunboat!"[59] Tillman Durdin of the *New York Times,* who was scarcely inclined to indulge in sensationalism, reported from Nanking that the ambassador's withdrawal to the *Luzon* had evoked a "storm of criticism" among Chinese officials who regarded it as further evidence of Washington's "exaggerated fear" of complications with the Japanese and disregard of Chinese interests and sensibilities.[60] Hallett Abend of the *Times* wrote from Shanghai that the Chinese press was so incensed that it was talking of taking some form of retaliation for the ambassador's actions.[61] Even the *Times* correspondent at Geneva cabled to say that he had never seen so much bitterness among the Chinese representatives at the League as had been produced by the *Luzon* incident.[62] The Chinese government itself went so far as to issue a semiofficial statement expressing its displeasure.[63]

But the agitation in China, however loud and vocal, was perhaps not as profound as that which occurred, unknown to the public, behind the closed doors of the State Department. Many of the leading officers of the Department, foremost among them the Secretary himself, felt that Johnson had made the administration look as though it was determined to "scuttle" out of China to appease the Japanese. This feeling indeed became sufficiently strong for some of the more isolationist-minded members of the Department to fear that the pendulum might swing too far in the opposite direction and that the administration might make some unnecessarily vigorous move to prove that its policy of withdrawal of its nationals from China was not part of an attempt to abandon all of its interests in the Far East for the sake of maintaining good relations with Japan.[64]

No doubt the Department's distress over the *Luzon* incident was intensified by the fact that (as related in connection with the Secretary's interchange with Grew in early September) it had come to believe that the American people had been horrified by such Japanese actions as the machine-gunning of the British ambassador and wanted the administration to impress their sense of moral outrage upon the Japanese government.[65] Probably for this reason, the State Department, on being notified by the Japanese government of its plan to bomb Nanking on September 21, had immediately sent a relatively strong note in reply.[66] The United States government, it said, felt that the bombing would jeopardize the lives of American nationals and of noncombatants generally, and it held the view that any bombing of an extensive area containing a large population which was engaged in peaceful pursuits was "unwarranted and contrary to principles of law and humanity." Moreover, it strongly objected to the creation of a situation in which the American ambassador and other agencies of the American government were confronted with the alternative of abandoning their establishments or being exposed to grave hazards. It therefore reserved all rights to claim damages which might result from the Japanese military operations in the Nanking area and appealed to the Japanese to refrain from any further bombing of that area. Furthermore, in addition to delivering the Department's note, Grew had tried for the first time to impress upon the Japanese Foreign Minister that, through her course of action in China, Japan was laying up for herself among the peoples of the world a liability of distrust and suspicion and popular antipathy which might result in her being "ostracized from the family of nations."[67] In regard specifically to the announced Japanese intention to bomb Nanking, the ambassador, according to his own report to Secretary Hull, said that the goodwill which both he and Hirota had been building up between their two countries was rapidly dissolving and that, while the American people were patient they were nevertheless easily aroused by some incident involving their legitimate interests abroad, as evidenced by the fact that the explosion of the *Maine* at Havana had been sufficient to provoke a war. "The force and directness of my statements," Grew told the Secretary, "left nothing whatever to Mr. Hirota's imagination."[68]

The Department presumably felt that its protests concerning the bombing of Nanking had the full support of the American people for, in a cable sent to Grew on September 27, which was devoted to a summary of press opinion, it said that, in so far as it was aware, the editorial comment in the United States had been solidly opposed to Japan's air raids over the Chinese capital. However, by this time another incident had occurred in regard to the protection of American citizens in China which was scarcely conducive to the Department's relaxing its policy on evacuation.

On September 22, perhaps in an effort to counteract the effects of the *Luzon* incident, Admiral Yarnell made public in China instructions which he had issued to his officers that constituted a definition of the "policy of Cincaf" (the Commander in Chief of the Asiatic Fleet) that was to remain in operation as long as the conflict between China and Japan lasted.[69] Most American citizens in China, it was said, were engaged in business or professions that were their only means of livelihood so that they were unwilling to depart unless compelled to do so by actual physical danger. It was therefore the duty of the United States naval force to offer all possible protection and assistance to American nationals where needed and while as a result such naval forces might be exposed to risks, the risks were likely to be slight and in any case had to be accepted. The vessels of the Asiatic Fleet could not be withdrawn without bringing "great discredit" upon the United States Navy.

Admiral Yarnell's definition of policy was clearly hard to reconcile with the President's previously reported comments that Americans who chose to stay in China did so at their own risk. Roosevelt—who had already left for his tour out west which was to culminate in the famous "quarantine" speech in Chicago—on reading of the admiral's statement in the newspapers, wired Secretary Hull to find out what had happened.[70] The Secretary explained that the Navy Department had been greatly perturbed by the admiral's action but that after prolonged consultation between Navy and State it had been decided that, as the admiral had made his instructions public in China, it would be useless to make a denial if correspondents inquired about it in Washington. The text had therefore been given out upon request, while at the same time Admiral Yarnell had been told that in case he wished in future to issue any declaration concerning the policy of Cincaf during the present emergency, he would have to secure the approval of the Secretary of the Navy. It was further decided that before granting approval, the Navy would consult with the State Department.[71]

The State Department, on its part, on September 29 redefined its own policy on the protection and evacuation of American nationals in a dispatch to Ambassador Johnson. The comprehensive instructions sent to the embassy on September 2, it declared, had contemplated American Foreign Service officers' bringing to the attention of our citizens in China the dangers to which they might be subjected as long as the Sino-Japanese conflict continued and advising them to withdraw while facilities for withdrawal were available.[72] The views expressed in those instructions, it was emphatically stated, remained "unaltered."

In short, in response to the demands of certain segments of the public, the State Department sought to solve the problem of the protection of American nationals in China by putting pressure upon them to return to the United States. This policy contrasted sharply with that which had been adopted by the Coolidge administration during the Chinese revolution of 1925-1928 at the critical moment when the Nationalists took Shanghai.[73] For then, despite the insistent demands of men such as Senator Borah to take all Americans out of Shanghai until the danger had passed, President Coolidge had announced that he did not believe in urging Americans with homes and businesses in Shanghai to leave that city. The Roosevelt administration felt, however, that it was necessary to give ground in the face of criticism, although—as will be discussed shortly—it was open to question whether that criticism was not more vocal than powerful.

THE CONTROVERSY OVER NEUTRALITY

The controversy that developed over the application of the United States neutrality legislation to the situation in the Far East after the Lukouchiao incident was especially complex because the whole problem of neutrality involved an unusually wide range of issues—political, psychological, economic, and legal. Moreover, by the time that the Lukouchiao incident occurred, the great debate over neutrality legislation had been going on in the United States for two years with the isolationists in Congress demanding a "rigid" or "mandatory" neutrality law that the President would have to invoke automatically and enforce against all belligerents, and the administration seeking "flexible" legislation which would leave as much as possible to the discretion of the Executive.[74] The isolationists in Congress had to a large extent had their way and obtained the kind of law they wanted in the Neutrality Acts of 1935 and 1936. However, as the Italian-Ethiopian conflict and the Spanish Civil War developed, the difficulties involved in attempting to legislate neutrality had become more and more evident. Consequently, the President himself, who had originally underestimated the vital significance of the neutrality issue, had become increasingly aware of the dangers inherent in any rigid neutrality law.[75] At the same time his chief antagonist on the neutrality question in Congress, Senator Nye, had reached a point by January 1937 where he faltered sufficiently in his devotion to the concept of strict neutrality to object to an embargo against the shipment of arms and ammunition to both sides in the Spanish Civil War because he did not want to hurt the Loyalist cause.[76]

The Neutrality Acts of 1935 and 1936 had been temporary and the latter was due to expire on May 1, 1937. Early in that year Congress therefore began to consider new legislation which was however not to have any time limit set upon its duration but was rather, as was generally stated, intended to be "permanent." The debate over the new law lasted from January almost until the deadline (May 1) and was marked by efforts of the isolationists to obtain support for a variety of mandatory provisions. But in the end it was felt by many that the isolationists had lost ground and that the law which was finally passed represented a considerable gain for those who favored permissive legislation.[77]

The most important parts of the Act of 1937 for our present purposes ⟨ were those which provided: (1) that the president upon finding that a state of war existed between foreign nations should proclaim such fact;[78] (2) that once the president had so proclaimed, it would automatically become unlawful to sell or transport arms, ammunition, and implements of war to any of the belligerents or to grant them loans or credits other than those customarily involved in "normal peacetime commercial transactions;" and (3) that the president should, at his discretion, establish lists of commodities that might thereafter only be exported to the belligerents on condition that their ownership passed into foreign hands before they left American shores and that they were transported in foreign ships.[79] The latter stipulation was the main innovation of the 1937 Act and constituted the so-called "cash-and-carry" plan.

The administration did not itself attempt to intervene actively in the congressional struggle which led to the passage of the 1937 law. The President was absorbed in his dramatic fight for the reorganization of the Supreme Court, and Secretary Hull, who had consistently opposed the rigid neutrality legislation of 1935 and 1936, had come to feel that he might do better if he left matters in the hands of the proadministration forces in the Senate and the House.[80] Close contact was however maintained between the administration and Congress by Judge R. Walton Moore who was himself an ex-congressman and as Assistant Secretary of State had served ever since 1935 as the chief go-between on neutrality issues for the Department and his erstwhile colleagues on Capitol Hill. While Judge Moore had in the past repeatedly urged the administration to make concessions to the advocates of inflexible neutrality legislation in Congress, his attitude evidently began to undergo a change in the early part of 1937.[81] In the first place, he became convinced, as he informed the President, that the importance of any neutrality law had been greatly minimized by the decision handed down by the Supreme Court in December 1936 in the so-called Curtiss-Wright case, in which it was specifically stated that in the conduct of international affairs the "very delicate, plenary and exclusive power of the President" did "not require as a basis for its exercise an act of Congress."[82] Second, the Judge, like many other observers, felt that the Neutrality Act of May 1, 1937, was relatively liberal and that the passage of the Act indicated a weakening of the position of the supporters of strict mandatory legislation. Indeed, he went further than this and believed that the attitude of the extreme isolationists was itself thawing as manifested by Senator Nye's explicit admission during the debate on the 1937 Act in Congress that it was essential to leave such questions as the determination of when a state of war existed to the discretion of the chief executive—an admission which the senator was to disregard later.

By the time of the Lukouchiao incident, there appeared therefore to be a degree of fluidity in the views of Congress toward the neutrality issue with the tide moving in favor of the administration but the isolationists still being prepared to proclaim many of the tenets which they had championed in the past. As a result, it was perhaps natural that immediately after the Lukouchiao incident, Congress passed through various apparently contradictory phases in regard to the application of the Neutrality law to the undeclared war between China and Japan.

The first pronouncement made by a member of Congress on the neutrality issue, after the outbreak of hostilities in the Far East, consisted of a statement issued by Senator Key Pittman on July 29 which appealed to the public not to be impatient and put pressure upon the President to reach a premature decision about whether or not to enforce the Neutrality Act against Japan and China.[83] The purpose of the Act, the senator said, was frequently misconstrued, its objective being neither to benefit nor to punish any other country but solely to ensure the peace of the United States and the safety of its citizens. In the present instance the President was endeavoring to the utmost of his abilities to protect the lives of our nationals in China and to bring about a cessation of hostilities. These peaceful and humane efforts would be endangered or even disrupted by any hasty invocation of the neutrality law. Moreover, in order to invoke the law the President would have to decide that a state of war existed between China and Japan, a decision which would prove erroneous under the interpretation intended by the Neutrality Act if an armistice was shortly declared.

It was generally assumed that Senator Pittman's statement was issued on behalf of the administration in order to apprise the public that Roosevelt had no intention of taking any action in regard to the Neutrality Act for the time being. Nevertheless, not only did the isolationists in Congress refrain from making any protest, but one of their most vocal spokesmen, Senator Lewis of Illinois, introduced Pittman's statement into the *Congressional Record* and on July 31 seconded it with a ringing speech in which he declared that to invoke the neutrality law, under the circumstances that existed in the Far East, would positively endanger the security of the United States:

I assert that the moment the President declared there was war within the meaning of the Neutrality Act, the next step is clear. It is that when the declaration is made . . . every form of trade becomes "illegal" and we are subject at once to our ships being seized and those American citizens who are upon the ships being arrested and detained and repressed and impressed in a manner after the order and processes of war.

The hour such a condition should arise America would find herself in conflict both with China and with Japan. Our country, desiring peace, would not only have destroyed the peace so far as the prospect of it with those countries is concerned, but we would open ourselves to the possibility of personal conflict. America would be at war with the Orient.[84]

However, some three weeks after Senator Lewis addressed these impassioned remarks to Congress, three other isolationist leaders, Senators Nye, Bone, and Clark, made public a pronouncement in which they called upon the President to apply the Neutrality Act to the undeclared war between China and Japan and sought to meet the main objections to invoking the Act that had been raised by Senators Pittman and Lewis.[85]

First, the Senators asserted, it should be recognized that the Neutrality Act was a "stay-out-of-war" law that Congress wanted the President to apply automatically in order to prevent his taking sides in any given conflict. If the occasion arose when the people of the United States wished to take sides—which meant readiness to go to war—the necessary steps should be taken, not by the executive branch of the government, but by Congress. Second, the existing neutrality legislation would not operate in the direction of involving the United States in the hostilities in the Far East. On the contrary, the circumstances were such that Japan would in all probability impose a blockade on China, in which case our neutrality law would avert critical "incidents" by prohibiting American ships from attempting to run the blockade with cargoes of arms and war materiel. Third, it was erroneous to state that the Neutrality Act would stop the President from "doing valuable things" in regard either to the protection of American nationals in China or the re-establishment of peace in the Far East. Those who raised the issue of protection seemed to fear that the Chinese people might so object to the enforcement of the Neutrality Act that they would retaliate against Americans in China while the Chinese government itself might feel justified in relaxing its efforts to safeguard them. This argument overlooked the fact that no government would condone any injury to American nationals knowing that to do so would be to invite war with the United States. As to the neutrality law's interfering with the President's efforts to bring about peace in the Far East, there was no objection to his calling the signatories of the Nine Power Treaty into consultation though it must be realized in advance that the only effective power behind such consultation was economic or military war which again was a subject for Congress to consider.

While the above points remained within the boundaries of the comments made by Senators Pittman and Lewis in that they dealt primarily with the effect that the enforcement of the neutrality law would have upon the United States, Senators Bone, Nye, and Clark also sought to anticipate the criticism that, under the prevailing circumstances, the neutrality law would operate in favor of Japan and against China. This, they said, was not the case. The prohibition against loans would act to Japan's disadvantage and reduce her trade with the United States so that it more nearly approached the level of China's. Moreover, while it looked on the surface as though the arms embargo would hurt China (which admittedly needed war supplies far more than Japan), in actual practice the embargo would not affect the situation as Japan could at any time blockade the Chinese coast and prevent arms shipments from passing whether the American neutrality legislation was or was not "on the books."

The Nye-Bone-Clark declaration evoked no visible reaction in the Senate but on August 19 twenty-four members of the House issued a brief pronouncement which declared that the Neutrality Act should be applied in the Sino-Japanese conflict for the sake of the security of the United States; that, as far as the belligerents were concerned, it would only tend to equalize their position; and that the Congress should not adjourn until the President had put the law into operation.[86] Nevertheless, Congress did adjourn within a few days. Moreover, neither the isolationists in the Senate nor the House were to make any serious effort subsequently to block the administration's adherence to a policy of noninvocation of the Neutrality Act in regard to China and Japan.

In sum, therefore, the isolationists in Congress presented a confused picture in that they first declared themselves against the invocation of the Neutrality Act, later loudly reversed their position, and in the end allowed the entire issue to simmer down to a point where it would not cause the administration any real embarrassment. But if confusion seemed prevalent among the isolationists in Congress it seemed even more prevalent in the press and the more vocal part of the public. As in relation to the issue of withdrawing our nationals from China, the press held conflicting opinions on the neutrality question which did not follow the customary ideological lines. Among the outstanding newspapers that were usually internationalist, the *New York Times* and the *San Francisco Chronicle* both opposed the use of the neutrality law in the Far Eastern dispute primarily on the grounds that it was an "unneutral neutrality law" which, contrary to the claims of some isolationist congressmen, would work to Japan's benefit.[87] They emphasized in particular that the cash-and-carry provisions would operate in favor of the Japanese who had both the funds and the ships to secure whatever commodities they wanted, while the Chinese did not. The *Chronicle* was particularly scathing in its attacks upon Congress and urged that body to repeal the Neutrality Act *in toto* and wake up to the fact that "just doing nothing is not the way to keep out of this war." On the other hand, the *Christian Science Monitor*, while adhering to its basically internationalist convictions to the extent of repeatedly calling for consultation under the Nine Power Pact, insisted that unless the President resorted to the Neutrality Act the United States would be dragged into war in the Far East.[88] Caught somewhere between these two extremes, the editors of the Scripps-Howard publications and of the *Milwaukee Journal* were unable to make up their minds. Thus the *Cleveland Press* (Scripps-Howard) at first asserted that as soon as the fighting between Japan and China developed into a genuine conflict, the Neutrality Act would have to be enforced; but after the holocaust of "bloody Saturday" in Shanghai, it agreed with the *New York Times* and the *San Francisco Chronicle* that the neutrality law should be held in suspense because it was "unneutral" and would help the Japanese.[89] Conversely, the *Milwaukee Journal* began by berating the Neutrality Act because it did not distinguish between the aggressor and the victim of aggression in the Far Eastern conflict and ended by asserting that the law should be invoked in the interests of American security irrespective of whether or not the Chinese would suffer.[90]

The customarily isolationist press on its side numbered in its front

ranks some of the most vigorous opponents in the United States to
the idea of applying the Neutrality Act to the Sino-Japanese dispute.
The Hearst publications objected to any recourse to the Act on
the basis that it would partially involve us in the undeclared war
between Japan and China, whereas we should follow a policy of
complete nonintervention.[91] The *Chicago Tribune* was wholly un-
bridled in its denunciation of the Act which it regarded as unfair
to China and as being in general a "war breeder" that, by dis-
criminating against weak nations, encouraged strong industrial powers
to attack them.[92] Among the leading journals reflecting isolationist
business opinion, the *Commercial and Financial Chronicle* also
vehemently condemned the existing neutrality legislation which it
had, in fact, opposed from the outset, as it belonged to the school
of thought that believed that the United States should not waive its
traditional neutral rights but should, on the contrary, "use all necessary force to maintain them," especially the right to trade.[93] In regard
to the Sino-Japanese conflict in particular, the *Chronicle* insisted that
to enforce the law would only endanger the United States. This
view was wholly shared by another outstanding business publication,
namely the *Journal of Commerce*, but was violently opposed by the
Wall Street Journal, which was indefatigable in its insistence upon
the necessity of the President's invoking the Act as a matter of law
and of policy.[94] From a legal point of view, it said, the law was as mandatory as any law could be and the President was therefore committed
to apply it in circumstances such as had developed in the Far East.
As to policy, there was "no halfway between yes and no"; the United
States must either be "neutral in word and deed," as the neutrality
law intended, or it must be prepared to intervene in foreign wars,
which essentially meant resorting to force to stop the aggressor.

As far as the more articulate sections of the public were concerned,
the controversy over the neutrality issue was most conspicuously
played out between the organizations which made up the American
peace movement in the 1930's. The energetic propaganda campaign
of the six peace societies, which in the summer of 1937 pooled their
activities in regard to the Far Eastern crisis under a joint strategy
board, has already been emphasized in connection with the problem
of the withdrawal of Americans from China. As suggested earlier,
the problem of withdrawal was, however, only of marginal interest
to most of the organizations involved in the peace movement, while
the question of neutrality had for some time been a central subject
of controversy. In fact, it is impossible to understand the cross
currents of opinion on neutrality that developed after the outbreak

of hostilities in China without some knowledge of the past history of the peace movement from which they emerged.

Following World War I, a large number of peace organizations had been exceedingly active in the United States.[95] These organizations differed in character in that some dealt exclusively with problems directly related to the cause of international peace while others engaged in more extensive programs that involved a wide variety of international and national topics; some worked to advance a definite point of view while others sought to maintain an unbiased position; some were religious, some secular. In addition, there were various schools of thought among the peace societies concerning the best methods to use to achieve their ends, with the result that certain groups employed high-powered publicity tactics while their more staid sister organizations relied upon long-term educational procedures.

For approximately a decade after the first World War, almost all the important peace societies in the United States had vigorously endorsed the concept of collective international action for the maintenance of peace and for the most part had advocated America's entry into the League of Nations. Even then they had supported the League with varying degrees of enthusiasm and had held conflicting views on many aspects of such questions as disarmament and the use of force in general. Nevertheless, in 1933 they made a great effort to unite and established an association, known as the National Peace Conference, which soon consisted of forty participating agencies that claimed a total membership of around fifty million.[96] The conference was designed to coordinate the programs of its constituent bodies, without however interfering with their individual activities, and to undertake joint projects on their behalf including nationwide educational campaigns that were to be conducted through such media as mass meetings, radio and publications programs, extensive correspondence, and conferences with government officials.

The National Peace Conference met its first great test when the debates over the neutrality issue started in Congress in 1935. The conference quickly recognized that as a result of the neutrality controversy its member societies, far from drawing closer together as had been hoped, were rapidly dividing into two groups, one of which continued to favor support by the United States of the economic and financial sanctions embodied in the League, while the other felt that, in order to avoid any possible involvement in war, the United States must adopt a policy of severing economic relations with both sides in a conflict. In an effort to bridge the gap between these two groups, the conference in late 1935 adopted as part of its program a plank which stated that the neutrality policy of the United States should be revised "in order that the risk of entanglement in foreign wars may be reduced and in order that the United States may not obstruct the world community in its efforts to maintain peace."[97] The conference also appointed a committee for the study of neutrality legislation under the chairmanship of Professor James T. Shotwell of the Carnegie Endowment for International Peace which in January 1936 published an elaborate report containing a proposed redraft of the existing neutrality law that was intended to translate into practical terms the compromise formula that had been embodied in the conference program.[98] Thus the redraft contained provisions that were designed on the one hand to extend the embargo on arms and ammunition in the existing Act to cover other essential war materials and on the other to authorize the President, with the consent of Congress, to lift embargoes against a state which had been attacked in violation of a treaty provided that the majority of nonbelligerent nations agreed that a treaty violation had occurred.

The committee's report did not succeed in reconciling the two factions within the peace movement. After considering the report, the National Peace Conference itself issued a statement saying that its members had been unable to agree. "Certain of the peace organizations," it said, "are staunch supporters of mandatory neutrality legislation whereas other groups are no less convinced that neutrality legislation should be made permissive in character."[99] This condition of affairs remained unaltered.

Immediately after the issuance of the conference statement, matters, in fact, grew considerably worse. In February 1936 an Emergency Peace Campaign was organized by a group of Quakers who were part of the American Friends Service Committee. In addition to the Friends, the prime movers in the campaign consisted of three organizations—the National Council for the Prevention of War, the Women's International League for Peace and Freedom, and the Fellowship of Reconciliation—which had certain features in common that by this time distinguished them from most of the other societies in the peace movement and that were ultimately to lead them to establish the joint strategy board which attracted so much attention after the beginning of the undeclared war in China.[100]

The National Council for the Prevention of War had been initiated at the time of the Washington Disarmament Conference by Frederick J. Libby who was a pacifist minister before World War I and who later became a Quaker. It was made up of thirty cooperating peace groups which, under Libby's tireless leadership, developed high-pressure propaganda techniques to a point where by 1936 it was distributing two million pamphlets annually and sending news releases fortnightly to over four thousand editors and other molders of public opinion as well as engaging in a multitude of other projects. The Women's International League for Peace and Freedom, though a relatively small organization (having a membership of around 12,000 in 1936), had been founded even earlier than the NCPW, dating from 1915. As it had been established by Jane Addams, it was a purely pacifist society. Its purpose was to mobilize public opinion in order to obtain legislative action and, among other matters, it made a great point of publishing the records of members of the House and Senate on peace issues and distributing them to their constituents. Throughout the 1920's, the Women's International League had proved second only to the NCPW in the energy with which it sought to disseminate its ideas. The Fellowship of Reconciliation had also originated in 1915 as a result of Jane Addams' activities and was therefore likewise wholly pacifist. In contrast to the Women's International League—with which it however at times joined forces for publicity purposes—it was a religious group which based its appeal upon religious tenets.

By the 1930's, these three organizations therefore had in common the fact that they had existed for a substantial period of time, that they had had a considerable amount of experience in the conduct of extensive and spectacular publicity programs, and that they were either entirely pacifist in conviction or had strong pacifist leanings. But in addition, after the emergence of the controversy over the neutrality issue in Congress, they developed an almost identical line of argument which they repeated seemingly without surcease in their publications.[101] As a result of the inequities created by the Versailles Treaty (so the argument ran) the world was divided between the "have" nations and the "have-nots," the former consisting of the large democratic powers and the latter of the fascist or dictator countries. By the very pressure of circumstances the "have-nots" would inevitably try to improve their condition through war unless some attempt was made to alleviate their distress. The United States should therefore adopt strict mandatory neutrality legislation as a means of announcing to all peoples that it would neither singly nor in conjunction with the other big democracies fight to maintain the "evil *status quo*" or use any form of coercion against the under-privileged nations. Once it had taken this step, the United States government should proceed to assume the leadership in an international effort to remedy the grievances of the "have-not" countries by peaceful change thereby eradicating war by eliminating its causes. It should furthermore unilaterally alter those aspects of its own policies which were augmenting international tension such as its provocative rearmament program, its unjust immigration laws, and the imperialistic privileges which it enjoyed abroad—notably the privilege of extra-territoriality in China. This argument was perhaps most effectively boiled down to its essence by Libby in the slogan "We support neutrality and peaceful change, not coercion and the *status quo*."

As a result of these views, the NCPW, the Women's International League, and the Fellowship of Reconciliation in 1935 supported the isolationists' efforts to obtain the most rigid neutrality legislation possible. Their support was in fact so vigorous that they were at times credited with playing a major part in the victory which the isolationists achieved over the administration on the neutrality issue and in strengthening the hand of the isolationists in Congress in general.[102] It was at this point that these organizations joined the Friends in the conduct of the Emergency Peace Campaign.[103] Within a short time the campaign managed to establish twenty regional offices in different parts of the country through which it carried on so-called "cycles" of brief, intensive propaganda programs in order to enlist public opinion to put pressure upon Congress and/or the administration to take some particular action. One of the main features of the programs was the holding of mass meetings which sometimes numbered as many as a thousand within two months. A cycle devoted to mandatory neutrality legislation took place in January and February 1937 while the controversy over a "permanent" neutrality law was raging in Congress.

By the time the undeclared war between China and Japan broke out, therefore, the societies which formed the spearhead of the Emergency Peace Campaign constituted one wing of the National Peace Conference. Opposed to them was a larger wing which included such big and well-known organizations as the League of Women Voters, the American Association of University Women, the National Federation of Business and Professional Women's Clubs, the YWCA, the National Committee on the Cause and Cure of War, and the General Federation of Women's Clubs. These organizations all belonged to the category of associations that were willing to take official stands on specific issues. However, owing to their size, their varied membership, and their manifold activities, they were inclined to act slowly and in the summer of 1937 they were still trying to adhere to a compromise formula on the neutrality issue such as was advocated by the National Peace Conference itself. Nevertheless most of them had shown, during the debates on the various neutrality acts, that they were averse to any legislation that did not distinguish between the aggressor and the victim of aggression and that they were moreover opposed to almost any manifestation of isolationism.[104] This wing of the National Peace Conference was furthermore strengthened by having among its leaders some of the most implacable foes of isolationism in the peace movement, such as Professor Shotwell and other officers of the Carnegie Endowment for International Peace, Clark M. Eichelberger of the League of Nations Association, and various members of the staffs of research organizations such as the Foreign Policy Association.

To confound confusion further, somewhere in between the pacifist societies that had made an alliance with the isolationists and the wing of the peace movement which was unalterably opposed to isolationism, stood the formidable administrative structure of the Protestant church. This was dominated by the Federal Council of Churches of Christ in America, which served as an interorganizational council for twenty-six denominations with a total membership of more than twenty-two million, and the Foreign Missions Conference of North America with its large constituency of missionary organizations. While already highly centralized, these two agencies coordinated their policies even further in 1936 by adopting a plan for constant, close collaboration on international questions and especially on matters related to the problem of peace.[105]

The church presumably followed a course midway between the extremes of the peace movement because of the conflict of opinion that existed among its own leaders and its membership as a whole. In any case, the Federal Council and the Foreign Missions Conference agreed with the pacifists in emphasizing that a substantial part of the blame for the chaotic conditions that had developed since the World War must be attached to the large democratic or "have" powers.[106] On the other hand, they were by no means as denunciatory of those powers, or as condoning of the dictator nations, as Libby and his associates. Likewise, they went part way with the pacifists in their demand for neutrality legislation but at the same time they emphatically stated that, while they were in favor of extensive neutrality legislation on the grounds that it might help to keep the United States out of war, they wished to disassociate themselves from those "misguided advocates of American neutrality" who were striving to isolate the United States from the rest of the world. Their own views, they said, were the "very antithesis of isolationism" as they believed, above all, in world organization. Indeed, both the Federal

Council and the Foreign Missions Conference in joint statements and in their separate publications repeatedly asserted that the only real solution to the problem of war was to create an international government to which the member states surrendered part of their sovereignty, including the police power with which to maintain world order.

In view of the important part which the neutrality issue had played in the recent history of the peace movement, it was inevitable that the question of applying the Neutrality Act to the undeclared war in China would create further agitation. No sooner had the war started than the peace groups which were active in the Emergency Peace Campaign began to bombard the administration and Congress with demands for the invocation of the Act.[107] Their demands were so insistent that some of the best informed contemporary observers believed that the isolationists in Congress shifted away from their initial policy of supporting the administration's decision not to enforce the law because they felt compelled to give in to the wishes of these peace societies at least temporarily.[108]

When, following the adjournment of Congress, Senator Pittman delivered his broadcast of August 23, he not only dealt with the question of the recall of Americans from China but also elaborated upon the arguments he had presented earlier against any hasty invocation of the Neutrality Act.[109] Perhaps more than any other point, the senator emphasized that it would be unwise to enforce the law in the Far Eastern conflict until there was genuine evidence of the existence of a state of war—evidence such as (he said) interference with the commerce of neutral nations.

The senator's example proved to be unfortunate as two days after his broadcast the Japanese declared a blockade of the China coast.[110] While the government at Tokyo asserted that the blockade would be limited to Chinese shipping and that neutral merchant vessels would only be stopped to check their identity, this seemed open to question as the Japanese naval commanders in China were stating simultaneously that they had the right to seize any goods in foreign boats that were customarily regarded as contraband in wartime.

Although Pittman's speech would therefore in any case have embarrassed the administration, further difficulties developed as it became known at the end of August that the S.S. Wichita—a ship operated by the American Pioneer Lines but owned and subsidized by the United States government—had sailed from Baltimore on August 27 carrying 19 Bellanca bombing planes which it intended to transport to China after a brief stop at the west coast. It was at this juncture that the establishment of the strategy board formed to coordinate the activities of the societies involved in the Emergency Peace Campaign plus two less well-known organizations (making six in all) was announced.[111] The efforts of the board were at once directed toward concentrating the attention of the public on the voyage of the *Wichita* as a glaring example of the need for an immediate enforcement of the Neutrality Act to keep us out of war in the Far East. In the first week of September, the board issued a flood of press releases, exhorting the President to "Stop the Bellancas!," which received such good coverage that they appeared daily on the front pages of some of the leading newspapers in the United States.[112]

In view of the administration's reaction to the board's efforts to secure the withdrawal of Americans from China, it was scarcely likely to be impervious to far more vigorous attempts to get the Neutrality Act enforced. On August 17 (the day that Senators Nye, Bone, and Clark issued their statement demanding the invocation of the Act) the President was asked at a press conference whether he intended to apply the neutrality law to the Far Eastern conflict.[113] Roosevelt's reply was that, as Japan and China had not as yet severed diplomatic relations and the entire situation in the Far East was in a state of flux, our neutrality policy was on a "24-hour basis." Nevertheless, a few days later he informed Hull that he was greatly concerned over developments and did not think he could postpone action much longer.[114]

Hull, on his part, was in almost continuous consultation with his aides who however could reach no agreement among themselves partly because they differed widely in their views toward isolationism and internationalism and partly because they held conflicting opinions concerning the effect of the Neutrality Act on Japan and China. Following the proclamation of a partial blockade by the Japanese and the unleashing of the propaganda campaign of the six peace societies over the *Wichita*, the Secretary urgently cabled Ambassadors Grew and Johnson in an effort to obtain further guidance; but he only obtained more contradictory advice. Grew urged the invocation of the neutrality law on the grounds that, in view of the Japanese blockade and a variety of other factors, the United States would not be able to carry on any substantial trade with China in any case and that a trickle of commerce was not worth the risks involved.[115] Johnson, on the contrary, was strongly opposed to putting the law into effect.[116] Any such action, he said, would anger the leaders of the Chinese government and "react dangerously for Americans in China." In substantiation of this argument he recounted a recent interview with Madame Chiang Kai-shek in which, after referring to various steps the United States had already taken and to the possible invocation of the neutrality law, she had said with "bitter resentment" that the United States "seemed to be going out of its way to put obstacles in the path of China engaged in a life and death struggle."

Johnson's observations concerning the likely effect of the imposition of the Neutrality Act on the attitude of Chinese officials were reinforced by Ambassador Wang, who, in an interview with Secretary Hull on September 10, remarked pointedly that China would be able to resist Japan successfully if she could only continue to get the facilities with which to fight from abroad.[117] The ambassador wanted to know what the United States government would do if the Japanese should stop an American ship and attempt to remove from it goods that belonged to the Chinese government. According to the official record of this interview, Hull

> . . . replied that we had not yet reached that point. The Secretary then explained to the Chinese Ambassador at some length the fact and the implications of the existence of the Neutrality Act, the public opinion and beliefs of certain sections of the American people which were responsible for the enactment of that act . . . and that we were operating on a 24-hour basis in regard to the question of invoking the act . . . The Secretary explained . . . we had to keep in mind not only the Neutrality Act but public opinion in this country. The Secretary said that he was endeavoring patiently to educate the American people in general away from adoption of a rigorous, storm-cellar, isolationist attitude but that he wished the Ambassador and his Government to realize the general situation in this country and the fact that the Secretary of State could not take action which would run definitely counter to the general state of public opinion.

Wang thereupon stated that he did realize the situation in the United States but that China was fighting for its very existence and for the principles of the Open-Door policy and that, in order to do so, it had to have supplies from friendly nations, especially the United States. The Secretary responded again that "the pressure from various groups in the United States" for immediate invocation of the Neutrality Act was causing the administration to proceed on a 24-hour basis and that it was impossible to tell "at what time we might have to make some further announcement of policy."

A further declaration of policy was actually made by the President four days later (September 14). Whether such a declaration should be issued and what form it should take continued to be a subject of controversy within the administration almost up to the last minute.[118] The factors with which the President and the Secretary were most

concerned were (a) that the Chinese government's hostility to the
use of the neutrality law might have dangerous repercussions for
Americans in China and (b) that to take no action concerning the
law would continue to arouse criticism at home.[119] As the most
immediate target of criticism remained the Bellanca planes en route
to China, it was decided on September 13 to inform the operators of
the *Wichita* that the ship could not leave San Pedro, California, where
it had docked, and to suggest that it should feign engine trouble to
account for its delay.[120] The following day the President proclaimed
that hereafter no merchant vessels owned by the United States government would be permitted to transport arms, ammunition, or implements of war to China or Japan and that any other ships flying the
American flag would engage in such trade at their own risk; the
question of applying the Neutrality Act was however to remain on
a "24-hour basis."[121] It was subsequently announced that the President's order had been specifically applied to the S.S. *Wichita* whose
cargo of planes had been unloaded.[122]

Having sought to conciliate its critics at home, the administration
sought also to allay the antagonism of Chinese officials. The day after
the President's declaration of policy was issued, Hornbeck had an
interview with Ambassador Wang in which, according to his own
record, he attempted to explain the administration's action:

I . . . said that we of course could not suppose or profess to suppose
that we were not aware that the Chinese would feel badly about our having
taken this step; but that we hoped that they would take account of the
reasons which led to our decision . . . I said that I assumed that the
Ambassador had observed the development of public opinion in this country
during recent years on the subject of trade in arms and munitions of war
and on the subject of discouraging warfare and keeping this country out
of war; I referred to the long period during which neutrality legislation was
in process of enactment, to the discussions, and to the Act itself; then, to
the demands which have come vociferously from various quarters since
July 7 that the Neutrality Act be put into effect; and to the fact that the
Administration has for more than two months refrained and is still refraining from putting the Act into effect. I said that the action taken yesterday
was taken essentially as a matter of domestic policy.

Hornbeck related further that Wang was impatient of his explanations and said that regardless of qualifying circumstances, the Chinese
people would be greatly disappointed at the United States government's action. Two days later, Wang called upon the Secretary
and expressed this disappointment officially and formally on behalf
of his government.[123]

The administration did not manage therefore to avert the anger of the Chinese government. But neither did it succeed in appeasing the six peace societies and their isolationist allies in Congress as quickly became evident. Representatives of the six peace societies met right after the bombing of Nanking on September 21 and issued a statement saying that, if despite this new demonstration of the existence of a state of war in the Far East, the President still refused to invoke the Neutrality Act he would be guilty of deliberate defiance of the will of Congress and the American people.[124] At about the same time the NCPW and the Fellowship of Reconciliation passed resolutions at their annual meetings again calling for enforcement of the Act.[125] Moreover, the strategy board of the six peace organizations continued to issue its full quota of press releases which were supplemented by vigorous editorials in their separate publications. In October the Emergency Peace Campaign published a leaflet, called "Deadly Parallels—A Warning to United States Citizens on Keeping This Country Out of War with Asia," in which it compared current developments with those that led up to the entry of the United States into the World War emphasizing, among other things, the maintenance of the right to trade and to extend loans and credits to belligerents. Further, in mid-October, Representative Tinkham cabled Secretary Hull that when Congress reassembled it should, in his opinion, "consider impeaching the President and yourself" for tearing into shreds the Neutrality Act which was the law of the land.[126] A few days later Hamilton Fish publicly endorsed Tinkham's statement.[127] While even newspaper editors who were wholly in favor of the enforcement of the Act regarded the idea of impeachment as a "wild threat," they nevertheless welcomed the Tinkham-Fish declarations as focusing public opinion further on the need to apply the neutrality legislation to the situation in the Far East.[128]

But if the isolationists and pacifists continued their activities they were not to be given a free hand for long. It has been said that, in addition to the fact that the larger and more diversified organizations in the peace movement normally moved with deliberate slowness, they were caught off base by the sheer momentum and forcefulness of the campaign concerning the neutrality law conducted by the NCPW and its associates after the outbreak of hostilities in China.[129] This in all probability was the case. Yet, as early as August 30, Harold Hinton noted in the New York Times that, to the relief of the State Department, there were signs of differences arising between the peace societies over the procedure to follow in regard to invoking the Neutrality Act.[130] On September 4, right after the strategy board of the six most vocal peace groups had been formed, a statement opposing the enforcement of the Act and denouncing it as an "unfair" piece of legislation was issued over the signatures of such prominent persons in the peace movement as Professors James T. Shotwell and Charles G. Fenwick, Dr. Mary E. Woolley, and the representatives of various religious associations who were pronounced opponents of any form of isolationism.[131] On October 1 a large rally was held in New York's Madison Square Garden by the American League Against War and Fascism which likewise condemned the neutrality law as "unneutral."[132] While the league was regarded as politically far to the left of most of the other peace organizations, it was nevertheless a well-known association with which many relatively conservative groups and individuals were willing to cooperate. In November the league held a congress which was reportedly the largest of its kind ever to be convened in the United States and which, according to outside observers, was marked by a "striking trend" away from neutrality.[133]

Indeed, by the beginning of 1938 the swing away from neutrality was sufficiently strong throughout the extensive anti-isolationist wing of the peace movement for many of the largest organizations to take a definite stand. The National Committee for the Cause and Cure of War held its annual meeting in January and voted to recommend to its eleven constituent agencies that, throughout the forthcoming year, they should put their major emphasis upon the "necessity of United States cooperation with other nations to eliminate war" including cooperation in financial and economic measures that were "designed to withhold aid to a treaty breaking nation."[134] Within the next months this resolution was carried out by the participating agencies which included such influential bodies as the League of Women Voters, the American Association of University Women, the YWCA, and the General Federation of Women's Clubs.[135]

In addition to these measures taken by established peace groups, a new association was formed in January 1938 which was called the *Committee for Concerted Peace Efforts* and which was composed of individuals who acted in a personal capacity but were high officials in many of the most important organizations that were affiliated with the National Committee for the Cause and Cure of War.[136] Under the leadership of Eichelberger, the *Committee for Concerted Peace Efforts* immediately engaged in a campaign through which it secured a thousand signatures for a manifesto demanding a revision of the Neutrality Act and urging the President to deny assistance to treaty violators.

While the peace movement therefore split into sharply defined lines, the Federal Council of Churches of Christ in America and the Foreign Missions Conference still found themselves unable to side with either the majority or the minority wing. On September 23, 1937, these two organizations issued a joint statement in which they declared that the church should lead in arousing public opinion to support the government in transforming a "policy of irresponsible isolationism" (which they defined as "futile . . . ignoble and unchristian") into "one of active participation in the organization of political and economic forces in the world for the purpose of establishing justice and good will."[137] In urging such a proposal, they said, there was however no thought of reliance upon military or naval force or such measures as were apt to lead to war.

This cautious pronouncement on the part of the Federal Council and the FMC reflected conflicts of opinion within the church and mission societies that proved too deep ever to be resolved. The contemporary religious press alone bears testimony to the strong cleavages in religious opinion.[138] The *Christian Century*, always outstanding for the decisive manner in which it championed its convictions, virtually conducted a one-man campaign for the application of the Neutrality Act to the conflict in the Far East.[139] On the other hand, many of the foremost denominational publications in the country remained silent— some of them stating explicitly that their readers were too divided to justify the adoption of any particular editorial policy—while others took a position that contrasted sharply with that of the *Christian Century*. The *Christian Century* itself stated that many religious persons regarded a belief in neutrality as "immoral" on the grounds that it "spelled cowardice and shameless national selfishness."[140] This seems if anything to have been an understatement. The *Churchman* (an independent journal of the Protestant Episcopal Church) not only attacked the concept of neutrality but also that of isolationism and of pacifism, asserting that it was doubtful whether even pacifism could be called truly Christian since it lacked "interest in any purpose of God except the saving of one's own soul."[141] Moreover, it asserted, there was nothing in the scriptures that commanded us "to turn China's other cheek to Japan. And it is possible for us to do this, even in our method of enforcing neutrality." The *Watchman-Examiner* (a national Baptist paper) declared that it should be said of nations as of individuals that "No man liveth to himself and no man dieth to himself"; those politicians who insisted that the United States was self-sufficient were dealing in ideas that were mere "cobwebs in the brain."[142] The *Christian Advocate* (a Methodist weekly) commented bluntly that theoretical pacifism was a piece of "philosophical dullness" that could only lead to international disaster.[143]

The religious press reflected not only a division among the rank-and-file of the religious community but also among its leaders. The situation among mission leaders in particular was complicated for a variety of reasons. There was inevitably a strong desire on the part of mission boards not to antagonize the Japanese because of the American missionary movement in Japan. Also, many missionaries, like other members of the church, clung to a profound faith in pacifism. But at the same time there was a considerable group of missionaries who were neither pacifist nor isolationist and who, because they had spent a large part of their lives in China and were deeply involved with the fate of that nation, were among the most determined advocates of sanctions against Japan.[144] As a consequence, not long after the start of the Sino-Japanese conflict, some of the missionaries who were home from China began to form committees to persuade the American government and people of the necessity of stopping Japanese aggression through the use of economic pressures. By the summer of 1938 matters had reached a point where two well-known China missionaries—Frank and Harry Price—felt that it was practical to found the *American Committee for Non-Participation in Japanese Aggression* which proceeded rapidly to carry its activities far beyond religious circles and vied in energy and spectacular performance even with the NCPW.

In view of all of the above developments, it is evident that the peace movement was in a state of ferment as a result of the Sino-Japanese conflict. By November 1937, when Congress reconvened, it should, however, have been apparent that those who wanted the Neutrality Act applied in the Far East were beginning to encounter formidable opposition. Nevertheless, according to those close to Hull at the time, the Secretary viewed the reopening of the neutrality debate in Congress with great apprehension and spent much time in seeing Senators and Representatives in order to explain the administration's position. Judge Moore, on the other hand, assured the President that he felt reasonably confident that there would not be "any serious division of opinion" in Congress concerning the course which the administration had taken. When, in mid-November, Congress did return to the neutrality question, the administration forces kept matters firmly in their own hands. Chairman McReynolds of the House Committee on Foreign Affairs delivered a speech, based upon a memorandum prepared by Judge Moore, which emphasized that the President had the legal right not to invoke the Neutrality Act and that, as the purpose of the Act was to keep the United States out of war, it would be folly to apply it in circumstances such as existed in the Far East. When all was said and done, even Hull seems to have become convinced that the administration had a surprising amount of support in Congress and among the public.

Taken as a whole the controversy over the enforcement of the Neutrality Act following the Lukouchiao incident was characterized by a veritable storm of confusion, caused by the many complexities involved in applying the neutrality law and, even more importantly, by the existing differences in political attitudes. The confusion essentially provided the administration with considerable leeway to act in any manner it wanted. It chose to follow its own inclination which was to avoid invoking the law—an inclination based in part on a desire not to antagonize the Chinese, for fear of retaliation against Americans in China, and in part, no doubt, on sympathy for China. But, as in the case of the withdrawal of Americans from China, the administration resorted to compromises under pressure notably when it stopped the *Wichita* and imposed limitations upon the transport of arms and ammunition to the Chinese. The pressures came primarily from isolationists in Congress and certain newspapers and a segment of the peace movement. Congressional opposition was faltering, however; the press was completely divided against itself (including the publications that represented business opinion); and while the peace societies with their strategy board admittedly had a moment of scarcely impeded triumph after the outbreak of hostilities in China, nevertheless it was virtually inevitable that the great groundswell of antineutrality feeling within the peace movement would rapidly gather momentum. As suggested at the end of the last section of this chapter, one may therefore question whether the administration did not concentrate upon isolationist opinion to such an extent that it lost perspective and overestimated the strength of pressures which were not as powerful as they appeared upon the surface.

Late in August, just as the controversy over the Neutrality Act began to attract attention, Ambassador Wang called on the Secretary of State in Washington.[1] Wang said that he had come on behalf of his government to tell the Secretary that China was thinking of either appealing to the League of Nations or of invoking the Nine Power Treaty but wanted to consult the State Department before taking either course, as it neither wished to put the United States in an embarrassing position nor meet with a diplomatic rebuff itself. The Secretary indicated that he appreciated the Chinese position and then asked whether his own statement of July 16 "would not more than cover the subject." The ambassador replied that it did as far as principle was concerned, but that his government was now looking for action. As the conversation proceeded and it became clear that the Secretary did not want to answer any further questions, the ambassador suggested that he might call again on the following day. Hull, however, turned this proposal aside with the statement that as soon as he had anything to tell the ambassador he would let him know.

From this point on matters were left to drift for about two weeks until on September 3 Wang, at his own request, came to see the Secretary again. The ambassador declared that the Chinese government had decided to invoke Article 17 of the Covenant at the forthcoming meeting of the League which meant in effect that the Japanese would be asked to submit the Sino-Japanese dispute to the Council of the League for settlement and that, if they refused to do so, they would be subject to the sanctions provided for in Article 16.[2] Wang added that his government hoped that the United States would give its moral support to the League in whatever action it decided to take. According to the official record of this interview, the Secretary thereupon

. . . commented on the fact that, although the American Government has expressed itself openly and vigorously on the subject of policy, other governments have remained mute. He asked: If they will not speak, how can it be expected that they will act? He said that, with us, Congress has passed a Neutrality Act. This is something that lies ahead of us. We are "on a twenty-four hour basis." If other governments will not even speak, what does China expect of us?

Hull suggested further that by introducing the question of sanctions the Chinese might be inviting a repetition of the League's experience during the Italian-Ethiopian affair which would amount to making "an advance backward." However, he said, he was merely expressing a personal point of view. The ambassador replied that, if that was the case, he hoped he could assume that the Secretary's comments did not indicate that the United States would refuse to give its moral support to the League. The Secretary remarked that the "Chinese must consider our record . . . must take notice of our historic position." Wang mentioned the record of 1932. The Secretary responded that sanctions were not attempted at that time.

A few days after his talk with Ambassador Wang, Hull cabled the newly appointed United States Minister to Switzerland, Leland Harrison, in order to acquaint him with the Department's current thinking concerning the Far Eastern crisis.[3] The Minister, Hull declared, should read the public statements which he (the Secretary) had issued on July 16 and August 23. Taken together these statements listed the principles which the American government considered "essential to peaceful intercourse between nations" and showed that such principles applied to the Pacific area as well as other parts of the world. The American government had maintained a "strictly fair and impartial course" as between Japan and China but it inevitably felt that these principles were being grossly violated. "It is a pity," the Secretary asserted, "that other nations have not more generally realized how such public utterances and the public reiteration of these principles would strengthen the principle of validity of treaties and foster the growth of a world-wide determination to resolve differences by peaceful means only."

The Secretary's first reaction to China's appeal to the League was therefore that the members of the League should do as the United States had done: let their policy rest upon moral statements which would form part of a great educative process designed to lead the world away from war. At the same time, Hull did not want to seem to be making any suggestions whatsoever to the members of the League in regard to the steps which they ought to take. He consequently sent supplementary instructions to Harrison in which he in effect reasserted the familiar thesis that the United States was determined to avoid allowing itself to be "pushed out in front" by the other interested powers and made into the unwilling leader of a concerted effort to stop Japanese aggression.[4] As he put the matter to Harrison, the United States had found in the past that members of the League tried to obtain assurances as to American action under hypothetical circumstances and, when the circumstances did not develop, we had at times discovered that we had made commitments far in excess of those of any other nation. Harrison was therefore to refuse "even to speculate" with the representatives of other governments at Geneva concerning the policy which the United States might adopt under certain given conditions. The Department could not but feel that it was "an eminently tenable position" that some fifty states should make up their minds and express themselves on a specific problem before any one state, which was outside the organization of the League, was asked to commit itself.

The Secretary himself quickly demonstrated his intention of remaining entirely aloof from developments at least until other Governments had decided upon and made known their policies. When approached by the Chinese to express his preference for one of several alternative courses, all of which were likely to have far-reaching consequences, Hull persistently replied that the United States would make no decisions as to whether or how to cooperate with the League unless and until that body presented it with some concrete proposal.[5]

The Chinese finally appealed to the Council on September 13 through their main spokesman at the League, Dr. Wellington Koo.[6] Although they invoked Articles 10, 11, and 17 for technical reasons, they gave every indication of intending to adhere to a policy of emphasizing Article 17 which, as already indicated, carried with it the threat of sanctions if the Japanese refused to cooperate with the League.

The Chinese move was followed by days of behind-the-scenes discussions at Geneva, the main point at issue being whether the Council should transfer the Chinese appeal to the Far Eastern Advisory Committee.[7] This Committee, it will be recalled, had been formed in the last stages of the Manchurian crisis but, as it had not met since 1934, there was doubt as to whether it was technically still in existence.[8] Nevertheless, it was felt by most of the League powers that its revival would have decided advantages. For the Committee included the representatives of more nations with interests in the Pacific area than the Council, and, even more significantly, there seemed a good chance that the United States would participate in its meetings as it had earlier when it allowed Hugh Wilson to attend as an observer. Moreover, the Committee was a highly flexible deliberative body which could make any recommendations it pleased and could therefore avoid getting entrapped in Article 17 more readily than the Council, if it so desired. However, the Chinese continued to insist upon Article 17.[9] In the end the matter was solved through a compromise in which it was agreed that the Council would refer the Chinese appeal to the Advisory Committee for immediate consideration while the Chinese would reserve the right to ask the Council to take action under Article 17 if they believed that developments required their doing so.[10]

Throughout these deliberations Leland Harrison adhered strictly to Secretary Hull's instructions not even to speculate upon the policy which the United States would follow and repeatedly stated that he could give no assurance whatever as to whether the administration in Washington would be willing to cooperate with the Advisory Committee if it was resuscitated to deal with the Sino-Japanese conflict.[11] Yet when finally confronted with the League's decision, the administration concluded that it could not very well alter the policy of cooperating with the Advisory Committee, which it had pursued at the time of the Manchurian crisis, without inviting a considerable amount of misunderstanding.[12] Harrison was therefore instructed to sit in on the meetings of the Advisory Committee on the same terms as had governed Hugh Wilson's attendance which meant as a silent nonvoting observer.[13] At the same time Hull made it plain that the United States was determined to maintain its policy of remaining aloof unless and until the members of the League had reached conclusions of their own. Harrison was told to deliver a note to Avenol which read in part:

> In the understanding of the American Government, the Advisory Committee was created to aid the members of the League in concerting their action and their attitude among themselves and with non-members for the carrying out of a policy recommended by the League. At present, until this Government is informed regarding the functions which the League will expect the Committee to perform, it is impossible for this Government to say to what extent it will be able effectively to cooperate.
>
> In order that there may be no misunderstanding with regard to this Government's position and no confusion or delay flowing from uncertainty, this Government feels constrained to observe that it cannot take upon itself those responsibilities which develop from the fact of their membership upon members of the League. It assumes that members of the League will arrive at their common decisions with regard to policy and possible courses of action by and through normal League procedures. This Government, believing thoroughly in the principle of collaboration among the states of the world seeking to bring about peaceful solutions of interna-

tional conflicts, will be prepared to give careful consideration to definite proposals which the League may address to it but will not, however, be prepared to state its position in regard to policies or plans submitted to it in terms of hypothetical questions.[14]

Hull's idea that the members of the League should reach a definite conclusion concerning the action they were willing to take in relation to the Far Eastern conflict without any hint as to what the United States was prepared to do, seemed to many League members unrealistic, especially as the Ethiopian crisis had only recently exhibited the practical difficulties involved in applying international pressures without knowing whether American policy would help or hinder their success.[15] Therefore, even before the convening of the Advisory Committee, there were indications that an effort would be made at Geneva to smoke out the United States government by putting it in a position where it would have to take an active part in the deliberations in contrast to merely being represented by an observer as on the Advisory Committee. On September 21, in a speech before the Assembly of the League, S. M. Bruce of Australia declared that nothing would be a greater mistake than to sidestep the issues presented by the Far Eastern conflict through the adoption of some meaningless formula and that therefore the League should try to "transcend the limitation of its membership" and arrange for a conference of powers primarily interested in the Pacific area—such as the signatories of the Nine Power Treaty—in which, not only League states but "great states outside of the League" would participate.[16] Subsequently, Lord Cranborne, representing the British, stated that Bruce's proposal for a conference of countries that were especially concerned with the Pacific area should constantly be kept in mind and that, if all the other nations agreed, Great Britain would certainly be willing to take part in such a meeting.[17]

Still, despite its desire for a conference of the signatories of the Nine Power Treaty, the British government did not want to alienate the administration in Washington. Lord Cranborne told Leland Harrison privately that Eden wanted to cooperate fully with Secretary Hull and do nothing which might cause him any embarrassment.[18] The British had consequently decided not to pursue the idea of a conference of the Pacific area powers for the time being, as they felt that such a suggestion might not be agreeable to Washington; instead, they intended to propose the establishment of a subcommittee which would be limited to the nations that were directly concerned with the Pacific area and which would therefore at least be a more efficient forum for discussion than the Advisory Committee as a whole.

Hull was fundamentally opposed to the British idea of a subcommittee.[19] As he informed Harrison in a lengthy cable, he remained convinced that the League powers should follow the example of the United States and seek to use the Sino-Japanese conflict as a means of impressing upon the world the necessity, not only of Japan and China, but of all nations maintaining the principles which were essential to the preservation of peace.[20] And he feared that the "universal character" of the issues involved might be obscured if they were dealt with by a subcommittee which was mainly limited to the countries that were party to the Nine Power Treaty. After reviewing once more the purpose and content of his own statements of July 16 and August 23, he went on to define the kind of a declaration which in his opinion the League powers should issue:

> I feel that there are certain principles upon which nations could take a position and upon which they could express themselves with regard to any particular situation or development which may arise, such as the developments now taking place in the Far East. Among those principles might be mentioned abstinence by all nations from the use of force in the pursuit of policy and from interference in the internal affairs of other nations; adjustment of problems in international relations by process of peaceful negotiation and agreement; upholding of the principle of the sanctity of treaties; respect by all nations for the rights of others; and performance by all nations of established obligations. These are broad basic principles upon which international relationships should be governed if peace is to be maintained.
>
> The developments occurring at present in China are and must be the concern of every nation in the world which hopes to base its relationships with other nations upon the principles set forth in my statement of July 16. I can see no reason why any and all nations could not take a position with regard to this conflict from the point of view of their own interest in the preservation of peace and the settlement of disputes by peaceful methods.

In conclusion, the Secretary reasserted that he did not wish to assume any initiative in regard to shaping the action which the League might take and that his comments were therefore purely for Harrison's guidance. Harrison was told, however, that in private talks with the representatives of other governments at Geneva he might refer to the principles set forth in the Secretary's statements of July 16 and August 23 in order "to discreetly foster" the idea that the whole question of the Sino-Japanese dispute should be dealt with "on the broadest possible basis."

Although Harrison did attempt to disseminate the Secretary's views to the extent permitted him, the subcommittee was finally organized along the lines which the British had originally proposed.

Meanwhile, various important developments had been taking place, among which was an effort by the Advisory Committee to persuade the Japanese to cooperate with its activities and the refusal of the Japanese to do so. In a note of August 25 the Japanese stated that the hostility of the Chinese government to Japan was the real cause of the present conflict between the two countries and that a solution could only be found by direct negotiations between Japanese and Chinese; the Japanese government therefore saw "no reason" to participate in the Advisory Committee's discussions.[21] Almost immediately after the receipt of this note at Geneva, the Advisory Committee adopted a resolution which condemned the Japanese bombardment of open towns in China and declared that no excuse could be made for such acts which inevitably aroused "horror and indignation" throughout the whole world.[22] On August 28 the committee's resolution was unanimously passed by the Assembly of the League with "warm applause" and was endorsed in an official statement issued by the State Department.[23]

On the same day that the Assembly acted, Chinese officials both at Geneva and Washington made a further effort to sound out the policy of the United States. In Geneva, Wellington Koo called on Harrison to say that his government recognized that, in view of the recent history of the League, that body would not agree to put the whole machinery of the Covenant into operation.[24] Nevertheless, Nanking hoped that the various members of the League would undertake certain measures, such as refusing credits to the Japanese, prohibiting the export to Japan of war supplies and war materials (among which he listed iron, steel, rubber, cotton, and wool), and conversely furnishing China with credits, munitions, and various commodities necessary for the continued conduct of hostilities. Koo wanted to know what Harrison thought about the possibility of getting such measures adopted, to which Harrison replied that he could express no opinion whatsoever and reminded Koo that the State Department's note to Avenol had stated that the United States would not answer any "hypothetical inquiry." In Washington, a member of the Chinese embassy told Maxwell Hamilton that the Chinese delegation at Geneva had been informed that the Advisory Committee might consider the imposition of an oil embargo against Japan and asked whether the United States would cooperate with any such movement.[25] But, like Leland Harrison, Hamilton merely referred his questioner to the State Department's assertion that it would only define its position if confronted with a definite proposal by the League.

The subcommittee of the Advisory Committee did not meet until

October 1, at which time it was given the task of drawing up proposals for submission to the Assembly of the League before the end of its current session which was to take place within four days. The sub-committee decided to draft a report that would include a summary of the facts related to the Sino-Japanese conflict and end with a con-cluding statement as to whether or not Japan's actions had been justified.[26] The draft when completed contained a long factual section which dealt respectively with the Marco Polo Bridge incident and sub-sequent developments in North China and Shanghai, Japan's obliga-tions under the terms of the Nine Power Treaty and the Kellogg-Briand Pact, and the policies pursued by both the Japanese and Chinese governments since the outbreak of hostilities as revealed in their official statements.[27] The final part of the draft read:

Conclusions: It is clear that the two countries take very different views as to the underlying grounds of the dispute and as to the incident which led to the first outbreak of hostilities.

It cannot, however, be challenged that powerful Japanese armies have invaded Chinese territory and are in military control of large areas, includ-ing Peiping itself; that the Japanese Government has taken naval measures to close the coast of China to Chinese shipping and that Japanese aircraft are carrying out bombardments over widely separated regions of the country.

After examination of the facts laid before it, the Committee is bound to take the view that the military operations carried on by Japan against China by land, sea and air are out of all proportion to the incident that occasioned the conflict; that such action . . . can be justified neither on the basis of existing legal instruments nor on that of the right of self-defense and that it is in contravention of Japan's obligations under the Nine Power Treaty . . . and under the Pact of Paris.

Although the draft thus denounced Japan's actions in China, thereby going considerably further than any individual nation had gone to date, it was accepted by the subcommittee without any delay or controversy.[28] Nevertheless, the question remained as to whether the League nations would go beyond a moral condemnation of Japan and agree to engage in any specific action to stop Japanese aggression. In order to force this issue, Dr. Wellington Koo, at a crucial meeting of the subcommittee on October 4, submitted a proposal which was designed to commit the Council to recommend to the various members of the League the adoption of certain measures which would, on the one hand, cut off aid to Japan and, on the other, assist China.[29] Lord Cranborne thereupon presented a counterproposal the gist of which was that the most immediately effective step the League could take would be to initiate consultation between the signatories of the Nine Power Treaty in order to seek a method of putting an end to the

Sino-Japanese conflict by agreement or, failing such a solution, to submit other proposals to the Assembly if it seemed desirable to do so.

Lord Cranborne subsequently told Harrison that the British regretted not having had time to consult the State Department but that they had felt compelled to revert to the idea of a conference of the signatories of the Nine Power Treaty so as to block Koo's attempt to force the Council's hand.[30] From many subsequent statements of British officials it is clear, however, that they were motivated at this point, as earlier, by the desire to shift the Sino-Japanese conflict away from the League to a meeting held under the provisions of the Nine Power Pact because they knew that such a meeting would almost certainly obtain the active participation of the United States.[31] In fact even before Lord Cranborne made his proposal concerning consultation between the signatories of the Nine Power Treaty, the British had again attempted to get some definite indication from Washington of what action, if any, it was willing to take in regard to the Sino-Japanese conflict. On October 1 the Foreign Office had sent a note to the State Department in which it declared that a strong feeling was developing in England in favor of some definite action to stop the hostilities in the Far East probably in the form of an economic boycott against Japan led by Great Britain and the United States.[32] The Foreign Office admitted that it was by no means certain that a boycott would achieve the desired end but asserted that it was in any case convinced that action by Great Britain alone would not be effective. It wanted therefore to know the attitude of the United States toward a possible boycott and whether the American government would be willing to explore the question further. At the time that Lord Cranborne spoke at Geneva, the State Department was in the process of considering its reply to the British note.

Lord Cranborne's suggestion of a Nine Power Conference led to dissension in the subcommittee.[33] Wellington Koo took the position that such a conference was an "excellent idea" but that it should be held in addition to, not in lieu of, League action. The situation, he said, was too urgent to permit of delay and moreover if the League did nothing it would be a "pathetic confession of its impotence, a disappointment to China, and to the millions supporting the League." Maxim Litvinoff supported Dr. Koo and argued further that sanctions might be effective even if undertaken only by some of the League Powers and that it was a mistake to assume they had to be universal. Bruce of Australia disagreed and, in keeping with his earlier comments, declared that the League by itself could do nothing and that the "cooperation of certain non-member powers . . . was absolutely necessary." The representatives of the other countries sided with Bruce and expressed their approval of the Cranborne proposal. After further discussion, it was decided to charge a drafting committee with the task of drawing up a second report which would take into consideration the suggestions made by both the British and the Chinese.

The drafting committee sought to go as far as it thought practicable toward reconciling the British and Chinese points of view. The text which it finally presented to the subcommittee met the demands of the British *in toto* by advocating that, as a first step towards a settlement of the Sino-Japanese conflict, the Assembly should invite the members of the League, who were signatories of the Nine Power Treaty, to initiate a conference of all the nations party to that treaty plus any other nations that had important interests in the Far East.[34] At the same time, in an attempt to fulfill some of the wishes of the Chinese, it was stated in a concluding paragraph that, pending the convening of the Nine Power Conference, the Assembly should recommend that the members of the League refrain "from taking any action which might have the effect of weakening China's power of resistance and thus increasing her difficulties in the present conflict."

When the final draft of the second report was presented to the subcommittee William Joseph Jordan, the delegate from New Zealand, immediately objected to the concluding paragraph on the grounds that it was too weak.[35] As a result, a phrase was added to the effect that the Assembly should also recommend that every member state consider how far it could go in extending aid to China individually. Wellington Koo proposed defining "aid to China" as "relating to the supply of materials and financial facilities"; but Lord Cranborne argued that any such amendment might prejudice action through the Nine Power Treaty as it was stronger than anything the United States has as yet shown a disposition to support. Dr. Koo's suggestion was consequently dropped. Jordan thereupon declared that he thought the members of the League should also be urged to "deter Japan from continuing its present form of aggression against China." This idea was likewise rejected.

The first and second reports were finally accepted by the sub-committee on the morning of October 5. As time was running short, they were passed by the Advisory Committee on the afternoon of the same day and submitted to the Assembly in the evening. The plan was to have the Assembly vote at once thereby enabling it to bring the current session to a close. But as many of the delegates complained that they could not take a stand on so important a matter without some time for consideration, the meeting was adjourned until the next day. Meanwhile the delegates learned that President Roosevelt had delivered a strong speech in Chicago in which he had referred to the possible quarantining of aggressors. According to subsequent newspaper stories, the President's speech influenced some of the League members to endorse the first report of the subcommittee although they had been hesitant to do so because of its denunciation of Japan's military operations in China. Whether the stories were correct or not, both of the subcommittee's reports were passed by the Assembly on October 6 without any further discussion.

To all appearances, Hull was pleased at the League's condemnation of Japan and may even have tried to prod it into action at the last moment, for he gave instructions to have the news of the President's Chicago speech telephoned to Geneva so that it would be brought to the attention of the delegates at the Assembly.[36] A cable sent to Harrison at the end of September suggests that at about this time Hull began to think that it would be a good thing if the League not only reaffirmed the general principles set forth in his own public declarations but also expressed its disapproval of Japan for having violated these principles.[37] In any event, Hull lost no time in supporting the League's action. Within a few hours after the adoption of the subcommittee's reports by the Assembly, the State Department gave out a press release which was intended to be firm (partly so that it would not be an anticlimax to the President's Chicago speech) and yet nonprovocative.[38] The Secretary's pronouncements of July 16 and August 23 were once more referred to as constituting the basis of American policy and the principles which, in the opinion of the United States government, were essential to the proper conduct of international relations were again enumerated. The main point, however, lay in the ending:

In the light of the unfolding developments in the Far East the Government of the United States has been forced to the conclusion that the action of Japan in China is inconsistent with the principles which should govern the relationships between nations and is contrary to the provisions of the Nine Power Treaty . . . and to those of the Kellogg-Briand Pact . . . thus the conclusions of this Government with respect to the foregoing are in general accord with those of the Assembly of the League of Nations.

Nothing was said in the press release or any other official American statement about the League's decision to convene a Nine Power Conference. Nevertheless, it was understood within the State Department that such a conference was now inevitable and that the United States could not decline to participate.

The day after the issuance of the press release Ambassador Saito came to see Secretary Hull to ask whether the United States had decided to alter its policy toward the Sino-Japanese conflict.[39] The Japanese, he said, had appreciated the "quiet and understanding way in which the American Government had hitherto proceeded" and they believed that relations between the United States and Japan had become increasingly friendly in recent years and should not be permitted to become otherwise. According to the record in the Department's files, the Secretary declared in reply,

. . . that the powers were naturally aroused over all this and naturally could not keep silent about it; that more than fifty powers had expressed themselves at the League; that we, as a signatory of the Nine Power Treaty and the Kellogg Pact, could not admit that the situation was none of our business and could not refrain from expressing the view that provisions of these agreements had been disregarded.

After some further talk Hull stated,

. . . that he greatly regretted the whole situation. He said that the powers would much rather give any country a clean bill of health than condemn or criticize it. He said that he himself would gladly walk from Washington to San Francisco if by doing so he could cause Japan and China to sit down and, with such assistance as anybody else might render, come to a peaceful solution.

As to the ambassador's inquiry concerning any change in American policy, Hull asserted that he had no "particular step" in mind but intended to follow the course which he had been pursuing.

Ambassador Saito's concern over developments in Washington was still not likely to be greater than, or perhaps as great as, that of Grew. As recently as October 2, Grew had again written the State Department to re-emphasize his basic conviction that if the administration continued to adhere to the methods which it had been using in dealing with the Sino-Japanese conflict, it would not sacrifice "an iota" of its "traditional position towards international law, principles and ethics" and would at the same time preserve its friendship with Japan; but that this friendship could only last just so long as the United States was "able to avoid arousing the antagonistic passions of the Japanese Government and people."[40] As Grew sent these comments to Washington by mail, they arrived long after the Department had issued its statement in support of the League's condemnation of Japan. On October 7 the ambassador described in his diary, with a poignant mixture of bitterness and humor, the effect of the Department's action upon the embassy in Tokyo:

It was today that we heard of the Department's espousal of the action of the League of Nations, following the President's Chicago speech of

October 5. The shock to us all was great. However, I called in the entire staff and told them that no matter what we individually might think or feel about the new tack taken by our Government—which was in effect widely at variance with our own carefully considered recommendations— we must take the utmost care (and our wives as well) not to utter a word outside of the Embassy which could give the impression that we were out of sympathy with the Administration's action. The members of the staff, I think unanimously, felt so bitter about this new development that I feared they would sputter about it outside . . .

This was the day that I felt my carefully built castle tumbling about my ears and we all wandered about the chancery, depressed, gloomy and with not a smile in sight. That afternoon . . . I went to the cinema. . . . And then I sank myself in *Gone With the Wind*—which is precisely the way I felt.[41]

Ambassador Grew's distress essentially arose from his belief that Hull's endorsement of the League's action represented a decision on the Secretary's part to adopt an entirely new policy which might soon result in the application of strong sanctions against Japan by the United States and the League.[42] But the record shows that Hull was not thinking in terms of using coercive measures against the Japanese. A memorandum written by Sumner Welles recounts the following conversation on the subject of sanctions which was held by Constantin Oumansky, then Soviet chargé d'affaires in Washington, and the Under Secretary on October 2:

Mr. Oumansky . . . remarked that while he understood the position of the United States very well and would be frank enough to say that if Russia were surrounded by the Atlantic and Pacific Oceans as the United States was, it probably would adopt the same policy . . . nevertheless our attitude was "very discouraging." To this observation I felt at liberty to say that in my judgment I thought no government in the world had adopted a policy based on a more vigorous insistence upon the need for recognition of the principles which should rightly govern international relations nor had any government equalled the United States Government in seeking every possible means of urging upon the two parties to the controversy the need for a peaceful settlement of the existing situation. I asked him to be good enough to explain what he meant by the term "discouraging." Mr. Oumansky then said that the United States could, of course, be helpful under existing circumstances by cooperating with other governments . . . through the imposition of military sanctions . . . I then said that if he anticipated cooperation by the United States through the imposition of military sanctions, he must have completely misunderstood the whole basis of the United States policy which was a policy based, under the terms of the existing neutrality legislation, on taking no sides in the present conflict . . . He then referred to cooperation in economic sanctions. I said that here again exactly the same question was raised, that the policy of this Government accepted overwhelmingly by public opinion in the United States was one of refraining from actions that could be regarded as unneutral, and that any action taken by this Government of an economic character would necessarily be action taken under the terms of the Neutrality Act, if such Act were ever applied.[43]

Similarly, the note which the State Department drafted during the first days of October, in response to the British inquiry about Washington's attitude toward an economic boycott against Japan, asserted in effect that the American government could not be expected to resort to sanctions as it must constantly keep in mind and be guided by the United States Neutrality Act which reflected the will of the American people.[44] In addition, a contemporary record relates that at a meeting of the Secretary and his aides on October 5, the consensus was that, if a Nine Power Conference were convened, it could not do more than reiterate the condemnation of Japan already embodied in the report of the subcommittee of the League.[45]

While Hull's censure of Japan made the deepest impression upon Ambassador Grew (perhaps because, as he indicated, it seemed a dramatic rejection of the policy which he had persistently recommended), the public at large was far more aroused over Roosevelt's "quarantine" speech. Was the President's address, it was being asked, solely an expression of indignation at the lawlessness of the so-called totalitarian states of Germany, Italy, and Japan; or was it, in effect, an announcement of the American government's intention to join with other powers in punitive action against the Japanese? If the latter was the case, what was the President's objective? Did he wish to uphold the principle of collective security as a means of ultimately realizing the ideal of permanent peace? Or did he hope to stabilize the immediate international situation by putting an end to the unrestrained drive for power of all three totalitarian countries or even of Japan alone? Unfortunately, in this instance the record provides no easy answers so that it has been necessary to make the study presented in the following chapter, which deals not only with the "quarantine" speech but also with Roosevelt's efforts in general to cope with the problem of war.

ROOSEVELT'S SEARCH FOR A PEACE PROGRAM

By the middle 1930's, Roosevelt had inevitably become greatly concerned over the international situation and the possibility of future
conflicts in Europe and Asia. Therefore, as already related, he began
to think in terms of finding some new method of solving the world's
problems which would be sufficiently bold and imaginative to dispel
the threat of war and establish a durable peace. This led him in the
summer of 1936 to entertain the notion that he might invite the heads
of all the large European nations to meet with him on board a battle-
ship where, seated around a conference table isolated from all other
influences, they would try to work out a blueprint for a "lasting
peace."[1] As he discussed the feasibility of such a project with a number of people, word of his idea spread and on August 26 Arthur Krock
published an article, together with the pictures of the leaders of five
European governments, on the front page of the New York Times
under a startlingly large headline which declared that ROOSEVELT
IF ELECTED MAY CALL KINGS DICTATORS AND PRESIDENTS
TO GREAT POWER CONFERENCE. The President, Krock said,
felt that he had made a "new discovery in world leadership" in what
he regarded as the greatest cause of mankind: the cause of peace. He
had invented a plan which involved calling a conference of the heads
of the most important states in order to devise a means of assuring the
peace of the world. While none of the details had yet been considered,
he was contemplating the presentation of a program which would in
general be patterned after the Pan-American agreements. The President had no intention of taking any action, however, until after the
forthcoming election campaign, as he was afraid that the Hearst
papers and the Chicago Tribune would attack him for launching a
foreign policy that was even worse than Wilson's effort to drag the
United States into the League of Nations.

Roosevelt subsequently by implication took the position that Krock's story was a figment of the writer's imagination and the project for a high-level meeting at sea was dropped.[2] But the President did proceed to carry out another scheme which, as described earlier, was to be his first concrete attempt to develop some sort of a peace plan. While he had actually set the wheels in motion for the convening of an extraordinary conference at Buenos Aires as early as January 1936, he waited until after his election in November to announce that he himself expected to attend the opening session. His trip to Argentina in December proved to be a triumphal tour which fulfilled his purpose of attracting widespread attention to the proceedings at the conference so that it became possible to impress upon the peoples of other continents that the program for the maintenance of peace which was to evolve from the deliberations at Buenos Aires was not intended to have only regional implications but rather to serve as a model for the whole world to follow.[3]

Of all the proposals advanced at Buenos Aires, the draft of a neutrality treaty submitted by the United States delegation probably created most agitation. The draft was introduced by Hull when, in his Eight Pillars of Peace speech, he posed the question: "Can we in the Conference work out for ourselves a common line of policy that might be pursued during a period of neutrality?"[4] The Secretary declared that an agreement embodying such a policy would be a "tremendous safeguard" to each of the American nations and "might be a powerful means of ending war." The draft itself provided that, in case of war on the continent of the Americas, the states not parties to the conflict would enforce measures similar to those incorporated in the existing United States neutrality law; in the event of war outside the Americas, the signatories would consult with a view (it was implied) to concerting their policies as neutrals *vis-à-vis* the belligerents.[5]

The United States proposal was an outgrowth of the general controversy of the times over neutrality and collective security.[6] At one extreme were the advocates of a collective security system of the Geneva variety who maintained that the outbreak of war anywhere was the responsibility of every nation and that countries that were not belligerents should, if necessary, resort to sanctions against an aggressor even though as a result they might be drawn into the hostilities. At the other extreme were the isolationists who favored the kind of neutrality that was embodied in the United States neutrality legislation of the 1930's, which was essentially based upon the principle that a government should concern itself with keeping its own people out of war and not with attempting to influence the conflict. In between these two schools of thought there existed a great variety of people holding many different opinions. Among them were those who believed that it must be possible to find a middle-of-the-road solution that would enable the nonbelligerents to have an impact upon the course of a war while at the same time protecting themselves from becoming involved in it. Within this group it was often argued that in order to reduce the risk of involvement the nonbelligerents would have to assume the status of neutrals and enforce whatever measures they adopted against both sides in a conflict equally. While neutral nations might find it difficult—or maybe even impossible—to discover a way of playing a decisive part in defeating an aggressor, they might at least be able to curtail the scope and duration of the hostilities if they operated collectively and followed a policy such as refusing to trade in war materials and perhaps other essential supplies with any of the belligerents. Moreover if an international agreement were concluded so that it were known in advance that all neutrals would automatically apply certain embargoes, it might prevent a potential aggressor from resorting to force. Also, to reduce the danger of their own involvement even further, it was thought that neutrals should disavow any intention of using military pressures and should in general adopt as unprovocative methods as possible. Many different kinds of methods were, however, regarded as unprovocative, even including at times a ban upon all commercial intercourse between neutrals and belligerents. Professor Philip C. Jessup, for example, in one of the most detailed studies of "techniques of neutral cooperation" to be published at the time, contended that a plan—which he himself favored—for neutrals engaging in "only interneutral trade," in contrast to the sanctions system of the League Covenant, would not tend to invite retaliation on the part of the belligerents because the renunciation of trade did not constitute an act of intervention in a war but rather of aloofness from it.[7]

The draft treaty which the United States presented at the Buenos Aires Conference was part of the effort to discover a middle-of-the-road course. In effect, it was an attempt to apply in practice the famous provision of the Saavedra Lamas Anti-War Pact accepted by the American Republics in 1933 which stated that, if war broke out between two or more of the American nations, the signatories that were not involved in the hostilities would "in their character as neutrals" adopt a "common and solidary attitude." In the end the United States draft was rejected by the delegates at Buenos Aires because some of the Latin American governments felt that it would conflict with their responsibilities as members of the League of Nations. Nevertheless, as a consequence of the United States proposal the general idea that the neutral countries of the Americas might, under certain circumstances, adopt a common neutrality policy was inserted in other agreements which were approved by the conference. Moreover, in the following years the Roosevelt administration, far from departing from the concept of collective neutrality, continued to try to implement it. The result was in part that the General Declaration of Continental Neutrality was adopted at the inter-American Conference at Panama in 1939. But, as in the meantime the threat of war in Europe had progressively increased and finally materialized, the administration in Washington went one step further and sought to get the American nations to manipulate their "continental neutrality" so that it would work to the advantage of the democracies against the Axis powers. This aim was actually achieved through the development of a policy which, though imposed upon all belligerents alike, by its very nature favored the war effort of the British and French.

Aside from considering the United States draft, the Buenos Aires Conference discussed a wide variety of other plans which aimed at enabling the nonbelligerents to deal with the problem of war short of reliance upon any of the more drastic forms of collective security or neutrality.[8] One consequence of these discussions was the passage by the conference, with extraordinary acclaim, of the Declaration of Principles of Inter-American Solidarity and Cooperation, which emphasized in particular the possibility of collective action by the American states in the face of a conflict outside of this hemisphere. The action was to be pacific but might or might not be neutral. The whole history of the declaration suggests, however, that, if unneutral, the pressures applied against the aggressor were to be relatively moderate. For the declaration was patterned after a well-known decree issued by Uruguay during the first World War for the purpose of organizing a united front of the American nations, that were not involved in the conflict, so that they would give moral support to the United States and the other American Republics that were fighting for the cause of democracy.[9] The kind of measures that were under consideration were the severance of diplomatic relations with Germany. Although the declaration was therefore not likely to involve the nonbelligerents in hostilities, in addition, in accordance with the whole Pan-American peace structure, it had a moral character which might also serve to prevent reprisals. For it declared in substance that the American nations formed a "moral union" which, if confronted with a war outside of this hemisphere, would act on behalf of the common interests of its members, prominent among which was their faith in the ideal of democracy. The collective action of the nonbelligerents was therefore invested with the high purpose of protecting and furthering the welfare of the "international American community" as a whole.

As far as the United States government was concerned, the most important part of the Buenos Aires Conference was, however, not any single agreement adopted by the delegates but the entire program for peace which resulted from the discussions. In the opinion of many United States officials, the main value of the program lay in what they termed its "constructive" and "comprehensive" approach, by which they meant that it sought to improve the political, social, and other conditions leading to war and treated them as interrelated problems. Even before the Marco Polo Bridge incident, Hull stated repeatedly that the application on a world-wide scale of a program similar to that which had been worked out at Buenos Aires was the best—if not the only—means of averting another World War; and after the incident he appears to have felt even more convinced than earlier that the key to the solution of the international crisis lay within the framework of the Buenos Aires Conference.[10]

The President attached as much significance as Hull to the Buenos Aires agreements. Nevertheless, he continued to explore other ways of stabilizing the world situation. When the Canadian Prime Minister, Mackenzie King, who was a close friend of Roosevelt's, visited Washington in early 1937, they had a long talk in which they discussed the possibility of creating a new world organization which might be called "Permanent Conference on Economic and Social Problems."[11] The main purpose of this body would be to demonstrate to the world that "collective security should not be identified with reliance upon force," whether in the form of military or economic sanctions, but rather with "reliance upon reason—public opinion." It was therefore not to concern itself with political problems but to investigate "fundamental" causes of war—that is, "economic and social injustices"—and expose them so that they could be cured by the pressure of an aroused public opinion. The President and Prime Minister agreed that, as this new method of dealing with international tensions proved its effectiveness, the League of Nations would inevitably change in the direction of seeking to preserve peace by peaceful means only and, as a result, would probably merge with the Permanent Conference to form one large international organization with a universal membership such as President Wilson had originally envisaged.

Roosevelt carried the scheme which he discussed with King a step further some two weeks later. It was at this point that Norman Davis was preparing to go to London for the International Sugar Conference and that the President instructed him to obtain the views of European statesmen on the trend of world events while he was abroad. In speaking to Davis before his departure, the President said that he might discreetly try to ascertain the reaction of European statesmen to the idea of possibly reorganizing the League of Nations so as to divest it of its political functions and transform it into a sort of Economic Council in which case "the United States ought to be able to go along."[12] But this was not the only kind of peace plan Roosevelt proposed. It will be recalled that he also told Davis to sound out European statesmen on the subject of a general agreement to "neutralize" the Pacific area which he regarded as a possible Far Eastern counterpart to the Buenos Aires agreements. In addition, Roosevelt wanted Davis to see if he could find a means of bringing the European governments together in a cooperative attempt to arrest the rapid deterioration of the international situation.

That Roosevelt was making increased efforts in the spring of 1937 to search for a plan by which peace might be maintained, was in no way remarkable. The President was widely regarded as having led his country out of the shadow of a fearful depression into a new economic era through courageous experimentation with the political and economic techniques of the New Deal. Consequently, as the international crisis deepened, many people believed that Roosevelt alone had the capacity to avert another World War. The early part of 1937 saw an upsurge of wishful thinking which gave rise to new rumors that the President intended to convene an international conference to settle the differences of the European powers before it was too late. By May the rumors had reached such proportions that Mussolini regarded it as expedient to declare, in a widely publicized interview, that he would greatly welcome Roosevelt's initiation of such a conference.[13] There can be no doubt that the President himself felt increasingly that the world was thrusting upon him the responsibility of solving its problems. When, for example, he was asked at a press conference whether he intended to respond to Mussolini's apparent desire for an international meeting, the President said that "almost everybody in Europe" felt that they were at the end of their tether so they naturally looked to him to pull a rabbit out of a hat; but, he added, not without poignancy, "I haven't got a hat and I haven't got a rabbit in it."[14] Somewhat later he wrote across the top of a memorandum which contained a proposal for a solution of the international situation that "so many leaders of nations in every part of the world" were appealing to him "to *do* something."[15]

Davis in his conversations with European statesmen concentrated largely upon an effort to get a movement under way whereby the leaders of various nations of the world would come together in an attempt to settle the problems which divided their countries.[16] Davis spoke first to the French Minister of National Economy, Charles Spinasse, who declared that animosity among the peoples of Europe was running so high that no European government would dare to take the initiative in making a move toward political or economic "appeasement"; nevertheless, if Roosevelt, with his enormous prestige, would set the wheels going there might be some prospect of success.[17] Spinasse and Davis agreed that in any move which was undertaken the political, economic, and disarmament problems would have to be tackled comprehensively. Davis next saw Anthony Eden who, while he favored the idea of a comprehensive approach, said that Great Britain could not propose any scheme for a general international agreement, as her doing so would be regarded as a sign of weakness and would thereby detract from the beneficial effect that her rearmament program was having upon Japan, Germany, and Italy. Like Spinasse, he thought that the initiative would have to come from President Roosevelt but he did not believe that the time was as yet quite ripe for action. Davis, on his part, declared repeatedly that he was absolutely certain that the President would not allow himself to become involved in the political controversies of the European powers but that he would be willing to participate wholeheartedly in a concerted effort to find a solution to economic questions and to the problems posed by the competitive construction of more and more armaments. In the end, it was decided that the United States and Great Britain would continue to exchange views about the possibility of reaching an international agreement—by convening a conference or by some other means—in the hope that the situation would have shaped itself so that some undertaking could be started in September. Subsequently Davis talked with Joachim Von Ribbentrop, then German Ambassador to Great Britain, who insisted that Germany desired a peaceful settlement of the international crisis and who also said that President Roosevelt as a "world figure with greater prestige than any living person" must take the initiative.

The most important interviews which Davis had during his stay in London were, however, his meetings with Neville Chamberlain who, while he expressed great sympathy with the general idea of trying to bring the European dictatorships and democracies closer together, strongly implied that he wished to pursue this objective in his own fashion. He explained that in his judgment "political appeasement" would have to precede "economic collaboration" and any further attempt to obtain a limitation of armaments. Moreover he told Davis that the British government had just instructed its ambassador in Berlin to impress upon Hitler that the British wanted to establish "more friendly relations and a sound basis for peace" as soon as they were convinced that Germany genuinely desired the same thing. Davis replied in effect that he did not question the British desire to reach an understanding with Germany; nevertheless he wondered whether in view of the critical state of the world it was practicable to postpone for much longer an effort to adjust the differences of the European powers on a wider scale than would be attained by discussions of purely political issues. Chamberlain, however, showed no disposition to change his mind on this point and instead reverted to the problem of the Far East which he said was still giving him great concern. This part of the Davis-Chamberlain talks has already been noted in an earlier chapter but, despite some repetition it seems worth reviewing its main features here. The Prime Minister reiterated the view he had expressed in his letter to Morgenthau, namely, that he feared if England should get into trouble with Germany, Japan would take advantage of the situation to attack British interests in the Pacific area. And he again suggested that this could be avoided by a firm Anglo-American stand in the Far East which, in his opinion, would cause the Japanese to abandon their hostile attitude in favor of cooperating with England and America to "promote peace and economic recovery in China and the Pacific." Davis' response was that if the Japanese were genuinely ready to cooperate on a "proper basis"—one which did not violate the integrity of China—"this might be a very constructive thing to do." Davis then brought up the President's proposal for "neutralizing" the Pacific area although he made no mention of Roosevelt's own connection with it. Chamberlain expressed considerable doubt about the wisdom of this suggestion, saying that he questioned "the practicability of trying to do anything so important before there should be an improvement in the political situation in Japan."

In addition to discussing means of solving the situation in Europe and Asia with Chamberlain, Davis raised the question of the possibility of the Prime Minister's coming to the United States so that he could talk with Roosevelt directly and received the impression that Chamberlain would be glad to do so if the matter could be conveniently arranged. There is no record of a conversation between the President and Davis on this subject after the latter's return home, but Roosevelt must have approved the idea of such a trip as on June 10 Davis wrote to the Prime Minister, on the President's behalf, to ask him to come to Washington around late September.[18] The President, Davis said, was ready to make arrangements immediately to have an agenda drawn up for their meeting. Davis stated further that he believed it might "become possible and advisable within a few months to make a concerted and comprehensive effort to achieve economic rehabilitation, financial stability, a limitation of armaments and peace" so that it would "seem most desirable for Great Britain and the United States to do what they can to . . . prepare the way for a broader move to establish more healthy . . . conditions in the world." But the Prime Minister replied that he did not believe that the time had yet arrived for meetings with the Germans and, if these materialized, they might provide "a valuable indication of the direction in which the lines of advance might run and in this way would be a useful preliminary to any conversation between the President and myself."[19]

By this time Roosevelt was apparently firmly convinced of the importance of a meeting with Chamberlain. For at the end of July he wrote personally to the Prime Minister to say that he appreciated his desire to make progress along other lines which would have a bearing upon the timing of his trip to the United States but that he would nevertheless like some suggestions as to any preparatory steps that might be taken to expedite his visit.[20] Chamberlain did not answer Roosevelt's letter until two months later, when he stated that, given the existing international situation, he was afraid that he could not suggest any way in which his meeting with the President could be expedited.[21] While conditions in Europe were less menacing than they had been a few months earlier, things were still "a long way from the resumption of cordial relations between the Totalitarian States and the democracies." Moreover, developments in the Far East had justified all the worst fears and there appeared little prospect of effecting any improvement through action by the Western powers.

The President was awaiting Chamberlain's reply at the time that he delivered his "quarantine" speech at Chicago so that he still had in mind getting under way some plan for securing peace by bringing the various powers together in a cooperative movement to achieve that end.[22] Indeed, only one day after the "quarantine" speech a new such plan—which was destined to attain considerable fame—was drafted by Sumner Welles.[23] Welles' thought was that it would be easier to get the democracies and the totalitarian states together to work out a broad program for the solution of political, economic, and armaments problems if they first succeeded in reaching an accord on less explosive issues. He therefore proposed trying to conclude an agreement concerning the fundamental rules which ought to govern international behavior such as certain rules of international law. Although Welles recognized that this project was exceedingly modest, he believed that, apart from all other considerations, it marked the limits to which the administration could go without awakening isolationist opposition at home, especially in Congress.

Welles discussed his plan with the President in the first week of October. Roosevelt seems to have reacted with enthusiasm but characteristically sought a means of imbuing the whole idea with a dramatic and human appeal. He therefore suggested holding a meeting of diplomatic representatives, accredited to Washington, at the White House on Armistice Day at which he would read a message outlining the proposal and appealing to the world for support in the interests of peace. Welles subsequently incorporated the President's suggestion in a detailed memorandum preparatory to action. But the entire undertaking was dropped before Armistice Day because Hull felt that it was too "pyrotechnical." It was nevertheless revived in early January 1938 in a manner which will be discussed later.[24]

All in all, the President's search for a plan that would reduce the danger of war in the immediate and distant future covered a period of time which started considerably before and continued after the "quarantine" speech. The most important feature of his plans was that they aimed at bringing the various powers together to settle their differences, an objective which Roosevelt for the most part assumed could best be achieved through the negotiation of an international agreement dealing with some of the basic causes of war.

At some point, however, Roosevelt also began to make groping efforts to find a technique of international organization which would provide a better solution than any as yet suggested to the question of how, if the outbreak of war proved unavoidable, nonbelligerents could have an influence upon the hostilities without becoming embroiled in them. The President developed a vague idea of his own to which he referred in talks with various people—talks that form part of the rest of this story—and in the "quarantine" passage of his Chicago speech. One of his reasons for returning to this idea on a number of occasions may well have been that he tended to follow a practice of giving expression to some half-formulated concept in the hope that others would be stimulated to improve upon it until it reached the point of furnishing a possible basis for action. At any rate, not only was Roosevelt's concept of a new technique for collaboration between nonbelligerents or neutrals vague, but, equally significantly, his plan for the use of it was also very nebulous.

Shortly after the Marco Polo Bridge incident, Eichelberger of the League of Nations Association sent the President a letter which indicates the substance of a conversation they had had about a week earlier.[25] Eichelberger wrote that he felt certain that some time before leaving the presidency, Roosevelt would find the occasion to fulfill the desire he had expressed during their talk of making a "dramatic statement" which would "not have the effect of 'simply another speech'" but would "lead the world on the upward path." Eichelberger suggested that such a statement should emphasize certain principles which the President had stressed as, for example, the need to establish economic and social justice throughout the world. "Once the world had accepted your principles," Eichelberger declared, "the denial of trade to the aggressor would be accepted by the American people. Instead of sanctions being voted piecemeal they would take the form of a denial of the economic benefits of the more nearly just international society to the nation that would make war."

On September 14, about a week before he was to leave on the trip that ended in the "quarantine" speech, Roosevelt had a talk with Ickes which the latter recorded in his diary.[26] The President, Ickes wrote, said that he was thinking of addressing a letter to all the nations of the world, except possibly the "three bandit nations" (Germany, Italy, and Japan) in which he would "suggest that in the future if any nation should invade the rights and threaten the liberties of any of the other nations, the peace-loving nations would isolate it." What the President had in mind was to "cut off all trade with any such nation and thus deny it raw materials." However, he did not intend to apply his plan to the situation in China and Spain as what had been done could not be undone; what he wanted was to evolve a "new policy for the future" in which case "it would be a warning to the nations that are today running amuck." Ickes on his part expressed approval of the President's scheme, as it offered a "method of keeping out of war ourselves" and preventing wars from occurring. The conversation ended with a discussion of whether Roosevelt's letter should be sent before or after his tour out west and with Ickes advising the President to wait until his return.

But only two days after speaking with Ickes, the President mentioned a plan to Morgenthau which did not include any reference to possible collective action against any aggressor and, in fact, had little in common with any of Roosevelt's other proposals. The President told Morgenthau that he continued to have a hunch about the international situation and thought he might publicly declare his readiness to act as a clearing house for peace between the governments of the world. Almost immediately thereafter he reiterated this statement to Hull. Both expressed their opposition to the President's embarking upon any such undertaking and, whether for this or some other reason, Roosevelt informed Morgenthau before he left for his western tour that he had changed his mind and had decided not to make any move that would call for any response or action from any other quarter, preservation of peace being a matter of long-term education.

The idea that Roosevelt should give a major foreign policy address during his trip across the country had first been suggested by Hull, who thought that something should be done to counteract the isolationism which he felt was rapidly increasing throughout the United States, especially in the middle west.[27] Roosevelt had readily accepted the Secretary's proposal and it was decided that the President would deliver the speech on the last day of his journey, at Chicago. Both men clearly had in mind that the address should also serve as a medium to convey to the world the revulsion felt by the American people to the outrages being committed by the "bandit nations." The original draft of the speech consisted of four memoranda, two of which were written (as far as can be learned) by Hull and Norman Davis while the remaining two were definitely written by Davis alone.[28] The memoranda as a whole were characterized by a strong tone of moral condemnation of Japan, Germany, and Italy (though these countries were not named) and described with great forcefulness the chaos being created by their brutal actions over wide areas of the globe. In addition, two points were made repetitively: that disorder in any part of the world could not fail to affect every nation and that peace-loving nations must make a concerted effort to uphold the "laws and principles" without which peace could not exist.

Roosevelt related subsequently that while traveling in his railroad car through the great western prairies he took out the memoranda which had been furnished him by the State Department and dictated his Chicago address; the dictation flowed with a readiness he rarely attained and he made few changes after re-reading the speech.[29] A comparison of the texts makes clear that Roosevelt used the four memoranda almost *in toto* and for the most part limited himself to editing them by rearranging and shortening sentences, so that they would conform to his own brilliantly vivid and terse style of writing, and by adding a few paragraphs largely for the sake of color. The President did, however, make two important changes in the section of the draft composed by Davis without Secretary Hull's collaboration. Davis, who was known for a tendency to express his feelings about the international situation with a lack of restraint unusual in statesmen, had written a characteristic passage which said that the United States was dedicated to certain principles "without which life would not be worth living" and that, if the time ever came when the American people were not willing to defend these principles to the utmost of their ability, they would cease to have the vitality and stamina to keep this nation alive.[30] Any such assertion could clearly be interpreted as meaning that, if pushed too far, the United States would fight. Roosevelt discarded this passage and in its place put his famous "quarantine" statement.[31] Under the circumstances, in doing so he may partially have been trying to tone down the original text while striking a note which, though vague, still sounded sufficiently strong to give pause to the totalitarian states. In any case he wrote:

It would seem to be unfortunately true that the epidemic of world lawlessness is spreading.

When an epidemic of physical disease starts to spread the community approves and joins in a quarantine of the patients in order to protect the health of the community against the spread of the disease.

The second change that Roosevelt made was in the ending of the speech. At the conclusion of his final memorandum, Davis had declared that "there must be positive endeavors to preserve peace" and had written an unusually moving statement to the effect that there was a tendency, in the welter of conflicting ideologies that were battling for control of the modern world, to overlook one basic truth: that "man, the human being . . . is the supreme end of society." One might have expected these lines to have a special appeal for the President in view of his own constant emphasis in political matters upon the overriding importance of the individual. But he set them aside and wrote his own ending instead:

There must be positive endeavors to preserve peace.

America hates war. America hopes for peace . . . Therefore America actively engages in the search for peace.

The President delivered the final text of the speech in Chicago on the morning of October 5. Immediately thereafter he went to lunch at the house of Cardinal Mundelein where he entered into a conversation in which he tried to define his "quarantine" idea further. Again, the record of his remarks is an indirect one, consisting of a letter written on the following day by Cardinal Mundelein to the Apostolic Delegate to the United States which said in part:

Yesterday the President of the United States delivered here in Chicago a strong and important address which may affect the future peace and tranquility of the world. Afterwards, in my own house, he continued discussion of the subject to which he had given considerable thought. He asked me whether he might invite participation of the Holy See in the movement and, as it is for the purpose of establishing permanent peace in a war-torn world, I answered that I thought he should. His intention in this case would be to send a special envoy to the Vatican . . . a man of ambassadorial rank . . .

His plan does not contemplate either military or naval action against the unjust aggressor nation, nor does it involve "sanctions" as generally understood, but rather a policy of isolation, severance of ordinary communications in a united manner by all the governments in the pact. It does seem that if an end is to be put to the present wave of lawlessness both in Europe and Asia, it must come from a united action of the civilized peoples of the world.[32]

Looking back over the events that began with the President's talk with Eichelberger, it is evident that the idea to which Roosevelt kept returning was, stated in its simplest form, that in case of war nonbelligerents might "quarantine" or isolate an aggressor thereby depriving him of the benefits of "ordinary communications" in the interests of the entire society of law abiding nations. This idea, as Roosevelt's subsequent remarks showed, was closely associated in the President's thinking with suggestions for possible collective action by neutrals or nonbelligerents such as had been made at the Buenos Aires Conference and elsewhere. In short, the President was trying to find a formula which would enable nonbelligerents to exercise an influence upon a war to the extent of actually defeating an aggressor while still limiting themselves to the use of methods which would not provoke reprisals that would involve them in hostilities. The President's "quarantine" idea was nonprovocative in that it contained features such as the moral overtones of the Pan-American agreements; but, on the other hand, it called for exceedingly drastic action on the part of the nonbelligerents without providing them with the protection that might be afforded by the much more positive safeguard of retaining the status of neutrals. Roosevelt never consistently faced up to the fact that his "quarantine" device departed from the principle of neutrality and at moments seems even to have persuaded himself that the common isolation of an aggressor by nonbelligerents was a form of neutral cooperation. This, however, required quite a *tour de force* so that the whole quarantining concept never reached the stage of providing a usable medium for action and although Roosevelt referred to it even after his Chicago speech none of the available evidence suggests that he ever really intended to push it. Indeed, he continued, as he himself emphasized, to grope for a genuinely satisfactory formula.

The theory that the President's "quarantine" idea was and remained a confused and unsuccessful attempt to solve the dilemma of how to restrict aggression without resorting to threatening measures such as sanctions is supported by two incidents that followed Roosevelt's Chicago speech. The day after his return from Chicago, the President held an off-the-record press conference which has since become famous.[33] The reporters, convinced that the President's references to a "quarantine" in his Chicago address had been carefully chosen to convey to the American people and the world that Roosevelt had decided to use sanctions—economic and perhaps military—against Japan, subjected him to many questions. His answers seemed to them meaningless, from which they concluded that, fearful of the almost hysterical attacks launched against his speech from certain quarters, the President was intentionally being evasive, having determined to beat a hasty retreat; but in retrospect Roosevelt's replies sound like a genuine attempt to explain what he had in mind. The main point which the President tried to make was that he was searching for a method of furthering the cause of world peace, that his "quarantine" concept was one of a variety of ideas related to this search, but that he was still in the process of seeking the right solution. The reporters were especially persistent in asking whether a "quarantine" concept was a sanction, to which the President responded by stating with considerable vehemence that "sanction" was a "terrible word" which should be thrown "out of the window" and by admonishing the correspondents not to "get off on the sanctions route" as he had "never suggested" sanctions. A reporter explained that by "sanctions" he meant "going further than moral denunciation" but the President declared: "That is not a definition of sanctions." When the same reporter said: "Are you excluding any coercive action? Sanctions are coercive," Roosevelt replied, "That is exactly the difference." When the reporter asked: "Better then to keep it in a moral sphere?" the President retorted "No, it can be a very practical sphere."

The correspondents also repeatedly questioned the President as to whether a "quarantine" was "neutral" and felt that on this point in particular his answers were so confused they must reflect a deliberate attempt to be misleading. But the key to Roosevelt's answers seems to lie in the fact that he had in mind techniques for neutral collaboration of the kind which the United States itself had suggested at the Buenos Aires Conference and in his tendency to regard his "quarantine" idea as similarly based upon the concept of neutrality. In general, the President said that it was "by no means" necessary that the method of international action he wanted to find would be "contrary to the exercise of neutrality." When asked whether he would not at least admit that a "quarantine" would essentially amount to a repudiation of the United States neutrality law, Roosevelt asserted, "Not for a minute. It may be an expansion." At another point when a correspondent, who from the outset had shown marked skepticism, said that in his opinion a "quarantine" was no longer neutrality, Roosevelt replied that "On the contrary, it might be a stronger neutrality." The President further declared: "There are a lot of methods in the world that have never been tried yet."

About two weeks after the President's press conference, Norman Davis, who was about to depart for Brussels, where he was to represent the United States at the Nine Power Conference which had been called as a result of the League's action, went to Hyde Park to receive his final instructions from Roosevelt.[34] In notes, written the day after their meeting, Davis recorded that the President "particularly objected to the word *sanctions* being used and said that this was a word that ought not to be used any more, some other word must be found." Roosevelt then asserted that every effort must be made at the Nine Power Conference to settle the Sino-Japanese conflict by mediation but that if none of these efforts succeeded, all of the countries that wished to stop the war and protect themselves from its consequences "or in other words the *so-called neutral nations,* should band together for their own protection against this contagion." One thing that might be considered was having the other powers agree to give to China every facility for acquiring arms, et cetera, although in that case the United States could do nothing because its laws would not permit. "Another alternative would be for *neutrals* to ostracize Japan, break off relations."[35]

Attached to these notes in Davis's files is a paper marked "Handed me by the President as of possible use." The paper contains what must be an excerpt from an article or book which states that "the principle of neutral cooperation, short of obligation to use force," as embodied in the Saavedra Lamas Anti-War Pact and reaffirmed at the Buenos Aires Conference, might "offer a useful formula for the United States at the present time" as it "suggests the possibility of a constructive program in which a group of neutrals, acting together, but without threat of force, might make their influence felt. If stressed by the President it could be made the instrument for a positive . . . policy."

If the President's remarks to the press and to Norman Davis showed among other things the extent to which his "quarantine" concept was loosely conceived, it cannot be emphasized too strongly that Roosevelt's idea of the use to which he wanted to put his "quarantine" device was equally ill defined. The furthest the President went in discussing a plan was in his talk with Cardinal Mundelein when he indicated that he had two purposes in mind: one of initiating a move-ment for the establishment of a "permanent peace" and the other of arresting the "present wave of lawlessness both in Europe and Asia." While he suggested that the first aim might be achieved by the conclu-sion of a universal pact involving some method of collective action designed to isolate an aggressor, Roosevelt apparently said nothing about any means of attaining the second objective. In speaking to Secretary Ickes, he had referred to the possibility of reaching an inter-national agreement from which the "three bandit nations" would be excluded. But he evidently abandoned this proposal nor was he likely to appeal to the Pope to assume the leadership of a political venture overtly directed against the governments of Germany, Italy, and Japan.[36] Moreover, in so far as he had a plan, the President was not very intent upon pursuing it for Cardinal Mundelein stated specifi-cally in his letter to the Apostolic Delegate that Roosevelt had not indicated what he intended to do next. It is in fact quite possible that in his conversation with Cardinal Mundelein, the President was not so much interested in advancing any specific scheme as in reaffirming his desire to establish closer relations with the Vatican through the appointment of an envoy, a matter with which he had been concerned for some time, as he believed that religious and lay leaders by pooling their influence could create a better spiritual climate in which peace was more likely to thrive.[37]

The detailed story of the "quarantine" speech seems therefore to indicate clearly that Roosevelt was not trying through his statements at Chicago to prepare the world for the enforcement of a policy of sanctions against Japan which he had already decided to adopt. Indeed, besides expressing the vigor of the reaction of his countrymen to the acts of aggression being committed in Europe and Asia and sounding a very general note of warning to the totalitarian states, the President probably wanted his Chicago speech to convey one message: that, in response to the outcry of the many people who were appealing to him to forestall the tragedy of another major war he was trying "to *do* something" in terms of uniting the world and opening the door to the possibility of unlimited peace. Roosevelt's own explanation of his speech was in essence that its significance lay in this message and in view of his long effort to find a peace plan which would involve a con-certed attempt on the part of all the powers to reach an agreement—especially a "constructive" agreement—there is little reason to doubt that he meant what he said. Thus when questioned at the press con-ference held after his return from Chicago about the meaning of his Chicago address as a whole, the President replied: "I don't know that

I can give you spot news because the lead is in the last line, 'America actively engages in the search for peace' . . . We are looking for some way to peace." When one of the correspondents then said that "foreign papers put it as an attitude without a program," the President answered: "It is an attitude and it does not outline a program but it says we are looking for a program." In addition, in a Fireside Chat on October 12, which was devoted to a discussion of his tour out west, Roosevelt, in referring to his remarks at Chicago, said that it was the duty of a president to think in terms of peace not only for one but for many generations and that peace must therefore be "sound and permanent," built on a "cooperative search" for peace by all nations desiring that end.[38] In conclusion he declared:

> The common sense, the intelligence of America agree with my statement that "America hates war . . . America hopes for peace, therefore America actively engages in the search for peace."

In response to the questions posed at the end of the last chapter, it may be said therefore that Roosevelt had not abandoned the hope to which he was so intensely committed, of securing peace by peaceful means. And that he definitely had not settled upon any policy of drastic action, let alone sanctions, either in order to support the general principle of restraining lawlessness by collective measures or to stop the advance of the totalitarian nations as a whole or of Japan individually.[39]

The Aftermath of the "Quarantine" Speech

Irrespective of what has been revealed by the record brought to light over the intervening years, it was only natural that at the time the "quarantine" speech should seem to many to be an indirect announcement that Roosevelt was about to apply sanctions against Japan. For the manner in which the President's delivery of the speech was followed in quick succession by the League's condemnation of Japan, its decision to convene a Nine Power Conference, and Hull's statement endorsing the League's action, created a widespread impression that Roosevelt's remarks about a "quarantine" and the measures taken by the League and the State Department were all parts of one piece of political strategy which had been carefully planned to lead up to the enforcement of sanctions against the Japanese. As the controversy over the "quarantine" speech was not only intense but lasted until well after the Brussels Conference, it could scarcely fail to have an impact upon men as concerned with the reactions of the public as many of the high officials in the Roosevelt administration.

In the end the estimate of the public's reaction to Roosevelt's references to a "quarantine" seems to have been fairly uniform in administration circles. Sumner Welles, for example, states in one of his books that the President "was dismayed by the widespread violence of the attacks" which his speech provoked.[40] Welles himself bitterly criticizes Hull and various other members of the Cabinet for their obviously deep-seated opposition to the speech and asserts that as a result a majority of the administration's spokesmen in Congress refused to give Roosevelt any support. In addition he writes that the "public, stimulated by isolationist leaders and the pacifist organizations" clamored against the "quarantine" proposal and that throughout the "entire country" there was "hardly a voice raised to express agreement with the President's views" except for a small segment of the press which had consistently supported internationalism.[41] Hull on his part says in his *Memoirs* that the "reaction against the quarantine idea was quick and violent" and set back by many months the administration's efforts to "conduct a constant educational campaign intended to create and strengthen public opinion toward international cooperation."[42] By way of proving the hostile character of the country's reception of the speech, he cites a few items beginning with a declaration issued by "six of the major pacifist organizations" to the effect that the President was pointing the "American people down the road that led to the World War." Judge Rosenman in his *Working With Roosevelt* also declares that the "reaction to the speech was quick and violent—and nearly unanimous."[43] The President, he asserts, was "attacked by a vast majority of the press" though there were "some notable exceptions of course, like the Washington *Post*." Moreover, he indicates that the messages which Roosevelt received after his delivery of the speech were mostly expressions of angry protest.

These estimates, coming as they do in part from the highest officials in the United States government, raise certain questions. Were they justified by the information which these officials had at their command? And, if this was not the case, what led them to the conclusion that the nation, speaking almost as one voice, repudiated Roosevelt's speech at Chicago?

In the first place, a survey of comments in a group of outstanding newspapers and periodicals, such as officials in Washington were reading, does not indicate any agreement with the judgment that the nation's immediate reaction to the speech was one of vehement antagonism. On the contrary, on October 6 the *New York Times* printed excerpts from sixteen editorials from all parts of the country under the headline "ROOSEVELT SPEECH WIDELY APPROVED."[44] The

Christian Science Monitor, on October 7, declared that observers were surprised at the degree of enthusiasm evoked by the speech with even papers that were normally hostile to the administration finding words of praise.[45] In a review of the week on Sunday (October 10), the *San Francisco Chronicle* wrote that the average citizen had responded to the President's message like a "cavalry horse to a bugle call."[46] It stated further that Roosevelt had appealed to the nation much as Woodrow Wilson had taken the case for the League to the country to "whip a little group of Senators"—only where Wilson had failed, Roosevelt had succeeded. *Time* magazine asserted at about the same time that the Chicago address had elicited more words of approval, ranging from enthusiastic to tempered, than anything Roosevelt had done in many a month.[47] He had regained the support of many persons whom he had alienated earlier and provided himself with an active peace issue which promised to remain popular unless it threatened to involve us in war. Meanwhile he kept the country guessing as to whether his proposed "quarantine" meant diplomatic pressures, voluntary boycotts, or economic sanctions.

There was therefore a marked tendency to assume at the outset that the country had received Roosevelt's remarks at Chicago, not only favorably but even enthusiastically. After a brief time, however, this tendency gave way to conflicting opinions. Some publications came to believe that the American people had initially supported the President's address only because they regarded it as an expression of moral indignation against Japan, Germany, and Italy which was, if anything, long overdue; but that much of this support changed either to skepticism or disapproval after the idea gained ground that Roosevelt's talk about a "quarantine" and a "concerted effort" on the part of peace-loving nations to maintain peace was really intended to pave the way for the adoption of a policy of vigorous sanctions against Japan at the forthcoming Nine Power Conference. *Newsweek,* for example, ultimately came to the conclusion that, while Roosevelt's pronouncement at Chicago originally "evoked favorable echoes" in the country, the boldness of his words and the subsequent actions of the State Department in regard to Japan frightened the isolationists so that American opinion soon began to turn.[48] Publications such as *Time,* however, thought that the nation remained firmly behind the President.[49] *Time* admitted that "Franklin Roosevelt's ringing, full-voiced abandonment of traditional United States isolationism at Chicago" had jolted the "isolationists and passive-peace advocates" and even diplomats like "Oldster Hull." But it nevertheless believed that both Roosevelt and Hull, while avoiding the use of the strong language that the

President had adopted at Chicago, had embarked upon a new foreign policy which they continued to pursue and which had the approval of the American people. In general it may be said that the comments under review agreed that the first widespread feeling of enthusiasm for the "quarantine" speech became tempered by a growing feeling of anxiety that, at the forthcoming Brussels Conference, Roosevelt might carry his new foreign policy to the point of actual warfare. On the other hand, there was no agreement as to whether this anxiety added up to a rejection of Roosevelt's "quarantine" speech as many people believed that it was possible to use punitive measures against Japan—up to and including various kinds of boycotts and embargoes—without their leading to war.

Turning from estimates of opinion to actual expressions of opinion, there is again reason to question the conclusion reached in administration circles. It is certainly true that the six peace societies attacked the President's Chicago address and in general continued the campaign which they had been conducting through their strategy board. Not only did they meet on the day following the address and issue a letter declaring that the President was pointing the "American people down the road that led to the World War"; but for many months after the speech they persistently resorted to the argument that Roosevelt was "hypocritical" in denouncing other nations as "lawless" when he himself refused to carry out the Neutrality Act which had been placed on the statute book with the overwhelming endorsement of the American people.[50] They also insisted that the whole approach to the international situation which Roosevelt revealed in his "quarantine" address was entirely unacceptable as it was based upon the "angel-devil theory"—that is to say, on the assumption that the world was divided into "peace loving" and "bandit" nations which, in their view, had nothing to do with reality as it existed.

Nevertheless, these criticisms, however arresting, were by no means the only opinions voiced by members of the peace movement. On the same day that the six peace societies met to issue their letter to Roosevelt, the large organizations which made up the National Committee on the Cause and Cure of War also held a meeting under the committee's auspices.[51] Carrie Chapman Catt, in a speech which dominated the gathering, hailed the "quarantine" address and the State Department's subsequent statement of moral condemnation of Japan as "the most hopeful effort for peace in twenty years" and urged the leaders of the various societies present to uphold the administration's new foreign policy. A resolution was thereupon passed expressing appreciation of the stand which the President and Secretary Hull had taken. In fact, October 1937 can be said to mark the end of a period in which the six more vocal peace organizations exercised a near monopoly over public attention as thereafter the wing of the peace movement, represented by such societies as the Committee on the Cause and Cure of War, closed ranks in order to come out in support of financial and economic measures against a "treaty breaking state."

As to the religious sector of the peace movement, on October 9 the heads of the Federal Council of Churches of Christ in America, acting in their official capacity, sent Roosevelt an open letter enthusiastically acclaiming his reaffirmation at Chicago of the principle of cooperation with other nations for the maintenance of law and order.[52] The letter further expressed approval of the State Department's announcement that the United States would attend the Nine Power Conference but, in accord with the previous policy of the council, stated that this approval did not imply support of concerted military action which might involve the United States in a general war. Both the council and the Foreign Missions Conference subsequently issued many statements, especially for circulation among their own constituents, which candidly declared that they were unable to take a position on the question of political and economic pressures against Japan as their members differed too widely on whether such pressures were ethically valid and on whether they were likely to be effective if not supported by the threat of military sanctions.[53] The Foreign Missions Conference did, however, suggest in the summer of 1938 that the churches might be justified in urging certain voluntary embargoes and boycotts on private individuals.[54] Actually there can be little doubt that even as early as the autumn of 1937 there was a powerful current of opinion among Protestant religious groups in favor of strong action, short of war, against Japan. It was stated in the October issue of the Council *Bulletin* itself that many churchmen favored economic pressures against Japan because they did not believe that the American people should support an aggressor and they regarded boycotts and embargoes as a "form of moral protest and social coercion."[55] Even such publications as the *Christian Century*, despite the editors' vigorous advocacy of neutrality for the United States, devoted much space in its October and November issues to articles by some of the most prominent clergymen in the United States arguing for economic sanctions against Japan.[56] It can therefore scarcely be said that the reaction to Roosevelt's Chicago address on the part of Protestant religious groups was "quick and violent—and nearly unanimous."

Among Catholic organizations, the Catholic Association for International Peace could hardly have been more outspoken in its support of the President's Chicago speech.[57] The Executive Committee of the Association issued a statement endorsing Roosevelt's address and stating that it was fully in accord with the view that a "concerted effort must be made to uphold the laws and principles of peace." Such a concerted effort, it said, "need not, and in our opinion, must not mean war." The international community had other methods of stopping aggression at its disposal, such as the discontinuance of commercial intercourse with the law-breaking nation and indeed the withholding of materials of war would in all probability be sufficient without resorting to the extreme of breaking off all trade relations.

One segment of public opinion did, however, respond to the President's "quarantine" speech quickly, vehemently, and almost uniformly—namely the businessmen, whose views were reflected in some of the leading commercial and financial publications in the United States. On the day following the speech the *Wall Street Journal* published a front-page editorial addressed to the President under the title: STOP FOREIGN MEDDLING; AMERICA WANTS PEACE. The *Journal* admitted that Roosevelt himself did not want war but indicated that this did not solve the problem.[58] An "innocent citizen," it said, watching a "street brawl" might either stay at a safe distance or intervene; however, if he chose to intervene he should not do so on the "fatuous assumption" that he would be immune to "blows and brickbats."[59] The President should therefore recognize that "the rule that the way to peace is to give all fights a wide berth" remained the one that peace lovers had found the most efficacious. The *Commercial and Financial Chronicle* similarly argued that if the "quarantine" speech was really intended to introduce a new foreign policy it could only end in a disastrous departure from isolationism.[60] American isolation, it declared, was a policy whose wisdom was enforced by the obvious facts of the world situation. The United States was not responsible for the political difficulties of the European and Asiatic powers and had no "superior wisdom" to apply to the solution of their problems. It should therefore remain aloof from international action which would only impair its independence, security, and welfare. The *Journal of Commerce*, on its part, warned that economic sanctions would have "grave implications" and that a blockade in support of such sanctions would be a "long step toward war."[61]

Business opinion as expressed in the above publications was, however, offset by labor opinion. Indeed, a passage in Hull's *Memoirs* seems characteristic of the whole tendency among officials to evaluate the reaction to the "quarantine" speech without due regard at times even to very obvious facts. Hull presents as evidence of the American people's solid hostility to the speech that the American Federation of Labor forthwith passed a resolution at its annual convention which declared that: "American labor does not wish to be involved in European or Asiatic wars."[62] But what actually transpired was that on October 7 William Green arose at the convention to support the President's "strong" stand at Chicago and to endorse the action of the State Department and the League in condemning Japan. An account of the meeting, printed on the front page of the *New York Times*, states that Green himself vehemently denounced Japan and then goes on to say:

"If I can have my way," shouted Mr. Green, "I will prevail upon this historic convention to join with our fellow workers in declaring . . . a boycott against this aggressive nation."
The applause was loud and long.[63]

Moreover, in response to Green's appeal, the A. F. of L. on October 13 passed a long resolution demanding a boycott of Japanese manufactured goods and calling upon "all of the free national trade union movements in other countries" to cooperate so that the "withdrawal of national purchasing power" might have an immediate effect upon Japan and prevent other nations from attempting similar acts of aggression.[64] On October 15 a similar boycott resolution was adopted by the C.I.O.[65] These boycott proposals did not, it should be noted, include raw materials such as silk (which would have been contrary to the interests of the American hosiery worker), and it has been generally assumed that they were most actively supported by labor groups that were facing competition from Japanese imports in the United States market.[66] Nevertheless, irrespective of the motives involved, the fact remains that the large labor organizations did not attack Roosevelt for his statement about a "quarantine" but, on the contrary, they themselves advocated economic action against Japan although, as Hull indicated, they did not want to see the United States drawn into a war with Japan through a boycott movement or otherwise.[67]

Another instance in which it may be said that official impressions were definitely at variance with measurable facts is that of the assessment of the messages that Roosevelt received after the delivery of the "quarantine" speech which Judge Rosenman characterized as highly unfavorable to the President.[68] The Judge may have seen some denunciatory telegrams as they came into the White House but, if so, these formed a small percentage of Roosevelt's mail which consisted overwhelmingly of expressions of approval.[69] Many came from individuals who had close personal or official connections with the President; but hundreds were written by simple persons, wholly unknown to Roosevelt, who wanted modestly to extend their encouragement. "Yours were the right words at the right time," one letter said; "I stand with the majority of citizens to support you. May this in its small way, help to hearten you."

As to editorial opinion, Lawrence Kramer's study of the editorial policies in eight representative newspapers shows six approving the "quarantine" speech and two opposing it.[70] Among the favorable papers were two published on the west coast: the *San Francisco Chronicle* and the *Los Angeles Times*. The *Chronicle* immediately welcomed Roosevelt's statements at Chicago on the assumption that they meant that the President had decided to join in cooperative economic sanctions against Japan. While it thought that the use of sanctions would require holding the fleet in readiness, it did not believe that the occasion would ever arise for military action. However, when a few weeks later the *Chronicle* became convinced that the hopes which it had placed in the "quarantine" speech were unjustified, it began to denounce Roosevelt. The President, it said, had made a "brave" speech at Chicago but there was no indication that he himself knew what he meant by it; he had "not thought it through" and was "not prepared to see it through." The *Los Angeles Times* reacted to the address by going through a similar process of expectation and disillusionment. It first supported Roosevelt on the basis that he was laying the ground for the adoption of economic and financial measures against the Japanese by the various powers at the forthcoming Brussels Conference. But when the conference convened and no such measures materialized, it asked sharply why Roosevelt had ever delivered an address at Chicago. What originally looked like a statesmanlike utterance, it said, appeared very different in the light of the lack of any effort to implement it.

In the middle of the country, the *Milwaukee Journal* expressed itself with even greater vehemence. Waiting until the close of the Brussels Conference, it let forth a blast describing the departing delegates as making for their home territories utterly beaten, their "tails between their legs." "Where do we go from here?" it asked, and declared, "Nowhere. There wasn't any bright new dream when the President spoke at Chicago . . . only rhetoric"; Roosevelt's words had not meant a "damned thing." The *Cleveland Press*, a Scripps-Howard paper, while hailing the "quarantine" speech and contending that it implied more than moral pressure, pursued a cautious policy, never definitely advocating any course.

On the east coast, the *Christian Science Monitor,* taking a far stronger position than earlier, acclaimed the principle which, in its opinion, the President had enunciated at Chicago, namely, that the United States could not remain neutral "between forces of order and disorder." As time went by, it stated that many people were beginning to feel "let down" because Roosevelt's "quarantine" suggestion was not leading to action and it repeatedly urged the administration to adopt a firmer policy at the Brussels Conference. As the conference ended it declared that Roosevelt had shown that he was more afraid of his isolationist critics than ever and that perhaps the whole trouble was that, while a large minority throughout the country had agreed with his "quarantine" speech, it was still only a minority. To most Americans, as well as to their government and the governments of the other Western powers, "interest in peace and order" was still not worth the risk of "effective collective economic action"; however, the day would come when this would change. In contrast to most of the above-mentioned papers, the *New York Times* was slow to commit itself to any definite point of view, perhaps because it was undergoing considerable soul-searching, involving a reconsideration of its whole editorial policy toward the Far Eastern crisis. At the outset it merely limited itself to expressing the profound hope that Roosevelt had decided to adopt a new internationalist policy and had launched it at Chicago. It soon warned, however, that the public was reading a meaning into the President's comments that he had not intended and that, if Roosevelt had a new foreign policy in mind, he had not thought it through either carefully or concretely. Throughout the Brussels Conference, the *Times* took an increasingly firm stand and when the conference was over, in an unusually forceful editorial, it blamed the isolationists and "blind peace groups" for so undermining the position of the United States in international affairs that no effort to cope with the totalitarian states, on the part of the democracies, could be successful.[71] A few weeks later—on the day before Christmas—the *Times,* in one of its rare dramatic gestures, declared itself in favor of withholding raw materials and credits from Japan.

While these six newspapers seem sufficiently representative to assume that their views, or equivalent ones in similar publications, came to the attention of members of the administration, it may be well to mention specifically the editorial policies of the outstanding Washington papers which Roosevelt (and no doubt other officials) frequently scanned.[72] The *News,* being a Scripps-Howard publication, followed the cautious policy already noted. The *Post* issued a sensational front-page editorial on October 6 endorsing Roosevelt's reference to a "quarantine" as a first step toward economic measures against Japan. The *Star* not only advocated such measures but asserted that, unless they were boldly applied, the signatories of the Nine Power Treaty would deserve nothing better than the contempt which they would certainly get from the Axis countries.[73] The *Times* and *Herald*, both Patterson papers, were in favor of a long-range, Anglo-American blockade of the Japanese.[74] In line with what has been said previously, it should be emphasized, however, that no matter what actions were recommended the publications under review believed— and repeatedly so stated—that these actions would not lead to war and that the President must not allow them to lead to war.

There is therefore reason to suppose that, if officials in Washington had read their newspapers with objectivity, they might not have been so convinced that the vast majority of editors throughout the country saw in the "quarantine" speech nothing but a cause for vituperation. An examination of the papers that were negative and of their impact upon the administration may throw some light upon the latter's attitude.

The two papers in Kramer's study that were found to be hostile were the *Chicago Tribune* and a Hearst publication. Nothing demonstrated the attitude of the *Tribune* better than its description of the scene of Roosevelt's delivery of the "quarantine" speech which, it should be explained, was part of a ceremony dedicating a new bridge at Chicago that was a PWA project:

> Those Chicagoans who went yesterday to see a bridge dedicated, those who gathered at the curbstones to see a President pass in a shower of ticker tape, and those who sat at their radios to hear some words of peace, these and many more found themselves last night the center of a world-hurricane of war fright. President Roosevelt came to Chicago to bless the bridge that spans two delightful and peaceful park systems.
> He talked war.[75]

Under such titles as "Whatever It's Called It's War" and "It's Britain's War," the Chicago *Tribune* throughout October and November published a large number of articles and editorials which were designed to bring two major themes home to the public: that a "quarantine" must mean economic sanctions and that economic sanctions under any name must mean war; that we were merely puppets of the British who were, once more, trying to use us to save their empire in the Far East.[76]

The same themes were emphasized by the Hearst press. But Hearst went much further. He issued a questionnaire to members of Congress which, leading off from the "quarantine" speech, asked whether we should take sides in the Sino-Japanese conflict or steer clear of all wars. The answers were published in a series of articles which began on October 17 and ran for about two weeks in the various Hearst papers.[77] The introduction stated that congressmen from the "Atlantic to the Pacific, from Canada to the Gulf" had "roared back their determination for today, tomorrow, and forever to keep the United States out of foreign wars."

Many of the published replies came from important political leaders, mainly well known isolationists. Senator Borah said he was utterly opposed to the United States' participating in sanctions against Japan which would be "just the same as initiating war." Senator Vandenberg declared that any move toward naming aggressors, using sanctions, et cetera, would lead us in the direction of entangling alliances—the one thing we were determined to avoid. Senator George of Georgia wrote that he would not under any circumstances favor action which might risk war with Japan. Senator Richard Russell asserted that, instead of policing the world to maintain peace, we should rely upon our neutrality legislation to "quarantine" us against war. Senator La Follette stated that he was opposed to anything which, by implication or otherwise, might ultimately require the United States to use force.

The statement which received the widest publicity was that issued on October 19, the eve of Norman Davis' departure for the Brussels Conference, by Hiram Johnson, who said in part:

> The natural public emotions, the detestation and indignation with which we view the actions of Japan are well nigh irresistible. They arouse the deepest sympathy for the Chinese and abhorrence of the Japanese; but this is far from embarking in the conflict.
> We want none of it. We want no union with welching nations who will receive us [at Brussels] with open arms and tell us we must lead mankind and save the world. There should be no mystery when lives are at stake and when a responsible ruler of a nation says that another nation must be "quarantined" because of its brutality and inhumanity; if that responsible ruler be of a democracy he should tell his people what he means by the word and how far he is going . . .
> The people should know when their ruler approaches war.[78]

Johnson stated further that the views of our "ambulatory Ambassador," Norman Davis, were well known and that if Davis followed his bent "he would return to America with the cheering news that England expects every American to do his duty." It was wholly obvious, he declared, that "Mr. Davis would not be going to Brussels, unless in advance a program had been agreed upon between England and this country." On the other hand, Johnson asserted that if nothing was accomplished at Brussels our conduct would be "deemed pusilanimous."

From the very beginning, the administration followed the attacks upon the "quarantine" speech closely, especially those which came from Hearst. At his press conference following his return from Chicago, Roosevelt made some remarks about excerpts from editorials around the country, referring presumably to those quoted in the *New York Times*. He failed, however, to mention that they were mostly in his favor but concentrated instead upon the editorial written by— to use his own words—"the old man of the seas—old man Hearst." This, he declared, was "the silliest ever . . . perfectly terrible— awful. Says it means this is getting us into war and a lot more of that." A few days later, Ickes recorded in his diary that the Hearst press was after Roosevelt "full cry" for his Chicago address and that the President had said he wanted to remind Hearst that he had been responsible for an absolutely unjustifiable war with Spain.[79] At about the same time, Pierrepont Moffat noted in his diary that Hearst was "alleged to be about to start a campaign against the idea of a 'quarantine.'"[80] When the campaign got under way, Roosevelt clearly showed his concern. On the day Norman Davis sailed for Brussels, the President issued a statement which was generally accepted as a reply to Senator Johnson's attack.[81] Obviously addressing himself to the accusation that Davis would not be going to Brussels unless we had an understanding with the British, Roosevelt asserted that we were "of course" entering the Nine Power Conference without any prior commitments. He also emphasized that the purpose of the meeting was to seek a *peaceable* solution of the Sino-Japanese conflict. At the same time the President dictated some instructions to guide Davis in his relations with the British—instructions which were in substance forthwith communicated to Anthony Eden by Ambassador Bingham. These started with:

It should be recognized by the British Cabinet that there is such a thing as public opinion in the United States, as well as in other nations.

That it is necessary for Mr. Davis and for his associates in the Nine Power meeting to make it clear at every step:

(a) That the United States is in no way, and will not be in any way, a part to joint action with the League of Nations.

(b) That the United States policy does not envisage the United States being pushed out in front as the leader in, or suggestor of, future action.

(c) That on the other side of the picture, the United States cannot afford to be made, in popular opinion at home, a tail to the British kite, as has been charged and is now being charged by the Hearst press and others.[82]

Given all the foregoing, it is hard to escape the conclusion that (1) any dispassionate estimate of the evidence at the administration's command did not justify the assumption that (to return to Welles' statement about the "quarantine" speech quoted at the outset) there was "hardly a voice raised to express agreement with the President's views; and (2) that the main factor which influenced many officials, from the President on down, was the same sensitivity to isolationist and pacifist criticism that they had shown earlier. The aftermath of the "quarantine" speech went far toward revealing the extent of that sensitivity. At the same time the attacks upon the address by isolationists and pacifists undoubtedly led many members of the administration to feel even more strongly than before that the United States government could not take any step toward participating in vigorous collective action against an aggressor unless and until it was wholly assured of the overwhelming support of the American people. Certain American statesmen did not share this view, outstanding among them being Norman Davis, who was rapidly becoming a more and more fervent advocate of collective security. But by and large the attitude of leading officials in Washington was such that, following the agitation over the President's Chicago speech, there was less chance than ever that the administration would reverse its previous policy toward Japan and agree to some sort of punitive measures undertaken jointly with other powers.

PREPARATIONS FOR THE CONFERENCE

Throughout October and November 1937 efforts to deal with the Sino-Japanese conflict moved along two parallel lines: the Nine Power Conference met without Japanese representation and engaged in prolonged discussions that ended in futility while simultaneously the Japanese attempted to open negotiations with Chiang Kai-shek outside the framework of the conference. As these two efforts remained curiously separate they will be treated separately here, attention being devoted first to the Nine Power Conference.

The second report adopted by the League of Nations Assembly on October 6 had stated that the Assembly should invite the members of the League, who were parties to the Nine Power Treaty, to initiate a meeting of the signatories of that treaty and other states with interests in the Far East in order "to seek a method of putting an end to the Sino-Japanese conflict by agreement."[1] No sooner had the report been accepted than the British began to plan for a Nine Power Conference and got in touch with the United States government to discuss some of the practical details involved.[2] The British suggested that the conference be convened in Washington but this idea was immediately rejected by the administration, which scarcely wanted to find itself in the forefront of the proceedings, and the President himself proposed Brussels as a suitable meeting place.[3] As to the form of the invitation to be extended to the various powers, the State Department said that in its opinion the invitation should be "couched in as broad language as possible" merely indicating the time and place at which the conference would be held, "coupled with the phrase in the Assembly resolution to the effect that the purpose was to seek a method of putting an end to the conflict by agreement."[4] The administration's wishes were followed and all the necessary arrangements were made with the Belgian government. A last minute obstacle arose in that the Belgians, unwilling to be responsible for the conference themselves, declared that in issuing the invitations they wanted to say that they were doing so "at the request of the American and British

Governments." The administration objected to any such phraseology because—as Hugh Wilson frankly stated to our embassy in London—it was determined that "nothing should be done that would seem to hitch us too definitely with the British and, above all, give the impression that we were following the British."[5] The phrase was therefore changed to read "at the request of the British Government and with the approval of the American Government." In addition to ironing out these difficulties, the British proposed that delegations "of the highest standing" be sent to the conference and expressed the hope that Secretary Hull would attend. Hull however replied that he could not possibly absent himself from Washington for so long a time and that the President had decided to send Norman Davis instead.[6]

Meanwhile officials in Washington were addressing themselves to the more fundamental problem of what the policy of the United States should be at the Nine Power Conference. The first step consisted of the discussions held by Hull and his principal advisers on the day that the League report was adopted, which indicated that the prevailing opinion in the State Department was that little could be accomplished at the conference other than to reaffirm the protests against Japan's actions already issued by the League and supported by the United States government. This was followed by the hiatus caused by the fact that the President did not return to Washington at once (having gone straight to Hyde Park from Chicago) and by the consequent bewilderment within the State Department itself as to whether or not the "quarantine" speech was intended to usher in a new foreign policy which might involve some sort of strong action against Japan. Norman Davis, who was in Washington, was privately expressing the hope that this was the case, declaring that while our interests in the Far East were not sufficiently important to justify a war, the principles of collective security might well be worth fighting for.[7] Some State Department officials agreed with him, while others decidedly did not. In any case, talk both for and against collective security simmered down when Roosevelt arrived back at the White House and word passed around the State Department that the President was thinking far more in terms of following a "constructive" policy at the Nine Power Conference than in terms of sanctions.[8]

Presumably spurred on by the President's attitude, an exceedingly interesting movement for a "constructive" peace in the Far East developed within the State Department. It appears to have originated as early as October 6 with a memorandum of Hornbeck's. In order to understand Hornbeck's proposals—and his later policy as well—

it is however necessary to consider for a moment his general approach to the developments following the outbreak of hostilities in China.

Hornbeck belonged to the internationalist group in the administration and was therefore not in sympathy with the general idea of remaining wholly aloof from foreign conflicts that was advocated by some of his colleagues in Washington and by Foreign Service officers such as Ambassador Grew. It will be recalled that shortly after the Marco Polo Bridge incident Hornbeck wrote a memorandum in which he specifically stated that the issue for China and Japan was whether the Japanese would gain control over an important part of China; but that the issue for other powers, especially the United States and Great Britain, was "whether the pursuit of national policy by force . . . is or is not to be objected to . . . and, if the answer is in the affirmative, then by what process?"[9]

Hornbeck himself had long maintained that, as a matter of principle, "the pursuit of national policy by force" should be opposed. He had taken this position at the time of the Manchurian crisis and in 1935 had emphatically differed with those Americans who insisted that the Italian-Ethiopian conflict was "none of our business," stating that the American people would have to realize some day that it was the "duty of all members of the community to endeavor to prevent breaches of the peace."[10] Hornbeck was moreover convinced that in order to "prevent breaches of the peace" the existing peace machinery would have to be supported by something more than moral pressures. He believed that for the most part a clear indication by several nations (including large powers such as England and America) that they would not tolerate aggression would be enough to stop a war but that in some instances action, even to the point of using armed force, might be essential and would be justified.

In accordance with these views, Hornbeck welcomed the President's "quarantine" speech as a sign that the United States was prepared to assume the leadership of a movement to take action in respect to Japan and the other "gangster" nations, and expressed the hope that the movement would go beyond moral condemnation of Japan. In a note, dated October 7, 1937, which appears in the records of the Nine Power Conference, he wrote:

> . . . we regard statements of principle and declarations of attitude as action. We set great store by public opinion. Among ourselves we find that public opinion is a powerful agency and that it is likely to determine and control policy. We therefore project our conception of the efficacy of public opinion into the field of·international relations . . . We think that if there is developed a widespread public opinion adverse to . . . the course which Japan is pursuing, this public opinion will cause Japan to desist

from that course. We make this a major premise in our reasoning on the subject of "action"—doing this, we may, if we are not very careful, again make the same error that we made in 1932 . . .

If we mean business and if we intend to be realistic, we must consider earnestly whether we are willing to do anything beyond and further than express opinions.[11]

The specific policy which Hornbeck advocated in his memorandum of October 6 was that, at the forthcoming Nine Power Conference, the various nations should devote themselves, first, to the adoption of "restrictive measures" against Japan, which would compel her to abandon her current course of aggression, and, second, to a consideration of "constructive" measures.[12] In regard to the latter, he stated that if the powers wanted to create a comparatively stable situation in the Far East they would have to go beyond the limits of the Nine Power Treaty and conceive of a settlement in terms of a broad group of commitments comparable to the agreements concluded at the Washington Conference. In fact Hornbeck suggested that, after proper preparation, a conference might be called which would have the scope and importance of the Washington Conference but instead of dealing largely with the problems of China, would concentrate on the problems of Japan in an effort to provide her with a sense of political and economic security that might put an end to her policy of imperialistic adventuring.

Hornbeck's suggestion of seeking a "constructive" peace in the Far East was further developed by Maxwell Hamilton in a long memorandum of October 12.[13] Hamilton's idea was in essence that it might be possible to relieve the economic and political tensions in Japan by reaching a settlement that would (a) meet Japan's desire for further access to raw materials and outlets for her manufactured goods and (b) ease Japan's fear of other countries (principally Soviet Russia), and of communism. In the economic field he thought an arrangement might be worked out which would give the Japanese a "greater share of the Chinese and other Far Eastern markets and resources." In the political field he envisaged the creation of an administration in Inner Mongolia which would recognize China's sovereignty but, at the same time, govern the area so that it would constitute a buffer state between the Soviet Union and China proper, thereby "tending to prevent the infiltration of communism from the Soviet Union into China."[14] As a matter of practical procedure, Hamilton suggested that the United States and the other interested governments might immediately develop a set of "constructive" peace proposals, such as he had outlined, which they would present to the Japanese. The Japanese would, no doubt, refuse to consider them; but the proposals should be held open until such time—perhaps three to six months hence—when Japan would have found through experience that the attempt to conquer and administer further large sections of China was costly and contrary to the best interests of the Japanese themselves. Then, it was to be hoped, the Japanese government would be ready to consider a "constructive" program for the stabilization of the Pacific area which would give practical application to the principles of policy set forth in Secretary Hull's statement of July 16.

Hamilton's memorandum was followed by prolonged meetings between Norman Davis, Secretary Hull, and leading State Department officials, to discuss the policy which the United States Delegation should adopt at Brussels. By this time it had been decided that Davis was to sail for Brussels, on October 20, accompanied by Stanley Hornbeck and Pierrepont Moffat. The meetings revealed that opinions within the State Department divided roughly into two schools of thought.[15] One felt that, if nothing was done to arrest Japan she would, after conquering China, go on to take the British and Dutch possessions in the Pacific and eventually attack the Philippines which would inevitably involve the United States in war. The other believed that Japan would never conquer China and would only exhaust herself in the effort; moreover if she should succeed, it would not make any great difference to the United States as she would have to continue to trade with us. In any case, the United States had no interest in the Far East that would justify a war; the Japanese could never successfully attack in this hemisphere and so they were not a menace to us.

Despite these sharp differences in points of view, the meetings finally settled down to a consideration of a "constructive" peace from which there emerged an outline of a broad program designed to solve some of the basic causes of friction in the Far East.[16] The theory governing the program was that a contribution toward a general settlement in the Far East should be made by Japan, China, and the interested foreign powers. Japan was to agree not to infringe Article I of the Nine Power Treaty and to remove her armies from Chinese soil in two stages: upon the signing of a general agreement, the Japanese were to reduce their troops in China to the number existing there before the Marco Polo Bridge incident; subsequently, within a period to be determined by all parties, Japan together with the other powers was to withdraw all her forces from China. China's contributions were, in part, to be economic, involving commitments to

(1) apply to all nations (thus including Japan) the principle of equality of treatment in the control, development, and export of raw materials; (2) enter into negotiations with the Japanese for a commercial treaty with the aim of facilitating trade with each other and assuring each other most-favored-nation treatment in their respective markets; (3) desist from and discourage anti-Japanese boycotts. At the same time the Chinese were to give certain guarantees for the safety of Japanese nationals in China, which might include the creation of zones to be policed by Chinese constabulary trained by foreign officers, including Japanese.

The concessions which the foreign powers were to make fell into two distinct categories, namely those benefiting Japan and those benefiting China. For the benefit of Japan, the powers—notably Great Britain, the United States, and France—were to undertake to deal with the Japanese, both in commercial and monetary matters, on a general basis of equality with special problems to be determined by mutual understanding. Specifically, the Powers were to commit themselves on a reciprocal basis not to impose any form of tax or other burden of a discriminatory character on the exports of raw materials and to pledge that, in any international restrictive scheme to which governments were parties, the governments of consuming nations— like Japan—would have adequate representation. For the benefit of China, the powers were to: (1) recall their troops, as previously noted, at the end of a period to be determined; (2) consider the relinquishment of extraterritoriality (with the possible creation of a special status for Shanghai); and (3) withdraw any objections to China's obtaining financial help for rehabilitation in the form of long-term loans.

In addition it was suggested that certain immediate political adjustments might be made to ease the situation in the Far East. These included the establishment of "some form of zones" along the Siberian border to keep the Japanese and Soviet armies apart and the creation of a regime in Inner Mongolia along the lines and for the purposes which Hamilton had described earlier. It was also definitely stated that there were some things which the United States would *not* do. The United States was not prepared to recognize Manchukuo, it was said; neither the League nor China itself had recognized it and the principle of nonrecognition of the fruits of aggression had been incorporated in other treaties as a basic policy of this country. Nor was the United States ready to make any concessions to Japan concerning immigration.

While all the above proposals were related to the terms of a possible Far Eastern settlement, two questions and answers were included in the Department's outline which dealt with the general policy that the United States should adopt at the Brussels Conference:

Q: Is the United States willing to engage in sanctions?
A: The scope and purpose of the Conference as evidenced thus far calls only for the putting an end to the conflict by agreement.
Q: Could the United States agree to any form of solution that infringed (a) China's territorial integrity or (b) the principles of the Nine Power Treaty?
A: No.

Only two copies of the Department's outlines were made, one of which was given to Secretary Hull and the other to Norman Davis.[17]

In the meantime the Secretary and Davis had been having some conversations with the President about the policy to be followed at Brussels. Unfortunately the only record of these talks consists of a very sketchy memorandum written by Davis after the lapse of a week or more which makes it difficult to determine what the President really said.[18] According to Davis' notes, however, the President indicated in general that he thought something would have to be done about the Far Eastern situation because a "great principle" was involved, namely, the principle of upholding the sanctity of treaties, which it was essential to maintain as otherwise international anarchy would ensue which, in itself, would endanger the security and stability of the United States. He therefore felt that a determined attempt should be made to bring about a truce between China and Japan and, if possible, to work out a constructive agreement; for merely to await the outcome of the situation would be dangerous, as it was already a disturbing factor in world peace and progress. The President, Secretary Hull, and Davis all agreed that every effort should be made to bring about a truce and a settlement but the question arose as to what the alternative might be if these efforts failed. Davis himself asked whether in that case the members of the American delegation to the conference should "pack up and come home and drop the matter," which "of course would be most disappointing, if not somewhat humiliating"; or whether they should consider a "concerted effort towards economic and other pressure upon Japan?" The President "felt that we could not quit . . . that we must then consider taking further steps." Secretary Hull and Davis pointed out that in the event it was "deemed advisable, if possible, to bring about coercion," it was most probable that the British and Dutch would decline to take any action unless the United States would agree to protect them with its navy. While, in all likelihood, the Japanese would come to terms if they were convinced that the powers meant "business," nevertheless it was "doubtful" if public opinion in the United States would support a policy of coercion. The President said that if, despite all efforts to bring about a cessation of hostilities and peace between China and Japan, the Japanese refused to be reasonable and persisted in their determination to dismember and conquer China, the public opinion of the world and of the United States would most probably demand that something be done.

On October 19 Davis went to Hyde Park for his final instructions, which he recorded more fully than the substance of his previous interviews with Roosevelt. Davis' account relates that he (Davis) showed the President the outline, which had been drawn up in the State Department, for a broad adjustment of the problems of the Pacific area, and that Roosevelt thought this "very good." The account then contains the passage which has already been quoted in part:

He [Mr. Roosevelt] felt that it was important that we try to generate a spirit of peace and goodwill at Brussels, and that if Japan refuses to come to the conference we should put various questions up to Japan as to what her objectives are, and so forth, which would become increasingly embarrassing and which would continue to mobilize public opinion and moral force. As long as such efforts are being made, there should be no discussion and no consideration of what the alternative steps should be. In case this effort failed, all of the countries which wish to stop this war and to protect themselves from its consequences, or in other words the so-called neutral countries, should band together for their own protection against this contagion. One thing that might be considered would be that in case Japan refuses all efforts of conciliation, the other powers would agree to give to China every facility for acquiring arms, and so forth, to defend themselves; although in this case the United States could do nothing because our laws would not permit. Another alternative would be for the neutrals to ostracize Japan, break off relations. This he said would not be practical unless the overwhelming opinion of the world would support it.

The support of the "overwhelming opinion of the world" formed the subject of most of the remainder of Roosevelt's instructions. The President paused in his talk with Davis at this point to dictate the memorandum which was to guide the United States representatives at the Brussels Conference in their relations with the British.[19] In the portion of the memorandum which has been cited earlier, Roosevelt emphasized that the British cabinet must recognize that "there is such a thing as public opinion in the United States" and asserted that Davis himself must make clear, at every step throughout the Nine Power Conference, that the administration did not want to be "pushed out in front as the leader in, or suggestor of, future action" nor did it wish to be made to appear, in the eyes of the

American people, as "a tail to the British kite." In addition, Roosevelt stated that the United States proposed to adopt as the basis for discussion at the Brussels Conference the policy which had proved "so successful among the twenty-one American Republics—no one nation going out to take the lead—no one nation, therefore, in a position to have a finger of fear or scorn pointed at it."[20] In amplification of this statement he declared that it was "especially important" for the British government to understand the manner in which the administration envisaged the proceedings at Brussels:

In the present Far Eastern situation it is visualized that whatever proposals are advanced at Brussels and whatever action comes out of Brussels, the proposals and the action should represent, first, the substantial unanimous opinion of the nations meeting at Brussels, and later the substantial unanimous opinion of the overwhelming majority of all nations, whether in or out of the League of Nations.

Because so much that happened subsequently hinged upon this interview between the President and Norman Davis it may be well, even at the risk of belaboring the obvious, to point out that Roosevelt's statements as recorded by Davis reduced themselves to a few, comparatively simple points. All possibilities of reaching a peaceful agreement were to be thoroughly explored at Brussels, including the State Department's plan for a "constructive" settlement. However, if the Japanese remained intransigent, some further action might be taken. Roosevelt did not define this action other than to throw out the suggestions that the other powers might facilitate the acquisition of arms by China or that the "neutral" nations might "ostracize Japan." In any case, the United States itself was not to initiate any proposals or take the lead in implementing them. Moreover, no measures whatever were to be adopted by the conference unless there was definite assurance in advance that they would have the endorsement of virtually all the nations represented at Brussels and the almost unanimous opinion of the peoples in the "overwhelming" majority of countries including those outside of the League (which presumably meant the United States in particular). In addition, Roosevelt wanted the conference to mobilize the public opinion and moral force of the world so they could be brought to bear against Japan.[21]

Needless to say, such instructions left much to be desired from the point of view of precision and clarity. And it is scarcely surprising to find that they led to an unfortunate amount of friction between Norman Davis and officials in Washington during the course of the Nine Power Conference. As matters developed, the central point at issue was whether the United States should or should not discuss sanctions at Brussels, Davis having understood that ultimately he might do so. It may therefore be well to draw the reader's attention here to the fact that Roosevelt's remarks concerning the possible use of sanctions were to say the least inconclusive both in terms of the type of sanctions he was willing to consider and the circumstances under which he was willing to consider them.

Perhaps confusion was further confounded because Davis departed for Brussels almost immediately after his talk with Roosevelt at Hyde Park and therefore did not have time to discuss the President's instructions with Hull or with Sumner Welles, who throughout the next weeks was to serve as Acting Secretary of State.[22] Be that as it may, there is no doubt that Davis and both his advisers, Stanley Hornbeck and Pierrepont Moffat, left for Brussels under the impression that the administration in Washington was prepared to have them take a firm stand against Japan whereas officials in Washington from the first gave no indication that this was what they had in mind.[23]

On October 12 Victor Mallet, the British chargé in Washington, called on Sumner Welles to say that Eden would like to know the "exact interpretation" which should be given to the President's "quarantine" speech and whether the United States was considering a joint economic boycott; he added that the Foreign Office intended to give the State Department a fuller expression of its views on this subject in the near future.[24] Welles replied that he could only assume that Eden's inquiry arose from the fact that the British government thought that Roosevelt had in mind "the immediate or imminent application of quarantine measures"; but "this was not the case." As far as the Brussels Conference was concerned, the President's intention was "to cooperate with the other signatories of the Nine Power Treaty for the purpose of trying to find a solution of the Chinese situation through an agreement satisfactory to all."

About a week later Mallet handed Hugh Wilson a note from the Foreign Office which explained in some detail the position of the Foreign Office in regard to a boycott.[25] In the opinion of His Majesty's Government, it was said, the initial objective of the Brussels Conference must be to reach peace by agreement. If the Japanese refused to attend the conference, however, this aim would be difficult to attain unless and until a considerable change occurred in Japan's military and economic position. The conference was therefore confronted with three possible choices of which the first two were: it could defer action in the hope that the necessary changes would occur in Japan; or, it could express moral condemnation of the Japanese without adopting or threatening to adopt any further measures. Both these policies, however, opened themselves to the obvious objection that they were tantamount to acquiescence in aggression and could only serve to encourage "peace breakers." Moreover, moral condemnation of Japan had the additional weakness that it would exasperate the Japanese to no purpose. The third possibility was to embark upon positive action in the form either of active aid to China or economic pressure against Japan. This being the situation, His Majesty's Government felt that it was necessary for both the United States and British delegations to go to Brussels in the full realization of the implications of such a course. So far as aid to China was concerned, it should be realized that grave practical difficulties would arise in any attempt to supply the Chinese with war materiel. Japan would undoubtedly extend her blockade of the Chinese coast to neutral ships which would confront the foreign powers with the necessity of either submitting to the blockade or keeping the sea routes open by armed force. As to economic measures against Japan, a preliminary investigation suggested that such measures might be effective if applied by the United States, all parts of the British Empire, and six or seven other countries and if they were extended to both imports and exports. However, even then it was questionable whether anything could be done in time to influence the outcome of the war, unless assistance were simultaneously given to China. But, irrespective of this consideration, it must be recognized that, if sanctions appeared likely to succeed, there would be a very real danger of the Japanese making war on one or more of the sanctionist powers or seizing the territory of some country from which they could obtain essential war supplies. No nation could therefore afford to enforce effective sanctions against Japan unless it was assured of the support of others in the event of retaliation by the Japanese. In addition the territorial integrity of third parties would have to be guaranteed. Should the powers, however, agree to make such advance commitments, the Japanese might (although, of course, there was no certainty about the matter) be deterred from resorting to drastic methods; moreover, if they were convinced that sanctions would eventually be successful, they might consider an early peace. In any case, His Majesty's Government was continuing to study the entire subject and would be happy to discuss its various aspects with the United States delegates at Brussels, if they agreed to such a discussion.

Wilson, on reading the British *aide-mémoire*, merely stated that the United States government was of the opinion that for the moment considerations such as the British were raising in regard to the third possible course of action "did not arise in a conference which had for its objective the finding of a solution of the conflict in the Far East by agreement."[26] About a week later, Ambassador Bingham openly expressed the administration's resentment of the British approach in a talk with Eden, in which he said that "the President felt that the attempt which had been made to pin the United States down to a specific statement as to how far it would go and precisely what the President meant by his Chicago speech was objectionable and damaging."[27] Furthermore, by this time Bingham had received a copy of the memorandum Roosevelt had dictated to guide Davis in his relations with the British. He therefore remarked additionally that the President wanted all the nations attending the Brussels Conference to participate equally and "felt that the British should not take the lead . . . nor should any effort be made by the British to push the United States in the lead." Eden replied that he thoroughly agreed and that "there would be no attempt whatever by the British to push the United States into such a position"—an assertion that he was to repeat many times before the conclusion of the meeting at Brussels.

While the British were thus broaching the issue of sanctions, the French raised the question of whether the United States and other members of the Brussels Conference would undertake to engage in action against Japan in case of a Japanese attack on Indochina. An interchange on this subject between Washington and Paris started in late October and continued after the Brussels Conference convened.[28]

By the middle of October, the Japanese had managed to close most of the Chinese ports. As a consequence, one of the few remaining lines of communication between China and the outside world was the railroad which ran across Indochina to Yunnan.[29] On October 19 Wellington Koo, then Chinese ambassador at Paris, informed the United States chargé d'affaires that the French government had prohibited the shipment of war material destined for China over the Indochina railroad for fear that the Japanese might take retaliatory measures.[30] Koo emphasized the serious effect which the French decision would have on China. He further expressed the view that the Japanese would not engage in any action against Indochina but that the French were so concerned over the situation in Europe that "they were leaning over backwards in being cautious regarding the Far East." Two days later Koo told Bullitt that he had impressed upon Foreign Minister Delbos that France's ban on the shipment of munitions over the Indochina railroad was "a question of life and death to

China" and had asked for a reconsideration of the problem.[31] Delbos had indicated that he would talk with Premier Chautemps.

Subsequently Bullitt himself discussed the issue of the Indochina railroad with Chautemps and Delbos, both of whom took the position that the French maintained thereafter.[32] The Japanese, they said, had given the French government to understand that unless the flow of war supplies to Chiang Kai-shek via Indochina ceased they might destroy the part of the Indochina railway that lay in Chinese territory and even seize Hainan and the Paracel Islands. Further, the Japanese had "politely" hinted that an attack on Indochina at some future date was not out of the question. Under these circumstances the French government had concluded that it must forbid the transport of munitions over the Indochina route. It was, however, prepared to reverse this decision on condition that the other signatories of the Nine Power Treaty would agree at the Brussels Conference to give France "physical support" if it became necessary to protect Indochina against military reprisals by the Japanese.

These developments were reported to Washington. On October 22 Sumner Welles cabled to Bullitt that by the President's direction he had spoken with Jules Henry, the French chargé d'affaires in Washington.[33] The President wanted Premier Chautemps to know that in his opinion the measures which the French government had taken in regard to the Indochina railroad might result in creating a situation which would be prejudicial to "the successful achievement of that solution by agreement" which the United States earnestly hoped would be attained at the Brussels Conference. Welles added that Henry had said he would send Roosevelt's message as secret. In response to the President's communication, Delbos told Bullitt that the French government had no desire whatsoever to prejudice the possibility of "a solution by agreement" when the Brussels Conference convened. He, however, redefined the French position in precisely the terms he had used earlier.[34]

As the time came close for the Nine Power Conference to open, one of the central issues was inevitably what the attitude of the Japanese would be toward sending a representative to Brussels. Ambassador Grew viewed the whole idea of the conference, and especially of American participation, with foreboding. In mid-October he wrote in his diary:

Our primary and fundamental concept was to avoid involvement in the Far Eastern mess; we have chosen the road which might lead directly to involvement . . . Once again I fear that we shall crawl out on a limb—

and be left there—to reap the odium and practical disadvantages of our course from which other countries will then hasten to profit. Such is internationalism today. Why, oh why, do we disregard the experience and facts of history which stare us in the face?[35]

Concerning the possibility of the Japanese attending the conference, Grew warned the State Department from the outset that he regarded the chances as very slim. On October 13 he cabled Washington that Japanese officials were stating privately that their government was "disinterested" in the forthcoming meeting at Brussels. The State Department responded that it was "considerably perturbed" at this news and asked Ambassador Grew to tell Hirota that the United States government was proceeding on the assumption that the Japanese would send a delegation to Brussels as Washington believed that the conference would "offer a useful opportunity for a reasoned and frank discussion of the difficulties, both present and underlying, of the situation with a view to seeking to arrive at a constructive solution by process of peaceful agreement."[36] Grew accordingly spoke to Hirota on the following day but received little satisfaction.[37] A week later he notified Washington that he had just learned in strict confidence that the Japanese Foreign Office had definitely decided to reject the invitation to come to Brussels because it felt that the conference was an outgrowth of the League resolution and the United States declaration of October 6 denouncing Japan and would therefore essentially be hostile to Japan's interests.[38]

On being told of this development by Sumner Welles, the President said that it was probably "too late for the United States" to take any action toward influencing the Japanese not to decline the invitation so that the best that could be done was to await the opening of the conference and then inform the Japanese that the meeting at Brussels had been called independently of the League resolution and did "not in any way arise out of the statement made by the Secretary of State on October 6th."[39] Thereafter the conference could renew its invitation to the Japanese to send a delegation to Brussels at which time the President would consider making a personal appeal to the Japanese Emperor.

Welles on his part decided, in consultation with other Department officials, that in order to re-enforce the moves suggested by the President, a cable might be sent to Ambassador Grew from the State Department in which it would be said that "our concept of the Conference was as described earlier" (to provide an opportunity for an exchange of views in order to arrive at a peaceful settlement) and "that it is not our idea that the Conference should undertake to declare Japan an aggressor."[40]

At the same time Welles tried to persuade the Germans to join in the Nine Power Conference to which they were to be invited as one of the nations which, though not a signatory of the Nine Power Treaty, was concerned with the Sino-Japanese conflict because of its substantial interests in the Far East. It was already known at this time that there was a strong faction in Germany which, despite that country's entente with Japan, was decidedly pro-Chinese and opposed to the continuance of the Sino-Japanese conflict.[41] Consequently, it was thought within the State Department that the Hitler regime might prove to be an important factor in bringing about a peaceful agreement between China and Japan. Welles, therefore, on being told by the German ambassador on October 21, that his government was under the impression that the meeting at Brussels had been called for the sake of "arraigning Japan," declared that so far as the United States was concerned that was "neither our attitude nor intention."[42] He thereupon repeated his constant thesis that the purpose of the United States was to achieve an agreement, acceptable to all, which would "result in a stabilization of peace in the Far East" and added that he felt the presence of Germany at the conference would be valuable.[43] Further, as the date for the opening of the Nine Power meeting approached, Ambassador Grew cabled that the Japanese would never submit to "collective mediation" because in their view it would contain an element of pressure.[44] He therefore suggested that the best policy for the Powers to pursue at Brussels was to appoint a few of the interested nations to keep in touch with developments so that, if the situation warranted, they could propose mediation either by themselves as a small committee or by one of their number. One of Welles' last acts before the start of the conference was to cable the draft of a long resolution to Norman Davis at Brussels which would have invited Germany, Great Britain, and the United States to hold themselves in readiness to explore, in cooperation with the Chinese and Japanese governments, means of attaining a peaceful settlement of the Sino-Japanese dispute when the proper moment arrived.[45] Although this resolution was never to see the light of day, it is significant in indicating how far removed the point of view of Washington was from those who wanted the Brussels Conference to serve as a line-up of the democracies against the dictatorships.

The diplomatic activities in Washington in the days following Norman Davis' departure for Brussels therefore point to one overriding conclusion: that the administration, on the one hand, rejected every approach which might lead to any consideration of coercive measures against Japan while, on the other, it made genuine efforts to be conciliatory to the Japanese. If any serious thought was given to a possible ultimate resort to sanctions, it does not appear on the record. The atmosphere in Washington was therefore very different from that which developed at Brussels as the delegates of the various nations began to arrive in that city and engage in a preliminary exchange of views.

THE CONFERENCE

The first talk which Norman Davis had upon his arrival in Brussels was with Anthony Eden. The character of the talk had already been foreshadowed by a prolonged debate in the House of Commons in which, in answer to urgent demands from the Opposition for economic sanctions against Japan, government spokesmen had made it very plain that the policy which Great Britain would pursue toward the Sino-Japanese conflict depended in the last analysis upon the United States.[46] It also became evident during the course of the debate that the President's words at Chicago had led many British statesmen to hope that the American government had decided to abandon isolationism. In a dramatic speech given just before his departure for Brussels, Eden himself implied that in his opinion the most important aspect of the Nine Power Conference was that it might prove the medium by which the United States returned to an active participation in international affairs. "I say without hesitation," he declared, ". . . that in order to get the full cooperation on an equal basis of the United States government in an international conference, I would travel, not only from Geneva to Brussels, but from Melbourne to Alaska, more particularly in the present state of the international situation."[47]

In his interview with Norman Davis, Eden said with great frankness that Great Britain felt herself seriously threatened by the forces of lawlessness which were gaining strength in Europe and Asia and was convinced that the only means of solving the international situation and preventing a general disaster was through the closest possible cooperation between England and America.[48] For this reason the British government, after the most careful consideration, wanted to assure the United States that it would engage in any action that America wanted to undertake in the Far East though it would go no further than the United States was prepared to go. The British government had been playing down its willingness to adopt so strong a

stand in part because it had not been able to judge what the administration in Wasington was ready to do. As far as the Brussels Conference was concerned, the British intended to base their policy squarely
upon American policy: they would second any initiative taken by
Davis but on the other hand would not embarrass him by suggesting
direct pressure against Japan, if the idea was unwelcome, even though
the British themselves were willing to join fully in such pressure. In
general, Great Britain would neither assume the lead in the conference nor attempt to push America out in front. At one point in the
discussion Davis said that it would seem as though, if Great Britain
and the United States undertook joint action against Japan and the
Japanese retaliated, America would have to bear the brunt of the
matter. But Eden insisted that this was not the case and asserted that,
although the bulk of the British Fleet had to remain in Europe, some
British ships could and would be sent to the Far East and that the
"moving around" of a few ships might, in fact, have a good effect upon
the efforts to find a peaceful solution of the Sino-Japanese conflict.

Following his talk with Eden, Davis had a long interview with
Foreign Minister Delbos which left him with the discouraging impression that the French had no intention of cooperating with the Brussels
Conference but were solely interested in attempting to secure a
political alignment of the United States, England, and France.[49]
Delbos insisted that it was entirely useless to try to accomplish anything through a meeting of eighteen nations such as had been convened at Brussels. He thought the only salvation for the world was to
establish a front of the democracies against the dictatorships and
suggested that Roosevelt should call a conference of the democratic
nations toward that end. In the meantime the French, British, and
American delegations at Brussels should recognize that there was
little hope of persuading Japan to agree to a peaceful settlement in
the Far East and should therefore proceed at once to discuss, outside
the framework of the Nine Power Conference, the measures they
would adopt if Japan rejected their efforts at mediation. Delbos declared that he was not in favor of sanctions against Japan but he was
in favor of aid to China and accordingly urged that consideration be
given to establishing some system of convoy or mutual protection of
French, British, and United States ships in Chinese waters and to
finding a means of solving the problem of the transportation of war
supplies through Indochina by assuring free entry and egress from
that country.[50]

Of the other delegates at the conference, Davis had the most significant discussion with Litvinov, who was participating in the delibera-

tions because it was felt that, even though the Soviet Union was not a signatory of the Nine Power Treaty, it should be represented at Brussels as a power with large interests in the Far East.[51] Davis had already received advance estimates of the position which the Soviet Union was likely to take from our embassy in Moscow. In August the USSR had concluded a nonaggression pact with China which had long been a subject of negotiation betwen the two nations.[52] In mid-October in a cable transmitted to Paris and sent from there by code in order to maintain the strictest secrecy, Ambassador Davies stated that he had just learned from Ch'en Li-fu, who was then in Moscow, that in August the Soviet government had also agreed to give Nanking a credit of 100,000,000 Chinese dollars for the purchase of war supplies and that the deliveries had already exceeded this amount.[53] Four hundred of the best Soviet bombing and pursuit planes had been shipped to China accompanied by forty instructors who were teaching the Chinese how to use them. Moreover, a Chinese military mission had been in the USSR for the past six months procuring supplies, and Ambassador Bogomolov had just returned from Nanking to negotiate some extensive arrangements with the mission. Despite these developments, the United States embassy in Moscow continued to maintain, in line with its earlier reports, that the Kremlin would not enter into any engagement to provide the Chinese with active military assistance or otherwise risk war with Japan. As to the Brussels Conference, the embassy stated that Soviet officials had been insisting that any moral action against the Japanese would be useless and that they would be willing to cooperate in economic and financial sanctions against Japan; at the same time they did not really expect the conference to accomplish anything and had no intention of making any proposals of their own.[54]

Davis therefore had no cause for surprise when Litvinov declared that the gathering at Brussels would be a waste of time unless the powers took a firm stand against Japan and that the Soviet Union would be quite willing to join with England and America in using coercive measures against the Japanese but that it wanted to be certain that it "would not be left with the bag to hold."[55] Litvinov argued that if Japan were made to realize that the United States, Great Britain, and the Soviet Union were really determined to bring about a cessation of hostilities in the Far East there would be no danger whatever of war. Concerning Russian policy in China, he said that the Soviet Union preferred to see a strong and prosperous China and had not interfered with any such development for years nor sought to promote communism among the Chinese. When asked by Davis whether, if the time came to work out a general settlement in the Far East, the Soviet Union would agree to stay out of Outer Mongolia if Japan stayed out of Inner Mongolia and a buffer state were created there, Litvinov replied that he was quite prepared to consider such an arrangement.

On the side of the Axis powers there were no German representatives at Brussels, as the Germans had finally declined to attend the conference on the grounds that it was too closely associated with the League to allow for German participation.[56] Nevertheless rumors persisted that the Hitler regime was not only anxious to put an end to the hostilities between China and Japan but was seeking to act as a mediator behind the scenes. The Italians, on their part, sent a delegation to Brussels but Davis seems to have made no effort to canvass their views presumably because he felt from the outset that they were "openly playing Japan's game."[57] The conference was in fact only a few days old when on November 6 the Italian government announced its adherence to the anti-Comintern pact which the Germans and Japanese had signed a year earlier.[58]

Davis did, however, talk to the delegates of some of the smaller powers upon whose activities at the conference President Roosevelt had set such great store. In particular he spoke with Paul-Henri Spaak who, as the representative of Belgium, was to serve as chairman of the conference, only to discover that he, as well as the Dutch delegate, was anxious to play as passive a role as possible in the forthcoming proceedings out of fear of becoming involved in a situation that would endanger his own country's interests and those of the other small European nations.[59]

The atmosphere at Brussels, in contrast to Washington, was therefore from the very outset one of discussing the possible use of sanctions against Japan. Davis sought to counter this by adhering to the line of argument which he assumed Roosevelt wanted him to follow.[60] Whether talking with Eden, Delbos, Litvinov, or any other members of the conference, he stated persistently that "a large section of public opinion in America felt that there was nothing in the Far East worth fighting about" and that the United States as a whole regarded the trouble between Japan and China as "only one part of a much larger problem, namely the protection of the world against law-breakers." In speaking with Delbos he further emphasized that he did not conceive of the issue at stake as a "struggle between the haves and have-nots, but between the law-abiders and the law-breakers." The United States, he said, in general believed that the conference should make every effort to find a peaceful solution to the Far Eastern conflict and should in particular attempt to mobilize the moral forces of the world to persuade Japan to come to an agreement with China. Until this had been earnestly tried and conclusively failed, he was not even willing to consider any other approach. However, if the conference did not succeed in getting Japan and China together in a settlement, all the interested Powers would have to determine whether they should try to exert any other kind of pressure to bring the conflict to an end. So far as the United States was concerned, future developments would largely be determined by the attitude of the American people as to what could or should be done.

Despite his efforts, Davis was soon convinced that his arguments were meeting with little response and that, with the exception of the British, none of the delegates at the conference believed in the possibility of dealing with Japan effectively through noncoercive measures or envisaged a strategy of arousing public opinion so as to have a moral impact upon Japan. His discouragement deepened as he found it difficult even to persuade Delbos and Spaak to agree to the holding of a public session of the conference as they believed that a series of keynote speeches would only show up the differences in the attitudes of the various delegations. Moreover they were strongly of the belief that the best policy was to establish a small committee to keep in touch with the Chinese and Japanese governments and, for the rest, to dissolve the conference as soon as possible.

Nevertheless, in the end an open session was convened on November 3. Norman Davis delivered the first speech, which unfortunately was the outgrowth of further difficulties.[61] For after spending days together with Hornbeck and Moffat in drafting the text and cabling it to the State Department, Davis had received back a completely altered version. In an accompanying message Sumner Welles had explained that, after consultations with the President and the Secretary, it had been decided that extensive changes were desirable because the address would largely determine public opinion in the United States and should therefore be written so that it could not be subject to misinterpretation. This distressed Davis greatly because he believed that the administration had promised him a free hand in dealing with procedural matters; but he finally decided not to make an issue of the incident and used the Department's draft with some re-editing.

The address, as delivered, mainly stated that the various powers had assembled at Brussels by virtue of the terms of the Nine Power Treaty which provided for "full and frank communication," but that they would in any case have had a real interest in the crisis which had developed in the Far East.[62] For, throughout the past decades, the peoples of all countries had been seeking a way of solving international conflicts by peaceful means recognizing that, granted the interdependence of the modern world, war wherever it occurred had universal repercussions. In the particular circumstances with which the conference was confronted, its objective must be to restore peace in the Far East and to make a constructive effort to create conditions that would render the use of force unthinkable in future.

Following Davis' address, Eden spoke briefly saying primarily: "I have listened with close attention to the speech made by the representative of the United States and the Government I represent is in full agreement with every word that he has said. He has so well defined our task . . . that I have little to add." Delbos thereupon seconded the views expressed by both Davis and Eden but in addition sounded a harsher note by stating that the members of the conference would be accomplices in the events taking place in the Far East if they did not try by every means to put an end to the "merciless massacres" occurring there which revolted both the heart and the mind. Litvinov also endorsed Davis' address but warned the conference against being lured into making the kind of peace which said to the aggressor "Take your plunder . . . and peace be with you" and to the victim of aggression "Love your aggressor; resist not evil." The Italian delegate, as might have been expected, denounced the conference, flatly declaring that it was wholly impotent and that the only thing it could do was to invite the Chinese and Japanese to settle their differences between themselves.

After the public session of the conference, the members spent several days in discussing a possible reply to the note in which the Japanese had refused to send any representatives to Brussels. The note, which had been issued on October 27, had corresponded with the advance information secured by Ambassador Grew in that it had declared that Japan would not participate in any meeting associated with the League resolution and the State Department's announcement of October 6.[63] But even more significantly the Japanese had asserted that their military operations in China were undertaken in self defense against the "fierce anti-Japanese policy" of the Chinese and consequently did not come within the "purview of the Nine Power Treaty"; and that moreover the entire Sino-Japanese problem could only be solved by direct negotiations between Japan and China. In addition, they had stated that any attempt to seek a solution at a gathering as large as that at Brussels, which contained countries that had practically no interests in the Far East, would merely serve to complicate the situation.

The conference's reply to Japan was sent on November 7.[64] In it the various delegates declared that, contrary to the contentions of the Japanese, they believed that the hostilities in the Far East were rightfully the concern of all the signatories of the Nine Power Treaty and, in fact, of the entire family of nations which was inevitably disturbed by any threat to the peace and security of the world. At the same time, in an effort to meet Japan's objection that the Brussels Conference was too large to be an effective agency for negotiation, the delegates offered to appoint a small committee to exchange views with representatives of the Japanese government if that government so desired.

With the dispatch of the reply to Japan, United States policy entered a wholly new phase. As none of the delegates at Brussels thought that the Japanese government would respond any more favorably to the second invitation to cooperate with the conference than it had to the first, the question was what to do next. Davis believed that he could go no further in fulfilling the President's instructions to try to attain a peaceful settlement and to crystallize public opinion vis-à-vis Japan, especially as by this time almost all the delegations at Brussels had clearly indicated that they wanted to adjourn the conference as soon as possible. He felt therefore that the moment had come to move on to what he believed to be the next stage of American policy as outlined by the President, namely, a discussion of coercive measures against Japan.

Before considering Davis' activities in connection with the problem of sanctions, however, the outcome of the discussion between Washington and Paris over the Indochina railroad should be noted.[65] On November 8, Ambassador Bullitt cabled the State Department that Delbos, who had returned to Paris from Brussels for a few days, during the course of a telephone conversation had stated that he would like immediate clarification of a matter which had arisen in respect to the Far East. According to Bullitt, Delbos said that when he had attempted to discuss with Norman Davis the issue of the protection of Indochina in case of Japanese reprisals, Davis had replied that the question was "so remote in the future that there was no use talking about it." He (Delbos) had therefore received the impression that the United States under no conditions would consider sending the American fleet to Far Eastern waters to defend Indochina. On the other hand, Jules Henry had cabled that he had a talk with the President on November 6 and that "the President had said that he regarded the situation of French Indo-China and the situation of the Philippines in much the same way and had given Henry the impression definitely that he would be inclined to extend the protection of the American fleet to French Indo-China." In conclusion Delbos stated that for obvious reasons he was intensely interested to know whether the impression he had derived from Davis or the impression Henry had derived from the President gave a correct picture of the view of the United States government.

In reply, on November 9, Welles sent Bullitt the following account of Roosevelt's meeting with Henry. The President, Welles said, had seen the French chargé when he paid a courtesy call at the White House a few days earlier to present Jacques Stern. During the brief conversation that took place, the President referred to the action of the French in regard to the shipment of munitions through Indochina and remarked that he thought "some of the great powers with territorial interests in the Far East were behaving 'like scared rabbits.'" His visitors responded by saying that, in view of the seriousness of the political conditions in Europe, the French government was not in a position to take measures comparable to those which might ordinarily be taken to defend its possessions in the Far East from possible aggression. They asked what the attitude of the United States would be if an attack on Indochina occurred. The President made it "very clear" that this was a "hypothetical question"; that, in his opinion an attack on Indochina was "such a remote contingency that it should not even be discussed at the present time." He added that, if such acts of aggression were committed, the repercussions would be so worldwide that, obviously, the United States could not remain unaffected. He made no other statement and "gave no impression directly or indirectly as to the possible extension of the protection of the American fleet." At the end of this account Welles wrote: "I have spoken to the President with regard to this question and this telegram is sent you with his authorization." (Indeed the original bears the notation: "O. K. FDR.") Welles stated further that he intended to talk with Jules Henry and request him to make the United States' position clear to Paris.

Bullitt discussed the content of the Welles despatch with Chautemps on November 10. As related in the ambassador's subsequent report to Roosevelt and Welles, the Premier said that it was quite true that France and England and the other democracies were behaving like "scared rabbits" but so nearly as he could see "the rabbit which was behaving in the most scared manner since there was no gun pointed toward it was the United States." On the same day Chautemps sent a personal message to Roosevelt to the effect that in his judgment the possibility of Japanese aggression against Indochina was not a "remote contingency." The Premier reaffirmed the French position, stating once more that his government would only reconsider its policy toward the transport of munitions to China if the members of the Brussels

Conference agreed to joint action in case of Japanese reprisals against Indochina. The President made no reply and the interchange between Washington and Paris on the subject of the Indochina railway was thus terminated.[66]

To return to the Brussels Conference, as indicated earlier, Norman Davis had arrived at a point where he thought he should move on to a consideration of the use of pressures against Japan. On November 10, therefore, he cabled Washington proposing certain kinds of sanctions.

Any account of the Brussels Conference would, however, be less than candid if it created the impression that up until November 10 Davis refrained entirely from talking about the question of sanctions or even from indicating that he personally believed that either punitive measures short of military action or the threat of such punitive measures would be necessary if the Western powers really intended to arrest Japanese aggression in China. Somewhat curiously, Davis seems to have been especially outspoken in interviews with newspapermen.

On November 5 Davis held an off-the-record press conference of which a report exists in his files that is presumably reasonably accurate as it is initialed by the State Department press officer who accompanied Davis to Brussels.[67] The report states that during a long interchange between the newspapermen and Davis, a correspondent asked whether there was not some risk that the American people would feel that the conference was being too easy on the Japanese as it had not even denounced Japan morally. Davis replied that there was "no use when you were trying to make peace with a fellow to call him names." When the correspondent remarked that it depended "on the sort of fellow you were dealing with," Davis agreed that "in dealing with a bully you had to use firm treatment." A reporter then inquired whether the United States was ready to administer firm treatment, to which Davis responded in essence that the administration's policy must ultimately depend upon the attitude of the American public. The issue at stake, he declared, was that of arbitrary action as opposed to law and order. The American people were beginning to understand that there were certain nations in the world which had nothing but contempt for the rights of others and that, if these nations were permitted to go on, no one would be safe. It was his belief, when he left home, that public opinion was veering; people were in a quandary between the desire to keep out of war and the realization that negative measures would not suffice to achieve this end. The administration was therefore searching for a means of solving the problem short of war and there was some feeling that the Brussels Conference might be helpful in this respect.

At this point in the discussion, a reporter asked Davis point blank whether he himself thought that the conference could restrain Japan by the exercise of moral influence. Davis replied that, while moral influence might have some effect, he questioned whether it would change Japan's course to any great extent. We learned at school, he said, that the only way of restraining a bully is to knock him down. If Japan came to believe that the United States, Great Britain, and some other powers were ready to act, she would give ground; but if she felt that no real pressure was going to be used against her and that she could get away with her Chinese venture, she would go ahead. A correspondent then wanted to know whether the other delegations at the conference had tried to find out how far the United States was prepared to go in promoting law and order and Davis stated that most of the delegations would be glad to learn that the United States "was prepared to uphold law and order with its entire fleet." At the same time he emphasized that the President himself was convinced that moral force was more effective than was generally realized and that the United States was determined to exhaust every possibility of a peaceful solution so that there was no use in worrying about the "next stage" yet. However, if the American people saw that every effort had been made to find a peaceful solution and that Japan still refused to listen to reason, they would "be ready to face the possibility of doing something else." If the powers made it clear that they really meant business, there would be little risk involved; war was not necessary.

Aside from such few but remarkably frank talks about sanctions outside the circle of United States officials at Brussels, Davis discussed the sanctions issue with Pierrepont Moffat and Stanley Hornbeck from the beginning of their mission. Moffat, who belonged to what was frequently called the "isolationist" wing of the State Department (or what he himself termed the "realistic" in contrast to the "messianic" wing) was opposed to taking any firm action against Japan.[68] Hornbeck, on the other hand, continued to advocate taking a strong stand against the Japanese and, even before the conference started, gave Davis a list of measures to be considered if the time came when there were definite indications that Japan would continue to refuse to cooperate with the delegates at Brussels or to substitute peaceful for forceful methods in dealing with China.[69] The measures which he specified included such matters as the nonrecognition of any new territory that Japan might gain through the current hostilities, the refusal of financial assistance to the Japanese, and a boycott of Japanese goods. Also on November 5 Hornbeck suggested to Davis a plan of procedure by which the conference would have drawn up the terms of an armistice and presented them to Japan and China with the understanding that, if the terms were not accepted by a certain date, the conference would consider the application of pressure through such means as "facilitating or impeding the acquisition of materials."[70] In addition both Davis and Hornbeck were sufficiently convinced by November 8 that the time was fast approaching for a discussion of coercive measures by the conference, for Hornbeck to talk over the question of sanctions with several of the delegates at Brussels though he did so on the stated basis that he was voicing his own and not his government's views. In a conversation on November 8 with Malcolm MacDonald of the British delegation, Hornbeck suggested that perhaps a boycott of Japanese goods by the powers at Brussels might be effective.[71] He explained further that he felt a boycott would be more advisable than an embargo because it was more likely to receive the support of manufacturing and labor interests in the sanctionist countries; moreover a boycott, by further diminishing Japan's already dwindling financial assets, might seriously damage the strength of the Japanese economic system which, in his opinion, was generally overestimated. Later in the same day in a conversation with Ludvig Aubert, the delegate from Norway, Hornbeck again raised the question of a boycott which led Aubert to declare that, according to his understanding, none of the smaller powers at the conference would want to participate in any measures of pressure against Japan.[72] Hornbeck thereupon said that "whether the Conference accomplished anything would depend on the willingness or unwillingness of the powers assembled to pay some price or take some risks"; if they felt that the possible cost outweighed the possible gains, then it must be assumed that their attitude toward the question of peace was still that it was "something merely to be talked about."

Anyone reading the record of the Brussels Conference today can therefore scarcely be surprised at Davis' submitting a plan for sanctions to Washington on November 10. Nor presumably would many of the delegations at Brussels have felt any very great astonishment if they had known about the matter. In fact, relative to such ideas as imposing a boycott, Davis' suggestions were moderate, partly, no doubt, because he had come to believe that, if a boycott was to be considered it should be made the subject of direct negotiations between the various interested Foreign Offices so that secrecy—which was virtually nonexistent at Brussels—could be maintained.[73] In any case, Davis limited himself to proposing what he himself called a "middle and halfway course," in which the members of the conference would have adopted a resolution agreeing to some or all of five points of which the two most important were

To refrain from "recognizing" changes in the situation in China which are inconsistent with or contrary to the provisions of the Nine Power Treaty;

To supplement the policy of non-recognition by agreeing to give no countenance to any form of assistance especially loans, credits, et cetera, to Japan in connection with the hostilities or for activities thereafter in development of anything which she may have gained thereby.[74]

The remaining points involved: taking no action which would discriminate against China in her military effort; taking no action toward persuading China to enter into an agreement involving unwilling concessions on her part; and giving no military aid to Japan in the event of her becoming embroiled with any of the other conference powers before reaching a settlement by agreement with China. In addition, Davis urged the President to recommend to Congress a repeal or suspension of the Neutrality Act, at least insofar as the Sino-Japanese conflict was concerned, mainly on the grounds that, if moral pressure proved to be ineffective against Japan and it was deemed advisable to adopt a more positive policy, the administration would find itself "embarrassed or impotent." He also suggested that Roosevelt consider asking for an appropriation for the construction of additional battleships in order to indicate that the United States was taking a serious view of the Far Eastern situation and the "general threat of international anarchy."

After forwarding these proposals to Washington, Davis had an important discussion with Eden and Delbos concerning the steps which might be taken if the Japanese rejected the second effort of the conference to bring them into negotiations for a peaceful settlement.[75] Delbos again asserted that the United States, Great Britain, and France should begin to consider how far they would ultimately go against Japan. Eden agreed saying that while he had every sympathy with the American idea of educating public opinion, the conference could not be kept in session indefinitely and the sooner it got down to "brass tacks" the better. Delbos, who in Davis' opinion had come to assume a far more cooperative attitude toward the conference, reiterated that France was prepared to go as far as the United States provided there was complete solidarity. He explained that by "solidarity" he meant, for example, that while France was willing to guarantee the possessions of others in the Far East, she would in return have to have a guaranty of Indochina. Eden likewise again defined the British position as being that England would go as far as America, adding that while boycotts and embargoes were "none too popular" in Great Britain as a result of the Ethiopian experiment, the government would nevertheless carry through such measures if necessary. Davis, on his part, stated that it was hard to foresee what the administration in Washington might feel free to do as its hands were tied by the Neutrality Act, which he sincerely hoped might be altered when Congress met. In any case, Congress was to reopen next week at which time the situation would be clarified, as any decisions of the American government would have to be guided by public opinion. It was thereupon agreed that if and when the Japanese refusal to the second invitation to the conference was received a general meeting of the conference would be held at which the speakers would re-emphasize that they wished to support the principle of international law and order and would undertake in particular to refute the Japanese thesis that Japan had the right to invade China in order to protect herself against "actual or potential communism." Following the general meeting, another communication to the Japanese would be drafted which would be stiffer than any sent so far. The conference was then to recess for about a week and reconvene in order to pass a final resolution. Considerable doubt was expressed, however, as to what the resolution should contain. Davis suggested that it might embody "a series of undertakings extending the principles of nonrecognition, including a refusal to extend loans and credits to enable the aggressor to profit by the fruits of the aggression" but added that this was his personal idea and that he was not speaking for his government.[76]

The expected rejection by the Japanese government of the second communication from the conference arrived on November 12 and, while based upon the same arguments as the first, was even more uncompromising in tone.[77] A general meeting of the conference was held on November 13, in which Davis, Eden, and Delbos, according to plan, spoke of the broad principles which they felt the conference must uphold.[78] The Chinese delegate, Dr. Wellington Koo, alone furnished cause for astonishment by departing from the indecisive and relatively passive policy which the Chinese had followed to date and addressing a direct appeal for sanctions to the conference. "Now," Koo said, "that the door to conciliation and mediation has been slammed in your face by the latest reply of the Japanese Government, will you not decide to withhold supplies of war materials and credit to Japan and extend aid to China? It would be, in our opinion, a most modest way in which you can fulfill your obligation of helping to check

Japanese aggression and uphold the treaty in question." Subsequently a declaration drafted by the American, British, and French delegates was circulated among the members of the conference.[79] In keeping with the intent of its framers to take a firmer stand, it reasserted that the Sino-Japanese conflict was the concern not only of the participants but of the entire world and declared that as a just and durable settlement could not be expected from direct negotiations between Japan and China the states represented at Brussels still hoped that the Japanese government would confer with them and accept their good offices. Meanwhile they would have to consider what their "common attitude" should be in a situation where one party to a treaty maintained, against the views of all the other parties, that the action which it had taken did not come within the scope of that treaty and that its provisions could therefore be set aside.

The declaration was adopted at a meeting of the conference on November 15.[80] While there was only one voice of outright dissent, namely that of the Italians, the larger Western powers received a shock when all three Scandinavian countries formally announced their determination to abstain from voting.[81] The Scandinavian delegates privately explained that their governments' position was that any commitment to adopt a "common attitude" against Japan might lead to the application of sanctions and that experience had shown that, in any effort to make sanctions effective, smaller countries suffered severely without receiving any compensations commensurate with their sacrifice.[82]

After the November 15 session, the conference recessed according to schedule, Eden and Delbos departing for home. No decision had as yet been reached, however, concerning the resolution which the conference was to pass as a final gesture at a closing meeting around November 24. Davis therefore settled down to work out an answer to this problem, as a result of which he found himself in the midst of a debate with the State Department that revealed the very deep gap between his own thinking and that of officials in Washington.

About the time that Davis' cable proposing possible coercive measures against Japan reached Washington, Hull returned to the capital. On November 12 he wired Davis that none of the measures he had recommended were acceptable to the administration and that, in any case, the United States was in no position to enter into an agreement with other countries to participate in any attempt to carry them out.[83] The Secretary stated further that he recognized that the conference could not stay in session much longer but that he felt it to be of the "utmost importance" for the delegates, before adjourning, to issue a public statement which would "serve as a dramatic appeal to all peace-seeking nations . . . to maintain the basic principles of peaceful international relationships not only with reference to the present situation in the Far East, but also in their broader bearing upon relations among nations in general." Moreover he wanted the various governments represented at the conference to make clear that they would continue to watch developments in the Far East and would hold themselves in readiness to explore, at any time, with China and Japan all peaceful methods of reaching an agreement on the basis of the principles and provisions embodied in the Nine Power Treaty.

Although Davis was apparently unaware of the matter, the Department did not just limit itself to the Secretary's message to Davis. A memorandum written by Sumner Welles on November 13 relates that Ambassador Lindsay called upon him on that day to clarify some of the points raised in reports which had been received from the British delegation at Brussels.[84] The memorandum states that Sir Ronald said that Davis, during his conversations with Eden, had apparently mentioned a great many possibilities for action such as that the President might have the Neutrality Act repealed, or that the powers might refuse both to recognize any territories gained by Japan through force and to extend credits to Japan in future for the development of such territories, or that an embargo might be enforced against Japanese goods. The ambassador furthermore indicated that he was especially puzzled because Davis had allegedly discussed a "possible fleet movement in the Pacific on the part of the United States, Great Britain and France" whereas the ambassador himself had not understood that the United States was prepared to consider military sanctions. Welles' memorandum then goes on to say:

> With specific regard to Mr. Norman Davis' conversations with Mr. Eden at Brussels, I said that I had no doubt that Mr. Davis had explored the whole field in a thorough manner with Mr. Eden and that it was for that reason that the topics mentioned by Sir Ronald Lindsay had been discussed . . . but that of course his [Mr. Davis'] mention of some of these topics could in no sense be construed as implying that this Government was prepared to take the action which had been discussed . . .
>
> Insofar as any consideration by the Conference of the imposition of economic sanctions was concerned, this Government did not believe that the Conference under present conditions was the proper agency for the determination of any such policy and most decidedly not at the present time. With regard to nonrecognition commitments, or an agreement not to extend credits for the development of territory acquired by force, etc., Mr. Davis had had it made clear to him that this Government was not favorably disposed to consider participation in such agreements and that Mr. Davis had been requested to submit any proposals of this character

which might come up to Washington for decision before making any commitments whatever with regard thereto. I reminded the Ambassador that, of course, he was well aware of the fact that there existed no legislation which would authorize the President to take part in any economic sanctions or in any of the other measures mentioned and that, lacking such authority from Congress, this Government could obviously enter into no commitments with regard thereto . . .

I said in view of this it seemed to me unnecessary to do more than to touch very lightly upon the question of fleet movements or the question of actual hostilities. I said that it seemed to me that those contingencies were remote and should not be considered at this time. I said the whole premise of this Government in going to the Brussels Conference was the keeping alive of the principles of the Nine Power Treaty and of international law and morality and, in a more practical sense, the making of every effort to promote a pacific solution by agreement.

Even without knowledge of Welles' talk with Ambassador Lindsay, it is evident that Norman Davis had good cause for concern. Pierrepont Moffat relates in his diary that Davis' first reaction to Secretary Hull's cable, flatly rejecting his recommendations for future action, was one of "pretty bitter disappointment."[85] Convinced that the President had been prepared to have him discuss sanctions at Brussels, Davis felt that he had been left "out on a limb." On second thought he decided that he could still persuade the administration to change its mind. He therefore wired the President and Secretary bringing them up to date on the attitude of Delbos and Eden concerning the necessity of considering some definite measures against Japan and went on to state that, in his opinion, the minimum step which the conference should take would be to pass a final resolution "calling for non-recognition of changes brought about by armed force, prohibition of government loans and credits and discouragement of private loans and credits."[86] If, he said, the final resolution was limited to Hull's suggestion of making an appeal to the peace-loving nations to uphold the principles of peace, he feared that it would be an "anti-climax" to the work of the conference if indeed it did not give aid and comfort to Japan. For to go on much longer without giving any indication that the Western powers intended "to do anything more than preach" would inevitably convince the Japanese that they could continue their present course without any danger of interference.

It is entirely evident in retrospect that there was no chance whatever of Davis' being able to influence the administration to change its mind. On November 15, Secretary Hull cabled that he felt any resolution looking toward the application of the policy of nonrecognition would be premature.[87] He further dismissed the remainder of Davis' proposals with a brief and decisive comment:

As to your suggested declaration against government loans and credits and the tightening of private loan and credits, you will recall that such measures are outside of the scope of the terms of the invitation to the Conference. You will further recall that the nations of the League assembled at Geneva definitely avoided the adoption of any such measures.

The next day Hull, referring to Davis' earlier recommendations concerning a possible repeal or alteration of the Neutrality Act, sent an even curter message which was limited to the statement that

There is no present prospect of a repeal or a suspension or a modification of the existing neutrality legislation and you should proceed on the assumption that no such action will occur.[88]

A few hours later, the Secretary wired once more:

Press reports from Brussels, especially during the last few days, have given and are continuing to give the impression that the other states there represented are willing and eager to adopt methods of pressure against Japan provided the United States would do so. The tenor of these reports is that the United States is solely responsible for determining what attitude the Conference will take in this respect.

I invite your attention to the fact that some 50 nations represented at Geneva are parties to a political instrument which provides expressly for the adoption, under certain circumstances, of means of pressure and when these nations met recently at Geneva to consider the present conflict between Japan and China, they definitely discarded the adoption of any such means and even took steps to avert public discussion of them. I invite your attention also to the purpose for which the Conference at Brussels was convened and to the fact that questions of methods of pressure against Japan are outside the scope of the present Conference.[89]

It is not surprising to find recorded in Pierrepont Moffat's diary that Davis was even more distressed by this series of communications than the initial dispatch from the Department repudiating his suggestions.[90] Apparently he drafted an unusually bitter reply to Washington but finally set it aside, having decided to surrender to the inevitable. On November 17 he consequently wired Hull: "I bow to your judgment and hope that it will be possible to make such a strong reaffirmation of the principles which underlie international relationships that it will not fall flat."[91] At the same time he found it impossible to refrain from countering Hull's main arguments against considering sanctions at Brussels.[92] None of the other principal powers, he said, shared the Secretary's view that a discussion of coercive measures fell outside the scope of the conference. The fact that the League nations assembled at Geneva had not adopted such measures in no way affected the proceedings at Brussels, as the League had not tackled the question of sanctions but specifically passed it on to be tackled at the conference. Moreover, before assessing responsibility for the unwillingness of the conference to do anything it was necessary to examine the record. Reviewing the record as he himself saw it, Davis wrote,

In broad outline the Conference has gone through several phases. Before and at its beginning there was in Europe in some quarters at least great expectation of American leadership; also probably hope and intention to push us out in front. At the Conference from the first and throughout other delegations, especially the British, the French, and the Russians, have advanced the view that nothing short of some form of pressure action would do any good and have taken the position that their Governments are prepared to embark upon some such action provided the United States would cooperate . . . However, I successfully declined to be put out in front and insisted that I would not discuss even the possibility of pressure measures until every possible effort had been made to bring Japan into negotiations. The Conference then proceeded with such an effort. When that effort had failed other representatives tried to induce me to discuss possible cooperative pressure measures. This I still declined to do except academically and in terms of some future possibility . . .

As regards other delegations whatever may be various motives and objectives of their Governments respectively, none has at any time suggested that the United States act alone or assume an outstanding responsibility. In their discussion of possible resort to pressure methods, what they have suggested has been cooperative effort. They have stated that their Governments are prepared to proceed toward and embark upon such measures if the United States can and will cooperate but that they cannot do so if we cannot and will not cooperate . . .

I understand perfectly and I accept without question your conclusion that with public opinion as it is at home you cannot adopt a position different from that which you are taking. Nevertheless we should not disregard the fact that whatever the reasons and however conclusive the explanations . . . inasmuch as other powers have advocated cooperative use of pressure and the United States has declined even to consider such a course the decisions made by the Conference, in the negative, will unquestionably be regarded as having been determined by the attitude of the United States . . .

I believe and I suggest that in whatever we say we should in order to be fair and to be on sure ground avoid discussion of "responsibilities" and refrain from attribution thereof to other powers.

Even the latter suggestion met with what can only accurately be described as an angry rebuff from the administration. The tone of the Department's cables indeed seems almost as significant as their content when it is remembered that Norman Davis was regarded as one of the most trusted advisors of the Roosevelt administration in general and of Secretary Hull in particular. Taking tone and content together one can only conclude that Washington had come to look at the proceedings at Brussels with an amount of anxiety that was, to say the least, acute. Moreover the anxiety was far from allayed even when

Davis assured the Secretary that he would cease to urge an acceptance of his views. For officials in Washington became more and more disturbed by public opinion in the United States which they believed to be increasingly critical of American policy at Brussels. And while they do not appear to have known about the press conferences which Davis had held at Brussels, they nevertheless tended to blame him for the adverse stories which the American newspapermen at the conference were sending home.

Part of the trouble was that when the conference recessed on November 15 there was a natural tendency on the part of the press to evaluate its accomplishments to date and that, as Congress was reconvening, these evaluations were likely to have an effect upon the forthcoming debates in the House and Senate.[93] As matters turned out, the administration became almost equally concerned over the criticism that it was doing nothing at Brussels and the criticism that it was doing too much.

Out of the many prominent newspapers in the United States that wanted to see the Brussels Conference adopt positive measures, the administration seems to have been especially worried over the attitude of the *New York Times,* which was rapidly moving in the direction of advocating sanctions against Japan. On November 12 Frederick T. Birchall, the *Times* correspondent in Brussels, wrote that, as all methods of peaceful persuasion had been exhausted, the conference was about to recess so that the delegates could find out whether their governments had decided to accept failure or to discuss taking action short of war against Japan.[94] There was a "distinct disinclination," Birchall said, among the delegates themselves to give up and go home though what this foreshadowed remained to be seen. On November 15, in an unusually bitter article, Birchall stated that, despite the hopeful atmosphere of the previous days, the declaration which had been passed by the conference before its recess was obviously a "swan-song" and as such could only serve as a demonstration that the democracies were not prepared to act against the dictatorships.[95] The American delegation at Brussels was "trying hard to be optimistic" but privately it must be wondering why it had ever come. At the same time, the *Times* asserted editorially that the results of the first stage of the Brussels Conference were "pitifully small" and that little more was to be expected from the second stage.[96] On November 21 Edwin L. James, in a column which touched off the most irate of the Department's dispatches to Davis, declared that the Brussels Conference had been a "fiasco" for which the United States was largely to blame.[97] He argued that the meeting had actually harmed the idea of collective security and that, since it was an outgrowth of the President's "quarantine" speech it constituted an American defeat. He further attacked the administration for having virtually inspired popular charges that the British were trying to "shove us out in front" at Brussels and declared that he could see nothing wrong with the British attitude which he defined as being that they did not want to take action against the Japanese alone but that if we were prepared to do anything they would go along.

On the isolationist side, the administration found cause for alarm in the position taken by the *Chicago Tribune,* the Hearst press, and ultimately certain congressmen. The *Chicago Tribune* (which during October and November published twenty-one editorials on the Far Eastern crisis) on November 17 addressed an editorial to Norman Davis entitled "Come Home To Us Now." Reviewing the history of the conference, the *Tribune* asserted that the delegates had fortunately refrained from discussions of sanctions or other warlike measures because Prime Minister Chamberlain was opposed to them, but that now the conference had recessed to give F.D.R. a chance to say what, if anything, was to be done along the lines of his Chicago speech. Japan was therefore "back on the Chicago bridge again" but as "nothing was meant by what was said on the bridge" Davis had better recognize that fact, take up his hat, and come home.

The Hearst press not only urged Davis' withdrawal from the conference but, as in its opposition to the "quarantine" speech, tried to work with the isolationists in Congress to strengthen its position. Three days after the conference opened, the Hearst newspapers announced that a demand was taking shape among a group of Senate leaders for the recall of Norman Davis.[98] This was immediately followed by attacks on the conference, proclaiming that the United States was forming "an alliance with death" by aligning itself with Great Britain, France, and the Soviet Union against Japan.[99] On November 14 it was said that rumors, to the effect that the British, French, and American delegates at Brussels were drafting a resolution involving a threat of sanctions against Japan, had so aroused the Senate that Borah was asking for Davis' withdrawal.[100] On the same day, the Hearst papers published a sensational article allegedly containing hitherto undisclosed minutes of an Imperial Conference held early in 1917 to plan how Great Britain could maneuver the United States into declaring war.[101] This disclosure, it was asserted, was exceedingly timely in view of the current machinations of the British in regard to the Sino-Japanese conflict and indicated once more that our delegates had no business to be at Brussels. A week later an editorial called "Quit

Brussels" concluded with the statement that: "The Brussels Conference is for us a DANGEROUS and UNJUSTIFIABLE venture, becoming more dangerous daily. Our delegation should be called home at once."[102]

Meanwhile Congress had reconvened on November 16 and the debate concerning the application of the Neutrality Act to the undeclared war in China had been resumed leading inevitably to comments upon the proceedings at Brussels. Senator Shipstead of Minnesota introduced into the Congressional Record an editorial from the *Philadelphia Record* which attacked the conference for having passed a declaration calling for a "common attitude" against Japan.[103] "Bearing in mind," the editorial said, "that any real 'police' work in the Orient will have to be done by the naval power of the United States, doesn't the line-up at Brussels suggest that Norman Davis had better pack up and come home quick?" Senator Shipstead's action was followed by a speech by Senator Lewis who criticized Davis personally for having joined in a declaration of censure against Japan and stated that the President's intention in sending a delegation to Brussels had been to create harmony and not to involve us in a conflict.[104] The senator declared,

If Japan is sincerely of the opinion that we have joined in an assault upon her and that we have proceeded to condemn her after calling her to court, but without hearing her, her natural instinct will be one of resentment and retaliation. That retaliation, let us understand, may take its course by an expression of conduct either as against the Philippines . . . or as against Hawaii or against one of the vessels of the United States.

In addition, Lewis said that now that it was apparent that the conference would be a failure the other delegates were "assuming to hold up the United States before the civilized world" as the one country responsible for whatever had transpired at Brussels. Under these circumstances he felt that the time had come "when our honorable President could most appropriately recall his representatives." Lewis' remarks were not only featured in the isolationist press but also appeared on the front pages of newspapers like the *New York Herald Tribune*, which carried a three column headline, NORMAN DAVIS RECALL PROPOSED, and asserted that the State Department was greatly troubled by a report that a petition was being circulated in Congress requesting Davis' return.[105]

In an effort to meet the criticism of both the internationalists and the isolationists, Hull sent Norman Davis another series of cables. In a dispatch, which has already been quoted in part, he instructed Davis to do what he could to correct the press reports that were creating the impression that the refusal of the powers to deal firmly with Japan was due to the attitude of the United States.[106] The Secretary not only charged that the League nations were actually to blame for the lack of action by the powers but also that some of these nations (notably Great Britain) were instigating the press reports in order to cover over their own unwillingness to do anything. Hard upon this communication, the Secretary informed Davis of the attacks upon him in the isolationist press.[107] "The President knows and I know," Hull said, "that these attacks are unfair and unjustified, but I fear that their continuation will undermine your position . . . I . . . believe that . . . it would be advisable to leave Brussels as soon as practicable after the recess." The Secretary asserted further that the Department could only keep within the scope of the policy that it had pursued from the beginning of the trouble in the Far East and that, moreover, it wished to emphasize two things: that at this moment the temper of the United States was not disposed to favor a course of pressure or threat; and that the longer Davis stayed at Brussels the greater the likelihood of his being accused of trying to further such a course. On November 20—the day after Lewis's speech in the Senate—the Secretary cabled again to say that the stories "alleging American responsibility for the 'failure of the Brussels Conference'" were still appearing in the press and that he might feel compelled to expose the record of the League powers unless they stopped disseminating these tales:

We have heretofore taken no public position as to this question of responsibility and hope to be able to avoid it. If we are driven to it, however, a strong case can be made from our own records of conversations and reports from Geneva, London and Paris to show that the states of the League assembled at Geneva made every effort to persuade Koo not to press for consideration of means of pressure provided by the Covenant and over a period of 2 or 3 weeks stoutly argued in private conversations about the difficulty, if not impossibility, of sanctions. The states of the League who are at Brussels should really be urging us to assume a share in the responsibility for nonapplication of sanctions rather than attempting, after their refusal to entertain the idea, to put the burden upon us. When the records show that they turned down sanctions at Geneva and when there is not a syllable of law to authorize our own Government to participate in sanctions, it is difficult for us from here to understand why the question of sanctions is a dominant theme of conversation at Brussels.[108]

Pierrepont Moffat, referring to this cable, states that "Stanley Hornbeck was so upset by what he called this 'stink-bomb' that he interrupted what he was doing and proceeded to draft a four-page telegram setting the Department aright."[109] The telegram turned out to be a brief resumé of the various phases through which the thinking of the American newspapermen at Brussels had passed since the opening of the conference, suggesting that the basic reason for the character of the news dispatches from Brussels was the simple fact that the correspondents were profoundly convinced that the policy which the United States was following was unwise, if not disastrous.[110] The American reporters, it was said, had virtually without exception come to Brussels with the belief that it was essential for the democracies to take a firm stand against the dictator governments. They had furthermore assumed that the conference had been called as a result of the President's Chicago speech and that the United States was prepared to take the leadership in concrete measures against Japan which would have the effect of restraining the dictatorships in Europe. They had consequently been disappointed by the United States policy of refusing to play a dominant part at Brussels and of concentrating upon a search for a peaceful solution to the Far Eastern conflict. Their hopes had, however, been somewhat revived when it was rumored that the conference intended to pass a strong resolution against Japan before undertaking to recess. But at this point Saburo Kurusu (then Japanese ambassador to Belgium), who had made a point of cultivating the American correspondents, had shown them a telegram from the Japanese embassy in Washington which stated that, as a result of pressure from various congressmen, the administration was not standing behind the American delegation at Brussels and that Davis would soon be instructed to "close down with some more resounding phrases and go home as speedily as possible." The embassy's telegram had moreover been re-enforced by stories carried by news agencies out of Washington declaring that there was a strong isolationist trend in the United States and that the administration was doing nothing whatever to combat it. In addition, before leaving for the conference recess, the other delegations had made clear that they would not take any further steps unless Washington was prepared to act. The correspondents had therefore become completely discouraged and bitterly complained that the United States was guilty of lack of fair play in raising the hopes of the peace-loving peoples of Europe, who felt that the dictators were merely biding their time to attack, and then failing to follow up its words with even a mild form of action. They had frankly stated that they could not in good conscience support the attitude of the American delegation at Brussels and that they would have to cable stories which would not be to its liking.

The upshot of the discussion of the press was that the Secretary of State himself asked the reporters in Washington to come to see him in small groups or individually so that he could explain the policy of the administration at Brussels and—in his own words—"give them a correct understanding of and perspective in regard to the whole matter."[111]

Meanwhile Hull had reverted to the idea that at the final session of the conference a statement should be issued which would constitute a "dramatic appeal" to the peoples of the world to maintain the principles vital to the preservation of peace. On November 17 the Department sent Davis the draft of such a statement which it was hoped might be adopted at the conference.[112] Taking exception to Davis' earlier comment that another moral pronouncement would only be an "anti-climax" to the work of the conference, the Secretary sought once more to give expression to the precepts which he continued to believe must guide his conduct of foreign policy:

I feel that each peace seeking nation . . . should make every effort to educate its people as to the urgent importance of the principles of peace and that each such nation should give its constant and earnest attention to building up . . . an understanding of the principles essential to orderly and healthy relations among the nations . . .
The essential first step in building for peace is development of an understanding and awareness on the part of the peoples and governments of all nations of the vital importance of the principles indispensable to normal international relationships.[113]

To Davis, however, the task of getting the conference to adopt a statement such as the Secretary had in mind did not seem an easy one.[114] The British in particular objected to what they regarded as a reiteration of moral generalities and favored instead a declaration of policy based on the nonrecognition of territorial gains by Japan supplemented by a prohibition of government loans and credits and a discouragement of private loans and credits.[115] Alternatively they thought that Great Britain and the United States might offer to mediate between Japan and China outside the framework of the conference— an idea which was suggested by renewed rumors of German mediation and indications that Japan might be willing to accept the good offices of Great Britain and the United States. Davis, however, intimated that a close association of England and America in an attempt to settle the Sino-Japanese conflict might be none too popular in the United States, especially as the Hearst newspapers were beginning a new attack upon the British with the publication of documents which they alleged to be the minutes of an Imperial Conference in 1917. As the British continued to put great pressure upon Davis to agree to the extension of an offer of Anglo-American mediation, he finally said that his governemnt wished to wind up the meetings at Brussels as soon as possible without committing itself to further action.

In the end the American and British delegations drew up two statements to be adopted by the conference, one in the form of a report of the deliberations which had taken place at Brussels, the other in the form of a declaration.[116] These two documents together reviewed the differences which had arisen between the Japanese and the nations assembled at Brussels and stated that as the attitude of the Japanese made any fruitful exchange of views impossible for the present the conference would be suspended for the time being. Nevertheless, it was said, the participating governments would continue to explore all peaceful methods of arriving at a just settlement and moreover hoped that the Chinese and Japanese would themselves bring hostilities to an early end and resort to peaceful processes. In addition emphasis was put upon the principles which Hull had insisted should be incorporated in any final statement issued by the conference.

The report and declaration were accepted by the conference at the closing session on November 24.[117] Speeches were made by the various delegates but again the only one of importance was a brief address by Wellington Koo, who declared frankly that the Chinese delegation did not regard the report and declaration as satisfactory and in fact looked upon them as a "mere reaffirmation of principles" which could not possibly cope with as grave a situation as existed in the Far East. He moreover expressed his regret that the conference had not seen fit to consider the concrete proposals concerning positive aid to China and restrictive measures against Japan which he had suggested at the meeting of November 13 and which, in his opinion, were indispensable to any successful effort to restrain Japanese aggression. In addition, after the conclusion of the conference, Dr. Koo candidly told the newspaper correspondents at Brussels that the Chinese delegates felt that the British had acted as their friends throughout the conference while the United States had let them down.[118]

Koo had indeed every reason to want the nations at Brussels to come to the support of China and every cause for concern at their failure to do so. For, although astonishingly little attention was paid to the matter at Brussels, the military situation in China had altered completely during the course of the conference, so that by the third week of November the Japanese armies were in control of the entire Shanghai area and were obviously preparing to embark upon a new campaign which had as its objective the taking of Nanking.[119] Moreover, the Chinese government had made it quite clear that it saw no hope of defending the capital as it had officially announced on November 20 that it was moving to Chungking where it would continue to carry on the conduct of the war. Following this announcement and just two days before the close of the Brussels Conference, the Chinese government had apparently made a further effort to persuade the administration in Washington to support some plan for aid to China. For, according to a memorandum of Hull's, the Chinese Ambassador in Washington called on him on November 22 to say that, although the Chinese government was departing from Nanking, it intended to "fight on to the last"; however it was in need of military supplies and wanted to know "if anything could be done by the other Governments in the way of cooperation along this line."[120] Hull goes on to relate:

I said that he, of course, was aware of the situation to date; that nothing was found possible at Geneva except some utterances or declarations, while the signatories of the Nine Power agreement assembled at Brussels with this knowledge fresh in their mind, and that the United States had entered this Conference along with the others with the knowledge and understanding that they were to convene there in order to explore all possible avenues of bringing about a constructive peace by agreement and, of course, these proceedings were to be short of either military force or economic coercion. I added everyone knew this and I assumed understood it and that that was the situation.

From the Chinese point of view, Hull's remarks shut the door on the possibility of any last minute action by the United States at Brussels— a matter which may have contributed to Koo's resentment toward American policy. From the point of view of the United States, the Secretary's comments showed that up to the very end of the meetings at Brussels he adhered to the administration's contention that the possibility of adopting economic or similar sanctions had been rejected by the League powers at Geneva and had never been considered as a subject for discussion at the Nine Power Conference.

According to the diary entries of Pierrepont Moffat for December, Norman Davis, in contrast to his usual resiliency, "brooded" over his experiences at Brussels long after his return to the United States and continued to make scathing comments to the Secretary, Sumner Welles, Hugh Wilson, and others whom he held responsible for the conduct of affairs at Washington throughout the duration of the conference.[121] In addition to his distress at having to carry out a policy which ran counter to his convictions, Davis felt that the administration had altered its views as the conference progressed, without giving him due notice, so that he advanced along the lines of the President's initial instructions only to be forced to beat a painful retreat. But, as has already been intimated, it is most unlikely that Roosevelt ever genuinely expected Davis to enter into serious deliberations concerning sanctions at Brussels. Insofar as it is possible to reconstruct the President's thinking from so meager a record, one may suppose that what

Roosevelt had in mind was that, *if* all the nations at Brussels were unanimously willing to adopt sanctions against Japan and *if* the general demand for sanctions became so strong that it even dispelled or drowned out isolationist opposition in the United States, he would be prepared to have the conference proceed to a consideration of coercive measures against Japan short of war. However it is hard to imagine that Roosevelt really believed that these near-miracles would come to pass. How difficult they were of achievement was demonstrated as soon as the conference opened by the determination of the smaller nations to avoid any active participation in the proceedings of the conference let alone in punitive action against Japan. Even more importantly, it became apparent before long that despite strong internationalist sentiment isolationist opinion in the United States was—as Davis himself said—not changing "an iota" as a result of the conference. Moreover, apart from the President, Sumner Welles, during the period when he served as Acting Secretary of State, at the outset of the conference made it plain that he did not expect sanctions to be discussed at Brussels and was averse to any such possibility. There was some feeling in the American delegation at Brussels that Sumner Welles was responsible for the policy that was formulated in Washington and that if Secretary Hull had been in charge matters might have been different. But there is nothing in the record to indicate that Hull upon his resumption of office was not willing to pursue the course which Welles had been following.[122] In fact, it was only after the Secretary's return that the administration went so far as to take the position (which was contrary to that of all the other large nations represented at Brussels) that the problem of sanctions definitely lay outside the scope of the conference and that, in any case, it was not a live issue as it had already been killed by the League powers. The chances are that, by this time at least (mid-November), Hull's concept of the conference was as he himself defined it: that it should serve as an agency for the education of the public toward a broader and more moral view of international relations in order to create the psychological foundations necessary for the maintenance of peace. And in all probability the President was of much the same opinion.

Aside from the controversy over sanctions the most important aspect of the Nine Power Conference, as far as American policy was concerned, was the constant emphasis put upon the theme that the real significance of the Far Eastern conflict went far beyond any immediate dispute between China and Japan and involved the whole issue of what Davis referred to as "the struggle between the law-abiders and the law-breakers." This theme was indeed so exclusively stressed by all the delegations at Brussels that almost no attention was paid to the concrete situation that existed in the Far East. Davis himself never even produced the outline drafted by the State Department looking toward a "constructive" and comprehensive settlement comparable to that attained by the Washington Conference in 1922 and in fact no specific terms were ever suggested at Brussels for a solution of the differences between China and Japan or between China, Japan and the powers.[123] This failure to consider the Far East *per se* goes far to explain why so many of the delegates at Brussels—emphatically including Davis—missed the significance of the movement which was afoot to open negotiations between China and Japan outside the framework of the conference itself.

Few good words have ever been said about the Brussels Conference. Among the many adverse criticisms one of the most apt was that written by Ambassador Grew in his diary at the time.[124] In general, Grew stated that he was greatly relieved by the developments at Brussels because he felt that the United States government was demonstrating that having gone on record with the President's "quarantine" speech and Hull's denunciation of Japan on October 6 it believed that nothing further could be done. But on the negative side the ambassador wrote that he could not understand why the Nine Power Conference had ever been convened as it was evident from the start that it "could never in the world agree to take *effective* measures" against Japan and therefore would only give renewed confidence to the Japanese militarists by showing up the "lack of unity and impotence of the Powers" so far as concerted action against Japan was concerned. "Why," the ambassador asked in brief, "can't statesmen think things through?"

EFFORTS AT A SETTLEMENT

The first efforts of the Japanese to open negotiations with China for a settlement of the Sino-Japanese conflict were made in the early days of August, approximately a month after the Marco Polo Bridge incident.[1]

The story has been told here of the events following the incident as they appeared to American officials. One of the developments which those officials did not perceive, however, was the division within the Japanese government concerning the advisability of carrying on a large-scale war against China at this time.

Baron Harada writing in the famous Saionji-Harada Memoirs in the second week of July stated that everyone was greatly concerned over the Sino-Japanese situation and was asking how Japan could escape from the predicament into which it had fallen in China.[2] Prime Minister Konoye, Foreign Minister Hirota, and indeed almost all of the important Ministers excepting the Minister of War, General Sugiyama, wanted to arrive at a settlement of the Lukouchiao incident, and the leaders of the General Staff shared this opinion. There had even been talk, Baron Harada stated, of sending Hirota to Nanking to get an agreement. But this had proved impossible because of the opposition of various elements in the army over whom the High Command itself did not have adequate control. Indeed, outside of the Minister of War, no one knew what the plans of the army were or, in general, just what was taking place.

Baron Harada's estimate of the situation is amply borne out by other evidence which forms part of the great volume of material connected with the proceedings of the IMTFE (International Military Tribunal for the Far East). The conflicts among the different sections of the army were especially complicated. The movement for a quick settlement of the Lukouchiao incident by peaceful agreement was supported, as Baron Harada indicated, by the highest officers in the General Staff led by Major General Ishihara, chief of the Operations Division. These men believed that Japan must prepare for a war with the Soviet Union and that she was in no position to engage in a struggle with China which would place her—to quote General Ishihara—in "as precarious a position as Napoleon in his Spanish campaign."[3] Moreover, they felt that the army was not ready for a major war with China. No military plans had been drawn up and at best only fifteen divisions would be available for service, an inadequate number especially if the Soviet Union should decide to enter the conflict on the side of the Chinese.[4] In addition, there appeared to be no means of supplying fifteen divisions with ammunition for longer than eight or nine months.

On the other hand, some of the young officers of the General Staff were in favor of using the Lukouchiao incident to launch an extensive military campaign in China and played an active part in attempting to undermine the policy of their superiors.[5] Even more importantly, the Japanese armies in Manchuria and Korea wanted an "all out" war and managed to impress their point of view upon the new commander of the Japanese garrison forces in North China who in July passed through Manchuria and Korea to take up his post in Tientsin. Nevertheless, some of the Tientsin army remained opposed to a prolonged conflict with China at this time and wanted to conclude a "cease fire." Because of the extraordinarily loose and divided structure of the Japanese government the pro-war elements among the armies in the field were, however, able to wield enormous power and exercised a great influence upon the Minister of War who, generally known to be a weak figure, was expected in any given circumstance to bend whenever sufficient pressure was applied.[6]

The first action of the Japanese government after the Lukouchiao incident was taken when the Cabinet on July 9 agreed to arrest the spread of the disturbances in China and seek a prompt settlement.[7] The next day the General Staff decided, however, that it was necessary to re-enforce the Japanese forces in North China and drew up a plan to send two brigades from Manchuria, one division from Korea, and three divisions from Japan proper, which it presented to the Japanese Cabinet on July 11. According to Baron Harada, Prince Konoye said that such a move would have the gravest international implications and that he would not accept it—a position which was also taken by the Foreign Minister and the Minister of the Navy.[8] Later in the day, however, the Prime Minister decided that, in view of the pressure from the army, he had better change his mind and the mobilization scheme was adopted; it was subsequently announced that re-enforcements would be sent to China. Meanwhile, news had reached Tokyo of the provisional agreement concluded on July 11 between the Mayor of Tientsin and a representative of the Japanese army in North China. As a consequence, it was decided that troops would be ordered to North China from Manchuria and Korea as planned but that three divisions in Japan proper would not be mobilized for the present. These shifts in policy naturally led to considerable confusion on the part of the public though Washington was greatly assisted by the confidential estimates of the United States military and naval attachés, which stated that while substantial contingents of Japanese troops were arriving in China, the popular idea of the numbers involved was exaggerated and that in the first weeks of July no forces had left Japan proper.

Concerning the tense days which followed July 11, it may be well to recall certain high points. The Chinese insisted that any settlement of the Lukouchiao incident must be negotiated between the Chinese and Japanese governments and not between the local Chinese authorities in the north and the officers of the Japanese army. They also asserted that they would not consider any agreement which violated the four points that the Generalissimo set forth as the minimum conditions that the Japanese must respect. In addition, the Chinese had, both through Sir Hughe Knatchbull-Hugessen and through direct communication with the Japanese, suggested the halting of all military activity and the restoration of the troops on both sides to the positions which they occupied before July 7. The Japanese on their part had insisted that the entire affair was a local matter and must be handled locally. Toward the end of July an agreement, reached at Peiping a few days earlier, had been signed at Tientsin and, despite all previous protestations, had been accepted by the National Government at Nanking. In the end, however, a new incident had occurred at Langfang. The Japanese had delivered an ultimatum and begun the mobilization of the three divisions in Japan proper whose mobilization orders had been withheld since July 11. Large-scale fighting started and led quickly to the conquest by Japan of the Peiping-Tientsin area.

While these developments were known to American officials, the continuing struggle within the Japanese government remained unknown. Nevertheless, the situation persisted whereby the government was torn between those who wished to seize the opportunity afforded by the clashes in North China to engage in a major military campaign and those who were opposed to such a policy. The pro-war elements among the armies in the field were pressing forward and apparently had forced the crisis after the Langfang incident. In early August, Prime Minister Konoye still did not know what the army intended to do and finally had to appeal to the Emperor who in turn spoke to the

War Minister. General Sugiyama stated that the campaign in North China would "definitely stop short of the line connecting the Yungting River and Paoting."[9]

At the same time, those who were opposed to an all-out military conflict with the Chinese began quite soon after the outbreak of hostilities to think in terms of a comprehensive political agreement. Grew, in a cable to the State Department on July 15, mentioned that a representative of the Foreign Office had informed the embassy that such an agreement might be concluded.[10] Various proposals for an extensive settlement were presented at a Five Ministers Conference on July 18, and subsequently Prince Konoye told Baron Harada that he would like to send Hirota to China, or even go himself, to open negotiations along the broad lines that the Ministers had discussed.[11] No action was taken, however, until the beginning of August, when the Ministers apparently decided that it was imperative to do something since the conquest of Peiping and Tientsin had been completed and they wished to forestall a further expansion of the war.[12] Moreover, they appear to have felt that having suffered a major defeat in North China the Nanking government might be more ready to come to terms.

As a consequence, on August 4 instructions were sent by Hirota to the Japanese consul general in Shanghai, Suemasa Okamoto, to arrange a meeting between Kao Tsung-wu, the director of the Bureau of Asiatic Affairs of the Chinese Foreign Office, and Shinichiro Funatsu, a Japanese businessman and former diplomat with whom Kao was well acquainted.[13] Funatsu was to attempt to pave the way for the opening of negotiations between the Chinese and Japanese governments. The meeting was, however, to take place in the utmost secrecy. Foreign Minister Hirota told Okamoto frankly that there was strong opposition to reaching a settlement among certain groups in the army and that only a few top officials of the General Staff knew what was taking place. "We are trying," he said, "to arrive at a decision first and then force it through."[14]

As matters transpired, Ambassador Kawagoe, who had been in the north, returned to Shanghai and insisted upon undertaking to meet Kao in place of Funatsu. On August 7 a detailed plan was adopted by the Ministers which was wired to the ambassador with the idea that he would present it to Kao. The plan consisted of two documents entitled respectively "Conditions for Truce Negotiations" and "Outline of the Plan for the Overall Adjustment of Sino-Japanese Relations."[15]

The first condition for a truce was the demand for the establishment of a new demilitarized zone which was to extend below Peiping and Tientsin.[16] Ambassador Kawagoe was told, however, that if the Chinese desired to fix a time limit for the termination of the demilitarized zone, the Japanese were "prepared to consider it."[17] In fact the theory from the outset seems to have been that a time limit of four or five years would be established and the Japanese always contended that the sole objective of creating a demilitarized zone was to prevent further clashes between Japanese and Chinese troops in this area during a period which was bound to be dangerous. Nevertheless the intent was not to do away with all demilitarized zones in the north but rather at the end of the four- or five-year term to replace the zone running south of Peiping and Tientsin with a more limited one, the boundary of which would be drawn about thirty kilometers below the Great Wall thereby more clearly approximating the demilitarized area as it existed before the Lukouchiao incident.

The Japanese on their part were willing to make concessions in North China. The Hopei-Chahar and East Hopei regimes were to be abolished and the areas involved were to be ruled in future by an administration controlled by the Nanking government. The leaders of the new administration were, however, to be friendly to Japan and to promote better Sino-Japanese relations, including economic cooperation. Ambassador Kawagoe was informed that the liquidation of the East Hopei regime was regarded as a particularly important measure which the army had agreed to with great reluctance only after being persuaded that it might help substantially to further negotiations. In addition to the above, the Japanese were prepared to abrogate the Tangku Truce and the Ho-Umetsu and Chin-Doihara agreements with the exception of the understandings that had been reached following the Tangku Truce which had, in essence, re-established communications and other forms of *de facto* relations with Manchuria.

As far as military matters were concerned, the Japanese stipulated that no truce would be possible unless the central armies of the Nanking government were removed from Hopei. Hirota explained to Ambassador Kawagoe that this condition was regarded as "only natural" as the Japanese government had taken the position all along that the presence of these armies in Hopei violated the Ho-Umetsu agreement. The Japanese on their side were willing to reduce their forces in North China to the number which they had maintained there before the Lukouchiao incident but not until the movement of the Nanking troops out of Hopei had been completed and the demilitarized zone had been established with only Paoantui to police it. The Japanese did not, in fact, wish to announce their decision to reduce their own contingents in North China until the terms of the truce had been carried out, although Ambassador Kawagoe was told that as a concession he might indicate that the Japanese intended to take such a step.

The "Outline of the Plan for the Overall Adjustment of Sino-Japanese Relations" dealt with subjects other than the immediate points of conflict in North China. China was to agree to recognize "Manchukuo" or, if this proved impossible, cease to make an issue of the matter. She was also to enter into an anti-Communist pact with Japan and pledge herself to prevent the spread of communism, especially in the demilitarized zone, and to suppress rigorously all anti-Japanese activities in China. If these terms were fulfilled the Japanese were ready to put an end to their attempts to exclude the influence of Nanking from Inner Mongolia and Suiyuan. Ambassador Kawagoe was also instructed to keep in mind as a bargaining point that Japan would, if necessary, agree to the abolition of the Shanghai truce agreement of 1932, which had in effect created a demilitarized zone in the Shanghai area. In regard to economic issues, in addition to accepting the general principle that there should be economic cooperation through the development of joint enterprises and similar media in North China, it was stipulated that the Chinese and Japanese governments should arrive at an understanding in regard to trade and other economic contacts and that China was to receive her freedom to control smuggling in the north.

There can be little doubt that the men who drew up these proposals for a settlement with China felt that they were offering the Chinese very generous terms, especially in regard to the restoration of North China to the administration of the central government. Baron Harada, in recording that proposals had been made for an extensive political agreement with China at a Five Ministers Conference on July 18, said that the aim was to create a "new" atmosphere between China and Japan.[18] The documents in which the terms for the settlement were set forth referred frequently to the necessity of reorienting Sino-Japanese relations on a basis which would be "unfettered" by all that had occurred in the past and provided that, after the conclusion of a truce, the Chinese and Japanese governments should issue a statement to the effect that they were entering "an era of a 'new deal' sincerely devoted to amity between the two countries."[19] On August 8 Foreign Minister Hirota in a final telegram to Ambassador Kawagoe said that the Lukouchiao incident should be fashioned into a turning point in Sino-Japanese relations leading to an understanding between the two countries which would be "a big stride forward."[20] The "broadminded policy" which the Japanese government had adopted, he declared, would "probably be beyond the expectation of the Chinese themselves" and was "worthy of winning the respect of the whole world."

Ambassador Kawagoe met with Kao on August 9 and informed him of the Japanese terms while stating that he had not yet been empowered to open negotiations formally but that his government wished to conclude a quick agreement.[21] According to the account of Japanese officials, Kao replied that such terms might present some difficulties but also offered some hope of success. In any case, Kao departed at once to consult with the government at Nanking. At this point, however, hostilities broke out in Shanghai and Kao did not return from the capital to carry on the discussions with Ambassador Kawagoe.[22]

No inkling of the foregoing developments reached American officials until the meetings of August 10 between Hirota and Ambassador Grew, when the Foreign Minister told Grew in strict confidence that on the preceding day Ambassador Kawagoe had presented Kao with a so-called "plan" for the adjustment of Sino-Japanese relations and that, as Kao had left to submit the proposal to Nanking, the Japanese government was now awaiting a response.[23] At the same time, it will be recalled, Hirota turned down the suggestion, which had originated with the British, that England and America should offer neutral ground on which Japanese and Chinese representatives might meet, in direct negotiation, with United States and British officials helping to smooth out problems as they arose.

The record indeed creates the impression that Hirota and his colleagues, who were trying to achieve a settlement with China, were not thinking at this time in terms of using the services of any third powers, perhaps because they started off with the expectation that negotiations with China would not be difficult in view of the concessions which they were willing to make. An added factor may have been the repeated assertions of the United States that it did not want to act as a "go-between" in the Sino-Japanese dispute to a large extent because it assumed that the Japanese would resent any effort by the Western powers to inject themselves into the situation and Ambassador Grew, supported by Ambassador Johnson, advised against our playing any active part in the Sino-Japanese conflict that might incur the hostility of either side.

In any event, after the failure of the Kawagoe-Kao talks, it was informally decided in discussions carried on within the Japanese government between the Foreign Office and the ministries of the army and the navy that, if the effort to reach a settlement with China was to be continued, it would be necessary to use the services of other governments.[24] These governments were, however, not to be permitted to engage in arbitration, mediation, or conciliation, all of which were regarded by the Japanese as forms of active intervention. They were merely to facilitate the conduct of direct negotiations between Japan and China through the exercise of their good offices.[25] Among other matters, the Japanese were increasingly anxious to avoid the appearance of submitting proposals for ending the war on their own initiative for fear that any such move would be interpreted as a sign of weakness and inability to continue fighting and it was thought that they could use third parties as a "smokescreen."

It may well have been for the sake of sounding out the possibility of the United States' acting as an intermediary to open negotiations with China, on the basis of the Japanese proposals of early August, that Hirota on September 1 told Ambassador Grew that he had fully explained Japan's objectives to the Chinese and that if Chiang Kai-shek would only accept the Japanese conditions he (Hirota) "could stop the war immediately."[26] Japan's conditions, he said, were three in number: (1) good relations with "Manchukuo" which, however, did not necessarily entail *de jure* recognition; (2) an improvement in the relations between Japan and China which necessitated a cessation of anti-Japanese hostilities and propaganda; (3) the withdrawal of Chinese troops from North China to be followed by the removal of Japanese forces. Concerning the third point, the Foreign Minister declared further that Japan "simply wanted to ensure a zone of peace and quiet on the frontier of 'Manchukuo.'" When Ambassador Grew asked, "Does that mean Japanese control of North China?" Hirota replied, "No, it does not," and added that "Japan visualized no political control."

Grew reported this conversation but it does not seem to have made any particular impression on American officials. In the weeks that followed pressures upon the Japanese government increased both as a result of political events abroad and the military situation in China. It was in the second week in September that the Chinese finally made a formal appeal to the League of Nations to consider the Sino-Japanese dispute which was followed by the convening of the Far Eastern Advisory Committee, the condemning of Japan's allegedly unjustifiable bombing of China, and the appointment of the League subcommittee which started its work on October 1. On the fighting front, the Japanese won signal victories in North China and by September 24 captured Paotingfu, thereby completing another major military campaign.[27] The elements in Japan that wanted a quick settlement therefore had reason to make another move in that direction in order to forestall action by the League and to prevent the Japanese military from launching a new campaign to penetrate further into China. The situation was made more difficult by the fact that some of the leaders of the Japanese armies in North China were now openly saying that they must at all costs advance to Nanking and that there was a growing feeling among the Japanese people that they must have some substantial recompense for the price paid in human lives and suffering for their military successes in China.[28]

Baron Harada recounts that Vice Minister of Foreign Affairs Horinouchi informed him around September 20 that the War, Navy, and Foreign Ministers were "in a great hurry" to conclude hostilities in China and wished to obtain the good offices of a third country.[29] On October 1 Prince Konoye, Hirota, and the two service Ministers met and approved a new plan for a settlement which in general was similar to that adopted in early August.[30] A few of the terms were however, more drastic. A demilitarized zone was to be established in the Shanghai area and the Nanking government was to recognize the regime of Prince Teh in Inner Mongolia. It was also said that, as the hostilities had expanded, the peoples' expectations of the "fruits of victory" had increased so that, while the Japanese government should hold to its "broadminded" policy toward China it might in addition have to consider demanding such tangible compensations as indemnities and certain mining, railroad construction, and other economic privileges in North China. As to the role of third powers, the principle was laid down that every effort must be made to avoid a conflict with other nations or in any way to invite their interference although negotiations could be carried on through them.

The evidence suggests that even before the October 1 plan was adopted, Foreign Minister Hirota entered into talks with Sir Robert Craigie concerning the possibility of the latter's acting as an intermediary between Japan and China.[31] The Foreign Minister told the ambassador that he would be willing to send a representative to China to open negotiations with the Nanking government on the basis of four points: China was to agree to (1) the establishment of a demilitarized zone in the north, (2) the maintenance of de facto relations with Manchukuo, (3) the control of anti-Japanese activities in China, and (4) the recognition of the principle of equal economic opportunity in North China. But, as Hirota did not wish to put Japan in a position of initiating peace proposals, it was decided that Sir Robert would convey these points to the Chinese as though they represented the Foreign Minister's personal views. According to the testimony presented to the IMTFE, the ambassador transmitted Hirota's conditions to Chiang Kai-shek, who expressed "bitter disapproval" of the creation of a new demilitarized zone although he raised no objections to the remainder of the terms.[32] No further exchange seems to have taken place between the Chinese and Japanese governments for the moment, no doubt for a variety of reasons, one of which was that difficulties arose in respect to Sir Robert's acting as a channel of communication.

Sir Robert Craigie's role in Japan's efforts to secure an end to the hostilities in China in the autumn of 1937 is in many ways obscure in part owing to the fact that the British government has not made public any documents for this period. An interesting memorandum in the State Department's files relates, however, that Sir Robert, on his way to Japan to take up his post as ambassador in August 1937, passed through Canada, deliberately avoiding Washington in order not to give the Japanese the impression that he was hatching a plan with United States officials for Anglo-American action against the Japanese.[33] While in Canada, Sir Robert explained some of his fundamental views concerning the situation in the Far East to the United States Minister. Until recently, he said, his government had felt that the "'civilian' and moderate" groups in Japan had been making steady progress and, despite the ever present danger of assassination, had become increasingly bold in their utterances, especially in regard to furthering the idea that the differences between Japan and China should be resolved by peaceful methods. This situation had so alarmed Japanese military groups that they felt impelled to put a stop to it and had consequently embarked upon their current military adventures in China. The only hope of avoiding large-scale military operations now was that the Chinese would have the good sense not to provoke the Japanese further. The situation was all the more regrettable because, if a period of political stability between China and Japan could be established, it ought to be comparatively easy to bring about an economic rapprochement for which the conditions were, in fact, "nearly ideal." Japan was primarily industrial while China was essentially agricultural so that the economies of the two countries were complementary. Meanwhile it was imperative to strengthen the hands of the moderates in Japan as much as possible. Undoubtedly there were large and influential groups out of sympathy with the current Japanese policy toward China. The military operations in China were costing a lot of money which would be reflected in an increase of taxes that was likely eventually to create an unfavorable reaction against the Japanese army leaders who in the long run might therefore lose some of their political power as a result of their present intransigence.

Under these circumstances, Sir Robert felt that Great Britain and the United States should do nothing to threaten the Japanese. He was especially convinced, he said, that England and America should not take joint measures against Japan since to do so would only help the Japanese military by giving them a chance to solidify the Japanese people behind them on the pretext that Anglo-American pressure was being brought to bear against their government. While there should be no appearance of a rift in Anglo-American relations, nevertheless Britain and the United States should pursue their policies independently. In conclusion, Sir Robert stated frankly that there was an important and influential group in the British Foreign Office which believed that the chief hope of curbing the Japanese lay in joint Anglo-American action and added laughingly that perhaps he should not have expressed his own opinions so freely as in some respects they were contrary to those held by his government.

After his arrival in Japan, Sir Robert entered into long policy discussions with Ambassador Grew in which he elaborated the ideas that he had briefly outlined in his talk with the United States Minister in Canada.[34] But although he engaged in these discussions during the time he was transmitting the Japanese proposals to Nanking, the British ambassador did not inform Grew of what was taking place. Indeed, there is no evidence to date that he even reported to his own government. The Japanese apparently wished to deal with Sir Robert on a wholly informal and unofficial basis and he in turn to all appearances felt committed to strict secrecy.[35]

Grew, on his part, continued to believe that the Japanese government was united in its desire to proceed with the war in China. Reviewing the ambassador's communications to Washington from the start of the hostilities in China, his first reference to this subject was in mid-July when he told the Department that there was a striking amount of agreement in Japan, concerning developments in China, which was "not a case of unwilling submission on the part of the Government to military initiative."[36] On the contrary, the Japanese cabinet, which was enjoying a high prestige and was entirely in command of the situation, had been giving its full support to the activities of the Japanese military in North China. Never, the ambassador said, during the years in which he had been stationed at Tokyo, had he seen Japanese officials so unanimous and so determined to withstand any weakening of their country's position in North China even at the price of extensive hostilities if necessary. During the succeeding months Grew reaffirmed at intervals his conviction that the Japanese government as a whole was in agreement on the conduct of the war. On October 6 he stated once more in a dispatch to the Department that he found "no evidence of there being any moderate element in Japan opposed to the carrying out of the Japanese military program in China."[37] In the same message he emphasized that, in his opinion, the objective of the Japanese was to reduce China to utter chaos and that until they had attained this goal they would not accept the good offices of any third party and then only to restore some degree of civil order.[38] As to the kind of a settlement the Japanese might ultimately demand, Grew remarked to the Department in late October that Japanese officials had never gone beyond indicating that they wanted an agreement based upon "Hirota's famous 'three points,'" which were so broad as to leave the matter of terms completely nebulous.[39] The ambassador thought that at the least the three points would be translated into concrete demands which would involve practically complete political and economic control of North China and might well be extended to include such conditions as the replacement of the Generalissimo with a pro-Japanese statesman, the appointment of Japanese advisers to all departments of the National Government, and the enlargement of the Japanese concessions in the various treaty ports in Central and South China.[40]

In China, in mid-October, the Generalissimo for the first time since the expansion of the hostilities in the north into a major conflict, broached the subject of a possible Sino-Japanese settlement in an interview with Nelson Johnson.[41] As Ambassador Johnson described the conversation to the State Department, General Chiang said "in the most positive way" that the American government should inform the Japanese government that China was determined to "fight to the point of extinction" rather than enter into direct negotiations with Japan without the participation of any outside power. China had learned by experience that she could put no faith in any promises made by Japan unless one or more third parties supported them as witnesses and guarantors. At the same time the Generalissimo declared "with equal force" that China was not only willing but anxious to accept a settlement with Japan based on international justice. "I inquired," Johnson told the Department, "whether he thought it conceivable that terms could be devised that would be acceptable to both the Chinese and Japanese governments and he said he thought such terms could be devised."

On the day of his talk with the Generalissimo, Johnson received the copies of several reports that Lockhart had sent to Washington from Peiping which indicated that Japan wanted to effect a settlement with China.[42] Lockhart declared that there were signs that Japan was not only seeking a solution to the North China problem but even to the whole Sino-Japanese situation for the near future. He felt that if there was a determination to carry on the struggle between Japan and China it lay in Nanking and not in Tokyo, and he suggested that the moment was opportune for other powers to try to bring Japan and China together in diplomatic negotiations. Writing to Nelson Johnson a week later, Lockhart stated that he was convinced that the Japanese would welcome a way out of their difficulties in China and the Chinese could get better terms now than in six months or a year.[43]

Ambassador Johnson apparently regarded the Generalissimo's remarks as merely cursory and definitely believed that Lockhart was misjudging the situation. Writing to Lockhart in late October, Johnson said that if the counselor's estimate of the Japanese desire for a settlement was correct it would indicate that Tokyo was satisfied with the territory it had gained in North China.[44] He could not personally believe that the Japanese would be content until they had "brought China to her knees." In other letters written at about the same time, the ambassador stated similarly that while Japan had conquered so much territory that her plan for the separation of the five northern provinces was virtually completed, the Japanese would not stop until they had wholly defeated China, at which point they would impose the most drastic terms of surrender or would entirely destroy the Nanking government. "Japan cannot draw back now whatever the end may be," the ambassador asserted; "Nothing but the collapse of Japan will save China."[45] In short, like Ambassador Grew, Johnson believed that there was no chance of the Japanese wanting to make an agreement with China until the war had reached its ultimate conclusion. Furthermore, by the beginning of November he thought that the conclusion was near at hand and that Chinese resistance would soon cease.[46]

On the other hand it should be said that even if Johnson had at any time felt that the Japanese were prepared to negotiate a settlement with China, he would still have been opposed to the Nanking Government's making anything but relatively minor concessions. He was convinced of the necessity of the Generalissimo's remaining in power if order and stability were to be maintained in China. And, in common with many foreign observers in the Far East at this time, the ambassador thought that any indication by Chiang Kai-shek of a willingness to capitulate to the Japanese would result in an enormous wave of popular feeling against him which would be used by his political opponents to drive him out of office.

As to specific peace terms, it is evident from Johnson's comments during the summer and autumn of 1937 that the conditions which he would have regarded as acceptable differed widely from those that the Japanese had in mind. In August the ambassador had objected to Grew's suggestion, made in response to an appeal from Hirota, that the United States might urge the Generalissimo to consider the plan for a settlement which the Japanese ambassador had presented to Kao of the Chinese Foreign Office because this plan was said to contain a demand for the suppression of anti-Japanese activities in China. Johnson's contention was that any such demand was unacceptable, since it would be used by the Japanese in the future, as it had in the past, to try to redirect the "whole form and purpose of Chinese nationalist education" as well as to create a positive attitude of opposition toward all developments that the Japanese were "pleased" to regard as communistic.[47] Several months later, Johnson forwarded to Washington a program for a peace settlement which a group of Chinese intellectuals had submitted to the Nanking government as of possible use by the Chinese delegation at the forthcoming Brussels Conference.[48] The program envisaged such concessions on the part of China as an agreement to establish a ten-kilometer demilitarized zone in the north and to respect the "demilitarized zone" in Shanghai which had resulted from the 1932 truce; the maintenance of *de facto* relations with Manchukuo; the conclusion of various economic arrangements which would give "friendly" consideration to Japanese needs; and the negotiation of a nonaggression pact with Japan similar to that in force between China and the Soviet Union, in order to meet Japan's insistence upon the adoption of an anti-Communist policy while preserving the principle that communism inside China was a domestic problem. The Japanese, on their side, were to consent to the restoration of North China to the control of the central government, the abolition of the conditions established by the Tangku Truce and other arrangements imposed upon China since 1933, and the limitation of the Japanese troops in China to the number and positions prevailing before the Marco Polo Bridge incident. Commenting upon these proposals to Washington, the ambassador remarked that while he thought they might be approved by the more moderate political leaders in China, he believed they would be bitterly opposed by others. That the ambassador himself regarded the proposals as too conciliatory is further indicated by the fact that on the very day that he forwarded the suggestions of the Chinese intellectuals to Washington he also cabled a peace plan to the State Department, which had been drawn up by Admiral Yarnell privately, with the observation that it was in accord with his own views of an acceptable settlement.[49] The plan basically provided for the recognition of Manchukuo by China but otherwise required all concessions to be made by Japan either alone or in conjunction with the Western powers that had so-called treaty rights in China. Japan was to withdraw from North China to the Great Wall and within one year of the signing of an agreement extra-territoriality was to be renounced by all the nations concerned, foreign troops were to be withdrawn from Peiping, Tientsin, and Shanghai, and the International Settlement was to be governed in a manner similar to the former British concession at Hankow. In line with all his previous statements, however, Johnson told the Department that he did not think Japan would agree to such conditions or, indeed, that it was possible to find any terms of peace which both China and Japan would regard favorably.

While the American ambassadors in Nanking and Tokyo were thus speculating upon the possibility or impossibility of terminating the hostilities in China, the Japanese government was doggedly persisting in its efforts to open discussions with Chiang Kai-shek on the basis of the plan drafted in August and revised on October 1. The difficulty which had arisen concerning the use of Sir Robert Craigie as an intermediary was that feeling against Great Britain was becoming strong in Japan as a result of the popular impression that the British were trying to organize an anti-Japanese front among the major Western nations. Moreover the hostility toward Great Britain was shared by the leadership of the General Staff of the Japanese army which, despite its desire to end the warfare in China, was vigorously opposed to cooperating in any way with the British and wanted instead to use the good offices of the German and Italian governments. As Hirota, on the other hand, had always been convinced that Germany and Italy carried little weight with China and that England exercised far more influence in Nanking than any other country, he wished to continue the conduct of the negotiations through Ambassador Craigie if possible, or, if this failed, through the United States.[50] After considerable discussion, a compromise was reached on October 22 and embodied in a formal document adopted by the Ministries of Foreign Affairs, War, and Navy, which defined the official attitude toward the role of third parties in connection with a settlement of the Sino-Japanese conflict.[51] The principle was reaffirmed that anything such as arbitration by other governments would not be tolerated and that any effort at mediation by the Brussels Conference would be rejected as the signatories of the Nine Power Treaty were bound to put Japan in the position of a defendant. Nevertheless, the good offices of any country that was "unbiased" would be welcome. If the

Chinese themselves suggested the services of Italy and Germany, it would be "execellent" but the assistance of England and America might also have its advantages. All of the foregoing was to be communicated to the Japanese ambassadors in the various countries involved with instructions to take appropriate measures. At the same time the ambassadors were to be warned against disclosing too quickly and too obviously that the Japanese government was seeking to open negotiations with China for fear of creating the impression that it was not able to continue the hostilities with China any longer owing to some internal weakness.

The policy adopted on October 22 was rapidly put into practice, as the Japanese were trying to forestall action by the Brussels Conference just as, to all appearances, they had attempted to effect a settlement with China in early October partly in order to prevent the League powers from making decisions adverse to Japan. On October 27 Hirota, in individual interviews with the British, American, German, and Italian ambassadors, handed them copies of the Japanese government's official refusal to attend the Nine Power Conference and at the same time sought to convey the idea that Japan wanted to enter into direct negotiations with China through the help of some third power serving as intermediary.[52] On October 29 and 30, Ambassador Yoshida in London called on Eden and Ambassador Bingham, respectively.[53] The ambassador said that the Japanese Foreign Minister had felt compelled to reject the invitation of the Brussels Conference but had nevertheless informed the British and American ambassadors in Tokyo that the Japanese government wished to bring about a cessation of war in the Far East and would welcome an opportunity to discuss the matter with them. Yoshida went on to explain that the military had dominated the political scene in Japan since 1930 and had precipitated both the Manchurian crisis and the present China incident. Moreover, they had managed to obtain the support of the Japanese people by subjecting them to a steady stream of propaganda. In the current situation the army had expected the military campaign, launched after the Marco Polo Bridge incident, to amount to no more than a short punitive expedition; but Chinese resistance had proved unexpectedly strong and as a consequence the military operations had become far more costly than originally anticipated, especially as the army was attempting at the same time to build up large and powerful forces to deal with the "Russian menace." Both public opinion and the Japanese government were therefore now in favor of ending the hostilities as soon as practicable. In view of these circumstances, Yoshida asserted, the main point he wished to make was that if the

Brussels Conference adopted a resolution condemning Japan outright it would be very difficult to conduct the peace negotiations which his government was eager to begin.

Two days after Ambassador Yoshida's talk with Ambassador Bingham, Yakichiro Suma told Joseph Ballantine in Washington that, in his opinion, it would be unfortunate if the Brussels Conference sought to interfere in the Sino-Japanese conflict as it would only stiffen Japanese public opinion and encourage China to prolong the hostilities. The best solution, he suggested, was for the United States to advise Nanking to seek direct negotiations with Japan for if Japan announced a readiness to reach an agreement it would be regarded as a sign of weakness.

Meanwhile Sir Robert Craigie and Ambassador Grew had sent the identical cable to their governments, in which they stated that the Japanese would regard any offer of good offices by a group of nations, such as the signatories of the Nine Power Treaty or the United States and Great Britain acting together, as an exercise of foreign pressure which would be resisted to the "last ditch."[54] The good offices of a single country (preferably Great Britain and the United States) might be acceptable to the Japanese government at some appropriate moment but the time was "not yet ripe." Therefore, in order to leave the door open for mediation in the future, the Brussels Conference should maintain as strict an appearance of impartiality as possible and should avoid making any decision which would tend to destroy the effectiveness of the assistance which some one nation might eventually be able to provide in attaining a Sino-Japanese settlement.

Why Ambassador Craigie did not regard Hirota's remarks at the time of Japan's rejection of the invitation to participate in the Nine Power Conference as a bid for a third party to serve as intermediary is not clear.[55] That Grew saw no particular meaning in the Foreign Minister's comments was on the other hand natural, since he remained unaware of the Japanese government's interest in a settlement.[56] It seems, therefore, in no way out of the ordinary to find that, on being told of Yoshida's talk with Bingham, Ambassador Grew cabled the Department that he was "astonished by Yoshida's statements" and that neither Hirota nor any other responsible official in the Japanese government had indicated any desire to discuss with American and British representatives the termination of hostilities in the Far East.[57] Furthermore, there was "no evidence" that apart from "big business"—which dared not be vocal—any substantial section of the population held opinions such as Yoshida had described. On November 6 Grew wired again concerning an article in the *New*

York Times, written by its correspondent in Tokyo, suggesting that "the thought is forming in Japan that it might be acceptable to the United States to open the way for peace discussions."[58] "We hope," Grew asserted, "that our Government will not suppose that the time is ripe for any such move."

Hirota's indirect appeal for third party assistance did, however, produce a response from the German ambassador in Tokyo, Herbert von Dirksen. As the United States ambassador in Berlin had continued to report, the German government remained divided in its attitude toward the Sino-Japanese war. Ribbentrop, who had great influence with Hitler, had from the outset favored Japan's military operations in China because of his sympathy for Japan which was largely based on ideological considerations and on what was aptly termed his "map-toying propensities."[59] In contrast, the German Foreign Office and the German embassies in both Tokyo and Nanking wished to see the hostilities in the Far East brought to a speedy conclusion.[60] In the first place, they felt that as a result of the Anti-Comintern Pact Germany might find herself unwillingly drawn into the conflict in the Far East as an ally of the Japanese. Second, it was argued that even if this danger was averted Japan's value to Germany would cease to exist if she became bogged down militarily in China, as she would no longer be either an actual or potential threat to the Soviet Union. Moreover, some of the leaders of the German Foreign Office shared the belief of Ambassador Trautmann at Nanking (who was himself very pro-Chinese) that attempts of the Japanese to force China to "suppress" communism were only driving her into the arms of Moscow.[61] In addition, there existed strong ties between Germany and China, as Germany had an important economic stake in China and a German military mission, under the leadership of the well known General von Falkenhausen, was serving as an advisory group to Chiang Kai-shek.

As early as the beginning of August Ambassador Dirksen had suggested to his government that in order to extricate herself from an awkward situation Germany might eventually attempt to mediate the Sino-Japanese dispute.[62] But nothing was done until late October when Foreign Minister Hirota indicated that Japan would like the German government to use its influence to open negotiations with Chiang Kai-shek.[63] The German Foreign Office thereupon decided that its envoys in Japan and China might transmit the Japanese proposals for a settlement to the Generalissimo provided it was understood that Germany was only assuming "the role of letter carrier." On November 3 Hirota handed Dirksen a list of terms which consisted of most of the principal demands for concessions from China that had been embodied in the plan adopted by the Japanese government on October 1 though none of the details were included. Concerning specific issues, it was primarily stated that a demilitarized zone should be established in North China, along a line south of Peiping and Tientsin; that another such zone should be maintained in Shanghai; and that Inner Mongolia should be autonomous. In regard to more general problems, the principles of "cessation of anti-Japanese policy" and a "common fight against Bolshevism" were to be reaffirmed. In discussing the all-important question of North China with Ambassador Dirksen, Hirota explained orally that "if peace were concluded at once" the Japanese government would agree to leaving the whole administration of North China to the Nanking government; however, if the hostilities continued, Japan would establish a separate regime in North China which would have to remain in existence even after the ultimate cessation of the war.[64]

Ambassador Dirksen informed his government that he thought the Japanese genuinely desired peace on the basis defined by Hirota but were just as seriously determined to continue fighting until "the final overthrow of China" if Nanking rejected their conditions.[65] The ambassador himself recommended transmitting the Japanese terms to the Generalissimo because he regarded them as "very moderate" and as affording the Chinese government a chance to make peace "without loss of face." As a consequence, Ambassador Trautmann submitted Hirota's proposals to Chiang Kai-shek on November 5.

In his account to Berlin of his interview with the Generalissimo, the ambassador reported that Chiang Kai-shek had said that it was, of course, possible to discuss some of the Japanese terms and to seek a friendly understanding concerning them but only if the Japanese were first willing to agree to restore the *status quo ante*.[66] Confidentially, and only for the information of the German government, the Chinese government would be swept out by the tide of public opinion if he agreed to such demands; there would be "a revolution in China." The Japanese were pursuing the wrong policy in making demands on China instead of seeking by a friendly gesture to lay the basis for good relations. If they continued the war, China would, of course, not have a chance to win a victory in the long run but neither would she lay down her arms. Should the Chinese government fall as a result of Japan's action, the only result would be that the "Reds" would gain the upper hand in which case it would be impossible for the Japanese to make any peace, as the Communists would never capitulate.

Ambassador Trautmann concluded his report with the following:

The Marshal said that it was almost impossible for him to take official cognizance of the Japanese demands because China was now the concern of the Powers at the Brussels Conference and they had the intention to work for peace on the basis of the Washington Treaty. I told him that the step I was taking meant nothing more than that we were informing the Chinese Government in confidence of the Japanese views on peace . . . The Marshal asked me to keep strictly secret the step I had taken today . . .

Irrespective of what Chiang Kai-shek thought of the Japanese terms, there was little chance of his entering into negotiations with Japan on a basis wholly unrelated to the Nine Power Conference at the very moment that the members of that conference were beginning their discussions at Brussels. In fact, only a few days before the Generalissimo's interview with the German ambassador, H. H. Kung, in response to a question concerning rumors of peace overtures, had told Johnson that the Chinese would not discuss any peace settlement with Japan before the meeting at Brussels took place.[67] The Chinese leaders could indeed scarcely have failed to reason that no matter what course they decided to pursue it was the better part of wisdom to cooperate with the delegates at Brussels as fully as possible. For if they continued the war, the logical policy was to renew the attempts they had been making to get the signatories of the Nine Power Treaty, and/or the League nations, to agree to assist China and to adopt punitive measures, such as economic sanctions, against Japan. On the other hand, if they decided to put an end to the hostilities through a settlement they were, as the Generalissimo repeatedly stated, determined not to enter into direct negotiations with Japan, in which case most of the nations that had participated in the Nine Power Treaty were certainly preferable as mediators to Germany which, though it had an interest in China, was nevertheless an ally of Japan's. If it was therefore only logical to want the closest association with the Brussels Conference, there is some reason to think that Chiang Kai-shek, despite his comments to Ambassador Trautmann, had not decided before the proceedings at Brussels started whether to urge aid for China and sanctions against Japan or to consider mediation under the best obtainable circumstances, and that he veered toward the former as a result of the atmosphere which developed during the proceedings themselves. It may be remembered that Ambassador Johnson cabled Washington that he had learned on good authority that no instructions had been sent to the Chinese delegates at Brussels as late as October 30.[68] Subsequently the ambassador told the Department that he had heard from the same sources that instructions had finally been cabled to the Chinese delegates and that they were not unlike the program drawn up by a group of intellectuals for use at the Nine Power Conference which Johnson had forwarded to Washington earlier.[69] Certainly the Chinese delegates at Brussels were exceedingly vague when questioned by Norman Davis on October 29 concerning the policy of their government.[70] Even at the opening session of the conference, Koo's address was so inconclusive that Pierrepont Moffat wrote in his diary that the general impression created by the speech was, "Well, he made some very telling points but after all we are not sure just what he was after."[71] In contrast, at the second general session on November 13, Koo astonished his audience by flatly appealing for coercive action against Japan. As November 13 virtually marked the high point of the trend at Brussels toward the adoption of sanctions against Japan, it is hard to suppose that the Chinese did not assume a tougher position in the expectation that sanctions might be forthcoming. In fact, in view of the persistent determination of the Chinese people to continue the war and in view of the constant talk of the possibility of agreeing to the use of strong measures against Japan which characterized most of the behind-the-scenes activity at Brussels, it would have been difficult for the Chinese government to make any serious move toward mediation if it had so desired. As it was, many Chinese officials seem to have hoped until almost the very end of the Nine Power Conference that the delegates would take some steps to intervene in the Far Eastern conflict on China's behalf. After the fall of Nanking in mid-November, the Chinese appeals for support took on an almost frantic quality. On November 19, for example, Wellington Koo gave the representatives of the United States, Britain, and France an *aide-mémoire* from Nanking which asked for a "joint forceful demonstration," such as a naval demonstration, against Japan.[72] In handing the *aide-mémoire* to Davis, Koo said that, whereas China had not really entertained any hope of aid from abroad until the Brussels meeting was called, that meeting had created considerable optimism which would be replaced by a "great sense of discouragement" if the powers failed to do anything. On another occasion, the Chinese delegates threatened that, unless the conference accomplished something toward assisting their country, the Nanking government might have to consider seriously accepting the offers which Germany and Italy were making to mediate the Sino-Japanese conflict.[73]

While the Chinese were desperately seeking intervention by the powers to enable them to carry on the war, the Japanese government was making a final urgent attempt to end the hostilities on the basis of the terms it had been proposing. Although continuing to reject the idea of mediation by the Brussels Conference, or by any individual nation or small group of nations that might be appointed to represent the conference, the Japanese maintained their determination to open direct negotiations with China through some intermediary.

At the time that Ambassador Trautmann transmitted the Japanese terms to Chiang Kai-shek there had been many rumors in the press to the effect that Germany was trying to bring about a peace agreement. But these stories had been denied by German officials and as a result were discounted by Grew and Johnson.[74] Nevertheless, while scarcely hopeful of success, Ambassador Grew decided that it would at least do no harm to try to find out from the Japanese what kind of terms they had in mind for a final agreement with China and whether "the widespread confidence of the Japanese Government in the disinterestedness and impartiality of the United States could in some way be profitably employed in the direction of peace."[75]

On November 8 (only three days after Trautmann's interview with the Generalissimo) Eugene Dooman, as Counselor of the American embassy, had consequently suggested to Sejiro Yoshizawa, the Director of the American Bureau of the Japanese Foreign Office, that perhaps the United States could pave the way for the opening of peace negotiations in the present situation, just as President Theodore Roosevelt had done in 1905 in connection with the Russo-Japanese war.[76] Yoshizawa replied that the military situation was in the process of change and that the situation had not as yet developed to the point which the Japanese were hoping for, namely, that the Chinese themselves would make peace overtures. Until this point had been reached, there would be little likelihood of the Japanese government's giving consideration to any proposed move toward peace involving the United States or any other third powers.

Precisely a week later, Yoshizawa told Dooman that he wanted to continue their conversation. But this time he spoke very differently, stating that Japan would be willing to consult with the United States or any other power with substantial interests in the Far East, either individually or collectively, as long as the exchange did not take place within the framework of a collective security structure such as existed at Geneva and Brussels. Yoshizawa then entered into a long discussion of the United States' role *vis-à-vis* the Far Eastern situation which was so similar in purport to the remarks that Hirota was to make to Ambassador Grew on the following day as to suggest the most meticulous planning by the Japanese of the moves in which they were engaging. Yoshizawa and Dooman parted with the understanding that they would seek the advice of their superiors. Dooman returned to the embassay at once but scarcely had time to report to Ambassador Grew before Hirota's secretary telephoned to request the ambassador to come to see the Foreign Minister early the next morning.

According to Grew's very careful account to the Department of his interview with Hirota, the Foreign Minister opened their talk by referring immediately to the draft resolution under consideration at the Brussels Conference that, he said, provided for "united action" against Japan, which presumably meant "some sort of economic boycott or other sanctions."[77] The Minister went on to declare that according to his information the United States government had not only initiated the Brussels Conference but had assumed the leadership in its proceedings. Rumors of the American activities at Brussels would inevitably soon appear in the Japanese press which would have a "most unfortunate effect on Japanese public opinion." The Japanese people had hitherto blamed Great Britain for attempting to organize a solid front against Japan but if current developments continued they were bound to hold the United States responsible. This would be unfortunate as previously America's position in the estimation of the Japanese had been such as to enable the United States government to "play the same role in helping to terminate the present hostilities as it had played in the Russo-Japanese war." The President's Chicago speech had temporarily modified the faith of the Japanese in the United States as the only country which had been "genuinely impartial during the Sino-Japanese conflicts"; but subsequent statements by the President had restored their confidence.

Grew's account goes on to say:

Mr. Hirota then said that the Japanese military movements in China are progressing favorably and there is no need for the army to go much further than it had already gone although they will be perfectly capable of doing so if they consider it necessary. In China's own interests now is the time to bring about peace. The Chinese Government is considering evacuating Nanking to some other capital and this, the Minister said, will be a very foolish move . . . If peace is made now the Japanese demands will be "reasonable" and not a foot of Chinese territory will be taken. If, however, the warfare continues, the present attitude of the Japanese Government will no longer apply and more drastic terms may result in view of the increased sacrifices involved.

If the United States wishes to help, the best thing it can do is to persuade the Chinese Government to open negotiations with Japan. As soon as there is some indication that such negotiations will be acceptable to the Chinese Government, Mr. Hirota would send a representative to Shanghai to talk with a representative of the Chinese Government either in public or in strict secrecy as the Chinese Government might wish.

In commenting upon the Foreign Minister's remarks to the Department, Grew said that he realized that a negotiated peace at the present moment might be regarded "as more in the interests of one of the combatants than of the other." Nevertheless, if one assumed that an early peace might be desirable from all points of view, there were various matters which appeared significant. Yoshizawa had indicated that the Japanese government was prepared to consult with the United States and Great Britain or other powers with interests in the Far East. He had also said that an opportunity to discuss terms with Chiang might be lost if the Chinese government was driven from Nanking into the remote and inaccessible interior of China; for the maintenance of world order would require the formation of a new Chinese regime in which case whatever remained of the Chinese government—whether it was still under the influence of Chiang or, as seemed more likely, had fallen into the hands of the radicals—would probably continue resisting indefinitely. Under these circumstances, Grew suggested, perhaps the situation was impending which he had envisaged some time earlier: the United States might be called upon for its services to prevent China from disintegrating completely.

In support of the Foreign Minister and Yoshizawa's comments in Tokyo, statements of the same general tenor were made by Ambassador Kurusu at Brussels, Suma in Washington, and Ambassador Yoshida in London. At Brussels, Kurusu approached various delegates, including those of the United States, with an urgent plea to postpone passage of the declaration which in effect recommended the adoption of a "common attitude" by the powers if Japan's intransigence continued.[78] Kurusu argued that the acceptance of such a resolution would foreclose the possibility of mediation by any nations other than Germany or Italy.[79] The delegates on their part thought that Kurusu was merely engaging in a maneuver to gain time and asked whether he was speaking on behalf of his government or on his own initiative. When he replied the latter, the matter was dropped—and, in fact, not even reported to Washington.

On November 16 Suma called on Hugh Wilson in Washington to say that he had received an account from Tokyo of Ambassador Grew's talk with Foreign Minister Hirota.[80] Suma proceeded to reiterate many of the points which the Foreign Minister had made and finally asked Wilson whether he thought "the American Government could play the role in this conflict that President Theodore Roosevelt had played in 1904." Wilson replied that he could only give an "instantaneous and unconsidered" answer but that personally he felt "it would be very difficult for us to make any suggestion, bound as we were by our own principles and the obligations of the Nine Power Treaty, which the Japanese Government in its present temper would consider for a minute." Suma responded that he "sincerely believed that if conversations could be begun with the Chinese, the world would be astonished at the moderation of the terms which Japan would be ready to accept." Unfortunately, the longer and more bitter the conflict, the more risk there was that "moderate terms would disappear from the minds of a fighting nation"; but if conversations could be begun now, it was not too late to reach a reasonable settlement.

At about the same time that Suma went to see Wilson, Yoshida called on Eden in London. The ambassador said that he had heard from Tokyo that a representative of the Japanese Foreign Office had told Sir Robert Craigie on November 15 that the Japanese Government would be disposed to accept an offer of good offices looking toward peace and that Hirota had made the "same suggestion" to Grew "in even more specific terms."[81]

There were undoubtedly several reasons for this extraordinarily intense "peace drive" on the part of the Japanese. According to their own statements, they wished to block the acceptance of the November 15 resolution by the Nine Power Conference. But presumably the elements in Japan that were opposed to a continuation of hostilities were even more concerned with the military situation in China where, the campaign for the conquest of Shanghai having just been completed, the crucial moment had arrived to decide whether or not the Japanese armies should push on to Nanking. The pro "peace" groups feared—as Yoshizawa frankly stated—that if the plans of the military to proceed to Nanking got underway and the capital was captured, the war would be prolonged indefinitely and that, in the process, Chiang Kai-shek would be overthrown in which event all semblance of law and order in China would disappear. As these same elements also continued to believe that China would only open negotiations with Japan through an intermediary, they felt it essential to renew appeals to the Western nations for a tender of good offices.

Despite the vigor of the Japanese government's efforts to convey the idea that they wanted American aid in achieving a quick settlement, United States officials again failed to understand the situation. The State Department, in answer to Grew's report of his conversation with Hirota, instructed the ambassador to inform the Foreign Minister that there was not "an atom of truth" in the allegation that the United States had taken the initiative in convening the Nine Power Conference and that the United States like all the other governments at Brussels, had done no more than share the common responsibility to exchange views in regard to the situation.[82] But the Department took no notice of Hirota's remarks about the possibility of negotiations between Japan and China. Ambassador Grew himself on hearing of Yoshida's comments in London told the State Department that he had definitely not received the impression that Hirota had sought to indicate that Japan would accept an offer of good offices by the United States although he thought the Foreign Minister might have been seeking to prepare the ground "for consultation with the United States to explore a possible path for peace."[83]

Meanwhile Sir Robert Craigie, who was in the process of altering his views concerning the best means of bringing about a settlement in the Far East, informed Grew that he had asked for authorization from London to inquire of the Japanese (a) what their attitude would be toward an Anglo-American offer of good offices and (b) whether the term "good offices" could be understood to mean that England and America would merely serve as intermediaries passing messages regarding peace terms from one combatant to the other until a basis had been found for direction negotiations.[84] Grew, in reporting this matter to the State Department, said that both he and the British ambassador feared that the Japanese idea of "good offices" was for other nations to bring pressure to bear on Chiang Kai-shek to enter negotiations, even against his will, which was obviously out of the question for either Great Britain or the United States. Nevertheless, a negotiated peace now would involve far less drastic terms than if delayed. As to a possible conflict between the procedure Sir Robert Craigie had in mind and the activities of the Brussels Conference, Grew stated that the British ambassador had explained that he envisaged no conflict but that, in any case, he would "deplore adherence to the principle of peace by collective action to a point where any prospect of peace lying outside of the Brussels Conference would be ruled out." Grew himself added that he would be "greatly interested" to know the Department's view on this point and drew attention to a recent dispatch to Washington in which he had expressed the opinion that: "Present evidence indicates that if our Government were to insist that efforts toward peace were to be made within the framework of a system of collective security, whether of the League or the Nine Power Treaty, force and only force could be effective."

Even before the receipt of Sir Robert Craigie's proposals in London, the British Foreign Office had instructed Ambassador Lindsay to tell the State Department that, on the basis of Yoshida's talk with Eden, the British government was prepared to join in an offer of Anglo-American good offices to Japan and China if the United States was willing.[85] On November 19, having by that time learned of Sir Robert's plan, the State Department informed Ambassador Lindsay in a formal *aide-mémoire* that as Foreign Minister Hirota's remarks to Ambassador Grew had been considerably less specific than those of Ambassador Yoshida to Eden, it seemed essential to clarify the Japanese position before taking any further steps.[86] In any event, the Department stated, it did not agree with Craigie's concept of England and America serving as intermediaries because intermediaries "would be called upon to transmit terms inconsistent with the Nine Power Treaty" and would appear to be "pressing such terms." The Department believed the British and American ambassadors in Tokyo should confine themselves to finding out individually whether the Japanese government genuinely desired to use the services of England and America to open conversations with China and, if this appeared to be the case, Washington and London should confer as to the form in which they would tender their good offices. In the Department's opinion, "it would be necessary to find some formula which would indicate clearly that the terms of settlement could not be recommended to China by either the United States Government or the British Government which would be inconsistent with the Nine Power Treaty."

Ambassador Craigie had not, however, waited for instructions from London but on seeing the Japanese Vice Minister for Foreign Affairs had inquired on his own initiative what the Japanese attitude toward a possible Anglo-American offer of good offices would be.[87] The Vice Minister had replied that the only acceptable kind of assistance from third powers would be an effort on their part to persuade the Chinese to enter into negotiations. Grew reported this development to Washington immediately and added his own comment which was that the present moment did not therefore appear opportune for any mediatory step by either the American or British governments, or both. The Department, which had just given Sir Ronald Lindsay the *aide-mémoire* described above, thereupon cabled Grew that it assumed the procedure which it had suggested to the British should not be attempted and that nothing further should be done.[88]

The British on their part did not take the Japanese Vice Minister's remarks very seriously and continued to believe that Great Britain and the United States might be instrumental in bringing about peace in the Far East. It was in fact at this point that the British delegation at Brussels made strong efforts to persuade Norman Davis to agree to

Anglo-American mediation outside the framework of the Nine Power Conference. Davis not only rejected this idea on the grounds already indicated but also because he believed that, as a matter of principle, England and America should not take any mediatory action unless delegated to do so by the conference as its agents.[89] Moreover, Davis' intense concentration upon the collective security issue and his consequent tendency to overlook the concrete situation in the Far East almost inevitably resulted in his giving little thought to the possibility of solving the Sino-Japanese conflict by some other means if the Brussels Conference failed. As he himself told the State Department when the conference was over, he had not really explored the subject of an eventual mediation or conciliation offer by the United States and Great Britain to China and Japan, if the efforts of the conference proved futile, "because of the strain of more pressing work."[90]

By the close of the Nine Power Conference the conquest of Shanghai by the Japanese was not only having an enormous impact upon the Chinese but was also affecting the interests of Great Britain and the United States in the International Settlement. According to Grew, Ambassador Craigie had consequently come to the conclusion that Great Britain and the United States should jointly follow a twofold policy of, on the one hand, putting pressure upon the Japanese even to the extent of engaging in a display of naval power while, on the other, suggesting that Japan and China might avail themselves of the services of England and America to open negotiations for a settlement.[91] Sir Robert Craigie's reasoning, as explained by Grew to the Department, was that the situation in Shanghai was leading to a "showdown" between the military and civilian factions in Japan as the commander of the Japanese armies in Central China was threatening to undermine the American and British position in that area—in part by seizing the customs service—while the government at Tokyo wished to keep on good terms with the Western powers that shared in the administration of the Settlement in the belief that it needed their economic and financial cooperation. The British ambassador thought, therefore, that the best means of strengthening the hands of the moderate groups in Tokyo was for Great Britain and the United States to demonstrate their determination to stand their ground at Shanghai as any sign of weakness would only increase the truculence of the Japanese militarists. At the same time he continued to believe that the moderates would also be assisted by the termination of hostilities which he presumed was still their goal. From what transpired subsequently, it would seem that Sir Robert Craigie's ideas had a great deal of influence upon British policy. As to Grew's own estimate of his

British colleague's views, he told the Department that he still had seen no evidence of any differences between the various elements in the Japanese government in regard to their policy in China and that, even if one were to assume such differences existed, any attempt at coercion by the powers would only succeed in driving the moderates into the camp of the extremists.

On November 23, Grew cabled to Washington the substance of a dispatch in which Sir Robert Craigie had suggested to his government that Great Britain and the United States might prepare the way for negotiations between China and Japan by initially acting as a "sort of 'post office,'" offering advice to either side when solicited.[92] Craigie, Grew said, stressed that once the ball was set rolling through the agency of Great Britain and the United States, its propulsion in the right direction might become easier and he therefore thought that a valuable opportunity might be lost if the British and American governments laid down too many conditions in connection with their tender of good offices. As Grew intimated, Ambassador Craigie was in essence taking exception to the State Department's previous assertion that whatever the circumstances the United States and Great Britain, before attempting to assist China and Japan to arrive at a settlement, would have to agree on some formula which would indicate clearly that they could not recommend terms to China that were inconsistent with the Nine Power Treaty. Concerning his own position on this issue, which was unquestionably central to the Department's thinking, Ambassador Grew said that the crux of the situation seemed to him to be:

granted on the one hand that we would not be willing to recommend peace terms inconsistent with the Nine Power Treaty, would we be willing to act in an effort toward peace merely as a nation having important interests in the Far East and as a friend of both combatants but bearing constantly in mind the provisions of the Nine Power Treaty and the determination to emphasize or to render compelling those provisions in the formulation of the final peace terms?

It is hard to suppose that Ambassador Grew intended this comment as anything but a suggestion that the administration should help to initiate an exchange between China and Japan looking toward a peace agreement without making too many advance demands and that, in lieu of such demands, it should attempt to exercise its influence during the course of the negotiations so that the ultimate settlement would be in harmony with the Nine Power Treaty. If this was, in fact, Grew's meaning, he was not understood by the State Department, judging by the statement which Sumner Welles was to make later to Ambassador Lindsay.

But before Welles and Lindsay were to return to the subject of good offices, the British ambassador on November 27 delivered a message to Welles from the Foreign Office in London which was obviously of great importance.[93] The message was in the form of a telegram which, according to notes taken by Welles from the original, stated that the British government had concluded that the Japanese were determined to disregard the interests of the Chinese Maritime Customs Service and, in fact, the interests in general of third parties in China. The British government took a "serious and anxious" view of this situation and wished to know whether the United States government shared its concern. If so, the British government further desired to know whether

the United States Government would be disposed to join with the British Government in strengthening the hands of the two Governments through supporting representations to be made with regard to the above questions "by an overwhelming display of naval force."

Should the United States government be disposed to consider such a possibility the British government wished to suggest "that the two Governments undertake immediately . . . staff conversations 'to consider appropriate and adequate combined steps.' "[94]

Welles immediately stated that in view of the unusual significance of this communication it would of course have to be referred to the President and the Secretary of State. Nevertheless, he went on to say on his own responsibility that during recent months competent British authorities had repeatedly advised American officials that "the British Government was not in a position to employ its naval forces in the Far East"; moreover, the whole policy of the British government, as explained by Ambassador Lindsay himself, "had been predicated upon its unwillingness to be drawn into a position with regard to the Japanese-Chinese controversy where the exercise of forceful measures might prove essential."[95] Therefore, unless British policy had undergone a change, the phrase "overwhelming display of naval power" would seem, under existing conditions, to imply an overwhelming display of United States naval force—a "very important fact" which the United States government would have to take into account in making any decision.

The United States government does not appear to have sent the Foreign Office any formal reply to its message but it is entirely clear from the events recorded below that it rejected the idea of entering into staff conversations at this time. Matters were allowed to slide until December 8, when Sir Ronald Lindsay again called on Welles, this time to discuss once more the question of extending Anglo-

American good offices to China and Japan.[96] According to a memorandum written by Welles, Ambassador Lindsay said that Sir Robert Craigie was continuing to insist that the Japanese government would be receptive to a suggestion from the United States and Great Britain of the use of their good offices. The British government therefore wanted to know the Department's opinion of Sir Robert's thesis that if and when good offices might be considered the British and American governments should not at the outset announce that they would refuse to convey terms from one combatant to the other that did not strictly conform to the Nine Power Treaty. Ambassador Lindsay declared further that "Mr. Grew had indicated to Sir Robert Craigie that he himself believed that, for reasons of expediency, a preliminary flat statement that the two Governments would refuse to transmit any proposals other than those in accordance with the Nine Power Treaty might not be necessary." Concerning his own response, Welles wrote,

In reply, I said to Sir Ronald Lindsay that my recollection was very clear that . . . Mr. Grew had indicated plainly that he felt it would be inadmissible for the two Governments to transmit peace proposals which were in any way counter to the provisions of the Nine Power Treaty and that he had felt that it would be essential for this position to be made clear to the Japanese Government. I said that . . . I considered it inconceivable that either the British Government or the United States Government would be willing to act as intermediaries in the reaching of a peace between China and Japan of a character contrary to the principles embodied in the Nine Power Treaty.

At this point Lindsay asserted that while the attitude of his government was fundamentally in accord with the views expressed by Welles, nevertheless as a practical matter it might be difficult for the Japanese Foreign Office to procure the assent of the Japanese army and navy to the good offices of the United States and Great Britain if, at the outset, the two governments made an "unqualified statement" to the effect that they would not serve as a medium of communication for terms which were not in keeping with the Nine Power Treaty. Welles replied that in negotiations of this character the policy of any government must of course be determined by circumstances as they developed but that in his opinion the only sound stand for Great Britain and the United States to take was to make their position "morally secure and perfectly plain" to Japan and China from the outset.

On December 13, the British made a final effort to get the State Department to adopt what they clearly regarded as a more realistic attitude. In a note which was again given to Welles by Ambassador Lindsay, the British suggested that the problem concerning the transference of proposals that were inconsistent with the Nine Power

Treaty might be overcome if Great Britain and the United States made it clear that they were in no way responsible for the proposals but were merely seeking to encourage an exchange of views which might eventually lead to a settlement.[97] It might be objected—the British said—that such a procedure would hardly amount to more than direct negotiations; but it seemed probable that if the Japanese were willing to communicate their terms to the British and American governments, they would frame them more moderately than in a direct approach to the Chinese government. Once aware of the conditions laid down by both parties, Great Britain and the United States could consult as to the "possibility or propriety of attempting to bring the [two] sides nearer together."

The British note was presumably written before news reached London or Washington of the sinking of the U.S.S. *Panay* on December 12. In handing the note to Welles, Lindsay referred to the *Panay* and reopened the subject of "secret and confidential staff discussions between Great Britain and the United States." This matter will be considered later in connection with the diplomatic crisis between the United States and Japan which followed the *Panay* incident and lasted until the end of December. The point here is that the British ceased at this time to urge an offer of Anglo-American good offices so that the entire issue was dropped. At any rate, by mid-December Germany had renewed its efforts to initiate negotiations to end the hostilities in the Far East and developments between Japan and China were rapidly moving toward a climax.

Apparently at the time of the intensive Japanese "peace drive" in mid-November Hirota told Ambassador Dirksen that he was ready to discuss a settlement with the Nanking government and that despite Japan's conquest of Shanghai the terms would not be more severe than those which had been presented to the Generalissimo through the German ambassador at Nanking a few weeks earlier; in particular, he said, the Japanese government still did not intend to demand the autonomy of North China.[98] The German government decided to inform Chiang Kai-shek of this new overture but delayed action presumably because it felt that the Chinese would be more likely to respond after the Brussels Conference closed. An interview was finally arranged for Ambassador Trautman with the Generalissimo on December 2.[99] According to a document published years later by Wang Ching-wei, which was purportedly part of the record of the Chinese Supreme National Defense Council, Chiang Kai-shek held a meeting of the leading Chinese generals just before seeing Ambassador Trautmann and informed them of the terms that the Japanese proposed in early November.[100] The generals indicated that they were in favor of reaching an agreement with Japan. The Generalissimo thereupon told Ambassador Trautmann that he would be willing to open negotiations on the basis of the conditions which the Japanese had outlined earlier and which Trautmann assured him remained unchanged.[101] Chiang Kai-shek specifically stated, however, that he could not accept the view that Japan was a victor imposing terms upon the vanquished. He stipulated, moreover, that he would not agree to any proposals that violated the sovereignty and administrative integrity of North China. On the other hand, when questioned by Ambassador Trautmann concerning the demand for the autonomy of Inner Mongolia, the Generalissimo said that an understanding could be reached with the Japanese on this subject and also expressed his willingness to appoint officials in North China that were friendly to Japan. The Generalissimo further asked that the Germans participate in the peace talks so that the Chinese would not be left to engage in direct negotiations with the Japanese. The German ambassador explained that while his government would do what it could to help China behind the scenes, it could not serve actively as a mediator but was simply offering its good offices.

On December 7 Ambassador Dirksen told Foreign Minister Hirota that the Chinese were ready to discuss a peace settlement.[102] Hirota replied that he would obtain the views of the army and navy but that he "doubted whether it would be possible to negotiate on the basis drawn up a month ago." The ambassador reminded the Foreign Minister that as late as mid-November he had said the Japanese terms remained the same. Hirota responded that the military events of the preceding weeks had altered the situation.

The facts of the matter were that the political situation inside Japan was rapidly undergoing a profound change. The Japanese armies in Central China were pushing toward Nanking and had penetrated the outer defenses of that city by the end of the first week in December, preparatory to its capture. The spectacular victories of the Japanese forces were inevitably increasing the power of the commanders in the field who were urging Tokyo to adopt a policy, not only of continuing the war, but of breaking off all relations with Chiang Kai-shek's administration and establishing in its stead a puppet regime completely under Japanese control.[103] Moreover, the so-called expansionist groups in the army had the support of the Japanese people, who by this time had been so aroused by war propaganda that anti-Chinese feeling was at a high pitch throughout Japan. In the face of these conditions, the more moderate elements in the Japanese government were in the process of surrendering to the extremists. Prince Konoye, who had been continuously vacillating under pressure from one side or the other, had virtually lost all control of the situation and was in one of his periodic moods of threatening to resign. Foreign Minister Hirota was in an intensely difficult—if not actually dangerous—position because the young officers of the General Staff and War Ministry had indirectly learned about the proposals for a settlement which Hirota had suggested to the Chinese and were reportedly threatening to "kill him."[104] The leaders of the General Staff alone remained firm in their original conviction that all military activity in Japan must be subordinated to the necessity of preparing for war with the Soviet Union and therefore continued to press for the termination of hostilities in China at the earliest possible moment and a settlement with the Chiang Kai-shek regime which would leave the Generalissimo in power.

Following Hirota's talk with Ambassador Dirksen, a new plan for an agreement with China was drafted by the Ministry of Foreign Affairs.[105] Severe in its terms, it was made even more severe at the request of several members of the Cabinet, including the War Minister, at a conference of December 14. The final text was adopted at a Liaison Conference between the Government and General Staff on December 20, but it was decided that instead of handing it to Ambassador Dirksen for transmission to the Chinese to give him only four very generally worded provisions. This decision was based upon the assumption that, if the Japanese government revealed all its conditions for a settlement and Chiang Kai-shek rejected them, it might be looked upon as a diplomatic defeat for Japan which would have violent repercussions domestically, given the warlike mood of the Japanese people.[106]

On December 23 Hirota informed Ambassador Dirksen that the Japanese government would enter into peace negotiations if China accepted four general conditions: the establishment of demilitarized zones and special regimes "wherever necessary"; the abandonment of her pro-Communist as well as her anti-Japanese and anti-Manchurian policies; the conclusion of an agreement for close economic cooperation between Japan, Manchuria, and China; and the payment of an indemnity.[107] The Foreign Minister stated further that if the Chinese consented to these basic terms and gave proof of their genuine intention to fulfill them, they were to send a delegation to negotiate at a place to be designated by the Japanese. In addition, the Chinese were to reply to Japan before the end of December.

Ambassador Dirksen stated frankly that the demands Hirota had outlined were far more drastic than those communicated to him in early November and that in his opinion it was "extremely improbable" that the Chinese government would accept them. He elicited a somewhat fuller explanation of some of the terms from Hirota but only on the understanding that the information provided to him was "very secret" and under no circumstances to be passed on to the Chinese. The stipulation in regard to the demilitarized zones, Hirota said, would require the creation of zones in Inner Mongolia, North China, and the Shanghai-Nanking area. A "special regime" was only contemplated for Inner Mongolia but the administration in North China was to have extensive powers of its own though still remaining under Chinese sovereignty. The Chinese would have to recognize Manchukuo and economic cooperation between Manchukuo, Japan, and China was to involve agreements on such items as tariff and trade.[108]

The German Foreign Office hesitated to hand such drastic proposals to Chiang Kai-shek but finally decided that having already committed itself to undertake the functions of a "letter carrier" it would do so.[109] Ambassador Trautmann went to see the Generalissimo on December 26 but, as Chiang Kai-shek was ill, gave the substance of the Japanese demands to H. H. Kung and Mme. Chiang Kai-shek, both of whom (according to the ambassador's account to Berlin) demonstrated the "deepest consternation."[110] Kung said subsequently that no nation could accept such conditions—"they might mean anything, ten special regimes, ten demilitarized zones."[111] In an effort to ameliorate the situation, Ambassador Dirksen, after receiving permission from Hirota, transmitted to the Chinese government some of the explanations of the terms which the Foreign Minister had given him confidentially stating that these were his own personal impressions of the concrete conditions which the Japanese had in mind.[112] He also induced the Japanese to extend the time limit for the Chinese reply to January 10.[113]

No Chinese reply had been received by January 10, however. In the meantime, the General Staff was more urgently than ever demanding a quick solution. In a last effort to reach an agreement between the General Staff and various factions within the government at Tokyo, a series of liaison and other conferences were held culminating in an Imperial Conference on January 11, conducted in the presence of the Emperor to give the decisions which had been reached earlier a stamp of finality.[114] The terms of the plan for a settlement which emerged were similar to those that had already been communicated to Ambassador Dirksen except that they were made even harsher by adding a provision for the stationing of Japanese troops in certain districts in North and Central China and in Inner Mongolia "for the purpose of security for the period of time deemed necessary." The basic principle governing the plan was that if the Chiang Kai-shek administration showed a sincere desire for reconciliation with Japan, the Japanese government would continue to negotiate with it and would, when the conditions of peace had been sufficiently fulfilled, rescind some of the "provisions of guarantee" such as the stationing of Japanese troops in China and the maintenance of demilitarized zones, et cetera; however, if the Chinese government demonstrated no desire to be conciliatory, Japan would sponsor the formation of a new central government in China and would "annihilate" the regime of Chiang Kai-shek. Thus the wishes of the General Staff were met to the extent that, if the Chinese reply proved satisfactory, negotiations with the Generalissimo were to continue.

On January 14, Ambassador Dirksen finally received the text of the Chinese reply from Ambassador Trautmann.[115] This stated briefly that after due consideration the Chinese government had found the new conditions presented by the Japanese "too broad in scope" and that it desired therefore "to be apprised of the nature and content" of the terms so that it could subject them to a careful examination and reach a definite decision. Ambassador Dirksen gave the Chinese note to Foreign Minister Hirota who said at once that he regarded it as wholly inadequate and no more than a "plain subterfuge" on the part of the Chinese to stall for time without any intent to consider seriously the Japanese proposals.[116] On learning of the Foreign Minister's remarks, Kung sent him an oral message on January 15 to the effect that the Chinese government had not meant to be "evasive" and still hoped to arrive at a genuine understanding with Japan.[117]

Kung's action, if it ever had a chance of exercising a moderating influence on Tokyo, was taken too late to receive any consideration. For only a few hours after Ambassador Dirksen handed Hirota the Chinese reply, on January 14, the Liaison Conference met and, overruling the opposition of the General Staff, decided to put an end to all negotiations with the Chiang Kai-shek government and to continue the war until China had been fully conquered.[118] Two days later, the Japanese government issued a formal statement in which it declared that it would henceforth cease to deal with the Chinese National Government and that it looked forward to "the establishment and growth of a new Chinese regime" with which it could effectively cooperate for the "building up of a rejuvenated China."[119]

In contrast to the extreme secrecy which surrounded the first effort of the Germans to serve as intermediaries, a considerable amount was known about the second effort from the very beginning. The Chinese

Foreign Office itself informed the American and other missions in China on December 3 that, as the Brussels Conference was over, the Chinese government "in principle" had accepted the good offices of the Germans.[120] Chinese officials seemed very uncertain, however, about what to do next and repeatedly approached United States officials, both in China and in Washington, for advice and also for information concerning the future policy of the United States. The Secretary of State himself took the lead in trying to impress upon the Chinese that they should not expect aid from the United States—a warning which was constantly repeated by other American authorities including Nelson Johnson.[121] At the same time, Johnson privately expressed the view that the Chinese had reached the end of their power to put up any effective resistance and that it was only a matter of time before they would enter into formal negotiations with the Japanese to get the best terms that circumstances would permit.[122]

By the third week in December, the Chinese were in fact showing signs of desperation, presumably having learned of the direction in which events were moving in Tokyo. On December 24, Chiang Kai-shek addressed a personal message to President Roosevelt in which he stated that while the Chinese were making the "supreme sacrifice" in man power and resources in combating the Japanese, they were not fighting only to defend themselves but also to defend the "principle of the sanctity of treaties especially the Nine Power Treaty."[123] The Generalissimo then went on to refer to the traditional policy of the United States in the Far East, with its interest in the maintenance of treaty rights and law and order, and appealed to the President to provide China with the assistance necessary to bring "the struggle for the cause of world peace . . . to a successful conclusion."

The Generalissimo's message was not handed to Roosevelt until December 31. By that time, the Japanese had presented the Chinese government with the four basic conditions upon which they were willing to reach a settlement. Nelson Johnson, who had been confidentially informed of the conditions, cabled them to Washington.[124] Johnson himself commented that while the Japanese proposals consisted on the surface only of broad principles they were sufficient to afford the Japanese military the opportunity they wanted of establishing "a very clear and complete domination of China."[125] President Roosevelt apparently agreed with Johnson's estimate for, on being told that he (the President) had been quoted in Nanking as having said that the Japanese terms were "very lenient," Roosevelt sent word to the Chinese ambassador in Washington that he regarded them as "utterly impossible."[126]

The opening days of January were filled with tension in the Far East while the Japanese government was awaiting the Chinese reply. As early as the first of January, the Chinese Vice Minister for Foreign Affairs told Ambassador Johnson that China could not accept the Japanese conditions as a basis for negotiations.[127] Again, on January 11, the Vice Minister asserted that all "important persons" in the Chinese government believed that "China had no choice but to resist Japan as long as possible" and that they believed additionally that as Japan advanced into the interior of China, Chinese resistance would become more effective and that "the United States and Great Britain would finally take joint action" to restrain the Japanese.[128]

The State Department made no move until January 12, when Hull, in reaction to reports that an Imperial Conference had been convened, sent Grew a cable which said,

It has occurred to the Department that possibly a useful purpose might be served if there could be conveyed to the Japanese Government at this time when the Imperial Conference has under consideration matters of the greatest import, mention of points as follows: that the eyes of the world are on Japan; that the nature of the decisions reached by the Conference may have a profound effect upon the welfare and prosperity of the whole world; that the fighting which has been going on in China in the past six months has seriously disturbed all normal and mutually beneficial activities in and with regard to China; that the fighting is producing political and economic and social dislocations and tensions which affect adversely not only China and Japan but other countries as well; that there is no way by which the countries of the world or even Japan can escape various adverse effects of and from the present conflict and that prolongation and further extension and intensification of the hostilities will inevitably . . . add to the chance of unfortunate international complications; that we are convinced that practical application of the principles set forth in my statement of July 16 would be in the best interests of Japan as well as other countries; and that we earnestly hope that the decisions of the Japanese Government will be fully in keeping with the best traditions of wise, high-minded and farseeing Japanese statesmanship.[129]

The Secretary added that Ambassador Grew should use his discretion as to whether to deliver the content of this cable to the Japanese government. If he did so, it should, however, be made clear that the United States government was not contemplating any mediation between Japan and China and that no part of the Secretary's communications should be so construed.

On January 14, the day that the Japanese secretly decided to break off relations with the Chinese government, Grew wired the Secretary that he had arrived at the conclusion that it would be better not to approach the Japanese government along the lines which Hull had suggested.[130] "I have little doubt," Grew said, "that the proposed representations by the American Ambassador seeking to influence or to modify the decisions of the Imperial Conference as contrasted with the protection of specific American interests would be interpreted at this moment as an effort to interfere with the prerogative of the Emperor."

At about the same time that Hull had wired Grew concerning the Imperial Conference, the State Department had drafted a letter which was to serve as the President's reply to Chiang Kai-shek's appeal for aid.[131] The letter, which reached the Generalissimo three days after the Japanese had publicly terminated relations with his government, scarcely offered the assistance which the Chinese had sought. The cause of peace, it declared, was one which the people and the government of the United States had "very much at heart." Constant study and thought was therefore being given to the ways and means by which the United States might "contribute more effectively toward promoting peace and facilitating international cooperation." It was to be hoped that out of the present conflict in the Far East, there would come a settlement which "by virtue of reasonable provisions, adequately considerate of the rights, legitimate interests and national integrity of all concerned," would provide a "basis for amicable relationships and an enduring peace."

On January 21, a final statement was made by Sumner Welles on the subject of American good offices in connection with the existing crisis in the Far East.[132] Kojiro Matsukata, who was in the United States on a kind of unofficial good will tour, came to see Welles to renew an appeal, which he had made earlier to Grew in Tokyo, for a proffer of good offices by the United States to China and Japan. Welles replied to Matsukata that it was his understanding that the German government had taken steps toward mediation a few weeks earlier and submitted Japanese peace proposals to the Chinese government which that government had found unacceptable. The United States government could not therefore take the initiative at this time and, in any event, if it were to embark upon an exercise of good offices it would have to be on the understanding that the terms were in keeping with the Nine Power Treaty. Matsukata (according to the official American memorandum on this interview) "appeared disconcerted" and said that if the United States "felt it must fall back on 'historical' ground . . . the problem was made very difficult." Welles responded that the American government "did not regard the Nine Power Treaty as being merely an 'historical' instrument" and repeated that the official American position was that the United States could act in the direction of mediation "only on the basis and in the light of its being understood that the settlement must be consistent with both the principles and the provisions of the Nine Power Treaty."

In conclusion, because of the very complex material which has been presented here, it may be well to summarize in the briefest possible form some outstanding points concerning the moves made by Japan to end the hostilities in China and the countermoves of the Chinese. The plan drawn up by the Japanese in August was largely based upon the idea that China should agree to a demilitarized zone in the North, the withdrawal of the central government troops from Hopei, and the general principles which had been covered in the past by Foreign Minister Hirota's so-called "three points": suppression of pro-Communist and anti-Japanese activities, Sino-Japanese economic cooperation, and better relations between China and "Manchukuo." In return, the control of North China was to be restored to the central government, the Japanese troops were to be reduced to the level prevailing before July, the demilitarized zone in the Shanghai area was to be abolished, and Japan was to cease attempting to undermine Nanking's authority in Inner Mongolia. The two latter concessions were withdrawn in October. Otherwise the August plan was retained as the basis upon which Japan sought to open negotiations until December, when the entire situation altered.

On the Chinese side, the Nanking government did not follow up the Japanese overtures in August because of the sudden extension of the war to Shanghai. Chiang Kai-shek responded to the second approach from Japan, which took place during the time that the Sino-Japanese dispute was under consideration at Geneva, by declaring his "bitter" opposition to any provision for a demilitarized zone. When the Japanese again sought to open negotiations, just as the Nine Power Conference was getting underway, the Generalissimo asserted that he could not possibly consider their proposals and that, in any case, the Sino-Japanese conflict was now the concern of the nations deliberating at Brussels. Following the close of the Brussels Conference, as Nanking was being threatened by the oncoming Japanese armies, the Generalissimo reversed himself and agreed to accept the Japanese terms as a basis for discussing a settlement.

As to the Japanese attempt to use third powers to serve as intermediaries, the first tentative efforts were made in early September and resulted in establishing contact with Nanking through Sir Robert Craigie at the end of the month. In late October, Foreign Minister Hirota made an indirect appeal to the ambassadors of the four nations whose good offices seemed most desirable to either one or another of the conflicting factions in Japan: England, America, Germany, and Italy. This led to the transmission of proposals to Chiang Kai-shek through the medium of the German government in early November. In the middle of November, when military developments were at an especially critical stage, Hirota again made guarded attempts to obtain the assistance of one or more of the four powers to open negotiations. On this occasion he seems to have been particularly anxious to obtain the help of the United States. In the end, however, the Germans renewed their efforts to act as a channel of communication.

It is obvious that by the time the Generalissimo consented to enter into discussions with Japan, the mood of the whole Japanese nation had so hardened that the government at Tokyo—even including the General Staff with its urgent desire to forestall a prolonged war—was no longer thinking in terms of reaching a settlement with China but rather of imposing conditions on the Chinese which were so extreme that no people with any power of resistance would have submitted to them. Even Japan's early proposals were considerably more severe than the Japanese themselves seemed to recognize. For while they involved substantial concessions on the part of Japan they also made substantial demands upon China. Furthermore they sought to perpetuate the general concepts embodied in Hirota's "three points," which had become anathema to the Chinese, partly because they had been used as political weapons by Japan in the past and partly because they were a symbol of the domineering attitude of the Japanese, who seemed simply to assume that the Chinese had always to give ground before them. Whether the Japanese would have moderated their terms in substance or tone if Great Britain and the United States, serving as intermediaries, had attempted to exercise persuasion or pressure (or—as the British wanted—both) is, of course, a highly speculative subject.[133] The balance between those forces in Japan that were for, and those that were against, the continuation of the war was a fine one and what might have been done depended no doubt in measure upon the proper timing. Perhaps one of the moments when the Japanese would have been most likely to be conciliatory was in the last stages of the battle for Shanghai, when Hirota greatly intensified his efforts to open negotiations with China in the apparent belief that, once the campaign for the capture of Nanking had started, it would be almost impossible to terminate the hostilities in the face of the heightened opposition within the Japanese army.

The question of the kind of an agreement which the Chinese government might have accepted again leads us into the area of guesswork. The Nationalist movement in China was at its height at the outbreak of the war and the demand for resistance to the Japanese was great throughout the country. Moreover, in the weeks after the Marco Polo Bridge incident there was considerable optimism in China about the ability of the Chinese armies to withstand the Japanese attack partly because it was thought that the Japanese government was in no position to send more than a limited number of divisions to China.[134] It would therefore have been very difficult for the Generalissimo to conclude any understanding with Japan that would not have endangered the existence of his government, even if (as was widely thought at the time) he had wanted to do so. This situation may well have continued to prevail in early August when the Japanese first approached the Chinese for an over-all settlement, even though by that time a vital part of North China had fallen to the Japanese. However, as the struggle for Shanghai progressed and the tide of military events turned disastrously against the Chinese, conditions inevitably underwent a great change and the only alternative to reaching an agreement seemed to be to permit the almost immediate conquest of China by Japan. It is therefore probable that at least by mid-November the Generalissimo would have entered into negotiations with Japan if the Brussels Conference had not raised his hopes of obtaining assistance from the West. And, as has just been indicated, it is possible that at this time the Japanese would have been relatively conciliatory. Nevertheless, having been severely defeated at the battlefront, the Chinese would certainly have had to make some definite concessions. The general nature of the concessions which they had in mind before the fall of Shanghai may perhaps be judged by the proposals which were drawn up by a group of Chinese intellectuals and, according to Nelson Johnson, were not dissimilar to the instructions sent to the Chinese delegates at Brussels as a possible basis for a peace Treaty. These concessions, it will be recalled, included such matters as a narrow demilitarized zone in North China and in the Shanghai district, *de facto* relations with Manchuria, a willingness to consider Japan's economic needs in the development of North China, and a Sino-Japanese nonaggression pact. Presumably, after the fall of Shanghai, the Chinese would have gone further toward meeting Japan's demands rather than continue fighting in view of the fact that the chances of being able to hold out and avert complete disaster appeared to be so exceedingly slim.

Concerning the attitude of the United States toward the moves and countermoves of Japan and China, it need hardly be re-emphasized that American officials failed to see what was taking place. That Grew was unaware of the trend of developments was probably owing in part to the extreme secrecy with which the elements in Japan that were opposed to the Sino-Japanese war operated for their own protection, and in part to ordinary human fallibility. Having once received the impression that the Japanese did not want any settlement with China until they had virtually subdued that country and that they would resent any outside interference, Ambassador Grew was not likely to keep pushing the subject of good offices under circumstances which might damage relations between the United States and Japan. Consequently, for the most part he took the position that the only way in which the United States could be useful would be to stave off the complete collapse of China after the Japanese had achieved their aims. When Grew finally did recognize that Japan wanted to terminate the war, it seems evident that, contrary to Sumner Welles' opinion, his sense of realism led him to suppose that the most practical approach was to try to get the Chinese and Japanese together without first insisting that the United States would not lend its good offices unless assured that the Japanese terms would conform to the Nine Power Treaty. In short, Grew shared the British view that Great Britain and the United States should exercise what influence they could after the negotiations started.

Nelson Johnson, while in agreement with some of Grew's estimate of the situation, would not have gone along with him all the way. By the time of the outbreak of the Sino-Japanese war, Johnson was convinced of the necessity of the Generalissimo's staying in power if China was to survive as a nation, and he believed that the Nationalist movement among the Chinese was so strong that any settlement containing genuine concessions to the Japanese would inevitably invite the overthrow of the Chiang Kai-shek regime. After several months of warfare, however, Johnson, like Grew, came to expect a quick and complete victory by the Japanese. But this did not lead him to think in terms of the United States' serving as an intermediary to help bring about a settlement between Japan and China and, if his advice had been sought by the State Department, he would probably have opposed a proffer of good offices because of his belief that, in the last analysis, the Sino-Japanese situation was not the responsibility of the United States.

The State Department in Washington, on its part, spoke its mind in a manner which left not a shadow of doubt as to its position. It would not, it said, pass messages to and from Japan and China unless the Japanese proposals were consonant with the Nine Power Treaty. At the same time the Department recognized that the Japanese were scarcely likely to write off their victories in China to the extent of making no claims upon the Chinese that would constitute a violation of that treaty. In view of these circumstances, one of the few ways in which the Department might have taken action was to suggest the type of "constructive" peace it had visualized in the draft for a settlement which had been drawn up within the Department in October for possible use by the American delegation at the Brussels Conference. For this draft would to a large extent have avoided discussion of the demands which the Japanese had made and were making upon the Chinese by seeking instead to remove the causes of Japanese aggression in China through compensations affected by the joint action of all the powers with interests in the Far East. Whether the compensations would have seemed sufficient to the Japanese to offset the major concessions to which they themselves would have had to agree, to conform to the terms of the draft, is decidedly open to question. The main point, however, is that the approach envisaged in the draft was never put to the test and the administration was left with the policy which it had pursued from the beginning, of insisting upon its unwillingness to take any step that might be interpreted as assenting to a move by Japan which was a breach of the Nine Power Treaty. In this instance such a policy severely circumscribed any attempts to explore the possibilities of a Sino-Japanese settlement.

THE CRISIS

On November 22, 1937, as the fighting between the Japanese and Chinese armies was drawing close to Nanking, Ambassador Johnson, at the request of the Chinese Minister for Foreign Affairs, moved to Hankow taking with him most of his staff.[1] Four officials of the embassy remained at the capital, however, in order to take care of official business until the moment arrived which made their departure absolutely essential. The United States gunboat *Panay* was ordered to stand by and evacuate the embassy personnel when the time came.

On December 9, as the Japanese troops were approaching Nanking, the embassy officers boarded the *Panay* accompanied by four other Americans and five foreigners among whom were several newspaper correspondents. The boat proceeded upstream and anchored several times, but finding itself surrounded by shellfire from Japanese shore batteries moved on again until, on December 12, it settled about twenty-eight miles above Nanking with a convoy of three Standard Oil Company tankers. Every time the *Panay* changed its location the Japanese authorities were notified through the United States Consul at Shanghai. Moreover Grew was informed of developments, with the result that he called upon the Japanese Minister of Foreign Affairs and requested that all necessary steps be taken to restrain the Japanese military in China from further endangering the lives of Americans by continuing to drop shells in the vicinity of the *Panay*.[2]

On the morning of December 12, the news was received in Washington that H.M.S. *Ladybird* had been fired upon by the Japanese and that one seaman had been killed and several wounded.[3] A few hours later, Ambassador Johnson cabled from Hankow that all attempts to establish contact with the *Panay* had been unsuccessful for several hours.[4] Around midnight another dispatch arrived from Johnson stating that George Atcheson, the senior diplomatic officer on board the *Panay*, had managed to reach Dr. Taylor, an American missionary at Anking, by telephone and informed him that the *Panay* had been bombed and sunk and that there were fifty-four survivors. Atcheson had stated further that the Standard Oil Company's ships were also sunk. Beyond this he had supplied few details.

Ambassador Johnson's message was quickly followed by a cable from Ambassador Grew, who said that the Minister for Foreign Affairs had just called upon him in person to tell him of the receipt of a Domei report to the effect that, "in following fleeing remnants of the Chinese Army," Japanese planes had bombed three Standard Oil vessels and had sunk the U.S.S. *Panay*.[5] The Minister had as yet obtained no official information but had come to the chancery immediately to offer the "profound apology" of the Japanese government to the United States government. Ambassador Saito in Washington had been instructed to convey expressions of regret to Secretary Hull, and the Navy and War Ministers were taking similar action in respect to the United States Navy and War Departments. Grew's dispatch concluded with the statement, "Hirota said, 'I cannot possibly express how badly we feel about this.'"

On the morning of December 13, before keeping a hastily made appointment to see Ambassador Saito, Hull went to the White House and gave the President all the facts which were so far available concerning the *Panay* disaster.[6] Roosevelt thereupon dictated the following memorandum for the Secretary:

Please tell the Japanese ambassador when you see him . . . :

1. That the President is deeply shocked and concerned by the news of indiscriminate bombing of American and other non-Chinese vessels on the Yangtze, and that he requests that the Emperor be so advised.

2. That all the facts are being assembled and will shortly be presented to the Japanese Government.

3. That in the meantime it is hoped the Japanese Government will be considering definitely for presentation to this Government:

    a. Full expression of regret and proffer of full compensation;

    b. Methods guaranteeing against a repetition of any similar attack in the future.

When Saito was received by Hull, the ambassador said that, owing to poor visibility, the airplanes attacking the *Panay* had mistaken it for a Chinese troopship but that, as Japanese officials had been informed by American authorities of the whereabouts of the *Panay*, this was a "very grave blunder" and his government wished to tender "full and sincere apologies."[7] The Secretary replied that "we here" in Washington had never been quite so astonished by any occurrence as by "this promiscuous bombing of neutral vessels upon the Yangtze." He then read to the ambassador the text of the President's memorandum and added that the United States government, after concluding an investigation of the facts involved in the assault upon the

Panay, would comment to the Japanese government in the light of its findings. Shortly after his talk with Saito, the Secretary sent a formal note to Ambassador Grew for presentation to Hirota which re-emphasized the points made by the President, stating that the United States expected an apology from Japan, "complete and comprehensive indemnifications," and "an assurance that definite and specific steps have been taken which will ensure that hereafter American nationals, interests and property in China will not be subjected to attack by Japanese armed forces or unlawful interference by any Japanese authorities or force whatsoever."[8]

But before the Secretary's note reached Tokyo, the Japanese government had itself dispatched a note to the State Department in which it continued to take the position that the attack upon the *Panay* had been "entirely due to a mistake" but that it nevertheless desired to extend its "sincere apologies."[9] A similar statement was made to the British concerning the shelling of the *Ladybird,* and moreover it was made clear that in respect to both incidents the Japanese government was prepared to pay indemnities and, after proper investigation, to punish those whom it found responsible.[10] In delivering the State Department's message to Hirota, Ambassador Grew pointed out that the Japanese communication was not fully responsive to the American demands, especially the request for assurances concerning the future safety of American nationals and their interests, and that he would therefore expect an answer.[11] The Foreign Minister said that he would make a prompt reply and added, "I wish to do everything in my power to maintain good relations with the United States."[12] Grew himself was convinced of the sincerity of the Japanese government in trying to make amends and moreover was deeply affected by the letters which were flowing into the embassy from Japanese in all walks of life who sought to convey their feeling of profound distress at the *Panay* disaster and their hope that it would not "irretrievably injure American-Japanese friendship."[13]

The initial exchanges between Japanese and American officials over the *Panay* crisis were paralleled by exchanges between British and American officials. Early on the morning of December 13 an urgent dispatch was received in the State Department from Johnson, the United States chargé to the United Kingdom, who stated that he had just seen Eden, at the latter's request, and that the Foreign Secretary had said that both he and the Prime Minister were greatly concerned over the attacks upon the *Panay* and the *Ladybird* which, in their opinion, could not possibly have been accidental.[14] They were about to send instructions to Sir Ronald Lindsay and hoped most earnestly that Hull would not take any action until he had heard what the ambassador had to say. While they were fully aware of the difficulties which the administration in Washington faced in making any move that might be interpreted as "joint action" with the British, nevertheless they attached great importance to being consulted in this instance and felt strongly that the more closely the steps taken by the American and British governments were "synchronized" the greater the effect upon the Japanese would be.

Later in the morning, Sir Ronald read to Sumner Welles the Foreign Office's instructions which by that time had arrived from London and which expressed even more forcefully than Eden had orally the British government's belief that the United States and Great Britain must act "jointly."[15] By way of reply Welles said that his government would probably demand complete guarantees against the recurrence of an incident similar to that of the sinking of the *Panay*; that it might adopt additional measures when all the facts were known; and that, in any event, the State Department would be glad to inform the Foreign Office before making any formal representations to the Japanese. The Under Secretary, however, deliberately omitted any reference to the British request for "joint action."[16] Nevertheless the ambassador himself at the end of their interview reverted to the important subject of possible staff conversations between the United States and British navies.[17] As Welles recorded the matter,

. . . , the British Ambassador said that he had a further instruction to communicate to me, which was that if this Government were prepared to discuss the possibility of secret and confidential staff discussions between Great Britain and the United States, he, the Ambassador, had instructions to arrange for such conversations immediately. The Ambassador added that it was because of his belief that such occurrences as the sinking of the U.S.S. *Panay* would occur that the British Government had made this suggestion. I told the Ambassador that I had taken careful note of this communication which he made to me, but that I had no response at this moment to make to him with regard thereto.

While Sir Ronald did not link the issue of staff talks with naval demonstrations as he had previously, Johnson in another cable from London on December 13 told the Department that Sir Alexander Cadogan had also sought to impress upon him the great importance of "British and American action being at least along synchronized parallel lines" and that in his (Johnson's) opinion what the British seemed in reality to want was "the moving of the fleet."[18] Johnson added that he felt the British were "not displeased" that American interests were so definitely involved in the incidents which had taken place in the Far East and that they hoped the reaction of the administration and the public in the United States would be sufficiently strong to result in some "positive action." The British did not believe that the end of the Sino-Japanese conflict was in sight and they feared that the hostilities might soon spread to Canton where their own interests predominated.

Despite the unusual urgency of the British request for joint, or carefully planned cooperative action, the United States government proceeded to act independently. Hull did not inform the British of the step he was taking before reading the President's memorandum to Ambassador Saito. Nor did he make any effort to consult with them in advance of sending the State Department's formal note of protest to the Japanese government, though the note was not dispatched until the evening of December 13. Moreover in wiring the text to Ambassador Grew for delivery, the Secretary specifically stated, "Before seeing Hirota inform your British colleague of intended action and text but do not thereafter await action by him."[19] Two days later in a further discussion of joint Anglo-American action with Sir Ronald Lindsay, Sumner Welles asserted that "concurrent or parallel action was preferable and equally effective" and added that, as of course the ambassador must recognize, he was "conveying the President's views in this regard."[20]

The British were very outspoken concerning their disappointment over the failure of the American government to respond to their appeals. Sir Ronald Lindsay delivered a message from Eden to Hull, which said that the Foreign Minister regretted that the State Department had "stepped out so far ahead" of the British in dealing with the Japanese and that he was convinced a "show of possibilities of force on a large scale" was necessary to restrain the Japanese military from committing further outrages against foreign nationals; unfortunately Great Britain did not have sufficient naval strength to make an adequate showing alone both in Europe and the Far East at this time although she hoped to remedy this situation within the next year.[21] Sir Ronald moreover expressed "a very great concern" over an article by Ferdinand Kuhn on the front page of the *New York Times* which, under the headline BRITAIN ABANDONS HOPE OF JOINT MOVE, stated in effect that Eden had sought to drag the United States into a joint naval policy that would have committed the American fleet to defend British interests in the Far East but that he had been unsuccessful.[22] The article went on to say that as Britain herself was too scared of Germany to send more than two battleships to the Pacific she had no alternative other than to face a "terrific loss" of prestige in Europe and Asia.

Following the first days of the *Panay* crisis, the British government ceased to speak of joint action to officials in Washington and according to reports in the press even the English newspapers, which had been filled with editorials asking for some sort of Anglo-American punitive measures against Japan, fell silent on this subject in the belief that any further effort to prod the United States would do more harm than good.[23] The crisis itself, however, was by no means over and indeed suddenly grew far worse.

It was impossible to get any detailed information concerning the sinking of the *Panay* until eye-witness accounts could be obtained. This did not occur until the first few survivors arrived by plane in Shanghai on December 15, to be followed two days later by the remainder on board the U.S.S. *Oahu*. The newspapers were then flooded with articles consisting not only of interviews with the survivors by Shanghai correspondents but also of vivid first-hand stories written by reporters who had themselves been on board the *Panay*.[24] Moreover Admiral Yarnell sent brief dispatches to Washington containing the results of his own investigations (which shortly thereafter were taken over by a special United States Naval Court of Inquiry) and on December 17 George Atcheson wired his preliminary report to the State Department.[25]

The facts as related by the survivors differed little in their essentials.[26] Far from the visibility having been poor—as the Japanese claimed—on the day the *Panay* was sunk, the weather had been clear · and still. The gunboat carried United States flags and had American colors conspicuously printed on its awnings; the Standard Oil tankers had similar marks of identification. The vessels were first hit by Japanese planes which released their bombs from a considerable height. Immediately thereafter a group of six planes power-dived at the *Panay* in succession, dropping bombs and machine-gunning the ship for about twenty minutes. Subsequently the Standard Oil boats were also attacked, the captain of one was killed, and the tankers themselves destroyed. As the *Panay*, having been repeatedly struck, began to sink rapidly it was abandoned and some of the wounded, including all of the officers, were carried into a marsh on shore where they were hidden among tall reeds. While the ship settled, two Japanese patrol boats appeared and opened fire; their officers then boarded the *Panay* for several minutes, although the United States flag was still in plain view. Later three Japanese bombers came down river and circled over the marsh where by now all the survivors were concealed. The action of the planes coupled with the previous action of the patrol boats convinced the survivors that the Japanese were searching for them to destroy all witnesses. They consequently waited until after dark before attempting to find shelter and then gradually made their way to a nearby village from which, on the following morning, George Atcheson was able to establish contact by telephone with Dr. Taylor at Anking. But before relief could be obtained, two of the wounded died.

It was apparently not until December 16 that officials in Washington began to recognize that the attack upon the *Panay* involved circumstances which they had scarcely envisaged. The advance accounts of eye-witnesses had by this time arrived and the President gave instructions to have them verified.[27] The facts as related were so appalling, however, that Hull cabled Ambassador Grew to tell Foreign Minister Hirota that, while the United States government was still awaiting complete information it was receiving fresh reports concerning the sinking of the *Panay* which presented a far more serious picture than earlier.[28] It would appear, the Secretary said, that the Japanese airplanes which had bombed the *Panay* had been flying at low altitudes; that Japanese army officers had machine-gunned and boarded the gunboat though its colors were clearly discernible; and that an effort had been made to exterminate all the survivors. There was therefore "very definite indication of deliberateness of intent" on the part of those who had been engaged in the assault.

Ambassador Grew cabled the State Department subsequently that he had spoken to Hirota in "the strongest possible way" in connection with the Secretary's message, and that the Foreign Minister, visibly upset, had said that he was "totally unaware" of the facts presented by Hull and would immediately take up the matter with the naval and military authorities.[29] While this sounded conciliatory, the comments of other Japanese officials did not. A representative of the Japanese navy told the United States naval attaché in Tokyo that the stories that the crew of a Japanese launch had machine-gunned the *Panay* and boarded the boat before it sank were contrary to the available evidence and to common sense.[30] Ambassador Saito called on Hull on December 17 to make a similar statement. But this was too much for the Secretary who, breaking through his self-restraint, said that if military officers in the United States acted as the Japanese had, they would be court-martialed and shot and that the question now was whether the Japanese government would deal properly with these "wild, runaway, half-insane" men.[31]

To make the situation worse, the foreign correspondents, who had remained in Nanking to witness the take-over of that city by the Japanese armies, arrived in Shanghai on board the U.S.S. *Oahu* together with the survivors of the *Panay*. As a result, the editions of the American newspapers which carried the accounts of the survivors also carried the first reports of the atrocities committed by the Japanese soldiers in the capital. A dispatch sent by Tillman Durdin to the *New York Times* stated, for example, that the Japanese had had a rare opportunity to win the confidence of the Chinese by restoring order to Nanking, but that they had engaged in wholesale looting, violation of women, and murder.[32] In an extraordinarily graphic passage Durdin wrote,

The killing of civilians was widespread. Foreigners who traveled widely through the city Wednesday found civilian dead on every street. Some of the victims were aged men, women and children . . .

Many victims were bayoneted and some of the wounds were barbarously cruel.

Any person who ran because of fear or excitement was likely to be killed on the spot . . . Many slayings were witnessed by foreigners . . .

Just before boarding the ship for Shanghai the writer watched the execution of 200 men on the Bund. The killings took ten minutes. The men were lined against a wall and shot. Then a number of Japanese, armed with pistols, trod nonchalantly about the crumpled bodies pumping bullets into any that were still kicking.

The army men performing the gruesome job had invited navy men from the warships anchored off the Bund to view the scene. A large group of military spectators apparently greatly enjoyed the spectacle.

The tension generated by the events which followed the *Panay* incident was probably at its height around December 17 and 18. It is, therefore, natural that the question of American policy received the most serious consideration at this time. Inevitably the issues which were uppermost were possible economic and/or naval action against Japan.

On the economic side, Secretary Morgenthau's account is so much more valuable than any other that it seems to justify the following summary, despite its length.[33] On December 14, the President said to Morgenthau that formerly the sinking of a naval boat would have been regarded as a declaration or cause of war but that this was no longer the case. Nevertheless, he would like to find out from some good lawyer, first, whether he had any authority to seize the possessions of the Japanese government and its citizens in the United States and hold them against payment for the damages done by Japan, and secondly, if he lacked this authority but went ahead anyhow, what could be done to him. The Secretary undertook to discuss these questions with Herman Oliphant, the General Counsel for the Treasury. Oliphant prepared a memorandum for Roosevelt on the following day in which he said that, pending further study of the matter from other angles, it would appear that under the 1933 amendment to the Trading with the Enemy Act the Chief Executive was authorized to find a national emergency existing, for example, by reason of the necessity to forestall acts and events which might plunge this nation into war, to quarantine a war situation which was endangering the United States, or to assure reparation in order to avoid the necessity of resort to force.[34] Upon such a declaration of national emergency, the President could prohibit transactions in foreign exchange, the withdrawal of bank credits in this country, or the export of gold or its proceeds owned by the Japanese government; the subject of private ownership would have to be examined further.

Roosevelt, reacting with enthusiasm to Oliphant's unusually imaginative suggestions, exclaimed that he had entirely forgotten about the Trading with the Enemy Act and asked Secretary Morgenthau to explore further the possibility of applying it along the lines Oliphant had indicated. The Secretary consequently met with a group of his advisers on the morning of December 17 and entered into a long discussion of technical problems the most important of which was that, granted the slightest opportunity, the Japanese would circumvent the proposed regulations by converting their assets into sterling. This difficulty seemed to necessitate, among other matters, obtaining the cooperation of the British and Secretary Morgenthau suggested sounding out Sir John Simon, then Chancellor of the Exchequer, by telephone. But some of those present felt that the entire plan was still too vague to warrant a talk with Sir John and asked Morgenthau whether, for example, he knew under what circumstances and for how long the regulations would be applied, to which he answered that he did not. During the course of further talk a political argument developed concerning the advisability of making a move such as that under discussion if it would lead to war. The Secretary with vehemence took the position that the country was ready for war and that he did not believe the American people should sit and wait until the Japanese progressively occupied the Philippines, Hawaii, and Panama. While this issue was still under hot debate, Morgenthau left to attend a cabinet meeting.

Returning to the Treasury after the cabinet meeting, the Secretary reported that the President had described the powers granted him under the Trading with the Enemy Act as defined in the Oliphant memorandum and had said, "We want these powers to be used to prevent war . . . After all, if Italy and Japan have evolved a technique of fighting without declaring war, why can't we develop a similar one?" As the meeting continued, the President kept reiterating that the British were way behind the times as they failed to realize that it was possible to use economic sanctions without declaring war and that he wanted to develop a modern technique to do just that. "We don't call them sanctions," he said, "we call them quarantines. We want to develop a technique which will not lead to war."

Morgenthau, himself quite excited about the idea of creating a new peace technique, thereupon put through his telephone call to Sir John Simon, having been authorized to do so by the President, who wanted the matter handled through the Treasury rather than through the State Department and kept as secret as possible. The Secretary outlined to Sir John the plan proposed in the Oliphant memorandum and explained that, while waiting for Japan's reply to our note concerning the *Panay*, the administration was exploring various steps it might take if the answer proved unsatisfactory. As anything like the Oliphant proposal would not be very effective without British cooperation, Morgenthau wanted to let Sir John know what was being talked about in Washington as he might care to think it over.

Sir John on his part indicated very clearly that he did not like to transact business over the telephone and that he had no desire to repeat the kind of misunderstanding that had occurred with Stimson during the Manchurian crisis. Nevertheless, he was prepared to discuss Morgenthau's suggestion with the Prime Minister.

After his conversation with Sir John Simon, Secretary Morgenthau saw the President again and found that, while he still wanted the Treasury to draft exchange regulations, he was "not in as great a hurry as he had been" and had "cooled off a bit." On the following day Roosevelt instructed Morgenthau to send Sir John Simon another message which said:

In pursuance my telephone conversation with you it is obvious that the subject is corollary to but an essential part of naval conversations and studies about to be made. The British Ambassador and your Foreign Office have been advised. With full concurrence of Secretary of State Hull we are asking the American officer who will shortly arrive in London to see you and obtain your views on the economic phase which I discussed with you by telephone.

The Treasury staff proceeded to formulate exchange regulations and, in addition, at the President's request investigated another scheme, namely the possibility of drawing up rules which might restrain the Japanese from using the Panama Canal. But Morgenthau was very disappointed because when the Treasury's work was completed Roosevelt showed no further interest in it. The Secretary was moreover further discouraged on hearing from Sir John Simon, who had spoken with both the Prime Minister and Eden. Sir John said the British would be happy to see the American officer who was coming to England. However, as far as the subject matter of his talk with Morgenthau was concerned, Great Britain had nothing comparable to the United States Trading with the Enemy Act, so that special legislation would be required. Furthermore, study and experience had convinced the Chamberlain government that in crises such as the present the economic factor could not be separated from the political and strategic. It was his personal belief that there were two kinds of economic pressure, gradual and long-range or immediate and drastic, and that the former served only as an irritant while the latter was indistinguishable from any other form of forceful action. All in all, Sir John's reply seemed to Morgenthau to add up to an emphatic rejection of the Treasury's approach.

This then is Secretary Morgenthau's story of the deliberations within the administration concerning possible economic measures against Japan. In respect to possible naval measures, the initial proposal for action was the British suggestion for a naval demonstration which the administration turned down apparently upon the decision of the President and Secretary Hull.[35] On December 14, Admiral Leahy, who ever since the outbreak of the Sino-Japanese conflict had been in favor of England and America joining together to wage war on Japan, urged the President to send the ships of the fleet to the navy yards without delay so that they could be cleaned and obtain fuel and stores preparatory to a cruise at sea.[36] But Roosevelt declared that he was not ready to take any such action. On December 17, the President discussed with Admiral Leahy the possibility of entering into staff talks with the British navy as the latter had suggested; also of sending some light cruisers to visit Singapore, at the time of the opening of the British naval base there in February, as a display of Anglo-American solidarity in the west Pacific.[37]

In addition, at a meeting of his cabinet on December 17, Roosevelt spoke of possible naval moves. In fact, in contrast to Secretary Morgenthau's description of the cabinet meeting, an account written by Secretary Ickes in his diary creates the impression that Roosevelt dwelt primarily on naval questions.[38] Ickes did record, however, that the President asserted he had wide powers under the Trading with the Enemy Act which, in effect, would enable him to "impose economic sanctions 'in order to prevent war,'" and that it was felt by the members of the cabinet that "if anything along this line were done, it should be after consultation and in cooperation with other democratic powers." As to the navy the President, according to Ickes, said that the American fleet could block Japan along a line running from the Aleutians to Hawaii, to Wake, to Guam, while the British could take over from there to Singapore. If such an operation were undertaken, Japan could be brought to her knees in a year; moreover it would be a "comparatively simple task which the navy could take care of without having to send a great fleet." (Ickes wrote subsequently that it was the President's belief that Japan "could be brought to terms without war" if the United States resorted to a naval blockade.) Roosevelt also referred to the subject of naval conversations with the British saying that such conversations had been conducted prior to the World War so that, when the United States entered the war, the naval plans were all ready. He further repeated a statement which he had made at an earlier cabinet meeting to the effect that he intended to deliver a special message to Congress in January asking for an even larger increase in the fleet than that provided for in the annual budget. At intervals throughout the discussion, Secretary of the Navy Swanson expressed his conviction that we should fight Japan immediately. But Roosevelt asserted that, while he wanted the same result as the Secretary, he "didn't want to have to go to war to get it."

As is evident from Morgenthau's story, within less than twenty-four hours after the Cabinet meeting the President decided upon a policy of sending a United States naval officer to England to engage in staff talks with the British. The task was assigned to Captain Royal E. Ingersoll, the director of the Navy's War Plans Division. Captain Ingersoll received his instructions from Roosevelt directly but apparently not until December 23.[39] The captain did not actually leave the United States until December 26, the very day that the *Panay* crisis was formally settled between America and Japan.[40]

Captain Ingersoll's mission did not therefore involve any consideration of retaliatory measures for the sinking of the *Panay*. Nor was it designed to effect any major preparations for the application of forceful pressure against Japan. The captain's instructions were to discuss various technical problems with the British related to their new naval construction program, and to investigate what steps might be taken if both England and America found themselves at war with the Japanese.[41] On his arrival in London, Ingersoll had an interview with Anthony Eden and thereafter devoted himself exclusively to an exchange of information and views with the officers of the War Plans Division of the British Navy.[42] During the course of the conversations the British emphasized their fear of being drawn into a war with the three Axis powers combined. In that case, they said, they would only be able to send to the Far East the naval vessels not needed for the defense of the British Isles themselves.[43] They also made plain that, in a conflict between the democracies and the dictatorships, they would hope for American naval aid against Japan in the Pacific in return for which, they pointed out, the United States could count on the British Navy to serve as a barrier against Germany in the Atlantic.[44] The most tangible outcome of the discussions was an informal understanding which provided "mutual assurance" that, in the event that the British and American fleets were "required to work together in a war against Japan," British naval vessels could use American waters and United States naval vessels could use the waters of the British Commonwealth.[45] As far as is known, the possibility of entering into any kind of formal agreement was not even considered; in any case, none was concluded.

In terms of planning for naval action against Japan, the results of Captain Ingersoll's mission were consequently as modest as its objectives. Moreover, only a few weeks after Captain Ingersoll's return to this country a new Orange Plan was adopted by the United States armed forces which placed less, rather than more, emphasis upon naval and military operations against Japan in our over-all defense policy.[46] About a month before the *Panay* incident the Joint Board had ordered the army and navy to discard the old Orange Plan and draw up a new one which would take into account the enormous changes that had occurred in the international situation as a result of such developments as the formation of the Axis alliance. But the army and navy had soon indicated that they could not find any basis for agreement. The navy, still almost exclusively preoccupied with the danger of an American-Japanese war, clung to the belief that the United States should throw its full naval power into an offensive operation in the Pacific designed to destroy the Japanese fleet. The army, on the other hand, increasingly convinced that America might have to fight not only Japan but several European powers as well, continued to advocate a defensive strategy in the Pacific which would enable the United States to divide its forces between the Pacific and the Atlantic if necessary. It was only after repeated efforts that the Joint Board succeeded in breaking the deadlock between the army and navy so that a compromise was worked out in which the navy agreed to modify its position. As a consequence the new Orange Plan for the first time departed from the Pacific orientation, which had dominated United States strategy for almost two decades, and put restrictions upon the navy's operation in the Far East in consideration of the possibility that it might be engaged in a conflict in Europe simultaneously. Furthermore the 1938 Orange Plan did not reflect any temporary change in the thinking of our strategists but, on the contrary, marked the beginning of a movement which rapidly led away from their past concentration upon the Far East so that within a few years both the army and navy were ready to accept the idea that the Atlantic theater of war must be accorded priority over the Pacific.[47]

While Captain Ingersoll's mission was inevitably largely naval, it will be recalled that Secretary Morgenthau had told Sir John Simon that the American officer who was about to come to England for staff talks would also be instructed to obtain the Chancellor's views on the prospects of possible Anglo-American economic cooperation against Japan. However, whether because he felt rebuffed by the British or for some other reason, Morgenthau later directed Captain Ingersoll to leave all initiative in regard to a meeting up to Sir John. The latter took no action so that Captain Ingersoll returned home without having seen him. As a result, Secretary Morgenthau was more convinced than ever that the British did not desire to make any move against the Japanese.

Nevertheless the British government was actually in the midst of reviewing the whole question of economic sanctions against Japan at the time of Captain Ingersoll's trip. In December a defense committee, which was working on a plan for the exercise of economic pressure against Germany in case of war, had been ordered to give priority to the study of a similar plan for possible use against Japan.[48] The committee was to make a more intensive examination of the situation than that which had been undertaken by another agency of the British government earlier, the results of which had been submitted to the State Department in October.[49] The new report took two months in the making, but in the end its findings were not very different from those which had emerged from the previous investigation. It declared that no economic sanctions would have any effect on Japan unless enforced by both the United States and the British Commonwealth. Even then an embargo on certain selected commodities would not seriously hamper the Japanese as they could obtain substitute supplies elsewhere. In fact the "cooperation of all countries conceivable in the existing circumstances" would still not be sufficient to prevent Japan entirely from acquiring the necessary raw materials. Basically the problem was therefore that only drastic measures would achieve the desired results and that, if these were adopted, the Japanese were likely to respond with such "grave counter measures" that war might ensue.

The decision to send Captain Ingersoll to London did not have any diplomatic repercussions during the *Panay* crisis itself, as the administration managed to keep it secret.[50] There were, in fact, no exchanges between the American and Japanese governments following Hull's note of December 16, as both were awaiting the results of the investigations into the *Panay* incident being conducted by their respective navies. The United States finally received a report from its own Naval Court of Inquiry on December 23 which confirmed all the most significant points of the stories that had been told by the survivors previously. In addition the court rendered an opinion to the effect that it was "utterly inconceivable" that the planes that had bombed the *Panay* were not "aware of the identity of the ship they were attacking."[51] Secretary Hull wired the findings of the court, but not its conclusions, to Grew for transmission to Hirota. But before his cable reached Tokyo, the Japanese had sent a formal note to the State Department in which, after once more tendering their apologies and offering to pay the proper indemnities, they described in detail the various steps which had been taken to safeguard the rights and interests of American nationals in future.[52] At the same time, they stated that their own investigations had only served to establish the fact that the sinking of the *Panay* had been "entirely due to a mistake."

The Japanese note arrived in Washington on Christmas Eve and the State Department replied on Christmas Day.[53] It indicated its satisfaction with the promptness with which the Japanese had originally admitted responsibility, expressed regret, and offered amends. Even more importantly it accepted the assurances given by the Japanese government in regard to the future protection of American nationals as "responsive" to the United States government's demands. Concerning the question of whether the attack upon the *Panay* had been intentional, the State Department restricted itself to saying,

With regard to the facts of the origins, causes and circumstances of the incident, the Japanese Government indicates in its note of December 24 the conclusion at which the Japanese Government, as a result of its investigation, has arrived. With regard to these same matters, the Government of the United States relies on the report of findings of the Court of Inquiry of the United States Navy.

After receiving the Department's note, Grew wired the Secretary that he had read it aloud to Hirota, who had said in return: "I heartily thank your Government and you yourself for this decision. I am very, very happy. You have brought me a splendid Christmas present."[54] At the close of the day, the ambassador wrote at greater length in his diary:

This was an eminently happy day and it showed the wisdom and good sense of two Governments which refused to be stampeded into potential war in spite of the tendency of the one side to "save face" at almost all costs, and in spite of an outrageous affront offered to the other . . . I thought that our Government's note was a masterpiece . . .

Equally masterly was the Japanese arrangement that its note should get to Washington on Christmas Eve . . . The Japanese could hardly have failed to realize that the Christmas spirit is strong in our country and that the thought "Peace on earth, good will toward men" must inevitably color and influence our decision. Anyway, I was so profoundly happy at the outcome that when I called on Hirota at noon I entered his room wreathed in smiles (a very different attitude from my call on him on December 17) and told him that I brought good news. When I had finished our note to him, his eyes were really filled with tears and he showed as much emotion as any Japanese is capable of showing . . . I think his relief must have been tremendous, as was mine. We have, for the moment, safely passed a difficult, a very difficult, hurdle.[55]

Yet, Grew recounted further, he left the Minister's house with the feeling that all sense of satisfaction over the settlement of the *Panay* incident might well be only temporary and that the "rock" upon which he had been trying to build a "substantial edifice of Japanese-American relations" had "broken down into treacherous sand." Other hurdles, perhaps even more difficult ones, were almost certain to present themselves and the patience of the American people was not inexhaustible. War between the United States and Japan would "not come through mere interference with or even destruction of our tangible interests in China, or yet from the breach of treaty rights, or the breaking down of the principles for which we stand," but it might come very easily "from some further act in derogation of American sovereignty or from an accumulation of open affronts."

That the *Panay* crisis was serious is not open to question. Yet there is reason to doubt even the measured judgment of those who believe that, for a brief moment, the President was ready to take vigorous action against the Japanese even to the point of risking war.[56] For, while it is true that immediately after the *Panay* incident Roosevelt wanted a legal opinion as to whether he had the authority to use certain kinds of financial sanctions, it is also true that the President simultaneously embarked upon a decidedly moderate course. He not only refused to consult with the British but deliberately proceeded without them although by doing so he virtually revealed to the Japanese that England and America were not uniting in any kind of cooperative front.[57] Moreover the President turned down both the British suggestion of an Anglo-American naval demonstration and Admiral Leahy's proposal concerning the preparation of the fleet. The nearest Roosevelt seems to have come to contemplating strong action against Japan seriously was when on December 17, the darkest moment of the *Panay* crisis, he discussed the possibility of resorting to any one of a wide variety of measures including sanctions such as Oliphant had enumerated, a naval blockade, staff talks with the British, the dispatch of some ships on a ceremonial visit to the British naval base at Sinapore, and the closing of the Panama Canal to the Japanese. Nevertheless, throughout these discussions the President repeatedly emphasized that he did not want to take any steps that might lead the United States into war. Oliphant's proposal apparently appealed to Roosevelt especially, because, like his own "quarantine" idea, it sought to devise a method of engaging in drastic punitive action without provoking an armed conflict.[58] But irrespective of intent, Oliphant's scheme was obviously very risky and there is no evidence that Roosevelt ever considered it more than tentatively.[59] In general, there is nothing to indicate that the President made up his mind to adopt any particular policy until he decided to agree to staff conversations with the British—a decision which, in effect, ended all talk of any immediate use of sanctions and provided for the whole issue of economic and naval pressure against Japan being discussed on the basis of planning for future contingencies. In addition, it should be said that, besides authorizing the Ingersoll mission, Roosevelt realized the proposal to send several United States naval vessels to Singapore. This did not occur until February 1938 when, as will be discussed below, it proved to be a very restrained gesture.

A further reason for supposing that Roosevelt did not, even momentarily, reach the point of deciding upon a showdown with Japan at the time of the *Panay* crisis, is that the President must have been very uncertain about the amount of support he would receive from the country. Brief surveys of editorial opinion made by the State Department at the beginning and again at the height of the crisis indicated no desire for strong action against Japan.[60] A more extensive review of the press shows that even newspapers like the *San Francisco Chronicle*, the *Los Angeles Times*, and the *Milwaukee Journal*, which had called for collective economic sanctions against an aggressor earlier, urged moderation following the attack upon the *Panay*.[61] Fundamentally their position was that the sinking of the *Panay* did not involve broad international issues, such as had been at stake at the Brussels Conference, but was more in the nature of an isolated episode. Moreover they felt that the traditional form of reprisals for such episodes was war, an outcome that they did not want in any case. The *New York Times* turned out to be the exception that proved the rule for it took an increasingly strong stand throughout the crisis until, on December 24, it issued its dramatic appeal for economic and financial sanctions against the Japanese to be enforced by the United States and Great Britain in concert.[62]

The isolationists in Congress for their part were so convinced that the primary reaction of the country to the *Panay* incident would be an upsurge of antiwar feeling that they immediately tried to push through measures which they had advocated unsuccessfully in the past. Only a few hours after the American newspapers carried word of the bombing of the *Panay*, isolationists arose in the Senate to renew their demands for the withdrawal of all Americans from China.[63] With virtually no opposition, isolationist spokesmen pointed out that, if the administration had followed their advice and recalled all American forces from China earlier, the assault upon the *Panay* would never have taken place. Senator Ashurst of Arizona declared that, if our troops and vessels remained in the "troubled sphere and troubled waters" of the Far East, they were bound to provoke incidents and that, under the circumstances, "no Senator would vote for war in the . . . Orient." Following the debate in the Senate, Senator Smathers of New Jersey made public a letter addressed to Hull in which he stated that, while he had no fear of the American people wanting a war over the attack upon the *Panay*, nevertheless he was greatly concerned over the possibility that their mood might change if United States citizens and boats remained in China where they would inevitably be involved in further catastrophes.[64]

While the Senate thus sought to revive the withdrawal issue, the House was not content with so limited a goal. The famous Ludlow Resolution for a war referendum had originally been introduced into the House in 1935 and sent to the Judiciary Committee, which deliberately failed to act upon it. Representative Ludlow had thereupon initiated a discharge petition. But 218 signatures were needed and he had only been able to obtain 74. Renewing his efforts in the spring of 1937 he managed, after several months, to raise the total to 205 but was unable to go any further. Matters rested there until the *Panay* incident occurred, at which point Representative Ludlow decided that the antiwar sentiment engendered by the incident was bound to be such that, by capitalizing upon it, he could get the thirteen additional signatures that he needed. His judgment not only proved correct but he attained his end in about twenty-four hours. As is well known, the Ludlow Resolution was finally voted upon in the House on January 10, 1938, and defeated by only a narrow margin.

RISING TENSIONS

The settlement of the *Panay* incident put to rest the question of an immediate war between the United States and Japan. But in most other respects the situation in the Far East grew worse, if anything, after the settlement had been concluded. The major political development between Japan and China has already been discussed in detail, namely the decision on the part of the Japanese government to make the "peace" terms so severe as to be virtually unacceptable and, finally, to break off relations with the Chiang Kai-shek government. As to the relations of Japan and the Western powers, the conquest of the Shanghai-Nanking area by Japanese troops and the establishment of the puppet provisional government at Peiping created many new difficulties.

One of the main sources of trouble was the Chinese Maritime Customs Administration, which was especially important to Great Britain and the United States because of its servicing of foreign loans.[65] Both the American and British governments were concerned over the maintenance of the integrity of the Customs Administration staff and the collection, safeguarding, and distribution of the revenues. Friction had already developed in Tientsin in October, when the Japanese began to deposit the revenues in a Japanese bank. But Shanghai presented a far more serious problem than Tientsin as, under normal conditions, over half of the funds collected by the customs for all of China came from Shanghai. Toward the end of November, the Japanese consul general at Shanghai announced to the foreign powers that he was engaging in negotiations with the local commissioner of customs but that they were to have no part in the discussions and that he would brook no interference from any quarter whatsoever.[66] The negotiations reportedly dealt primarily with the question of the bank of deposit but the Japanese military authorities made clear that they did not feel in any way bound to respect China's financial obligations to foreign creditors. Late in December, the commissioner of customs at Tientsin told Sir Frederick Maze, the British Inspector-General of Customs, that the provisional government at Peiping was about to replace the customs staff at Tientsin with its own agents, seize the customs houses, and take possession of the funds.[67] The British feared that if any such plans went through in Tientsin, the Japanese would begin to institute similar measures throughout all the ports in China under their command. This fear seemed to be substantiated when, a few days thereafter, the Japanese consul general in Shanghai informed the commissioner of customs that the Japanese proposed to take control of the customs houses in that city.[68] Early in January, Sir Frederick Maze told British and American officials in the strictest confidence that he expected soon to be faced with the choice of having to declare his allegiance to a new puppet regime which would claim jurisdiction over all of China or having to resign, in which event he would be replaced by a Japanese.[69] Simultaneously, matters went from bad to worse in the north where the provisional government proclaimed a series of reductions in the prevailing customs tariffs with the obvious intent of benefiting the Japanese and further endangering the interests of foreign governments and bondholders.[70]

From the beginning of the dispute over the customs both Great Britain and the United States had made repeated representations to the Japanese.[71] But the American government had limited itself to reasserting its great concern lest the security of the customs revenues and the functioning of the Customs Administration be impaired. The British, on the other hand, had advocated and supported certain plans for the solution of the customs issue and had sought to take an active part in the negotiations being conducted in Shanghai.[72] When, therefore, these negotiations seemed to have reached an impasse in January 1938, they managed to have them transferred to Tokyo where Hirota was likely to be less obdurate than the Japanese officials in the field.[73] Between February and May, Sir Robert Craigie worked out a *modus vivendi* with the Japanese government which was to be applied for the duration of the Sino-Japanese hostilities.[74] He found, however, that he had to make such far-reaching concessions to the Japanese that the final agreement was subjected to bitter attacks from many quarters; most importantly it was never accepted by the Chinese and was greeted with a disapproving silence in Washington.[75] Nevertheless, many of its provisions governed the relations of the Japanese government and the foreign powers in regard to the customs throughout the following years, the net effect being to leave control of the collection and deposit of the revenues in Japanese hands. Moreover, while the agreement was intended to ensure the servicing of foreign loans and indemnities secured on the customs revenue, it proved inadequate in this respect.

Paralleling their drive to undermine the Customs Administration, the Japanese engaged in a movement to increase their hold on the International Settlement at Shanghai which also achieved critical proportions in the weeks following the *Panay* incident.[76] During the fighting between the Japanese and Chinese in Shanghai, the Japanese forces had occupied about half of the Settlement, consisting of the northeast area which contained approximately sixty per cent of the total industries in the Settlement (including some of the largest foreign holdings) and all the wharves capable of accommodating boats big enough to engage in international trade. It had been assumed that, after the retreat of the Chinese armies, the Japanese would return the northeast districts to the authority of the Shanghai Municipal Council so that normal conditions could be restored. But, on the contrary, the Japanese military retained control and, by imposing a wide variety of regulations, prevented any genuine revival of industrial and commercial activities. Moreover, by a constant interference with the operations of the municipal police they encouraged the growth of crime which reached formidable proportions and made the maintenance of law and order impossible.

In addition, the Japanese sought to make their influence felt in the areas of the Settlement still under the effective rule of the Shanghai Municipal Council. Late in November, the Japanese consul general at Shanghai handed Cornell Franklin, the American Chairman of the Council, a note demanding the suppression of all anti-Japanese organizations and activities in the Settlement, the closing of Chinese government offices and the eviction of officials such as Dr. T. V. Soong, and the prohibition of Chinese censorship of various forms of communication.[77] Only a few hours after this event the council received a message from the Japanese military commander in Central China, stating that unless the Japanese demands were met he would be compelled to take action.[78] At the same time the Japanese announced that they would take over or supervise the operations of the Chinese postal, telegraph, and radio services and install censors in the offices of the three foreign cable companies at Shanghai. On December 3, in an effort to impress the Chinese population of Shanghai with their strength, as a warning against engaging in any anti-Japanese movement, the Japanese staged a parade through the Settlement in opposition to the expressed wishes of the American and British governments and the Shanghai Municipal Council.[79] During the course of the parade, a bomb was thrown at the marchers. Although no one was seriously injured, the Japanese military attaché subsequently tried to force the commissioner of police in the Settlement to guarantee that no such incident would recur and threatened, in case of future trouble, to take "appropriate" measures.[80] Higher authorities later stated that the attaché had acted on the basis of a mistake. Nonetheless the Japanese presented Franklin with a new set of demands on January 5, 1938, claiming that the bombing incident had demonstrated the inability of the council to enforce the law. The demands were for: a reorganization of the municipal police force so as to increase the number, rank, and power of the Japanese personnel; the appointment of a Japanese secretary for the council, who was to participate in all decisions and undertakings on a par with the existing American secretary general and the British secretary; and the placing of Japanese in controlling positions in all sections of the municipal administration.[81] Orally, the Japanese also indicated that they wanted a larger representation on the Shanghai Municipal Council.[82] Faced with this challenging situation, the United States government itself took a hand. The State Department cabled Gauss at once that, in its opinion, attempts by the Japanese "to interfere with or encroach upon the administrative functions of the Council should be opposed by the Council, and the Consular Body if its assistance is requested."[83] While it might be advisable to increase Japanese participation in the administration and policing of the Settlement, any step toward this end should be undertaken in accordance with "law, treaty rights, and considerations of justice and efficiency" rather than in response to the "wishes of any one power supported by military force." Gauss, who thereafter took an active part in the deliberations, sought to impress upon the Japanese the impossibility of the council's considering their proposals so long as they were framed in the form of "demands."[84] The eventual outcome was that the council, in March, agreed to make most of the changes urged by the Japanese with the understanding that the Japanese themselves would simultaneously restore the northeast sections of the Settlement to the full authority of the council.[85] While Gauss had been very much in accord with this arrangement, he expressed his disappointment with the results to the Department at the end of the year.[86] For he felt that the council had fulfilled the promises made in March while the Japanese not only retained control of the northeast districts but forced the council into making new concessions.

In addition to difficulties over the customs and the International Settlement, the British and American governments were increasingly concerned over "incidents" involving various forms of maltreatment of their citizens in China. Despite the assurances which the Japanese had given, at the time of the *Panay* settlement, that they would respect the personal and property rights of Americans in China in the future, violations of these rights grew more numerous after the capture of Nanking. Also, on a number of occasions the United States flag was reportedly torn down and burned or otherwise mutilated.[87]

Episodes involving the British were even more frequent and indeed had not let up since the extraordinary attack upon Sir Hughe Knatch-bull-Hugessen in August.

As a consequence of all these developments, Sir Robert Craigie sought to persuade Ambassador Grew to join with him in urging their respective governments to take some kind of strong action against Japan in order to bring about a satisfactory solution of the problems related to the customs, the tariff, the International Settlement, and the various affronts to British and American nationals.[88] Craigie argued that, while admittedly Britain's tangible interests in China were greater than those of the United States, nevertheless America could not be entirely indifferent to Japan's efforts to drive her out of Asia. In a talk on January 7, Sir Robert suggested recommending to London and Washington engaging in an Anglo-American naval demonstration in which a substantial part of the British fleet would be moved to Singapore and of the American fleet to Hawaii. He thought a show of strength would have the desired effect but that if the Japanese remained intransigent it would be necessary to establish a blockade from Singapore to the Panama Canal. In a further conversation some three days later, Sir Robert modified his position and proposed recommending that the British and American governments should first consult with a view to agreeing upon some form of joint action if Japanese interference with their interests in China became intolerable and should thereafter quietly notify Hirota that such action would be undertaken if their representations continued to be disregarded. Grew said that in his opinion any attempt on the part of the British and American fleets to threaten Japan would inevitably result in war and that he himself was increasingly convinced that the American people would not fight merely to protect their material interests in China; consequently, if he made any recommendations to Washington at all it would be to suggest possible Anglo-American consultations for the purpose of being prepared for future emergencies but not to propose any action at this time. Returning for a more conclusive discussion of this subject with the British ambassador on January 18, Grew was surprised to hear Sir Robert Craigie say in effect that he was no longer interested and would do nothing further until he saw how the negotiations over the Chinese customs problem worked out. Ambassador Grew felt that the change in Craigie's attitude might have been brought about by a report from the Foreign Office that the United States was not sympathetic to his ideas. While this seems unlikely in retrospect, it is probable that Sir Robert had considerable information (lacking to Grew) about the interchanges

which had taken place between the British and American governments, including Captain Ingersoll's interviews with the British navy,
and that he made at least some of the recommendations to the Foreign
Office which he talked over with Ambassador Grew.[89]

Whether as a result of advice from Sir Robert Craigie or not, Ambassador Lindsay called on Sumner Welles in Washington on January 8 to tell him that news had just been received of the beating of
some British police officers by Japanese soldiers in the International
Settlement.[90] Should the incident turn out upon investigation to
seem sufficiently serious to warrant action, the British government
might make "an announcement of the completion of naval preparations." Upon being asked by Sumner Welles to explain this phrase,
Lindsay stated that it was "to be regarded as a step prior to mobilization and as implying that the British navy was on a war footing save
for the completion of naval complements which latter was a step that
would be undertaken solely as a result of mobilization." Sir Ronald
wanted to know whether, if the British government did decide to make
an announcement of this character, the United States government
would be prepared to state that certain units of its fleet were proceeding toward Hawaii in the course of naval maneuvers or that
certain units were being moved from the Atlantic to the Pacific. Welles
replied that this was an inquiry which could only be answered by the
President.

Two days later a meeting was held between the President, Secretary
Hull, Sumner Welles, and Admiral Leahy, at which it was decided
that, if the British declared the "completion of naval preparations,"
the United States navy would dock its ships for cleaning and
advance the date of its annual spring maneuvers, which had already
been announced for mid-March.[91] It was also agreed that the fleet
should be sent to Honolulu, although it is not clear whether this was
to take place during the maneuvers, which in any event customarily
centered on Hawaii, or somewhat earlier.[92] As far as can be ascertained, immediately after this meeting the President sent a message
to the British explaining what the United States was prepared to do.[93]
On January 13 the British replied that they had arrived at the conclusion that instead of resorting to naval measures they would
send a stiff protest to the Japanese government concerning the latest
incident at Shanghai.[94]

The motives behind the decision to agree to the original proposal
of the British are not spelled out in any available document but they
presumably had some of their roots in the controversy which was
taking place in the State Department at this time. In January 1938,

Secretary Hull had a number of prolonged meetings with top State Department officials for the sake of subjecting the administration's foreign policy to a thorough review. The Secretary indicated that his own attitude toward the Axis countries was rapidly hardening, as he felt that Japan's policy was growing increasingly "desperate and dangerous" and that the Japanese were working in close association with the Germans and the Italians who were embarking upon a far-reaching program to impose their will upon the rest of the world. He therefore argued that Great Britain and the United States would have to have recourse to the only effective countermove which was to give an unmistakable demonstration of firm unity between England and America. In the Far East he thought the United Kingdom and the United States should enage in some kind of parallel naval measures and, following the British decision not to complete fleet preparations short of mobilization, he advocated having the British send some ships to Singapore when the American navy would be holding its spring maneuvers in Hawaii. As to Europe, the Secretary proposed that England and America should manifest their closeness by concluding monetary, trade, and other economic agreements and by cooperating in further schemes for the limitation and reduction of armaments. Germany and Italy should be given a chance, at the appropriate moments, to participate in various aspects of both the economic and disarmament programs. But, if they refused to collaborate or if the programs themselves failed, Great Britain and the United States would have to recognize that the only remaining possibility was to rely upon their combined strength.

Sumner Welles objected to the Secretary's views on the grounds that they would not prove workable. He insisted that any movement by the British and American fleets in the Far East would not be effective unless undertaken on such a large scale that war would be inevitable and that, in any case, the American people would not support close cooperation with the British. Leaving these points aside, he felt that the policy which the Secretary had in mind could only be developed over a long period of time during which Germany and Italy would have committed additional acts of aggression thereby further endangering the situation in Europe and inciting the Japanese to go ahead in Asia.

In contrast to the Secretary's suggestions, Welles urged a revival of the plan which he had drawn up following the President's "quarantine" speech and which Roosevelt had subsequently discarded because of Hull's conviction that it was too "pyrotechnical."[95] Welles was in favor of retaining the part of his plan that called for a meeting of the representatives of other governments at the White House, at which the President was to propose negotiating an international agreement concerning such subjects as the broad principles that ought to govern the conduct of international relations. But he wanted to make some changes in procedure so as to limit the actual drafting of the agreement to the representatives of a number of smaller powers and the United States. For he feared that if the larger European nations were involved the American people would immediately become apprehensive lest their government was allowing itself to be drawn into the political controversies of the totalitarian states and the democracies.[96] On January 10, Welles wrote a memorandum outlining the new procedure he believed should be followed and the line of reasoning behind his desire to resuscitate his plan at this particular time. His main point was that Great Britain and France were currently trying to reach a practical understanding with Germany and Italy on the colonial issue, security, and similar problems, and that parallel negotiations of the kind he visualized, carried on under the initiative of the United States, might lend "support and impetus" to their efforts. Unlike Hull's scheme, Welles's was therefore designed to produce an immediate effect by speeding up the movement for conciliation which the British and French already had underway. Regarding the Far East, Welles intimated in the last paragraph of his memorandum that a realistic approach might be to hope that a rapprochement in Europe would moderate Japanese aggression:

Finally, if Germany and Italy solve their practical problems with Great Britain and France, it would seem probable that their present support of Japan will be very greatly weakened—at least to an extent sufficient to obligate Japan to make peace with China upon terms not inconsistent with the principles of the Nine Power Treaty.

During January the administration made various moves involving the navy which were obviously in keeping with Hull's school of thought. Up until at least January 19 it worked on a program for the simultaneous appearance of British naval vessels at Singapore and American naval vessels at Hawaii during the United States fleet maneuvers in March. Discussions on this subject must have been held with the British.[97] On January 13, it announced that several United States cruisers, en route home from Sidney, would attend a "fete" for the opening of the Singapore naval base.[98] But in the end the March war games were held as usual and accorded only routine attention by the press.[99] And when the American cruisers arrived at Singapore for the inauguration ceremonies in mid-February every possible effort was made to impress upon the public that their visit had "no international significance."[100] One can only assume that the policy which the administration had originally intended to follow was reduced to a minimum because of certain unexpected developments. The President had announced in December that he would ask for authorization for a larger navy at the beginning of the next year and accordingly sent a special message to Congress on January 28. Unfortunately for the administration, two days earlier there were some leaks to the press concerning Captain Ingersoll's voyage to England and, while these leaks would undoubtedly have stirred up trouble with the isolationists in Congress under any circumstances, the situation was made worse by the President's request for a larger navy. Rumors that Captain Ingersoll had gone to London to establish a basis for special Anglo-American naval cooperation in the Far East immediately went the rounds, causing the State Department grave concern.[101] Reporters were told by Department officials that Captain Ingersoll had no other purpose in England than to find out what methods the British were using to figure tonnages in the construction of their new battleships, as questions had been raised concerning their methods by American naval designers.[102] According to the *New York Times,* "high diplomats," when asked whether some form of Anglo-American naval collaboration was being contemplated, stated with a gesture toward Capitol Hill: "We are not that crazy." When the hearings on the new naval bill opened at the beginning of February, Admiral Leahy was repeatedly questioned about Ingersoll's talks with the British and even about the forthcoming visit of American cruisers to Singapore.[103] Under these conditions, the administration was not likely to engage in any conspicuous demonstrations of Anglo-American unity.

While these events were unfolding, the administration was also pursuing the line of policy advocated by Sumner Welles. A message incorporating Welles's revised plan was sent to Prime Minister Chamberlain on January 11. The story of the subsequent developments has frequently been told, but the precise manner in which it related to the administration's policy toward the existing situation in the Far East deserves somewhat more attention than it customarily receives.[104] Chamberlain responded by expressing his fear that if the plan which Roosevelt had outlined were presented to all the powers immediately Hitler and Mussolini might use it as an excuse to block the progress toward appeasement which the British had laboriously made throughout the preceding months in diplomatic exchanges with their governments. The Prime Minister suggested that the President might care to stay his hand until the outcome of the negotiations between Britain and France on the one side and Germany and Italy on the other were further advanced. At the same time, Chamberlain revealed that as a part of these negotiations he was prepared to recognize the Italian conquest of Ethiopia if in return Mussolini was ready to make a contribution toward the "restoration of confidence and friendly relations."

The administration in Washington lost no time in letting Chamberlain know that it had little sympathy for his willingness to consider abandoning the principle of nonrecognition in connection with Ethiopia. On January 17 the President sent the Prime Minister a note, drafted in the State Department, the substance of which was explained by Secretary Hull to Sir Ronald Lindsay on the same day.[105] Hull said that the administration was fully aware of the difficulties which England faced in Europe and did not have the remotest desire to inject its views into the negotiations between the United Kingdom and Italy. However, he wanted to make plain the United States government's profound concern over the "movement for destruction" instigated by Japan in the Far East and that

our opposition to this entire movement rests primarily on moral concepts and considerations and, in turn, upon the sanctity of agreements and the preservation of international law, both of which rest upon this moral foundation; that, of course, in addition we are strongly opposed to the course of Japan in violating all laws of war and humanity, the whole unjustifiable and outrageous nature of which is patent to both the thinking and the unthinking.

Hull stated further that the principle of nonrecognition had carefully been kept alive because it was of "universal importance as a factor and agency in the restoration and stabilization of international law and order." If any great power, such as Great Britain, should suddenly abandon that principle to the extent of recognizing the Italian conquest of Ethiopia, for example, its actions would be capitalized upon by desperado nations and heralded as a virtual ratification of the opposing policy of violating and wrecking treaties. At this critical juncture in the Far East, Japan would feel that the powers were acknowledging its right to ignore and destroy solemn treaties, and a universal precedent would have been established. The American people would feel "let down" and might well relax their present support of the administration's policies in the Pacific. While there were admittedly difficulties in maintaining a policy of nonrecognition, nevertheless the United States government had always assumed that any attempt to modify or interrupt this policy would only be made by an agreement entered into by all or most of the nations of the world according to peaceful and orderly proceedings.

Relative to the Far East, the Secretary was therefore saying that the

United States government objected to any recognition of Italy's seizure of Ethiopia because (1) on the practical level it would encourage Japanese aggression and (2) on the moral level it would condone Japan's violations of the principle of respect for international law. As a corollary to the second point, the Secretary did not wish the British to do anything which would lessen the American people's sympathy with the determination which the administration had always shown to refuse assent to Japan's course.

On January 21, at Eden's instigation, Prime Minister Chamberlain reversed his position and told Roosevelt that he would welcome his taking the initiative in regard to the plan he had proposed. But the President decided to delay action and, although he continued to work on the Welles plan for some time, he never again discussed it with other governments. No doubt he felt increasingly that the moment was unpropitious, as within a month Eden resigned over his chief's Italian policy and shortly thereafter Hitler took over Austria.

The controversy concerning any possible changes in our policy designed to affect the Far East, directly or indirectly, therefore produced few results. Meanwhile, the Chinese were seeking financial aid from the United States. Morgenthau, more than ever convinced that the cause of world peace was closely tied in with that of China and that Hull was following far too timid a course, decided to do what he could by continuing his own brand of "monetary diplomacy."[106] At the beginning of November he had responded to the first wartime petition from the Chinese to purchase twenty million ounces of silver. After the fall of Shanghai, eager to supply the Chinese with the means to purchase war materials which he felt they desperately needed, Morgenthau asked the President for authorization to purchase fifty million ounces more and to extend the existing foreign exchange agreement for another year. Roosevelt referred him to Secretary Hull who, according to Morgenthau's version of the story, in scarcely veiled fashion indicated his opposition. The President thereupon himself expressed considerable annoyance with Hull's dilatory tactics and instructed Morgenthau to go ahead. An arrangement was consequently made with the Chinese, although the Treasury in order to avoid trouble with the State Department expressly stated that the purpose of the silver purchase was the stabilization of the dollar, thereby circumventing the question of helping the Chinese to attain war supplies.

While in all probability, as on similar occasions in the past, the State Department had another side to this story, it is clear that Hull remained opposed to an outright loan to China. Immediately after the

Brussels Conference, the Chinese had indicated their desire for a $500 million loan from the British, American, and French governments to buy arms, ammunition, and implements of war. On January 3, 1938, the Chinese ambassador called on Secretary Hull to discuss this subject further.[107] Hull, according to his official account of this talk, was most emphatic in defining his own position:

> I . . . said . . . that only Congress could authorize a loan in any amount by the Government; that I could not undertake to speak for Congress in regard to possible legislation authorizing a loan; that, in the circumstances, I would not be frank, as I always desired to be, if I offered any comment . . . except that this is a matter which comes under the authority and jurisdiction of Congress. The Ambassador . . . suggested that perhaps the President and the executive branch might have influence with Congress in carrying out a program such as he was proposing. I replied that in some and possibly many instances this would be true, but that the Congress itself is giving increasing attention to our foreign affairs and especially to conditions in the Pacific area, and that it would have definite opinions in regard to the question of a loan and hence would not be susceptible of influence by the opinions of the executive or other branches of government . . . The Ambassador sought to induce me to say that the matter was still under advisement and that there were possibilities of a different decision in the future. To this I again promptly brought him back to my statements which I have just recorded and I made the matter most definite by a further statement that I was not called upon to speak except as to the present; that I have spoken definitely as to the present; and that the future would have to take care of itself.

In addition to Secretary Hull's rejection of the Chinese appeal for a loan, the State Department at this time drafted the answer to the request for "effective assistance" which Chiang Kai-shek had sent to the President on the last day of December.[108] Quite possibly the Generalissimo's note had originally been timed so as to pave the way for the loan proposal. In any case, the reply finally sent to Chiang, by conspicuously avoiding any mention of possible help to China, was obviously designed to reaffirm that the United States government would not take any action at this time beyond the silver purchases made by the Treasury.

Alongside of the issue of aid to China, another basic problem involved in our Far Eastern policy continued to be pushed to the fore in the early days of 1938—the question of the withdrawal of American troops and citizens from China. Only a few days after the *Panay* and *Ladybird* incidents, the British government had informed the administration in Washington that it was contemplating the recall of its embassy guard from North China if the Japanese should grant *de jure* recognition to the puppet regime which had just been established at

Peiping.[109] The State Department replied that it felt that any move of this kind would be premature. But on January 17 Secretary Hull told Sir Ronald Lindsay that he understood the British wanted to get their forces out of Peiping and Tientsin and reduce their military contingents in Shanghai and that the United States was now prepared to consider similar measures. The Secretary went on to say that the problem was just how and when the evacuation of these troops should be made in order "to avoid the appearance of scuttling on the one hand and at the same time possibly to permit synchronization with any naval movements which might occur on the part of our two countries." After some further discussion with the British, the State Department announced, on January 31 and February 4, respectively, that it had decided to withdraw (1) the reinforcements sent to Shanghai at the outbreak of the Sino-Japanese war and (2) the Fifteenth Infantry stationed at Tientsin; the latter were to be replaced by two of the four companies of marine guards presently at Peiping.[110] The Chinese ambassador, apparently somewhat surprised at these developments, called on Hull to inquire concerning the significance of the removal of the Infantry from Tientsin in particular.[111] The Secretary answered that before the fighting had started in China in July the administration had been discussing the evacuation of these forces as the War Department felt it was not a "wholesome policy" to keep troops out of the United States for an indefinite period and, moreover, they were no longer of any great use in Tientsin. Under ordinary circumstances they would therefore have been brought home no later than was now planned so that it should be evident that the decision to recall them at this time had "no significance."

While it was most certainly true that the War Department—and indeed the President himself—had long wanted to withdraw its men from North China, nonetheless, in view of previous developments it seems probable that the Department's final decision was in part affected by the attitude of Congress.[112] Following the letter sent by Senator Smathers to Hull immediately after the *Panay* incident, the Senate continued to demand the evacuation of all Americans from China. Early in January Vice President Garner forwarded a Senate resolution to the Secretary asking for information concerning the number of United States citizens, military and civilian, in China and the approximate amount of American capital invested in that country.[113] Hull replied to Senator Smathers by restating the Department's thesis that in regard to the protection of nationals in China the administration must adhere to a middle-of-the-road course.[114] Many Americans, he said, had established themselves in China over several generations and they could not be expected to "suddenly disavow and cut themselves off from the past" nor could the United States government which had undertaken to safeguard them "suddenly disavow its obligations and responsibilities"; at the same time, United States officials were earnestly advising American citizens, who were in zones of danger, to leave China. The Secretary advanced the same arguments in his response to the Vice President.[115] But the letter sent to Senator Smathers on December 19 stated positively that the Department did not regard the present as affording an opportune moment for the evacuation of United States armed forces from China while the answer to Garner, written on January 8, indicated that some of those forces were about to be recalled. Presumably therefore the Department reversed its earlier stand at this point.

The main significance of the Secretary's message to Garner lay, however, in those passages which went beyond the discussion of the problems related to the protection of our nationals in China. For Hull decided to use this chance of addressing the Senate to put before the American people a succinct statement of what he felt to be the essence of his Far Eastern policy at this time. The relevant paragraphs read:

The interest and concern of the United States in the Far Eastern situation, in the European situation, and in situations on this continent are not measured by the number of American citizens residing in a particular country at a particular moment nor by the amount of investment of American citizens there nor by the volume of trade. There is a broader and much more fundamental interest—which is that orderly processes in international relationships be maintained. Referring expressly to the situation in the Far East, an area which contains approximately half the population of the world, the United States is deeply interested in supporting by peaceful means influences contributory to preservation and encouragement of orderly processes. This interest far transcends in importance the value of American trade with China or American investments in China; it transcends even the question of safeguarding the immediate welfare of American citizens in China . . .

In the present situation in the Far East, the Government of the United States is affording appropriate protection and assistance to American nationals, as this Government has always done. The American Government is also upholding principles, as it has always done. It has asked and is asking that the rights of the United States and the rights of our people be respected, and at the same time it has sought and is seeking to avoid involvement of this country in the disputes of other countries.

The principles which the Government of the United States is following in its international relationships are set forth in the statement which I made on July 16, 1937. A copy of this statement and a copy of a further statement which I made on August 23 are enclosed . . . We are directing our whole thought and effort toward making effective the policies, especially the policy of peace, in which this country believes and to which it is committed.

Among the various developments connected with American policy that followed the *Panay* crisis, the most important was the growth of the feeling in Washington that the international situation was becoming increasingly dangerous. The circumstances of the attack upon the *Panay* seemed definitely to indicate that the Japanese military— described by Hull as "wild, runaway, half-insane men"—were getting out of control. Moreover, the boldness with which the Japanese were attempting to destroy British and American interests in China suggested a new readiness to challenge the Western powers without restraint. In addition, it was felt that as a result of the expansion of the Anti-Comintern Pact and other events Japan was constantly drawing closer to Germany and Italy, who in turn seemed prepared to pursue their unlimited ambitions for conquest at any cost.

Consequently, renewed efforts were made within the administration to find a fresh means of dealing with all three Axis powers that would prevent them from precipitating a general war. As the policies proposed by Secretary Hull and Sumner Welles show, the emphasis was upon Europe. But there were those, including the Secretary himself, who thought it might be advisable to engage in some kind of parallel naval action with the British in the Pacific as a warning to Japan. There was, however, never any intention of exerting genuine pressure upon the Japanese, and the only measure put into operation (the visit of some naval vessels to Singapore) was relatively insignificant. Our policy toward Japan therefore remained unaltered. Nor was there any shift in the direction of aid to China. The net result was that up until the time when relations between Japan and China were formally terminated, the administration continued to rely upon the issuance of policy pronouncements, such as that addressed to Vice President Garner, which were basically a repetition of the Secretary's statements of July 16 and August 23.

This volume has dealt intensively with American policy in the Far East during the period that started with the Tangku Truce and ended in January 1938, when the first phase of the undeclared war in China was terminated by the severance of relations between the Japanese and Chinese governments. The following is presented as a brief review of the broad trend of our diplomacy during these years.

The events of the Manchurian crisis had, it is felt, a significant influence upon the United States government's subsequent policy. Stimson's initial objective in respect to the crisis was to strengthen the movement for the establishment of universal order that had developed since the World War. His concern with that movement was readily understandable within the context of the time. Before the World War the creation of an organization like the League of Nations had seemed little more than a vague and highly idealistic goal. Yet immediately following the war, the League had come into existence and in many respects had achieved remarkable results during the 1920's. It had moreover been supplemented by the conclusion of various multilateral agreements designed to provide solutions to the problem of war. Many people therefore felt that a system for the establishment and maintenance of peace had been created which for the first time in history offered some promise that the world might achieve international order. As a result they regarded Japan's invasion of Manchuria as primarily significant because it constituted the first great attack upon the peace system that had evolved in the postwar years; further, they believed that the way in which other nations responded to Japan's action would go far to determine whether that system would be progressively strengthened or gradually destroyed.

Stimson's efforts during the early months of the Manchurian crisis were to a large extent directed toward supporting the League. Although he failed at times to supply the League with all the assistance that it wanted, he certainly had no intention of weakening its stand. Rather, he was concerned with warding off what he regarded as the attempts of the League when engaged in any joint undertaking with the United States to shift the burden of responsibility upon this country, thereby forcing it into a position of leadership. Moreover, in some respects his views differed from those of the League, notably in that he placed more emphasis upon the necessity of exhibiting tolerance toward the Japanese in the hope that, with outside support, the moderates in the Japanese government would be able to control the extremists.

After the fall from power of the moderates in Japan, Stimson felt that the situation in the Far East had taken a radical turn for the worse. His objective remained the strengthening of the peace system but it seemed evident that this aim could not be achieved by the tactics he had used to date. At the same time the Secretary recognized that few lines of action were open to him if for no other reason than that President Hoover was opposed to the use of any measures stronger than moral sanctions. Faced with new and increasingly serious evidence that Japan was determined to continue its invasion of Manchuria in defiance of the whole world, he however believed that some quick move was necessary to indicate that the "peace loving nations" were willing to adopt a definite stand against Japan's efforts to undermine the peace structure. He consequently decided to take unilateral action immediately, which meant assuming the initiative he had hitherto left to the League, and issued his note of January 7, 1932, in the hope that other countries would follow suit thereby refusing to recognize any gains Japan might achieve in violation of the Paris Pact as an expression of their disapproval of Japan's acts of aggression. Soon after it became apparent that other countries were not going to fall in line as he desired, Stimson began to consider making a second statement which would be similar to his note of January 7. However, this statement, which ultimately became his letter to Senator Borah, was to emphasize the Nine Power Treaty over and above the Paris Pact in order to implement another major aspect of Stimson's policy which was his desire to maintain the strong ties that he felt existed between the United States and China. Convinced that, primarily as a result of the American missionary movement, Americans had a deep and idealistic attachment to China which was not to be found among other peoples, he wished to reaffirm the faith of the United States in the principles of the Nine Power Treaty at a moment when the Chinese, subjected to defeat and humiliation, were in great need of encouragement. In its final form the letter to Senator Borah also contained the suggestion that the treaties concluded at the Washington Conference were indivisible, which was intended as a warning to the Japanese that the United States might feel free to disregard the restrictions imposed upon her naval power by the Washington Conference agreements if Japan continued to disregard the provisions of the Nine Power Treaty.

In the last phase of the Manchurian crisis, Stimson devoted himself to persuading the League to adopt a firm position on the basis of the Lytton report. He attempted, however, to remain in the background, insisting that the League must not revert to its tendency to transfer its responsibilities to the United States. When the League finally censured Japan and agreed to apply the nonrecognition doctrine to Manchukuo, the Secretary felt that a "momentous event" had occurred which represented a "great step forward" in the postwar effort to abandon the "jungle law of international diplomacy" that had existed before 1914.

It is doubtful whether many members of the American government shared Stimson's optimistic estimate of the League's action. In general, as the Roosevelt administration took office most American officials connected with the making of our Far Eastern policy seem to have been in agreement on three main points concerning the Manchurian crisis. First, contrary to Stimson, they did not believe that the Manchurian crisis had resulted in strengthening the postwar movement to establish world order; in fact, some officials were convinced that that movement had been totally discredited. Secondly, they felt that the Manchurian crisis had left the United States in a very precarious position in relation to Japan. In their estimation the conquest of Manchuria and the ousting from power of the moderates in Tokyo meant that the Japanese were determined to fulfill their expansionist ambitions at almost any cost. Granted a bellicose Japan, they thought that there not only existed the possibility of an ultimate clash between Japan and the United States but that such a possibility had been made substantially more real by the increase in anti-American feeling among the Japanese which had resulted from the Manchurian crisis. Thirdly American officials appear almost uniformly to have concluded that the Manchurian crisis had demonstrated the dangers of the United States' engaging in action against Japan either unilaterally or in cooperation with other nations. They had in particular been impressed by the precautions which the American government had repeatedly felt compelled to take during the Manchurian crisis to avoid being pushed into a position of leadership which entailed risks that it did not want to incur.

The views of American officials relative to the Manchurian crisis commenced to have an effect upon the trend of our policy in the Far

East at the very outset of the Roosevelt administration. The initial stage of the struggle for North China, ending in the Tangku Truce, marked a transition period for the United States in which ideas that had governed our diplomacy during the Stimson era began to give way to a new set of concepts that were to predominate throughout the next years. In particular, the emphasis which had been placed upon the necessity of supporting the peace system began to be shifted to another objective: the avoidance of a conflict between the United States and Japan. In keeping with this objective, it was decided that if any joint measures were adopted by outside powers to arrest Japan's penetration of North China, the United States should leave the initiative to others and participate only in a relatively inconspicuous role; even more importantly, it was felt that it would be in the best interests of America to take no action whatever.

The aspects of American policy that began to emerge at the time of the Tangku Truce became progressively evident during the incident involving the Amau declaration. The views of policy-making officials in Washington relative to the whole problem with which the Amau doctrine was concerned—the establishment of a strong China— were on the whole well defined. They continued to believe in the theory underlying the Nine Power Treaty that the soundest way of attaining peace in the Pacific area was to create a strong China capable of maintaining a balance of power in the Far East. At the same time they thought that the transformation of China into a strong state could not be accomplished by the Chinese without substantial outside assistance. They were in favor of the kind of technical aid that the League was providing for China but basically were convinced that no country still on the threshhold of industrialization could hope to modernize unless it obtained large-scale financial help from abroad.

On the question of whether the Kuomintang was capable of achieving the reconstruction of China the opinions of officials in Washington differed from those of the leading American Foreign Service officers in China. Men such as Nelson Johnson had become increasingly disappointed at what they regarded as the failure of the Nationalist regime to fulfill much of the promise of the political tutelage period. As a result, by 1934 their dispatches to Washington reflected an almost unrelieved sense of discouragement. The main burden of their criticism was that the leadership of the Kuomintang had deteriorated so that it was unable to carry out the task of unifying the country and that the party as a whole had lost the revolutionary fervor necessary to effect the reforms essential for the rehabilitation of China. Officials in Washington on the other hand tended to judge the Kuomintang less severely. They were disturbed by the constant military and political conflicts among its leaders which they felt inevitably jeopardized any effort at national reconstruction. But they nevertheless believed that the Kuomintang had made decided progress in the political tutelage period, especially in light of the magnitude of the problems with which it was confronted, and that although China's future might still be uncertain it was by no means devoid of promise.

The views maintained by officials in Washington contrasted sharply with the actions taken by the United States government following the Amau declaration. The most important moves made by the State Department initially consisted of: the Department's assertion to the British that if any cooperative measures were undertaken in protest against the Amau declaration the United States might participate but that it did not want to be thrust into a position of leadership; Hull's *aide-mémoire* which was sent to the Japanese on April 29 and which he himself subsequently described to the Japanese ambassador as a message issued in a "respectful and friendly spirit"; and the Secretary's comments on his *aide-mémoire* to the press, which amounted to an appeal to try to promote better relations between the United States and Japan. But an even more significant step was taken by the State Department after the agitation over the Amau declaration had to a large extent subsided when Hull asked the Far Eastern Division to re-examine our policy on aid to China to see if any changes should be made in view of the objections which the Japanese had raised. For, as a consequence, the Department arrived at the conclusion that at least for the present the United States government should refrain from giving the Chinese any financial assistance in no matter what form. It reached this conclusion for various reasons, among them being that the Chinese already owed substantial sums to the United States government and its nationals which they were making no apparent effort to repay. But it was largely influenced by a determination to avoid taking any action that might lead to the development of further friction between the United States and Japan. Moreover, the State Department subsequently decided that if, at some time in the future, the United States did furnish the Chinese with financial assistance, it would have to do so in cooperation with other powers including Japan. It therefore requested the American group of the Consortium, which was on the verge of dissolution, to remain intact so that, should the opportunity ultimately present itself, the various Consortium groups would be able to collaborate in helping China.

In sum, the main views entertained by officials in Washington were that the internal development of China was a matter of high importance; that China had entered upon a new period in its history in which, after years of turmoil, it had a chance of attaining national reconstruction; but that no country could expect to become a strong state in the modern world unless it obtained extensive foreign support. All of these ideas pointed in the direction of the United States' aiding China. But the Amau declaration led the State Department to advocate a contrary course based—as has already been indicated—upon the concepts which had been tentatively suggested at the time of the Tangku Truce, namely, that within the foreseeable future the primary aim of our Far Eastern policy should be to avert trouble with Japan and that the best means of achieving this objective was for the most part to adhere to a strategy of inaction.

The naval talks of 1934 seemed to American officials both in the State Department in Washington and the embassy in Tokyo, to provide a further indication of the possibility of war between the United States and Japan. The fear of such a war was most strikingly expressed in the letter that Ambassador Grew sent to the Secretary of State on December 27, 1934, in which he asserted in substance that the Japanese, driven by a fierce and blind chauvinism, would probably attempt to gain control over most of the western part of the Pacific area and might even suddenly try to seize some of the island possessions of the United States, such as Guam. The ambassador's comments had a marked influence in Washington, if only because they set forth ideas which had prevailed in the State Department for some time but had not as yet been stated in so definite or comprehensive a manner. The net result was that, after the failure of the naval conferences, the Department attached considerably more significance to the development of naval power. It felt primarily that the United States should be prepared to defend itself in case an attack by Japan eventuated but, in addition, it hoped that the mere existence of a strong American navy would deter the Japanese from ever launching such an attack.

In the year 1934, the moral aspect of the State Department's policy in the Far East was also demonstrated. Because of the manner in which he approached Hull, Ambassador Saito's proposal that America and Japan should issue a joint statement of policy seemed part of a scene from an *opéra bouffe*. Yet the Secretary's response was very significant. Hull objected to the ambassador's proposal for two reasons: One was that in his opinion for the United States government to sign a statement containing the provisions outlined by Ambassador Saito would have been tantamount to an outright declaration that America was willing to sanction Japan's efforts to attain what the Secretary frequently referred to as the "overlordship of the Orient." The other was that any bilateral agreement between Japan and the United States suggested a tie of intimacy between the two countries which carried with it the connotation that America approved Japan's purposes and policies. The Secretary's position was therefore basically that the United States did not have the moral right to engage in any action that either directly or indirectly appeared to endorse Japanese aggression. The moral stand taken by Hull became part of the State Department's policy. However, in considering the moral aspect of American diplomacy, it is important to recognize that the State Department drew a sharp distinction between endorsing Japanese aggression and accepting it without opposition. This distinction was defined by Hornbeck, who had devoted considerable thought to the matter, in the memorandum of April 1935, in which he pointed out that to "acquiesce" passively in Japan's encroachments on China was different from actively giving "assent" and indicated that the former was morally justifiable while the latter was not.

Thus by 1934 the objective of preventing a clash with Japan, a strategy which emphasized on the one hand refraining from action in the face of Japan's current involvement in China and on the other the strengthening of our naval power, and the moral considerations which have just been noted characterized the trend of American policy in the Far East. But before discussing the events which took place after 1934, a word should be added about certain aspects of the naval talks conducted in that year which further suggested the general direction in which American policy was moving. As has already been related in some detail, the position taken by the United States at the naval meetings was squarely based on the thesis that the principles of the Washington Naval Treaty should be maintained because they provided the United States and Japan with equality of security by limiting the fleet of each nation so that it could operate only on its own side of the Pacific Ocean. In adopting this stand, the United States demonstrated a willingness to retain restrictions on its naval power which went far to curtail its ability to support the Nine Power Treaty by forceful measures and, indeed, seemed to indicate that it had little intention of doing so. At the same time Secretary Hull reaffirmed that he would not, even by implication, endorse Japan's efforts to destroy the Nine Power Treaty through his refusal to negotiate with the Japanese under conditions which he believed suggested a participation by the United States in their denunciation of all the Washington Conference agreements.

In 1935 the United States was confronted with two major developments in the Far East: the deterioration of the economic situation in

China as a result of our silver policy and a dramatic resurgence of Japan's efforts to get control of China. By the end of 1934, it will be recalled, it had become evident that the impact of our silver policy on China was having disastrous consequences. The Chinese currency system seemed on the verge of collapse—a collapse which, it was predicted, might bring with it not only economic chaos but the political ruin of the Nanking regime. Anti-American feeling was rising and was likely to increase progressively as conditions in China worsened. According to the statements of leading Chinese officials, the Japanese were trying to capitalize on the situation with the result that the Nanking government might soon have to choose between cooperation with—which meant complete submission to—Japan or the extension of Japanese control over a large part of China.

Under these circumstances it was apparent that the United States would have to take some kind of action. The controversy that developed between the Treasury and State Departments was over the form which that action should assume. The State Department at the outset argued vigorously for a radical change in our silver policy and against the procedure recommended by the Treasury, which was to provide China with financial assistance. Its attitude no doubt stemmed in part from the antipathy which existed within the Department to the silver legislation in general. But the Far Eastern specialists in the Department were especially concerned over the fact that, in their opinion, the Nanking government did not have the capacity to carry out a reorganization of its currency and that, consequently, if the United States supplied the Chinese with funds to engage in monetary reforms, it would soon find itself deeply involved in China's domestic affairs. Beyond that, Secretary Hull and his advisers on the Far East wished to adhere to the policy that they had decided upon at the time of the Amau declaration, which decreed that in view of the opposition of the Japanese the United States should not by itself undertake to furnish China with financial help. When it became evident that the President and Morgenthau would not make any significant change in our silver policy, the State Department suggested that the United States should consider assisting China in cooperation with other nations including Japan. This suggestion was followed to the extent of the United States government's expressing a willingness to support the initiative and leadership of the British, who wished to explore the possibility of aiding the Chinese in conjunction with the United States, France, and Japan. Secretary Morgenthau, however, objected to collaborating with the British. He feared that a situation would develop in which the representatives of other countries would embarrass the administration in Washington by advancing proposals for drastic alterations in our silver policy which, for domestic political reasons, it would be compelled to reject. But even more fundamentally, Morgenthau believed that the entire trend of the policy which the United States government was pursuing in the Far East should be reconsidered. The United States, he insisted, should cease to concentrate upon trying to avoid a conflict with Japan, and acting on its own should embark upon a vigorous effort to strengthen China irrespective of the effect upon our relations with the Japanese. As the State Department held to its position, it looked for a while as though an impasse had been reached. After the Chinese issued their currency decree of November 1935, however, the United States Treasury concluded the first of a series of agreements involving the purchase of Chinese silver. Secretary Morgenthau thereby instituted what he himself called his "monetary diplomacy," which, in the long run, was undoubtedly of great service to the Chinese and which he came to regard as one of the most important contributions he made during his years in office. The State Department, while attempting to keep a careful watch on Morgenthau's "monetary diplomacy" agreed to it because it was limited to a particular kind of financial transaction to which the Japanese raised no objections. The State Department felt, therefore, that Morgenthau's efforts did not interfere with the mainstream of the policy which it had been following and from which it did not want to depart.

Both in 1935 and 1936 that policy was put to a severe test by the renewal of Japanese aggression in China. Despite all the details contained in the large number of reports written by American Foreign Service officers on the Sino-Japanese struggle during those years, one overriding conclusion emerged, namely, that Japan was inexorably advancing toward its aim of securing control of China. There were presumed to be differences between the military faction, which represented the extremists in Japan, and the Foreign Office, which represented the moderates. The military were seen as attempting to take over China by a process of territorial partition starting with the alienation of the northern provinces. As long as they appeared to have a chance of dividing China by such methods as the establishment of puppet regimes, the Japanese armies would not, it was thought, resort to force. Moreover, it was hoped that the Japanese civilians still retained the will and the power to prevent an outright military invasion of China. The Japanese Foreign Office was regarded as determined to negotiate with the Nanking government on the basis of Hirota's three-point program. However, this program, in the opinion of American Foreign Service officers, was far from being as innocuous as its vague phraseology might suggest. It was felt that, on the contrary, the realization of Hirota's "three principles" would gradually have the effect of transforming China into a colony, economically, politically, and militarily dependent upon Japan and devoid of all connection with other powers. Whether the blatantly aggressive tactics of the Japanese military or the ostensibly restrained procedures of the Japanese Foreign Office prevailed, the final outcome, if the Japanese were successful, would therefore be the same: the subjugation of China. By the end of 1935 the situation between Japan and China had reached the point where both our embassies in Peiping and in Tokyo were inclined to assume that this outcome was, in fact, all but inevitable—a position which they did not modify until the autumn of the following year.

American policy toward the Sino-Japanese struggle during 1935 and 1936 was first discussed in the interchange which occurred at the outset (January 1935) involving Hornbeck and Hull, and, finally, the President. Although the decisions reached were regarded as tentative, one need only bring them back to mind to recognize that the rules of conduct they embraced continued to serve as a guide for the administration during the next two years. The United States, it was agreed, should watch the situation developing between the Chinese and Japanese closely and, whenever necessary, ask for information from both sides; for the rest, it should refrain from action and as far as possible from comment without, however, creating an impression of indifference.

Subsequently the American government showed itself very reluctant to engage in any move regarding the various crises that arose, whether in connection with Japan's encroachments on North China or negotiations such as were conducted by General Chang Chun and Ambassador Kawagoe relative to Hirota's three points. Perhaps the United States would have elected to remain entirely silent if it had not been for the British. However, when the British undertook to register quite vigorous protests with the Japanese government, the United States was inclined to make some corresponding gesture if only to preserve the tradition of an Anglo-American parallel policy in the Far East, which it regarded as an important instrument of our diplomacy. At any rate, American officials held a number of conversations with Japanese officials in Washington and Tokyo. But every effort was made, as the State Department itself explained on several occasions, to handle these conversations as tactfully as possible. For the most part the American officials involved, in accordance with the precepts laid down initially, avoided commenting upon developments and limited themselves to requesting information and indicating that the United States was not lacking in interest in what was taking place. The only time an exceptional note was injected into these talks was when Secretary Hull, in his interview with Yoshida in June 1936, expressed the opinion that to all appearances Japan was trying to attain exclusive economic domination first of China and then of other countries, which would eventually entail political and military domination as well. Hull's remarks as a whole, however, constituted another step in his general endeavor to meet the growing threat of aggression in Europe and Asia by educating both individual statesmen and the general public to an understanding and acceptance of the fundamentals of peace. In his comments to Yoshida, the Secretary emphasized that one of the avenues to peace lay in international cooperation of the kind he was attempting to promote through his reciprocal trade agreements. In addition to remarks made by American officials to Japanese officials in private, the Secretary issued his public statement of December 1935. Even more than his assertions to Yoshida, this pronouncement was intended as an appeal for greater comprehension and support of the cause of peace. The Japanese themselves apparently thought that Hull spoke in such general terms that his words provided no occasion for resentment in contrast to the specific and sometimes sharp representations made by the British.

The current of American policy, therefore, continued to flow in channels which by this time were well established. The United States government interfered in the Sino-Japanese controversy to only a minor degree and on the whole maintained a position which was at times described within the confines of the State Department as "playing no favorites" between the disputants. The main reason for not altering American policy itself remained unchanged, being clearly the desire of the administration to stabilize our relations with Japan. However, since despite an official attitude of impartiality there existed a large reservoir of sympathy for the Chinese within the administration, much thought was given to the effect of our policy on China. It was often contended that if the United States took a definite position against Japan and exercised nonmilitary pressures (coercion admittedly being out of the question) the consequences might actually be harmful to the Chinese. The anger generated by Stimson's diplomacy would almost inevitably be revived with the result that the Japanese people and especially their military leaders might well become even more chauvinistic and belligerent. It was also argued that under any circumstances it was useless for the United States to engage in measures short of war as the only means of stopping the Japanese was through military action. But in the case of many internationalists, both in and out of the administration, this argument seems to have been at least partially a rationalization. For they became strong advocates of the use of measures short of war against Japan when, after the Marco Polo Bridge incident, the paramount issue was once again the establishment and maintenance of world order.

From the viewpoint of the United States, the most important conclusion to be drawn from the events of 1935 and 1936 was that the trend of our policy was in fact so fixed that, as has been suggested in previous chapters, it was not likely to be changed unless some new and vitally important element was introduced into the situation. The Mac-Murray memorandum and the pertinent dispatches written in the winter of 1935-1936 by Ambassadors Grew and Johnson show that American officials were already accepting as a possibility, if not a probability, that the struggle between Japan and China would continue in its present form and result in the Japanese achieving all they wanted in the near future. The question raised among American officials was not, however, whether the United States could forestall this eventuality but rather whether it should subsequently enter into some agreement or agreements with the Japanese which might, hopefully, render its position *vis-à-vis* Japan less dangerous.

Yet the events which dominated the closing months of the year 1936 unexpectedly challenged the view that the subjugation of China by Japan was both inevitable and imminent. The reports of American Foreign Service officers, which had for so long been devoid of any note of optimism in regard to China, suddenly adopted a new tone. Beginning with the Suiyuan campaign, they were filled with descriptions of the success being achieved by the Chinese people in attaining unity, the growth of the popular determination to resist Japan, and the transition from defeatism to hope through which the country was passing. Nevertheless, American officials seem frequently to have been unaware of even the major developments that were contributing to the ferment in China. A case in point is the interpretation by officials, both in China and in Washington, of the Sian incident as a play for personal aggrandizement on the part of Chang Hsueh-liang comparable to the act of an old-fashioned warlord or an ordinary "gangster." Even admitting that various aspects of the Sian incident are still obscure, there was certainly enough evidence available to the United States government at the time to indicate that the capture of the Generalissimo involved the most important issues facing the nation and could not reasonably be regarded as a venture undertaken by the Young Marshal merely for selfish gains.

Moreover, the favorable reaction of American Foreign Service officers to developments in China was not matched by any practical support from the United States of the kind which the Chinese were seeking—economic assistance. The American government, the American banking group in the Consortium, and the American industrial community, each for its own reasons, remained reluctant to participate in China's reconstruction as other governments and nationals were doing. The first sign of a possible change of major significance in the American position came when in July 1937 the Export-Import Bank indicated its willingness to consider the extension of substantial credits to China. By then, however, the situation in the Far East was in the process of being radically transformed and the administration soon arrived at the decision to postpone all action indefinitely.

The confusion concerning the Chinese Communists that existed among American officials in the early and mid-1930's has been discussed at some length in chapter VII, partly because of its current interest. The examination of the documents which formed the basis of this chapter seemed repeatedly to suggest that the confusion was caused by a particular set of circumstances. With few exceptions American Foreign Service officers in China had little more than a superficial knowledge of the Chinese Communist movement owing primarily to the many obstacles which either hampered or prevented the ferreting out of information and owing also to their own lack of enterprise. The specialists on China within the State Department at home were unable to make up for the deficiencies of the officers in the field for the simple reason that as human beings they were influenced by the intellectual atmosphere in the United States at a time when few people as yet saw the need for any genuine understanding of communism. In turn, the inadequacies of the China specialists were not rectified by the experts on the Soviet Union in the State Department whether because of a lack of coordination or an inclination to view communism in China as a peripheral subject. Whatever the causes of the confusion, the immediate consequence was that American officials were ill-prepared first to recognize and then to interpret the extension to China of the united front policy promulgated in Moscow. As, following the Sian incident, there was more and more talk of a "reconciliation" between the Communists and the Kuomintang, our embassy in China saw the action of the Chinese Communists as another example of the "tremendous growth" of the "ideal of national unity" affecting all Chinese political factions.

The spring of 1937 was also marked by the discussion which arose within the administration over the problem of fortifying the Pacific islands. This discussion, together with the manner in which the administration handled the entire fortifications issue, assumes particular significance in retrospect. The President's plan for the neutralization of the Pacific islands had important implications. Admittedly, Roosevelt in all likelihood did not expect his neutralization scheme to be incorporated in a treaty in precisely the form in which he initially conceived it. Nevertheless the mere fact that he advanced such a proposal shows that as late as the eve of the Sino-Japanese war he was still thinking in terms of solving the problems of the Pacific area not by the exercise of pressure against Japan but by negotiating a multilateral agreement to which it would be a party. Moreover, the agreement which Roosevelt envisaged was bound to be regarded not only as a friendly gesture toward the Japanese but an exceedingly friendly gesture. For it required the Western powers to disarm most of their territories in the Pacific in return for a pledge from Japan that it would do likewise. Since, as critics of Roosevelt's neutralization idea pointed out, experience had demonstrated that Japan was not likely to observe its pledges, the chances were that the President's scheme would operate overwhelmingly in its favor.

In any event, Roosevelt's plan elicited little support within either the American or British governments and was gradually set aside. In addition, no agreement on the fortifications issue was concluded with the Japanese. On the other hand, no steps were taken in respect to the construction of defenses in the Pacific area that could reasonably lead to dissension between the United States and Japan. Thus, even in relation to a matter of great military significance, the administration held to the passive position which it had been maintaining in the Far East.

Shortly after the President had advanced his neutralization plan, Neville Chamberlain suggested that the United States and Great Britain might reach some sort of an understanding with Japan which would help to prevent the outbreak of a general war in the Pacific area. In connection with these developments, the State Department indicated on several occasions that it was in favor of awaiting the time when it would be possible to conclude another comprehensive settlement comparable to that achieved at the Washington Conference. What the Department evidently had in mind was an agreement that would both reaffirm the general principles embodied in the Nine Power Treaty and deal with specific problems like those with which the Washington Naval Treaty had been concerned. Before the summer of 1937, Department officials seem to have entertained little hope of being able to negotiate such a settlement with Japan for a long time, perhaps even within the next decade. But by June 1937 they were more optimistic about the possibility of Japan's cooperating with other powers in the interests of peace.

All optimism was, however, quickly dispelled. In July 1937 the phase of the struggle between Japan and China that had been marked by an absence of extensive fighting came to an end. The outbreak of a major armed conflict in the Far East created a situation analogous to that which had prevailed during the Manchurian crisis. As a consequence, the American government was again confronted with the question of whether to adopt the isolationist view that the United States should not intervene in disputes between other nations or whether to take the internationalist position that an act of aggression anywhere should be dealt with by all the "law-abiding" members of the community of nations for the sake of preserving world peace. It was evident, however, that if the administration chose the second of these alternatives it would have to contend with even greater difficulties than those which beset Stimson. The international machinery for the maintenance of peace, created after the World War, had progressively deteriorated since the Manchurian crisis and within the United States itself isolationism had become more widespread. At the same time the whole problem of suppressing aggression had assumed a far greater urgency owing to the possibility of war in Europe which might be joined with the struggle in Asia.

In the first months of the Sino-Japanese conflict, Hull emerges as the most conspicuous figure in the conduct of our diplomacy. The Secretary showed at once that he intended to adopt a policy that, like Stimson's, would have as its primary purpose the furtherance of the internationalist cause which would also serve to counter the spread of war in Europe. The most important step that Hull took initially was the issuance of his statements of July 16 and August 23. These statements were intended, first, to lay down the thesis that any war was essentially the concern not only of the parties to the dispute but of all countries interested in the maintenance of world peace and, secondly, to declare that this thesis applied specifically to the situation in the Far East. Hull deliberately refrained from stating which party was the aggressor in the conflict in the Far East and insisted that he was adhering to a policy of "strict impartiality." Nevertheless, he undoubtedly felt that he was making quite a drastic move in proclaiming a doctrine which ran counter to the basic tenet of isolationism and which established a theoretic foundation for action by the United States in respect of the disputes of others.

Hull also revealed, perhaps more clearly than was recognized at the time, the nature of the action that he intended to take for the present, which was essentially one of moral suasion. In his statement of July 16, the Secretary enumerated the principles which, in his opinion, had to be respected if universal peace was to be preserved. In a passage, which he himself repeated verbatim on a number of important occasions thereafter, he listed such precepts as "abstinence by all nations from the use of force," "adjustment of problems in international relations by process of peaceful negotiation," "respect by all nations for the rights of others," and observance of the "sanctity of treaties." The Secretary sent his July 16 statement to all of the governments of the world requesting an expression of their views. By doing so he sought to prod other statesmen into arousing their peoples to express disapproval of the breach of the peace that had occurred in the Far East which meant, at least by implication, of Japanese aggression. World public opinion, he believed, would operate as a moral sanction toward dissuading the Japanese from continuing their attack upon China. In addition, Hull hoped to achieve certain long-term results. Consonant with his faith in the efficacy of moral education, he thought that by engaging in a prolonged and persistent campaign of reiterating the "principles upon which peace alone can exist" he could gradually awaken the conscience of peoples everywhere to the point of supporting vigorous action against any nation that violated those principles. In particular, he felt that through such a process of enlightenment— and perhaps only through such a process—he could lead the American people themselves away from isolationism. Hull also believed that, if an awareness of the importance of moral values became more widespread, the rulers who entertained false nationalistic ambitions for their countries might resist the temptation to resort to aggression or, failing this, might be prevented from embarking upon military adventures by the opposition of their own people. Long-term as these results might be, the Secretary apparently trusted that he could make sufficient progress toward their attainment to avert the catastrophe of a war in Europe.

Hull's activities during the late summer of 1937 constituted an effort to carry forward the policy initiated in his statements of July 16 and August 23. In this connection, it is of interest to remember the entries in Pierrepont Moffat's diary, which relate that the Secretary wished to issue still a third moral pronouncement in September and only relinquished the idea with considerable reluctance upon the earnest counsel of his advisers. Certainly the Secretary's behind-the-scenes activities during the debates on the Sino-Japanese case at the League were almost exclusively directed toward getting the states represented at Geneva to make a declaration which would have amounted to a restatement of the principles which he had already enunciated and a renewed expression of disapproval of any country that transgressed them. At first Hull wanted the League to adhere to the "strict impartiality" which he had continued to observe, and refrain from explicitly putting the blame for the breach of the peace in the Far East upon Japan; but as the proceedings at Geneva progressed he seems to have changed his mind on this point. In the end the League did censure the Japanese, though for its own reasons it based its disapprobation on Japan's violation of the Kellogg-Briand Pact and the Nine Power Treaty rather than the general moral precepts which the Secretary thought should be made the focus of attention. Hull immediately endorsed the League's action but also doggedly held to his own brand of moral denunciation by seizing the opportunity to repeat the principles, which he had been proclaiming, and to assert that the Japanese had ignored these fundamental rules of conduct as well as the terms of the specific agreements cited by the League.

Hull thus consistently adhered to his strategy of moral suasion. At the same time he made every effort to avoid any situation which might result in the United States government's having to take a stronger stand against Japan. In the period before the League considered the Sino-Japanese dispute, the British approached the State Department with as many as half a dozen different proposals for attempting to terminate the fighting in China through some form of Anglo-American cooperation. Hull rejected the British plans for a variety of reasons but foremost among them was certainly the fear that they might entail the exercise of considerable pressure against the Japanese. After the League took official cognizance of the Sino-Japanese conflict, the Secretary adamantly refused to associate himself with the proceedings at Geneva in any but the most perfunctory way. Evidently haunted by memories of the Manchurian crisis, he was determined not to be drawn into a discussion in which other powers might seek to make the United States assume the leadership of a movement directed against the Japanese. Again, at the beginning of October, Hull turned aside the British suggestion for an exploration of the possible use of a boycott against Japan and all but stated that the American government would not resort to economic sanctions. Indeed, a few days later the Secretary frankly told the Japanese ambassador that while he had felt fully justified in supporting the censure of Japan, voted by more than fifty nations at the League, he was not considering any departure from the policy which he had been pursuing since the outbreak of hostilities in the Far East.

If Hull was the central figure in the conduct of our policy in the first months of the Sino-Japanese war, he was dramatically supplanted by the President in early October when Roosevelt delivered his "quarantine" speech at Chicago. The President's own statements leave no doubt that, like Hull, his main aim in dealing with the Sino-Japanese conflict was to strengthen the internationalist movement and to forestall the advent of an armed clash in Europe which might merge with that in Asia. The question of the President's strategy, however, requires closer scrutiny and takes us back to the story of Roosevelt's search for a peace plan.

The main elements of the story which were emphasized in detail in the discussion presented earlier, can be briefly summarized. The President embarked upon his effort to find a peace plan well before the commencement of the fighting in China. From early 1936 to his enthusiastic espousal of the Welles plan immediately following his Chicago address, Roosevelt considered a whole series of schemes that contained certain fundamental differences. Some had as their goal the establishment of a "lasting peace," others the elimination of the immediate threat of war on either a world-wide or regional basis, while still others were designed to fulfill both these objectives. Even more importantly, they relied upon a wide variety of methods to attain their ends.

In general, however, the plans which sought to meet the immediate situation provided for the use of conciliatory measures. As in the case of the President's proposal for the neutralization of the Pacific islands, they tended to call for the conclusion of a multilateral agreement which would remove some of the problems leading to the existing international tension. But in the summer of 1937 Roosevelt also spoke on a number of occasions of the idea of quarantining an aggressor, which he incorporated in his Chicago address. To all appearances, the President was looking for an answer to the much discussed problem of how to develop a better method of collective action against an aggressor than that provided for in the Covenant of the League which, it was felt, was likely to result in a general war. More specifically, the President hoped to find a method of international organization which would enable the "peace-loving" members of the international community to oppose an aggressor without resorting to military sanctions or otherwise involving themselves in hostilities. For the reasons previously indicated, Roosevelt seems to have thought that his concept of quarantining or isolating an aggressor was a step in the right direction. But the President's concept was so rudimentary that he may well have advanced it more as a suggestion that in his opinion held considerable promise than one which he himself regarded as furnishing a practical basis for action. In any event, Roosevelt never decided upon any plan for applying his "quarantine" idea. At times, he indicated that it might be incorporated in a treaty to be signed by all the countries of the world which would lay the foundations of a "lasting peace," presumably by discouraging would-be aggressors. At other times, he mentioned the possibility of excluding Germany, Italy, and Japan from such an agreement as a warning to them not to engage in acts of international violence. In the latter connection the President stated, however, that he was thinking in terms of deterring the "three bandit nations" in the future rather than of stopping Japan's current assault upon China, since what had been done could not be undone. All in all, Roosevelt advanced one proposal after another with bewildering rapidity. Moreover, he never stopped considering plans which were based upon the kind of conciliatory approach he had favored from the outset. In the end he settled upon the program suggested by Sumner Welles which involved the negotiation of a multilateral agreement dealing with relatively noncontroversial issues such as certain rules of international law. The main purpose of this program was to secure the participation of Hitler and Mussolini in an undertaking that might improve their relations with the democracies and thereby lead to a subsequent effort to solve some of the major causes of friction. In the case of the Far East, it was thought that if it proved possible to reduce the tensions in Europe, Germany and Italy might withhold their support of Japan at least to the extent of forcing that country to conclude a peace with China on terms that did not violate the principles of the Nine Power Treaty. However, the Welles plan was also soon to be laid aside although it was revived in the following year in the brief but famous episode that included its rejection by Prime Minister Chamberlain.

The story of Roosevelt's search for a peace plan consequently points to the conclusion that up to the beginning of October 1937 the President did not have any definite strategy for dealing with the international situation in general, much less the Sino-Japanese conflict in particular. While at times he may have hoped to discover a magic solution and been impatient with the slow methods adopted by his Secretary of State, the fact of the matter seems to be that he had not devised any alternative course and, in regard to the crisis in the Far East, was prepared to support the policy Hull was following.

At the beginning of October censure of Japan was therefore to all appearances as far as either the President or the Secretary intended presently to go. Among the many factors influencing their attitude, public opinion has been emphasized in this study because of its apparent importance. Like the administration, the American people as a whole ostensibly felt that for the United States the main issue involved in the struggle in Asia was whether to follow an isolationist or an internationalist course. The problems which proved to be most controversial were the protection of our nationals in China, the possible application of the Neutrality Act to the hostilities in the Far East, and the President's "quarantine" speech. The groups that expressed themselves with the greatest vigor consisted of congressmen, sections of the press, and representatives of organizations that largely belonged to the peace movement.

Throughout the discussion of the questions of protection and neutrality, there was sufficient division of opinion among both the isolationists and internationalists to allow the administration considerable latitude to act as it chose. As a consequence, additional troops were sent to China to provide adequate safeguards for American citizens and the Neutrality Act was not invoked. However, at such times as vigorous opposition to the measures undertaken by the government developed on the isolationist side, especially in the wing of the peace movement that was currently advocating many isolationist tenets, the extreme sensitivity of the administration to adverse criticism became strikingly evident. While by no means fully retreating, both the President and Hull made substantial concessions.

The administration was similarly responsive to the outcries of isolationists following the President's "quarantine" speech. Hull has testified to his own great distress at what he regarded as the widespread violent denunciation of the address and, according to others, Roosevelt was scarcely less disturbed. The effect of their concern upon our subsequent policy toward the Far Eastern crisis is essentially an imponderable factor. But certainly as the Brussels Conference approached the administration seemed, if anything, more determined than ever to avoid making any move that might invite an isolationist attack. The memorandum that Roosevelt dictated before the opening of the conference to guide Norman Davis in his relations with the British was nothing if not a powerful injunction to remain within the bounds prescribed by isolationist sentiment with its anti-British bias. Moreover, in his instructions regarding our policy as a whole at Brussels, Roosevelt went far toward stating that he did not want to take any strong action against the Japanese unless and until isolationist opinion in the United States altered radically. Further, it is apparent from the dispatches sent to Davis that throughout the Brussels Conference both the President and Hull paid the closest attention to the isolationist criticism to which the administration as a whole and Davis in particular was subjected. In chapter XI, which deals with public opinion, the question has been raised of whether, in their desire to avoid a political struggle, the President, Hull, and the administration in general did not pay undue attention to all signs of isolationist opposition while overlooking important manifestations of internationalist support (a case in point being their evaluation of the country's reaction to the "quarantine" speech). This is a question which does not lie within our province in reviewing the trend of American policy. It is, however, one that needs further exploration, as historians of the Roosevelt era fully recognize.

The test of whether the administration would or would not go beyond the policy that it had been pursuing since the start of the war in China came at the Brussels Conference. The preparatory stage of the conference was dominated by the President's instructions to Norman Davis. In retrospect, these instructions are primarily important because they indicate that Roosevelt's position remained the same in that he had no means of dealing with the conflict in the Far East beyond the use of the kind of moral suasion that Hull favored. The President's directions to Davis were clear in so far as they stated that at the outset of the conference every effort must be made to bring about a settlement of the conflict between Japan and China and that the pressure of world public opinion must be brought to bear on the Japanese to assist in the attainment of this end. But when it came to the question of what should be done, if the attempt to secure a settlement failed, Roosevelt had no definite proposals. While he spoke of possible punitive action against Japan and mentioned that the conference might consider a general attempt to "ostracize" the Japanese, he never amplified these points. Moreover, he hedged by laying down conditions that there was virtually no hope of fulfilling. Any action, he said in substance, that was decided upon by the conference must represent the almost unanimous opinion of the people in the "overwhelming majority" of the nations of the world. There can be no doubt that Davis understood the President to mean that if it proved impossible to persuade Japan to come to terms with China he was prepared to join with the other powers at Brussels in adopting a program of sanctions. But one may surmise that owing to the confused nature of the President's remarks Davis read into them more than was there. This likelihood is even greater since Davis himself was convinced that, if the Japanese remained intransigent, it was imperative for the conference to demonstrate that the "law-abiding" nations of the world were determined to put an end to aggression, if necessary even at the cost of fighting a war.

The Brussels Conference would in any event have been a challenge to the administration to determine whether it would exceed its present policy. For the other large powers represented at Brussels went much further than had been anticipated in Washington in urging a consideration of the use of coercive measures against Japan. But the real challenge came from Davis himself when he asked Washington to submit a resolution to the conference which included provisions for the application of the nonrecognition doctrine and of financial sanctions against Japan, and to recommend to Congress the suspension or repeal of the Neutrality Act. The situation was not entirely lacking in irony since Davis must have thought that his proposals not only lay within the boundaries of his instructions but were very modest compared to the President's idea that it might be possible to "ostracize" Japan. In any event, there followed the administration's rejection of Davis's suggestions, Davis's appeal for a reconsideration of his plan, and finally Hull's assertion that the United States government would not go beyond the policy which it had been pursuing since the beginning of the trouble in the Far East.

The intensity of feeling on the administration's side was demonstrated by the unusual bitterness that the State Department injected into its exchange with Davis. The main points were that the Department insisted that a consideration of coercive measures did not fall within the scope of the conference which had been called for the sole purpose of negotiating an agreement between Japan and China. Davis countered by saying that none of the other interested governments shared this view. The Department then declared that the question of punitive measures had been debated by the members of the League in September and decided in the negative; it therefore had no place in the present discussions. Further, the Department charged that the other countries represented at Brussels were attempting, largely through inspired stories in the press, to place the blame upon the United States for the failure of the conference to impose sanctions upon Japan when the blame was really theirs, since they had already demonstrated their unwillingness to entertain the idea of taking any action. Davis replied in effect that the Department's claims did not conform to the realities of the situation. The issue of sanctions, he said, had purposely been left open by the members of the League when they met at Geneva; moreover, since the beginning of the proceedings at Brussels most of the other nations had consistently maintained the position that they would resort to "pressure methods" against Japan if the United States would cooperate. The Department, however, held to its opinions and even threatened to issue a public statement proving its contentions.

The net result of the Brussels Conference was that the administration not only repudiated any thought of altering its course but Hull reasserted his belief that much could be accomplished by adhering to his policy of reiterating the principles which must govern international relationships if peace was to prevail. Throughout the latter part of the conference the Secretary persistently urged the delegates at Brussels to issue a declaration comparable to his statements of July 16 and August 23 and eventually succeeded in having a reaffirmation of some of the principles he had enunciated earlier incorporated in the final pronouncement of the conference.

Another fundamental aspect of the administration's policy was put to the test by the efforts of the Japanese to reach an agreement with China outside the framework of the Brussels Conference or any organized group of nations operating on the basis of the right of collective intervention in international disputes. It is evident from the material made available since the war that for a variety of reasons the government at Tokyo genuinely wanted to negotiate a settlement with Nanking and to use the good offices of other nations— especially Great Britain, the United States, and Germany—for that purpose. Although the chances that Japan and China would have come to terms are small, the possibility cannot be discounted. It has been suggested that the likelihood of a settlement might have been increased by a well-timed move on the part of Great Britain and the United States to serve as intermediaries. If so, the position adopted by the United States becomes all the more significant. At any rate, that position was that the administration in Washington would not undertake to convey peace proposals between China and Japan unless assured by the Japanese in advance that the terms they would offer would conform to the principles of the Nine Power Treaty. To lay down any such condition, however, went far toward precluding action since little hope was entertained that the Japanese would accept it. The American attitude differed sharply from that of the British, who contended that the important factor was to get the negotiations under way after which various influences might conspire to bring about a satisfactory outcome; furthermore, that the American and British governments could safeguard their own integrity by announcing that they were merely trying to facilitate an exchange of views between the belligerents but were not responsible for whatever proposals were advanced. But officials in Washington did not modify their stand nor is there any reason to suppose they would have done so even if circumstances had not changed. For the administration was evidently convinced that to associate itself in any way with negotiations which might terminate in an agreement that was incompatible with the principles of the Nine Power Treaty would be to grant the Japanese a measure of the moral support for their aggression in China which it had long been determined to withhold.

With the sinking of the gunboat *Panay* in December 1937, the possibility arose that the American government might completely reverse the current of its policy in the Far East and engage in vigorous, retaliatory measures which would result in war with Japan. But such a possibility appears to have remained remote. The attack upon the *Panay* was an extraordinary affront to the United States and therefore inevitably a great shock to the country as a whole. Some high officials, primarily naval officials, advocated an immediate showdown with the Japanese on the grounds that it was only a matter of time before a clash would occur between the United States and Japan and that there was more to lose than to gain by postponing it. However, as far as could be judged the American people, whether internationalist or isolationist minded, did not regard the *Panay* incident as a justifiable cause for war as there was no proof that the Japanese government had been directly implicated. At the outset the President explored many different ways of dealing with the situation, some of which were very drastic, such as the possible seizure of Japanese assets, the feasibility of which he asked Morgenthau to investigate. But in discussing the *Panay* crisis at the cabinet meeting, which was held when matters were at their worst, Roosevelt indicated that he neither wanted to go to war with Japan nor to adopt measures that ran the risk of precipitating a war and—at least in the writer's judgment—he probably never departed far from this position. Certainly the measures which were put into practice were exceedingly moderate. The most important of these was the dispatch of Captain Ingersoll to England on the mission on which he engaged in staff talks with the British. As we now know, however, the talks were conceived from the first as a modest undertaking and produced relatively insignificant results.

The main feature of the days following the *Panay* crisis was the fact that while the administration's concern over the possibility of a general war between the democracies and the dictatorships increased, no real change was effected in American policy. A search for a fresh solution of the international situation was renewed. But the plans which were discussed continued to be temperate, the underlying idea being for the most part to make a further effort to bring the European powers together and to undertake some limited naval move in the Pacific which would be designed as a display of Anglo-American cooperation *vis-à-vis* Japan. In the end, for a variety of reasons, little of consequence was achieved.

Meanwhile, Japan and China were absorbed in the acute controversy which terminated in the severance of relations between their governments in mid-January, bringing to a close the first stage of the Sino-Japanese conflict. American officials watched events approach their denouement with a heavy sense of foreboding that the Chinese were heading into disaster as their armies appeared on the verge of collapse while conditions had reached a point where a settlement with the Japanese was obviously impossible except on terms of abject surrender. The only move which the administration seems to have seriously contemplated, however, was a last-minute appeal to the Japanese government to modify its actions. A message to this effect, it will be remembered, was actually drafted by the State Department but was not submitted to the authorities in Tokyo on the advice of Ambassador Grew.

It is apparent that there were differences between the policy of the Roosevelt administration in the period preceding and following the Marco Polo Bridge incident. Before July 1937 our relations with the countries of East Asia were mainly influenced by the views of members of the Far Eastern Division of the State Department and certain Foreign Service officers. Subsequently, policy was formed on the highest level of the United States government. In advance of the outbreak of fighting in the Far East, the administration dealt with the struggle between China and Japan as though it was in large measure confined to those two countries although admittedly it had serious implications for the security of the United States in the long run. But after the development of a full-scale war in the Far East, the President and Secretary of State themselves were convinced that the Sino-Japanese conflict involved broader issues which were intimately connected with the welfare of all nations, and furthermore, that Japan's attack upon China might precipitate a concerted effort on the part of the Axis powers to overwhelm the European democracies. As a consequence of their assumption that the character of the Far Eastern crisis had changed, the aims of

American policy shifted automatically. Nevertheless the administration's method of procedure remained to a remarkable extent the same. In the making of specific decisions, officials in Washington returned again and again to the conclusion that they should avoid any action or should hold action to a minimum. The degree of passivity which the United States government maintained is the feature of our record in the Far East in the mid-1930's that is most likely to seem astonishing in retrospect. For with the benefit of hindsight it is evident that the events which culminated in the second World War were closing in upon peoples everywhere with a terrible rapidity.

BIBLIOGRAPHY · NOTES · INDEX

BIBLIOGRAPHY

At the outset of the Notes to many of the foregoing chapters, there are references to some of the basic works on the particular topic under consideration. It is felt, therefore, that only a few additional comments need be made here concerning the large body of material that is available in connection with United States policy in the Far East from 1933 to 1938.

The primary sources take precedence over all else. Foremost among them are the State Department papers, published and unpublished. For such times as our Far Eastern policy was to a large extent left to American officials who specialized on China and Japan, Ambassador Grew's diary and Ambassador Johnson's correspondence and memoranda are of particular value. The former is the more important because of the quality of Mr. Grew's reporting and because of the influence which he exercised in Washington.

For the period when policy was formed in the main by the highest officials in the United States government, the Franklin D. Roosevelt papers are indispensable. Often frustrating, as the President was temperamentally averse to formal written records, an exploration of the files at Hyde Park can nevertheless prove an exciting and rewarding experience. In respect to the occurrences in which Norman H. Davis played an active part, Davis' own papers are of great interest. These documents were made available to the writer through the kindness of the Council on Foreign Relations when they were still in its possession, stored in the attic and as yet unorganized. While they include much that can be obtained elsewhere, they also contain some unique items as might be expected from the position of unusual trust that Davis enjoyed in the Roosevelt administration. Revealing stories about day-to-day interchanges between officials involved in major policy decisions can often be found in the diary of Jay Pierrepont Moffat, although his concern with the Far East was essentially limited.

Selections from the Grew and Moffat diaries are available in book form. In addition, a number of leading members of President Roosevelt's official family have published their own version of events. Cordell Hull's memoirs deserve study but the reader may be disappointed by their failure to provide a more critical appraisal of the Secretary's actions. John M. Blum's *From the Morgenthau Diaries* (based upon the fabulous collection of letters, memoranda, verbatim records of meetings and conversations, et cetera, accumulated by the Secretary of the Treasury while in office) often presents a very different interpretation from Hull's. The same is true of the various books produced by Sumner Welles which should, however, be used with a degree of caution as they appear to have been written from memory, at least in part. *The Secret Diary of Harold L. Ickes* is famous for its inaccuracies but may nevertheless prove an excellent guide if one proceeds with appropriate caution.

Contemporary newspapers and magazines offer an invaluable means of recreating the climate of thought in the 1930's which even to the historically minded often seems strangely elusive. The number of such publications that were read during the course of working on this volume proved too large for their inclusion in the bibliography. Yet the historian cannot hope to cover more than a tiny fraction of the material of this nature which is available so that the problem is, above all, one of selection. In attempting to get some indication of editorial opinion in the general press in the United States, it is necessary to examine newspapers of outstanding importance which were issued in different parts of the country and which represented different political points of view. Lawrence I. Kramer, Jr.'s, "A Study of Editorial Opinion in Eight Newspapers in the United States on the Far Eastern Crisis, 1933-1938" was based on the following carefully chosen publications: the *Chicago Tribune, Christian Science Monitor, Cleveland Press, Los Angeles Times, Milwaukee Journal, New York Times, San Francisco Chronicle,* and *San Francisco Examiner.* For any sampling of the religious press it is essential to read leading Catholic and Protestant journals. Among the former, *Catholic Action* and *The Commonweal* devote considerable attention to international issues. Any selection of Protestant periodicals should include publications of different denominations such as the Congregational *Advance,* the Methodist *Christian Advocate,* the Episcopalian *Churchman,* and the Baptist *Watchman-Examiner.* A study, however limited, of the business press should involve a careful scrutiny of the *Commercial and Financial Chronicle, New York Journal of Commerce,* and *Wall Street Journal.* Of the magazines which specialized on the Far East and were issued in the United States in the decade of the 1930's, *Asia* and *Pacific Affairs* were among the best known. Of the American magazines published in China, *The China Weekly Review* was the most important.

Various contemporary books which contain discussions of current international problems are also useful in reconstructing the atmosphere of the prewar days. Foremost among them are the Council on Foreign Relations' *The United States in World Affairs*; the Institute of Pacific Relations' *Problems of the Pacific*; and the Royal Institute of International Affairs' *Survey of International Affairs*. T. A. Bisson's *Japan in China*, a detailed account of the Sino-Japanese crisis of the mid-1930's published in 1938, is remarkably successful in bringing to life the spirit of the times.

More general accounts of the struggle between Japan and China in the mid-1930's, written considerably later, are available in the standards texts on the Far East. Among these *The Far East* by Paul H. Clyde should receive special attention because of the author's exceptional interest in and contribution to the study of American Far Eastern policy.

Many of the books about Roosevelt which have appeared since the President's death review the early phases of his foreign policy. The parts of that policy which were directly connected with China and Japan are briefly surveyed in A. Whitney Griswold's *The Far Eastern Policy of the United States* and Foster Rhea Dulles' *China and America*; but there are few relevant monographs. One notable advance has been made, however, namely the publication of Louis Morton's work on the United States army and navy's strategic plans for the Pacific area. Among the subjects which await further investigation is the role played by American bankers in the triangular relationship of the United States, China, and Japan.

In addition, it is to be hoped that in future we may obtain a more complete picture of American Far Eastern policy from 1933 to 1938 as it appeared to officials of other governments. In this connection the American primary sources are quite revealing but should be supplemented. As far as the Japanese are concerned the records of the International Military Tribunal for the Far East and the private recollections of statesmen, such as the Saionji-Harada Memoirs, have already yielded significant information which has been used to advantage by Robert J. C. Butow, F. C. Jones, Yale Candee Maxon, and Richard Storry among others. Our knowledge, moreover, should be greatly increased by the publication of *Taiheiyō Sensō e no Michi* (*The Road to the Pacific War*), a history of Japanese foreign policy from 1931 to 1941 being issued by the Nihon Kokusai Seiji Gakkai (Japan Association of International Politics). Consisting of seven volumes, this series has been written by a group of Japanese scholars who had access to a wide variety of sources including the archives of the Japanese Ministries of Foreign Affairs, War, and Navy, and diaries hitherto withheld from the public. As far as British and Chinese officials are concerned, the situation is less promising. Relatively few of the documents of the British and Chinese governments or the personal papers of their leaders are as yet available for the period under discussion.

UNPUBLISHED SOURCES

Clifford, Nicholas R. "British Policy in the Far East 1937-1941," unpub. diss., Harvard University.

Davis, Norman H. Papers, Division of Manuscripts, Library of Congress.

Department of Commerce. Archives, Washington, D. C.

Department of the Navy. Archives, Washington, D. C.

Department of State. Archives, Washington, D. C.

Forbes, W. Cameron. Papers, Houghton Library, Harvard University.

Grew, Joseph C. Diary, Houghton Library, Harvard University (Parts of Grew's diary are published in his *Ten Years in Japan*, New York: Simon and Schuster, 1944).

Hinton, Harold C. (untitled, unpublished manuscript).

Johnson, Nelson T. Papers, Division of Manuscripts, Library of Congress.

Kramer, Lawrence I., Jr. A Study of Editorial Opinion in Eight Newspapers in the United States on the Far Eastern Crisis, 1933-1938. This study was written in connection with the present volume and was given by Mr. Kramer to the author.

Leahy, Joseph P. "The China Policy of Charles Evans Hughes," unpub. diss., Duke University.

Leahy, William D. Papers, Division of Manuscripts, Library of Congress.

Moffat, Jay Pierrepont. Diary, Houghton Library, Harvard University (Parts of Moffat's diary are published in *The Moffat Papers: Selections from the Diplomatic Journals of Jay Pierrepont Moffat*, ed. by Nancy Harvison Hooker, Cambridge, Massachusetts: Harvard University Press, 1956).

Roosevelt, Franklin D. Papers, Franklin D. Roosevelt Library, Hyde Park, New York.

Saionji-Harada Memoirs. Exhibits 56 and 57 of the International Military Tribunal for the Far East.

Stimson, Henry L. Diary, Yale University Library.

Yarnell, Harry E. Diary, Division of Manuscripts, Library of Congress.

PUBLISHED SOURCES

Adler, Selig. *The Isolationist Impulse*, London and New York: Abelard-Schuman, 1957.

Allen, G. C., and Audrey G. Donnithorne. *Western Enterprise in Far Eastern Economic Development*, New York: Macmillan, 1954.

Almond, Gabriel A. *The American People and Foreign Policy*, New York: Praeger, 1960.

Alsop, Joseph, and Robert Kintner. *American White Paper*, New York: Simon and Schuster, 1940.

American Association of University Women. *Journal of the American Association of University Women* (quarterly), Washington, D. C.

American Chamber of Commerce of Shanghai. *Bulletin* (monthly).

American Economic Mission to the Far East, *American Trade Prospects in the Orient*, New York: National Foreign Trade Council, 1935.

American Union for Concerted Peace Efforts, *Manual for Organization*, New York: 1939.

Atwater, Elton. "Organizing American Public Opinion for Peace," *Public Opinion Quarterly*, April 1937.

Baldwin, A. W. *My Father: The True Story*, London: Allen and Unwin, 1955.

Baldwin, Hanson W. *Great Mistakes of the War*, New York: Harper, 1949.

Bardens, Dennis. *Portrait of a Statesman*, New York: Philosophical Library, 1956.

Bassett, R. *Democracy and Foreign Policy*, London: Longmans, Green, 1952.

Beard, Charles A. *American Foreign Policy in the Making 1932-1940*, New Haven: Yale University Press, 1946.

Beloff, Max. *The Foreign Policy of Soviet Russia 1929-1941*, London: Oxford University Press, 1947-1949 (2 vols.).

Bemis, Samuel Flagg. *A Diplomatic History of the United States*, New York: Henry Holt, 1936.

—— *The Latin American Policy of the United States*, New York: Harcourt, Brace, 1943.

Bertram, James M. *First Act in China: the Story of the Sian Mutiny*, New York: Viking, 1938.

Bisson, T. A. *America's Far Eastern Policy*, New York: International Secretariat, Institute of Pacific Relations, 1945.

—— *Japan in China*, New York: Macmillan, 1938.

Bloch, Kurt. *German Interests and Policies in the Far East*, New York: International Secretariat, Institute of Pacific Relations, 1939.

Blum, John Morton. *From the Morgenthau Diaries*, Boston: Houghton Mifflin, 1959.

Borchard, Edwin M., and William P. Lage. *Neutrality for the United States*, New Haven: Yale University Press, 1937.

Borg, Dorothy. *American Policy and the Chinese Revolution 1925-1928*, New York: American Institute of Pacific Relations and Macmillan, 1947.

—— "Notes on Roosevelt's 'Quarantine' Speech," *Political Science Quarterly*, September 1957.

Borton, Hugh. *Japan's Modern Century*, New York: Ronald Press, 1955.

Brandt, Conrad, Benjamin I. Schwartz, and John K. Fairbank. *A Documentary History of Chinese Communism*, Cambridge, Massachusetts: Harvard University Press, 1952.

Burns, James MacGregor. *Roosevelt: The Lion and the Fox*, New York: Harcourt, Brace, 1956.

Butow, Robert J. C. *Tojo and the Coming of the War*, Princeton: Princeton University Press, 1961.

Bywater, Hector C. *Sea-Power in the Pacific*, Boston: Houghton Mifflin, 1934.

Campbell-Johnson, Alan. *Eden, the Making of a Statesman*, New York: Ives Washburn, 1939.

Cantril, Hadley, ed. *Public Opinion 1935-1946*, Princeton: Princeton University Press, 1951.

Cohen, Bernard C. *The Influence of Non-Governmental Groups on Foreign Policy Making*, Studies in Citizenship Participation in International Relations, Boston: World Peace Foundation, 1959.

Chang Kia-ngau. *China's Struggle for Railroad Development*, New York: John Day, 1943.

Chennault, Claire Lee. *Way of a Fighter*, New York: Putnam, 1949.

Ch'ien Tuan-sheng. *Government and Politics of China*, Cambridge, Massachusetts: Harvard University Press, 1950.

Chow Tse-tung. *The May Fourth Movement*, Cambridge, Massachusetts: Harvard University Press, 1960.

Churchill, Winston S. *The Gathering Storm*, Boston: Houghton Mifflin, 1948.

Cianfarra, Camille M. *The Vatican and the War*, New York: Dutton, 1944.

Clyde, Paul H. *The Far East*, Englewood: Prentice Hall, 1958.

────── *Japan's Pacific Mandate*, New York: Macmillan, 1935.

Cole, Wayne S. *America First*, Madison: University of Wisconsin Press, 1953.

Condliffe, J. B. *China To-day: Economic*, Boston: World Peace Foundation.

Connally, Tom. *My Name Is Tom Connally*, New York: Crowell, 1954.

Conover, Helen F., comp. *Islands of the Pacific: A Selected List of References*, Washington, D. C.: Library of Congress, 1943.

Cooper, Alfred Duff. *Old Men Forget*, London: Rupert Hart-Davis, 1953.

Council on Foreign Relations. *The United States in World Affairs*, New York: Harper (annual survey published in each succeeding year).

Craigie, Sir Robert. *Behind the Japanese Mask*, London: Hutchison, 1946.

Dallin, David J. *Soviet Russia and the Far East*, New Haven: Yale University Press, 1948.

Davis, George T. *A Navy Second to None*, New York: Harcourt, Brace, 1940.

Davis, Norman H. "The Disarmament Problem," *Foreign Affairs*, April 1935.

DeConde, Alexander, ed. *Isolation and Security*, Durham: Duke University Press, 1957.

Dennett, Tyler. "Calm Settles on the Far East," *Current History*, July 1934.

────── "Japan Seeks American Agreement," *Current History*, May 1934.

────── "Japan Takes Her Stand," *Current History*, June 1934.

Department of the Army, United States, Office of the Chief of Military History. *Command Decisions*, New York: Harcourt, Brace, 1959.

Dimitroff, Georgi. "The Fifteenth Anniversary of the Communist Party of China," *Communist International*, October 1936.

Dirksen, Herbert von. *Moscow, Tokyo, London*, London: Hutchison, 1951.

Drummond, Donald F. *The Passing of American Neutrality 1937-1941*, Ann Arbor: University of Michigan Press, 1955.

Dull, Paul S., and Michael Takaaki Umemura. *The Tokyo Trials: A Functional Index to the Proceedings of the International Military*

Tribunal for the Far East, Ann Arbor: University of Michigan Press, 1957.

Dulles, Allen W., and Hamilton F. Armstrong. *Can America Stay Neutral?* New York: Harper, 1939.

Dulles, Foster Rhea. *China and America,* Princeton: Princeton University Press, 1946.

Ellinger, Werner B., and Herbert Rosinski, comp. *Sea Power in the Pacific 1936-1941* (a selected bibliography of books, periodicals and maps), Princeton: Princeton University Press, 1942.

Emergency Peace Campaign, Philadelphia. *Deadly Parallels,* 1937.

———— *News Bulletin* (monthly).

———— *No-Foreign-War Crusade,* Handbook, 1937.

———— *Program for Government Action to Keep Us Out of War and War Out of the World* (undated: early 1937 ?).

Epstein, Israel. *The Unfinished Revolution,* Boston: Little, Brown, 1947.

Everest, Allan Seymour. *Morgenthau, the New Deal and Silver,* New York: Columbia, King's Crown Press, 1950.

Fairbank, John K. *The United States and China,* Cambridge, Massachusetts: Harvard University Press, 1958.

Farley, James A. *Jim Farley's Story,* New York: McGraw-Hill, 1948.

Federal Council of Churches of Christ in America, New York. *Bulletin* (monthly, except July and August).

———— *Information Service* (weekly, except July and August).

Feiling, Keith. *The Life of Neville Chamberlain,* London: Macmillan, 1946.

Feis, Herbert. *The Road to Pearl Harbor,* Princeton: Princeton University Press, 1950.

———— *Seen From E. A.,* New York: Knopf, 1947.

Fellowship of Reconciliation, *Fellowship, Journal of the Fellowship of Reconciliation,* New York (monthly, except July and August).

Fenwick, Charles G. "The Inter-American Conference for the Maintenance of Peace," *American Journal of International Law,* April 1937.

Ferrell, Robert H. *American Diplomacy in the Great Depression,* New Haven: Yale University Press, 1957.

———— *Peace in Their Time,* New Haven: Yale University Press, 1952.

Fey, Harold E. *World Peace and Christian Missions,* New York: Friendship Press, 1937.

Field, Frederick V. *American Participation in the China Consortiums,* Chicago: University of Chicago Press, 1931.

Foreign Missions Conference of North America, New York. *Bulletin* (monthly).

———— *Information Service* (weekly).

———— Report of the 45th Annual Meeting, 1938.

———— Report of the 46th Annual Meeting, 1939.

Franklin D. Roosevelt and Pius XII: Wartime Correspondence, New York: Macmillan, 1947.

Freidel, Frank. *Franklin D. Roosevelt,* Boston: Little, Brown, 1952-1954-1956 (3 vols.).

Friedman, Irving S. *British Relations with China 1931-1939,* New York: International Secretariat, Institute of Pacific Relations, 1940.

Fundamental Laws of the Chinese Soviet Republic, New York: International Publishers, 1934.

Garner, James Wilford. *Studies in Government and International Law,* Urbana: University of Illinois Press, 1943.

Documents on German Foreign Policy 1918-1945 from the Archives of the German Foreign Ministry, Series D, Washington, D. C.: United States Government Printing Office, 1949-1956.

Gilchrist, Huntington. "The Japanese Islands; Annexation or Trusteeships," *Foreign Affairs,* July 1944.

Godley, Shirley. "W. Cameron Forbes and the American Mission to China (1935)," *Papers on China,* East Asian Research Center, Harvard University, December 1960.

Gosnell, Harold F. *Champion Campaigner: Franklin D. Roosevelt,* New York: Macmillan, 1952.

Great Britain (London, His Majesty's Stationery Office):
  History of the Second World War Series:
  The Economic Blockade, W. N. Medlicott, in *History of the Second World War,* United Kingdom Civil Series, 1952.
  The War Against Japan, Vol. I: The Loss of Singapore, Major General S. Woodburn Kirby, in *History of the Second World War,* United Kingdom Military Series, 1957.

Great Britain, Parliamentary Debates, House of Commons.

Grew, Joseph C. *Ten Years in Japan,* New York: Simon and Schuster, 1944.

―――― *Turbulent Era,* Boston: Houghton Mifflin, 1952 (2 vols.).

Griswold, A. Whitney. *The Far Eastern Policy of the United States,* New York: Harcourt, Brace, 1938.

Handlin, Oscar, and others, ed. *Harvard Guide to American History,* Cambridge, Massachusetts: Harvard University Press, 1955.

Hanwell, Norman. "China Driven to New Supply Routes," *Far Eastern Survey,* November 9, 1938.

―――― "France Takes Inventory in China," *Far Eastern Survey,* September 20, 1938.

Hinton, Harold B. *Cordell Hull,* New York: Doubleday Doran, 1942.

Hoe, Y. C. "The Programme of Technical Cooperation Between China and the League of Nations," Paper presented at the Institute of Pacific Relations Fifth Biennial Conference, Banff, Canada, August 1933.

Hooker, Nancy Harvison, ed. *The Moffat Papers,* Cambridge, Massachusetts: Harvard University Press, 1956.

Hoover, Herbert. *The Memoirs of Herbert Hoover: Vol. II 1920-1933,* New York: Macmillan, 1952.

Hornbeck, Stanley K. *Contemporary Politics in the Far East,* New York: Appleton, 1916.

Horowitz, Solis. *The Tokyo Trial,* International Conciliation pamphlet, New York: Carnegie Endowment for International Peace, November 1950.

Hsu, Shushi. *How the Far Eastern War Began,* Shanghai: Kelly and Walsh, 1938.

―――― *The North China Problem,* Shanghai: Kelly and Walsh, 1937.

Hull, Cordell. *The Memoirs of Cordell Hull,* New York: Macmillan, 1948 (2 vols.).

Ickes, Harold L. *The Secret Diary of Harold L. Ickes*, New York: Simon and Schuster, 1953-1959 (3 vols.).

Icklé, Frank William. *German-Japanese Relations 1936-1940*, New York: Bookman, 1956.

Inter-American Conference for the Maintenance of Peace, International Conciliation pamphlet, New York: Carnegie Endowment for International Peace, 1937.

Inter-American Conference for the Maintenance of Peace; Proceedings, (stenographic), Buenos Aires, 1937.

Jessup, Philip C. "The Argentine Anti-War Pact," *American Journal of International Law*, July 1934.

————— *Elihu Root*, New York: Dodd, Mead, 1938 (2 vols.).

————— "The Inter-American Conference for the Maintenance of Peace," *American Journal of International Law*, January 1937.

————— *Neutrality, Its History, Economics, and Law, IV: Today and Tomorrow*, New York: Columbia University Press, 1936.

Johnson, Walter. *The Battle Against Isolation*, Chicago: University of Chicago Press, 1944.

————— *William Allen White's America*, New York: Henry Holt, 1947.

Johnstone, William C. *The United States and Japan's New Order*, New York: Oxford University Press, 1941.

Jones, F. C. *Japan's New Order in East Asia 1937-45*, London: Oxford University Press, 1954.

————— *Shanghai and Tientsin*, New York: American Council, Institute of Pacific Relations, 1940.

Kao, Ping-shu. *Foreign Loans to China*, New York: Sino-International Economic Research Center, 1946.

Kennan, George F. *American Diplomacy 1900-1950*, Chicago: University of Chicago Press, 1951.

Kiang, Wen-han. *The Chinese Student Movement*, New York: Columbia, King's Crown Press, 1948.

Knatchbull-Hugessen, Sir Hughe. *Diplomat in Peace and War*, London: John Murray, 1949.

Knauer, Frederick J. "American Neutrality Reconsidered," *Columbia Law Review*, January 1936.

Lamont, Thomas W. *Across World Frontiers*, New York: Harcourt, Brace, 1951.

Langer, William L., and Everett S. Gleason. *The Challenge to Isolation*, New York: Harper, 1953.

League of Nations (Geneva). *Appeal by the Chinese Government: Report of the Commission of Enquiry*, 1932.

————— Council Committee of Technical Cooperation Between the League of Nations and China:

Report of the Technical Agent of the Council on his Mission to China from date of his Appointment until April 1st, 1934.

Annexes (reprinted Shanghai; *North China Daily News and Herald*), 1934.

Report of the Secretary of the Council Committee on his Mission to China, January-May 1935, 1935.

————— *Official Journal.*

———— *Official Journal: Special Supplements* 112, 169, 177.

———— Permanent Mandates Commission of the League of Nations: *Minutes of the 22d session November 3 to December 26, 1932.*
Minutes of the 26th session, October 29 to November 12, 1934.
Minutes of the 27th session, June 3 to 18, 1935.

———— *Ten Years of World Cooperation,* 1930.

———— *The Present Condition of China* (Documents Prepared by the Japanese Government and Communicated to the Commission of Enquiry Appointed by the Council of the League of Nations in Pursuance of Its Resolution of December 10, 1931) Doc. A, Appendix No. 3.

League of Nations Secretariat, "Memorandum of the League of Nation's Activities in the Pacific," Prepared for the 1936 Conference of the Institute of Pacific Relations, 1936.

———— "A New Procedure in International Life," Prepared for the 1939 Conference of the Institute of Pacific Relations, 1939.

Leavens, Dickson H. "American Silver Policy in China," *Harvard Business Review,* Autumn 1935.

———— "Silver in Recent Sessions of Congress," *Finance and Commerce,* October 9, 1935.

Levi, Werner. *Modern China's Foreign Policy,* Minneapolis: University of Minnesota Press, 1953.

Levy, Roger, and Andrew Roth. *French Interests and Policies in the Far East,* New York: International Secretariat, Institute of Pacific Relations, 1941.

Lewis, Cleona. *America's Stake in International Investments,* Washington, D. C.: Brookings, 1938.

Lin, W. Y. *The New Monetary System of China,* Shanghai: Kelly and Walsh, 1936.

Liu, F. F. *A Military History of Modern China, 1924-1949,* Princeton: Princeton University Press, 1956.

Liu, James T. C. "German Mediation in the Sino-Japanese War 1937-1938," *Far Eastern Quarterly,* 1949.

Lockwood, W. W., ed. *Our Far Eastern Record,* vol. I, New York: American Council, Institute of Pacific Relations, 1940.

Lowe, Chuan-hua. *Facing Labor Issues in China,* Shanghai: China Institute of Pacific Relations, 1933.

Madden, John T., Marcus Nadler, and Harry C. Sauvain. *America's Experience as a Creditor Nation,* New York: Prentice-Hall, 1937.

Mao Tse-tung. *Red China; President Mao Tse-tung Reports on the Progress of the Chinese Soviet Republic,* New York: International Publishers, undated; London: Martin Lawrence, 1934.

———— *Selected Works of Mao Tse-tung,* New York: International Publishers Library, 1954-1956.

Martin, Percy Alvin. *Latin America and the War,* Baltimore: Johns Hopkins Press, 1957.

Masland, John W. "American Attitudes Toward Japan," *Annals of the American Academy of Political and Social Science,* May 1941.

———— "Missionary Influence Upon American Far Eastern Policy," *Pacific Historical Review,* September 1941.

————— "The 'Peace' Groups Join Battle," *Public Opinion Quarterly*, December 1940.

————— "Pressure Groups and American Foreign Policy," *Public Opinion Quarterly*, Spring 1942.

Maxon, Yale Candee, *Control of Japanese Foreign Policy*, Berkeley and Los Angeles: University of California Press, 1957.

Michael, Franz H., and George E. Taylor. *The Far East in the Modern World*, New York: Henry Holt, 1956.

Miff, P. *Heroic China*, New York: Workers Library, 1937.

Moley, Raymond. *After Seven Years*, New York: Harper, 1939.

Moore, Harriet L. *Soviet Far Eastern Policy 1931-1945*, Princeton: Princeton University Press, 1945.

Morison, Elting E. *Turmoil and Tradition*, Boston: Houghton Mifflin, 1960.

Morison, Samuel Eliot. *The Rising Sun in the Pacific 1931-April 1942*, vol. III: *History of the United States Naval Operations in World War II*, Boston: Little, Brown, 1955.

Morton, Louis, "Army and Marines on the China Station: a Study in Military and Political Rivalry," *Pacific Historical Review*, February 1960.

————— "Pearl Harbor in Perspective, A Bibliographical Survey," in *United States Naval Institute Proceedings*, April 1955.

————— "War Plan Orange," *World Politics*, January 1959.

National Christian Council (China), Shanghai. Minutes of meetings of the N. C. C.

————— *Bulletin* (irregular).

National Committee for Cause and Cure of War, New York. *Delegates' Worksheet*, published for annual meetings.

————— *News Bulletin* (monthly).

National Council for the Prevention of War, Washington, D. C., *Press Information* (press releases).

————— *Peace Action* (monthly).

National Federation of Business and Professional Women, *Independent Woman*, Baltimore (monthly).

National League of Women Voters, *News Letter* (irregular), Washington, D. C.

National Peace Conference, New York. *National Peace Conference Information Bulletin*.

————— *Washington Information Service*, Washington, D. C.

National Peace Conference, Directory, Personnel, Aims, Activities, International Conciliation pamphlet, New York: Carnegie Endowment for International Peace, 1937.

National Study Conference of the Churches and the International Situation, *The Conflict in Asia*, Philadelphia: February 1940.

North, Robert C. *Moscow and Chinese Communists*, Stanford: Stanford University Press, 1952.

Ohaka, Keishi, ed. and comp. *Japanese Trade and Industry in the Meiji-Taisho Era*, translated by and adapted by Okaya Tamotsu, Tokyo: Obunsa, 1957, in Century Cultural Council Series, *A History of Japanese-American Cultural Relations (1853-1926) 1*.

Orchard, John. "Transport Facilities in China's Defense," *Far Eastern Survey*, November 5, 1937.

Otsuka, Reizo. "The Red Influence in China," Paper prepared for the Sixth Conference of the Institute of Pacific Relations, Yosemite National Park, California, 1936.

Perkins, Dexter. *The New Age of Franklin Roosevelt*, Chicago: University of Chicago Press, 1957.

—— "Was Roosevelt Wrong?" *Virginia Quarterly Review*, Summer 1954.

Phillips, William. *Ventures in Diplomacy*, Boston: Beacon, 1952.

Pomeroy, Earl S. "American Policy Respecting the Marshalls, Carolines, and Marianas 1898-1941," *Pacific Historical Review*, February 1948.

—— *Pacific Outpost*, Stanford: Stanford University Press, 1951.

Pratt, Sir John T. *War and Politics in China*, London: Jonathan Cape, 1943.

Pratt, Julius W. *A History of United States Foreign Policy*, Englewood: Prentice-Hall, 1957.

Presseisen, Ernst L. *Germany and Japan*, The Hague: Martinus Nijhoff, 1958.

Price, Willard. *Japan's Islands of Mystery*, New York: John Day, 1944.

Pringle, J. M. D. *China Struggles for Unity*, Harmondsworth, England: Penguin Books, 1939.

Problems of the Pacific, 1933, Proceedings of the 5th Conference of the Institute of Pacific Relations, Banff, Canada: London, New York, Toronto; Oxford University Press, 1934.

Problems of the Pacific, 1936, Proceedings of the 6th Conference of the Institute of Pacific Relations; Yosemite National Park, California, London, New York, Toronto: Oxford University Press, 1937.

The Public Papers and Addresses of Franklin D. Roosevelt, compiled and collated by Samuel I. Roseman, Vol. 2 1933, Vol. 3 1934, Vol. 4 1935, New York: Random House, 1938; Vol. 5 1937, New York: Macmillan, 1941.

Puleston, W. D. *The Armed Forces of the Pacific*, New Haven: Yale University Press, 1941.

Pusey, Merlo J. *Charles Evans Hughes*, New York: Macmillan, 1951 (2 vols.).

Quigley, Harold S., and George H. Blakeslee. *The Far East*, Boston: World Peace Foundation, 1938.

Rauch, Basil, *Roosevelt from Munich to Pearl Harbor*, New York: Creative Age Press, 1950.

Religious Directory. New York: Joseph F. Wagner, 1943.

Remer, C. F. *Foreign Investment in China*, New York: Macmillan, 1933.

The Revolutionary Movement in the Colonies: Thesis Adopted by the Sixth World Congress of the Communist International, New York: Workers Library Publishers, 1932.

Roosevelt, Eleanor. *This I Remember*, New York: Harper, 1949.

Roosevelt, Elliott, ed. *F. D. R. His Personal Letters 1928-1945*, New York: Duell, Sloan and Pearce, 1950 (2 vols.).

Roosevelt, Franklin D. "Our Foreign Policy. A Democratic View," Foreign Affairs, July 1928.

—— "Shall We Trust Japan?" *Asia*, July 1923.

Rosenman, Samuel I. *Working with Roosevelt*, New York: Harper, 1952.

Royal Institute of International Affairs, *Documents on International Affairs*, London: Oxford University Press (published annually).

———— *Survey of International Affairs*, London: Oxford University Press (annual survey published in each succeeding year).

Salter, Arthur S. *China and Silver*, New York: Economic Forum, 1934.

Schwartz, Benjamin I. "On the Originality of Mao Tse-tung," *Foreign Affairs*, October 1955.

Seeley, Evelyn. "—'And There Is No Peace,'" *Independent Woman*, January 1936.

Selle, Earl Albert. *Donald of China*, New York; Harper, 1948.

Sherwood, Robert E. *Roosevelt and Hopkins*, New York: Harper, 1948.

Smith, Holland, and Percy Finch. *Coral and Brass*, New York: Scribner's, 1949.

Smith, Sara R. *The Manchurian Crisis 1931-1932*, New York: Columbia University Press, 1949.

Snow, Edgar. *Random Notes on Red China 1936-1945*, Chinese Economic and Political Studies, Harvard University (distributed by Harvard University Press, Cambridge Massachusetts, 1957).

Soong, Mayling (Madame Chiang Kai-shek) *Sian: A Coup D'Etat* and Chiang Kai-shek, *A Fortnight in Sian: Extracts from a Diary*, Shanghai: China Publishing Company, 1937.

Sprout, Harold, and Margaret Sprout. *Toward a New Order of Sea Power*, Princeton: Princeton University Press, 1940.

Stimson, Henry I., and McGeorge Bundy. *On Active Service*, New York: Harper, 1947.

Stone, William T., and Clark M. Eichelberger. *Peaceful Change, the Alternative to War*, Headline Books, New York: Foreign Policy Association, 1937.

Storry, Richard. *The Double Patriots*, Boston: Houghton Mifflin, 1957.

A Study of Neutrality Legislation, Report of the Committee of the National Peace Conference, International Conciliation pamphlet, New York: Carnegie Endowment for International Peace, 1936.

Tamagna, Frank M. *Banking and Finance in China*, New York: International Secretariat, Institute of Pacific Relations, 1942.

———— *Italy's Interests and Policies in the Far East*, New York: International Secretariat, Institute of Pacific Relations, 1941.

T'ang Leang-li. *China's New Currency System*, Shanghai: China United Press, 1936.

Tansill, Charles Callan. *Back Door to War*, Chicago: Henry Regnery, 1952,

Tate, Merze. *The United States and Armaments*, Cambridge, Massachusetts: Harvard University Press, 1948.

Tawney, R. H. *Land and Labour in China*, New York: Harcourt, Brace, 1932.

Thomson, James C., Jr. "Communist Policy and the United Front in China 1935-1936," *Papers on China*, East Asian Research Center, Harvard University, December 1957.

Tompkins, Pauline. *American-Russian Relations in the Far East*, New York: Macmillan, 1949.

Tully, Grace. *F. D. R.: My Boss*, New York: Scribner's, 1949.

Tupper, Eleanor, and George E. McReynolds. *Japan in American Public Opinion*, New York: Macmillan, 1937.

United States (Washington, D. C.: United States Government Printing Office):

Congress. *Congressional Record*.

———*Hepburn Report*, 76th Congress, 1st session, House Document No. 65, 1938.

——— *Hearings before the Committee on Naval Affairs*, House of Representatives, on H. R. 2880, 76th Congress, 1st session, January 25-February 17, 1939.

——— *Hearings before the Committee on Naval Affairs*, Senate, on S. 830, 76th Congress, 1st session, March 6-14, 1939, 1939.

——— *Decline and Renaissance of the Navy 1922-44*, Prepared by Senator David I. Walsh, Chairman of the Committee on Naval Affairs, Senate, 78th Congress, 2d session, 1944.

——— *Hearings before the Joint Committee on the Investigation of the Pearl Harbor Attack*, 79th Congress, 1st session, 1946.

——— *Report of the Joint Committee on the Investigation of the Pearl Harbor Attack*, 79th Congress, 2d session, 1946.

Department of State. *Foreign Relations of the United States: Diplomatic Papers*, Volumes on the Far East:

1931, Vol. III (1946)
1932, Vol. III and IV (1948)
1933, Vol. III (1949)
1934, Vol. III (1950)
1935, Vol. III (1953)
1936, Vol. IV (1954)
1937, Vols. III and IV (1954)
1938, Vols. III and IV (1954-1955).

——— *Papers Relating to the Foreign Relations of the United States: Japan 1931-1941*, 1943 (2 vols.).

——— *Peace and War: United States Foreign Policy, 1931-1941*, 1943.

——— *Report of the Delegation of the United States to the Inter-American Conference for the Maintenance of Peace*, Buenos Aires, Argentina, December 1-27, 1937, Department of State Conference Series, No. 33, 1937.

——— *The Conference of Brussels November 3-24, 1937*, Department of State Conference Series, No. 37, 1938.

——— *The London Naval Conference of 1935*, Department of State Conference Series, No. 24, 1936.

——— *The Practical Accomplishments of the Buenos Aires Conference*, Address by Sumner Welles before the Academy of Political Science, Department of State Conference Series, No. 29, 1937.

Department of War. United States Army in World War II:

Campaign in Marianas, Philip A. Crowl, 1960 in *U.S. Army in World War II: Vol. IX The War in the Pacific.*

Chief of Staff: Prewar Plans and Preparations, Mark Skinner Watson, 1950 in *U.S. Army in World War II: Vol. I War Department.*

Strategic Planning for Coalition Warfare, 1941-1942, Maurice Matloff and Edwin M. Snell, 1953 in *U.S. Army in World War II: Vol. III War Department.*

United States Department of Commerce, Bureau of Foreign and Domestic Commerce, Office of the Commercial Attaché, Shanghai, *China Monthly Trade Report.*

Varg, Paul A. *Missionaries, Chinese, and Diplomats*, Princeton: Princeton University Press, 1958.

Vinacke, Harold M. *A History of the Far East in Modern Times*, New York: Appleton-Century-Crofts, 1959.

Vinson, John Chalmers. *The Parchment Peace: The United States Senate and the Washington Conference 1921-1922*, Athens: University of Georgia Press, 1955.

Wagner, Augusta. *Labor Legislation in China*, Peking: Yenching University, 1938.

Wales, Nym. *The Chinese Labor Movement*, New York: John Day, 1945.

Walters, F. P. *A History of the League of Nations*, London: Oxford University Press, 1960 (1 vol. ed.).

Wan Ming, and Sin Kang. *Revolutionary China Today*, Speeches at the 13th Plenum of the Executive Committee of the Communist International, New York: Workers Library Publishers, 1934.

Wang, Ching-wei. *China's Problems and Their Solution*, Shanghai: China United Press, 1934.

Wang Ming. *The Revolutionary Movement in the Colonial Countries*, New York: Workers Library Publishers, 1935.

Ware, Edith, E., ed. *The Study of International Relations in the United States*, New York: Columbia University Press, 1938.

Weizsacker, Ernst von. *Memoirs of Ernst von Weizsacker*, London: Gollancz, 1951.

Welles, Sumner. *Seven Decisions That Shaped History*, New York: Harper, 1950.

———— *The Time for Decision*, New York: Harper, 1944.

———— *Where Are We Heading?* New York: Harper, 1946.

Wilbur, Ray Lyman, and Arthur M. Hyde. *The Hoover Policies*, New York: Scribner's, 1937.

Wilson, Hugh R. *Diplomat Between Wars*, New York: Longmans, Green, 1941.

Woodhead, H. G. W., ed. *China Year Book*, annual, Shanghai: *North China Daily News and Herald.*

Woodward, E. L., and R. Butler, eds. *Documents on British Foreign Policy*, 3rd series, 1949-1955.

Wu, Aitchen K. *China and the Soviet Union*, New York: John Day, 1950.

Yakhontoff, Victor A. *The Chinese Soviets*, New York: Coward-McCann, 1934.

Yuan, Tung-li. *China in Western Literature*, New Haven: Yale University Press, 1958.

Zacharias, Ellis M. *Secret Missions*, New York: Putnam's, 1946.

NOTES

CHAPTER I. THE MANCHURIAN INCIDENT AND THE TANGKU TRUCE

1. *Foreign Relations of the United States* 1932, IV, 271. This series of papers, published by the State Department, will be referred to hereinafter by the initials *FR*; the numerals signify, in order, the year covered by the documents, the volume, and the page number on which the dispatch begins.

2. *FR Japan* 1931-1941, I, 17. This is a special volume in the series, *Foreign Relations of the United States.*

3. The following account of the Manchurian crisis is intended as no more than a "cursory look at the record" to bring out certain points which were to have an effect upon subsequent policy. It is largely based on Henry L. Stimson's writings, secondary sources, which will be cited in subsequent notes, and some of the documents in the *FR* series.

4. *FR* 1931, III, 43.

5. This comment is intended to reflect Stimson's point of view. It should be recognized, however, that there were those who felt that the Secretary did not support the League properly and that the failure of the League to settle the Manchurian controversy at the outset was due to Stimson's lack of prompt and adequate cooperation with Geneva. One of the most effective exponents of this school of thought is Sara R. Smith, who in 1949 argued her case in a monograph entitled *The Manchurian Crisis 1931-1932.*

6. *FR* 1931, III, 154, 164, 167, 178.

7. *Ibid.,* 205; also 177, 220.

8. *FR Japan* 1931-1941, I, 27.

9. *FR* 1933, I, 248; Henry L. Stimson, *The Far Eastern Crisis* (1936), p. 66; see also account of the Gilbert episode in Robert H. Ferrell's *American Diplomacy in the Great Depression* (1957), p. 142. Ferrell has colorful quotations from Stimson's diary.

10. *FR* 1933, I, 248.

11. *FR* 1931, III, 366 and *FR Japan* 1931-1941, I, 36 contain interesting telegrams dealing with the pros and cons of supporting the League resolution from the American viewpoint. Here again, Sara Smith argues that the United States failed the League.

12. *FR* 1931, III, 407; also 452.

13. *Ibid.,* 444; also 452.

14. *Ibid.,* 488, 499; also 504.

15. *Ibid.,* 504.

16. *Ibid.,* 488.

17. *FR Japan* 1931-1941, I, 60.

18. For a discussion of Stimson's attempts to strengthen the hands of the liberals in Japan and his discouragement over the failure of those attempts, see the Secretary's own comments in *The Far Eastern Crisis*, Pt. III, Sec. I; also Henry L. Stimson and McGeorge Bundy, *On Active Service* (1947), Chap. IX, Sec. 2.

19. Ferrell, *American Diplomacy*, p. 153.

20. This often quoted phrase appears in Stimson, *The Far Eastern Crisis*, p. 92.

21. Herbert Hoover, *The Memoirs of Herbert Hoover, Vol. II* (1952), p. 373.

22. Stimson and Bundy, *On Active Service*, p. 235.

23. Official text, *FR Japan* 1931-1941, I, 76.

24. Stimson and Bundy, *On Active Service*, p. 236.

25. The incident of the British communiqué gave rise to a controversy that appears to have no end. For Stimson's views as expressed in 1936, see *The Far Eastern Crisis*, Pt. III, Sec. III. The British position was set forth in a letter to the London *Times* written in 1938 by Sir John T. Pratt, who was adviser on Far Eastern Affairs in the Foreign Office during the Manchurian crisis. (This letter is reprinted in Sir John's *War and Politics in China* [1943], p. 274.) It is evident from Bundy's comments, however, that Sir John's explanation in no way altered Stimson's opinions. (Stimson and Bundy, *On Active Service*, p. 238.)

26. *FR* 1932, III, 256.

27. The Nine Power Treaty, it will be recalled, had specifically stated that its signatories would "provide the fullest and most unembarrassed opportunity to China to develop and maintain for herself an effective government." (Article I, paragraph 2.)

28. Stimson constantly referred to the Johnson cable. See, for example, *FR* 1932, III, 287, 341, 440. In the memorandum on page 440 he said that Johnson's messages were the "chief compelling motive of my letter to Borah."

29. *The Memoirs of Herbert Hoover*, Vol. II, p. 375.

30. *FR* 1932, III, 383.

31. *FR* 1932, III, 278, 294, 335, 341. The record of these telephone conversations makes extraordinary reading. Among other factors, one is constantly impressed by the inadequacy of the transatlantic telephone as a means of communication at that time. At one point, for example, Stimson referred to Charles Evans Hughes, and Sir John inquired as to whether he was talking about "a Japanese." It is interesting that, after the sinking of the *Panay*, Sir John refused to discuss important diplomatic matters over the telephone with Washington precisely on the grounds that the use of the transatlantic telephone had helped to create misunderstandings at the time of the Manchurian incident. (See Chap. XVI on the *Panay* crisis.)

32. Article X read: "The Members of the League undertake to respect and preserve as against external aggression the territorial integrity and existing political independence of all Members of the League. In case of any such aggression or in case of any threat or danger of such aggression the Council shall advise upon the means by which this obligation shall be fulfilled."

33. Stimson repeatedly stressed that the League could only invoke

the Covenant and that what was needed—in the President's opinion as well as his own—was a strengthening of the Paris Pact and the Nine Power Treaty. (See, for example, *FR* 1933, III, 335 and 341.)

34. *Ibid.*, 352.

35. Norman Davis papers (hereinafter referred to as the Davis papers). Quoted in Foreign Office memorandum dated April 30, 1935. See also references to this memorandum in Pratt's *War and Politics in China*, pp. 272, 282.

36. In December 1934, Norman Davis during the course of a week-end at Lord Lothian's remarked that, according to his recollection, in 1932 the United States had suggested to the British that their governments should jointly call a conference of the signatories of the Nine Power Treaty to settle the Manchurian crisis. According to some of those present, he also stated that, while we had run out on the British in 1919 by not accepting the Covenant of the League, they had run out on us in 1932 by not supporting the proposal for a Nine Power Conference. These comments created a considerable furor in British official circles with the consequence that Davis asked Stimson to relate just what had happened. This led Stimson to write the confidential memorandum cited above, which is dated March 15, 1935. There was further correspondence on this subject, including the Foreign Office memorandum of April 30, 1935 (see note 35) and a curious letter signed J. S., apparently from Sir John Simon. All these documents are in the Davis papers.

37. For original draft and final text, see *FR Japan* 1931-1941, I, 80, 83.

38. See below for further discussion of the argument that the Washington Conference treaties were interrelated.

39. *Documents on International Affairs 1932*, Sec. C, on "The Sino-Japanese Dispute" contains an unusually large number of documents relative to the Manchurian crisis covering the period from September 1931 to March 1933. The March 11, 1932, resolution is on p. 284.

40. The Lytton report was published by the League under the title *Appeal by the Chinese Government: Report of the Commission of Enquiry*, 1932. The League also issued an official summary.

41. Stimson Diary, entry of January 12, 1933. The only parts of Stimson's diary read in connection with the present study were those dealing with events leading up to the advent of the Roosevelt administration.

42. *FR* 1932, IV, 287.

43. *Ibid.*, 300, 303.

44. *Survey of International Affairs 1933*. Arnold Toynbee, in describing the meeting of the Assembly, states that a "'class difference' between the attitude of the Great Powers and the attitude of the smaller countries made itself apparent." Stimson himself was greatly impressed by this point and also by Toynbee's whole account of the Manchurian crisis.

45. *FR* 1933, IV, 405, 424.

46. Ferrell in his *American Diplomacy* gives an account of the meeting between Stimson and Roosevelt that emphasizes the part of the discussion that dealt with the Manchurian situation. (See Chap. 14, "A Meeting at Hyde Park.") At a news conference on January 17, 1933, in response to an effort on the part of the reporters to get him to state his views on the

Far Eastern crisis, Roosevelt, borrowing a pencil from one of the correspondents, wrote:

Any statement relating to any particular foreign situation must, of course, come from the Secretary of State of the United States.

I am, however, wholly willing to make it clear that American foreign policies must uphold the sanctity of international treaties. That is the cornerstone on which all relations between nations must rest.

(*FR Japan* 1931-1941, I, 109.)

47. *FR* 1933, III, 48.

48. *Ibid.*, 46. See also *FR Japan* 1931-1941, 107, 108.

49. *FR* 1933, III, 53.

50. *Ibid.*, 54, 59, 61.

51. The report was issued as Special Supplement No. 112 to the *Official Journal* of the League of Nations. The general principle laid down in respect to the government of Manchuria was that the "maintenance and recognition of the existing regime in Manchuria" would be "incompatible with the fundamental principles of existing international obligations" but that, at the same time, there should be no return to the "*status quo* existing before September 1931." (Pt. IV, Sec. III.)

52. Stimson Diary, entry of February 24, 1933.

53. For Hoover's opinions on sanctions and his differences with Secretary Stimson on this subject, see *The Memoirs of Herbert Hoover*, Vol. II, Chap. 48; Stimson and Bundy, *On Active Service*, Chap. IX; Elting E. Morison, *Turmoil and Tradition* (1960), pp. 390, 394.

54. See for example *FR Japan* 1931-1941, I, 99 and 102 and Joseph C. Grew's *Ten Years in Japan* (1944), p. 39.

55. *FR* 1932, IV, 705 with enclosure.

56. *Ibid.*, 289.

57. *FR* 1933, III, 195.

58. *Ibid.*, 209; Stimson Diary, entry of Feb. 24, 1933.

59. Text in *FR Japan* 1931-1941, I, 115.

60. An excellent description of the atmosphere inside the State Department at this time is to be found in the diary entries of Pierrepont Moffat, who had been made Chief of the Division of Western European Affairs in 1932. The Moffat Diary will be referred to as such in subsequent notes, but the reader should distinguish between this and *The Moffat Papers*, a published selection from the diaries.

61. There had been a widespread rumor that Roosevelt on becoming President would appoint Norman Davis as Secretary of State. Moffat records that Davis told him early in March that he was entirely reconciled to having "missed out" on the appointment. Apparently Hull before accepting the post told Davis that he would only consider it if he could count on Davis' assistance, especially in representing the United States at Geneva in regard to the disarmament problem. (Moffat Diary, entry of March 1, 1933).

62. For a review of the events connected with the arms embargo resolution, see the State Department memorandum printed in *FR* 1933, I, 369.

63. Stimson's remarks to the committee were intended to be secret. But one of the committee members asked for his notes which were accidentally given to a newspaper reporter later. (*FR* 1933, I, 361.)

64. Stimson's speech was delivered at the Council on Foreign Relations and was originally published as a Special Supplement to Vol. XI, No. 1 of *Foreign Affairs* (Oct. 1932). At the beginning of 1933, the Secretary was considering the possibility of writing an article for *Foreign Affairs* reviewing the fundamental principles which had governed his foreign policy. Moffat records that Stimson said his main interest had been in the development of the peace machinery which he felt was best exemplified in the Covenant of the League and the Paris Pact. The Covenant he regarded as a highly logical document, almost Latin in concept; the Paris Pact, on the other hand, he looked upon as pliable and vague, very like the common law in that it depended for its growth upon precedent. The Pact, he maintained, had been the cornerstone of the Hoover administration's foreign policy and he had made every effort to further its development. (Moffat Diary, entries of Jan. 30 and Feb. 10, 1933.)

65. *FR 1933*, I, 369.

66. Moffat Diary, entry of March 20, 1933.

67. *Ibid.*, entry of March 22, 1933.

68. R. Bassett, in his *Democracy and Foreign Policy* (1952), discusses this episode in detail in Chap. XIX. For a different point of view, see Toynbee's account in the *Survey of International Affairs*, for 1933, p. 512.

69. *FR 1933*, III, 204.

70. *Ibid.*, 210, 215, 219, 220, 238; *FR Japan 1931-1941*, I, 117, 118.

71. *Ibid.*, 238, 239.

72. *Ibid.*, 239.

73. *Ibid.*, 257, 260.

74. *Ibid.*, 265.

75. Among the contemporary accounts of the Disarmament Conference which recall the spirit of the times is Toynbee's in the 1933 volume of the *Survey of International Affairs* and Walter Lippmann's, in the volume for the same year, of *The United States in World Affairs* series.

76. The Germans had asked for a specific promise that the new disarmament convention would replace the military clauses of the Versailles Treaty and give them equality of status in armaments with the other powers.

77. Davis papers, letter to Pierrepont Moffat, dated March 29, 1933. See also Hugh R. Wilson's *Diplomat Between Wars* (1941), p. 285.

78. The way had been paved for the acceptance of these ideas earlier. (See *FR 1933*, I, 25, 89.) The views of the American delegation are well defined in a letter to Walter Lippmann written by Allen Dulles, who accompanied Davis to Geneva. Dulles argued that a "new doctrine of neutrality" was the inevitable outcome of the Kellogg-Briand Pact, as Stimson had already indicated, but that the new doctrine should be restricted to Europe. (Davis papers, letter dated May 30, 1933.)

79. *FR 1933*, I, 89, 93; see also 113.

80. *Ibid.*, 102; Moffat Diary, entries of April 18, 19, 20, 1933.

81. *FR 1933*, I, 102; Moffat Diary, entries of April 22, 24, 25 and May 14, 20, 23, 25, 1933. Moffat gives a vivid picture of developments at this time. Apparently, during MacDonald's visit, policy was made at the White House. Thereafter, almost all of the responsibility was left in the hands of the few specialists in the State Department who had been dealing with the disarmament problem. Hull, in sharp contrast to the account in

his memoirs, seems to have remained strictly on the sidelines. (*The Memoirs of Cordell Hull* [1948], I, 223ff.)

82. FR 1933, III, 106, 124.

83. Roosevelt suddenly issued a statement on May 16. Hitler had unexpectedly announced that he was reconvening the almost forgotten Reichstag and that, on May 17, he would deliver a major foreign policy speech before it. It was generally feared that the speech would constitute an announcement that Germany intended to withdraw from the Disarmament Conference at once and carry out a large rearmament program. In the hope of influencing Hitler to be more conciliatory, Roosevelt addressed an appeal to fifty-four nations endorsing the plan for disarmament which MacDonald had presented at Geneva in March. In addition, the President threw out the suggestion that

all the nations of the world should enter into a solemn and definite pact of non-aggression: That they should solemnly reaffirm the obligations they have assumed to limit and reduce their armaments, and, provided these obligations are faithfully executed by all signatory powers, individually agree that they will send no armed force of whatsoever nature across their frontiers. (Text in *The United States in World Affairs*, 1933, appendix V (a).)

Whether correctly or not, it was widely believed at the time that Roosevelt's speech did achieve its goal of making Hitler take a more moderate stand for the moment.

84. *Survey of International Affairs 1933*, p. 275.

85. *Ibid.*

86. FR 1933, I, 365.

87. *Ibid.*, 369.

88. *The Memoirs of Cordell Hull*, I, 229.

89. Johnson papers, letter dated Jan. 10, 1933.

90. *Ibid.*, letter dated only January 1933.

91. *Ibid.*, letter dated July 16, 1936.

92. *Ibid.*, letter dated June 8, 1934.

93. Grew Diary, entry of Jan. 27, 1933.

94. Grew, *Ten Years in Japan*, pp. 78ff.

95. FR 1933, III, 287, 289, 291, 293, 303. (These references cover the story of both the Japanese and Chinese efforts to get Sir Miles Lampson and Nelson Johnson to mediate the Sino-Japanese dispute.)

96. Roosevelt papers, PSF, China 1933-1935, Box 10.

97. FR 1933, III, 314.

98. *Ibid.*, 327.

99. Roosevelt papers, PSF, China 1933-1935, Box 10; see memorandum attached to Under Secretary of State Phillips' letter of May 9, 1933, entitled "Manchurian Situation" with subtitle "The Tientsin-Peiping Area," and memoranda attached to unsigned note sent to Howe dated May 8, 1933; also FR 1933, III, 325, 327. All the quotations in the following paragraph in the text are taken from the memorandum attached to Phillips' letter.

100. Hornbeck felt that the Manchurian crisis had demonstrated that the American people had a greater devotion to the principles embodied in the postwar peace agreements than other peoples and that they were

more concerned over Japan's violations of these principles. (*FR* 1934, III, 189.)

101.   Concerning our material interests, Hornbeck said "The United States has not much to lose. The principles of our Far Eastern policy and our ideals with regard to world peace may be further scratched and dented (they have been considerably so in this connection) and our trade prospects may be somewhat further impaired; but from the point of view of material interests there is nothing there [i.e., in North China] that is vital to us." (Roosevelt papers, PSF, China 1933-1935, Box 10, memorandum attached to Phillips' letter of May 9, 1933.)

102.   *FR* 1933, III, 327; also 290.

103.   Hornbeck added that Hugh Wilson and Norman Davis "share our view in that connection."

104.   *FR* 1933, III, 336. Text in cable to Nelson Johnson.

105.   *FR* 1933, III, 325, 338, 340, 341, 347, contain Johnson's cables in respect to the North China situation. The Department's response concerning the airplane incident is on p. 334 of the same volume.

106.   The *New York Times* articles are quoted in T. A. Bisson's *Japan in China* (1938), p. 43.

107.   This is the phrase used by Bisson (*Japan in China*, p. 44). Probably the best account of the Tankgu Truce is still that which was published in 1937 by Shushi Hsu in his book, *The North China Problem* (Chap. I).

108.   Grew papers, letter to Secretary of State, dated May 11, 1933.

109.   Grew, *Ten Years in Japan*, p. 96; see also p. 89.

110.   *FR* 1933, III, 702.

111.   Grew, *Ten Years in Japan*, p. 93.

112.   Grew Diary, entry of Oct. 5, 1933.

113.   Grew, *Ten Years in Japan*, p. 99.

114.   *FR Japan* 1931-1941, I, 123; Grew papers, conversation memoranda.

115.   *FR Japan* 1931-1941, I, 123.

116.   *Ibid.*, 125.

117.   Grew Diary, entry of Oct. 27, 1933.

118.   *FR Japan* 1931-1941, I. The text of Hirota's message appears on p. 127 and is immediately followed by the text of Hull's reply.

119.   The Johnson papers contain digests of a series of memoranda, written by Johnson, under the general title "The Far Eastern Situation and Peoples Involved"; in the series were papers on "The Chinese Mind," "The American Mind," "The Character of China Before the Revolution," "China and World Peace," and "American Policy." The digests were made in the State Department and sent to Johnson by Hornbeck on Jan. 2, 1934.

120.   Johnson papers, letter dated Aug. 29, 1933.

121.   Johnson papers, memoranda as cited in note 119; letter to Roy Howard, dated Aug. 29, 1933; letter to Nicholas Murray Butler, dated July 9, 1934; letter to Stanley Hornbeck, dated April 12, 1934. These are only some of the instances in which Johnson explained this theory in detail. The writer of this volume has tried to adhere as closely as possible not only to the concepts but to the words and phrases that Johnson repeatedly used. By way of explanation it should perhaps be added that where he had certain fixed beliefs (such as those described here) he returned to

them frequently and expressed them, over a period of years, in much the same way.

122. Johnson papers. See for example letter to Roy Howard, dated Aug. 29, 1933.

123. Johnson papers, enclosed in letter to Stanley Hornbeck, dated April 12, 1934.

124. Johnson papers, letter to Assistant Secretary of State, Judge R. Walton Moore, dated Aug. 15, 1934.

125. Johnson papers, letter dated June 1, 1933.

CHAPTER II. THE CHALLENGE OF THE AMAU DOCTRINE

1. Among the many books dealing with this period are such general surveys as *The Far East* (1958) by Paul H. Clyde (Chaps. 29 and 31), *The Far East in the Modern World* (1956) by Franz H. Michael and George E. Taylor (Chap. XII), *The United States and China* (1958) by John K. Fairbank (Chaps. 10 and 11), and the more specific study of *The Government and Politics of China* by Ch'ien Tuan-sheng.

2. Chang Tso-lin was killed when, on retreating to Mukden, his train was dynamited at the instigation of the Japanese. Chang Hsueh-liang, known as the "Young Marshal," accepted the authority of the Nanking government against the will of the Japanese, who had hoped to exercise control over his activities. He thereafter became one of the chief targets of Japan's hostility. His troops were driven out of Manchuria by the Japanese in 1931.

3. Chiang Kai-shek had been president but gave up this post to Lin Sen, who held it until his death in 1943. The presidency, however, was shorn of any real power. The Generalissimo himself retained the important positions of Commander-in-Chief and Chairman of the Military Council through which he had control of the army.

4. Edgar Snow, *Red Star Over China* (1938), p. 165.

5. *Ibid.*, p. 166.

6. The Japanese, as indicated in Chapter I, insisted that, since the Washington Conference, the Chinese had demonstrated they were incapable of creating a strong nation; therefore, the principles of the Nine Power Treaty should be discarded.

7. *Appeal by the Chinese Government: Report of the Commission of Enquiry*, Chap. I (p. 13).

8. *FR 1933*, III, 171.

9. *Ibid.*, 491.

10. Johnson papers, letters to: Kermit Roosevelt, dated Dec. 22, 1933; O. Edmund Clubb, dated Aug. 30, 1934; Roy Howard, dated Jan. 13, 1934; and Hunter Miller, dated Jan. 3, 1934.

11. State Department files 893.00/12842.

12. Roosevelt papers, PSF, China 1933-1935, Box 10.

13. State Department files 711. 93/302.

14. Sun Yat-sen, *San Min Chu I*, p. 10.

15. Y. C. Hoe, "The Programme of Technical Cooperation between China and the League of Nations" (1933).

16. *Problems of the Pacific 1933*, Selected Documents, IV. "Chinese Government Economic Planning and Reconstruction" by Gideon Chen.

17. Hoe, "Technical Cooperation," p. 23.

18. *Ibid., Problems of the Pacific 1933*, p. 366.

19. *Report of the Technical Agent of the Council on his Mission in China*, p. 37.

20. *Annexes to the Report to the Council of the League of Nations of its Technical Delegate on his Mission in China*, No. 8 on National Health Administration and No. 9 on education. J. M. D. Pringle's *China Struggles for Unity* (1939), pp. 106ff., summarizes some of the work of the educational mission and its results.

21. *Annexes to the Report to the Council of the League of Nations of its Technical Delegate on his Mission in China*, No. 6.

22. *Ibid.*, p. 180.

23. *Ibid.*, p. 175.

24. *Ibid.*, pp. 171, 196.

25. *Ibid.*, p. 229; *Report of the Technical Agent of the Council on his Mission in China*, pp. 31-33.

26. A memorandum, prepared by some of the members of the League of Nations Secretariat for the Institute of Pacific Relations conference of November 1939, defined this point clearly:

The system of technical collaboration evolved during the last decade between the League of Nations and China has initiated a new procedure in international relations . . .

The basic principle involved in this procedure is, briefly, that a State facing serious problems at home and desiring expert advice from abroad may apply to an international institution . . . and be assured of receiving the best technical assistance without impairment of its national prestige or danger of unexpected political consequences. ("A New Procedure in International Life," p. 1.)

27. The Japanese appear to have been especially concerned over the possibility that the League might serve as an instrument for the international financing and conduct of a big reconstruction effort in China. It should be remembered that the League played such a role in Austria following the first World War and in other countries subsequently. At the time that the Assembly was about to draw up a resolution based upon the Lytton report, Sir Eric Drummond tentatively suggested that the resolution might provide for the establishment of a committee of the interested powers to devise a plan for the reconstruction of China. Drummond's idea was that a committee of this kind would (1) strengthen the Chinese government and encourage the Chinese people in general and (2) put pressure on the Japanese since they would wish to participate in the committee but would be told that they could not do so usefully until they had settled the Manchurian controversy. Norman Davis, in a talk with Drummond, expressed doubts about the advisability of injecting so complicated a question as that of the reconstruction of China into the Assembly resolution. First, he felt that it would be a tacit admission of Japan's claim that its action in Manchuria was justified by the lack of a stable government in China. Secondly, he believed that a committee "would not be able, in any reasonable time at least, to work out a plan for the reconstruction of China as it would require substantial financial assistance which could not now

be secured"; it was, therefore, "unwise" to hold out hopes to the Chinese which might not be realized. (*FR* 1932, IV, 336.)

For contemporary discussions of other schemes similar to that which Sir Eric Drummond had in mind, see *Problems of the Pacific* (1929), p. 372. At the 1929 conference of the Institute of Pacific Relations, one of the members of the Chinese delegation, who was a leading Chinese banker, urged the appointment by the League of an International Commission on the Economic Development of China to formulate a plan for the rehabilitation of China and take charge of the raising of funds from Chinese and foreign investors. (Also discussed in Hoe, "Technical Cooperation.")

28. The *North China Herald,* for example, stated in a long editorial that some of the schemes proposed by the League's experts in China were realistic while others were no more than "admirable counsels of perfection." Concerning the latter, it said: "They have been equivalent in their practicability to the advice of a Harley Street physician who tells a labouring man to send away his sick wife to the Riviera for six months." ("True Cooperation," July 26, 1933, editorial.)

29. Johnson papers, letter to Kermit Roosevelt, dated Dec. 22, 1933.

30. *Appeal by the Chinese Government: Report of the Commission of Enquiry,* p. 23.

31. Stimson, *The Far Eastern Crisis,* Appendix IV, p. 282.

32. The text of this well known letter appears in many places, among them being the *Report of the Technical Agent of the Council on his Mission in China,* Introduction.

33. League of Nations, *Official Journal,* Sept. 1933, p. 1058.

34. *FR* 1933, III, 499.

35. *Ibid.,* 497.

36. Besides its membership on the Advisory Committee, the United States government, since the early 1920's, had increasingly made use of "unofficial observers" who cooperated more and more actively in the technical work of the League. By 1930, American experts were members of several committees of the League's Communications and Transit Organization, Health Committee, Committee on Intellectual Cooperation, Committee of Experts for the Progressive Codification of International Law, Financial Committee, Fiscal and Economic Committees, and Advisory Commission for the Protection and Welfare of Children and Young People. (League of Nations, *Ten Years of World Cooperation* (1930), p. 9.)

37. *FR* 1933, III, 197.

38. *Ibid.,* 498.

39. *Ibid.,* 500.

40. As quoted on page 6 in the *Report of the Technical Agent of the Council on his Mission to China,* the Committee passed a resolution which read in part:

The appointment of the technical agent requested by the Chinese Government is of a purely technical and entirely nonpolitical character . . .

The duties of the technical agent shall be:

(1) To supply information on the working of the technical organizations of the League and on the manner in which these organizations may be utilized for the purpose of cooperation in the reconstruction of China;

(2) To transmit to the Secretary-General of the League of Nations, for sub-

mission to the competent organization or organizations, any request for technical cooperation which he may receive from the Chinese Government;

(3) To afford the Chinese Government such assistance as it may desire with a view to securing the cooperation of such experts as that Government might wish to engage for a technical service connected with the work of reconstruction, and,

(4) To assist the National Economic Council in co-ordinating on the spot the activities of the experts of the League's technical organizations . . .

The Committee . . . desires to state that it will in future remain at the Council's disposal for the purpose of:

(a) Considering any questions in relation to the League's technical cooperation in the reconstruction of China that may be laid before the Council by the Chinese Government;

(b) Examining the statements and reports received from the technical agent and discussing all questions relating to the discharge of his duties which the Committee may deem it desirable to consider.

41. *FR* 1933, III, 502.

42. According to an expert of the Chinese Ministry of Economic Affairs, "Excise tax was assigned as security, with cigarettes, flour, cotton thread, matches, tobacco and liquor stamp duty helping to meet the bill. There was also a five per cent customs for additional flood relief revenue as second security." Ping-shu Kao, *Foreign Loans to China* (1946), p. 26.

43. *New York Times*, June 5, 1933, p. 1, "$50,000,000 Lent to China to Buy Cotton and Wheat."

44. *China Weekly Review*, June 24, 1933, p. 139, "Some Reflections on the Fifty Million Dollar Cotton Loan;" *North China Herald*, June 21, 1933, p. 442, "American Loan to China."

45. *FR* 1933, III, 495; State Department files 711.93/302 (part of this document may be found in *FR* 1933, III, 643).

46. The Second or New Consortium as organized in 1920 consisted of four national Groups: American, British, French and Japanese. Frederick V. Field in his *American Participation in the China Consortiums* (1931), lists the banks that were members of the different Groups (p. 165). Since its inception, the Consortium had prevented the negotiation of certain loans but had not made any loans of its own.

47. See speech by Frederick W. Stevens, representative of the American group, made in China in 1922 in an effort to counteract Chinese criticisms of the Consortium. (Cited in Field, *American Participation in the China Consortiums*, pp. 175, 181.)

48. For Hornbeck's comments on this point, see later in this chapter.

49. *FR* 1933, III, 495.

50. *Ibid.*

51. *Ibid.*, 501.

52. *Ibid.*, 505.

53. State Department files 711.93/302.

54. Keishi Ohaka, ed. and comp., *Japanese Trade and Industry in the Meiji-Taisho Era*, Pt. VI, Chap. II, deals with the increased American business in Japan following World War I and touches on the part played by J. P. Morgan and Co. (p. 450). For public attacks upon Lamont for helping Japan at China's expense see the *China Weekly Review*, "How Morgan Power Was Felt in Far Eastern Politics" (June 24, 1933, p. 140). "Is Japan

Blocking 'Consortium' Loans to China?" (April 7, 1934, p. 203), "Morgan and Co. and the Japanese 'Hands-Off' Doctrine" (June 30, 1934, p. 171).

55. Johnson papers, letter from Thomas W. Lamont, dated Nov. 3, 1933; FR 1934, III, 414; also 377 and 378.

56. FR 1933, III, 502.

57. Ibid., 508.

58. Ibid., 512.

59. Japanese press summaries are to be found in FR 1933, III, 388, 509; current issues of the China Weekly Review and the North China Herald also carried many references to articles in Japanese newspapers.

60. North China Herald, "League Help for China," July 26, 1933, p. 123.

61. Ibid., Aug. 2, 1933, p. 168, "Mr. Soong's Activities."

62. FR 1933, III, 508.

63. Ibid., China Weekly Review, July 29, 1933, p. 346, "Tokyo Warlords Worry about Upton Close, the League, and Loans to China."

64. Roosevelt papers, PSF, China 1933-1935, Box 10, dated Aug. 2, 1933.

65. The credit was thought not to violate the letter of the Consortium agreement as it did not involve any public bond issue.

66. Roosevelt papers, PSF, China 1933-1935, Box 10, dated Aug. 2, 1933.

67. Memorandum also dated Aug. 2, 1933.

68. State Department files 711.93/302.

69. Ibid., section marked "Comment."

70. FR 1933, III, 512.

71. FR 1934, III, 414; Johnson papers, letter from Thomas W. Lamont, dated Nov. 3, 1933.

72. Johnson papers, letter from Thomas W. Lamont, dated Nov. 3, 1933.

73. FR 1933, III, 444.

74. FR 1934, III, 377, 379; text of statement in North China Herald, June 6, 1934, p. 333, "New Finance." The corporation was a syndicate of leading Chinese government and private banks. See also Frank M. Tamagna, Banking and Finance in China (1942), pp. 181, 186, 188, 201, 353. G. C. Allen and Audrey G. Donnithorne, Western Enterprise in Far Eastern Economic Development (1954), p. 118.

75. FR 1934, III, 421.

76. Report of the Technical Agent of the Council on his Mission in China, see various sections dealing with these subjects.

77. Annexes to the Report to the Council of the League of Nations of its Technical Delegate on his Mission in China, Nos. 4 and 5.

78. Sir Arthur S. Salter, China and Silver (1934).

79. FR 1934, III, 408.

80. Ibid., 395.

81. Ibid., 373.

82. For Dr. Soong's statement on this, see China Weekly Review, March 31, 1934, p. 169, "T. V. Soong Makes Report on Cotton and Wheat Loan."

83. F. F. Liu, *A Military History of Modern China, 1924-1949* (1956), Chap. 10.

84. For summary of developments see *FR* 1934, III, 288; see also *FR* 1932, III, 582, 636, 643, 680.

85. The Department of Commerce had transmitted messages between the Chinese government and members of the Jouett group (*FR* 1934, III, 288).

86. *FR* 1933, III, 455.

87. *Ibid.*, 285, 300; *FR* 1934, III, 315; Frank M. Tamagna, *Italy's Interests and Policies in the Far East* (1941), p. 19; Claire Lee Chennault, *Way of a Fighter* (1949), p. 36.

88. *FR* 1934, III, 315; Johnson papers, letter to Roy Howard, dated July 27, 1934.

89. *China Monthly Trade Report*, March 1, 1937, p. 7.

90. *Ibid.*, p. 128.

91. *FR* 1934, III, 372.

92. *FR* 1933, III, 388; China Weekly Review, Aug. 5, 1933, p. 391, "Japan's Initial Attempt to Assert Her 'Monroe Doctrine' Apparently Has Failed," and Sept. 19, 1933, p. 99, "League's Technical Aid to China; Dr. Rajchman and T. V. Soong"; *North China Herald*, Aug. 9, 1933, "Sino-American Air Treaty Bogey."

93. See for example *FR* 1933, III, 388; and *FR* 1934, III, 44.

94. *FR Japan* 1931-1941, I, 223, 228, 230; *FR* 1934, III, 112, 115, 117, 123, 160, 181.

95. *FR Japan* 1931-1941, I, 230; *FR* 1934, III, 141.

96. *FR Japan* 1931-1941, I, 227; *FR* 1934, III, 160, 181; Joseph C. Grew, *Turbulent Era* II (1952), section beginning p. 957 and Grew, *Ten Years in Japan*, diary entry beginning p. 128.

97. *FR Japan* 1931-1941, I, 227.

98. *FR* 1934, III, 160.

99. Grew, *Ten Years in Japan*, p. 130.

100. *FR* 1934, III, 117, 123, 160, 180.

101. Monnet had formerly occupied a high post in the League of Nations.

102. Toward the end of 1933 the American Curtiss-Wright Corporation announced plans for the construction of an airplane assembly plant to be set up in Hangchow. T. A. Bisson, *America's Far Eastern Policy* (1945), p. 39.

103. *FR* 1934, III, 143.

104. *Ibid.*, 121, 122, 125, 131, 135, 141.

105. *Ibid.*, 126.

106. State Department files, Hornbeck memorandum dated April 24, 1934, entitled "Problem Presented by Statement of the Spokesman of the Japanese Foreign Office."

107. *FR* 1934, III, 165; long report by Ambassador Bingham on British policy in connection with Amau declaration. For the ambassador's explanation of the British shift in policy see Chap. III.

108. State Department files 793.94/6700.

109. For subsequent British policy see note 179.

110. State Department files 793.94/6700, memorandum dated April 28, 1934.

111. *FR Japan* 1931-1941, I, 231.

112. *FR* 1934, III, 153.

113. State Department files 711.93/324.

114. In the summer of 1934, Colonel Jouett sent President Roosevelt a letter suggesting that he write the Generalissimo and Dr. H. H. Kung to say that he had been following the work of the American aviation group in China with interest and hoped for its continuation. Jouett urged Roosevelt to concern himself with this matter on the grounds that Italy was about to get a clear field to dominate Chinese aviation. Roosevelt gave instructions to have "a nice letter of thanks" sent to Jouett. Otherwise neither the President nor the Secretary of State seems to have taken any action and Jouett's contract was not renewed. (*FR* 1935, III, 177, 339; see also 18, 21, and Johnson papers, letter to Willys Peck, dated Jan. 30, 1935 and letter to Clarence Gauss, dated Feb. 19, 1935.)

115. *FR* 1934, III, 436.

116. Rogers' cable dealt in part with the silver question (see Chap. IV) and he recommended that, if the price of silver was to be raised, "simultaneous consideration" should be given to a loan.

117. *FR* 1934, III, 383.

118. *Ibid.*, 128.

119. *Ibid.*

120. *Ibid.*, 145; see also 395, 410. Avenol felt that the Japanese had as yet produced no evidence to show that Rajchman was engaged in political activities. Gilbert however concluded later that a program of technical assistance for China was almost inevitably linked with political questions and that Rajchman, while adhering to the letter of his mandate, nevertheless engaged in projects that extended "beyond the mere technical field."

121. *FR* 1934, III, 150; *North China Herald*, May 23, 1934, p. 254, "League Cooperation with China."

122. *FR* 1934, III, 150.

123. *Ibid.*, 165; Irving S. Friedman, *British Relations With China: 1931-1939* (1940), p. 44; *North China Herald*, May 16, 1934, p. 214, "Reactions to Rajchman Report."

124. *FR* 1934, III, 381.

125. *Ibid.*

126. *Ibid.*, 408.

127. *Ibid.*, 388.

128. *Ibid.*, 390.

129. *Ibid.*, 393.

130. *Ibid.*, 391, 392, 421.

131. Act passed June 1934.

132. In his book entitled *Across World Frontiers*, which was published in 1951, Thomas W. Lamont wrote (p. 263):

For a long time after my return to the United States [from China in 1920] I continued to descant upon the Chinese people, upon their virtues and upon the glowing future which I felt lay before them. In recent years, however, I have been one of the thousands of Americans who have been disappointed and begun to despair—I hope that is far too strong a word—over China's political and economic future. Contrary to all expectations there has been no group powerful enough to establish stable government untainted by corruption. Nor has anyone seemed to care about democracy.

So far as I can see, in no respect is the political situation of China better today than it was when I studied the country briefly a quarter century ago . . .

On my visit it was Dr. Sun Yat-sen, the leader of high renown, who wanted $25,000,000 to equip an army and crush his opponents. Now it is his younger brother, Marshal Chiang, who asks for America to equip his rabble armies to the same end in order to crush his opponents coming down from the North, the so-called Communist armies. Much as I detest Communism and the police state (which seems to be its outward and visible sign), I still believe that the Northern armies may be ranked as Chinese first and Communist second, and that in any event they are not to be won over merely by force of arms.

Today as in the past, the opposing forces sway hither and thither over the countryside. And all the time the people of the land continue to suffer for lack of conservation improvements, agricultural machinery and all the equipment that might give them a chance for a half way normal existence.

133. Johnson papers, letter dated Nov. 3, 1933.

134. Johnson papers, letter dated Jan. 18, 1934.

135. *FR* 1934, III, 412, 420.

136. The deliberations within the American group were not made public.

137. See *FR* 1934, III, 145 for comments by Avenol on situation in respect to the possibility of the Amau declaration being discussed by the Far Eastern Advisory Committee.

138. From time to time press summaries were sent to Foreign Service officers abroad when it was felt that they should be informed of newspaper opinion in connection with some particularly critical event. The newspapers that were cited usually consisted of a few of the best known papers for the most part published in large eastern cities such as New York, Boston, Philadelphia, and Washington.

139. Mr. Kramer's manuscript (hereafter referred to as Kramer ms.) was done in connection with this study. It was supplemented by a paper, written for the Regional Studies Program at Harvard University, entitled "The Amau Statement: America's Response to a Challenge."

Kramer summarized the editorials in the following internationalist newspapers: *New York Times, Christian Science Monitor, Los Angeles Times, Cleveland Press, Milwaukee Journal*, and the *San Francisco Chronicle*. Some of these publications were classed as "liberal" in their attitude toward domestic affairs; others were not. Of the isolationist press, he dealt with the *Chicago Tribune* and the Hearst papers.

Unless otherwise indicated, the interpretations of editorial opinion are my own.

140. Kramer ms., p. 4.

141. *Ibid.*, p. 7.

142. *Ibid.*, p. 15.

143. *Ibid.*, p. 8.

144. *Ibid.*, p. 17.

145. *Ibid.*, p. 23.

146. *Ibid.*

147. *Ibid.*

148. *Ibid.*
149. *Ibid.*, p. 24.
150. *Ibid.*
151. *Ibid.*, p. 9.
152. *Ibid.*, p. 15.
153. Eleanor Tupper and George E. McReynolds, *Japan in American Public Opinion* (1937), sections beginning pp. 359 and 385.
154. Kramer ms., p. 29.
155. *Ibid.*, p. 27.
156. *Ibid.*, p. 29.
157. *Ibid.*, p. 30.
158. *Ibid.*, p. 25.
159. *Ibid.*, p. 31.
160. *Ibid.*, p. 19.
161. *Ibid.*, p. 33.
162. Tupper and McReynolds, *Japan in American Public Opinion*, p. 390.
163. Kramer ms., p. 33.
164. *Ibid.*, p. 32; Tupper and McReynolds, *Japan in American Public Opinion*, p. 389.
165. Tupper and McReynolds, *Japan in American Public Opinion*, pp. 342, 388.
166. Kramer, Lawrence I., Jr., "The Amau Statement: America's Response to a Challenge," p. 30.
167. *Ibid.*, p. 31.
168. *Ibid.;* Tupper and McReynolds, *Japan in American Public Opinion*, p. 388.
169. A reading of the files of the *New York Times* suggests that, with the exception of the dispute over Rajchman, little news was printed in papers in the United States concerning the reconstruction of China. This formed a sharp contrast to the English language press in China.
170. Following the delivery of Hull's *aide-mémoire* to the Japanese government, Ambassador Grew cabled the State Department that a high official of the Foreign Office had said that he regarded the American memorandum as "frank and friendly" and as characterized by a "tone . . . entirely different from that used by Mr. Stimson." (*FR 1934*, III, 152.) In his diary entry of May 1, 1934, Grew wrote that he had not liked to repeat this criticism of Stimson but had done so because it showed how much "tone" meant to the Japanese. Ambassador Grew also sent Secretary Hull a letter expressing his own admiration of the *aide-mémoire* which he described in his diary as "wholly admirable, absolutely called for by the circumstances, drafted in masterly fashion, perfectly clear in substance, moderate and friendly in tone." (See Grew's *Ten Years in Japan*, p. 133. For Hirota's attitude toward the *aide-mémoire*, see the second conversation between Saito and Secretary Hull, below.)
171. *FR 1934*, III, 650; see also *The Memoirs of Cordell Hull*, I, 281ff. and *FR Japan 1931-1941*, I, 237.
172. *Ibid.*, 233.
173. See below.

174. Text of the document appears in *FR Japan* 1931-1941, I, 232, and in *FR 1934*, III, 653.

175. *Ibid.* In a memorandum to the President, Hull stated specifically that his notes gave only the substance of his statement to Saito. The notes may even have been prepared in advance to furnish a basis for the Secretary's comments. In any event, by their very nature they do not indicate the tone of Hull's remarks but they do give the impression that he spoke far more sharply that he had earlier. Hull's statement took up one by one the eight points whch the ambassador made in his memorandum. After the conclusion of his formal statement, the Secretary continued the conversation informally, emphasizing in particular that if Japan and the United States wanted to convince each other of their peaceful intentions, they must do so by "acts rather than words."

176. *The Memoirs of Cordell Hull*, I, Chap. 20.

177. *Ibid.*, 278.

178. In *The Memoirs of Cordell Hull*, I, 282, the Secretary expresses his indignation at the insistence of the Japanese propagandists of the time that Japan's claims regarding "special interests" in its area of the Pacific were comparable to the claims of the United States under the Monroe Doctrine. "Japan," the Secretary states, "violently and fraudulently misrepresented the idea of the Monroe Doctrine, deliberately forgetting that that doctrine did not give us the right to conquer and occupy or dominate sections of the Western Hemisphere or close them off to the trade of other nations. And she ignored the basic concept of the Monroe Doctrine, which was to preserve the security and independence of the nations of the Western Hemisphere . . . There was no resemblance at all between the Japanese 'Monroe Doctrine' and our own."

In this connection, see also Stanley K. Hornbeck's *Contemporary Politics in the Far East* (originally published in 1916), where he discusses "Japan's Monroe Doctrine for Asia" within the context of an earlier period. (Chap. XVIII.)

179. *The Memoirs of Cordell Hull*, I, 281.

180. *FR 1934*, III, 661.

181. *The Memoirs of Cordell Hull*, I, 284.

CHAPTER III. NAVAL POLICIES

1. Among the many useful books on American naval policy are George T. Davis, *A Navy Second to None*, written from a prewar point of view (1940), and Merze Tate, *The United States and Armaments*, written from a postwar point of view (1948).

2. Frank Freidel, *Franklin D. Roosevelt: The Apprenticeship*. In this volume, the first of his series on Roosevelt, Freidel deals extensively with the President's years as Assistant Secretary of the Navy.

3. "Shall We Trust Japan?" *Asia* magazine, July 1923.

4. "Our Foreign Policy. A Democratic View," *Foreign Affairs*, July 1928. See also Freidel, *Franklin D. Roosevelt*, Vol. 2, pp. 236ff.

5. Two books which contain unusually interesting material on the activities of peace organizations, et cetera, and on public opinion in general in connection with disarmament in the 1920's are John Chalmers

Vinson, *The Parchment Peace: The United States Senate and the Washington Conference, 1921-1922* (1955), which deals primarily with the Senate and the Washington Conference of 1921, and Robert H. Ferrell, *Peace In Their Time* (1952), which deals with the Kellogg-Briand Pact.

6. Davis papers, October 1934 report.

7. *The Public Papers and Addresses of Franklin D. Roosevelt* (compiled and collated by Samuel I. Rosenman [1938]), Vol. 3 (1934), p. 172.

8. The debate on the Vinson-Trammell bill in Congress indicates that the main argument in favor of the bill was that preparedness prevents wars. (Congressional Record, 73d Congress, 2d session.)

9. *Ibid.*, p. 3688.

10. *FR 1934*, I, 222-230.

11. The memorandum written by Davis subsequently seems to be the only record of this talk in existence. Davis papers.

12. *FR 1934*, I, 259. In order to ensure a "candid and free discussion," no official minutes were made of this or the following Anglo-American Naval meetings in the summer of 1934. However, there are unofficial notes in the Davis papers.

13. For a discussion of the technical problems involved in the cruiser question, see *FR 1934*, I, 266, 267, 272, 282, and minutes of the Technical Committee in the Davis papers.

14. See especially Davis' notes on his lunch with the Prime Minister, June 20, and with Simon and Baldwin, July 16; letter to Pierrepont Moffat dated July 4 (all in Davis papers). Also *FR 1934*, I, 279, 287.

15. Davis made notes on his lunch with the Prime Minister, June 20, Davis papers.

16. Davis papers, Davis' letter to Atherton, dated September 12.

17. *FR 1934*, I, 238; see also *ibid.*, III, 65, 168ff., 232, and Moffat Diary, entry of May 21, 1934.

18. *FR 1934*, I, 279; see also *ibid.*, 276, 284 for Department's views.

19. Moffat Diary, entry of June 26 and 28, 1934.

20. *FR 1934*, I, 277.

21. *Ibid.*, 284; Moffat Diary, entries of June 28, 1934 and July 2, 1934.

22. Roosevelt papers PCF Naval Conference 1933-35, Box 3. This view was frequently repeated by MacDonald; see for example, notes of the meeting of June 27, 1934, Davis papers, and *FR 1934*, I, 344.

23. *FR 1934*, I, 289, 290, 294.

24. *FR Japan 1931-1941*, I, 253; see also *ibid.*, 249; *FR 1934*, I, 217, 306, 307, 309.

25. *The Moffat Papers*, p. 6.

26. The story of the drafting of the letter is in the Moffat Diary, entries of Sept. 28, and Oct. 3, 4, 5, 1934. Text of the letter is in *FR Japan 1931-41*, I, 282. See also the press conference which the President held on Oct. 5, 1934—the day the letter was finally drafted, Roosevelt papers, PPF I 1-P Press Conferences Box 201.

27. This point runs through the Department's cables and also the Moffat diary. See also Davis papers, Moffat's letter to Davis, dated Nov. 3, 1934.

28. The Japanese proposed (a) what they termed a "common upper limit" for all the navies involved which would cover the total tonnage regard-

less of the type of ship, and (b) the abolition of "offensive" categories of ships—categories which, as they defined them, included most of the types which the United States regarded as essential for its needs. They were prepared to agree to a "common upper limit" lower than the tonnages of the American and the British fleets at the time. For the first meeting (Oct. 24) between the Japanese and Americans, see *FR Japan* 1931-41, I, 254; for later meetings, *FR 1934*, I, 317, 323. Fuller accounts of all these meetings are to be found in the Davis papers.

29.   Davis papers, Davis letter to the President, dated Oct. 31, 1934.

30.   Davis papers, Roosevelt letter to Davis, dated Nov. 9, 1934.

31.   Davis papers, Davis letters to the President, dated November 6 and December 14, 1934; Davis notes on talk with Simon, dated November 1, 1934. Also *FR 1934*, I, 328, 351.

32.   *FR 1934*, I, 334.

33.   *Ibid.*, 333.

34.   The Secretary's point of view is well recorded in Moffat's diary. Moffat, who together with Stanley Hornbeck, drafted most of the telegrams that were sent to Davis, during the naval talks, was in constant contact with Hull. Even during the weeks that the Secretary was away in order to recover from an illness he gave instructions as to how the telegrams should be drafted through constant phone messages to Washington. See especially Moffat Diary, entries of Oct. 24, Nov. 13, Nov. 22, Dec. 1-2, 1934. Among the more important cables reflecting Hull's views are those in *FR 1934*, I, 327, 353, 355, 361, 364, 380, 391.

35.   *FR 1934*, I, 307, 322; see also Grew Diary, entries of Oct. 16, Nov. 13, 1934, and *FR 1935*, III, 827. The President himself apparently believed that the Japanese could not afford a naval race, perhaps as a result of Grew's reports. See Davis papers, Roosevelt letter to Davis, dated Nov. 9, 1934.

36.   *FR 1934*, I, 353, 355, 364, 391.

37.   For the Secretary's reaction to public opinion see Moffat Diary, entries of Nov. 3, Nov. 10, Nov. 28 and 29, 1934. In order to offset the isolationist criticism which began to develop after Nye's attack on the administration's policy, Hull asked Norman Davis to make a public statement redefining the issues for the press. Davis consequently delivered a speech, which came to be regarded as one of the best statements of America's case in the naval controversy, before the Association of American Correspondents in London. The text of the speech is in *FR Japan* 1931-41, I, 269. The story of the drafting of the speech, its reception in the American press, et cetera, is in the Moffat Diary, entries of December 1-6, 1934. In January 1935 Davis gave an address on "The Disarmament Problem" which dealt at length with the naval problem. (Reprinted in *Foreign Affairs*, April 1935.)

38.   *FR 1934*, I, 351, 356, 361.

39.   *FR 1934*, I, 415; Davis papers, Davis letter to Moffat, dated December 18, 1934, and Noel Field letter to Moffat, dated November 6, 1934.

40.   *FR 1934*, I, 368, 381, 388. These references contain the official accounts of the meetings at which Davis and the British discussed these points.

41. *FR* 1934, I, 402; *FR Japan* 1931-1941, I, 272.
42. *FR* 1934, I, 380, 390.
43. Moffat Diary, entries of December 29 and 30, 1934; *FR* 1934, I, 415.
44. *FR* 1934, I, 420.
45. Press conference of December 21, 1934, Roosevelt papers PPF 1-0 Press conferences, Box 201.
46. December 3, 1934.
47. December 24, 1934.
48. December 20, 1934.
49. The Davis papers have good material on Hull's despair at the passage of the first neutrality act and his feeling that Roosevelt was not supporting him.
50. *FR* 1935, I, 103, 105.
51. *Ibid.,* 145, 150.
52. *The London Naval Conference 1935,* Department of State Conference Series No. 24, contains the record of the conference.
53. *FR* 1936, I, 32.
54. *Ibid.,* 35; see Hornbeck's memorandum disagreeing with this, *ibid.,* 36.
55. *Ibid.,* 38.
56. Congressional Record, 74th Congress, 2d session, p. 7430.
57. For memorandum see *FR* 1935, III, 821. Grew's comments on the writing of the memorandum are in his diary entries of December 27, 1934, and March 18, 1935.
58. *FR* 1935, III, 829. A somewhat earlier memorandum (November 17, 1934) based on the same theme is in the Johnson papers.
59. *FR* 1934, III, 189; see also *FR* 1934, I, 230, *FR* 1935, III, 855.
60. Johnson papers, memorandum of April 13, 1935.

CHAPTER IV. THE UNITED STATES SILVER POLICY AND THE FAR EAST

1. For details see below.
2. For an account of these developments, see Allan Seymour Everest, *Morgenthau, The New Deal and Silver* (1950). Everest's book is of particular importance because he had access to Morgenthau's diaries. *The United States in World Affairs,* 1934-1935, is useful as a contemporary account of the political aspects of the Roosevelt administration's silver policy. Much has been written on the technical aspects and on the impact of the administration's silver policy on China. W. Y. Lin, *The New Monetary System of China* (1936), is, for example, a helpful monograph. See also reference to John Morton Blum's *From the Morgenthau Diaries* (1959) in note 9.
3. *FR* 1934, III, 424, 428; *Finance and Commerce,* February 28, 1934, p. 239.
4. *FR* 1934, III, 440, 442, 445, 447, 450; Dickson H. Leavens, "American Silver Policy on China," *Harvard Business Review,* Autumn, 1935, p. 53. For earlier representations on behalf of the Chinese government, see *FR* 1934, III, 423.
5. *FR* 1934, III, 441, 444, 449, 451.
6. *Ibid.,* 455.

7. *Ibid.*, 456; Roosevelt papers PSF China 1933-1935, Box 10.

8. Johnson papers, memorandum dated Dec. 15, 1934.

9. Everest, p. 9; research memorandum of John Morton Blum's, herein-after referred to as JMB memo. (Since the writing of this chapter, Mr. Blum has published his *From the Morgenthau Diaries, Years of Crisis 1928-1938*. Chap. V, Sec. 4, deals with the repercussions of our silver policy in China and should be read by all those concerned with this subject.)

10. *FR* 1934, III, 457.

11. *Ibid.* The note was purposely sent through the Federal Reserve Bank of New York rather than by diplomatic channels to make it look as nonpolitical as possible.

12. *Ibid.*, 461; Everest, p. 108; *Finance and Commerce*, Jan. 16, 1935, p. 64.

13. *FR* 1935, III, 526.

14. Roosevelt papers OF 150 China 1933-1935, Box 1.

15. Everest, p. 108.

16. *FR* 1934, III, 461; *FR* 1935, III, 527.

17. See Chap. V for a detailed account of these events.

18. *FR* 1935, III, 532.

19. *Ibid.*, 37.

20. *Ibid.*, 45.

21. *Ibid.*, 533.

22. *Ibid.*, 535.

23. Part of document referred to in *FR* 1935, III, 597, footnote 9.

24. *FR* 1935, III, 539.

25. Everest, p. 109.

26. *FR* 1935, III, 540. Roosevelt apparently wanted to avoid inter-national consultations in which the issue of our silver policy might be raised. (JMB memo.)

27. *FR* 1935, III, 542.

28. Talks with State Department officials.

29. Everest, pp. 107, 118; JMB memo; talks with a Chinese govern-ment official.

30. JMB memo.

31. *FR* 1935, III, 542.

32. *Ibid.*, 547, 553, 554.

33. *Ibid.*, 545; see also 564, 567, 569.

34. Document referred to in *FR* 1935, III, 597, footnote 9.

35. *Ibid.*, 555, 556, 558.

36. *Ibid.*, 560.

37. *Ibid.*, 564.

38. *Ibid.*, 563.

39. *Ibid.*, 95.

40. *Ibid.*, 95, 567, 570.

41. The various consuls were asked to report to the Department "any manifestations of anti-American feeling . . . and particularly any develop-ments tending toward a boycott of American goods." *Ibid.*, 584, 588, 589. See also in Johnson papers, talk with Hopkins of the Shanghai Power Company, dated Feb. 13 and 16, 1935; and American Chamber of Commerce of Shanghai *Bulletin*, No. 207, dated April 1935.

42. *FR* 1935, III, 566, 580; Frank M. Tamagna, *Banking and Finance in China* (1942), p. 126.

43. Tamagna, *Banking and Finance in China*, p. 103.

44. Everest, p. 106.

45. As indicated in Chap. V.

46. Pratt, *War and Politics in China*, pp. 235ff.

47. *FR* 1935, III, 591.

48. *Ibid.*, 605, 614; JMB memo.

49. The State Department prepared several memoranda in which it stated its case, the most important of which dealt with the problem of Anglo-American cooperation. These were discussed at a meeting between Morgenthau and Hornbeck on July 9. *FR* 1935, III, 596, 599; and document referred to 597, footnote 9.

50. *Ibid.*, 595, 596, 606, 612, 613.

51. *Ibid.*, 614.

52. *Ibid.*, 328.

53. For the conflict between Congress and the administration, see Dickson H. Leavens, "Silver in Recent Session of Congress," reprinted in *Finance and Commerce*, October 9, 1935, p. 382; *United States in World Affairs*, 1934-1935, p. 46. It is apparent from the record that Roosevelt sought throughout to avoid international discussions that would inevitably involve criticism of our silver policy (see, for example, note 26 of this chapter).

54. *FR* 1935, III, 612, 618, 619, 631.

55. Johnson papers, interviews of Oct. 2, and 28; see also interview of Nov. 4.

56. *Ibid.*, talk with H. H. Kung, dated May 15, 1935; see also interview with J. Lossing Buck, dated May 13, 1935, and *FR* 1935, III, 580.

57. Johnson papers.

58. For Johnson's attitude toward the Leith-Ross mission see, for example, in the Johnson papers, the letter to the Secretary cited in note 57 of this chapter; letter to Roy Howard, dated Aug. 15, 1936; letter to Hornbeck, dated Aug. 25, 1936; letter to Lamont, dated July 15, 1935; memorandum on interview with Dr. Soong, dated April 26, 1935; also *FR* III, 569, 591.

59. Pratt, *War and Politics in China*, p. 237, and comments to the writer by Sir Frederick Leith-Ross. The United States government said it had no power to make a ruling similar to that of the British but American banks ultimately did turn over their silver holdings to the Chinese government voluntarily. *FR* 1936, III, 629, 631, 637; *FR* 1936, IV, 462; *Finance and Commerce*, Jan. 8, 1936, p. 31. T'ang Leang-li in his *China's New Currency System* (1936), pp. 87 and 95, says the silver holdings of the foreign banks in Shanghai amounted to approximately $40 million, of which about seventeen and a half million were held by four British banks and a little over five million by two American banks and the American Express Company.

60. Everest, p. 111; JMB memo; *FR* 1935, III, 628, 632.

61. *FR* 1935, III, 632; for these negotiations I have relied upon Everest; JMB memo, and *FR* 1935, III, 637.

62. Everest, p. 111.

63. Text is in *FR* 1935, III, 641.

64. T'ang Leang-li has a good account of the Japanese efforts to block the currency reforms, *China's New Currency System*, pp. 86, 87, 95. See also *FR* 1935, III, 642.

65. *FR* 1935, III, 631, 640, 642, 645; *FR* 1936, IV, 490 (text of Leith-Ross statement on leaving China); Pratt, *War and Politics in China*, p. 236.

66. For Morgenthau's statement see *New York Times*, Feb. 14, 1936, p. 25.

67. Everest, p. 112.

68. The following is based upon Everest's account of the negotiations unless otherwise indicated.

69. *FR* 1936, IV, 466.

70. *Ibid.*, 467.

71. The dollar exchange seems not to have been used by the Chinese; see Everest, p. 117.

72. Text in *FR* 1936, III, 482; Dr. Kung also issued a statement which is on the same page.

73. *FR* 1936, III, 480. Hornbeck does not appear to have seen the full agreement, however. (*Ibid.*, 499.)

74. *FR* 1935, III, 645; *FR* 1936, IV, 495.

CHAPTER V. FURTHER JAPANESE ENCROACHMENTS ON CHINA

1. *FR* 1935, III *The Far Eastern Crisis*, Chap. I *in passim*. There are many good secondary sources dealing with the outstanding events related in this chapter, some of which will be found in the bibliography. A deliberate attempt has been made, however, to emphasize in these notes references which would give the picture as it appeared to American officials and other contemporary observers.

2. Roosevelt papers OF 150 China 1933-45, Box 1.

3. Note attached to the memorandum.

4. *FR* 1935, III, 34.

5. *Ibid.*, 79.

6. *Ibid.*, 79, 81, 90, 91, 134. Because of the length of Johnson's memoranda it had been necessary to concentrate on only a few of the ideas which he set forth so that the above does not adhere closely to his presentation.

7. Of the various themes covered in these memoranda the one which Johnson probably emphasized most frequently was that Japan intended to wipe out every bit of Western influence in China.

8. *FR* 1935, III, 60, 81, 90, 92, 125, 159, 160.

9. *Ibid.*, 139.

10. For some of the more significant reports see *FR* 1933, III, 421, 424, 434, 458; *FR* 1934, III, 32, 297; *FR* 1935, III, 49, 106.

11. Our embassy in Tokyo, departing from the restraint which customarily characterized its reports, stated definitely in November 1934 that, in its opinion, the position of the Soviet Union had been so improved that there was little danger of attack from Japan (*FR* 1934, III, 297). This view was supported by Ambassador Bullitt in Moscow (*FR* 1935, III, 5). Bullitt was convinced that the United States should do what it could to prevent an armed conflict between the Soviet Union and Japan because, as he said, "if there is a war, someone may win it." If the Soviets won, a

Communist China would be inevitable; if Japan won, China would fall under Japanese rule. (*FR The Soviet Union* 1933-1939, 294.) The ambassador also believed that the USSR regarded a clash between the United States and Japan as its one great hope and that anyone who expected the Russians to assist us, if such a clash occurred, was indulging in "wishful thinking." In April 1936 he predicted that in case we had to fight Japan, the Soviets would avoid becoming our ally until Japan had been thoroughly defeated and would then merely join us in order to use the opportunity to acquire Manchuria and "sovietize" China. (*FR The Soviet Union* 1933-1939, 226.)

Ambassador Grew felt that one of the most important influences in strengthening the position of the Russians against the Japanese, so that war no longer seemed an imminent threat, was the recognition of the USSR by the United States. Before recognition took place, the Japanese Foreign Office indirectly sought to impress upon our embassy in Tokyo that the Japanese military feared an Anglo-American-Russian combine against Japan and that, if anything occurred to substantiate their fears, the army would probably nullify the improvement in the relations with other countries which Hirota had been able to bring about. (*Ibid.* 20.) As a consequence, the State Department assured the Japanese that our recognition of the Soviet Union had "nothing whatever to do with the Far East." (*FR* 1933, III, 463.) In Grew's view the Japanese nevertheless remained very anxious about the American-Russian *rapprochement* and for the first time showed signs of uncertainty as to the role the United States might play in case of a Russo-Japanese war. This uncertainty, in the ambassador's estimation, was likely to be the strongest factor in restraining Japan from attacking the Soviet Union. (*FR* 1934, III, 32. See also Stalin's talks with Ambassador Bullitt concerning America's position if war should break out between the Soviet Union and Japan, *FR The Soviet Union 1933-1939*, 53, 55.)

12. *FR* 1935, III, 148.
13. *Ibid.*, 508.
14. *Ibid.*, 509.
15. *Ibid.*, 512; see also 524 for a typical statement by the State Department of the difficulties encountered in pursuing a parallel policy with the British.
16. *Ibid.*, 513.
17. *Ibid.*, 517.
18. By the time the Senate and the President had acted in appointing Johnson as ambassador, President Lin Sen had left Nanking for the summer so that he could not receive Johnson's letter of credence until September 17.
19. *FR* 1935, III, 197, 244, 514, 517.
20. Two excellent sources of information concerning these developments, written close to the event, are Shushi Hsu, *The North China Problem* and Bisson, *Japan in China.*
21. *FR* 1935, III, 187.
22. *Ibid.*, 196, 199, 229, 237, 239. For the press see, for example, the *New York Times*, May 29, 1935, p. 43, "Japan Threatens War Unless China Accepts Demands"; May 31, 1935, p. 1 "Japan Threatens Invasion of China."
23. *FR* 1935, III, 230.
24. *Ibid.*, 196, 249.
25. *Ibid.*, 230.

26. *Ibid.*, 237, 239, 241.

27. *Ibid.*, 253. Chinese Minister gave the State Department similar information. See also 232, 249.

28. *Ibid.*, 241.

29. *Ibid.*, 249.

30. *Ibid.*, 252.

31. *Ibid.*, 248, 253.

32. *Ibid.*, 256.

33. *Ibid.*, 286.

34. Presumably Phillips still thought that the Chinese government wished to minimize matters but subsequent events, as seen below, suggest that this was not the case.

35. *FR 1935*, III, 262.

36. *Ibid.*, 267.

37. *Ibid.*, 287.

38. *Ibid.* In its review of developments in the first six months of 1935 in China, the legation staff likewise reported that our silver policy had aroused much criticism in China which was "perhaps augmented by the silence of the United States in the face of recent Japanese aggression and by the growing feeling in China that America's traditional sympathy had little practical application." (*Ibid.*, 306.)

39. Shushi Hsu, *The North China Problem*, Chap. IV.

40. *FR 1935*, III, 234, 255, 256, 263, 270, 274, 277.

41. *Ibid.*, 277.

42. Shushi Hsu, *The North China Problem*, p. 19.

43. *FR 1935*, III, 280.

44. See for example *New York Times*, June 30, 1935, Sec. IV, p. 2, "China Yields Again."

45. *FR 1936*, IV, 89. Shushi Hsu, *The North China Problem*, pp. 22ff. and Bisson, *Japan in China*, pp. 55ff.

46. *FR 1935*, III, 257.

47. *Ibid.*

48. *Ibid.*, 313, 306.

49. *Ibid.*, 262.

50. Grew, *Turbulent Era* II, p. 982. In this reference Grew indicates that he did, however, have some information to the effect that the immediate situation was not out of hand, which apparently meant that the Japanese military would not advance into North China.

51. *FR 1935*, III, 244.

52. See Chap. III.

53. *FR 1935*, III, 855.

54. American officials almost always spoke of the events of the early summer of 1935 in terms of the developments which had taken place in Hopei and do not seem to have devoted a great deal of attention to the developments in Chahar.

55. This statement was repeated later.

56. One also gets an impression in reading the documents of this period that there was an element of self-deception in the State Department's attitude toward the events in North China as though, wholly persuaded that it should follow a given course, it did not wish to take account of new and decidedly disturbing circumstances.

57. See for example *FR* 1935, III, 320, 335, 365, 403, 407.

58. A translation of the Tada pamphlet was printed in the *China Weekly Review*, November 2, 1935, p. 306.

59. *FR* 1935, III, 355, 360.

60. *Ibid.*, 365, 379.

61. *Ibid.*, 365, 379, 392.

62. *Ibid.*, 390.

63. *Ibid.*, 396, 397, 402, 403, 406.

64. *Ibid.*, 404. *New York Times*, October 31, 1935, p. 9, "Japan Is Seeking China Show-down."

65. There were slight variations in the principles as defined by different people. (See, for example, *FR* 1935, III, 404, 429.) Hirota's definition to Grew was: cessation of anti-Japanese activities; recognition of the existence of Manchukuo, and regularization of factual relations such as communications, transit, customs, et cetera; Sino-Japanese cooperation to combat the spread of communism. The recognition of Manchukuo, he said, need not imply *de jure* recognition however. (*FR* 1936, 759.)

66. *FR* 1935, III, 404, 429, 460.

67. Willys Peck, in Washington in the early summer of 1935, wrote a long and interesting memorandum on the pro-Western and pro-Japanese factions within the Nanking regime. (*Ibid.*, 207.)

68. *Ibid.*, 256. See also *New York Times*, November 3, 1935, "Review of the Week."

69. *FR* 1935, III, 421, 422, 423. *New York Times*, see for example, November 11, 1935, p. 1, "Shanghai Chinese Evacuate Chapei, Fearing Japanese," Subhead: "Tokyo Expects North China To Set Up Independent Regime In A Few Days"; November 17, 1935, "Review of the Week."

70. *FR* 1935, III, 422, 423.

71. *Ibid.*, 423, 425.

72. See for example *New York Times*, Nov. 21, 1935, p. 1, "North China Split Suddenly Off."

73. *FR* 1935, 442. See also *China Weekly Review* Jan. 25, 1936, p. 258, "Major General Doihara Asia's Greatest Plotter."

74. *FR* 1935, III, 438; *New York Times*, Nov. 25, 1925, p. 1, "New State Set Up in North China in Pro-Tokyo Coup."

75. *FR* 1935, III, 431.

76. *Ibid.*, 444.

77. *Ibid.*, 446, 447, 453, 457, 460.

78. *Ibid.*, 475.

79. *Ibid.*, 479, 482, 485.

80. *Ibid.*, 480. For student movement see also 491, 495, 496, 497, 498. Of contemporary publications the *China Weekly Review* devoted a large amount of space to the activities of the students. Bisson (*Japan in China*, pp. 113ff.) gives many details concerning developments in the student movement in December 1935.

81. Bisson, *Japan in China*, p. 107, footnote 36, quoted from the *New York Sun*, Dec. 18, 1935.

82. *FR* 1935, III, 502.

83. Johnson papers: letters to Hornbeck, dated Dec. 3, 1935, to Stimson, dated Dec. 9, 1935.

84. *FR 1935*, III, 400, 403, 407; letter to Roy Howard in Johnson papers, dated Dec. 31, 1935. Dr. Hu in particular had created something of a sensation by abandoning the pacifism which had made him virtually the only Chinese leader to express approval, in print, of the Tangku Truce at the time it was signed.

85. Johnson papers, letter to Stanley K. Hornbeck, dated Dec. 3, 1935.

86. Johnson papers, letter dated Feb. 24, 1936. This letter was approved by Johnson before it was sent.

87. Grew, *Ten Years in Japan*, p. 159.

88. *Ibid.*

89. *FR 1935*, III, 353.

90. For a typical expression of Johnson's attitude in this connection see Johnson papers, his letter to Roy Howard, dated June 19, 1936.

91. *FR 1935*, III, 458.

92. *Ibid.*, 434.

93. *Ibid.*, 448.

94. *Ibid.*, 459, 463.

95. *Ibid.*, 460.

96. *Ibid.*, 469.

97. *Ibid.*, 464.

98. The statement was to be released by the press the following day.

99. See for example the *New York Times*, Dec. 6, 1935, p. 1, "U.S. And Britain Warn Japan On North China Activities; Hull Cites Treaty Rights."

100. *The Memoirs of Cordell Hull*, I, 446.

101. *FR 1935*, III, 474.

102. Hull was convinced that the Italian-Ethiopian conflict had caused the North China crisis, demonstrating that aggression anywhere had "awful repercussions"—in his words—even in remote parts of the world. (*The Memoirs of Cordell Hull*, I, 438, 440.)

103. Kramer ms., section beginning p. 36.

104. *FR 1935*, III, 34.

105. *Ibid.*, 278.

106. *Congressional Record*, 74th Congress, 2d session, Vol. 8., Pt. 2, p. 1703.

107. This quotation and following references to the press are all based on Kramer ms., section beginning p. 36.

108. The memorandum is in the State Department files. (711.93/383.) There are several notes attached showing that it was used, even in the postwar years, as a means of occasionally briefing officials on the Far East. George F. Kennan refers to the memorandum in his book on *American Diplomacy 1900-1950* (1951). MacMurray himself informed me of the circumstances that led him to undertake the memorandum.

109. Much of the material in the historical sections is related in my *American Policy and the Chinese Revolution 1925-1928* (1947).

110. MacMurray believed "The essence of our traditional Far Eastern policy was that China, with its vast potentialities for economic development, was the crux of the whole problem." (MacMurray memorandum section I, "The Aftermath of the Washington Conference," paragraph 1.)

111. In this connection MacMurray's thesis was that, even a decisive

victory over the Japanese would not work to our advantage because (a) a "virile people," such as the Japanese, were "not made tractable by defeat and humiliation" as the Germans and the Russians were presently demonstrating and (b) the elimination of Japan from Far Eastern politics would only result in the substitution of the Soviet Union which would be at least "an equally unscrupulous and dangerous" contestant for the "mastery of the East."

112. In November 1954 MacMurray stated in a letter to me that his memorandum was not written with reference to any of the specific policies of the Roosevelt administration. He does not appear to have seen the documents relative to our Far Eastern policy since his own departure from China or to have discussed that policy with his colleagues in the State Department.

MacMurray's letter dealt primarily with a correspondence which he had with Roosevelt that was found in the Hyde Park archives; Roosevelt papers, OF 20 State Department January-June 1937. The correspondence shows that, at the beginning of his second term in office, the President asked MacMurray to return to China as ambassador, replacing Johnson. MacMurray replied that he would prefer to stay at his present post in Turkey and, although Roosevelt urged him to reconsider, the offer was tacitly dropped. In respect to this episode MacMurray wrote in his letter of November 1954 that he had never understood the President's action as he had insisted to Roosevelt that he would scarcely be *persona grata* to Chiang Kai-shek and his principal advisers; Roosevelt had given "no hint" of any new policy or approach he might have had in mind. Since during his years as Minister in China MacMurray's views had been sharply at variance with the opinions of most Chinese leaders and of his own government, it is indeed hard to interpret this move on the President's part. The whole incident is made more obscure by the fact that some of Hull's closest advisors have stated that they had no knowledge that any change of ambassadors was ever contemplated and felt certain that the Secretary had not been informed.

113. *FR* 1936, IV, 1.

114. *FR* 1936, I, 24, 25.

115. *FR* 1936, IV, 3.

116. *Ibid.,* 7.

117. *Ibid.,* 42. Grew did not see the MacMurray memorandum until Nov. 1937 when MacMurray was on a brief mission to Tokyo. Writing of it in his diary, entry dated Nov. 20, 1937, the ambassador said:

It is a masterly work and I only wish that every officer, from the President down, who has anything to do with our Far Eastern policy could read and study it, for it gives both sides of the Sino-Japanese picture accurately and objectively and would serve to relieve many of our fellow countrymen of the generally accepted theory that Japan has been a big bully and China the downtrodden victim . . . MacMurray's summing up . . . is admirably and soundly presented.

See also among Grew's papers the letter to MacMurray dated Nov. 24 1937, which should be taken in conjunction with the interchange between Ambassador Grew and the State Department related in Chapter X.

118. *FR* 1937, IV, 5, 11.

CHAPTER VI. A TURNING POINT IN THE SINO-JAPANESE STRUGGLE

1. *FR* 1936, IV, the section beginning on p. 706 has good background material. Again it should be emphasized that there are many excellent books that discuss the developments related here but that these notes refer largely to sources which depict events as they were known at the time.

2. Grew was particularly affected by the assassination of former Premier Saito, as evidenced by some very moving passages in his diary. (Grew, *Ten Years in Japan*, pp. 171, 172, 174.)

3. *FR* 1936, IV, 777, analysis made by the staff of the United States embassy in Tokyo.

4. *Ibid.*, 761; Grew, *Ten Years in Japan*, p. 178.

5. *FR* 1936, IV, 759; Grew, *Ten Years in Japan*, p. 179.

6. *FR* 1936, IV, 87, 95.

7. *FR* 1936, IV, "The Far Eastern Crisis," Chap. II deals largely with the smuggling operations in China. There is also a good account, drawn mostly from contemporary sources, in Friedman's *British Relations With China* (pp. 71ff.).

8. Friedman, p. 73, footnote 18. Contains data on loans to be serviced.

9. *FR* 1936, IV, 134.

10. Friedman, *British Relations With China*, p. 76.

11. *FR* 1936, IV, 141, 157, 196.

12. *Ibid.*, 141.

13. *Ibid.*, 142, 171, 172, 186, 189.

14. *Ibid.*, 129, 220.

15. *FR Japan* 1931-1941, I, 241.

16. *The Memoirs of Cordell Hull*, I, 363ff. Hull tells of his reciprocal trade agreements program in Chaps. 26, 27, and 37 of his memoirs. One of his beliefs at this time was that the Italian-Ethiopian war might have been averted "if Italy's exports had approximated the pre-crisis volume." (p. 521). Recounting a conversation which he had with the Italian ambassador in Washington at the height of the Italian-Ethiopian conflict, he wrote: "I mentioned to Rosso that during the past three years I had almost worn myself out physically in an effort to aid in world-economic rehabilitation so that Italy and other countries would have an adequate amount of international trade to afford contentment to their respective populations. 'You can imagine the deep disappointment I feel,' I told him, 'at the effort to renew the practices that all nations have recently undertaken to abandon—that of military aggression.'" (p. 438)

17. Hull had an additional point in mind. A sharp rise in the export of certain types of cotton cloth from Japan to the United States had so aroused the opposition of the American textile industry that Hull feared his entire reciprocal trade agreements program might be in jeopardy. He had consequently appealed to the Japanese government to make an arrangement whereby it would restrict the export of these commodities to the United States. In his talk with Yoshida the Secretary sought to impress upon the ambassador that such an arrangement would be but a "slight contribution" that Japan could well afford to make to so universally important an undertaking as his effort to bring about the recovery of trade. Hull had also talked

with the Japanese ambassador along the same lines. (*FR* 1936, IV, 878; see also *FR* 1935, III, 1004, 1011, 1018, 1038. Earlier talks with Japanese statesmen concerning his reciprocal trade agreements are in *FR* 1934, III, 806, 807; *FR* 1935, III, 951, 970.)

18. *FR* 1936, IV, 273; Grew Diary, entry of Aug. 26, 1936.

19. *FR* 1936, IV, 150, 153, 161, 174, 231. On May 20 the State Department cabled our embassy in China that at a press conference the Under Secretary "in response to a question whether this Government had taken any steps to determine whether Japan's action in strengthening its garrison in North China violated the Boxer Protocol replied that in his opinion the Secretary's public statement on December 5, 1935, covers the situation." (*Ibid.*, 162.)

20. *Ibid.*, 111, 124, 125, 151, 167, 174, 192, 231.

21. On October 18, 1936, Dr. Sung signed an agreement establishing a Sino-Japanese aviation corporation which shortly thereafter began to operate lines between Tientsin and various cities in Manchukuo. In the same month he concluded another agreement with Japan the terms of which were not known but which presumably laid the foundations for certain economic projects to be undertaken jointly. (*Far Eastern Survey*, March 3, 1937, p. 54, C.T.C. "Establishment of North China Air Network Under Way" and Nov. 17, 1937, p. 261, Rockwood Chin, "Cotton Mills, Japan's Economic Spearhead in China." Bisson gives the terms of the more general agreement as rumored at the time in his *Japan in China* (p. 188).

22. *FR* 1936, IV, 231.

23. Kiang Wen-han *The Chinese Student Movement* (1948), p. 107. For an account based on contemporary sources see Bisson, *Japan in China*, 136ff.

24. See Chapter VII for further reference to the Shansi campaign of the Communists.

25. *FR* 1936, IV, "The Far Eastern Crisis," Chaps. II and III include many documents on the conflict between the Southwest and Nanking. Details of the conflict are also related in the *Survey of International Affairs 1936*, Pt. VII (11) (a) and Bisson, *Japan in China*, 138ff.

26. *FR* 1936, IV, 272 (incident at Chengtu) 292, 294, 297 (Pakhoi) 302, 306, 315, 323 (Shanghai).

27. The movement is not mentioned in the embassy's semiannual report (*FR* 1936, IV, 231) nor are there any significant references to it in the published documents. The latter point might be accounted for by the fact that the published documents are selected to tell certain specified stories. Nonetheless if there is material of significance in the files dealing with the National Salvation Movement it is reasonable to suppose that some of it would have been printed as throwing light upon one aspect of the Far Eastern crisis which is dealt with at length in *FR* 1936, IV, 1-459.

28. Members of the consulate general at Tientsin wrote in many dispatches of the activities of the students. On one occasion a translation of a forty-nine page pamphlet issued by the students was forwarded to the Department. (State Department file 893.00/13546. Other reports in the files that are of considerable interest are classified as 893.00/PR Tientsin/91, 92, and 94. The latter received the rating of excellent.)

29. *FR* 1936, IV, 231.

30. *Ibid.*

31. *Ibid.*, 253.

32. Johnson papers, letter dated Aug. 20, 1936. Strawn had represented the United States at the Special Conference on the Chinese Customs Tariff and had served as chairman on the Commission on Extraterritoriality in China in 1925 and 1926. He had subsequently made many speeches describing conditions in China as utterly chaotic. (Dorothy Borg, *American Policy and the Chinese Revolution 1925-1928* (1947), pp. 183ff.)

33. Johnson papers, letter dated Aug. 3, 1936.

34. *FR 1936*, IV, 316, 321, 333, 345, 347, 351, 360, 404, 410.

35. The Japanese demands were also said to include insistence upon the negotiation of a Sino-Japanese customs convention, with lower tariffs on certain specified items, and the establishment of direct air communications between Shanghai and Japan. The Japanese version as given to Grew was somewhat different as Hirota told the ambassador that while Tokyo was asking for the appointment of more Japanese advisers by the Nanking government these were to involve "purely economic and not political or military advisers."

36. The Japanese were especially disturbed about the communist issue since the large body of Chinese Communists who had been in Kiangsi had settled in the Northwest where they were obviously in a far better position to make trouble for the Japanese.

37. *FR 1936*, IV, 339; see also 246.

38. Some of the more important documents related to the Suiyuan campaign are in *FR 1936*, IV, 386, 387, 388, 403, 409, 431, 453. A good account is in Shushi Hsu, *The North China Problem*, Chap. IV.

39. *FR 1936*, IV, 404, 410, 411.

40. The Chinese issued an unofficial statement which is reprinted in Shushi Hsu, *The North China Problem*, Appendix B.

41. *FR 1936*, IV, 453.

42. Johnson papers, letter dated Oct. 19, 1936.

43. *Ibid.* Letter to William Allen White, dated Nov. 3, 1936.

44. *FR 1936*, IV, 319, 321, 324, 341.

45. The Minister stated specifically that the "part of the Kuomintang in which Feng Yu-hsiang was outstanding . . . had communistic tendencies." (*Ibid.*, 341.)

46. This was another instance when American officials complained about the British disregard of the "principle of cooperation" between the United States and Great Britain in the Fast East. (*Ibid.*, 319.)

47. *Ibid.*, 333.

48. *Ibid.*, 330.

49. *Ibid.*, 331.

50. *Ibid.*, 321, 325, 332.

51. *Ibid.*, 335, 338, 340.

52. *Ibid.*, 324, 340, 341.

53. *Ibid.*, 343.

54. See Chap. V.

55. The ambassador said that his talk with the President was limited to two topics: whether Grew would remain at his post in Tokyo if Roosevelt were reelected to a second term in November and questions related to the

salaries of Japanese nationals employed by the embassy in Tokyo. (Grew Diary, entry dated Oct. 1936, p. 2908.)

56. Johnson papers, letter to Willys Peck, dated December 1, 1936.

57. *FR* 1936, IV, 393.

58. See also *FR* 1937, III, 44, last paragraph.

59. *Ibid.*, 36. Hornbeck wrote Johnson a personal letter in response defending American policy as having "moved along parallel lines and abreast of the attitude and action of Great Britain in reference to China." (*Ibid.*, 44.)

60. Grew Diary, entry of Dec. 1, 1936. Johnson, in reporting his talk with the Generalissimo in March 1937, suggested that Chiang Kai-shek's remarks might have been motivated by the representations made by the British concerning the Chang Chun-Kawagoe meetings the preceding autumn. For Amau's comments see Grew's *Ten Years in Japan*, p. 205. Grew's report appears in *FR* 1937, III, 1.

61. Text as translated and sent to the State Department, *FR Japan 1931-1941*, II, 153. The secret clauses are in Max Beloff's *The Foreign Policy of Soviet Russia* 1929-1941 (1947-1949), Vol. I, II, p. 170, footnote 1, quoted from De Witt C. Poole, "Light on Nazi Foreign Policy," *Foreign Affairs*, October 1946.

62. *FR Japan 1931-1941*, II, 157. This is one of the many instances when, in private talks with American officials, Japanese diplomats went out of their way to indicate approval of American policy and imply disapproval of the British. The Vice Minister told Erle R. Dickover that the only governments he was notifying in advance, concerning the forthcoming announcement of the Anti-Comintern Pact, were the British and American governments. He had given this information to the British, he said, because questions had been raised in the House of Commons; he wished to give it to the United States because Japan "greatly valued its friendship."

63. Tupper and McReynolds, *Japan in American Opinion*, section beginning p. 421.

64. *FR* 1937, I, 404.

65. *FR* 1937, III, 1; Frank William Icklé, *German-Japanese Relations 1936-1940* (1956), p. 46. Icklé says that Grew soon drew the conclusion that Japan had aligned itself with the Fascist powers, that is, the Rome-Berlin axis. This may well be the case though in the semiannual report sent to Washington by Grew on January 1, 1937 it is asserted that "there is no good reason to believe that Japan is purposely aligning herself with a Fascist bloc." The theory that Japan was joining in a fascist front with both Germany and Italy was, however, being advanced as in early December arrangements were made involving a recognition by Japan of the Italian annexation of Ethiopia and a *de facto* recognition by Italy of Manchukuo. (*FR* 1937, III, 1, section on Italy; also *FR* 1936, IV, 400, 403.)

66. This view was expressed in contemporary surveys such as *The United States in World Affairs, 1936*, section beginning p. 57, and the *Survey of International Affairs, 1936*, introduction by Arnold J. Toynbee.

CHAPTER VII. VIEWS OF AMERICAN OFFICIALS ON THE CHINESE COM-MUNISTS AND THE SIAN INCIDENT

In this chapter all references to numbers of documents, unless otherwise indicated, are to papers in the State Department files, which are in the National Archives in Washington, D.C. The writer did not see documents which are still confidential, but since these form a small percentage of the vast quantity of material which is available for this period and since, in the opinion of Department officials who generously helped with this study, there is no reason to suppose that they contain any unusual or especially valuable information, in all probability they would not substantially alter the picture as presented here.

1.   It is still difficult to find a good consecutive account of the Chinese Communist movement during the years dealt with in this chapter and the author is therefore especially indebted to Dr. Harold Hinton for permission to read the manuscript of a brief history of the Chinese Communist move-ment on which he is still working.

2.   File 893.00b/771. See also 893.00b/813.

3.   File 893.00b/857.

4.   File 893.00b/857 attachment. The consul general at Shanghai also took the unusual step of sending a copy of the study to the Secretary of State directly. (893.00b/923.)

5.   File 893.00b/927.

6.   Yang Chien's articles created considerable excitement in China and Willys Peck paid a special call on the author to find out where he had obtained his information. Yang explained that he had been opposed to the government's ban on the publication of all data indicating the extent of communist activities in China, believing that such a ban created a false sense of security among the Chinese people as a whole. He had therefore learned what he could about the Communists from documents captured from them during the course of the annihilation campaigns and from visits to the war areas, et cetera. Subsequently, he had managed to persuade the government to allow him to publish this material in articles. The picture of the Chinese Communists which Yang gave to Peck during the course of their conversation was that they were orthodox Leninists who had a large and loyal following among the Chinese peasants and possessed an army that was superior in training and morale to that of the government. (File 893.00b/835. Attached is a pamphlet with Yang's articles.)

For a later account of the Chinese Communist movement which was circulated in the west, see Reizo Otsuka, "The Red Influence in China," written in August 1936 for the Sixth Conference of the Institute of Pacific Relations, Yosemite National Park, Calif.

A copy of the Japanese study of communism in China was left with Willys Peck by General McCoy, when the latter was in China in 1932 in connection with his work as a member of the Lytton Commission. In a letter to General McCoy, written in July of that year, Peck commented that he knew nothing to disprove the factual statements made by the Japanese. However, he added, his impression was that the Japanese were too pessimistic in their evaluation of the situation in China in general and overemphasized the success of the Chinese Communists. (File 893.00b/972. The Japanese study appears in "The Present Condition in China," which was presented by the Japanese Foreign Office to the Lytton Commission, as Appendix A-3.)

7. The report contained mistakes such as that Chou En-lai had been executed in Shanghai in 1932. This type of error was easy to fall into, as there were many erroneous rumors about the Communists in circulation at the time.

8. For the comments of the consul general at Shanghai and the replies he received, see File 893.00b numbers 927, 947, 968 (Johnson's response).

9. Note attached to File 893.00b/927.

10. A somewhat similar memorandum had been written by another member of the East European Division after receiving the pamphlet containing Yang Chien's articles in July of the previous year. The memorandum stated that the division would be pleased to have a Foreign Service officer in China write a fairly extensive study of Moscow's direction and control of communist activities in China, citing adequate sources. (File 893.00b/835.)

11. The discouraging reception given the Hankow report in Washington was to some extent counterbalanced two years later when the Department expressed the hope that the author of the report would continue to provide Washington with dispatches on the subject of Chinese communism from time to time. (File 893.00b/1060.)

12. File 893.00b/1064. The report as printed in the *Chinese Workers Correspondence* appears in Victor A. Yakhontoff's *The Chinese Soviets*, Appendix A, p. 9. This book, published in 1934, was an attempt to compile the material on Chinese Communism available outside the communist areas of China.

13. *Ibid.*

14. File 893.00b, numbers 1066, 1070, 1072.

15. For exchange of communications, see File 893.00b, attachments on numbers 1066 and 1071.

16. The dispatches were returned to the files of the Far Eastern Division stamped so as to indicate the offices to which they had been routed. If comments were made, they were usually in memoranda that were attached, although remarks were occasionally written in the margin of the text.

17. The State Department files contain many dispatches concerning the Fukien revolt of 1933, the most interesting being the legation reports which discuss the role of the Communists in the revolt (see especially File 893.00, numbers 12610, 12680).

18. Before the Long March, the Chinese Communists had seized and held as captives a number of American missionaries. In December 1934, two American missionaries, Mr. and Mrs. John Stam, were taken by the Communists in Southern Anhwei and were brutally killed. The question of the protection of American nationals was therefore a critical one. (For official dispatches on the case of Mr. and Mrs. Stam, see FR 1934, III, 479-490.) Moreover, it was impossible to forget the many other periods in Chinese history when the United States government had been engaged in protecting United States citizens in China, including the large-scale evacuation of Americans from the interior from 1925 to 1928 when the Communists did much to channel the revolution in an anti-foreign direction. (See Borg, *American Policy and the Chinese Revolution 1925-1928*, pp. 290-295 and Chap. XIII.)

19. File 893.00/12324 A. During the Long March the amount of space given to an account of the Communists' activities varied greatly, the Hankow monthly reports sometimes devoting as much as 24 out of 30 pages to the Communists while the embassy report itself was more likely to devote 2 or 3 out of approximately 15 pages to the Communists and twice that number to the Sino-Japanese situation. (File 893.00 PR Hankow/91 to 102; 893.00 PR/87 to 98.)

20. Except for the monthly reports, the dispatches on the Long March are classified under the number 893.00 and are mainly in boxes 7126-7129.

For an account of the political developments within the Chinese Communist movement during the Long March, including the events which brought Mao Tse-tung to power, see Robert North's *Moscow and Chinese Communists* (1952), pp. 166, 174. None of these developments were referred to in the dispatches of American Foreign Service officers, except for mention of a "disagreement between Mao and Chu Teh on the one hand and Hsu Hsiang-chien on the other" which the members of the Hankow consulate general stated, in November 1935, was being reported by the Nanking government, although, they added, they themselves were skeptical of the reports. File 893.00 PR Hankow 1103.

21. File 893.00/12929 enclosure.

22. File 893.00/12929.

23. File 893.00/113161.

24. File 893.00/12966. For other typical reports, File 893.00 numbers 12983, 13011, 13341, 13391.

25. File 893.00, numbers 12948 and 12984, deal with Kiangsi; numbers 13037, 13071, 13138 are typical dispatches relating the Generalissimo's reorganization of Kweichow, Yunan, and Szechwan.

26. Abridged version of speech and discussion, *Communist International*, Sept. 20, 1935 (Vol. XII, No. 17-18), p. 1188; for part dealing with China, see p. 1212. Also in *Inprecorr*, Aug. 20, 1935 (Vol. 15, No. 37), p. 971. For interpretation see Beloff, *The Foreign Policy of Soviet Russia* I, 191, 221, and David J. Dallin, *Soviet Russia and the Far East* (1948), p. 128.

For guidance on the various English language versions of the speeches at the 7th Congress which had a bearing on Chinese affairs and for a discussion of some of the most important Chinese communist declarations on the united front policy, cited below, the author is indebted to Professor C. Martin Wilbur of Columbia University for permission to use the draft of a chapter on the united front policy of the Chinese Communists which he has not yet published.

27. *Inprecorr*, Nov. 11, 1935 (Vol. 15, No. 60), p. 1488. Like Dimitrov, Wang Ming did not include Chiang Kai-shek and the leadership of the Kuomintang in the united front at this time.

28. Wang Ming, *The Revolutionary Movement in the Colonial Countries* (pamphlet, Workers Library Publishers) pp. 49, 51.

29. Aug. 9, 1935. The chief interest of the American press in the congress was in whether its proceedings constituted a violation by the Soviet Union of its pledge of noninterference in the internal affairs of the United States, given at the time of the United States' recognition of the USSR. The Roosevelt administration felt that it did and protested to Moscow in late

August 1935. (See *FR The Soviet Union 1933-1939*, section beginning 218; comment on press in particular is in dispatch printed on 241.)

30. Beginning with August 1935, the speeches, discussions, resolutions, etc., of the 7th Congress appeared in issues of *Inprecorr* for many months. For list of pamphlets, see inside cover of Wang Ming's *The Revolutionary Movement in the Colonial Countries;* typical advertisement appears on inside cover of these pamphlets, of the *Communist International,* and of *The Communist,* the monthly magazine of the Communist Party of the United States.

31. *FR The Soviet Union 1933-1939*, section beginning 218 dealing with the 7th Congress.

32. *Ibid.*, 224.

33. *Ibid.*, 244. That leading officials of the East European Division agreed with Bullitt's analysis of the united front policy seems evident from the memorandum of a conversation between the Assistant Chief of the Division and the Soviet ambassador published on 260.

34. The articles appeared in the following numbers of *Inprecorr:* Dec. 21, 1935 (Vol. 15, No. 70), p. 1728; Dec. 28, 1935 (Vol. 15, No. 71), p. 1751; Jan. 11, 1936 (Vol. 16, No. 2), p. 16; Jan. 25, 1936 (Vol. 16, No. 6), p. 149; Feb. 8, 1936 (Vol. 16, No. 8), p. 223. The article in *The Communist International* was printed in the February 1936 issue (Vol. XIII, Special Number), p. 107.

35. Jan. 11, 1936 (Vol. 16, No. 2), p. 39. The evolution of the "united front from above" policy is related in detail by James C. Thomson, Jr., in a paper entitled "Communist Policy and the United Front in China 1935-1936," (*Papers on China*, vol. 11) which has been of great assistance in the writing of this chapter. Thomson discusses all of the articles written by Wang Ming in this period and compares them with the statements issued by the leadership of the Chinese Communist Party in China. He concludes that while Moscow wanted a "united front from above" policy for its own purposes, Mao Tse-tung and other Chinese communist leaders only accepted this policy reluctantly, believing that it was against the interests of the Chinese Communist Party. (See also Benjamin Schwartz, "On the Originality of Mao Tse-tung," *Foreign Affairs*, Oct. 1955, p. 67, and Dallin, *Soviet Russia and the Far East*, pp. 129, 131.) Although this point is an exceedingly interesting one, it has not been discussed in the above context, as most foreign observers knew too little about the united front policy to notice whether there were differences between the views being expressed in China and the Soviet Union. (For additional comment, see note 64 of this chapter.) The article published in the Jan. 11, 1936 *Inprecorr* had been printed in a Paris newspaper in November 1935. (See footnote 59 of Thomson's paper.)

36. *Inprecorr*, Feb. 8, 1936 (Vol. 16, No. 8), p. 223; *Communist International*, Feb. 1936 (Vol. XIII, Special Number), p. 118.

37. *Communist International*, Feb. 1936 (Vol. XIII, Special Number), p. 122.

38. Aug. 3, 1935 (Vol. 15, No. 32), p. 830. Also *China Today*, Sept. 1935, p. 236.

39. Nov. 31, 1935 (Vol. 15, No. 64), p. 1595. Also *China Today*, Dec. 1935, p. 58 and the *Communist International*, Feb. 1936. (Vol. XIII, Special Number), p. 218. Professor Wilbur states that the latter translation differs

from the earlier ones and has certain curious distortions. (See note 26 of this chapter.)

40. March 14, 1936 (Vol. 16, No. 23), p. 377.

41. *China Today*, p. 41; 893.00/13696 enclosure. In his manuscript, cited in note 26 of this chapter, Wilbur gives an abstract of a twenty-page document adopted by the Central Political Bureau of the Chinese Communist Party at a meeting at Wayaopao (North Shensi) on December 25, 1935, entitled "The Resolutions of the Chinese Communist Party regarding the immediate political situation and the tasks of the Party." This envisages a far-reaching change in the program of the Chinese Communists and presumably was the basis for the March manifesto of the Central North China Bureau of the Chinese Communist Party. At the same Wayaopao meeting, Mao Tse-tung delivered a report "On the Tactics of Fighting Japanese Imperialism." (*Selected Works of Mao Tse-tung*, I, 175.) However, as far as I have been able to ascertain neither the "Resolutions" nor Mao's speech were available in the West at the time. (For further discussion of these documents see Thomson, "Communist Policy," pp. 115-117.)

42. Based upon a statement of an official of the State Department who examined these documents for the writer.

43. July 13, 1935, 213; signed "W. B."

44. Johnson papers, letter dated Dec. 31, 1935. Years later (Oct. 1942), when the Communist Party of the United States charged that "reactionary officials in the State Department" were encouraging Chiang Kai-shek to keep his best troops out of the war with Japan in order to liquidate the Chinese Communist armies, the Department replied in effect that it had at no time given such advice and added, "This Government has in fact viewed with skepticism many alarmist accounts of the 'serious menace' of 'communism' in China. We have, for instance, as is publicly and well known, declined to be moved by Japanese contentions that presence and maintenance of Japanese armed forces in China were and would be desirable for the purpose of 'combatting Communism.'" *FR China* 1942, 243, 248.

45. 893.00/13425.

46. 893.00 PR/94. The Shansi campaign has been referred to in Chap. VI.

47. 893.00b/1089 enclosure. The *Post* may have secured *Inprecorr* from the police of the International Settlement at Shanghai who sometimes furnished interested foreigners with copies. (893.00 PR Shanghai/39.)

48. 893.00b/1089. Here again it should be recognized that the primary interest in Wang Ming's article on the part of Gauss and Peck (and also of the *Shanghai Evening Post and Mercury*) lay in the fact that the Communists were altering their foreign policy so as to release foreign missionaries they had captured and cease their attacks upon foreigners in general.

49. 893.00/13464; also printed in *FR* 1936, IV, 112.

50. The term "First International" appears in the original as well as the published version and is therefore not a typographical error in the latter.

51. 893.00b/1089.

52. 893.00/13769 enclosure. *Communist International*, Jan. 1937, p. 68.

53. *Inprecorr*, Sept. 26, 1936 (Vol. 16, No. 44), p. 1208; *Communist International*, Oct. 1936, p. 1341. See also Georgi Dimitroff's article in celebration of the 15th anniversary of the Communist Party of China immedi-

ately preceding Wang Ming's in both references. Both articles were reprinted in a pamphlet entitled "China: The March Toward Unity" published in May 1937 by the Workers Library Publishers. For quotations in this paragraph, see Section IV.

54. 893.00b/1091.

55. 893.00/13696. The Foreign Service officer was commenting upon the March Manifesto of the Central North Bureau of the Chinese Communist Party which has been referred to earlier in this chapter and which he enclosed in his dispatch. The manifesto was still based upon the idea of a "united front from below" and virtually called Chiang Kai-shek a traitor.

56. 893.00b/1091.

57. Final paragraph. (In version published in "China: The March Toward Unity," p. 118.)

58. 893.00/13769 enclosures. Edgar Snow's interviews were also printed in *The China Weekly Review*, Nov. 14 (p. 377) and 21 (p. 430) 1936. For Snow's own estimate of the effect of the publication of these interviews, see *Red Star Over China* (Pt. 11, Chap. 6). In this book (first published in 1938), Snow does discuss the character of the united front policy and the influence of the Comintern upon the policies of the Chinese Communists in general reaching the conclusion that the "political ideology, tactical line, and theoretical leadership of the Chinese Communists had been under the close guidance, if not positive direction, of the Communist International." (Pt. 11, Chap. 3, next to the last paragraph.)

It should be recognized, however, that Snow was primarily intent upon telling the public what he had seen and heard on his historic trip into the Communist areas of China so that his book consists far more of an account of the concrete operations of the Chinese Communists inside China than a consideration of the ideological connection between the Chinese Communists and the Comintern. The same may be said of James M. Bertram's *First Act In China: the Story of the Sian Mutiny*, which was also published in early 1938.

(The Department's files also contain the text of a long address given by Snow in February 1937, which was forwarded to Washington by the consul general in Shanghai with the comment that, while the address was written from a standpoint sympathetic to the aspirations of the Chinese Communists, it constituted the most authoritative, comprehensive and up-to-date account of the Communist movement in China that the consul general himself had as yet seen. 893.00/14044 with enclosures.)

59. See, for example, 893.00 numbers 13716, 13726.

60. The Second Secretary of the embassy, for example, made a trip to Kansu in November 1936 and reported that he received the impression that the Nanking government had ceased to fight the Communists because it recognized that they would be strong allies in case of war with Japan. (893.00/13746.) The Third Secretary reported, on the other hand, that the situation between the Communists and Chang Hsueh-liang, on one side, and the government, on the other, was constantly growing more tense. (893.00/13769.) This report has as an enclosure a copy of an important interview held by Nym Wales with Chang Hsueh-liang on October 3, 1936, in which the Young Marshal stated that he was loyal to the Generalissimo but was convinced that the unification of the country was essential for

resistance to Japan and that he believed in cooperation with the Communists if they were sincerely prepared to aid in such resistance.

61. The newspapers which have been used include the *North China Daily News and Herald*, the *China Weekly Review*, the *New York Times*, the *Christian Science Monitor*, the *Chicago Tribune*, the *San Francisco Chronicle*, the *Los Angeles Times*, and a number of others. Useful accounts written subsequently are Bertram's *First Act in China*; Snow's *Red Star Over China*, Pt. 12; and Bisson's *Japan In China*, Chap. 5. The volume written by the Generalissimo and Madame Chiang Kai-shek and published in the spring of 1937, are essential reading for anyone interested in this famous incident (Soong, Mayling, *Sian: A Coup d'Etat* and Chiang Kai-shek, *A Fortnight in Sian: Extracts From a Diary*).

62. For the text of this important telegram, see Bertram, *First Act in China*, p. 125. The U.S. embassy at Peiping somehow obtained the full text and cabled it to the Department on December 20 with the statement that, as far as it had been able to ascertain, the complete text had not been published in China. (*FR 1936, IV*, 440.)

63. The *China Weekly Review* stated that Spilwanek had additionally denied any responsibility for the Chinese Communists, declaring that Moscow had no connection with them. (Feb. 27, 1937, p. 456.)

64. The Department's files contain two different copies of the *Izvestia* editorial, one sent from the embassy in Moscow (893.00/13947), the other from the embassy in Peiping. (893.00/13913.) The latter was handed to Johnson by Spilwanek and was apparently the version distributed by *Tass* in China. There are some variations in the texts, the version forwarded by Ambassador Johnson omitting, among other things, the italicized sentence in the following quotation: "Inasmuch as the Nanking Government conducts a policy of resistance to Japanese aggression, the United Popular Front struggle against Japan is regarded by all participants, not as a front against Nanking, but as a front together with Nanking. *This was recently stated bluntly by Mao-t'un [sic], the President of the Chinese Soviet Government, in his interview with Edgar Snow which was pubilshed in the American-Chinese China Weekly Review.*"

It is possible that this omission reflected a desire on the part of Moscow not to produce the impression in China at this time that it was closely associated with the Chinese Communists who were not mentioned in any part of the text of the *Izvestia* or *Pravda* editorials forwarded to the Department from the embassy in China.

In any case, it is clear that Spilwanek went out of his way to tell United States officials, after the Sian incident, that he was certain the Generalissimo had not made any concessions in regard to the Chinese Communists at Sian and that Nanking would probably soon renew its military campaigns against them. (893.00 numbers 13979 enclosure, 13986 enclosure, 14073.) What the Soviet Union's motive was in taking this position must be a matter of conjecture as long as our knowledge of the role which it played in the Sian incident remains obscure. Interesting new light has, however, been thrown upon this subject by Edgar Snow in a mimeographed manuscript issued in 1957 and entitled *Random Notes on Red China (1936-1945)*, in which the first section is devoted to "New Data on the Sian Incident." Some of this material indicates that the Chinese Communists may have planned to hold

Chiang Kai-shek prisoner at Sian, and bring him to trial and disgrace, but abandoned this scheme on receiving a telegram from Stalin which stated that unless they used their influence to release the Generalissimo they would be denounced by Moscow as "bandits" and publicly repudiated (page 2).

65. The dispatches begin with 893.00/13753. Quite a number are published in *FR* 1936, IV, from 414 on.

66. 893.00/13774.

67. Johnson papers, letter from Willys Peck to Nelson Johnson, dated Dec. 19, 1936.

68. 893.00/13809A; see also *FR* 1936, IV, 439, footnote 14.

69. *FR* 1936, IV, 419.

70. *Ibid.*, 423.

71. *Ibid.*, 438.

72. *Ibid.*, 434.

73. *Ibid.*

74. *FR* 1937, III, 12.

75. There are two versions of this memorandum in the Department's files: 893.00 numbers 13772 and 13847.

76. PSF China 1936, Box 19, Roosevelt papers.

77. Johnson papers, letter dated Dec. 22, 1936. On Jan. 12, 1937, Johnson wrote an official report of the Sian incident but this had virtually no interpretative comments. (893.00/13980; copy in Johnson papers filed as letter to Secretary of State.)

78. Johnson papers; filed as letter to Secretary of State, dated Jan. 26, 1937.

79. Johnson papers, letter dated Feb. 6, 1937. Hornbeck's letter is also in the Johnson papers (dated Jan. 4, 1937). The Department files contain memoranda of a number of conversations held by American officials with prominent representatives of other countries following the Sian incident. The ambassador's remarks concerning the Young Marshal's personality are obviously based upon the memorandum of a talk between Willys Peck and a member of the Executive Yuan in which the latter discussed Chang Hsueh-liang in some detail. (893.00/13979.)

80. For first statement, see note to Nelson Johnson, dated Dec. 14, 1936; for telegram see attachment to Hornbeck's memorandum, dated Dec. 22, 1936, in Roosevelt papers, PSF China 1936, Box 19.

81. Johnson papers, letter dated May 11, 1937. For earlier views, see Johnson papers, letters to Roy Howard, dated Dec. 22, 1936, and to William Castle, dated Jan 26, 1937.

82. The following statements are based on articles in the contemporary issues of the *North China Daily Herald* and the *China Weekly Review*.

83. Based on an examination of the *Christian Science Monitor*, the *Chicago Tribune*, the *Los Angeles Times*, and other papers.

84. The most important editorials of the *North China Daily News* appeared in the issues of: Dec. 23, 28, 29, 1936; Jan. 12, 24, Feb. 3, March 3, 17, 23, Sept. 27, 1937, and were reprinted in the weekly edition of the *News* (the *North China Herald*), which always carried the leading editorials published in the *News* during the course of the preceding week. Two important articles were reprinted in the *Herald* on Dec. 30, 1936 (p. 528) and Jan. 6, 1937 (p. 8).

85. The *China Weekly Review,* Jan. 9, 1937, p. 185.

86. See especially editorials of Jan. 30, Feb. 27, March 20, 1937.

87. See for early dispatches 893.00/13833 and *FR* 1937, III, 10; for conflicting stories 893.00 numbers 13972, 13983, 13979 (enclosed memorandum of Jan. 6 talk with member of Executive Yuan), 1400; *FR* 1937, III, 1823, 1824; on talk of Ambassador Johnson with Kuomintang official, *FR* 1937, III, 27 and later statements of Nanking officials 893.00/14075, *FR* 1937, III, 79, 125. In April, Earl Leaf, the United Press correspondent at Tientsin who had made a trip to Yenan, gave the Tientsin consulate general a considerable amount of information about the Kuomintang-Communist rapprochement. (893.00/14122 enclosure; see also *FR* 1937, III, 79, 107.)

88. Official memorandum 893.00/14068 enclosure.

89. Johnson papers, letter to General William Crozier, dated March 23, 1937.

90. *FR* 1937, III, 87.

91. *Ibid.,* 111.

92. The quotation is from an account of Stuart's speech in the *China Weekly Review* (Feb. 27, 1936, p. 456).

93. For Kennan's reports, see 961.93/1583; 961/94 numbers 953 and 965; *FR* 1937, III, 21, 91.

94. Following the outbreak of the Sino-Japanese War, the United States embassy in Moscow primarily emphasized that the Soviet Union had no intention whatever of allowing itself to be drawn into the conflict in the Far East, despite the signing of the Sino-Soviet Non-Aggression Pact of August 1937, and merely hoped that China would so weaken Japan that the latter would no longer constitute a danger to the Soviet Union. In November 1937, it ascribed the mysterious disappearance in Moscow of Dimitri Bogomoloff, the Soviet Ambassador to China (who was rumored to have been arrested and perhaps executed), to his probably having encouraged the Nanking government to expect Soviet aid without realizing that no such aid would be forthcoming. (761.93, numbers 1604, 1614, 1632; 761.94/1005.)

In regard to the Sino-Soviet Non-Aggression Pact, the United States consul general at Shanghai had cabled the Department as early as April 1937 that Bogomoloff had confidentially told Anthony J. Billingham of the *New York Times* (apparently for repetition to interested American officials) that the Soviet Union had decided to support the Nanking government as "the stabilizing and paramount force" in China and that conversations were currently underway for the conclusion of a Sino-Soviet agreement. (*FR* 1937, III, 69. In this cable the consul general made the rather astonishing suggestion that the Soviet government might be carrying on negotiations for a Sino-Soviet agreement "through the medium of the Communist leader, Chou En-lai.")

CHAPTER VIII. THE PACIFIC ISLANDS

1. The story of how Article XIX was negotiated is of course related in many places. There is a good account in Harold and Margaret Sprout's *Toward a New Order of Sea Power* (1940), pp. 166ff., and a more detailed and up-to-date account in Earl S. Pomeroy, *Pacific Outpost* (1951), Chap.

IV. Werner B. Ellinger, and Herbert Rosinski, comp., *Sea Power in the Pacific, 1936-1941* (1942), is a useful bibliography on the general subject; also Helen F. Conover, *Islands of the Pacific: A Selected List of References* (1943).

2. The question of the Senate's relations to the Washington Conference is well told in Vinson, *The Parchment Peace;* for references to Article XIX, see especially pp. 169, 199, and 206.

3. A convenient copy of the text is printed in the Sprouts' *Toward a New Order of Sea Power*, Appendix B, and reads:

The United States, the British Empire and Japan agree that the *status quo* at the time of the signing of the present Treaty, with regard to fortifications and naval bases, shall be maintained in their respective territories and possessions specified hereunder: (1) The insular possessions which the United States now holds or may hereafter acquire in the Pacific Ocean, except (a) those adjacent to the coast of the United States, Alaska and the Panama Canal Zone, not including the Aleutian Islands, and (b) the Hawaiian Islands; (2) Hongkong and the insular possessions which the British Empire now holds or may hereafter acquire in the Pacific Ocean, east of the meridian of 110° east longitude, except (a) those adjacent to the coast of Canada, (b) the Commonwealth of Australia and its territories, and (c) New Zealand; (3) The following insular territories and possessions of Japan in the Pacific Ocean, to wit: the Kurile Islands, the Bonin Islands, Anami-Oshima, the Loochoo Islands, Formosa and the Pescadores, and any insular territories or possessions in the Pacific Ocean which Japan may hereafter acquire.

The maintenance of the *status quo* under the foregoing provisions implies that no new fortifications or naval bases shall be established in the territories and possessions specified, that no measures shall be taken to increase the existing naval facilities for the repair and maintenance of naval forces, and that no increase shall be made in the coast defenses of the territories and possessions above specified. This restriction, however, does not preclude such repair and replacement of worn-out weapons and equipment as is customary in naval and military establishments in time of peace.

4. Merlo J. Pusey considers Hughes' attitude toward the question of fortifying the Pacific islands in his biography, *Charles Evans Hughes* (1951), in some detail; in this connection, Chap. 43, "Opening the Mandated Islands," pp. 476ff., is of particular interest.

5. Paul H. Clyde in his book *Japan's Pacific Mandate* (1935), Chap. III, discusses the manner in which Japan received a mandate over the former German islands and quotes Article 4 of the mandate, which states: "The military training of the natives, otherwise than for purposes of internal police and the local defense of the territory, shall be prohibited. Furthermore, no military or naval bases shall be established, or fortifications erected in the territory."

6. The United States had to make separate arrangements with Japan concerning the mandates, as she was not a signatory of the Versailles Treaty or a member of the League of Nations.

7. The various arrangements made by Hughes are listed in a State Department memorandum printed in the Report of the Army Board which investigated the Pearl Harbor disaster. They included: the extension to the mandated islands of the Japanese-American Treaty of Commerce and Navigation of 1911 which had provisions for the citizens of each country, with their ships and cargoes, to visit places open to commerce on the territories of the

other; and an interchange of notes in which the Japanese promised that the "usual comity" would be extended to nationals and vessels of the United States in regard to visiting the mandates. (See also Pusey, *Charles Evans Hughes*, p. 449.)

8. Ellis M. Zacharias, *Secret Missions* (1946), p. 40. Captain Zacharias gives a dramatic account of the American officer who, as the story goes, was in the service of the Naval Intelligence and was inspecting the Japanese mandated islands for military preparations when he died mysteriously on Palau in 1923. According to this version, a United States Naval officer, sent to recover the body, himself returned to Japan mentally deranged. (Chap. 5, "The Strange Case of 'Colonel X.'" See also Holland Smith, and Percy Finch, *Coral and Brass*, 1949, p. 56.)

9. *FR* 1939, III, 256, 257.

10. *Ibid.*, 258, 259, 261; these pages contain all the documents pertaining to this incident that are referred to here. See also the testimony of Captain Edwin T. Layton before the Army's Pearl Harbor Board. (Hearings of the Board, Vol. 28, 1959.)

11. There was one further episode involving plans of the United States Navy to send a Naval Observatory Expedition to the Marianas to observe a solar eclipse in 1934. The State Department, late in 1932, sounded out the Japanese to see if they would give permission for access to Saipan. The Japanese replied that they would be glad to send American scientists down in Japanese ships. As Grew remarked in his diary, the Japanese thus solved the "awkward question" of American scientists visiting the island with the "wisdom of Solomon," as the scientists would be "honored guests but mighty carefully chaperoned guests too." (*Ten Years in Japan*, p. 85. See also the statement in regard to this matter made to newspaper correspondents by a State Department officer at the time that the Japanese were being questioned by the Mandates Commission in November 1932, to the effect that the administration had not pressed the issue of entry to Saipan as the Navy Department had subsequently decided it did not want to send a scientific expedition. *New York Times*, Nov. 6, 1934, p. 4.)

12. Permanent Mandates Commission of the League of Nations. *Minutes of the 22nd session, Nov. 3 to Dec. 6, 1932*, 114ff. The meeting at which Ito appeared was secret, but the minutes were released in January 1933 (*New York Times*, Jan. 25, 1933).

13. The argument over whether Japan had fortified the mandated islands continued after the outbreak of the war and was discussed in detail at the Tokyo War Crimes Trial. (IMTFE *Proceedings* pp. 9067-9159; pp. 11189-11202 *passim;* pp. 26466-26515, p. 381115.) In a volume of the U.S. Army's official history published in 1960 the author states, "Whether or not Japan made any active effort to fortify or garrison the mandates before 1933 remains in doubt although their policy of excluding foreign visitors . . . raised suspicions. In any event after her withdrawal from the League and before the outbreak of hostilities it is certain that Japan embarked upon a program of military construction in the area." (Philip A. Crowl, *Campaign in Marianas* (1960), in series entitled *The U.S. Army in World War II.*)

14. Permanent Mandates Commission of the League of Nations. *Minutes of the 22nd session, Nov. 3 to Dec. 6, 1932*, p. 319.

15. *Ibid.*, pp. 179, 299.

16. Permanent Mandates Commission of the League of Nations, *Minutes of the 26th session, Oct. 29 to Nov. 12, 1934,* pp. 89-94.

17. *Ibid.*, p. 206.

18. Permanent Mandates Commission of the League of Nations, *Minutes of the 27th session, June 3 to 18, 1935,* p. 201.

19. Willard Price states that the controversy over the fortifications of the mandates between the commission and the Japanese government was also published in the European press. (*Japan's Islands of Mystery* [1944], p. 29.)

20. *FR* 1933, III, 750.

21. Grew, *Ten Years in Japan,* p. 85.

22. The State Department has never given a full account of its dealings with the Japanese government on the subject of entry into the mandated islands. It has been severely criticized for responding to a demand for an account by the Senate Naval Affairs Committee, in 1939, with an inadequate, if not actually misleading, statement of developments and moreover insisting upon the meager information which it imparted being kept secret. (The statement appears in a document issued by Senator David I. Walsh, Chairman of the Senate Naval Affairs Committee, in 1944 under the title of "The Decline and Renaissance of the Navy 1922-1944." For an example of criticisms, see Earl S. Pomeroy's article, "American Policy Respecting the Marshalls, Carolines, and Marianas 1898-1941," in *Pacific Historical Review,* Feb. 1948, p. 8.)

In 1944 the State Department, upon again being asked—this time by the Army Board investigating the Pearl Harbor attack—for information concerning requests by the administration for access to the mandates, again responded with a brief and sketchy memorandum. The Army Board, however, felt that in any case it had sufficient knowledge of the situation to justify the inclusion in its final report of a devastating attack upon the State Department's policy in which it contended that, if the Department had insisted upon Japan's living up to the treaty provisions which entitled Americans to visit the mandated islands, the "entire naval and military structure" that the Japanese erected in the Pacific islands "might have been made impossible." As it was, the Japanese managed for "nearly twenty years" to exclude visitors to the islands and "during this time built up army, navy, and air installations of tremendous strategical value." All in all, the Board stated, our policy had been based upon "a combination of fear of the Japanese and an obsession not to give offense to the Japanese." (The State Department's memorandum is printed on p. 21 of the Board's report and the Board's comments appear on pp. 19 and 20.)

23. *FR* 1934, III, 664.

24. *Ibid.*, 683; see also 681.

25. Huntington Gilchrist has stated that between 1932 and 1936 the visits of foreign ships "of any description" to the mandated islands was so rare as to average one a year. ("The Japanese Islands; Annexation or Trusteeships?" in *Foreign Affairs,* July 1944.) Some foreign private citizens, including Americans, did however visit the islands in the mid-1930's. Among these was Paul H. Clyde, who was invited to take a trip to the islands by the Japanese government in 1934 and who, in a book which he published in the following year, said he had seen no evidence of fortifications.

(*Japan's Pacific Mandate*, p. 222.) Willard Price also managed to get to the mandates, although with great difficulty, in this period, but contrary to Clyde, saw things which made him suspect that Japan was building military installations. Price did not, however, state his suspicions publicly until 1944, when he issued his book, *Japan's Islands of Mystery.* For discusssions of fortifications, naval bases, et cetera, see, for example, p. 30.

At the Japanese War Crimes Trials, correspondence between officials of the NYK Steamship Co. was introduced to the effect that all applications for passage to visit the mandated islands had to be referred by the company to the Japanese Foreign Office and Navy Department so that the government could secretly control all entries to the islands. (Refer to citations in note 13 of this chapter.)

26. *FR* 1936, IV, 984.
27. *Ibid.*, 985.
28. *Ibid.*, 986.
29. *Ibid.*, 989; Grew, *Turbulent Era*, II, p. 1029.
30. *FR* 1936, IV, 990.
31. *Ibid.*
32. *Ibid.*, 991.
33. *Ibid.*
34. *Ibid.*, 992.
35. *Ibid.*

36. In its statement to the Army's Pearl Harbor Board, the State Department asserted that after 1936 a more restrictive policy was adopted (presumably by the navy) in regard to the admission of Japanese public vessels to "the Aleutians and Alaska" so that they were only allowed to enter Dutch Harbor and, on two occasions, because of special circumstances, the Pribiloff Islands; moreover, visits were not permitted to the "territorial waters of the western Aleutian Islands." No further diplomatic action seems to have been taken by the State Department which indeed stated specifically in its letter to the Senate Committee on Naval Affairs in 1939: "With regard to the questions whether the terms of the treaty had been violated by Japan . . . the Government of the United States has at no time raised any question with the Japanese Government in regard to the obligations of Japan to the United States with respect to the Japanese mandated islands." (Walsh, "The Decline and Renaissance of the Navy," p. 8.)

Various persons have testified, from time to time, to friction between the State and Navy Departments over the issue of visiting the mandates. High-ranking naval officers declared repeatedly before the naval committees of the House of Representatives and the Senate in 1939 that Japan had consistently refused to allow our ships access to the mandates and affirmed, with remarkable candor, that the United States had not been able to obtain any information concerning the islands. It was these statements which led Senator Hiram Johnson to insist upon the State Department's providing the Senate Committee with an account of its efforts to achieve access to the mandates. Whatever the implications of their statements may have been, the naval officers did not, however, enter into any direct criticism of the State Department's policy at this time. But during the post-Pearl Harbor investigations, Admiral W. S. Pye, one of the outstanding officers in the Navy, who drafted the Basic War Plan for the Pacific, testified that for about twenty years before the war the Navy Department had asked the State Department to get permission for some of our ships to visit the mandated islands but that the "State Department never stood up to our rights" so that permission was always refused. Captain Layton of the Naval Intelligence, when a witness before the Army Board, definitely stated that there had "long been existing differences between the Navy Department and the State Department as to American naval vessels calling in the Marshall Islands." Captain Zacharias in his book, *Secret Missions*, stated that in 1935, when he was head of the Far Eastern section of the O.N.I. in Washington, the State Department was opposed to pressing the issue of the right of American naval vessels to enter into the mandated islands and even advised against asking for permission for them to do so. "It was largely," Zacharias wrote, "the shackles which our prewar diplomacy placed on our peacetime intelligence that forced us to embark on a difficult total war without even elemental information on the enemy." (Hearings Before the House Committee on Naval Affairs, pp. 66, 81, 477, and Hearings Before the Senate Naval Affairs Committee, pp. 46, 71; hearings of the Army Pearl Harbor Board, Vol. 27, p. 552, Vol. 28, p. 1589.)

37. Minutes of the meeting of Nov. 14, 1934, *FR* 1934, I, 334 dialogue beginning 340 and continued 342.

38. The "middle course" is discussed above, Chapter III.

39. *FR* 1934, I, 351.

40. *FR* 1936, I, 122. The Japanese subsequently turned down the British proposal regarding Article XIX. (*United States in World Affairs 1936*, p. 38, footnote 12.)

41. *FR* 1936, I, 124.

42. *FR* 1936, IV, 220; *FR* 1936, I, 131. Davis' position in respect to concluding a new agreement with the Japanese on the fortifications question is also explained in a letter that he wrote to Hornbeck on March 23, 1937, which appears in his files and in *FR* 1937, III, 974.

43. *FR* 1936, I, 130; Davis papers, memorandum of Robert Pell's, dated Nov. 6, 1935.

44. Harold L. Ickes, *The Secret Diary of Harold L. Ickes* (1953-1959), Vol. II, *The Inside Struggle*, p. 7.

45. *Ibid.*, p. 51.

46. *FR* 1937, III, 954.

47. *Ibid.*, 973.

48. The memorandum was written by Maxwell Hamilton but was the product of discussions within the Far Eastern Division and represented the ideas of its leading officials.

49. *FR* 1937, III, 972, footnote 95; letter to Stanley K. Hornbeck, dated March 31, 1937, Grew Diary, p. 3127.

50. Memorandum of telephone conversation of March 19, 1937, between President Roosevelt in Warm Springs and Norman Davis in New York (Davis papers).

51. *FR* 1937, III, 975.

52. Memoranda of conversation with Chamberlain, April 26, 1937 (two versions of the same conversation, Davis papers).

53. Davis papers, memorandum of conversation with Anthony Eden, April 9, 1937.

54. The strategic planning of the army and navy in regard to the Pacific is discussed in detail in "War Plan *Orange*" by Louis Morton (*World Politics*, Jan. 1959). There are also helpful brief references in some of the volumes of *The U.S. Army in World War II*, especially *Chief of Staff: Prewar Plans and Preparations* (1950) by Mark Skinner Watson (p. 414) and *Strategic Planning for Coalition Warfare 1941-1942* by Maurice Matloff and Edward Snell (pp. 1ff.).

55. The Joint Board of the Army and Navy repeatedly sought to resolve the controversy between the army and navy planners by working out a program which presented a compromise.

56. The Hepburn Board's recommendations and detailed discussions of these recommendations and the administration's bill will be found in the following references: *Hepburn Report*, 76th Congress, 1st session, House Document No. 65; *Hearings Before the Senate Committee on Naval Affairs* on S 830, March 6-14, 1939, 76th Congress, 1st session; *Hearings Before House Committee on Naval Affairs* on HR 2880, Jan. 25-Feb. 17, 1939, 76th Congress, 1st session.

57. Pomeroy, *Pacific Outpost*, p. 131; *Hearings Before the Senate Naval Affairs Committee*, p. 70.

58. *New York Times*, Jan, 21, 1931, p. 1, "Roosevelt Backs New Base at Guam."

59. *Ibid*. There appears to have been considerable confusion about what the President said originally, but it is reasonably clear that he told the press, through Stephen Early, that he had not seen the Guam item in the bill.

60. Pomeroy has a good description of the highlights of the congressional debate on the administration's bill in his *Pacific Outpost* (pp. 128ff.).

61. Whitney H. Shepardson and William O. Scroggs, *The United States in World Affairs*, 1939, p. 122; *New York Times*, Jan. 15, 1939, p. 1, "Guam Arming Plan Stirs Rising Clash."

62. The classic statement of Congress's point of view is given in Senator Walsh's *The Decline and Renaissance of the Navy*. The Senator was Chairman of the Senate Naval Affairs Committee.

63. *United States Naval Institute Proceedings*, Aug. 1939, p. 1198, *Professional Notes*.

64. William L. Langer and Everett S. Gleason, *The Challenge to Isolation* (1952), p. 150.

65. See for example Merze Tate, *The United States and Armaments* (1948), p. 195.

66. *New York Times*, Jan. 15, 1939, p. 1, "Guam Arming Plan Stirs Rising Clash"; Jan. 17, 1939, p. 9, "Japanese Press Warn Against Fortifying Guam"; Jan. 18, 1939, "Roosevelt Checks Alarm Over Guam."

67. An account of the agreements reached at the Buenos Aires Conference and other plans which the President devised for the maintenance of peace is given in Chap. XIII.

CHAPTER IX. END OF A PERIOD OF "PEACE"

1. *FR 1937*, IV, 581, 582.
2. Accounts of the events in Japan as they appeared to contemporary

observers are to be found in Bisson, *Japan in China*, pp. 228ff. and Chap. VII; Harold S. Quigley and George H. Blakeslee, *The Far East* (1938), pp. 100ff.

3. Some of the embassy's analyses of the situation appear in *FR* 1937, IV, 1, 48, 96, and *FR* 1937, III, 48.

4. *FR* 1937, IV, 592.

5. Johnson papers, letter to Hugh Wilson, dated May 13, 1937. Grew sent a copy to Nelson Johnson which suggests that he also sent one to Washington.

6. Friedman, *British Relations with China*, p. 60.

7. Kurt Bloch, *German Interests and Policies in the Far East* (1939), p. 24.

8. State Department files 811.51693/74.

9. In connection with the Forbes mission, I have read a substantial number of the documents which form part of the Forbes collection but have relied heavily upon the paper written by Shirley Godley entitled "W. Cameron Forbes and the American Mission to China (1935)." (*Papers on China* (1960), Vol. 14, East Asian Research Center, Harvard University). Mrs. Godley made a thorough study of Forbes' journal and letters.

10. The difficulties which the National Foreign Trade Council met in organizing the mission were recounted in various letters to the State Department. (State Department files, American-Chinese Trade Commission 693.11/1, 5, 8, 13, 15, 21, 29).

11. No doubt the Department's anxiety was increased because the Japanese raised so many objections that the plan of sending an economic mission to the Far East was almost abandoned. (State Department files, American-Chinese Trade Commission 693.11/17).

12. Godley, "W. Cameron Forbes," Sec. 2. Forbes collection: *Journal*, p. 237 (interview with Chiang Kai-shek), p. 261 (interview with T. V. Soong and H. H. Kung), p. 267 (letter to Chiang Kai-shek); letter to J. Grant Forbes, August 5, 1935. Forbes's account of his interview with the Generalissimo is a particularly amusing example of his lack of knowledge of even the most elementary facts concerning China and the difficulties which resulted.

13. *FR* 1937, IV, 490 (quoted at end of Sir Frederick Leith-Ross' statement).

14. Forbes collection: letter to J. Grant Forbes, dated August 5, 1935; letter to E. P. Thomas, dated October 26, 1936. Also American Trade Prospects in the Orient, Report of the American Economic Mission to the Far East (1935), pp. 57, 60.

15. Godley, "W. Cameron Forbes," Sec. 4. An elaborate plan for a bank was drawn up (Forbes collection: *Journal*, p. 313). The most interesting documents concerning the tin and railway project are the following letters in the Forbes collection: E. P. Thomas to H. L. Hughes, dated July 22, 1935; Forbes to H. M. Bixby, dated May 11, 1936, to Li Tsung-jen, dated May 21, 1936, to Myron C. Taylor, dated May 25, 1936, and to J. Grant Forbes, dated December 2, 1936.

16. For an account of French's activities see State Department files 893.51/6050, 60, 63, 64; American Chamber of Commerce of Shanghai

Bulletin, No. 217, February 1936; Department of Commerce files, folder on Trade Promotion 1939-40, French memorandum February 1939.

17. State Department files 893.51/6113.

18. State Department files R.G. 84, American consulate general, Shanghai, p. 851 (1936); Forbes collection, letter to H. M. Bixby, dated May 11, 1936.

19. Forbes collection, letter to H. M. Bixby, dated May 11, 1936.

20. State Department files, 893.51/6138.

21. See for example *FR* 1936, IV, 574, 576.

22. Chang Kia-ngau *China's Struggle for Railroad Development* (1943), Pt. III, Chaps. 1, 2, 3; Friedman, *British Relations With China*, p. 83, footnote.

23. *FR* 1936, IV, 586, 588, 590, 591; Chang Kia-ngau, *China's Struggle*, pp. 153, 154, 156, 160.

24. *FR* 1936, IV, 473, 590.

25. *FR* 1935, III, 607; Johnson papers, letters from Hornbeck to Ambassador Johnson, dated March 2, 1936 and May 8, 1936. Forbes wrote in a personal letter in May 1937 that his plan for a credit organization was still in abeyance. Officials in Washington, he said, were friendly but dwelt on the "obstacles and impediments and difficulties" to an extent that so far had prevented any constructive action. Nevertheless he felt that the issues involved were "so important" and the need "so great . . . that some day it will force itself through and over these impediments and get going on a big scale and any one who can advance the day . . . will be a benefactor." (Forbes collection, letter to N. F. Allman, dated May 17, 1937).

26. Johnson papers, letter dated July 17, 1936.

27. The most comprehensive story of the developments related in the text is in Chang Kia-ngau, *China's Struggle*, Part II. The *Far Eastern Survey* carried some useful articles such as "Boxer Fund Aids British Railway Supply" by J. R., dated March 12, 1936; "Sino-British Railway Loan Sets Precedent" by W. W. L., dated August 26, 1936; "Latest Sino-German Railway Deal One of Several" by R. G. S., dated January 20, 1937; "Revitalizing British Interests in China" by Kate Mitchell, dated June 23, 1937; "Railway Strategy in China, New Style" by Chen Han-seng and Miriam Farley, dated July 21, 1937. The number of articles alone indicates the importance being attached to these events.

28. In March 1936 the Chinese Minister of Railways indicated to the United States commercial attaché in China that he would like to have American interests participate in the construction of a railway to run from the southwest corner of Kwangtung to Hunan and in the expansion of a line, already started, that was to connect Nanking with Canton. (State Department files 893.51/6122).

29. For German activities see Bloch, *German Interests*, p. 26; Liu, *A Military History of Modern China: 1924-1949*, p. 101. For British activities see Tamagna, *Banking and Finance in China*, p. 111.

30. "China Association, London," *British Chamber of Commerce Journal*, January 1937.

31. *FR* 1937, IV, 581, 592. State Department files 033.1190 Warren Lee Pierson/11. Julean Arnold, the United States commercial attaché, had for many years been devoting himself to the promotion of United

States trade with China. In early 1935 he had tried to interest United States railways and the Export-Import Bank in the sale of equipment to China but had found them "pathetically" unresponsive. (Bureau of Foreign and Domestic Commerce files, 520-China, railways 1932-1936).

32. *FR 1937*, III, 111.
33. Johnson papers, letter to Hornbeck, dated April 19, 1937.
34. *FR 1937*, IV, 581, 584, 585, 586.
35. Chang Kia-ngau, *China's Struggle*, p. 144.
36. *Ibid.*, pp. 13, 14, 93, Pt. II, Chaps. 9, 11.
37. *FR 1937*, IV, 568.
38. *FR 1936*, IV, 469.
39. *FR 1937*, IV, 576; also 571.
40. Roosevelt papers, PSF, Morgenthau 1937, Box 24. The President edited the note himself and returned it to Secretary Hull with the comment that he thought it went "much too far" in regard to the Consortium. "I do not think," he declared, "that it is necessary for us to give approval at this late date to the old Consortium agreement, especially in the way it has worked out." (*FR 1937*, IV, 576).
41. *FR 1937*, IV, 570, 586.
42. *Ibid.*, 590, 591. Lamont added, "In the case of America the existing group is almost completely debarred from offering securities under our present laws . . . On the other hand it is quite probable that the existing Managing Committee in America might well succeed in organizing an offering group of first-class Houses that might be interested in future Chinese business, although not immediately."
43. *FR 1937*, IV, 590.
44. *Ibid.*, 619; Chang Kia-ngau, *China's Struggle*, Pt. III, Chaps. 9, 10, 11.
45. *FR 1937*, III, 102; *FR 1937*, IV, 603, 605.
46. *Ibid.*, 608.
47. *Ibid.*, 612, 616, 617, 618, 619.
48. *Ibid.*, 610, 611; Blum, *From the Morgenthau Diaries*, p. 479; Everest, *Morgenthau, The New Deal and Silver*, p. 117.
49. Blum, *From the Morgenthau Diaries*, p. 457.
50. *FR 1937*, I, 98.
51. Morgenthau tells the following story. At lunch at the White House in February 1937 he said that the President was the only person who could stop the world from drifting into a war. Mr. Roosevelt replied: " 'I had Hull, Norman Davis to lunch and Davis said, the only person who can save the situation is Roosevelt and then I said to Davis how, and Davis said by sending a secret envoy to Europe.' Roosevelt paused. 'Another Colonel House.' " The President added that "Hull's philosophy" was that he would increase world trade through his trade treaties and take up the slack of unemployment as individual countries gradually disarmed. The Secretary responded that he was "not in disagreement with Hull" but that this policy would take five years to be effective and war might well break out within the next five months. It was at this point that Morgenthau obtained the consent of the President to send a message to Chamberlain. (In his diary Morgenthau wrote that he did not think that Hull and Norman Davis

would make an effective move toward disarmament because they "just don't have guts enough.") (Blum, *From the Morgenthau Diaries*, pp. 457ff.).

52. Davis papers, conversation of April 26, 1937. There are two memoranda on this conversation in the Davis papers.

53. *FR* 1937, III, 975. See also Yoshida's talk with Norman Davis on April 23, 1937, in which the ambassador made many of the same statements. (Davis papers.)

Yoshida's idea was basically one which was frequently set forth at the time. He believed that the only solution to Japan's economic problems was a return to the so-called Shidehara policy. This meant the promotion of trade with all nations and in particular with China through the development of that country's vast potential market.

54. On June 23 our embassy in Tokyo wired that Dooman had just been told by a Japanese official that a recent Domei report, which had originated in London, concerning the outline to be submitted to the British was "substantially accurate." Briefly summarized, the embassy said, the report was as follows:

(a) The Japanese Government will emphasize the adjustment of trade relations (presumably this refers to desire of Japanese for removal of quotas on Japanese imports into British Colonies and assurance that special restrictions will not be imposed upon Japanese goods entering British markets);

(b) Possibility of declaration by Japan that "it has no territorial ambitions in China and is ready to respect British vested interests in that country."

It would seem, however, that both the British and Japanese continued to contemplate discussion of some sort of collaboration in a project or projects related to the economic rehabilitation of China. (*FR* 1937, III, 115, 602, 605; also *FR* 1937, IV, 291.)

55. *FR* 1937, III, 126, 154, 158, 164, 178, 291.

56. See, for example, *FR* 1937, III, 102; *FR* 1937, IV, 605.

57. *FR* 1937, III, 82, 83.

58. *Ibid.*, 95.

59. *Ibid.*, 103. The Department emphasized in the strongest possible terms the "unfortunate" experience that the United States had had with the Lansing-Ishii agreement.

60. *FR* 1937, I, 102. Hull tells of the drafting of the memorandum in *The Memoirs of Cordell Hull*, I, 532ff. The President's estimate of the memorandum was very different, however, for in approving the draft he attached a note to Sumner Welles saying that he could not possibly object to the statements it contained. "They are completely pious—I can think of no other characteristic" he observed. (Roosevelt papers, PSF Great Britain 1937.)

61. Another consideration was that the effort to adjust China's loans had continued so that by the summer of 1937 settlements had been reached concerning the most important debts owed to American citizens. Moreover the terms of the Hukuang loan agreement had been more favorable to the American bondholders than had originally been expected.

62. *The Memoirs of Cordell Hull*, I, 532.

CHAPTER X. THE OUTBREAK OF UNDECLARED WAR IN CHINA

1. Shushi Hsu, *How the Far Eastern War Began* (1938). Chapter II contains a discussion of the legal problems involved in the North China situation in 1937 as related to the Boxer Protocol.

2. For the League of Nations' version of the Marco Polo Bridge incident see *FR Japan* 1931-1941, I, 384; the American version *FR 1937*, III, 432; the Japanese version *FR Japan* 1931-1941, I, 318; the Chinese version, *FR 1937*, III, 148.

3. Detailed accounts of the developments in North China following the Marco Polo Bridge incident appear in Shushi Hsu, *How the Far Eastern War Began;* Bisson, *Japan in China,* Chap. I; *Survey of International Affairs,* 1937, I, Pt. III (d) (2); and F. C. Jones, *Japan's New Order in East Asia* (1954), Chap. II.

4. *FR Japan* 1931-1941, I, 313.

5. Grew papers, letter dated July 10, 1937.

6. *FR 1937*, III, 136.

7. *Ibid.,* 156; also 141, 145.

8. *Ibid.,* 146.

9. *Ibid.,* 138.

10. *Ibid.,* 142.

11. *Ibid.,* 161.

12. *FR Japan* 1931-1941, I, 314.

13. *FR 1937*, III, 189, 190.

14. *FR Japan* 1931-1941, I, 172, 323.

15. *FR 1937*, III, 139, 206; *FR Japan* 1931-1941, I, 322.

16. *FR 1937*, III, 154, 162; The Department supported Johnson's decision (*ibid.,* 204, 205).

17. *Ibid.,* 206, 229, 246; also 204, 255.

18. *Ibid.,* 211.

19. *Ibid.,* 187.

20. Grew, *Turbulent Era,* II, 1050; *Ten Years in Japan,* p. 230.

21. *FR 1937*, III, 206.

22. The text is reprinted in *FR 1937*, III, 216.

23. *FR 1937*, III, 196.

24. *Ibid.,* 198; text 205.

25. *Ibid.,* 198.

26. *Ibid.,* 210.

27. *Ibid.,* 213, 220, 226.

28. *Ibid.,* 221.

29. *Ibid.,* 231.

30. *Ibid.,* 243.

31. *Ibid.,* 256.

32. For a further discussion of the relationship between the Roosevelt administration's search for a peace plan and the Buenos Aires Conference, see Chap. XIII and my article entitled "Notes on Roosevelt's 'Quarantine Speech'" in the *Political Science Quarterly,* September 1957.

33. *FR 1937*, III, 132.

34. *Ibid.*

35. *Ibid.,* 142.

36. *FR Japan* 1931-1941, I, 318.
37. *Ibid.*, 316.
38. *Ibid.*, 320.
39. *FR* 1937, III, 143, 151.
40. *Ibid.*, 158.
41. *Ibid.*, 159, 160.
42. *Ibid.*, 159.
43. *Ibid.*, 160.
44. *Ibid.*, 164.
45. *Ibid.*, 162.
46. *Ibid.*, 164.
47. *Ibid.*, 206, 224.
48. Hull states in his memoirs: ". . . on July 16, after consultation with the President I issued a formal statement of our position. This was based chiefly on the 'Eight Pillars of Peace' program I had presented at Buenos Aires in 1936, but it contained the fundamental principles of international conduct I had inserted in the Democratic platform of 1932 and proclaimed at Montevideo in 1933 and in numerous addresses elsewhere." (*The Memoirs of Cordell Hull*, I, 535.)
49. *FR* 1937, I, 699.
50. The replies appear in *FR* 1937, I, 697-802.
51. *Ibid.*, 791.
52. *The Memoirs of Cordell Hull*, I, 536.
53. *FR* 1937, I, 697.
54. In regard to talk at this time of invoking the Nine Power Treaty, see *FR* 1937, III, 189.
55. In *The Memoirs of Cordell Hull*, I, p. 498, Hull rephrased this principle to read: "Peoples must be educated for peace. Each nation must make itself safe for peace."
56. *FR* 1937, III, 226.
57. *FR Japan* 1931-1941, I, 330; *FR* 1937, III, 236. There was some suspicion in Washington that the Japanese ambassador was not transmitting the Secretary's remarks to him to Tokyo.
58. *FR* 1937, III, 238.
59. *Ibid.*, 235.
60. Eden stated in the House of Commons on July 21 that so long as the present situation existed in North China, the British government would not open the general conversations with Japan which it had been considering since the spring of 1937 and that it had so informed the Japanese. (*Ibid.*, 240.)
61. *Ibid.*, 257.
62. *Ibid.*, 278.
63. *Ibid.*, 277.
64. Grew Diary, entry of July 28, 1937.
65. *FR* 1937, III, 291.
66. *Ibid.*, 345, 529.
67. *Ibid.*, 271, 272; *FR* 1937, IV, 238, 239.
68. *Ibid.*, 274.
69. *FR Japan* 1931-1941, I, 334.
70. *FR* 1937, III, 286, 289, 319, 328, 339.

71. *Ibid.*, 297.
72. *Ibid.*, 305.
73. *Ibid.*, 327.
74. *Ibid.*, 340.
75. *Ibid.*, 349.
76. *Ibid.*, 368; *FR Japan* 1931-1941, I, 368.
77. *Ibid.*, 372, 384.
78. *Ibid.*, 374.
79. *Ibid.*, 385.
80. *Ibid.*, 395.
81. Shushi Hsu, *How the Far Eastern War Began*, p. 87.
82. F. C. Jones, *Shanghai and Tientsin* (1940), pp. 55, 57.
83. *Survey of International Affairs* 1937, I, 204.
84. *FR* 1937, III, 116.
85. *Ibid.*, 123, 126.
86. *Ibid.*, 314, 321.
87. Jones, *Shanghai and Tientsin*, p. 59; *FR* 1937, III, 362.
88. *FR* 1937, III, 375, 395, 407.
89. See 1937, Report 53.
90. *FR* 1937, III, 352.
91. *Ibid.*, 352.
92. *Ibid.*, 354.
93. *Ibid.*, 369, 375, 376.
94. *Ibid.*, 379, 380, 390.
95. *Ibid.*, 380.
96. *Ibid.*, 394.
97. *FR Japan* 1931-1941, I, 346.
98. *Ibid.*, 352; *FR* 1937, III, 346.
99. *FR* 1937, III, 394, 397, 414; *FR Japan* 1931-1941, I, 353.
100. *FR* 1937, III, 419.
101. *Ibid.*, 101.
102. *Ibid.*, 442.
103. *FR Japan* 1931-1941, I, 342; *FR* 1937, III, 400, 410.
104. *FR* 1937, III, 397.
105. *Ibid.*, 409.
106. *Ibid.*, 426.
107. *Ibid.*, 440.
108. *Ibid.*, 440.
109. *Ibid.*, 450.
110. *Ibid.*, 449.
111. *Ibid.*, 455.
112. *Ibid.*, 456.
113. *Ibid.*, 464.
114. *Ibid.*
115. *Ibid.*, 472.
116. *FR Japan* 1931-1941, I, 355.
117. Moffat Diary, entry of August 27.
118. *FR* 1937, III, 460.
119. *Ibid.*, 471.
120. Sir Hughe describes this incident with characteristic British under-

statement and humor in Chapter 10 of his *Diplomat in Peace and War* (1949), adding touches such as the following: "The Japanese made one other effort to show concern at the incident. They sent a Secretary from their embassy in Peking by air to Pei-tai-ho with a message to my wife. But my wife had already left for Shanghai. My children received the Secretary and gave him lunch. I understand that the meal was somewhat icy. The Japanese secretary brought it to a close by rising and explaining that he must be back in Peking early that afternoon as the aeroplane was required to bomb Nant'ai."

121. *FR* 1937, III, 486.
122. Grew Diary, entry of August 27, 1937.
123. Moffat Diary, entry of August 27, 1937.
124. An August 25, Grew had cabled (*FR* 1937, III, 469):

In conversation with the British Chargé d'Affaires on August 23 the Vice Minister for Foreign Affairs asked why the United States had not supported the British proposal for neutralization of Shanghai as had the French. Dodds replied that question should be addressed to me but that he understood our attitude was determined by the belief that Japan had already closed the matter by rejection.

I report this otherwise trivial circumstance to add to many which show how minutely the Japanese Government is scrutinizing our attitude and acts with regard to China and Japan, and how the American Government's restraint and consideration of all circumstances is noted and appreciated.

125. *Ibid.*, 505.
126. *Ibid.*, 525.
127. Johnson papers, letter dated November 10, 1937.
128. Grew Diary, entry of August 27, 1937.
129. For Hull's ideas regarding this principle see his *Memoirs*, I, 425.

CHAPTER XI. PROTECTION AND NEUTRALITY

1. *FR* 1931, III, 1013ff.
2. *FR* 1935, III, 700ff.
3. *FR* 1936, IV, 541; 1937, III, 132; *The Secret Diary of Harold L. Ickes*, II, 186.
4. *FR* 1936, IV, 531, 534, 541.
5. *FR* 1937, IV, 420; William C. Johnstone, *The United States and Japan's New Order* (1941), Chap. 7.
6. *New York Times*, July 22, 1937, p. 10.
7. Congressional Record, 75th Congress, 1st session, p. 8156.
8. *Ibid.*, p. 8178.
9. *Ibid.*, p. 8158, Senate Resolution 170. Senator Pittman persuaded Lewis to send the resolution to the Secretary of State instead of the Secretary of War. Hull replied on August 17 that, in view of recent developments it seemed to him "axiomatic" that the presence of our forces in North China was in the best interests of the United States. (*FR* 1937, IV, 264.)
10. Congressional Record, 75th Congress, 1st session, p. 8579, House Resolution 304.
11. *The Secret Diary of Harold L. Ickes*, II, 186, 192.
12. *New York Times*, Aug. 14, 1937, p. 1.
13. Congressional Record, 75th Congress, 1st session, p. 8940.

14. *Ibid.*, p. 2166.

15. *FR* 1937, IV, 256.

16. *FR* 1937, III, 420, 421, 423.

17. Hornbeck argued that Shanghai was a unique port, developed by international effort, which was of immense economic and political importance to the Far East and the whole world. The United States should therefore not abandon its responsibilities in connection with the common world interests that existed there, unless the other foreign powers involved in the situation were also prepared to undertake such an abandonment.

18. *The Moffat Papers,* Diary entry of Aug. 17, 1937.

19. Roosevelt papers, press conferences.

20. *New York Times,* Aug. 18, 1937. See article by Harold Hinton and AP dispatch.

21. *FR Japan* 1931-1941, I, 349.

22. *New York Times,* Aug. 19, 1937; *Cleveland Press,* Aug. 22, 1937.

23. Aug. 20, 21, 23.

24. Aug. 6, 17, 24.

25. Aug. 31.

26. Aug. 18, 20.

27. For further discussion of these peace societies, see below.

28. See, for example, contemporary issues of the *New York Times.*

29. *New York Times,* Sept. 1, 1937, p. 3. John W. Masland, "The 'Peace' Groups Join Battle" (*Public Opinion Quarterly,* Dec. 1940) and "Pressure Groups and American Foreign Policy" (*ibid.,* Spring 1942). See also press releases of the board.

30. Hinton was close to the State Department and later became Hull's biographer.

31. *New York Times,* Sept. 3, 1937, p. 3.

32. Bisson, *America's Far Eastern Policy,* p. 68; *Our Far Eastern Record,* Vol. I (1940), edited by W. W. Lockwood, has a section on all of the polls of this period, pp. 44ff. One wonders whether the wording of the question in the poll published on October 5 did not suggest an affirmative answer to many people.

33. *New York Times,* Sept. 6, 1937, p. 1.

34. Sept. 11, 1937, p. 29.

35. Sept. 8, 1937, p. 1.

36. Text appears in *China Weekly Review,* Sept. 11, 1937, p. 29.

37. *Ibid.,* p. 17.

38. *Ibid.*

39. Sept. 15, 1937, pp. 407, 409.

40. *North China Herald,* Sept. 15, 1937, p. 428.

41. Kramer ms., pp. 57-133ff.

42. Sept. 8, 1937.

43. *New York Times,* Aug. 24, 1937, p. 1 (text of speech, p. 3).

44. *FR* 1937, IV, 306.

45. Leahy papers, Aug. 29, 30, 31, Sept. 1, 2.

46. *FR* 1937, IV, 282.

47. *Ibid.,* 301.

48. *Ibid.,* 315.

49. *Ibid.,* 335.

50. Unless otherwise indicated, the information concerning missionaries in these paragraphs is based upon material in the Missionary Research Library contained in a file marked "China Communications Prior to Series B." This includes the Secretary's letter of September 4 and official reports of the Foreign Missions Conference.

51. See for example China Bulletin No. 8 of the Board of Foreign Missions of the Methodist Episcopal Church, Oct. 13, 1937; Frank W. Price, "Christian Morale in War-torn China" in *The Missionary Review of the World,* Jan. 1938; and the Information Service published by the Department of Research and Education of the Federal Council of Churches of Christ in America, Vol. XVI, No. 33, Oct. 16, 1937.

52. For estimate concerning 1937 period see John W. Masland, "Missionary Influence upon American Far Eastern Policy" in the *Pacific Historical Review,* Sept. 1941, p. 288; for the earlier period see my *American Policy and the Chinese Revolution,* p. 361.

53. *China Weekly Review,* Oct. 9, 1937, p. 13.

54. *China Annual Economic Report 1937,* Office of the U.S. Commercial Attaché, Shanghai.

55. *FR 1937,* III, 513.

56. *FR Japan 1931-1941,* I, 499.

57. *FR 1937,* IV, 351; *New York Times,* Sept. 22, 1937, p. 1.

58. *FR 1937,* IV; for Department's instructions allowing Johnson to act on his own discretion see page 342.

59. Sept. 25, 1937.

60. Sept. 21, 1937, p. 1.

61. *Ibid.*

62. *Ibid.,* Sept. 22, 1937, p. 10.

63. *Ibid.,* Sept. 21, 1937, p. 1.

64. For description of reaction within the Department, see *The Moffat Papers,* Diary entries of Sept. 21, 23, 24, 25.

65. See Chap. X.

66. *FR Japan 1931-1941,* I, 504; see also *ibid.,* 502.

67. *Ibid.,* 500.

68. Grew, *Turbulent Era,* II, 1150.

69. *FR 1937,* IV, 352, 363.

70. *Ibid.,* 362.

71. *Ibid.,* 363.

72. *Ibid.,* 360.

73. Borg, *American Policy and the Chinese Revolution,* p. 271.

74. Among the seemingly endless writings on the subject of neutrality, the contemporary accounts which have been especially useful in connection with the material presented here are the chapters dealing with neutrality in *The United States in World Affairs* for the years 1935, 1936, 1937, 1938.

75. There is a series of documents in the Davis papers which is very interesting as a record of the view of State Department officials on the President's attitude during the passage of the Neutrality Act of 1935. For a senatorial opinion, see Tom Connally, *My Name is Tom Connally* (1954, pp. 211ff.). There is valuable material in recent books on Roosevelt's handling of the neutrality issue at various stages, especially in Langer and

Gleasons's *The Challenge to Isolation* (Chap. 6, Sec. 3) and James Mac-Gregor Burns's *Roosevelt: The Lion and the Fox* (1956, Chap. 13).

76. On January 8, 1937, Congress passed a special act imposing an embargo on the shipment of arms and ammunition to both sides in the Civil War. In 1938 Senator Nye went so far as to introduce a resolution into Congress to repeal this act. *The United States in World Affairs 1938* (p. 161) reflects the astonishment felt at the time at the Senator's action.

77. *The United States in World Affairs, 1937*, Chap. 3, Sec. 3; James Wilford Garner, *Studies in Government and International Law* (1943), p. 538; Edwin M. Borchard and William P. Lage, *Neutrality for the United States* (1937).

78. This became one of the most highly controversial parts of the Act, the issue being whether the President had to declare that a state of war existed under circumstances such as were presented by the outbreak of hostilities after the Lukouchiao incident, or whether he could so declare at his discretion.

79. *Peace and War, United States Foreign Policy 1931-1941* (1943), p. 353, has the text of the Act.

80. Hull, in his memoirs, devotes a great deal of attention to the passage of the various neutrality acts and the political factors involved. (See Vol. I, Chaps. 29, 33, and 36 in particular; also pp. 490ff. for the special act regarding Spain.)

81. Herbert Feis, in his valuable account of American policy toward the Ethiopian crisis in *Seen From E. A.* (1947), p. 235, states of Judge Moore:

> The warnings of the kindly and elderly ex-member of Congress who . . . reported the opinion and wishes of that body [to the State Department] had great weight in critical discussions. He always advised against any stroke that might provoke the group that placed the Neutrality Resolutions on the books. (Not long afterward his amiable wish to go along with the views of old friends on the Hill contributed toward the easy consent of the Department to an amendment to the Neutrality Resolution that prevented the sale of arms to the Spanish government . . .).

82. Judge Moore expressed his views in memoranda to the President. (Roosevelt papers: OF Neutrality 1561 and PSF R. Walton Moore 1937, Box 24.)

83. Congressional Record, Vol. 81, p. 7862, 75th Congress, 1st session.

84. *Ibid.*, p. 7918.

85. *Ibid.*, Appendix, p. 2187.

86. *Ibid.*, p. 2196.

87. *New York Times*, July 31, Aug. 19, 24, 31, Sept. 16; *San Francisco Chronicle*, July 29, Aug. 20, Sept. 2, 11, 20.

88. Aug. 20 and 27, Sept. 2, 16.

89. Aug. 14, 17.

90. Aug. 3, 20, Sept. 17, 21.

91. *San Francisco Examiner*, Sept. 1, 9.

92. Aug. 3, 17, 19, 24.

93. Aug. 21, 28, Sept. 4.

94. *Journal of Commerce*, July 30, Aug. 27, Sept. 16; *Wall Street Journal*, Aug. 17, 20, 28, Sept. 1, 3, 17, Oct. 7.

95. The organizations which made up the American peace movement in the 1920's are dealt with in a highly informative though irreverent fashion by Ferrell in his *Peace in Their Time* (see especially Chap. 2 and Chap. 16, Sec. 4). Vinson has an interesting account of the activities of the peace societies at the time of the Washington Conference in his *The Parchment Peace*, pp. 130ff. and 175ff. Masland's articles on the peace movement in the 1930's are of great value, especially "The 'Peace' Groups Join Battle," "Pressure Groups and American Foreign Policy," and "Missionary Influence Upon American Far Eastern Policy." In the following account the author, in addition to using a considerable amount of primary source material, has relied heavily upon Masland's articles though probably differing somewhat in point of view.

96. For a list of the member organizations, see *Directory of the National Peace Conference. Personnel and Activities, 1937.* More detailed accounts of the organizations which made up the peace movement as a whole in the mid-1930's will be found in *The Study of International Relations in the United States* (1938), edited by Edith E. Ware. The *Directory* also describes the purpose and activities of the conference.

97. *Directory of the National Peace Conference*, section on "Statement of Principles."

98. *A Study in Neutrality Legislation*, International Conciliation pamphlet series, No. 316, Jan. 1936.

99. *Ibid.*, p. 21.

100. These organizations are discussed in the references cited in notes 95 and 96.

101. See especially Libby's editorials in *Peace Action*, the monthly publication of the NCPW, and the editorials in *Fellowship*, the journal of the Fellowship of Reconciliation which, in November 1937, made an arrangement to become the organ of the Women's International League for Peace and Freedom as well. From this date on, therefore, *Fellowship* also carried editorials by Dorothy Detzer, the energetic Executive Secretary of the League.

102. Masland states that Dorothy Detzer was an "inveterate lobbyist" who almost single-handed persuaded Senator Nye to introduce into Congress the resolution calling for the famous investigation of the munitions industry which had such a great influence upon the subsequent neutrality legislation. (See "The 'Peace' Groups Join Battle," p. 665.) It must be understood, however, that while the three organizations under discussion vigorously supported the isolationists in Congress on specific issues, they themselves constantly claimed that they were internationalists because of their belief in international cooperation for peaceful change and the establishment of a just international order.

103. Details concerning the organization and activities of the Emergency Peace Campaign can be found in *No-Foreign-War Crusade*, a handbook published by the Campaign in 1937. See also Elton Atwater's article, "Organizing American Public Opinion for Peace" (*Public Opinion Quarterly*, April 1937).

104. Masland, "The 'Peace' Groups Join Battle," section on Neutrality Laws.

105. Luman J. Shafer, "What Should be the Bearing of the Foreign

Missionary Enterprise on World Peace?" Foreign Missions Conference of North America, 1938, *Report of the 45th Annual Meeting*.

106. Based largely upon articles, reports, et cetera, published in the reports of the annual meetings of the Foreign Missions Conference of North America, the monthly *Bulletin* and weekly *Information Service* issued by the Federal Council of Churches of Christ in America, and a wealth of material in the files of the Missionary Research Library in New York. The quotations in this paragraph are from an editorial paragraph entitled "Keep Out of War" in the Federal Council's *Bulletin*, Feb. 1936. Especially good statements on the kind of world organization that the Federal Council and the FMC believed should be developed are in the *Bulletin's* editorial for May 1938 and in an article on "The Churches and The International Crisis," in its issue of November 1938.

107. National Council For The Prevention of War, *Press Information*.

108. *The United States in World Affairs, 1937*, p. 203.

109. *New York Times*, Aug. 24, 1937, p. 1 (Text of speech, p. 3).

110. On Aug. 25 the Japanese announced a blockade of about 800 miles of China's coast which they extended on Sept. 5 to include virtually the whole coast. (For details see *Survey of International Affairs*, 1937, I, 226; and *FR* 1937, IV, 436, 449.)

111. The six societies were the Emergency Peace Campaign, the NCPW, the Fellowship of Reconciliation, the Women's International League for Peace and Freedom, World Peaceways, and the Committee on Militarism in Education. World Peaceways was the youngest of the peace societies and operated by publishing spectacular advertisements that mainly depicted the horrors of war. The Committee on Militarism in Education was opposed to compulsory military training in the schools and consisted mainly of a staff of two young men whose "nuisance value" in needling Congressmen was, however, regarded as substantial. (Evelyn Seeley, "—'And There Is No Peace,'" *Independent Woman*, Jan. 1936.)

112. See, for example, the *New York Times*. Many of the board's press releases appear in the NCPW's *Press Information*.

113. Roosevelt papers, PPF 1-P.

114. *The Secret Diary of Harold L. Ickes*, II, 199.

115. *FR* 1937, III, 515.

116. *Ibid.*, 516.

117. *FR* 1937, IV, 456.

118. Moffat papers, Diary entry of September 7 (see also entries of Aug. 16, 30, 31) on talks with State Department officials who attended daily conferences with Secretary Hull at this time.

119. Talks with Department officials.

120. *FR* 1937, IV, 527.

121. *FR Japan* 1931-1941, II, 201.

122. *FR* 1937, IV, 533.

123. *FR* 1937, III, 531.

124. "The Mandatory Neutrality Law Should Be Operative," *Christian Century*, Oct. 6, 1937, p. 1220.

125. *Fellowship*, Oct. 1937, p. 11; NCPW *Press Information*, Oct. 11.

126. *New York Times*, Oct. 14, p. 16.

127. *Ibid.*, Oct. 17, p. 40.

128. See, for example, the *Christian Century*, Oct. 27, 1937, p. 1317.

129. Masland, "The 'Peace' Groups Join Battle," p. 669.

130. Page 2.

131. *New York Times*, Sept. 5, p. 1.

132. *Ibid.*, Oct. 2, 3. In November 1937, this organization changed its name to American League for Peace and Democracy.

133. Federal Council of Churches of Christ in America *Information Service*, Jan. 1, 1938, article on "Congress for Peace and Democracy." According to this article the American League for Peace and Democracy adopted a new constitution at this Congress which provided that it would in future have no affiliation with political parties which was assumed to mean that it would no longer have any "official relation" to the Communist Party. Masland states that although quite a number of the peace societies of this period (especially the pacifist societies) were frequently "smeared" as Communist, they remained free of outside influence or control except for the American League for Peace and Democracy. ("The 'Peace' Groups Join Battle," section on Pacifist Organizations.)

134. National Committee for Cause and Cure of War, *Delegate's Worksheet*, Thirteenth Conference, 1938, Number 4, p. 2.

135. "Roll Call of Presidents of Member Organizations," in *Delegate's Worksheet*, Thirteenth and Fourteenth Conferences (1938 and 1939); *Journal of the American Association of University Women*, April 1938, pp. 175, 177; *Independent Woman*, Jan. 1938, p. 36. In May 1938 the American Association of University Women formally withdrew from the NCPW because it had become "increasingly identified" with the mandatory neutrality group of the peace movement. (*Journal*, Oct. 1938, "AAUW Withdraws From NCPW.")

136. The Committee later changed its name to the American Union for Concerted Peace Efforts. (See its *Manual for Organization* published in 1939 which relates its history, purposes, activities, etc.) In 1939 it led to the establishment of the Non-Partisan Committee for Peace Through Revision of the Neutrality Law. (Walter Johnson, *The Battle Against Isolation* (1944), Chap. 2, and *William Allen White's America*, p. 515.)

137. Foreign Missions Conference of North America, *Report of the 45th Annual Meeting*, 1938, Appendix.

138. The religious publications in the United States, together with their circulation, are listed in the *Religious Press Directory*. The *Directory* also makes some analytical comments such as that the readers of the religious press number tens of millions; that an abnormally large proportion renew their subscriptions from year to year; and that surveys have shown that they belong primarily to the middle class with 80 per cent owning automobiles and 60 per cent owning their own homes.

139. See especially editorials of Aug. 11, Sept. 1, Oct. 6 and 27.

140. Editorial of March 17, 1937.

141. Oct. 20.

142. Aug. 26.

143. Jan. 6, 1938.

144. Masland in his article on "Missionary Influence Upon American Far Eastern Policy" takes the position that almost all officers of the mission boards favored economic pressure against Japan and that the missionary

movement as a whole was in large measure responsible for the molding of an organized public opinion in the United States which demanded a strong policy against Japan in the years prior to Pearl Harbor. Paul A. Varg, however, in his book, *Missionaries, Chinese, and Diplomats* (1958, pp. 266ff.), adopts a very different point of view, stating that although some of the China missionaries advocated boycotts, embargoes, et cetera, they were never able to win over the leadership of the Foreign Missions Conference, much less the church. "Those who may seek," he says, "for some indication of pressure on the part of the organized representatives of foreign missions for a firmer course in dealing with Japan will find no evidence supporting such a thesis in the written records." (p. 269.)

CHAPTER XII. THE SECRETARY AND THE LEAGUE OF NATIONS

1. *FR 1937, IV, 3.*
2. *Ibid.,* 11.
3. *Ibid.,* 13.
4. *Ibid.,* 15.
5. *Ibid.,* 18, 20.
6. *Ibid.,* 18.
7. *Ibid.,* 20.
8. For earlier discussion of the Far Eastern Advisory Committee, see Chap. I of this volume.
9. *FR 1937, IV, 20, 22.*
10. *Ibid.,* 20.
11. *Ibid.*
12. *Ibid.,* 24; *The Moffat Papers,* p. 150.
13. *FR 1937, IV, 24.*
14. *Ibid.*
15. For an extraordinarily interesting account of the problems involved in the League's applying sanctions against Italy without any foreknowledge of whether American action would strengthen or nullify them, see Feis's *Seen From E. A.,* "Episode Number Three," which deals with the Ethiopian crisis. In respect to the attitude of other nations toward taking action in regard to Japan without any indication of what the United States intended to do, see the debates in the House of Commons referred to in Chap. XIV of this volume. Also Pratt's *War and Politics in China,* pp. 243ff. Pratt was currently Adviser on Far Eastern Affairs in the British Foreign Office (a post which he held for thirteen years) and one of the British representatives on the Advisory Committee. (League of Nations Official Journal, Special Supplement No. 177, p. 7).
16. *FR 1937, IV, 26.*
17. *Ibid.,* 46. League of Nations Official Journal, Special Supplement, No. 177, p. 17.
18. *FR 1937, IV, 29.*
19. *The Moffat Papers,* September 23, 1937.
20. *FR 1937, IV, 32;* also 44.
21. *Ibid.,* 35.
22. *Ibid.,* 37.
23. *Ibid.,* 40, 41.

24. *Ibid.*, 44, 51.
25. *Ibid.*, 38.
26. *Ibid.*, 48, 50. Harrison also attended the meetings of the subcommittee as an observer.
27. *FR Japan* 1931-1941, I, 384.
28. *FR 1937*, IV, 52, 53, 54.
29. *Ibid.*, 54.
30. *Ibid.*, 63.
31. See Chap. XIV.
32. *FR 1937*, III, 560, 569.
33. *FR 1937*, IV, 54.
34. *FR Japan* 1931-1941, I, 394; *FR 1937*, IV, 58.
35. *FR 1937*, IV, 59.
36. *The Moffat Papers*, p. 154. There seems to be no doubt that the Secretary gave instructions to have Harrison informed by telephone of the President's speech. But at least some of the Secretary's aides disagree with Moffat's account of Hull's reaction to the speech; see Chap. XIII, note 42, of this volume.
37. *FR 1937*, IV, 42.
38. *FR Japan* 1931-1941, I, 397. Because of the tendency of the Roosevelt administration to react sharply to evidences of public opinion, it should be noted that a Gallup poll was published on October 4 in which the question was asked: "In the present fight between China and Japan are your sympathies with China, Japan, or neither side?" Of those who answered, 59 per cent said "China" in contrast to approximately 43 per cent who replied to the same question two months earlier. In general, however, the polls concerned with the outbreak of the Sino-Japanese conflict are more interesting for their possible influence upon the administration than for the picture of public opinion they reveal because, taken over the long run, they are highly contradictory. Thus, the August 1937 poll indicated that 55 per cent of those questioned had no sympathy for either China or Japan. A year later the question was asked: "Which of the recent foreign military aggressions disturbed you most?" and those polled were given a list that included such events as "Japan's invasion of China," "Germany's seizure of Austria," and "Outside Intervention in Spain." The highest response (30 per cent) was to "Japan's invasion of China." (*Public Opinion 1935-46*, pp. 1074, 1081, "Compilation of Polls," Hadley Cantril, ed. The contradictory nature of these polls was commented upon at some length by *Fortune* in its "Fortune Quarterly Survey," July 1938, p. 80.)
39. *FR Japan* 1931-1941, I, 397.
40. *FR 1937*, III, 574.
41. Grew, *Turbulent Era*, II, 1166, footnote 44.
42. *Ibid.*, 1167, footnote 46.
43. *FR 1937*, III, 569.
44. *Ibid.*, 582.
45. For further reference to this meeting, see Chap. XIV.

CHAPTER XIII. THE PRESIDENT AND THE "QUARANTINE" SPEECH

1. *The Memoirs of Cordell Hull*, I, 646.

2. See note concerning the Krock article in Elliott Roosevelt (ed.), *F.D.R. His Personal Letters 1928-1945* (1950), I, 649. On January 9, 1937, in a letter to Ambassador Dodd in Berlin, the President wrote with characteristic humor: "That story by Arthur Krock was not wholly crazy. If five or six heads of the important governments could meet together for a week with complete inaccessibility to press or cables or radios, a definite, useful agreement might result or else one or two of them would be murdered by the others! In any case, it would be worthwhile from the point of view of civilization!" (*Ibid.*, 648.)

3. Contemporary publications are full of the worldwide impact of the President's trip to Buenos Aires. Thus the *New York Times* said on December 2 that Roosevelt's "instincts led him right." His presence at Buenos Aires made the conference a world event rather than a regional gathering. And while nothing the President said at the conference was directly addressed to Europe, no European government could "fail to take note of every word spoken by such a man at such a place in such a time." (Editorial entitled "The President's Speech.") There are interesting comments on the European reaction in *The United States in World Affairs*, 1936, p. 207, and *Survey of International Affairs*, 1936, p. 823.

4. *Peace and War: United States Foreign Policy 1931-1941*, p. 342.

5. Text of the draft is in *Documents on International Affairs*, 1936, p. 77.

6. Frederick J. Knauer, "American Neutrality Reconsidered," in the *Columbia Law Review*, January 1936, p. 505, surveys many of the ideas current at the time. A very colorful demonstration of different views held by different people is to be found in the proceedings of the Committee on Neutrality at the Buenos Aires Conference recorded in the stenographic reports of the Conference published under the title of *Inter-American Conference for the Maintenance of Peace, Proceedings.*

7. Philip C. Jessup, *Neutrality, Its History, Economics, and Law, IV: Today and Tomorrow* (1936), p. 187. Jessup thought that total nonintercourse, while theoretically possible, was not practical for the present and suggested that a beginning might be made by neutrals agreeing to the adoption of common measures for withholding shipments of arms, ammunition, and implements of war from the belligerents.

8. For pertinent material on the Buenos Aires Conference, in addition to the proceedings cited in note 6, see *The Report of Delegation of the United States to the Inter-American Conference for the Maintenance of Peace*, which among other matters contains the official texts of the treaties, resolutions, etc., passed at the conference; Professor Charles G. Fenwick's article on "The Inter-American Conference for the Maintenance of Peace," in the *American Journal of International Law*, April 1937, p. 210 (Professor Fenwick was a member of the United States Delegation to the Conference); *The Memoirs of Cordell Hull*, I, Chap. 35; Sumner Welles, *The Time for Decision* (1944), pp. 205ff. and *Seven Decisions That Shaped History* (1950), pp. 103ff.; Samuel Flagg Bemis, *The Latin American Policy of the United States* (1943), Chap. XIV, Sec. 3.

9. Percy Alvin Martin, *Latin America and the War* (1925), p. 361.

10. For an expression of Hull's views before the Marco Polo Bridge incident, see for example the extraordinarily comprehensive statement of his opinions which appears in a memorandum of a talk that he had with Prime Minister Mackenzie King of Canada, printed in *FR 1937*, I, 641.

11. Roosevelt, *F.D.R. His Personal Letters*, I, 664.

12. Memorandum of telephone conversation between the President and Norman Davis, March 19, 1937. (Davis papers.)

13. *FR 1937*, I, 655. The same volume contains papers on the German reaction to Roosevelt's calling a world conference to stabilize the European situation (29, 638, 640, 649).

14. Press conference of July 13, 1937, Roosevelt papers.

15. Roosevelt papers, PSF State Department 1933-1938, marked: "F.D.R.'s first draft."

16. The following accounts of Davis' conversations with European statesmen are all based on memoranda in his files.

17. It must be recognized that the word "appeasement" was consistently used at this time and did not have the unpleasant connotations it acquired after the Munich settlement.

18. Davis papers. A draft appears also in the Roosevelt papers, PSF Great Britain 1933-38, Box 7.

19. Davis papers.

20. *FR 1937*, I, 113.

21. *Ibid.*, 131.

22. Chamberlain's letter was not delivered to the President until October 14 (see *FR 1937*, III, 608, footnote 24).

23. *FR 1937*, I, 665. Welles's own account of his plan appears in *The Time for Decision*, p. 64, and *Seven Decisions that Shaped History*, Chap. I. See also the discussion of the Welles plan in Langer and Gleason, *The Challenge to Isolation*, p. 22.

24. See Chap. XVI.

25. Roosevelt papers, OF State Department, Box 6.

26. *The Secret Diary of Harold L. Ickes*, II, 213.

27. *The Memoirs of Cordell Hull*, I, 544.

28. For a detailed discussion of these memoranda and the manner in which Roosevelt used them, see my "Notes on Roosevelt's 'Quarantine Speech,'" in the *Political Science Quarterly*, September 1957. The four memoranda are in both the Roosevelt and Davis papers, although there are some differences in the texts and also in the accompanying letters and notations (see note 30).

29. William Phillips, *Ventures in Diplomacy* (1952), p. 207.

30. The passage which the President omitted read in full:

It is my determination to pursue a policy of peace . . . We recognize, however, that if we are unable or unwilling to defend our rights and interests we will lose the respect of other nations and we will also lose our own self-respect.

This nation was dedicated to certain principles which our forebears considered to be of greater value than life itself and without which life would not be worth living. If the time ever comes when we are no longer willing or able to defend to the utmost of our ability the principles which are the foundation of freedom and progress we will sacrifice our great national heritage and will cease to have the vitality and stamina to keep this nation alive.

The original memorandum, which exists in the Davis files and which the President may or may not have seen, contains an even stronger version of this passage: "We recognize, however, that a policy of peace at any price will not ensure peace . . . This nation was born fighting for certain principles which our forebears considered to be of greater value than life itself."

It should be added that the only part of the first two memoranda which the President did not use was a paragraph that laid itself open to the same interpretation.

31. The "quarantine" simile may have been suggested to the President by the fact that one of Davis' drafts prominently featured the sentence: "War is a contagion." Secretary Ickes, however, thought that Roosevelt took the simile from a talk in which he (the Secretary) said that neighbors had a right to "quarantine" themselves against the spread of an infection such as existed in the international situation. Welles has still a different version. In any case, it is a simile quite often found in political speeches and writings of the time dealing with the issue of collective security. (*The Secret Diary of Harold I. Ickes*, II, 221; Welles' version is in Samuel I. Rosenman, *Working with Roosevelt* (1952), p. 164.)

32. Roosevelt papers, special file on foreign policy statements.

33. Samuel I. Rosenman, ed., *The Public Papers and Addresses of Franklin D. Roosevelt, 1937* (1941), p. 414. On the same day the President also saw William Phillips, who was in the United States on a short leave of absence from his post as ambassador in Rome. In his *Ventures in Diplomacy* (p. 206), written many years later, Phillips states that during the course of their conversation he asked Roosevelt what he meant by a "quarantine" and the President said that, in dictating the text of his speech he had "searched for a word which was not 'sanctions' and had settled upon a 'quarantine' as a 'drawing away from someone.'" Phillips felt that the President, in developing his thought further, showed a "willingness to go very far in drawing away." But Roosevelt's comments do not seem to have added up to anything very concrete for Phillips merely says that the President seemed to him to be taking a "new position" which showed a "disposition to favor the so-called peace-loving countries as against Japan, Italy, and Germany, the three bad boys." Moreover, as the ambassador apparently devoted much of the time to telling the President about the benefits that Mussolini was bringing to Italy, it is hard to evaluate how much Roosevelt's remarks reflected his reaction to the ambassador's statements.

34. Davis papers.

35. Italics inserted in both these quotations.

36. For a discussion of the Pope's policy at this time and how far he was likely to go in interfering in the temporal conflicts of other governments, see Camille M. Cianfarra, *The Vatican and the War* (1944). Also for the kind of relationship the President did ultimately establish with the Vatican in regard to the international situation, see *Franklin D. Roosevelt and Pius XII: Wartime Correspondence* (the introduction by Myron C. Taylor describes this relationship very well).

37. Langer and Gleason, *The Challenge to Isolation*, section on "A Special Mission to the Vatican," beginning on page 347.

38. Rosenman, comp. and coll., *The Public Papers and Addresses of Franklin D. Roosevelt, 1937*, p. 429.

39. One further point should be mentioned. Sumner Welles, writing in the 1950's, said that in the summer of 1937 the President was far more preoccupied with the Far East than with Europe and that Roosevelt had, on several occasions, talked to him about the possibility of stationing units of the American and British navies at certain points in the Pacific to enforce an embargo against Japan. Welles stated further that as he was in Europe during most of September 1937 he knew little about the writing of the "quarantine" speech but believed the President had in mind the embargo and quasi blockade he had mentioned earlier.

However, Welles' recollection closer to the event does not bear out the thesis that the Chicago address reflected Roosevelt's determination to use sanctions against Japan but instead supports the interpretation that the President was thinking of some program to stabilize the world situation. For in 1944 Welles wrote:

Partly because of the issues involved in the Spanish war, and partly because the real nature of Hitlerism was becoming increasingly apparent, the President determined to make a vigorous effort to persuade public opinion that in its own interest the United States should propose some constructive plan for international action to check the forces of aggression before they succeeded in engulfing the world. For this effort he selected the very heart of isolationism—the city of Chicago.

Welles then went on to quote the "quarantine" speech. (See Welles's *Seven Decisions That Shaped History*," pp. 8, 13-14, 70-75, 91-93; *The Time for Decision*, p. 61. There is a letter from Welles on the "quarantine" speech in Rosenman's *Working with Roosevelt*, p. 164.)

40. Welles, *Seven Decisions That Shaped History*, p. 13.

41. Welles, *Time for Decision*, p. 63.

42. *The Memoirs of Cordell Hull*, I, 545. There are different opinions as to Hull's initial reaction to the "quarantine" speech. Pierrepont Moffat wrote in his diary (*The Moffat Papers*, p. 153) on October 5, 1937:

Two more meetings in the Secretary's office today. We were polishing off the last draft of our reply to the British *aide-mémoire* regarding a boycott when the ticker service brought in the text of the President's Chicago speech. We had known that he was to make a speech along these general lines and in fact many notes had been prepared for him by Norman Davis and the Department, but he dramatized them in a way we had little expected and the sentence regarding the quarantine of nations was a surprise. The Secretary was delighted at the speech and the majority thought it would be strongly approved by the public.

However, another member of the meeting in the Secretary's office states that he remembers Hull as having expressed himself "in terms of vexation and misgiving" and that there was a decided division of opinion among those present as to whether or not the public would approve the speech. In view of the fact that, as already related, the Secretary did give immediate instructions to have the President's address brought to the attention of the nations assembled at the League, there is, however, some reason to suppose that his initial response to the speech was at least partially favorable. And one may hazard the guess that his subsequent severely critical attitude was not unconnected with his feelings of dismay at the furor created by the speech in the isolationist press.

43. Rosenman, *Working with Roosevelt*, p. 166.

44. Page 17.

45. Page 1. Article by the Washington Bureau of the *Monitor*.

46. Magazine section, p. 3.

47. Oct. 18, p. 19. The article was obviously written before the President's Fireside Chat of October 12.

48. Dec. 20, p. 11.

49. Nov. 1, p. 17.

50. National Council for the Prevention of War, *Press Information*, Oct. 7, 1937, issue has an open letter to the President; for examples of attacks upon the President, see *Press Information*, Oct. 16, 1937; Dorothy Detzer's article on "Neutrality at the Special Session," in *Fellowship*, Nov. 1937; and the "Statement on the Far East," issued by the Fellowship of Reconciliation in *Fellowship*, Oct. 1938.

51. *Independent Woman*, Nov. 1937, p. 338.

52. Text is in the *Bulletin* of the Federal Council of Churches of Christ in America, Nov. 1937, p. 10.

53. See statements issued or distributed by Federal Council in Council's *Information Service*, Feb. 12 and June 18, 1938; "The Conflict in Asia," memorandum distributed by the Council dated Feb. 1940; Masland, "Missionary Influence Upon American Far Eastern Policy," p. 292; Varg, *Missionaries, Chinese, and Diplomats*, pp. 266ff.

54. *Foreign Missions Conference of North America, 1939, Report of the 46th Annual Conference*, Appendix, 46.

55. "The Churches and the Far Eastern Situation," p. 9.

56. See especially the articles in the Nov. 10, 1937, issue, which attracted considerable attention.

57. Text of statement in Federal Council of Churches of Christ in America, *Information Service*, April 2, 1938.

58. The *Wall Street Journal*, printed editorials against the "quarantine" speech on Oct. 6, 7, and 9 and then, for some reason, refrained from further comment on this or other matters related to the Far Eastern situation.

59. Oct. 7, 1937.

60. Oct. 16, 1937.

61. Oct. 8, 1937.

62. *The Memoirs of Cordell Hull*, I, 545.

63. October 8, 1937, p. 1.

64. *New York Times*, Oct. 14, 1937, p. 1.

65. *Ibid.*, Oct. 15, 1937, p. 1.

66. John W. Masland, "American Attitudes Toward Japan," in the *Annals of the American Academy of Political and Social Science*, May 1941, section on labor.

67. See Green's speech quoted in *New York Times*, Oct. 8, 1937, p. 1.

68. Rosenman, *Working With Roosevelt*, p. 166.

69. There are several boxes of mail on the "quarantine" speech in the Roosevelt papers at Hyde Park.

70. The following paragraphs are based upon Kramer's manuscript with additions and analyses by me.

71. See Libby's "We Reply to the New York Times," (*Peace Action*, Dec. 1937). Libby said that the Brussels Conference had failed not because the "peace groups" had undermined the United States' position but because

the delegations at Brussels had prejudged Japan before the conference started, thereby making mediation impossible.

72. Roosevelt's scrapbook at Hyde Park is full of clippings from the Washington press and Grace Tully, the President's secretary, says that he customarily read or scanned four Washington newspapers daily. Of the total of eleven papers which Miss Tully (in *F.D.R.: My Boss* [1949]) states Roosevelt looked at every day, giving special attention to the editorial pages, only four opposed the "quarantine" speech.

73. Oct. 7, 1937.

74. Oct. 10 and 12, 1937, respectively. The *New York Daily News*, also a Patterson paper, had come out on Oct. 3 for a blockade such as that advocated by the *Times* and *Herald* a few days later. (Magazine section, p. 6.)

75. Page 1. The banner headline across the page stated: EUROPE APPLAUDS ROOSEVELT.

76. The titles referred to were printed, respectively, over an article (p. 1) and an editorial on Oct. 8, 1937.

77. In the *San Francisco Examiner*, for example, the articles were printed much of the time on page 1.

78. *San Francisco Examiner*, Oct. 20, 1937, p. 1.

79. *The Secret Diary of Harold L. Ickes*, II, 227.

80. *The Moffat Papers*, p. 155.

81. *New York Times*, Oct. 20, 1937, p. 15.

82. *FR 1937*, IV, 85.

CHAPTER XIV. THE BRUSSELS CONFERENCE

Author's Note: Since the completion of this study a second volume of Anthony Eden's memoirs has been published (*The Memoirs of Anthony Eden, Earl of Avon, Facing the Dictators*). The later chapters are devoted to a discussion of the events leading up to Eden's resignation in February 1938 including the Brussels Conference, the Panay crisis, the Ingersoll mission, and the Welles plan. No startling new light is thrown on United States policy but much valuable information is provided.

1. *FR Japan 1931-1941*, I, 394.

2. *FR 1937*, IV, 64-83 *in passim*.

3. *Ibid.*, 67.

4. *Ibid.*, 65.

5. *Ibid.*, 81.

6. *Ibid.*, 75.

7. Moffat Diary, entry of September 29, 1937.

8. *Ibid.*, entry of October 7, 1937.

9. *FR 1937*, III, 279, previously mentioned in Chap. X.

10. Johnson papers, memoranda of July 31 and August 1, 1935.

11. Davis papers, memorandum of October 7, 1937.

12. Davis papers, memorandum of October 6, 1937.

13. *FR 1937*, III, 596.

14. The report of the Lytton Commission following the Manchurian crisis had made a similar suggestion concerning Inner Mongolia.

15. Davis papers, memorandum on Norman Davis' talk with the President at Hyde Park, October 20, 1937. See also *The Moffat Papers*, p. 157.

16. Davis papers, undated memorandum.

17. Davis papers, mentioned in memorandum on Davis' talks with the President, October 20, 1937.

18. The memorandum which Davis wrote on October 20 covered all of his talks with the President concerning the Brussels Conference.

19. The memorandum appears in *FR 1937*, IV, 85 and the Davis papers.

20. One of the main points which had been insisted upon at the Buenos Aires Conference was that of the unanimous acceptance of all measures.

21. In respect to the subject of public opinion, see *FR 1937*, IV, 160. (For an interpretation which differs radically from my own understanding of the President's policy toward the Brussels Conference see two articles by John McVickar Haight, Jr., which have appeared since this chapter was written: "France and the Aftermath of Roosevelt's 'Quarantine' Speech," *World Politics*, January 1962, and "Roosevelt and the Aftermath of the Quarantine Speech," *The Review of Politics*, April 1962. Dr. Haight believes that Roosevelt steadfastly sought to implement a policy of vigorous action against Japan until the final stage of the Brussels Conference; then, he contends, the President was forced to back down for a number of reasons including the hesitancy of Hull and the opposition of Congress.)

22. Davis wrote the record of his conversations with Roosevelt on the boat going to Europe and did not mail it to Sumner Welles until November 1. (See Davis papers, letter to Sumner Welles, dated November 1, 1937.)

23. *The Moffat Papers*, p. 157.

24. *FR 1937*, III, 600.

25. *FR 1937*, IV, 89.

26. *Ibid.*, 92.

27. *Ibid.*, 114.

28. The part of the discussion between Washington and Paris that took place after the opening of the Brussels Conference is dealt with later in this chapter.

29. For background information on China's lines of communication see Roger Levy and Andrew Roth, *French Interests and Policies in the Far East* (1941), section beginning p. 56; also the *Far Eastern Survey*, "Transport Facilities in China's Defense," by John E. Orchard, November 5, 1937; "France Takes Inventory in China," September 28, 1938, and "China Driven to New Supply Routes," November 9, 1938, both by Norman D. Hanwell.

30. *FR 1937*, III, 623.

31. *Ibid.*, 629; see also 639.

32. *Ibid.*, 629, 634, 637.

33. *Ibid.*, 632.

34. *Ibid.*, 637.

35. Grew, *Turbulent Era*, II, 1167, footnote 67.

36. *FR 1937*, IV, 77.

37. *Ibid.*, 80.

38. *Ibid.*, 100.

39. *Ibid.*, 101; also 108.

40. *Ibid.*, 101.

41. *FR 1937*, III, 625.

42. *FR 1937*, IV, 97.

43. *FR 1937*, III, 648.

44. *FR* 1937, IV, 124.
45. *Ibid.*, 123.
46. Parliamentary Debates, House of Commons, Vol. 327, beginning col. 57 and Vol. 328, Debate on the Address (see especially Vol. 327, col. 165, Chamberlain's speech; Vol. 328, col. 298, Cranborne's speech; and Vol. 328, col. 583, Eden's speech).

The emphasis put upon the United States as the determining factor in whether or not Great Britain would take action against Japan created a good deal of excitement in the United States and led to many comments in the press, some of which will be related later. The administration in Washington was inevitably disturbed by this attempt of the British to shove the United States "out front" and was particularly agitated over a press agency report cabled to Washington on the evening of November 1, which quoted Eden as having stated in the House of Commons that the Brussels Conference was initiated by the United States. Upon instructions from the President, Sumner Welles immediately telephoned to the United States embassy in London; the embassy explained that the report was incorrect and that Eden had merely said that the idea of holding the conference in Brussels had first been suggested by the United States. Frantic efforts were thereupon made to have the story corrected in time to prevent the original version from being printed in the morning newspapers in the United States. (*FR* 1937, IV, 138, 140, 145.)

47. Prime Minister Chamberlain intimated in his speech in the House of Commons that he personally did not expect the United States to take any action in regard to the conflict in the Far East, and that consequently the British would not do anything themselves. This led newspapers such as *The Chicago Tribune* (as noted later in this chapter) to assume that it was really the British who were restraining the United States. Feiling quotes Chamberlain as having said in regard to the possibility that the "quarantine" speech meant that America might consider sanctions against Japan, that "it is always best and safest to count on nothing from the Americans but words." Keith Feiling, *The Life of Neville Chamberlain* (1946), p. 325.

Concerning Eden's speech, Sir John Pratt has written in his *War and Politics in China* (p. 244):

If America had been willing to give a strong lead and to continue to play a leading part, England, although she already had her back to the wall in Europe, would have been prepared to run considerable risks in the Far East; for the mere fact that America had come out of her isolation and was playing a leading part by England's side in world affairs would have had a sobering effect on aggressors everywhere ... In order that there should be no mistake about this, Mr. Eden, in a speech in the House of Commons, used a picturesque phrase which sank into men's minds and has not been forgotten. He said that in order to secure the cooperation of America he would fly not only from London to Geneva but from Melbourne to Alaska.

48. *FR* 1937, IV, 145; *The Moffat Papers*, p. 163. Moffat's diaries, especially if both the published and the unpublished parts are used, are an excellent source of information concerning the Brussels Conference. However, it must be remembered that Moffat drafted many of the cables which Davis sent from Brussels and that the cables and his personal writings are therefore likely to represent the same point of view.

49. *FR 1937*, IV, 157, 162; *The Moffat Papers*, p. 169; Moffat Diary, November 3, 1937.

50. For a statement of Chautemps' views see Bullitt's cable to the State Department on November 10. (*FR 1937*, IV, 172).

51. Davis papers, Davis-Litvinov interview of Nov. 8, 1937; *FR 1937*, IV, 89, 95, 98, 99.

52. For the views of the United States embassy in Moscow on the pact, see Chap. VII, note 94, of this volume.

53. *FR 1937*, III, 616.

54. *FR 1937*, IV, 87, 100, 102, 116, 119, 129; also State Department files 761.94/1005.

55. Davis papers, talk of Nov. 4, 1937.

56. *FR 1937*, IV, 117, 120, 121.

57. *Ibid.*, 157.

58. *FR 1937*, I, section beginning 605.

59. *FR 1937*, IV, 157; *The Moffat Papers*, p. 165.

60. *FR 1937*, IV, 145; *The Moffat Papers*, pp. 165, 169.

61. *FR 1937*, IV, 134; Moffat Diary, entry of Oct. 31, 1937. Some of the earlier versions of the speech are in the Davis papers.

62. *The Conference of Brussels, Nov. 3-24, 1937*, pp. 21ff. contains addresses at opening session of the conference.

63. *Ibid.*, p. 9.

64. *Ibid.*, p. 51; *FR 1937*, IV, 164; *The Moffat Papers*, pp. 171, 172. Roosevelt's idea of telling the Japanese that the conference was not an outgrowth of the League resolution and the Secretary's statement of October 6 was discarded by the State Department itself. (*FR 1937*, IV, 143).

65. For this exchange between Washington and Paris over the problem of the Indochina railway see *FR 1937*, III, 666, 672 and *FR 1937*, IV, 170, 172.

66. In his final communication to the President, Chautemps stated that the French government had, however, decided to temporize by permitting munitions purchased prior to October 30 to be shipped over the Indochina railroad. (*FR 1937*, III, 672). Actually this decision had been made some time earlier. (see *FR 1937*, III, 634, 637).

[John McVickar Haight, Jr., in his two articles on the aftermath of Roosevelt's "quarantine" speech"—see note 21 of this chapter—uses as a source some documents which form part of an article I had not seen previously: "Roosevelts Kriegswille gegen Japan. Enthullungen aus den Akten des Quai D'Orsay," *Berliner Monatshefte*, February 1943. The documents consist of French Foreign Office papers which were captured by the Nazis and were translated into German. They include two dispatches from Jules Henry to Delbos reporting on the chargé's talk with President Roosevelt on November 6.

Partly because of their vagueness, Henry's dispatches are likely to give rise to a variety of interpretations. The main issue is whether they indicate that Roosevelt was determined to take a strong stand against Japan. Although it is obviously impractical to analyze, or even summarize, these documents in detail here, I would like to consider them briefly.

In the first dispatch (dated November 7) Henry starts by relating Roosevelt's remarks concerning the problem of the Indochina railroad. According to the chargé, the President referred to the French ban on the transport of munitions via Indochina. Henry on his part observed that, in imposing the ban, his government had no doubt been prompted by considerations of national security. Roosevelt replied that he quite understood the point of view of the French but was under the impression that they were perhaps giving way to unfounded fears. He made some further comments the meaning of which seems to have been that, in the existing situation, moral considerations were the most important. The President then went on to say:

"Does one not realize in France that a Japanese attack on Hong Kong or Indochina or on the Dutch East Indies would mean an attack on the Philippines?

"Were this to happen, our common interests would be in danger and we would have to protect them together."

In his second dispatch, written on November 18, Henry declares that in his opinion Sumner Welles in all probability had learned of his (Henry's) meeting with the President from Bullitt's cables and had thereupon persuaded Roosevelt to make the "correction" which was communicated to Paris on November 9. Referring to his own earlier account of his talk with the President, the chargé asserts that Roosevelt "in fact expressed himself as I reported."

As I interpret these documents they do not reflect a determination on the part of the President to take a vigorous position in opposition to the Japanese. To all appearances the President was not discussing the possibility of American cooperation in the defense of Indochina in terms of a situation which he thought might be imminent. There is therefore little reason to doubt Roosevelt's own assertion to the effect that he was only talking about what might happen if an assault upon Indochina should someday materialize. Moreover the President did not give the French anything in the nature of assurances of American support in case the need ever arose for the protection of Indochina. Indeed, in his second dispatch, Henry carefully explains that Roosevelt's comments about Indochina represented the President's personal views. Furthermore, he warns that owing to the isolationist attitude of the American people, among other factors, there is no way of knowing how far the President would be willing to go toward transforming his personal opinions into official policy until a major international crisis arose.

In addition it should be noted that Roosevelt was not suggesting that the French should undertake any measure which he regarded as strongly anti-Japanese. As the President himself stated subsequently, he thought it was in effect unneutral to curtail the flow of munitions to China while the Japanese remained free to obtain supplies at will.]

67. The memorandum in the Davis papers is marked as the record of a press conference held at the Metropole, Brussels, November 5.

68. *The Moffat Papers*, pp. 183 (with footnote 50), 184; Moffat Diary, entry of January 31, 1938.

69. Davis papers, memorandum dated Nov. 2, initialed by Hornbeck.

70. Davis papers. This memorandum is not signed but seems definitely to have been written by Hornbeck. See also Hornbeck's memorandum of Nov. 29, 1937 in the Davis papers in which he states that there is no reason why the Japanese should consider an armistice suggested by outside powers

unless the terms are highly favorable to Japan or the sponsors are prepared to penalize the Japanese for not accepting the suggested provisions.

71. Davis papers. The memorandum of this conversation is written by Hornbeck himself. For confusion concerning some of his earlier remarks, see a conversation between Hugh Wilson and Ambassador Lindsay on November 6. The ambassador said that Eden had reported to his government that "Stanley Hornbeck . . . stated that the Government of the United States had already prepared certain plans for bringing pressure on Japan, plans, Hornbeck . . . added, which are so confidential that they should not, as yet, be spoken about. Hornbeck also spoke of the need of educating public opinion." On seeing an account of Lindsay's remarks later Hornbeck declared that this was a "beautiful example" of the way in which statements became distorted and that he had said "nothing about 'the Government of the United States' or about 'plans' or about 'anything so confidential that they should not, as yet, be spoken about.'" He had merely stated that the American delegation had "certain ideas on the subject of ways in which pressure might conceivably be brought to bear upon Japan." (FR 1937, IV, 160, with footnote 74.)

72. Memorandum by Hornbeck in Davis papers.

73. FR 1937, IV, 175; The Moffat Papers, p. 176.

74. FR 1937, IV, 175.

75. Ibid., 177; The Moffat Papers, p. 174. The French Minister returned to Brussels on November 9. He subsequently showed Norman Davis the cable in which Henry had reported on his meeting with Roosevelt on November 6. Delbos however made no mention of the account of that meeting given by Welles to Bullitt and, presumably, to Henry on November 9. It would appear therefore that he had not as yet been informed about the latest exchanges between Washington and Paris.

76. The reference is to Moffat's account of what Davis said and not a direct quotation. The Moffat Papers, p. 177.

77. Text in The Conference of Brussels, p. 53.

78. Ibid., p. 55.

79. FR 1937, IV, 182, 183.

80. The Conference of Brussels, p. 65.

81. Ibid., p. 67.

82. The Moffat Papers, p. 178; Moffat Diary, entry of Nov. 15, 1937.

83. FR 1937, IV, 180.

84. Ibid., 152. (This cable inadvertently was not printed in chronological order.)

85. FR 1937, IV, 182.

86. Ibid., 183, 185. Davis said that he envisaged the resolution in terms of a common declaration of individual policies as he realized that the United States would probably not be in a position to enter into an agreement with other countries to carry out joint measures.

87. Ibid., 187.

88. Ibid., 193.

89. Ibid., 197.

90. Moffat Diary, entry of Nov. 17, 1937; The Moffat Papers, p. 184.

91. FR 1937, IV, 200.

92. Ibid., 200, 212.

93. The administration does not appear to have been concerned with any particular polls during the course of the Brussels Conference. The most pertinent poll would have been the one already quoted which was published on October 4 and showed that 59 per cent of those who furnished any reply stated that their sympathies in the Sino-Japanese conflict lay with China. Of the 59 per cent, a large majority (63 per cent) said that their sympathy for China was, however, not sufficient to keep them from buying goods made in Japan. (*Public Opinion 1935-1946*, p. 1081.) As with the other polls relative to the Far Eastern conflict, this presented a confused picture as, in a *Fortune* poll in April 1938, 57 per cent voted in favor of boycotting Japan by refusing to buy Japanese goods although, as the editors of *Fortune* themselves pointed out, the shift could not be explained upon the basis of any perceptible reaction by the American public to any of the events which had occurred in the meantime. ("Fortune Quarterly Survey," *Fortune*, July 1938, p. 80; Lockwood, *Our Far Eastern Record*, p. 47.)

94. Page 1.

95. Page 2.

96. "Brussels: the First Stage."

97. Sunday editorial section, p. 3.

98. *The San Francisco Examiner*, p. 3, "Senate Leaders to Challenge Foreign Policy."

99. *Ibid.*, editorial, p. 1, "An Alliance with Death."

100. *Ibid.*, Section 1, p. 2.

101. *Ibid.*

102. Nov. 23, 1937.

103. Congressional Record, 75th Congress, second session, Vol. 82, Appendix 94.

104. *Ibid.*, p. 173.

105. Nov. 20, 1937.

106. FR 1937, IV, 197.

107. *Ibid.*, 203.

108. *Ibid.*, 117.

109. *The Moffat Papers*, p. 186.

110. FR 1937, IV, 221.

111. *Ibid.*, 224.

112. *Ibid.*, 205.

113. *Ibid.*, 217.

114. The statement was sent in double code and was so long that it took nine hours to decipher. It was accompanied with instructions that Davis should assist in drafting a report on the basis of the resolution without, however, taking any initiative or "position of special leadership" in regard to the report. As Moffat suggested in his diary, these were indeed difficult instructions to carry out. (*The Moffat Papers*, p. 185.)

115. FR 1937, IV, 219; Moffat Diary, entries of Nov. 15, 19, 20; *The Moffat Papers*, p. 185.

116. *The Conference of Brussels*, pp. 76, 78.

117. *Ibid.*, pp. 69ff. Two days before the final session, Norman Davis phoned Washington to tell Hull that he thought the Report and Declaration would be approved by all the delegations except the Chinese, concerning whom he said, "They like the statement of principles but unfortunately

that doesn't stop Japan from killing their people. They are naturally dissatisfied." Davis then went on to warn the Secretary that the Report and Declaration would get a "sour press" as they were too "tame" for the correspondents. Hull characteristically suggested that Davis should draw the attention of the correspondents to the "principles" involved but Davis replied, "Newspapermen don't think principles are news." Hull agreed and indicated that the trouble was that most people did not understand the value of principles. "You might as well," he said, "be talking to a child about the A.B.C.s as to be talking to them [i.e., the public] of principles. We have got to organize and educate each country . . . before you can talk to them." Davis declared that he was trying "to get the American newspapermen to realize that"; but this seemed to the Secretary a dangerous course and he repeated several times that Davis should be careful not to give the press the impression that an effort was being made to change public opinion in order to promote a peace. (Davis papers, memorandum of Hull-Davis telephone conversation, Nov. 22, 1937).

118. Moffat Diary, entry of Nov. 23, 1937.

119. A good account of the military developments in China is given in the *Survey of International Affairs, 1937*, I, section beginning on page 213.

120. *FR* 1937, III, 706. After the conference, Dr. Koo apparently prepared a list of China's needs at Hornbeck's request which included war materiel and a loan. (See Chap. XVI of this volume; *FR* 1937, IV, 231; memoranda in Davis papers on Chinese delegation letter paper, dated Nov. 27, 1937.)

121. Moffat Diary. See entry of Dec. 14, 1937, for example.

122. Hull's account in his *Memoirs* (Vol. I, Chap. 39) also in no way indicates that he disagreed in any way with the policy which had been laid down in his absence; quite the contrary. It should be said in passing that Hull's *Memoirs* do not add any important information concerning the Conference as they chiefly repeat the official report submitted to the State Department by Davis on December 16. (Davis papers.)

123. There exists in the Davis papers an interesting memorandum evaluating the conference which was written toward the end of November, presumably by Hornbeck. It points out that very little had been done by the delegates to exhaust the possibilities of bringing about peace between Japan and China through conciliation, as the conference never attempted to examine any aspect of the situation in the Far East but merely limited itself to asking Japan to confer.

124. Grew Diary, entry of Nov. 12, 1937. It was in the third week of November that MacMurray paid a brief visit to Tokyo and left with Grew a copy of the memorandum he had written in the autumn of 1935 which so aroused the ambassador's enthusiasm. (See Chap. V, note 117.)

CHAPTER XV. JAPANESE EFFORTS AT A SETTLEMENT

1. While nothing can of course replace a reading of the primary sources related to Japan's efforts to effect an early settlement of the Sino-Japanese conflict, the writer wishes to acknowledge a very genuine debt to Dr. F. C. Jones whose book *Japan's New Order in East Asia 1937-45* (1954) made the use of these exceedingly complicated primary materials much easier in connection with the events related here.

2. Saionji-Harada Memoirs, p. 1824.

3. Based upon Shinkichi Eto's article, regarding Japan's policy in connection with the termination of the Sino-Japanese war, published in *Taiheiyo senso shuketsuron*. Part of this article, which will be referred to hereafter as "Japan's Policy to Terminate the War with China," was translated for the writer by Yoji Akashi.

4. *Ibid.;* IMTFE (Proceedings, p. 20660).

5. Saionji-Harada Memoirs, p. 1822; Yale Candee Maxon, *Control of Japanese Foreign Policy* (1957), p. 122.

6. Saionji-Harada Memoirs, p. 1887; Shinkichi Eto, "Japan's Policy to Terminate the War with China."

7. IMTFE *Judgment*, p. 686, Proceedings, p. 29684.

8. Saionji-Harada Memoirs, p. 1818.

9. *Ibid.*, 1846, 1926; Maxon, *Control of Japanese Foreign Policy*, p. 121.

10. FR 1937, III, 177.

11. Saionji-Harada Memoirs, p. 1832. Tanaka told virtually the same story in testifying before the IMTFE—see Proceedings, p. 20698. The terms said to have been suggested at the Five Ministers Conference were: (1) creation of a demilitarized zone in North China, (2) the liquidation of the autonomous regimes in North China, and (3) the development of plans for Sino-Japanese economic cooperation in North China.

12. IMTFE Exhibit 3275 (Proceedings, p. 29918). They wanted specifically to reach a settlement before the three divisions that were being mobilized in Japan proper were dispatched to China which, according to schedule, was to take place on August 20.

13. IMTFE Exhibit 3275 (Proceedings, p. 29918) and 3276 (Proceedings, p. 29926).

14. IMTFE Exhibit 3280 (Proceedings, p. 29935).

15. The plans adopted are in IMTFE Exhibit 3735; the telegrams sent to Okamoto are Exhibits 3280 A (Proceedings, p. 29938); Exhibit 3280 B (Proceedings, p. 29941); Exhibit 3280 C (Proceedings, p. 29943); Exhibit 3280 D (Proceedings, p. 29946).

16. The Japanese were prepared to make various concessions if the Chinese objected to the first line which the Japanese negotiators proposed but the line was definitely to include "the strategically important hills on the right bank of the Yungting and Hai Rivers and all important points such as Tientsin and Taku." Exhibit 3280 B (Proceedings, p. 29946).

17. IMTFE Exhibit 3280 (Proceedings, p. 29946).

18. Saionji-Harada Memoirs, p. 1832.

19. IMTFE Exhibit 3274 (Proceedings, p. 29917).

20. *Ibid.*, Exhibit 3280 (Proceedings, p. 29935).

21. *Ibid.*, Exhibit 3274 (Proceedings, p. 29925); FR 1937, III, 368.

22. FR 1937, III, 167 has Chinese side.

23. *Ibid.*, 368.

24. IMTFE Proceedings, p. 29695.

25. *Ibid.*, Proceedings, p. 29788.

26. FR Japan 1931-1941, I, 359.

27. Bisson, *Japan in China*, p. 292. At the IMTFE trials, General Torashiro Kawabe of the General Staff testified that the Central Command hoped to stop the hostilities in China every time a single military operation

was brought to an end and secretly prepared plans to do so. This was the case following the operations in Tientsin, Paoting, Shanghai, and Nanking. (IMTFE Proceedings, p. 21999.)

28. Saionji-Harada Memoirs, pp. 1884, 1888.

29. *Ibid.*, p. 1885.

30. IMTFE, Exhibit 3262 (Proceedings, p. 29684).

31. Proceedings, p. 29740; Saionji-Harada Memoirs, p. 1890.

32. Saionji-Harada Memoirs, p. 1902.

33. *FR* 1937, III, 401. Sir Robert, it will be recalled, had earlier been hopeful that Japan and China would conclude a nonaggression pact which he wanted to see followed up by a similar agreement between Great Britain, the United States, and Japan. (See Chap. V.)

34. *FR* 1937, III, 591, 612.

35. See Sir Robert Craigie's own comments in his book, *Behind the Japanese Mask* (1946), p. 50; American Foreign Service officers in the Far East in general felt that their British colleagues had much more leeway to act on their own than American officials. Grew referred upon a number of occasions to Sir Robert Craigie's taking action in regard to possible negotiations for a settlement between China and Japan without instructions from the Foreign Office. (See, for example, *FR* 1937, III, 687, 700.) In this connection, it should be noted that even Grew permitted Dooman to approach the Japanese Foreign Office in regard to possible American mediation without informing the State Department. (See note 76.)

36. *FR Japan* 1931-1941, I, 320.

37. *FR* 1937, III, 591.

38. *Ibid.;* Grew, *Ten Years in Japan*, p. 221.

39. *FR* 1937, IV, 122; also 80 and Grew, *Ten Years in Japan*, p. 223.

40. *FR* 1937, III, 628.

41. *FR* 1937, IV, 75.

42. *FR* 1937, III, 605, 611; also 641 and 645.

43. Johnson papers, letter dated Oct. 29, 1937.

44. *Ibid.*, letter dated October 23, 1937.

45. *Ibid.*, letter to Dr. Gilbert Grosvenor, dated Nov. 8, 1937; also letters to Karl F. Baldwin, Oct. 28, 1937, Roger Greene, Nov. 8, 1937, and Ambassador Grew, Nov. 10, 1937.

46. *FR* 1937, III, 268, 654.

47. *Ibid.*, 374.

48. *FR* 1937, IV, 150.

49. *FR* 1937, III, 654.

50. IMTFE Proceedings, pp. 29699, 29794, 29798.

51. *Ibid.*, Exhibit 3268.

52. *Ibid.*, Proceedings, p. 29699.

53. *FR* 1937, IV, 26.

54. *Ibid.*, 24.

55. It has been suggested that Ambassador Craigie may have regarded Hirota's remarks as a request for good offices but thought it necessary to await developments at Brussels. It is clear that under any circumstances the British government could not act alone as an intermediary at this time as Japanese animosity against Great Britain had reached such a point that, according to Grew, Ambassador Craigie feared a possible blockade of Hong

Kong. (*FR* 1937, IV, 136.) Norman Davis' feeling was that Craigie wanted to keep the United States from serving as sole mediator, as he wished Great Britain to perform this task ultimately, thereby improving Anglo-Japanese relations.

56. Grew states in his diary (p. 3515) that the original draft of the identical cable was written by Ambassador Craigie but that he (Grew) objected because the British ambassador had enumerated the peace terms which the Japanese might demand. Grew asked to have this passage omitted on the grounds that it was "pure speculation" and might be misleading.

57. *FR* 1937, IV, 134.

58. *FR* 1937, III, 662.

59. *Ibid.,* 625. Presumably Davis thought this accounted for the statement in the cable that the time had not "yet come" for an offer of good offices by any one power. Certainly Sir Robert's ultimate goal was better relations between England and Japan in order to stave off possible hostilities between the two countries in the Far East which he believed would prove an open invitation to Hitler to attack Great Britain in Europe. (See Craigie, *Behind the Japanese Mask,* pp. 49ff.)

60. Documents on German Foreign Policy 1918-1945 from the Archives of the German Foreign Ministry, Series D (referred to hereafter as German Documents), p. 743; *Memoirs of Ernst von Weizsacker* (1951), p. 116; Herbert Von Dirksen, *Moscow, Tokyo, London* (1951), p. 189.

61. German Documents, p. 754.

62. *Ibid.,* p. 754.

63. *Ibid.,* p. 773.

64. *Ibid.,* p. 776.

65. *Ibid.,* p. 778.

66. *Ibid.,* p. 780.

67. *FR* 1937, III, 649.

68. *FR* 1937, IV, 149.

69. *Ibid.,* 169.

70. Davis papers, two memoranda dated Oct. 29, 1937, concerning talks between the Chinese and American delegations.

71. *The Moffat Papers,* p. 168.

72. *FR* 1937, IV, 214; also 199.

73. *Ibid.,* 199, 231; Moffat Diary, entry of Nov. 15, 1937. In addition to the appeals made by the Chinese delegation at Brussels, it was on the day before the conference closed that Ambassador Wang came to see Hull to ask if anything could be done by the powers represented at Brussels to furnish the Chinese with military supplies and the Secretary indicated clearly that he did not expect any action to be taken. (See Chap. XIV.)

74. Grew, *Ten Years in Japan,* p. 222. Grew also said later that he knew the German ambassador had taken Hirota's suggestion seriously that third powers should persuade Chiang to negotiate for peace and had informed his government accordingly but that "nothing came of it." (*FR* 1937, III, 687).

75. Grew, *Ten Years in Japan,* p. 223; *FR* 1937, III, 690.

76. It was understood that this talk was to be entirely unofficial so that it was not reported to Washington until November 18, when Yoshizawa consented to the State Department's being informed. On November 18 a com-

plete account of this and Dooman's subsequent conversation with Yoshizawa was sent to Washington by mail, arriving there on December 16. (*FR 1937, III*, 690.)

77. *FR* 1937, IV, 189. This was the resolution, actually adopted on November 15, which ended with the assertion that if Japan continued to refuse to cooperate with the conference the states represented at Brussels would have to consider what their "common attitude" should be toward a nation which set aside provisions of a treaty that the other parties held to be operative under the existing circumstances.

78. Moffat Diary, entry of Nov. 15, 1937.

79. Kurusu made this statement on the same day the Chinese spoke of mediation by Germany and Italy as a solution which they might have to consider seriously unless the conference accomplished something by way of aiding China. Pierrepont Moffat wrote in his diary that thus the "threat" of German and Italian mediation had been made twice on the same day. (Moffat Diary, entry of Nov. 15, 1937.)

80. *FR* 1937, IV, 194.

81. *FR* 1937, III, 687.

82. *FR* 1937, IV, 196.

83. *FR* 1937, III, 688.

84. *Ibid.*, 687.

85. *Ibid.*, 699.

86. *Ibid.;* the *aide-mémoire* on page 698 was printed in error. The correct one is in the Department files and was used by the writer.

87. *FR* 1937, III, 700.

88. *Ibid.*, 701.

89. *FR* 1937, IV, 219.

90. *Ibid.*

91. *FR* 1937, III, 792; Sir Robert also suggested certain financial sanctions. (*Ibid.*, 775.) Subsequent developments are discussed in Chap. XVI of this volume.

92. *FR* 1937, III, 714.

93. *Ibid.*, 724.

94. The quotation marks indicate phrases quoted by Welles from the original British telegram.

95. Langer and Gleason, in *The Challenge to Isolation*, p. 28, speak of the "suspicion that Ambassador Lindsay did not always convey the substance of Washington conversations faithfully" to London. Conversely, in his talks in Washington the ambassador does not always seem to have fully reflected his own government's point of view. At the same time Welles himself shared the tendency within the State Department—which appears to have been surprisingly strong—of interpreting events in a way that would seem to corroborate the opinions held in Washington.

96. *FR* 1937, III, 775.

97. *Ibid.*, 800.

98. German Documents, p. 793.

99. Harada recorded early in November that after the failure of the Trautmann talk with Chiang Kai-shek, Ambassador Dirksen advised waiting until the Brussels Conference was over before making any further move. Saionji-Harada Memoirs, p. 1928.

100. As this document has been used by Wang and others to discredit Chiang Kai-shek, its validity is of course open to question. However, the details are so in accord with the story as related in the German documents that it seems reasonable to suppose that it may be authentic. The version used here is a translation from Po-ta Ch'en, *Chiang Kai-shek Enemy of the People*, Chap. IV, Sec. 3. See also James T. C. Liu's article, "German Mediation in the Sino-Japanese War 1937-1938," published in *The Far Eastern Quarterly*, 1949, p. 160. Liu used Wang Ching-wei's book published in Shanghai in 1939.

101. German Documents, pp. 787, 797.

102. *Ibid.*, p. 799.

103. A Provisional Government of the Republic of China was established in Peiping on December 14, 1937.

104. Saionji-Harada Memoirs, p. 1962. (The army apparently intercepted some messages between the German government and Ambassador Dirksen.)

105. Eto, "Japan's Policy to Terminate the War with China."

106. IMTFE Exhibit 21428; Saionji-Harada Memoirs, p. 1999.

107. German Documents, p. 802.

108. Hirota explained the terms to Grew in much the same manner as he had to Dirksen on Jan. 10, 1938. (*FR* 1938, III, 10.)

109. German Documents, p. 805.

110. *Ibid.*, p. 809.

111. *Ibid.*, p. 810.

112. *Ibid.*, p. 811.

113. *Ibid.*, p. 814.

114. IMTFE Exhibit 3265 (Proceedings, p. 29853).

115. German Documents, p. 815.

116. *Ibid.*, p. 816.

117. *Ibid.*, p. 817.

118. IMTFE Proceedings, pp. 29858, 29863.

119. *FR Japan* 1931-1941, I, 437.

120. *FR* 1937, III, 752.

121. *Ibid.*, 773, 750, 777, 790, 796.

122. Johnson papers, letter to Harold M. Bixby, dated Dec. 7, 1937; also *FR* 1937, III, 777.

123. *FR* 1937, III, 832.

124. *Ibid.*, 842.

125. *Ibid.*, 844

126. *Ibid.*, 847, footnote 64.

127. *FR* 1938, III, 2.

128. *Ibid.*, 12.

129. *Ibid.*, 16.

130. *Ibid.*, 22.

131. *Ibid.*, 36. Also *The Memoirs of Cordell Hull*, I, 567.

132. *FR* 1938, III, 44.

133. That the Japanese were not immune to pressure is evident from their reaction to the proceedings at the League in October and Brussels in November.

134. According to information supplied by Eto, there was a regulation

in Japan which stipulated that twice as many divisions of the Japanese army should be retained at home as were permitted to go abroad. It was probably with something of this nature in mind that Falkenhausen informed Berlin in July that China's military prospects were decidedly favorable as Japan probably would not send a large part of her army to China and could not win a genuine victory without doing so. As matters developed, the Japanese broke their own regulation and did send a far larger proportion of their troops to the mainland than had been anticipated. By November, Falkenhausen's optimism had disappeared and it was part of German strategy to use him to impress upon the Generalissimo the gravity of the military situation and the consequent necessity of entering into negotiations with Japan to end the hostilities. The Germans themselves were especially fearful that a long drawn out war would create complete disorganization in China which would mean that "Bolshevism would come to China." (German Documents, pp. 783, 784.)

CHAPTER XVI. THE *Panay* CRISIS

1. *FR Japan* 1931-1941, I, 517.
2. *FR* 1937, IV, 485, 486, 497; *FR Japan* 1931-1941, I, 520.
3. *FR* 1937, IV, 487.
4. *Ibid.*, 488, 489 (contain both cables from the ambassador).
5. *FR Japan* 1931-1941, I, 521.
6. *Ibid.*, 522.
7. *Ibid.*
8. *Ibid.*, 523.
9. *Ibid.*, 524.
10. *FR* 1937, IV, 502.
11. *FR Japan* 1931-1941, I, 526.
12. *Ibid.*
13. *FR* 1937, IV, 502; Grew, *Ten Years In Japan*, p. 236.
14. *FR* 1937, IV, 490.
15. *FR* 1937, III, 798.
16. At this point in the conversation the British ambassador reverted to a discussion of the possibility of the United States and Great Britain offering their good offices for a settlement of the Sino-Japanese conflict.
17. See Chap. XV.
18. *FR* 1937, IV, 494.
19. *FR Japan* 1931-1941, I, 523.
20. *FR* 1937, IV, 503.
21. *Ibid.*, 499.
22. *Ibid.*, 503.
23. *New York Times*, Dec. 17, 1937, p. 1, "*Panay* Attack Deliberate." See also the reviews of the British press sent to Ambassador Grew by the State Department, Grew papers, vol. 1937, pp. 53, 69. Special mention was made of the *Yorkshire Post*, which was owned by Mrs. Eden's family and was therefore presumed to express the Foreign Secretary's views.
24. The *London Times* correspondent had been on board the *Panay* and a Chinese correspondent for the *New York Times*.
25. *FR* 1937, IV, 505.

26. See the reports of the survivors in the *New York Times*, for example.

27. Roosevelt papers, PSF Navy Department 1937, Box 18.

28. *FR Japan* 1931-1941, I, 527.

29. *Ibid.*, 528.

30. *FR* 1937, IV, 507, two dispatches.

31. *FR Japan* 1931-1941, I, 527.

32. Dec. 18, 1937, p. 1, "Butchery Marked Capture of Nanking."

33. Blum, *From the Morgenthau Diaries*, section on "The *Panay*" beginning p. 485; certain details supplied by Blum in talks with the writer.

34. Roosevelt papers PSF Treasury 1937, Box 24.

35. The instructions to go ahead without the British which Secretary Hull sent to Grew were cleared with the President. *The Memoirs of Cordell Hull*, I, 561.

36. Admiral Leahy believed that a war between the Western powers and Japan was inevitable and that, while we would find it difficult to defeat the Japanese by ourselves, we could easily do so in conjunction with the British. The Sino-Japanese War seemed to him to present an excellent opportunity to win a victory over Japan with the least cost.

37. Leahy papers.

38. *The Secret Diary of Harold L. Ickes*, II, 272, 275, 279. Concerning his own views, Ickes wrote: "Pacifist though I am, I am becoming imbued with the idea that sooner or later the democracies of the world, if they are to survive, will have to join—armed issue—with the fascist nations. This will mean that America and Japan will be at war, and if that ever is to happen, aren't we strategically in a better position now than we will be after Japan has strengthened her hand militarily and perhaps replenished her treasury with the spoils of China?"

39. Leahy papers.

40. *Ibid.*

41. *Command Decisions*, Chap. I, "Germany First: The Basic Concept of Allied Strategy," by Louis Morton, p. 11.

42. *Ibid.*; Watson, The U. S. Army in World War II, *Chief of Staff: Prewar Plans and Preparations*, p. 92; Samuel Eliot Morison, *The Rising Sun in the Pacific* 1931-April 1942 (1955), p. 48; *Pearl Harbor Attack. Hearings before the Joint Committee on the Investigation of the Pearl Harbor Attack*, 79th Congress, 2d session, Pt. 9, pp. 4272ff.

43. *The War Against Japan*, Vol. 1, *The Loss of Singapore*, by Major General S. Woodburn Kirby, p. 17. See the following pages for shifts in British plans. Also Documents on British Foreign Policy, 1919-1939, 3d series, Vol. VIII, pp. 320, 455, Appendix I.

44. *Command Decisions*, Morton, p. 12.

45. Watson, *Chief of Staff*, p. 93. In *The Rising Sun in the Pacific*, p. 49, Samuel Eliot Morison says that Ingersoll and the corresponding officer in the British navy agreed in January 1938 to recommend cooperation in case of war on the basis of the Royal Navy's basing a battle force on Singapore, if the Japanese moved south, with the United States Fleet concentrating at Pearl Harbor.

46. For previous reference to Orange Plan, see above.

47. Langer and Gleason, writing of the "now famous Plan Dog concept" advanced by Admiral Stark in 1940, state: "Plan Dog reiterated the now

widely accepted view of the Army as well as of the Navy that future strategic planning . . . should be based on the assumption that if and when the United States became involved in war against the three Axis powers, the wisest course would be to anticipate 'an eventual strong offensive in the Atlantic as an ally of Britain and a defensive in the Pacific.'" (Langer and Gleason, *The Undeclared War*, p. 222.)

48. W. N. Medlicott, *The Economic Blockade*, in *History of the Second World War* (1952), pp. 14, 383.

49. See Chap. XIV of this volume.

50. There were "leaks" to the press later which are mentioned below.

51. *FR Japan* 1931-1941, I, 542 Report, 547 Opinion.

52. *Ibid.*, 549.

53. *Ibid.*, 551.

54. *Ibid.*, 552.

55. Grew, *Ten Years In Japan*, p. 239.

56. Blum in *From the Morgenthau Diaries* states that the *Panay* incident "showed that the President was prepared, albeit only emotionally and momentarily, to force the issue in the Far East." (p. 492). This would appear to reflect Secretary Morgenthau's view. Langer and Gleason are of the opinion that the attack upon the *Panay* brought the United States to the "verge of war." (*The Challenge to Isolation*, p. 24.)

57. This point was commented upon in the press at the time. See, for example, the article by Hugh Byas in the *New York Times,* December 16, 1937 ("Japanese Air Chief Ousted," p. 1), in which he states that the Japanese newspapers were full of reports that the United States would not cooperate with Great Britain and that, as such cooperation was the only eventuality which could cause the Japanese serious concern, they were "relatively tranquil over the present affair."

58. There were obviously many differences between Oliphant's "quarantine" idea and Roosevelt's, among them being that according to Oliphant's plan the United States would at best have been acting in conjunction with Great Britain and a few other powers while the President had envisaged the United States as acting as a member of a worldwide community of "neutrals."

59. That the administration itself felt the Oliphant plan might quickly lead to a shooting war is evident from the fact that further discussion of it was entrusted to Captain Ingersoll on the grounds that it was essentially part of the naval problem.

60. Grew papers, 1937, Vol. 45, p. 63.

61. Kramer ms.

62. See Chap. XIII of this volume.

63. Congressional Record, 75th Congress, 2d session, p. 1356. See also, *New York Times,* Dec. 14, 1937, p. 18, "Congress Leaders Decry Jingoism."

64. *New York Times,* Dec. 14, 1937, p. 1, "U. S. Demands Full Satisfaction With Guarantee Against Further Attack." Smather's letter is quoted in this article.

65. Good accounts of the difficulties which developed over the Customs administration may be found in Friedman, *British Relations with China,* sections beginning pp. 111 and 118, and Johnstone, *The United States and Japan's New Order,* pp. 109ff.

66. It was at this point that the British first suggested a possible naval demonstration and staff talks. (See Chap. XV of this volume.)

67. *FR 1937*, IV, 906, 909.

68. *Ibid.*, 912.

69. *FR 1938*, III, 627.

70. *Ibid.*, 634, 638.

71. See, for example, *FR 1937*, III, 880, 887, 891, 911.

72. *Ibid.*, 879, 883, 887.

73. *Ibid.*, 911, 914.

74. Craigie, *Behind the Japanese Mask*, p. 53.

75. Among the most important features of the agreement were provisions depositing all revenues collected by the customs at ports in areas under Japanese control in the Yokohama Specie Bank. Foreign loan quotas were, however, to be remitted to the Inspector-General of Customs to meet the servicing of foreign loans and indemnities secured on the customs. The text of the communiqué issued by the British government describing the agreement appears in Friedman, *British Relations with China*, p. 119. See also *FR 1938*, III, section beginning page 626 and especially texts 678, 685, 688, and statement of the American position, 694-701. The British communiqué contained a sentence which read: "It is further understood that the Governments of the United States and France do not propose to raise any objections to the temporary application of these arrangements . . ." By mistake, this sentence had not been cleared with the United States government which, in fact, objected to it. For criticisms of the agreement, see Friedman, *British Relations with China*, p. 121, and Johnstone, *The United States and Japan's New Order*, p. 110.

76. *Survey of International Affairs*, 1937, I, 317; Jones, *Shanghai and Tientsin*, Chap. IX.

77. *FR 1937*, III, 704, 705, 707.

78. *Ibid.*, 717.

79. *Ibid.*, 742, 743.

80. *Ibid.*, 756, 760, 761, 765, 767.

81. *FR 1938*, III, 116.

82. *Ibid.*, 123.

83. *Ibid.*, 119.

84. *Ibid.*, 123.

85. *Ibid.*, 123, 126, 129, 130.

86. *Ibid.*, 139.

87. *FR Japan 1931-1941*, I, 565.

88. For this series of talks between Craigie and Grew, see the Grew papers, *Conversations 1937-1938*, pp. 182, 196, 208. See also the very long memorandum Grew sent Hornbeck on April 12, 1938, discussing his own views in detail. (Grew papers.) Hornbeck had written the ambassador asking him to respond to the following question: "Were the American Government to take definite steps in the field of positive pressure, such as disposal of naval force in a manner threatening to Japan or an application of embargoes in a manner which would adversely affect Japan, for the purpose, declared or implied, of compelling Japan to refrain from abuse of American nationals and violation of American rights in regard to property and other matters in China, what would be likely to be the results in terms of official

action by the highest responsible and effective authorities of the Japanese state?"

89. Sir Robert's remarks show very clearly that he had considerable information from the Foreign Office about exchanges with the United States. It is, however, very difficult to make out whether the views he expressed to Grew reflected those of the British government and if so, to what extent.

90. *FR* 1938, III, 7. The following quotations are from the Welles memorandum in this reference.

91. Leahy papers. For announcement of naval maneuvers, see *New York Times,* Oct. 17, 1937, Pt. II, p. 3, article entitled "For Record War Games" and Dec. 11, 1937, p. 11, "Pacific War Games Expanded by Navy."

92. Leahy papers.

93. This message has been lost in the State Department files but its purport was to all appearances along the lines indicated here. See *FR* 1938, III, 19.

94. *Ibid.*

95. See Chap. XIII of this volume. The documents drawn up by Welles in January appear in *FR* 1938, I, section beginning p. 115.

96. Hull argued that the smaller powers were far too frightened to act.

97. See note 105 of this chapter and Hull's reference to naval action in his talk with Sir Ronald Lindsay on January 17 (*FR* 1938, III, 31).

98. Leahy papers; *New York Times,* Jan. 14, 1938, p. 2, "U. S. Cruisers To Go To Singapore."

99. *New York Times,* March 2, 1938, p. 19, "Fleet Problem 19 Will Start March 14," March 13, 1938, sect. VIII, p. 38, "Pacific Game Goes Grimly On," by Hanson Baldwin, March 15, 1938, p. 10, "Fleet Manoeuvres on Wartime Basis."

100. *Ibid.,* Feb. 15, 1938, p. 9, "British Navy Opens Its Singapore Base."

101. *The Moffat Papers,* Jan. 26, 1938.

102. *New York Times,* Jan. 27, 1938, p. 13, "Navy Message Key to Foreign Policy."

103. *Ibid.,* Feb. 3, 1938, p. 6, "Leahy Denies Navy Has Tie to British"; Feb. 5, 1938, p. 1, "Navy Chief's Talk To British 'Secret'"; Feb. 6, 1938, E, p. 7, "Europe Weighs U.S. Navy Plan." See also Hull's letter to Pittman, *FR Japan* 1931-1941, I, 448.

104. The best account is probably Langer and Gleason, *The Challenge to Isolation,* p. 22. See also Sumner Welles' *Seven Decisions That Shaped History,* Chap. I; *The Memoirs of Cordell Hull,* pp. 579ff.; Feiling, *The Life of Neville Chamberlain,* p. 336; Winston S. Churchill, *The Gathering Storm* (1948), pp. 251ff. The documents published by the State Department are in *FR* 1938, 1, section beginning p. 115 with some additional versions of the Welles plan among the Roosevelt papers at Hyde Park.

105. The reply (*FR* 1938, I, 120) sent by Roosevelt to Chamberlain read in part:

I must confess that I am concerned by the statement of the Prime Minister that His Majesty's Government under certain contingencies "would be prepared for their part, if possible with authority of the League of Nations, to recognize the *de jure* Italian conquest of Abyssinia." I take it, of course, for granted that the

THE PANAY CRISIS | 649

Prime Minister has given due consideration to the harmful effect which this step would have, especially at this time, upon the course of Japan in the Far East and upon the nature of the peace terms which Japan may demand of China. At a moment when respect for treaty obligations would seem of such vital importance in international relations, as proclaimed by our two Governments only recently at the Brussels Conference and at the time when our two Governments have been giving consideration to measures of cooperation in support of international law and order in the Far East, as well as their legitimate and legal rights in China, I cannot help but feel that all of the repercussions of the step contemplated by His Majesty's Government should be most carefully considered.

Secretary Hull's memorandum recording his comments to Lindsay is in *FR* 1938, I, 133.

106. Blum, *From the Morgenthau Diaries*, pp. 483ff.; Everest, *Morgenthau, The New Deal and Silver*, pp. 120ff.

107. *FR* 1938, III, 519. For earlier request for a loan see Chap. XIV of this volume.

108. See Chap. XV.

109. For British note and Department's reply, *FR* 1937, III, 814, 816.

110. Bisson, *America's Far Eastern Policy*, p. 75; press release *FR Japan* 1931-1941, I, 448. For a discussion with the French respecting the effect of the withdrawal of troops from Tientsin upon the Boxer Protocol, see *FR* 1938, III, 75, 77, 86. The Secretary of State took the position that: "Our decision now to reduce and redistribute our troops in north China does not involve modification of our treaty position in north China. We are continuing to maintain armed forces in both Peiping and Tientsin in accordance with our rights and responsibilities under the Boxer Protocol of 1901."

111. *FR* 1938, III, 74.

112. See Chapter XI of this volume.

113. *FR Japan* 1931-1941, I, 429.

114. The text of Hull's reply is in Bisson, *America's Far Eastern Policy*, Appendix, p. 172. The six peace societies which had been so active in demanding the withdrawal of United States citizens and troops from China continued their campaign. See especially the open letter from the Women's International League for Peace and Freedom addressed to Secretary Hull on December 15 and the Secretary's reply a few days later. *Fellowship*, Feb. 1938 issue.

115. *FR Japan* 1931-1941, I, 429.

INDEX

Abend, Hallett, 331
Addams, Jane, 343
Addis, Sir Charles, 63-65, 69, 266
Africa, 27
Alaska, 20, 239, 244, 249, 607 n. 36
Alden, U.S.S., 240
Aleutians, 239, 497, 607 n. 36
All-China Conference of Soviets, 199
Amau, Eiji, 75, 77, 78, 128, 193
Amau Doctrine, 46-99, 121, 128, 136; background of, 46-55; declaration of, 55-92, 100, 104, 167, 169, 256, 522, 523, 524, 526; U.S. policy toward, 81-82, 523
American Association of University Women, 344, 351, 623 n. 135
American business in China, 256-275; in Shanghai, 122-123, 325, 583 n. 41
American Committee for Non-Participation in Japanese Aggression, 353
American Economic Mission to the Far East, 258-259, 610 nn. 11, 15. *See also* Forbes, W. Cameron
American Federation of Labor, 392
American Friends Service Committee, 342. *See also* Friends
American League for Peace and Democracy, *see* American League Against War and Fascism
American League Against War and Fascism, 351, 623 n. 132
American-Oriental Banking Corporation, bankruptcy of, 130
American people, attitude toward "bandit nations," 380-381, toward Japan, 311, 312, 317; aversion to armament, 103, 118; concepts different from Japanese, 118; interest in China, 15, 89; and League of Nations, 2; opposition to bilateral declarations, 97; reaction to *Panay* crisis, 542, to U.S. naval policy, 106, 110; and treaties, 118
American Samoa, 244
American trading houses on the China coast, 43
American Union for Concerted Peace Efforts, *see* National Council for the Cause and Cure of War

Anglo-American cooperation (proposed or effected), 78, 91, 104, 136-137, 167, 273, 294, 297, 316, 376, 451-452, 484, 488-490, 494-496, 499, 508-510, 523, 535, 584 n. 49, 593 n. 46, 646 n. 57; naval talks, 100-115, 121, 129, 241-242, 489-490, 495-498, 502, 524; parallel policy, 292-293, 510-512, 518, 528, 594 n. 59; proposed mediation, 448, 468-470, 471-473; proposed naval measures, 395, 469, 471, 490, 495-499, 508, 510, 543; staff talks, 471, 489-490, 495, 497-498, 502; unity, 111, 131, 271, 510
Anglo-French negotiations with Italy and Germany, 512-513
Anglo-Japanese alliance, 104; trade relations, 271; treaty plan, 272
Anti-American feeling, in China, 122, 130, 526, 583 n. 41; in Japan, 4, 5, 20-21, 39, 40, 521
Anti-Comintern Pact, 194-195, 459, 518, 594 n. 62
Apostolic Delegate to U.S., 381
Argentina, 370
Arita, Hachiro, 177, 179, 181, 189, 191, 193, 593 n. 45
Ariyoshi, Akira, 160
Armament, limitation of, *see* Disarmament
Arms embargo, 22-26, 32, 335, 342; U.S. resolution on, 24, 29-30
Arms race, 270
Army Board, 606 n. 22
Arnold, Julean, 611 n. 31
Article XIX, *see* Washington Conference agreements, and Article IX of Naval Treaty
Ashurst, Senator, 503
Atcheson, George, 146-147, 150, 486-487, 492
Atherton, Ray, 129
Atlantic, U.S. military strategy in, *see* Orange Plan
Aubert, Ludvig, 424
Australia, 108, 244, 245
Austria, 514, 571 n. 27

HARVARD EAST ASIAN SERIES